T5-BQA-612

Human Resource Management

Sixth Edition

Human Resource Management

R. WAYNE MONDY, SPHR
McNeese State University

ROBERT M. NOE, SPHR
East Texas State University

In Collaboration with
SHANE R. PREMEAUX
McNeese State University

Prentice Hall, Inc.

Acquisitions Editor: *Natalie Anderson*
Senior Project Manager: *Alana Zdinak*
Marketing Manager: *Jo-Ann DeLuca*
Production Editor: *Neil Saunders, Monotype Editorial Services*
Interior Design: *Maureen Eide*
Cover Design: *Jeanette Jacobs*
Design Director: *Patricia Wosczyk*
Copy Editor: *Monotype Editorial Services*
Proofreader: *Monotype Editorial Services*
Permissions Editor: *Monotype Editorial Services*
Photo Researcher: *Monotype Editorial Services*
Manufacturing Buyer: *Vincent Scelta*
Assistant Editor: *Lisamarie Brassini*
Editorial Assistant: *Crissy Statuto*
Production Coordinator: *David Cotungo*
Cover Art: *Illustration by Paul Schulenburg*

A Simon & Schuster Company
Upper Saddle River, NJ 07458

Printed in the United States of America

10 9 8 7 6 5 4 3 2 1

ISBN 0-13-229832-5

Prentice-Hall International (UK) Limited, *London*
Prentice-Hall of Australia Pty. Limited, *Sydney*
Prentice-Hall Canada Inc., *Toronto*
Prentice-Hall Hispanoamericana, S. A., *Mexico*
Prentice-Hall of India Private Limited, *New Delhi*
Prentice-Hall of Japan, Inc., *Tokyo*
Simon & Schuster Asia Pte. Ltd., *Singapore*
Editora Prentice-Hall do Brazil, Ltda., *Rio de Janeiro*

To My Daughters:

Alyson Lynn and Marianne Elizabeth

RWM

To My Grandchildren:

Michael, Lillie, Robert, and Margaret Vaughan

RMN

To My Wife:

Elizabeth Anne Premeaux

SRP

TABLE OF CONTENTS

PART TWO ■ HUMAN RESOURCE PLANNING, RECRUITMENT, AND SELECTION

CHAPTER 5 Human Resource Planning

PART THREE ■ HUMAN RESOURCE DEVELOPMENT

CHAPTER 8 Organization Change and Human Resource Development

CHAPTER 10 Career Planning and Development

CHAPTER 11 Performance Appraisal

PART FIVE ■ SAFETY AND HEALTH

CHAPTER 14 A Safe and Healthy Work Environment

PART SIX ■ EMPLOYEE AND LABOR RELATIONS

CHAPTER 15 The Labor Union

CHAPTER 16 Collective Bargaining

PREFACE

The sixth edition of *Human Resource Management* continues to offer a practical and realistic approach to the study of human resource management. While the book is essentially pragmatic, it is balanced throughout by current human resource management concepts. A common theme—the interrelationships among the various human resource functions—runs throughout the book. Each of these functions is described from the standpoint of its relation to the total needs of human resource management. The book is written primarily for students who are being exposed to human resource management for the first time. It puts the student in touch with the real world through the use of numerous illustrations and company material showing how human resource management is practiced in today's organizations.

Features of the Book

We have included the following features to promote the readability and understanding of important human resource management concepts:

- A model (see Figure 2-1) is developed that provides a vehicle for relating all human resource management topics. We believe that the overview provided will serve as an excellent teaching device.
- "Key Terms" are listed at the beginning of each chapter. In addition, every key term appears in bold print the first time it is defined or described in the chapter.
- "Chapter Objectives" are listed at the beginning of each chapter to highlight the general purpose and key concepts of the chapter.
- A caselet (short case study) involving human resource management is provided at the beginning of each chapter to set the tone for a discussion of the major topics included within the chapter.
- Real company examples and material are featured throughout the book to illustrate how a concept is actually used in organizations. A minimum of five company examples are included in each chapter.
- A brief exercise called "HRM in Action" is included in the body of each chapter. These exercises are designed to permit students to make decisions regarding "real world" situations that could occur in the business world. A debriefing guide is provided in the *Instructor's Resource Manual*.
- Each chapter concludes with a "Summary," distilling the major points covered in that chapter.

- "Questions for Review" appear at the end of each chapter to test the student's understanding of the material presented in the chapter.
- As a special new feature to this edition, a *Human Resources Management Simulation* by Smith and Golden is included for each chapter. "HRM Simulation" provides students with the opportunity to practice managing an organization's human resources functions. With a simulation, students have the opportunity to make decisions, see the effects of those decisions, and then try it again. Players get "hands-on" experience at manipulating key human resources variables in a dynamic setting.
- Another new feature to this edition is "ABC Video Case," based on clips from an ABC television program, which appear in each chapter. These interesting video cases allow students to tie information contained in the text to actual business situations.
- Two "HRM Incidents" are provided at the end of each chapter. These short cases highlight material covered in the chapter.
- A comprehensive exercise called "Developing HRM Skills: An Experiential Exercise" is provided at the end of each chapter from Chapter 2 onward. These exercises provide for considerable class participation and group involvement. A comprehensive debriefing guide is included in the *Instructor's Resource Manual*.
- To ensure the text remains as current as possible, all the footnotes have been updated wherever appropriate. The citations for these footnotes appear at the end of each chapter in "Notes."
- A list of "References" is provided at the back of the book to permit additional in-depth study of selected topics.
- A "Glossary" of all the key terms featured in the chapters appears at the back of the book.

Improvements to the Sixth Edition

The previous editions of this book have all enjoyed considerable success. Many of our adopters provided us with suggestions for improving the sixth edition. All the topics have been updated to provide the most recent coverage available. Here is a list of the topics that have been added to this new edition:

- Because of the impact of the multinational environment on human resource management, new major multinational topics are highlighted in each chapter under the heading "A Global Perspective."
- New sections on the "Changing Role of the Chief Human Resource Executive" and a list of trends that will affect how work is done in the future appear in Chapter 1.
- "Managing the Diverse Workforce" in Chapter 2 now includes topics on women in business, workers of color, older workers, contingency workers, leased employees, persons with disabilities, immigrants, and young persons with limited education or skills.

- A new section on the Adarand Constructors v Pena Supreme Court decision has been incorporated in Chapter 3.
- There is also a new section on "The Small Business."
- Major sections on "Reengineering" and "Job Design" have been added to Chapter 4.
- Chapter 5 includes a new section on "Downsizing."
- Additional material on contingent workers, recruitment data bases, and automated applicant tracking systems is featured in Chapter 6.
- New topics in Chapter 7 include a discussion of resume preparation for college graduates, drug testing, testing for AIDS, behavior description interviewing, potential interviewing problems, and personal reference and background investigation checks.
- Chapter 8 contains new material on computer-based training, distance learning, and videoconferencing, as well as a new section on the "Job Training Partnership Act."
- "Total Quality Management," "Team Building," and "Self-Directed Teams" have become major new sections in Chapter 9.
- The environment as it affects career planning, steps that should be taken to promote a new career path, and methods of adding value to retain present jobs are three new topics that have been added to Chapter 10.
- A section on the "Legal Implications" of performance appraisal appears for the first time in Chapter 11.
- Material on the Family and Medical Leave Act of 1993, determinants of executive compensation, workplace flexibility, regular part-time work, and modified retirement is included in Chapter 13.
- New sections on "Cumulative Trauma Disorders," "Workplace Violence," and "Smoking in the Workplace" have been added to Chapter 14, as well as information about stress abatement through ergonomics.
- Chapter 15 discusses the North American Free Trade Agreement (NAFTA), the General Agreement on Tariffs and Trade (GATT), and the proposed mega merger of the United Auto Workers, the United Steel Workers of America, and the International Association of Machinists into the United States' largest union.
- In Chapter 19, the section on "Technology Affecting Human Resource Management" has been substantially revised.

All these revisions reflect the latest in HR practices. They have been presented in such a way to promote and stimulate student interest. Numerous company examples demonstrate how "textbook" concepts are actually being used in leading-edge organizations. We sincerely hope that students of human resource management derive as much pleasure from reading the book as we did in writing it.

Acknowledgments

The assistance and encouragement of many people is normally required in the writing of any book. It was especially true in the writing of the sixth edition of *Human Resource Management*. Although it would be virtually impossible to list every person who assisted in this project, we feel that certain people must be credited because of the magnitude of their contribution. We especially appreciate the efforts of the professionals who reviewed this edition.

We would also like to thank Marthanne Lamansky, Kendra Ingram, Julie Du, Rajiv Rajian, and Anita Platt, all very competent and professional individuals, who were always available to ensure that our deadlines were met. As with the previous editions, the support and encouragement of many practicing HRM professionals have made this book possible.

We also appreciate the input of our Senior Project Manager, Alana Zdinak; our Editor, Natalie Anderson, and Assistant Editor, Lisamarie Brassini; and Jo-Ann DeLuca, Marketing Manager at Prentice Hall. Neil Saunders at Monotype Editorial Services has also been an integral member of our publishing team.

Human Resource Management

CHAPTER 1

Human Resource Management: An Overview

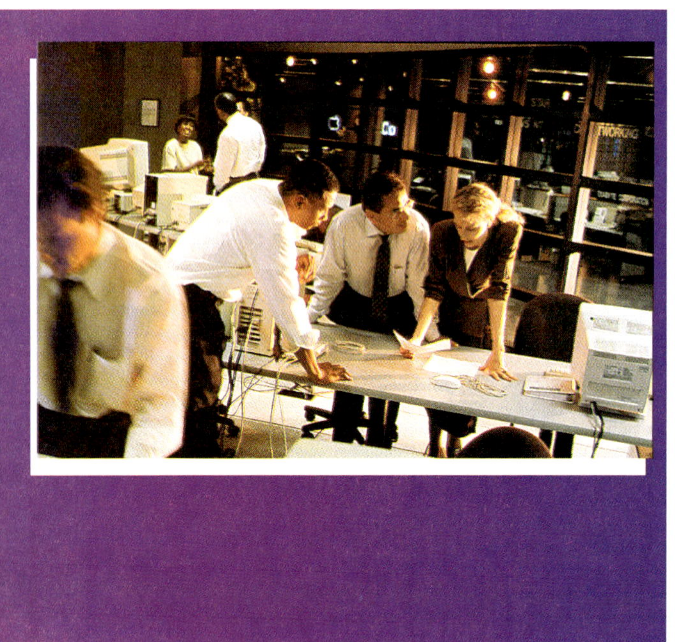

KEY TERMS

CHAPTER OBJECTIVES

1. Distinguish between human resource management and the human resource manager. Describe the functions of human resource management.
2. Describe the changes that have taken place in the human resource field in recent years. Define human resource executive, generalist, and specialist. Describe the changes that occur in the human resource function as a firm grows larger and more complex.
3. Express the nature of professionalization of human resources and the direction it has taken. Define ethics and relate ethics to human resource management.

As David Curtis, vice president of human resources for Nelson Enterprises, headquartered in New York City, rose to leave the executive meeting, he realized his job would be even busier than usual during the next six months. Nelson Enterprises produces high tech components for both government and private industry, and greater production capacity is needed to meet industry demands. A decision to open a new plant in Mobile, Alabama, had been made at the meeting. David and other members of the council had analyzed numerous sites and had determined Mobile most closely met their needs. When the plant is completed in a year, 500 new employees must be available and trained. In addition, 75 employees at the New York facility will be transferred to Mobile. It is David's responsibility to ensure qualified new workers are hired and trained, and the transferred workers are effectively integrated into the workforce.

Carl Edwards is the supervisor of ten Baby Giant convenience stores in Sacramento, California. As the Baby Giant chain is relatively small (forty stores), it has no human resource department. Each supervisor is in charge of all employment activities for his or her store. Carl must ensure only the best people are recruited for positions as store managers, and then he must properly train these individuals. If one of the managers fails to report for an assigned shift, and Carl cannot find a replacement, he is expected to work the shift. It is Friday afternoon, and Carl is hurriedly attempting to locate a replacement because one store manager quit without giving notice.

Judy Lynley is the industrial relations manager for Axton Pneumotives, a small manufacturer of pumps located in Bangor, Maine. The sixty-five machine operators in the firm are unionized. Judy has been negotiating with union leaders for five weeks with little success. The union members have threatened to walk off the job if the contract is not resolved by midnight. However, if Judy's firm agrees to all the union's demands, it will no longer be competitive in the industry because of the higher wage level.

David, Carl, and Judy have one thing in common; they are deeply involved with some of the challenges and problems related to human resource management. Managers of human resources must constantly deal with the often volatile and unpredictable human element that makes working in this field very challenging. Managing people in organizations is becoming more complex than ever because of rapidly changing and increasingly complicated work environments.

In the first part of this chapter, we distinguish between human resource management and the human resource managers. Next, we review the human resource management functions. Then, we present topics related to the evolution of human resource management, the globalization of human resource management, and the changing world of the chief human resource executive. We make a distinction among human resource executives, generalists, and specialists, and we discuss the human resource function in organizations of different sizes. Finally, we discuss professionalism and ethics in this dynamic discipline.

HUMAN RESOURCE MANAGEMENT AND THE HUMAN RESOURCE MANAGER

The field of human resource management changed dramatically in recent years, which created a greatly expanded role for the human resource manager. As human resource leaders brainstormed the profession's future, one stated, "Yesterday, the company with access to the most capital or the latest technology had the best competitive advantage. Today, companies that offer products with the highest quality are the ones with a leg up on the competition. But, the only thing that will uphold a company's advantage tomorrow is the caliber of people in the organization."[1] In order to understand this development, we must make a distinction between human resource management and the human resource manager.

Human resource management (HRM) is the utilization of human resources to achieve organizational objectives. Consequently, managers at all levels must concern themselves with human resource management. Basically, through the efforts of others, managers get things done which require effective human resource management. In a manufacturing firm, for instance, the production manager meshes physical and human resources to produce goods in sufficient numbers and quality, the marketing manager works through sales representatives to sell the firm's products, and the finance manager obtains capital and manages investments to ensure sufficient operating funds. These individuals are called *line managers* because they have formal authority and responsibility for achieving the firm's primary objectives. Although involved in human resource management, they are not human resource managers. They are primarily responsible for specific functional areas of the business. Carl Edwards, the convenience store supervisor in Sacramento, California, fully understands the challenges a line manager faces with human resources because he will have to work Friday night if he cannot find a replacement.

A **human resource manager** is an individual who normally acts in an advisory or *staff* capacity, working with other managers to help them deal with human resource matters. In previous editions of this book, the term *personnel manager* denoted the individual who performed staff functions similar to those now performed by the human resource manager. This evolving change in terminology reflects the expanded role of HRM and an increasing awareness that human resources are the key to a successful organization. Although only cosmetic in some instances, this change has been substantive in most cases. Thus, it reflects a new and continually expanding role for the human resource manager. The current functions of many chief human resource managers is epitomized by a senior banking executive who states, "I am now a strategic partner with line management and participate in business decisions which bring human resources perspectives to the general management of the company." Human resource management has moved away from the transactional, paper-pushing, hiring/firing support function it has been and is becoming a bottom-line decision maker. Indeed, the phrase that is used most often is that of a strategic partner.[2] Explains Tim Hattis, senior vice president of human resources for Novell Inc. in San Jose, California, "Being a strategic partner means understanding the business direction of the company, including what the product is, what it's capable of doing, who the typical customers are and how the company is positioned competitively in the marketplace."[3] Thus, the role of the human resource executive is increasingly focused on being a strategic business partner and decision maker.[4]

The human resource manager is primarily responsible for coordinating the management of human resources to help the organization achieve its goals. Jane Kay, former vice president of employee relations for Detroit Edison Company, states, "The human resource manager acts more in an advisory capacity, but should be a catalyst in proposing human relations policies to be implemented by line managers." A senior vice president for American General Life Insurance Company once stated, "The real human resource management game is played by the line manager. The human resource manager's role is to develop policies and programs—the rules of the game—and to function as a catalyst and energizer of the relationship between line management and employees." There is a shared responsibility between line managers and human resource professionals. The distinction between human resource management and the human resource manager is clearly illustrated by the following account:

> Bill Brown, production supervisor for Ajax Manufacturing, has just learned that one of his machine operators has resigned. He immediately calls Sandra

Williams, the human resource manager, and says, "Sandra, I just had a Class A machine operator quit down here. Can you find some qualified people for me to interview?" "Sure Bill," Sandra replies. "I'll send two or three down to you within the week, and you can select the one that best fits your needs."

In this instance, both Bill and Sandra are concerned with accomplishing organizational goals, but from different perspectives. Sandra, as a human resource manager, identifies applicants who meet the criteria specified by Bill. Yet, Bill will make the final decision as to whom is hired because he is responsible for the machine operator's performance. His primary responsibility is production. Hers is human resources. As a human resource manager, Sandra must constantly deal with the many problems related to human resources Bill and the other managers face. Her job is to help them meet the human resource needs of the entire organization. In some firms, her function is also referred to as personnel, employee relations, or industrial relations.

HUMAN RESOURCE MANAGEMENT FUNCTIONS

Today's human resource problems are enormous and appear to be ever expanding. The human resource manager faces a multitude of challenges, ranging from a constantly changing workforce to coping with the ever present scores of government regulations. Because of the critical nature of human resource issues, they are receiving increased attention from upper management. Many report directly to the president or CEO, and others have progressed to the top level.

Human resource managers develop and work through a human resource management system. As Figure 1-1 shows, six functional areas are associated with effective human resource management: human resource planning, recruitment, and selection; human resource development; compensation and benefits; safety and health; employee and labor relations; and human resource research. A major study conducted for the Society for Human Resource Management confirmed these areas essentially constitute the field of human

HRM IN ACTION

—HOW HUMAN RESOURCE MANAGEMENT IS PRACTICED

Sections entitled "HRM In Action" and "HRM Incidents" are included in all chapters. These sections permit you to make decisions about situations that could occur in the real world. They are designed to put you on the spot and let you think through how you would react in typical human resource management situations. "Developing HRM Skills: An Experiential Exercise" (included in all but this chapter) permits students to see how they would react in simulated *real-life* situations. Each exercise enables you to analyze how well you will deal with the subject matter.

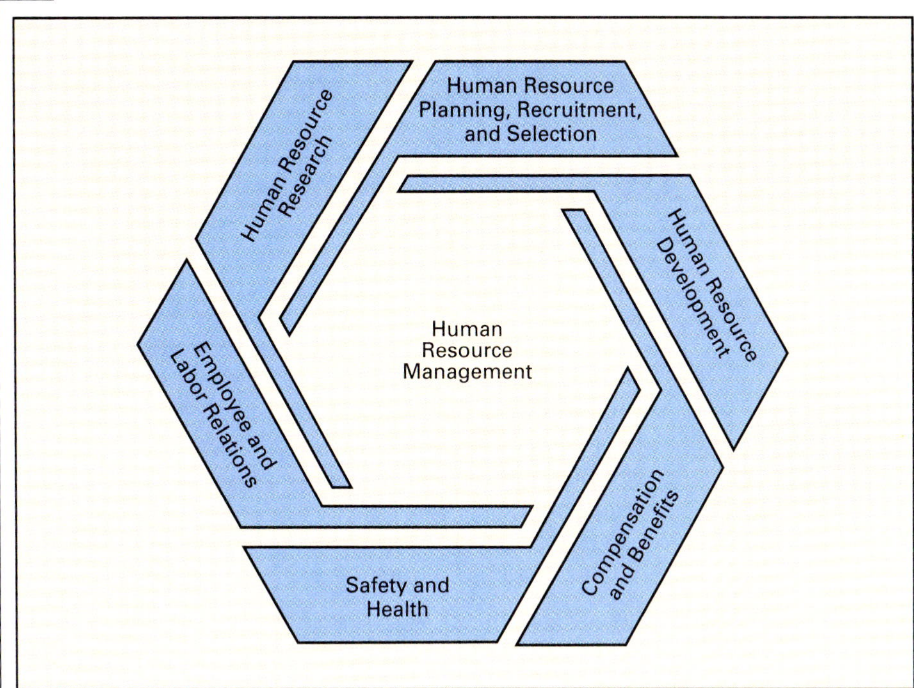

FIGURE 1-1
The Human Resource Management System

resource management.[5] Sound management practices are required for successful performance in each area. We discuss these functions next.

Human Resource Planning, Recruitment, and Selection

An organization must have qualified individuals in specific jobs at specific places and times in order to accomplish its goals. Obtaining such people involves human resource planning, recruitment, and selection.

Human resource planning (HRP) is the process of systematically reviewing human resource requirements to ensure the required numbers of employees, with the required skills, are available when needed. Recruitment is the process of attracting individuals in sufficient numbers and encouraging them to apply for jobs with the organization. Selection is the process through which the organization chooses, from a group of applicants, those individuals best suited both for open positions and for the company. Successful accomplishment of these three tasks is vital if the organization is to accomplish its mission effectively. Chapters 5, 6, and 7 are devoted to these topics.

Human Resource Development

Human resource development (HRD) helps individuals, groups, and the entire organization become more effective. Human resource development is needed because people, jobs, and organizations are always changing. In addition, continuous improvement in processes is mandatory for the firm to remain competitive. The development process should begin when individuals join the firm and continue throughout their careers. Large-scale HRD programs are referred to as organization development (OD). The purpose of OD is to alter the environment within the firm to help employees perform more productively.

Other aspects of HRD include career planning and performance appraisal. Career planning is a process of setting human resource goals and establishing the means to achieve them. Individual careers and organizational needs are not separate and distinct. Organizations should assist employees in career planning so that the needs of both can be satisfied. Through performance appraisal, employees and teams are evaluated to determine how well they are performing their assigned tasks. Performance appraisal affords employees the opportunity to capitalize on their strengths and overcome identified deficiencies, thereby becoming more satisfied and productive employees.

Throughout this text, but especially in the HRD chapters, we use the term operative employees. **Operative employees** are all workers in an organization except managers and professionals, such as engineers, accountants, or professional secretaries. Steel workers, truck drivers, and waiters are examples of operative employees. Chapters 8, 9, 10, and 11 are devoted to human resource development.

Compensation and Benefits

The question of what constitutes a fair day's pay has plagued management, unions, and workers for a long time. A well thought-out compensation system provides employees with adequate and equitable rewards for their contributions to meeting organizational goals. As used in this book, the term compensation includes all rewards individuals receive as a result of their employment. The reward may be one or a combination of the following:

- *Pay:* The money a person receives for performing a job.
- *Benefits:* Additional financial rewards other than base pay include paid vacations, sick leave, holidays, and medical insurance.
- *Nonfinancial rewards:* These are nonmonetary rewards, such as enjoyment of the work performed or a pleasant working environment.

Although compensation includes all rewards shown above, the increasing importance of benefits warrants separate treatment. We discuss many aspects of compensation in Chapter 12 and address benefits in Chapter 13.

Safety and Health

Safety involves protecting employees from injuries caused by work-related accidents. Health refers to the employees' freedom from illness and their general physical and mental well-being. These aspects of the job are important because employees who work in a safe environment and enjoy good health are more likely to be productive and yield long-term benefits to the organization. For this reason, progressive managers have long advocated and implemented adequate safety and health programs. Today, because of federal and state legislation, which reflect societal concerns, most organizations have become attentive to their employees' safety and health.[6] Chapter 14 is devoted to the topic of safety and health.

Employee and Labor Relations

Since 1983, union membership has fallen 6 percent, to 16.6 million, or 15.8 percent of the workforce—the lowest level since the Great Depression. Subtracting government employees, unions represent only 11 percent of the private industry workforce, a figure that by 2000 could plunge to 4 percent or 5 percent.[7] Even so, a business firm is required by law to recognize a union and bargain with it in good faith if the firm's employees want the union to represent them. In the past, this relationship was an accepted way of life for many employers. But according to a survey of labor-management relations, preventing the spread of unionism and developing effective employee relations systems are now more important to some managers than achieving sound collective bargaining results.[8] Chapters 15, 16, 17, and 18 are devoted to the coverage of employee and labor relations issues.

Human Resource Research

Human resource research has been increasingly important, and the trend will likely continue. The human resource researcher's laboratory is the entire work environment. Studies may involve every HRM function. For instance, a study related to recruitment may suggest the type of workers most likely to succeed in a particular firm. Or research on job safety may identify the causes of certain work-related accidents.

The reasons for problems such as excessive absenteeism or too many grievances may not be readily apparent. When such problems occur, human resource research can shed light on their causes. In Sweden, the labor force is highly educated and well trained. But the country's high income tax rates reduce the motivational power of pay, even incentive type pay. Research at Sweden's Volvo factory revealed the Swedes objected to the grime of the typical automobile factory. The close supervision and machine-paced work on the assembly lines were also sore points. So Volvo built more pleasant and colorful factories, where teams of workers were allowed largely to manage themselves. Each team assembles a substantial portion of a car, which is moved from area to area. In the new Volvo plants, morale and productivity are better and absenteeism is lower than in the older factories.[9] Human resource research is clearly an important key to developing the most productive and satisfied workforce possible. As you will see in Chapter 19, numerous quantitative methods are used in human resource research.

Interrelationships of HRM Functions

The functional areas of HRM are not separate and distinct; they are highly interrelated. Management must recognize decisions in one area will affect other areas. For instance, a firm that emphasizes recruiting and training of a sales force while neglecting to provide adequate compensation is wasting time, effort, and money. In addition, if management is truly concerned about employee welfare, it must ensure a safe and healthy work environment. An added benefit may be keeping the firm union free. The interrelationships among the six HRM functional areas will become more obvious as we address each topic in greater detail.

THE EVOLUTION OF HUMAN RESOURCE MANAGEMENT

One of the major changes in business in recent years has been the increased respect and responsibility afforded human resource professionals.[10] In fact, in 1990, the job of human resource manager was identified as one of fifteen fast-track careers.[11] Human resource managers are now expected to provide the direction necessary to meet the many human resource problems and challenges that continue to arise. For example, within the next decade, the content of more than half of all existing jobs is likely to change, and 30 percent of all existing jobs will be eliminated by technological advances.[12] When robots were introduced in the automobile industry, there was a major decrease in the demand for workers who welded or painted, but their introduction created a demand for technicians who could program, install, and service the robots.[13] Human resource professionals will have to respond positively to such trends while keeping an alert eye on their organizations' overall goals.

Not many decades ago people engaged in human resource work had titles such as *welfare secretary* and *employment clerk.* Their duties were rather restrictive and often dealt only with such items as workers' wages, minor medical problems, recreation, and housing.[14] *Personnel,* as human resources was most commonly called, was generally held in low esteem as a profession, and its organizational position was typically near the bottom of the hierarchy. "In the past," says John L. Quigley, former vice president administration for the Dr Pepper/7-Up Companies, Inc., "the personnel executive was the 'glad hander' or 'back slapper' who kept morale up in a company by running the company picnic, handling the United Fund drive, and making sure the recreation program went off well." Those days are over in most organizations. The human resource manager's position is no longer a *retirement* position given to managers who cannot perform adequately anywhere else in the organization. Firms have now learned that the human resource department can have a major impact on the organization's overall effectiveness and profitability.

Because of the impact that human resource professionals have on organizational success, careers in human resources are projected to increase by 22 percent by the year 2000. Salaries are also advancing.[15] As might be expected, salaries of corporate human resource executives depend largely on the size of the organizations employing them. The average salary for top executive human resource managers at firms with over 10,000 employees was $196,000, including benefits and incentives. The average salary of human resource managers in firms with between 1,300 and 3,500 employees was $113,000 when benefits and incentives were added to the base salary. For firms with under 250 employees, the salary was $109,000 with benefits and incentives included.

The type of work performed also has a major effect on the pay levels in large companies. Labor relations and international HR enjoy the highest salaries while development and employee relations are the lowest.

Education evidently is a major factor in determining the salaries for human resource positions. According to one survey, the median income for all human resource practitioners is 24 percent higher if the employee has earned a bachelor's degree and 10 percent higher still if the employee holds a graduate degree. Length of experience also affects the income of human resource practitioners.[16]

A GLOBAL PERSPECTIVE

Twenty years ago many U.S. multinational corporations had operations in Canada but not in many other countries. Today most international corporations are becoming truly global. American companies still regularly do business in Canada, but increasingly they are doing business in Hong Kong, Singapore, Japan, the United Kingdom, France, and Germany, to name a few. More and more U.S. multinational corporations are showing interest in doing business in former Eastern Bloc countries. This interdependence of national economies has created a global marketplace in which worldwide products and services are bought and sold. The globalization of the marketplace has created special challenges for human resource professionals in the decade of the 1990s.[17]

Among the most serious of the human resource challenges in the global job marketplace is the growing mismatch between emerging jobs requiring higher level skills, and the skill levels of the people available to fill them. In the case of American multinationals, human resource management is becoming an even greater challenge because, according to the Commission on Workforce Quality and Labor Market Efficiency, "Unless government and business undertake a vast increase in their investment in human capital, U.S. companies will not be able to hire the types of workers they need to compete in international markets."[18] It may well be time for U.S. businesses and education to join forces to prepare children and the workforce to meet the demands of the future. Although skills are declining, the demand for those skills has never been greater. To compete in the new worldwide marketplace, the U.S. economy must be based on high technology industry and the U.S. worker, therefore, requires higher skill levels. The Secretary of Labor's Commission on Achieving Necessary Skills (SCANS) was established to study the relationship between education and work. According to the Commission, just as a consumer expects that products will work, a business should expect someone coming out of school is prepared to work. In order to examine these kinds of issues and submit recommendations, the Society for Human Resource Management created a task force. According to these human resource professionals, "To succeed as a nation, the U.S. must prepare their children to compete in a world economy." The United States must also prepare 27 million citizens who are illiterate and retain 30 million who are already employed.[19]

Coping with human resource problems, such as educational and skills limitations of the workforce, is very complex. American human resource professionals must cope with global problems by educating or reeducating much of the American labor force, by carefully reviewing the human resource situation in the host country, by planning to cope with the limitations of the labor situation, and by taking advantage of the strengths of the host country's labor force.

The global human resources role is, and should be, a natural extension of the positive orientation toward global human resource management and the recognition of the strategic role that must play. Melissa DeCrane of the Corporate Resources Group believes that international expertise is a very real asset for human resources people because every company is challenged by the global marketplace. However, Lauren O'Leary of Baxter World Trade Corporation is not so sure that human resource management is becoming global. She believes that human resource people need to be more aware of international human resource issues, but their focus is usually domestic.[20] Effectively dealing with global human resource issues is essential for success in the global marketplace. "A Global Perspective" is presented in each chapter.

THE CHANGING WORLD OF THE CHIEF HUMAN RESOURCE EXECUTIVE

The work of the chief human resource executive is affected greatly by top management's human resource priorities, and the major changes occurring in management responsibilities and organizational relationships. There is a growing recognition that people are the greatest competitive weapon. This attitude is changing dramatically the role of human resources in U.S. companies. As a result, the HR function ten years from now will likely be very different from the one that existed a decade ago.[21] Jim Alef, executive vice president and head of human resources for First Chicago Corporation in Chicago, Illinois, stated, "If you take a look at the sources of sustainable, competitive advantage during the last decade, the only one that has endured has been the quality of the people who work for you."[22] These individuals are experiencing a dramatic pace of change in business. Change brings with it new buzzwords, which are having a profound impact on the way individuals work. *Mobility, empowerment, teams, virtual offices, telecommuting, downsizings, restructuring, increased global competition, technological advances, contingency,* and *reengineering,* to name but a few, have made the job of the human resource professionals more complex than ever before. Consider Table 1-1, which lists some of the *OUTs* and *INs* of human resources, and you will have a brief insight into why the profession itself is in a great deal of flux.[23] The only thing certain is that the job of human resource professional is continuously evolving. Yesterday's solutions may not be sufficient for today's challenges.

HUMAN RESOURCE EXECUTIVES, GENERALISTS, AND SPECIALISTS

There are various classifications within the human resource profession you need to recognize and understand. Among them are human resource executives, generalists, and specialists. An **executive** is a top-level manager who reports directly to the corporation's chief executive officer (CEO) or to the head of a major division. A

Change has made the job of the human resource professionals more complex than ever before.

TABLE 1-1
What the Future Holds: A List of Trends That Will Affect How Work Is Done in the Future

OUT:	Job titles and labels such as "employee," "manager," "staff," and "professional."
IN:	Everyone a business person, an 'owner' of a complete business process, president of his/her job.
OUT:	Chain-of-command, reporting relationships, department, function, turf, sign-off, work as imposed-from-above tasks.
IN:	Self-management, responsiveness, proactivity, initiative, collaboration, egalitarianism, self-reliance, standards of excellence, personal responsibility, work as collection of self-initiated projects and teams.
OUT:	Stability, order, predictability, structure, better-safe-than-sorry.
IN:	Flux, disorder, ambiguity, risk, better sorry-than-safe.
OUT:	Good citizenship—show up, good soldier, 9-to-5 in cubicle, don't make waves, wait for someone else to decide your fate, work in same organization for thirty years, retire with gold watch.
IN:	Make a difference—add value, challenge the process, four hours or eighteen hours per day, job site wherever the action is, learn from mistakes, career mobility and fluidity, work your tail off and be intensely loyal to Company X for one year or ten years, and then move on to Company Y a better, more marketable person.

Source: Adapted from Oren Harari, "Back to the Future of Work," *Management Review* 82 (September 1993): 35.

generalist, who often is an executive, performs tasks in various human resource-related areas. The generalist is involved in several, or all, of the six human resource management functions. A **specialist** may be a human resource executive, manager, or nonmanager who is typically concerned with only one of the six functional areas of human resource management. Figure 1-2 helps clarify these distinctions.

The vice president of industrial relations shown in Figure 1-2 specializes primarily in union-related matters. This person is both an executive and a specialist. The human resource vice president is both an executive and a generalist, having responsibility for a wide variety of functions. The manager of compensation and benefits is a specialist, as is the benefits analyst. Whereas an executive is identified by position level in the organization, generalists and specialists are distinguished by their positions' breadth of responsibility.

The distinction between generalists and specialists should be even clearer after studying the Monsanto example in Figure 1-3. It lists the type of general work assignments at various levels in the organization for both generalists and specialists. Also interesting are the "two bits of advice" Monsanto gives generalists and specialists. Career development at the departmental and corporate levels varies considerably. The lines between these assignments for generalists and specialists blur at times, and the career paths for both may not always be "up."

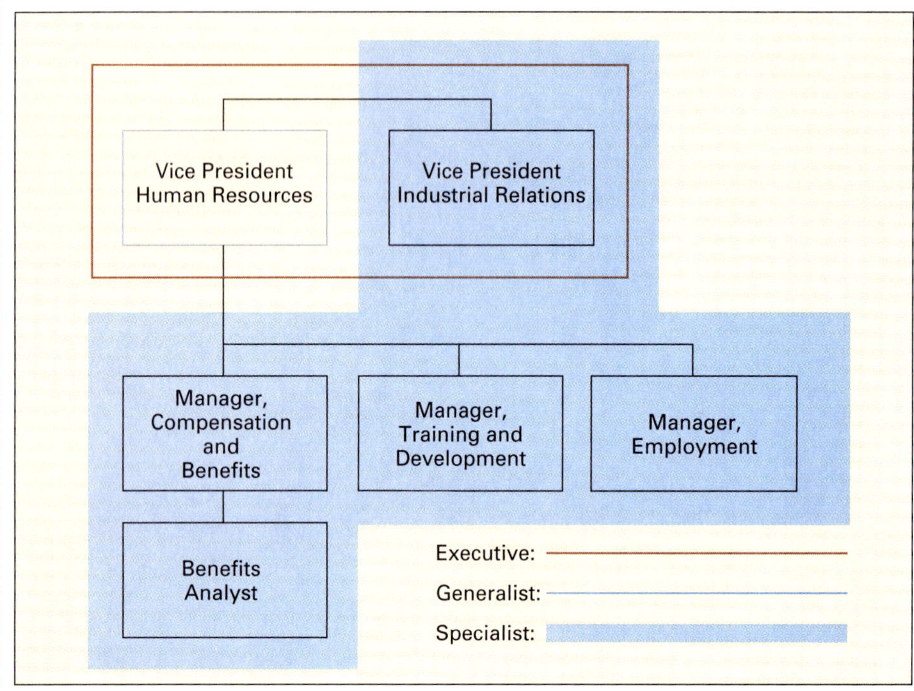

FIGURE 1-2
Human Resource Executives, Generalists, and Specialists

THE HUMAN RESOURCE FUNCTION IN ORGANIZATIONS OF VARIOUS SIZES

As firms grow and become more complex, the human resource function becomes more complex and its function achieves greater importance. The basic purpose of human resource management remains the same, but the approach followed in accomplishing its objectives often changes.

Small businesses seldom have a formal human resource unit and HRM specialists, as Figure 1-4 shows. Rather, other managers handle human resource functions. The focus of their activities is generally on hiring and retaining capable employees.

Some aspects of the human resource function may actually be more significant in smaller firms than in larger ones. For instance, if the owner of a small business hires her first and only full-time salesperson, and this individual promptly alienates the firm's customers, the business might actually fail. In a larger firm, such an error would be must less devastating. As a firm grows, a separate staff function may be required to coordinate human resource activities. In a larger firm, the person chosen to do so will be expected to handle most of the human resource activities, as Figure 1-5 implies. For a medium-sized firm, there is little specialization. A secretary may be available to handle correspondence, but the human resource manager is essentially the entire department.

When the firm's human resource function becomes too much for one person to handle, separate sections often are created and placed under a human resource manager. These sections will typically perform tasks involv-

Starting Assignment

Specialist	**Generalist**
Work for a supervisor in an area such as labor relations, employment, training, or benefits. This would be at a larger location, where the function is broken down into areas of specialty.	Work for a supervisor or superintendent in several areas. You might be responsible for training, communications, employment, benefits, and safety. This would be at a smaller location with two or three personnel professionals on the staff.

Later Assignments

Specialist	**Generalist**
Manage one or two areas of responsibility, such as labor relations, training, and development, a combination of employment and benefits. Again, this would be at a larger location.	Manage the total human resource function: For a sub-unit within the location (such as for the maintenance department, or for a geographic area within the location), for a smaller Monsanto location, or for a larger location.

Operating Company/Staff Department

Specialist	**Generalist**
Manage one or two functions, such as human resource planning, compensation, recruiting, or an entire company or staff department.	Manage the total human resource function for a sub-unit within a company (e.g., a division) or for the entire company or staff department.

Corporate

Specialist	**Generalist**
Work in or manage an entire area of expertise for the corporation, such as labor relations, equal employment opportunity, development, or benefits.	Manage the total corporate human resource function.

Two bits of advice:

- Do not get hung up on whether you begin your career as a specialist or generalist. The lines between generalist and specialist are not as neat as the chart would indicate. For example, as an employment "specialist," you would become involved daily with questions of labor relations, compensation, human resource planning, equal employment policy, and much more! Or as a small plant "generalist," you would have to learn the basics of several specialties. Also, the overwhelming odds are you will get both types of exposure—specialist and generalist—in your career.
- Career development will not always be "up." It's to the professional's advantage to get as much experience and exposure as possible—and many times, this will mean lateral moves into different areas of specialty.

FIGURE 1-3 Career Development at Monsanto

Source: Used with the permission of the Monsanto Company.

HRM IN ACTION

—A DEAD-END JOB?

"Scotty, I know that you are the human resource manager, and I really appreciate your concern for my career, but the position you are offering me as assistant human resource director is, in my opinion, a dead-end job. Recruiters just find employees to fill vacant positions. They don't get involved in other areas of the company, so my achievements could go unnoticed, and I'd be stuck there forever. Also I have heard top management only cares about marketing, production, and finance, not human resources. I appreciate the thought, Scotty, but don't put me in a dead-end job."

How should Scotty respond?

ing human resource development, compensation and benefits, employment, safety and health, and labor relations, as depicted in Figure 1-6.

In still larger firms, the human resource function takes on even more responsibility, permitting even greater specialization. Figure 1-7, an organizational chart for Champion International Corporation, illustrates this condi-

FIGURE 1-4
The Human Resource Function in a Small Business

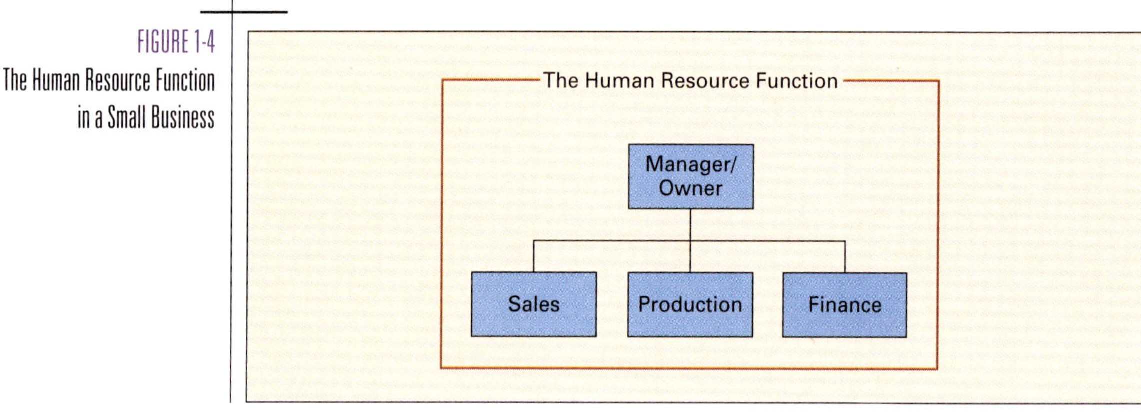

FIGURE 1-5
The Human Resource Function in a Medium-Sized Business

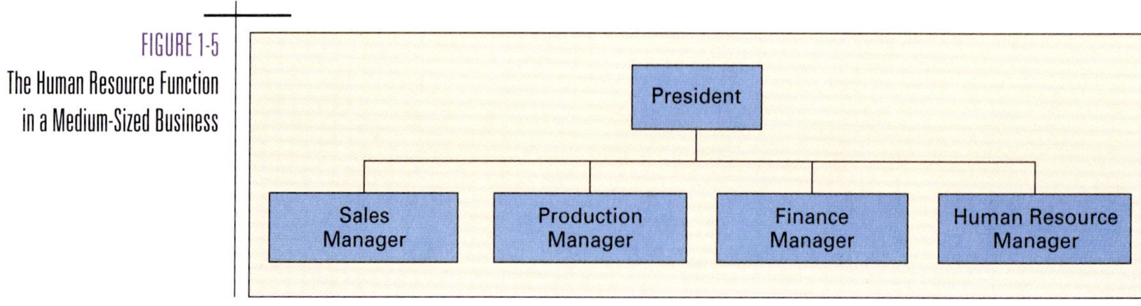

FIGURE 1-6
The Human Resource Functions in a Medium-Large-Sized Firm

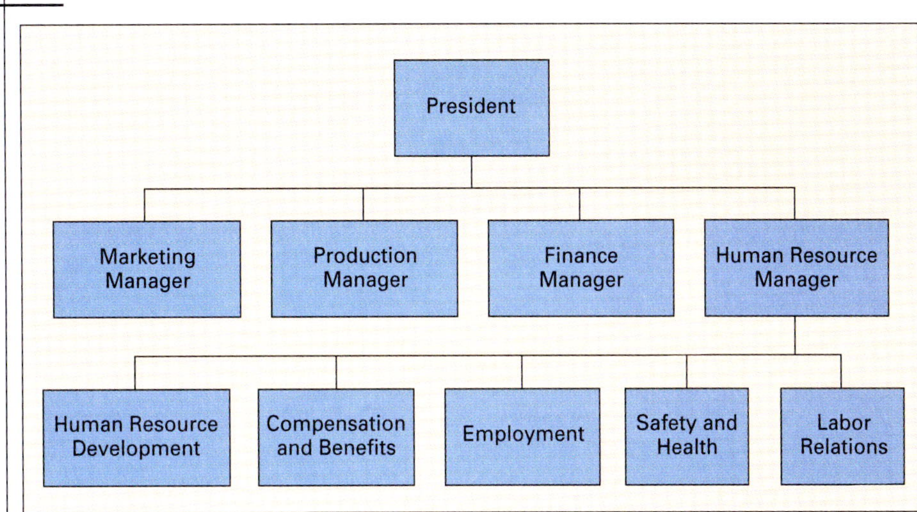

tion. The unit responsible for compensation, for example, will most likely include some specialists who concentrate on hourly wages and others who devote their time to salary administration. The employee relations vice president works closely with top management in formulating corporate policy.

FIGURE 1-7
The Employee Relations Organization Champion International Corporation

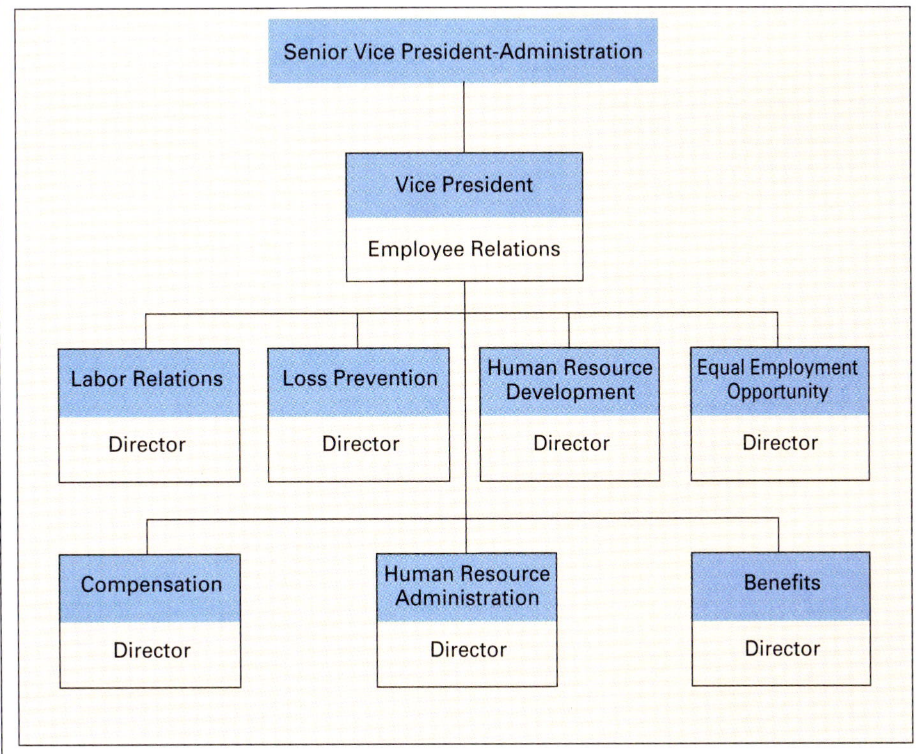

Source: Used with permission of Champion International Corporation.

Table 1-2 outlines the duties and responsibilities of Champion's employee relations executive. As you can see, the scope of such a position is quite broad, ranging from coordinating, recommending, and implementing plans to auditing performance.

PROFESSIONALIZATION OF HUMAN RESOURCE MANAGEMENT

A **profession** is characterized by the existence of a common body of knowledge and a procedure for certifying members of the profession. Performance standards are established by members of the profession (self-regulation) rather than by outsiders. Most professions also have effective representative organizations that permit members to exchange ideas of mutual concern. These characteristics apply to the field of human resources, and several well-known organizations serve the profession. Among the more prominent are the Society for Human Resource Management, the Human Resource Certification Institute, the American Society for Training and Development, the American Compensation Association, the National Human Resources Association, and the International Personnel Management Association.

Society for Human Resource Management

The largest national professional organization for individuals involved in all areas of human resource management is the Society of Human Resource Management (SHRM), which was formerly called the American Society for Personnel Administration (ASPA). The name change, which became official in 1990, reflects the increasingly important role human resource manage-

TABLE 1-2
Champion International Corporation
Corporate Employee Relations

Charter:

To provide operating and staff management with professional centralized services that will assure the competence and continuity of the company's human resources

Scope:

- To provide expertise and centralized services
- To coordinate plans, recommendations, implementation, and review of corporate projects
- To recommend general policies
- To establish functional procedures for designated activities
- To audit performance and compliance with general policies and procedures for designated activities

Objectives:

- To provide direction and support to each functional director and his or her department
- To require quality and excellence in total performance of function
- To assure that professional positions are occupied by competent people who can and do respond to the company's needs and requirements

Source: Used with permission of Champion International Corporation.

ment plays in the overall bottom line of organizations. The basic goals of the society include defining, maintaining, and improving standards of excellence in the practice of human resource management. Membership consists of 55,000 individuals; there are currently more than 437 local chapters and numerous student chapters on university campuses across the country.[24]

Human Resource Certification Institute

One of the more significant developments in the field of HRM has been the establishment of the Human Resource Certification Institute (HRCI), formerly the Personnel Accreditation Institute (PAI), an affiliate of SHRM.[25] Founded in 1976, HRCI's goal is to recognize human resource professionals through a certification program.[26] This program encourages human resource professionals to update their knowledge and skills continuously. Certification indicates they have mastered a validated common body of knowledge. The advantages of human resource certification were outlined a number of years ago by a former national president of ASPA, Wiley Beavers.

> First, we would benefit at the college and university level. The development of the body of knowledge required for successful practice in the various areas of personnel would provide invaluable assistance in curricula design. The breakdown of the field into its specialties would also allow students to focus on career directions earlier in their education.
>
> Second, young practitioners would have sound guidelines and information covering areas in which they should be boning up and could avoid the mistakes many of us older types make.
>
> Third, senior practitioners would be encouraged to update their knowledge. (Don't know how many of them will be interested in certification. There will be an appreciable reaction along the lines of: "I don't need to take tests to prove I know what I'm doing. I have already proven it by the job I'm doing." And they will be right in about 50 percent of the cases.)[27]

American Society for Training and Development

Founded in 1944, the American Society for Training and Development (ASTD) has grown to become the largest specialized professional organization in human resources. Its membership exceeds 55,000, and it has more than 155 local chapters.[28] The membership consists of individuals who are concerned specifically with training and development. The society publishes *Training and Development,* a monthly journal, to encourage its members to remain current in the field.

American Compensation Association

The American Compensation Association (ACA) was founded in 1955 and currently has a membership that exceeds 15,000.[29] The ACA consists of managerial and human resource professionals who are responsible for the establishment, execution, administration, or application of compensation practices and policies in their organizations. The ACA's quarterly journal, which contains information related to compensation issues, is the *ACA Journal.*

National Human Resources Association

Founded in 1950, the National Human Resources Association (NHRA), formerly the International Association for Personnel Women (IAPW), was established to expand and improve the professionalism of women in human resource management. Its membership consists of human resource executives in business, industry, education, and government. The NHRA has approximately 1,500 members.[30]

International Personnel Management Association

The International Personnel Management Association (IPMA) was founded in 1973 and currently has more than 6,500 members. This organization seeks to improve human resource practices by providing testing services, an advisory service, conferences, professional development programs, research, and publications. It sponsors seminars and workshops on various phases of public human resource administration. The organization's journal, *Public Personnel Management,* is published quarterly for those involved in public agency human resource administration.[31]

ETHICS AND HUMAN RESOURCE MANAGEMENT

Professionalization of human resource management created the need for a uniform code of ethics. **Ethics** is the discipline dealing with what is good and bad, or right and wrong, or with moral duty and obligation. According to one survey, more companies in the United States are stressing ethical conduct in business. One major reason for this change is employees are better educated and well versed in the realities of the workplace.[32] Apparently, the attitude has changed from "Should we be doing something in business ethics?" to "What should we be doing in business ethics?"[33] Every day, individuals working in human resources must make decisions having ethical implications. Ethical dilemmas, such as whether a manager should recommend against a woman applicant for employment strictly because she will be working exclusively with men, occur frequently and must be correctly addressed. These issues must be dealt with on the basis of what is ethically correct, not just from the standpoint of what will most benefit the organization in the short run.

There are many kinds of ethical codes, and most professions have their own. An example is SHRM's Code of Ethics shown in Figure 1-8. A growing number of firms are establishing ethical codes and communicating these codes to all employees.[34] Few of the numerous codes that exist in our society conflict in principle. They vary primarily in the extent to which they are applied under particular circumstances. It is vitally important that the human resource manager understand those practices which are unacceptable and make every attempt to act ethically in dealing with others.

SCOPE OF THIS BOOK

Effective human resource management is crucial to every organization's success. In order to be effective, managers must understand and competently practice human resource management. We designed this human resource management book to give you the following:

FIGURE 1-8
SHRM Code of Ethics

As a member of the Society for Human Resource Management, I pledge myself to:

- Maintain the highest standards of professional and personal conduct.
- Strive for personal growth in the field of human resource management.
- Support the Society's goals and objectives for developing the human resource management profession.
- Encourage my employer to make the fair and equitable treatment of all employees a primary concern.
- Strive to make my employer profitable both in monetary terms and through the support and encouragement of effective employment practices.
- Instill in the employees and the public a sense of confidence about the conduct and intentions of my employer.
- Maintain loyalty to my employer and pursue its objectives in the ways that are consistent with the public interest.
- Uphold all laws and regulations relating to my employer's activities.
- Refrain from using my official positions, either regular or volunteer, to secure special privilege, gain or benefit for myself.
- Maintain the confidentiality of privileged information.
- Improve public understanding of the role of human resource management.

This Code of Ethics for members of the Society for Human Resource Management has been adopted to promote and maintain the highest standards of personal conduct and professional standards among its members. Adherence to this code is required for membership in the Society and serves to assure public confidence in the integrity and service of human resource management professionals.

Source: Reprinted from *Who's Who in HR 1992 Directory,* 4. Copyright 1992, The Society for Human Resource Management, Alexandria, Virginia.

- An insight into the role of human resource management in today's organizations.
- An understanding of human resource planning, recruitment, and selection.
- An awareness of the importance of human resource development.
- An appreciation of how compensation and benefits programs are formulated and administered.
- An understanding of safety and health factors as they affect a firm's profitability.
- An opportunity to view employee and labor relations from both unionized and union-free standpoints.
- An understanding of the role of research in human resource management.

- An appreciation of the global dimension of human resource management.

Students often question whether the content of a book corresponds to the realities of the business world. In writing and revising this book, we have drawn heavily on the comments, observations, and experiences of human resource practitioners as well as our own extensive research efforts. We cite the human resource practices of leading business organizations to illustrate how theory can be applied in the real world. Our intent is to enable you to experience human resource management in action.

This book is organized under seven parts as shown in Figure 1-9; combined, they provide a comprehensive view of human resource management. As you read this book, we hope you will be stimulated to increase your knowledge in this rapidly changing, expanding, and challenging field.

FIGURE 1-9
Organization of This Book

SUMMARY

Human resource management (HRM) is the utilization of the firm's human resources to achieve organizational goals. Human resource managers normally act in an advisory (staff) capacity, working with other managers regarding human resource matters. Human resource managers have primary responsibility of coordinating the firm's human resource actions through a well-conceived human resource management system that embraces the six functional areas of effective human resource management: human resource planning, recruitment, and selection; human resource development; compensation and benefits; safety and health; employee and labor relations; and human resource research.

An organization must have qualified individuals available at specific places and times to accomplish its goals. Among the tasks involved in accomplishing this objective are human resource planning, recruitment, and selection.

Human resource development (HRD) is designed to assist individuals, groups, and the entire organization in becoming more effective. These programs are needed because people, jobs, and organizations are always changing. Development should begin when individuals join a firm and continue throughout their careers. Large-scale HRD programs are referred to as organizational development (OD). Other aspects of HRD are career planning and development and performance appraisal.

An effective compensation and benefits system rewards employees adequately and equitably for their contributions to the organization. As used in this book, the term compensation includes all rewards that individuals receive as a result of their employment.

Safety involves protecting employees from injuries caused by work-related accidents. Health refers to employees' freedom from illness and their general physical and mental well-being.

A business firm is required by law to recognize a union and bargain with it in good faith if the firm's employees want the union to represent them. However, union-free firms typically strive to satisfy their employees' work-related needs in order to make union representation unnecessary for individuals to achieve their personal goals.

Every human resource management function needs effective research. This need is particularly strong today because of the rapid changes taking place in the HRM field.

Within the human resource profession are executives, generalists, and specialists. Executives are top-level managers who report directly to the corporation's CEO or to the head of a major division. A generalist, who often is an executive, performs tasks in many human resource-related areas. A specialist may be an executive, a manager, or a nonmanager who is typically concerned with only one of the six functional areas of HRM.

As firms grow and become more complex, changes are required in the way human resource functions are implemented. The basic purpose of human resource management remains the same, but the approach followed in accomplishing its objectives often changes.

A profession is characterized by the existence of a common body of knowledge and a procedure for certifying members of the profession. Among the more prominent professional organizations in the field of human resources are the Society for Human Resource Management, the Human Resource Certification Institute, the American Society for Training and Development, the American Compensation Association, the National Human Resources Association, and the International Personnel Management Association.

Professionalization of human resource management created a need for a uniform code of ethics. Individuals working in human resources must constantly make decisions having ethical implications. Most professions, organizations, and individuals subscribe to ethical codes of one type or another.

QUESTIONS FOR REVIEW

1. Justify the statement "All managers are involved in human resource management."
2. Distinguish between human resource management and the human resource manager.
3. What human resource management functions must be performed regardless of the organization's size?
4. By definition and example distinguish among human resource executives, generalists, and specialists.
5. How does implementing human resource functions change as a firm grows? Briefly describe each stage of the development.
6. Define profession. Do you believe that the field

of human resource management is a profession? Explain your answer.

7. Define ethics. Why is ethics important to the field of human resource management?

HRM SIMULATION

Available for use with your text is the *Human Resource Management Simulation* by Jerald R. Smith and Peggy A. Golden. In this simulation you will be acting as the human resource director (or a general manager) of a moderate size organization, making the types of decisions required of a modern human resource department. The simulation gives life to the text material. You will not only read about the decisions that HR people make, but you will also make those decisions.

You will be organized into teams and implement your HR recommendations in an ongoing simulation. There is no single winning strategy! Instead, there are many successful strategies depending on the specific plans your team makes and the diligence with which you implement them. You will make decisions in the following four categories: overall strategy, human resource operating decisions, financial, and behavioral. Have fun!

ABC VIDEO CASE

REVOLUTION AT WORK: SATURN TAPE 1, NUMBER 1

In the last eleven years, General Motors (GM) laid off nearly 80,000 workers and closed fifty plants. Cars, surroundings, jobs, and attitudes changed because workers were sent around the world to see other companies' secrets of success. After eight years and nearly four billion dollars expended to create a better relationship between management and labor, GM got rid of the symbols that separated the two camps. No longer is the white shirt and tie a symbol of authority. Teams were created that decided what parts to buy, whom to hire, and when to stop production if something did not look quite right. "We begin by assuming that they do want to do a good job," said Skip LeFauve, President, Saturn Corporation. "That they really do care about what they are doing. And it is the leadership's job to show them what it is they need to do in order to be successful."

Employees work on salary, with bonuses linked to productivity. Gone are the "old-world" concepts of hourly wages and time clocks. For the first time in American automotive history, workers and managers are partners. Workers are strongly encouraged to take courses that foster the team spirit by making them rely on each other. In addition, workers are paid to spend 5 percent of their time taking classes in everything from "Listening and Assertion" to "Managing Conflict." "It is the combination of the social skills and the technical skills that make the whole Saturn team member," said LeFauve.

HRM INCIDENT 1

—A DAY TO REMEMBER

The day was one of the happiest in Ed Beaver's life. He had been told he was being promoted to corporate vice president for human resources from his present position as human resource manager for his firm's large New York plant. As he leaned back in his office chair, he felt a deep sense of accomplishment. He thought back to the day fifteen years earlier when, fresh out of college, he had joined Duncan Foods as an assistant compensation specialist.

He had always wanted to be in human resources, but he got his degree in business management because the university did not have a human resource curriculum. Ed remembered how tense he was when he arrived at work that first day. College graduates were rarely given the opportunity to start work directly in human resources in those days, and he was the youngest employee in the department.

Ed learned his job well, and the older workers quickly accepted him. Three years later he was promoted to the position of compensation manager. Immediately after the promotion he was given the task of designing a new pay system for operative employees. As he remembers, "Designing the system wasn't difficult. Convincing the employees the new system was better than the old one was the real chore." But he overcame that obstacle.

A few years later Ed moved up again. He was chosen to become the new human resource manager for a small Duncan plant outside Chicago. The move required a major adjustment for his family. At the time Ed's wife remarked, "I sure hated to move in the middle of the school year. And we'd just begun to enjoy our new house." Ed was able to find another house that the family came to like just as well, and the children adjusted quickly. The job was certainly no bed of roses. Six months after Ed arrived he led negotiations for a new union contract. He worked night and day for months to develop a contract acceptable to the company and the union. Successful signing of the new agreement was one of his most satisfying experiences.

Four years later Ed was asked to accept the position of human resource manager for the large New York plant, which employed five times as many workers as the Chicago plant and had many different types of problems. After a family discussion, the Beavers were off to new adventures in the Big Apple.

Now Ed's reminiscing had come to an end. He began to realize the challenge that the new job presented to him. As vice president of human resources for Duncan Foods, he would be responsible for the human resource management activities for fifty plants and warehouses employing 13,000 people. What an overwhelming responsibility he faced! Human resource management had changed greatly during the previous fifteen years, and the rate of change seemed to be accelerating. Ed wondered about these problems and the role he would play in solving them as the new vice president for human resources.

Questions

1. Trace Ed's progression to vice president of human resources. Do you believe this progression qualifies him for the job?
2. What problems do you imagine Ed will face in his new role that he did not have to deal with as plant human resource manager?
3. What future challenges do you think Ed will confront in the field of human resources?

HRM INCIDENT 2

—LEARN WHAT THEY REALLY WANT

Marsha Smith was exceptionally happy the day she received word of her appointment as assistant human resource director at Nelson Electronics in Boise, Idaho. Marsha had joined the company as a recruiter three years earlier. Her degree from the University of Missouri was in human resource management, and she had four years' experience as a human resource specialist with Nelson Electronics.

As she walked to her office, she thought about how much she had learned while working as a recruiter. During her first year with Nelson, she went on a recruiting trip to Southern Idaho College, but found its placement director was extremely angry with her company. She was visibly upset when the placement director said, "If you expect to recruit any of our students, you people at Nelson had better get your act together." When she questioned the placement director, she learned that a previous recruiter had failed to show up for a full afternoon of scheduled interviews with Southern's students. Marsha's trip ended amicably, though, and she eventually recruited a number of excellent employees from the college.

She learned another important lesson when the production manager asked for some help. "I need you to find an experienced quality control inspector," he said. "I want to make sure the person has a degree in statistics. Beyond that, you decide on the qualifications." Marsha advertised the position and checked through dozens of resumes in search of the right person. She sent each promising applicant to the production manager. This process went on for six months with the production manager giving various obscure reasons for not hiring any of the applicants. Finally, the production manager called Marsha and said, "I just hired a QC person. He has a degree in history, but he seems eager. Besides, he was willing to work for only $1,500 a month."

Marsha learned more with each passing day. She felt that one of her greatest accomplishments was improving the firm's minority recruitment program. She was able to do so, in part, because one of her closest friends in school had become a leader in the Black Chamber of Commerce. With his advice, she was able to develop a recruiting program to attract blacks to Nelson Electronics.

As Marsha began to clean out her desk, she suddenly realized the learning process was really just beginning. As assistant human resource director, she would be responsible not only for matters related to recruiting, but also for all aspects of human resource management. It was a little scary, but she felt ready.

Questions

1. What lessons can be learned from each of the three situations described?
2. How will the problems Marsha faces as an assistant human resource director differ from those she handled as a recruiter?

NOTES

1. Shari Caudron, "HR Leaders Brainstorm the Profession's Future," *Personnel Journal* 73 (August 1994): 54.

2. Ibid.

3. Ibid.

4. Ibid., 54–62.

5. Walter W. Tornow, Janis S. Houston, and Walter C. Borman, "An Evaluation of the Body-of-Knowledge," *Personnel Administrator* 34 (June 1989): 140.

6. The key law in the area of health and safety is the Occupational Safety and Health Act of 1970. This act is discussed in Chapter 14.

7. Aaron Bernstein, "Why America Needs Unions But Not the Kind It Has Now," *Business Week* (May 23, 1994): 70.

8. Alexander B. Trowbridge, "A Management Look at Labor Relations," in *Unions in Transition* (San Francisco: ICS Press, 1988): 414.

9. Jonathan Kapstein and John Hoerr, "Volvo's Radically New Plant: The Death of the Assembly Line?" *Business Week* (August 28, 1989): 92–93.

10. Alexander B. Trowbridge, "A Management Look," 414.

11. Michele Morris, "15 Fast-Track Careers," *Money* (June 1990): 122.

12. Eric G. Flamholtz, Yvonne Randle, and Sonja Sackmann, "Personnel Management: The Tenor of Today," *Personnel Journal* 66 (June 1987): 64.

13. Elizabeth McGregor, "Emerging Careers," *Occupational Outlook Quarterly* 34 (Fall 1990): 22.

14. Henry Eibirt, "The Development of Personnel Management in the United States," *Business History Review* 33 (August 1969): 348–349.

15. Charlene Marmer Solomon, "Managing the HR Career of the 90's," *Personnel Journal* 73 (June 1994): 64.

16. Steven Langer, "Human Resources: Who Makes What?" *Personnel Journal* 69 (February 1990): 106.

17. Mike Fergus, "Employees on the Move," *HRMagazine* 36 (May 1990): 44.

18. Stephen B. Wildstrom, "A Failing Grade for the American Workforce," *Business Week* (September 11, 1989): 22.

19. Michael J. Lotito, "A Call to Action for U.S. Business and Education," *Employment Relations Today* (Winter 1992/1993): 379–387.

20. Stephenie Overman, "Is HR a Weak Link in the Global Chain?" *HRMagazine* 38 (June 1994): 67–68.

21. Shari Caudron, "HR Leaders Brainstorm the Profession's Future," 54.

22. Ibid.

23. Charlene Marmer Solomon, "Managing the HR Career of the 90's," ibid.

24. Carol A. Schwartz and Rebecca L. Turner (eds.), *Encyclopedia of Associations,* 29th ed., vol. 1: National Organizations of the United States, part 1 (Detroit: Gale Research Company, 1995): 324.

25. Juanita F. Perry, "Accredited Professionals Are Better Prepared," *Personnel Administrator* 30 (December 1985): 48.

26. Details of the HRCI are shown in the Appendix to this chapter.

27. Wiley Beavers, "Accreditation: What Do We Need That For?" *Personnel Administrator* 18 (November 1975): 39–41.

28. Carol A. Schwartz and Rebecca L. Turner (eds.), *Encyclopedia of Associations,* 925.

29. Ibid., 142.

30. Ibid., 324.

31. Ibid., 144.

32. Alan Weiss, "Seven Reasons to Examine Workplace Ethics," *HRMagazine* 36 (March 1992): 71.

33. Bill Leonard, "Business Ethics Touch HR Issues, Survey Finds," *HR News* 10 (June 1991): 13.

34. Patricia Buhler, "How Can We Encourage Ethical Behavior?" *Supervision* 52 (January 1991): 3.

APPENDIX

PROFESSIONAL CERTIFICATION

The Human Resource Certification Institute (HRCI) is an affiliate of the Society for Human Resource Management (HRM). Since its inception in 1976, the HRCI has granted certification to many human resource professionals.

The number of certified individuals will likely increase substantially as the benefits of certification become more apparent.

The HRCI's program provides two levels of certification: Professional in Human Resources (PHR) and Senior Professional in Human Resources (SPHR). These two levels recognize degrees of expertise and responsibility.

ELIGIBILITY

The HRCI grants certification after an applicant has:

1. verified current full-time professional exempt experience in the HR field as a practitioner, educator, researcher, or consultant.
2. passed a comprehensive written examination to demonstrate mastery of knowledge.

To earn the basic generalist designation, Professional in Human Resources (PHR), an individual must have:

1. four years of professional HR exempt experience *or* two years of professional HR exempt experience and a bachelor's degree *or* one year of professional HR exempt experience and a graduate degree. Degrees must be earned from a higher education institution accredited by a generally recognized college or university accrediting association.
2. passed a comprehensive examination.

To earn the senior generalist designation, Senior Professional in Human Resources (SPHR), an individual must have:

1. eight years of professional HR exempt experience *or* six years of professional HR exempt experience and a bachelor's degree *or* five years of professional HR exempt experience and a graduate degree. Degrees must be earned from a higher education institution accredited by a generally recognized college or university accrediting association.
2. passed a comprehensive examination.

Definitions

The credentialing program established and administered by the HRCI is intended for those professionals who are currently working in the field. While the work need not always be exclusively in the HR field, it is expected work in the field be the dominating thrust. Therefore, the following general definitions apply:

Practitioner: One whose duties are those normally found in the typical HR/personnel activity.

Educator: One whose principal area of instruction is in the HR/personnel field in a higher education institution.

Researcher: One whose research activities are restricted primarily to the HR/personnel field.

Consultant: One whose consulting activities are predominantly in the HR/personnel field.

The HRCI defines professional HR exempt experience as "work that would meet the test for 'exempt' as defined by the Fair Labor Standards Act and its amendments."

EXAM COMPOSITION

Functional Areas

1. Selection and placement
2. Training and development
3. Compensation and benefits
4. Health, safety, and security
5. Employee and labor relations
6. Management practices

The content of HRCI's comprehensive examinations is divided up (by percentage) as follows:

Functional Content Area	PHR Level	SPHR Level
Compensation and benefits	21%	18%
Employee and labor relations	18%	19%
Selection and placement	20%	15%
Training and development	12%	12%
Health, safety, and security	7%	7%
Management practices	22%	29%

In addition:

- Both exams have a four-hour time limit.
- Both exams have 250 multiple-choice questions with each question having four possible answers.
- Passing or failing is based on the examinees' scaled score for the total test. A scaled score of at least 500 is needed to pass.
- Questions unanswered are counted as incorrect.

Recertification

Certification is earned by individuals who demonstrate their mastery of the defined body of knowledge. The human resources field, however, is not static. Rapid changes require new and more sophisticated knowledge and behaviors by human resource professionals who wish to grow and develop with their field. Recertification is a method certified individuals can use to demonstrate their accomplishments in keeping abreast of these changes and to update their knowledge in the field.

Recertification is required within three years of certification. Each subsequent recertification period is also for three years. There are two ways to become recertified. Testing is one method. The other method involves continuing one's educational and professional experience.

Certification examinations are given on the first Saturday of each May and December at designated test sites. Applications must be submitted to the HRCI at least nine weeks in advance of the examination date. For additional certification information, contact the Human Resource Certification Institute, 606 North Washington Street, Alexandria, VA 22314.

CHAPTER 2

The Environment of Human Resource Management

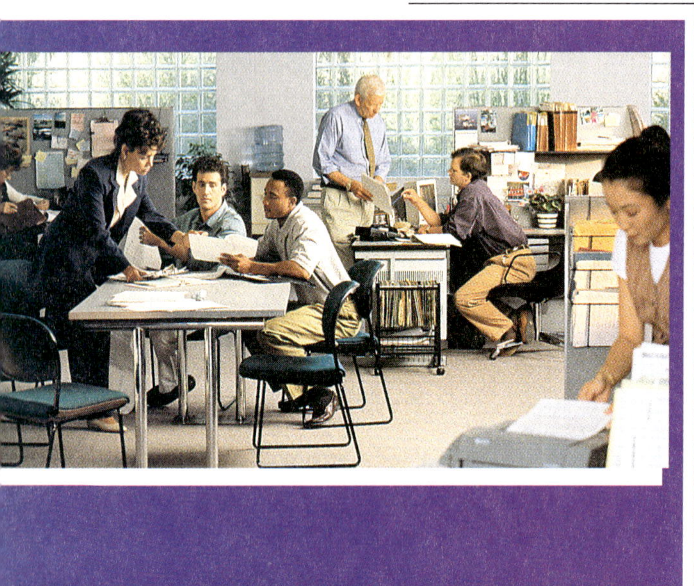

KEY TERMS

External environment	32	Internal environment	45
Social responsibility	34	Mission	46
Union	35	Policy	46
Shareholders	35	Corporate culture	47
Proactive response	38	Informal organization	48
Reactive response	38	Multinational corporation (MNC)	51
Managing diversity	39		

CHAPTER OBJECTIVES

1. Identify and describe the environmental factors that affect human resource management.
2. State and describe the external environmental factors that affect human resource management. Distinguish between a proactive and a reactive response to the external environment.
3. Describe the diverse workforce that management now confronts.
4. Explain the importance of small business in today's work environment.
5. Identify and describe the internal environmental factors that affect human resource management.

As Wayne Simmons, vice president of human resources for Lone Star Manufacturing, returned to his office from the weekly executive staff meeting, he was visibly disturbed. Lone Star, a producer of high-quality telecommunications equipment, is headquartered in Longview, Texas, and has manufacturing plants throughout Texas, Louisiana, and Oklahoma. Wayne had just heard a rumor than an overseas firm had developed a new manufacturing process which had the potential to cut costs substantially. Should this report prove true, customers might switch to the cheaper product. The three plants in the Longline Division that produce similar products would then be in serious trouble. The Longline Division had been expanding rapidly, but Wayne knew demand for Lone Star's products was far from automatic. If the new technology was superior, he also knew Lone Star might have to cut back production severely or even close the three plants in the Longline Division. These plants are located in areas already experiencing high unemployment because of the depressed price of crude oil. Plant closings would have a devastating effect on the economies of their respective communities. A few workers could be transferred to other locations, but most would have to be laid off. Thus, Wayne is now keenly aware of ways in which the external environment can have an impact on Lone Star Manufacturing's operations.

In this chapter, we first identify the environmental factors that affect human resource management. Then, we describe the means by which specific external environmental factors can influence human resource management. Next, we describe the diverse workforce that management now confronts and explain the importance of small business in today's work environment. Then, we discuss some of the major internal environmental factors that can affect human resource management.

ENVIRONMENTAL FACTORS AFFECTING HUMAN RESOURCE MANAGEMENT

Many interrelated factors affect human resource management. Such factors are part of either the firm's external environment or its internal environment (see Figure 2-1). The firm often has little, if any, control over how the external environment affects management of its human resources. These factors impinge on the organization from outside its boundaries. Moreover, important factors within the firm itself also have an impact on how the firm manages its human resources.

Certain interrelationships tend to complicate the management of human resources. For instance, human resource professionals constantly work with people who represent all organizational levels and functional areas. Therefore, they must recognize the different perspectives these individuals bring to HRM if they are to perform their human resource tasks properly.

Understanding the many interrelationships implied in Figure 2-1 is essential in order for the human resource professional to help other managers resolve issues and problems. For instance, a production manager may want to give a substantial pay raise to a particular employee. The human resource manager may know this employee does an exceptional job; he or she should also be aware granting the raise may affect pay practices in the production department and set a precedent for the entire firm. The human resource manager may have to explain to the production manager that such an action is not an isolated decision. They may have to consider alternative means of rewarding the employee for superior performance without upsetting the organization's reward system. Perhaps the human resource manager can point to a higher paying position the employee is qualified to fill.

Whatever the case, the implications of a particular act must be considered in light of its potential impact on a department and the entire organization. Human resource managers must realize the overwhelming importance of the big picture, rather than concentrating on a narrow phase of the company's operation. The basic HRM tasks remain essentially the same regardless of the source of the impact. However, the manner in which those tasks are accomplished may be altered substantially by factors in the external environment.

THE EXTERNAL ENVIRONMENT

Those factors that affect a firm's human resources from outside its boundaries make up the **external environment**. As illustrated in Figure 2-1, external factors include the labor force, legal considerations, society, unions, shareholders, competition, customers, technology, and

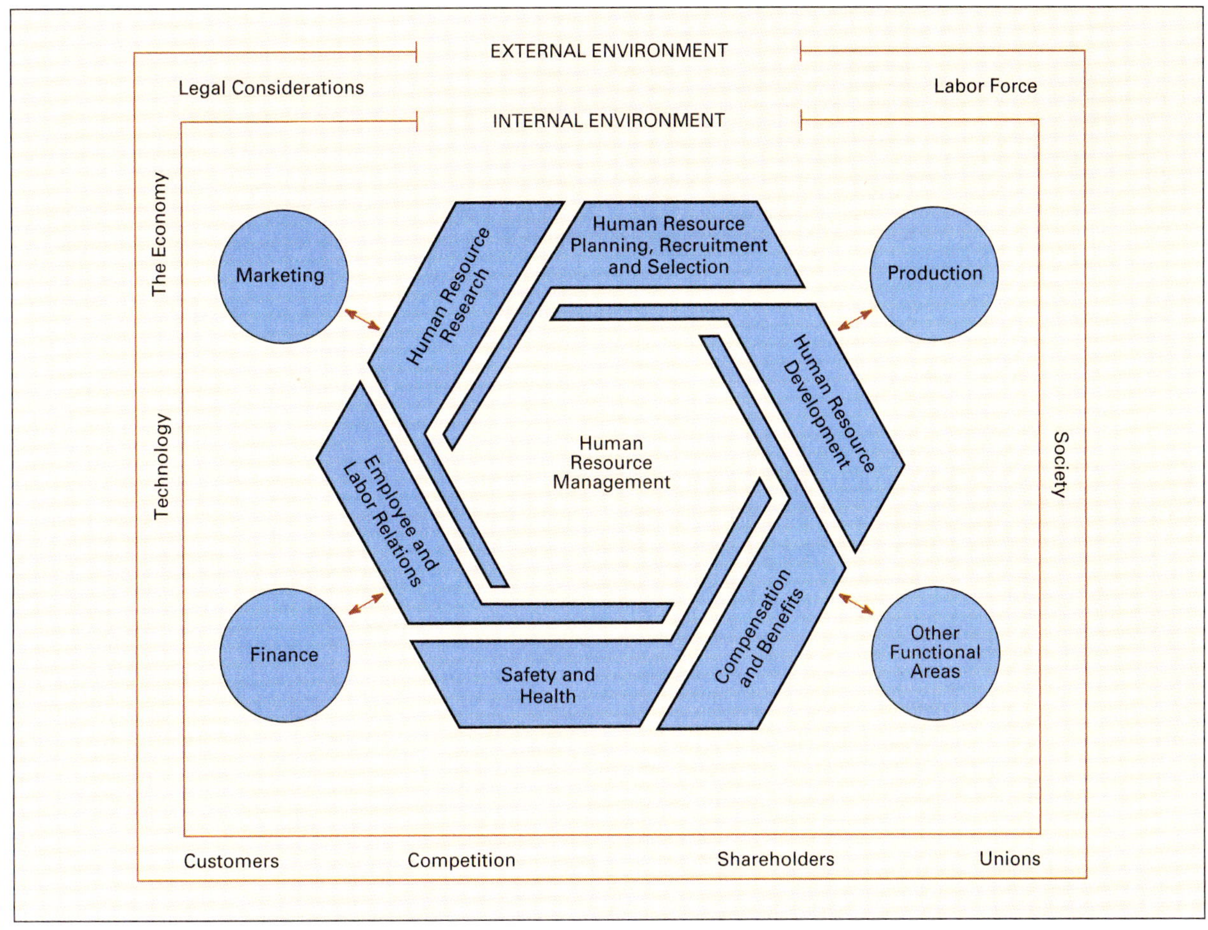

FIGURE 2-1 The Environments of Human Resource Management

the economy. Each factor, either separately or in combination with others, can place constraints on the human resource manager's job. Thus, the HR manager must always try to identify and consider the impact of such factors.

The Labor Force

The labor force is a pool of individuals external to the firm from which the organization obtains its workers. The capabilities of a firm's employees determine to a large extent how well the organization can perform its mission. Since new employees are hired from outside the firm, the labor force is considered an external environmental factor. The labor force is always changing, and this inevitably causes changes in the workforce of an organization. In turn, changes in individuals within an organization affect the way management must deal with its work force. In short, changes in the country's labor force create dynamic situations within organizations. This topic will be discussed later in this chapter under the heading "Managing the Diverse Workforce."

Legal Considerations

Another significant external force affecting human resource management relates to federal, state, and local legislation, and the many court decisions interpreting this legislation. In addition, many presidential executive orders have had a major impact on human resource management. These legal considerations affect virtually the entire spectrum of human resource policies. We highlight in Chapter 3 the most significant of these considerations, which affect equal employment opportunity. Laws, court decisions, and executive orders affecting other human resource management activities will be described in the appropriate chapters.

Society

Society may also exert pressure on human resource management. The public is no longer content to accept, without question, the actions of business. Individuals and special interest groups have found they can effect change through their voices, votes, and other actions. The influence of activists is obvious by the large numbers of regulatory laws that have been passed since the early 1960s. To remain acceptable to the general public, a firm must accomplish its purpose while complying with societal norms.

The general public's attitudes and beliefs can affect the firm's behavior because those attitudes and beliefs often directly affect profitability. When a corporation behaves as if it has a conscience, it is said to be socially responsible. **Social responsibility** is an implied, enforced, or felt obligation of managers, acting in their official capacities, to serve or protect the interests of groups other than themselves. Many companies develop patterns of concern for moral and social issues. They do so through policy statements, practices, and the leadership of morally strong employees and managers over time. Open-door policies, grievance procedures, and employee benefit programs often stem as much from a desire to do what is right as from a concern for productivity and avoidance of strife.[1]

You may well ask, "Why should a business be concerned with the welfare of society? Its goal is to make a profit and grow." Obviously, a business must make a profit over the long run if it is to survive. But you should also remember another basic point: If a firm does not satisfy society's needs, then it will ultimately cease to exist. A firm operates by public consent to satisfy society's requirements. Although such issues relate to the organization as a whole, you can easily see how human resource managers might be expected to become involved in them. The organization is a member of the community in which it operates. Just as citizens work to improve the quality of life in their community, the organization should also respect and work with the other members of its community. For instance, a high unemployment rate among a certain minority group may exist within the firm's service area. A philosophy of hiring workers who are capable of being trained in addition to qualified applicants may help to reduce unemployment for that group. In the long run, this philosophy will certainly enhance the firm's image and may actually improve profitability.

In recent years, companies have been struggling with how they will compete in the new global environment. Companies are constantly looking for new ideas that will make them more efficient. Workforces are being trimmed. In fact, for the first eight months of 1993, an average of 2,389 American workers lost their jobs daily. Even firms on the rebound are not rehiring. Instead, they are seeking other ways to get the job done. In view of this new environment, some firms are questioning whether or not efficiency and social responsibility can be married.[2] For example, IBM once had the reputation of never laying off workers. This reputation has been shattered with layoffs in recent years. In view of these layoffs, it would be reasonable to question whether or not IBM can afford to do many of the things that gained them the reputation for being socially responsible. Resource utilization may need to be thoroughly analyzed to determine if a certain *socially responsible* action actually assists the firm in remaining competitive in this ever-expanding global environment. Only time will tell how the concept of social responsibility fares in this new environment.

Unions

Wage levels, benefits, and working conditions for millions of employees now reflect decisions made jointly by unions and management. A **union** is a group of employees who have joined together for the purpose of dealing with their employer. Unions are treated as an environmental factor because, essentially, they become a third party when dealing with the company. In a unionized organization, the union rather than the individual employee negotiates an agreement with management.

Although unions remain a powerful force, union membership as a percentage of the nonagricultural workforce slipped from 33 percent in 1955 to 15.8 percent today. When government employees are subtracted, unions represent a mere 11 percent of the private industry workforce.[3] This trend is expected to continue for a number of reasons, and as the power and influence of unions decline further, the emphasis will likely shift to a human resource system that deals directly with the individual worker and his or her needs.

Shareholders

The owners of a corporation are called **shareholders**. Because shareholders have invested money in a firm, they may at times challenge programs considered by management to be beneficial to the organization. Managers may be forced to justify the merits of a particular program in terms of how it will affect future projects, costs, revenues, and profits. For instance, $50,000 spent on implementing a management development program may require more justification than stating, "Managers should become more open and adaptive to the needs of employees." Shareholders are concerned with how such expenditure decisions will increase revenues or decrease costs. Thus, management must be prepared to explain the merits of a particular program in terms of its economic costs and benefits.

Stockholders are wielding increasing influence. There are frequent stockholder lawsuits against managers and directors, claiming they failed to look out for stockholder interests. For instance, when Medco merged with Merck, unhappy shareholders filed five suits alleging that the Merck deal was designed to enrich top executives at other shareholders' expense. Medco dismissed the suits as nonsense although Martin J. Wygod, Medco's chief executive officer, stacked the Medco Board with his pals who have made millions from generous stock options.[4]

Competition

Unless an organization is in the unusual position of monopolizing the market it serves, other firms will be producing similar products or services. A firm must maintain a supply of competent employees if it is to succeed, grow, and prosper. But other organizations are also striving for that same objective. A firm's major task is to ensure it obtains and retains a sufficient number of employees in various career fields to allow the firm to compete effectively. A bidding war often results when competitors attempt to fill certain critical positions in their firms. Because of the strategic nature of their needs, firms are sometimes forced to resort to unusual means to recruit and retain such employees. The poster shown in Figure 2-2 exemplifies the extreme approaches some organizations have used to recruit qualified workers.

Customers

The people who actually use a firm's goods and services also are part of its external environment. Because sales are crucial to the firm's survival, management has the task of ensuring its employment practices do not antagonize the customers it serves. Customers constantly demand high-quality products and after-purchase service. Therefore, a firm's workforce should be capable of providing quality goods and services. Sales are often lost or gained because of variances in product quality and follow-up service. These conditions relate directly to the skills, qualifications, and motivations of the organization's employees.

Technology

The rate of technological change is accelerating, and as a result, few firms operate today as they did even a decade ago. A major concern to those in HRM is the effect technological changes have had and will have on businesses. During the next decade, one of the most challenging areas in human resource management will be training employees to keep up with rapidly advancing technology. Products that were not envisioned only a few years ago are now being mass produced, substantially enlarging the tasks of all managers, including human resource managers. New skills are typically not in large supply; as a result, recruiting qualified individuals in areas that demand them is often difficult.

As technological changes occur, certain skills also are no longer required. This situation necessitates some retraining of the current workforce. As we mentioned in Chapter 1, within the next decade, more than half of all existing jobs are expected to change and another 30 percent to be eliminated as a result of technological advances.[5] Furthermore, it has been estimated by the year 2000, 75 percent of all jobs will involve the use of computers.[6] For instance, the traditional role of the secretary has changed substantially since the advent of word processing. Rather than writing or dictating a letter to

FIGURE 2-2
A Recruitment Poster

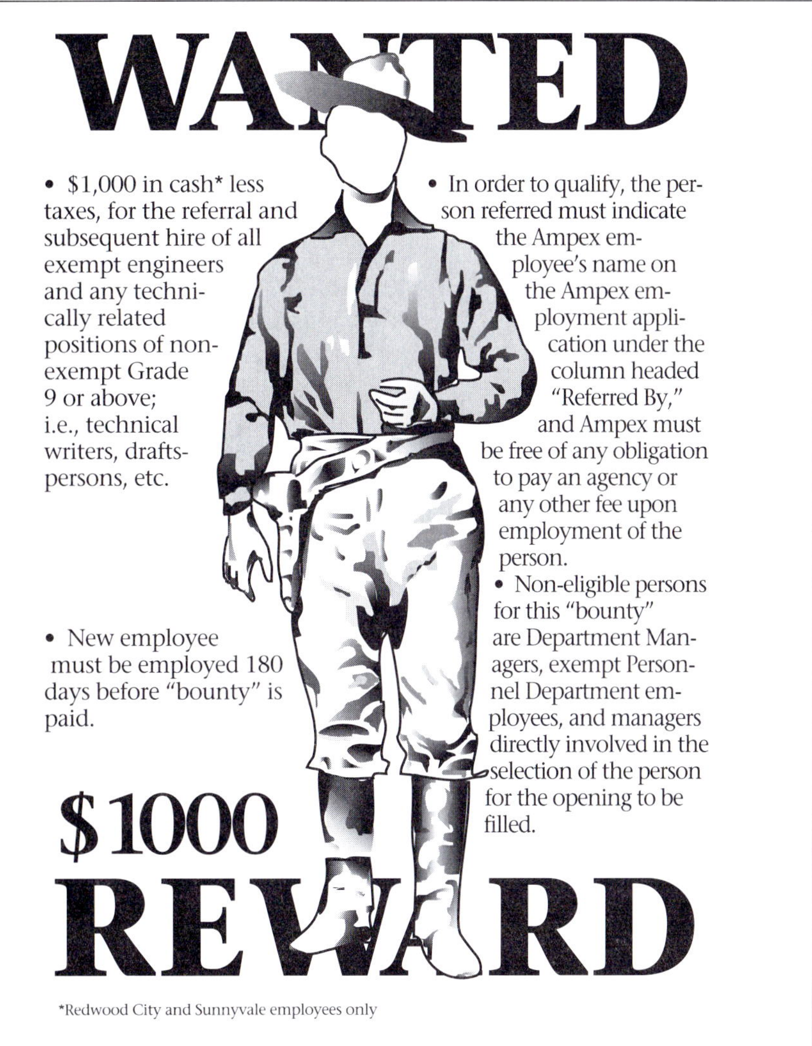

give to a secretary, more and more managers are entering their letters utilizing word processors and then printing them out.

WANTED
• $1,000 in cash* less taxes, for the referral and subsequent hire of all exempt engineers and any technically related positions of non-exempt Grade 9 or above; i.e., technical writers, draftspersons, etc.
• In order to qualify, the person referred must indicate the Ampex employee's name on the Ampex employment application under the column headed "Referred By," and Ampex must be free of any obligation to pay an agency or any other fee upon employment of the person.
• Non-eligible persons for this "bounty" are Department Managers, exempt Personnel Department employees, and managers directly involved in the selection of the person for the opening to be filled.
• New employee must be employed 180 days before "bounty" is paid.
$1000
REWARD
*Redwood City and Sunnyvale employees only

The trend toward a service economy also affects the type and amount of technology needed. While the number of manufacturing jobs has been decreasing, the number of service industry jobs has dramatically increased. By 1993, 80 percent of the new jobs in the United States were in service-related industries.[7]

The Economy

The economy of the nation, on the whole and in its various segments, is a major environmental factor affecting human resource management. As a generalization, when the economy is booming, it is often more difficult to recruit qualified workers. On the other hand, when a downturn is experienced, more applicants are typically available.

Complicating this situation even further is the fact that one segment of the country may be experiencing a downturn, another a slow recovery, and another a boom. Such was the situation existing in the early 1990s. Some of the northeast states were facing a downturn; Houston, Texas, was gradually recovering; and Salt Lake City, Utah, was booming.[8]

THE EXTERNAL ENVIRONMENT: PROACTIVE VERSUS REACTIVE

Managers approach changes in the external environment proactively or reactively. A **proactive** response involves taking action in anticipation of environmental changes. A **reactive** response involves simply responding to environmental changes after they occur. For example, while the Americans with Disabilities Act (ADA) of 1990 was weaving its way through Congress, some companies had already implemented its anticipated provisions. Managers of these companies were being proactive. Those who waited until the law went into effect to even plan the required changes were being reactive.

Organizations exhibit varying degrees of proactive and reactive behavior. When the Occupational Health and Safety Act (OSHA) was enacted, some firms did only what the letter of the law required. Others went far beyond that and allocated significant resources to create a safe and healthful environment for employees. The response to Title VII of the Civil Rights Act of 1964 provides another example. Prior to passage of that law, many firms were inactive with regard to equal employment opportunity. However, many of these same companies later became aggressive in promoting equal opportunity. Convinced that the national agenda was to eliminate discrimination in employment based on race, color, sex, religion, or national origin, they went beyond the explicit requirements of the law. Human resource managers have discovered a proactive attitude reduces the level of damaging discrimination suits.[9]

A firm may be either reactive or proactive in any matter, legal or otherwise. For example, reactive managers may demonstrate concern for employee welfare only after a union organizing attempt starts. Proactive managers try to spot early signs of discontent and correct the causes of that discontent before matters get out of hand. Proactive managers prevent customer complaints rather than *handle* them. In the markets they serve, proactive managers tend to set the prices competitors must match. They install scrubbers on exhaust stacks before environmental groups begin picketing the plant and before federal regulators file suit. In all matters, proactive managers initiate rather than react. When an unanticipated environmental change occurs, proactive managers go beyond what the change forces them to do.

MANAGING THE DIVERSE WORKFORCE

From McDonald's to Holiday Inn, from AT&T to Levi Strauss, managers are learning not only to understand their *kaleidoscopic workforce,* but also to effectively manage diverse environments. Diversity management presents new challenges in the workplace. Not only are more businesses expanding their operations overseas, but many workers in the United States are working alongside individuals whose cul-

Diversity management presents new challenges and opportunities in the workplace.

tures differ substantially from their own, and more ethnic minorities are entering the workforce. Managers must be knowledgeable about common group characteristics in order to manage diversity effectively. **Managing diversity** is having an acute awareness of characteristics common to a culture, race, gender, age, or sexual preference while at the same time managing employees with these characteristics as individuals.[10] This philosophy recognizes that individuals of a particular culture may have unique general characteristics. However, in the work environment, employees are treated as individuals while still taking into consideration cultural differences.

By 1995, the U.S. labor force is projected to be about 129 million people, 14 percent more than the 1984 level of 114 million. Size alone, however, does not tell the whole story. The labor force now includes more women and older persons than ever before. Employees with disabilities are being included in increasing numbers. Many immigrants from developing areas, especially Southeast Asia and Latin America, are joining the labor force.

The issue of diversity is one reality of being globally competitive. Today it would seem socially irresponsible to proclaim in an advertising brochure that "none but white women and girls are employed," but in 1908 that is just what was included in a Levi Strauss brochure. In fact, today Levi Strauss has taken the moral high ground in terms of being socially responsible by developing a diverse workforce. Levi Strauss appears to be exceptionally responsible in this area and is currently recognized as "one of the most ethnically and culturally diverse companies in the United States, if not the world." In 1992, 56 percent of the company's 23,000 person U.S. workforce belonged to minority groups. Fourteen percent of Levi Strauss' top managers are nonwhite and 30 percent are female. In another step up the social responsibility ladder, Levi Strauss is doing its best to eliminate the "glass ceiling," which may have prevented some qualified minorities and women from being promoted into the company's top ranks. Promoting diversity makes good business sense for Levi Strauss and has allowed the company to design and develop merchandise for diverse markets, which it may have not understood or appreciated in the past. Levi Strauss credits the Dockers line of casual pants, now worth more than $1 billion a year, to Argentine employees.

Both diversity and social responsibility are often costly and time consuming, but Levi Strauss chief executive officer Robert B. Haas believes that harnessing diversity will continue to benefit the company well into the future. According to Levi Strauss executives, "Standing firm . . . sends an important message to employees of all races and lifestyles."[11]

The challenge for managers in the coming decades will be to recognize that people with common, but different characteristics from the mainstream, often think differently, act differently, learn differently, and communicate differently. Because every person, culture, and business situation is unique, there are no simple rules for managing diversity, but diversity experts say that employees need to develop patience, open-mindedness, acceptance, and cultural awareness. Only by such measures can productivity be maximized.[12]

Women in Business

Today half the entry level management positions consist of women; this is up from 15 percent 15 years ago.[13] Because of the critical mass of talent, many believe that the 1990s will be the decade women in mass break through to upper level management. In fact, a recent survey of 400 top female executives revealed that the percentage of women who hold the title of executive vice president more than doubled over the past decade, from 4 percent to 8.7 percent.[14] In the same study, it appears that women no longer see careers and family as mutually exclusive. Sixty-nine percent of the women polled were married, and 63 percent had children.

Because of the number of women who are entering the workforce, there are an increasing number of nontraditional households in the United States. These households include those headed by single parents, and those in which both partners work fulltime. Women who formerly remained at home to care for children and the household, today need and want to work outside the home. In fact, women are expected to account for more than 60 percent of labor force growth during the period from 1984 to 1996. If this valuable segment of the workforce is to be effectively utilized, organizations must fully recognize the importance of addressing work/family issues.[15]

Some executives, such as Marion O. Sandler, CEO and president of Golden West Financial Corporation, believe that not a lot of progress has been made in terms of women moving up in business. He also believes that, "It's the power structure that doesn't allow women entry." Carleton S. Fiorina, Network Systems vice president for strategy and market development at AT&T, disagrees. Fiorina believes that her sex has not been a disadvantage. According to Fiorina, "There's a lot of discussion that men won't give adequate clout or power to women. Women share an equal burden for that. No one can expect to be handed power."[16] However, regardless of whether women have been at a disadvantage in business, it is apparent businesses are having to adapt to employees' requirements for flexibility and innovation in child care services, benefit plans, and work practices.

Traditionally, child care needs were viewed as being outside the realm of the business world—a responsibility workers had to bear and manage alone. This was particularly difficult for single parents, but even working parent couples generally cannot afford a full-time live-in housekeeper. For many workers, child care has been managed with the help of family or friends. The need for alternative arrangements is evidenced by the fact that in 1950, only 12 percent of women with children under age six were in the labor force. That figure has now risen to almost 60 percent.[17]

Today business has begun to see that providing child care services and workplace flexibility may influence workers' choice of employers. Many companies have begun providing day care services for employees. Some companies located in the same building or facility provide joint day care service. Other companies, such as IBM, provide day care referral services. More and more companies provide paid maternity leave, and some offer paternity leave. Still other firms give time off for children's visits to doctors, which can be charged against the parents' sick leave or personal time. Managers need to be sensitive to the needs of working parents. At times, management also needs to be creative in accommodating this most valuable segment of the workforce.

The increasing number of dual career couples presents both challenges and opportunities for organizations. Some firms have revised their policies against nepotism to allow both partners to work for the same company. Other firms have developed policies to assist the spouse of an employee who is transferred. When a firm wishes to transfer an employee to another location, the employee's spouse may be unwilling to give up a good position or may be unable to find an equivalent position in the new location. Some companies are offering assistance in finding a position for the spouse of a transferred employee. Overall, the trend is toward *nontraditional* households, and firms must develop programs to accommodate employees' needs.

Workers of Color

Workers of color often experience stereotypes about their group (Hispanics, African Americans, Asians, etc.). At times, they encounter misunderstandings and expectations based on ethnic or cultural differences. Members of ethnic or racial groups are socialized within their particular culture. Many are socialized as members of two cultural groups—the dominant culture and their racial or ethnic culture. Ella Bell, professor of organizational behavior at MIT, refers to this dual membership as *biculturalism*. In her study of African American women, she identifies the stress of coping with membership in two cultures simultaneously as bicultural stress. She indicates that *role conflict*—competing roles from two cultures—and *role overload*—too many expectations to fulfill comfortably—are common characteristics of bicultural stress. Although these issues can be applied to many minority groups, they are particularly intense for women of color. This is because this group experiences dynamics affecting *both* minorities and women.[18]

Socialization in one's culture of origin can lead to misunderstandings in the workplace. This is particularly true when the manager relies solely on the cultural norms of the majority group. According to these norms, within the American culture it is acceptable—even positive—to praise an individual publicly for a job well done. However, in cultures that place primary value on group harmony and collective achievement, this method of rewarding an employee causes emotional discomfort. Employees feel that, if praised publicly, they will *lose face* within their group.

Older Workers

The U.S. population is growing older, a trend that is expected to continue through the year 2000. Life expectancies continue to increase, and the baby boom generation (people born from the end of World War II through 1964) had only half as many children as their parents did.

In addition, the trend toward earlier retirement appears to be reversing itself. This may have been due to the 1986 amendment to the Age Discrimination in Employment Act. With certain exceptions, firms cannot force employees to retire because of age, no matter how old they are. Many older persons do not want to retire, or even slow down. As many as one-third of retirees want to return to full- or part-time work.[19]

As the workforce grows older, their needs and interests may change.[20] Many become bored with their present careers and desire different challenges. The *graying* of the workforce has required some adjustments. Some older workers favor less demanding full-time jobs, others choose semiretirement, and still others prefer part-time work. Many of these individuals require retraining as they move through the various stages of their careers.

Contingency Workers

In the late 1980s and early 1990s, many companies drastically reduced their workforce. As the economy began to recover, often full-time workers were not hired. As companies downsize and reorganize, many of them are employing contingency workers—employees hired by companies to cope with unexpected or temporary challenges. This workforce consists of part timers, freelancers, subcontractors, and independent professionals.[21] These workers are usually paid less than full-time workers and almost never receive benefits. Some predictions have contingency workers making up approximately 50 percent of the workforce by the year 2000. Unlike in previous years, many of the temporary workforce are professionals, comprising about 20 percent of the total contingency workforce.

Of course, the use of contingency workers is not without disadvantages. Contingency employees tend to be less dependent on the firm and, therefore, less committed to it. In addition, companies have discovered contingent workers require more training and closer supervision. Otherwise, high turnover and low productivity are the result.

Leased Employees

Leased employees are individuals provided by an outside firm at a fixed hourly rate, similar to a rental fee, often for extended periods. Using this approach, a firm formally terminates some or most of its employees. Then, a leasing company hires them, usually at the same salary, and leases them back to the former employer, who becomes the client. The employees continue to work as before, with the client supervising their activities. The leasing company, however, assumes all responsibilities associated with being the employer, including personnel administration.

Use of employee leasing is growing. Currently, about 75,000 employees are being leased. It is estimated 20 percent of the 4.4 million businesses in the United States with fewer than 35 employees will be attracted to employee leasing, resulting in 10 million leased employees by the year 2000. Larger companies have also begun using employee leasing to a greater extent. It provides them with a body of well-trained, long-term employees that can expand or contract as business conditions dictate.[22]

Persons with Disabilities

According to one estimation, there are approximately 36 million disabled employees in the United States, not including mentally handicapped persons.[23] A handicap, or disability, limits the amount or kind of work a person can do or makes its achievement unusually difficult. More common disabilities include limited hearing or sight, limited mobility, mental or emotional deficiencies, and various nerve disorders. Studies indicate that handicapped workers do as well as the unimpaired in terms of productivity, attendance, and average tenure.[24] In fact, in certain high turnover occupations, handicapped workers have had lower turnover rates. The Americans with Disabilities Act (ADA), passed in 1990, prohibits discrimination against *qualified individuals with disabilities* and will be discussed in detail in Chapter 3.

A serious barrier to effective employment of disabled persons is bias or prejudice. Managers should examine their own biases and preconceived attitudes toward such persons. Many individuals experience anxiety around workers with disabilities, especially if the disabilities are severe. Fellow workers may show pity or feel a disabled worker is fragile. Some even show disgust. The manager can set the tone for proper treatment of workers with disabilities. If someone is unsure about how to act or how much help to offer, the disabled person should be asked for guidance. Managers must always strive to treat employees with disabilities as they treat other employees and must hold them accountable for achievement.

HRM IN ACTION

—WHAT TO DO?

Duane Roberts, a paraplegic, has just been assigned to your division as a radio dispatcher for your delivery trucks. The personnel department has given you only limited information about Duane. But you know he is thirty-two years old and has held similar jobs before. You are in the dispatching office when you see a person you assume to be Duane coming up the sidewalk in his wheelchair. You think he might have a problem getting through the double glass doors in his path, which open against his direction of travel.

How would you handle the situation?

Immigrants

In the 1980s, 8.7 million people immigrated to the United States. Large numbers of immigrants from Asia and Latin America have settled in many parts of the United States. Some are highly skilled and well educated and others are only minimally skilled with little education. They have one thing in common—an eagerness to work.[25] They have brought with them attitudes, values, and mores particular to their home country cultures.

In the 1970s and 1980s, after the end of hostilities in Vietnam, Vietnamese immigrants settled along the Mississippi and Texas Gulf Coast. At about the same time, thousands of Thais fleeing the upheaval in Thailand came to the Boston area to work and live. New York's Puerto Rican community has long been an economic and political force there. Cubans who fled Castro's regime congregated in southern Florida, especially Miami. A flood of Mexicans and other Hispanics continues across the southern border of the United States. The Irish, the Poles, the Italians, and others who came here in past decades have long since assimilated into—and indeed have become—the culture. Newer immigrants require time to adapt. Meanwhile, they generally take low paying and menial jobs, live in substandard housing, and form enclaves where they cling to some semblance of the cultures they left.

Wherever they settle, members of these ethnic groups soon begin to become part of the regular workforce, and break out of their isolation in certain occupations. They begin to adopt the English language and American customs. They begin to learn new skills and to adapt old skills to their new country. Human resource managers can place these individuals in jobs appropriate to their skills with excellent results for the organization. As corporations employ more foreign nationals in this country, managers must work to understand the different cultures and languages of their employees.

Young Persons with Limited Education or Skills

Each year thousands of young, unskilled workers are hired, especially during peak periods, such as holiday buying seasons. These workers generally have limited education, sometimes even less than a high school diploma. Those who have completed high school often find their education hardly fits the work they are expected to do. Most, for example, lack familiarity with computers. Many of these young adults and teenagers have poor work habits; they tend to be tardy or absent more often than experienced or better educated workers.

Although the negative attributes of these workers at times seem to outweigh the positive ones, they are a permanent part of the workforce. There are many jobs they can do well. And more jobs can be *de-skilled,* making it possible for lower skilled workers to do them. A well-known example of deskilling is McDonald's substitution of pictures for numbers on its cash register keys. Managers should look for ways to train unskilled workers and to facilitate their formal education further.

THE SMALL BUSINESS

During the 1980s in the United States, small and midsized companies created 80 percent of the jobs.[26] Every year approximately 400,000 such businesses are established.[27] Since 1988, companies employing fewer than 100 workers have accounted for more than 90 percent of all job growth.[28] Every year thousands of individuals, motivated by a desire to be their own boss, to earn a better income, and to realize the American dream, launch a new business venture. These individuals, often referred to as entrepreneurs, have been essential to the growth and vitality of the American free enterprise system. Entrepreneurs develop or recognize new products or business opportunities, secure the necessary capital, and organize and operate the business. Most people who start their own business get a great deal of satisfaction from owning and managing their own firm. Historically, it has been estimated that four out of five small businesses fail within five years. However, in a recent study it was found that over half survived in one form or another.[29]

Almost every large corporation began as a small business. Many small businesses are so successful they become big businesses. For example, Steven Jobs and Steve Wozniak, the founders of Apple Computer Company, began making personal computers in Wozniak's garage. From this meager beginning, Apple Computer evolved into a major personal computer maker.

There is no commonly agreed upon definition of what constitutes a small business. The Small Business Act of 1953 defines a small business as one that is independently owned and operated and not dominant in its field. Basically, a small business is one in which the owner-operator knows personally the key personnel. In most small businesses, this key group would ordinarily not exceed twelve to fifteen people. Regardless of the specific definition of a small business, this category certainly makes up the overwhelming majority of business establishments in this country.

The environment of managers in large and small businesses is often quite different. Managers in large firms may be separated from top management by numerous managerial layers. They may find it difficult to see how they fit into the overall organization. They often know managers one or two layers above them, but seldom those higher up. In some large companies, supervisors are restricted by many written guidelines, and they may feel more loyalty to their workers than to upper management.

Managers in small businesses often identify more closely with the goals of the firm. They can readily see how their efforts affect the firm's profits. In many instances, lower level managers know the company executives personally. These supervisors know the organization's success is closely tied to their own effectiveness.

THE INTERNAL ENVIRONMENT

The internal environment also exerts considerable pressure on human resource management. Factors that affect a firm's human resources from inside its boundaries comprise the **internal environment**. The primary internal factors include the firm's mission, policies, corporate culture, management style of upper managers, employees, the informal organization, other units of the organization, and unions. These factors have a major impact in determining the interaction between HRM and other departments within the organization. This interaction has a major effect on overall organizational productivity, so it is vital that the interaction be positive and supportive of the firm's mission.

Mission

Mission is the organization's continuing purpose or reason for being. Each management level should operate with a clear understanding of the firm's mission. In fact, each organizational unit (division, plant, department) should clearly understand objectives that coincide with that mission.

The specific company mission must be regarded as a major internal factor that affects the tasks of human resource management. Consider two companies, each having a broadly based mission, and envision how certain tasks might differ from one firm to the other. Company A's goal is to be an industry leader in technological advances. Its growth occurs through the pioneering of new products and processes. Company B's goal is one of conservative growth, which involves little risk taking. Only after another company's product or process has proven itself in the marketplace will Company B commit itself.

Company A needs a creative environment to encourage new ideas. Highly skilled workers must be recruited to foster technological advancement. Constant attention to workforce training and development is essential. A compensation program designed to retain and motivate the most productive employees is especially important.

The basic tasks of human resource management are the same for Company B, but the mission dictates that they be altered somewhat. A different kind of workforce will likely be needed. Highly creative individuals may not want to work for Company B. Perhaps because the mission encourages little risk taking, most of the major decisions will be made at higher levels in the organization. Thus, management development at lower levels in the organization may receive less emphasis. The compensation program may reflect the different requirements of this particular workforce. As this comparison indicates, a human resource manager must clearly understand his or her company's mission.

Policies

A **policy** is a predetermined guide established to provide direction in decision making. As guides rather than as hard-and-fast rules, policies are somewhat flexible, requiring interpretation and judgment in their use. They can exert significant influence on how managers accomplish their jobs. For instance, many firms have an *open door* policy that permits an employee to take a problem to the next higher level in the organization if it cannot be solved by the immediate supervisor. Knowing that their subordinates can take problems to a higher echelon tends to encourage supervisors to try harder to resolve problems at their levels.

Many larger firms have policies related to every major operational area. Although policies are established for marketing, production, and finance, the largest number of policies often relate to human resource management. Some potential policy statements that affect human resource management are as follows:

- Provide employees with a safe place to work.
- Encourage employees to achieve as much of their human potential as possible.

- Provide compensation that will encourage a high level of productivity in both quality and quantity.
- Ensure current employees are considered first for any vacant position for which they may be qualified.

Because policies have a degree of flexibility, the manager is not necessarily required to adhere strictly to the policy statement. Often the tone of a policy guides managers as much as the actual words. Consider, for instance, a policy that ensures that "all members of the labor force have equal opportunity for employment." This policy implies more than merely adhering to certain laws and government regulations. Confronted with this policy, the human resource manager will likely do more than merely conform to the law. Perhaps the manager will initiate a training program to permit hiring of minorities or women who are not immediately qualified to perform available jobs. Rather than just seeking qualified applicants, a firm actively implementing this policy goes beyond the minimum required by law.

Corporate Culture

When being considered as an internal environmental factor affecting human resource management, corporate culture refers to the firm's social and psychological climate. **Corporate culture** is defined as the system of shared values, beliefs, and habits within an organization that interacts with the formal structure to produce behavioral norms.[30] Managers can, and should, determine the kind of corporate culture they wish to work within and strive to make sure that kind of culture develops. Dennis L. Nowlin, manager of executive development at 3M Corporation, said his company was challenged with "managing a large firm with the value system of a small business." Nowlin added, "We work in a highly technical organization with many technical, research and development, and manufacturing specialists. . . . My personal vision is to get every manager within 3M thinking from a general management perspective."[31] We discuss corporate culture in considerable detail in Chapter 9.

Management Style of Upper Managers

Closely related to corporate culture is the way in which the attitudes and preferences of one's superiors affect how a job is done. This situation deserves special emphasis here because of the problems that can result if the managerial style of upper level managers differs from that of lower level managers. In general, a lower level manager must adapt to the style of the boss. It is hard to be open and considerate when the boss believes in just giving orders and having them followed. A lower level manager's concerns about involving employees in decision making and giving them freedom may be seen as a lack of decisiveness. Even the company president must deal with the management style and attitudes of superiors, in this case, the board of directors.[32] The president may be a risk taker and want to be aggressive in the marketplace, but the board may prefer a more conservative approach.

Employees

Employees differ in capabilities, attitudes, personal goals, and personalities. As a result, behavior a manager finds effective with one worker may not be effective with another. In extreme cases, employees can be so different it is virtually impossible for them to be managed as a group. In order to be effective, the manager must consider both individual and group differences. A supervisor of experienced workers, for instance, may pay little attention to the technical details of the job and more to encouraging group cooperation, while a supervisor of inexperienced workers may focus mainly on the technical aspects of the task.

Informal Organization

New managers quickly learn there are two organizations they must deal with in the firm—one formal and the other informal. The formal organization is usually described by an organization chart and job descriptions. Managers know the official reporting relationships. But an informal organization exists alongside the formal one. The **informal organization** is the set of evolving relationships and patterns of human interaction within an organization that are not officially prescribed. Such informal relationships are quite powerful. Assume, for instance, top management has expressed total commitment to equal employment opportunity. An all-male or all-white work group may still resist the assignment of women or blacks to the group. Unwanted workers may be ostracized or refused the usual friendly assistance in adapting to a new job. In extreme cases, derogatory jokes may be told within earshot of such employees. This kind of behavior places the supervisor in a difficult position, caught between formal policy and aggressive action arising from the informal organization.

Other Units

Managers must be keenly aware of interrelationships that exist among divisions or departments and should use such relationships to the best advantage. Some of these possible relationships are presented in Figure 2-3. The human resource department helps maintain a competent workforce; the purchasing department buys materials and parts. Because one department precedes another in the flow of work, that department's output becomes the other department's input. Most managers soon discover cooperation with other departments is necessary if the job is to get done efficiently. Managers who fail to develop positive relationships with other managers may jeopardize the productivity of several departments.

Unions

Upper management typically negotiates labor-management agreements, but managers throughout the organization must implement the terms of the agreements. In most instances, agreements place restrictions on the manager's actions. For example, a manager may want to shift a maintenance worker to an operator's job temporarily; but if the labor-management agreement specifies the tasks that can and cannot be performed in each job, the supervisor may not be able to make the temporary assignment.

A GLOBAL PERSPECTIVE

In the 1980s, the need for adapting business practices to different national environments was not fully appreciated. Today, if exports and imports were combined, they would total almost 25 percent of the U.S. economy. This figure is up from only 16 percent just 10 years ago.[33] Global competition, air travel, satellite communication technology, and wage differentials have made doing business abroad both necessary and feasible. Companies have responded by establishing more and more operations overseas.

Unfortunately, American managers have tended to fall back on their own limited experiences, treating an assignment in Hong Kong, Sydney, or Paris much like a stint in Dallas or Atlanta.[34] Today managers commonly recognize that this way of doing business is unacceptable and that, in fact, the challenge of multinational operations is not easily met. This is especially true with regard to the challenges of human resource management. According to Ellen Brandt, a human resources consultant and journalist, "Human resources executives must acquire a global perspective and global skills."[35] Unfortunately, the number of human resource professionals with a truly global perspective and effective global skills are quite limited. This is often even more of a problem for midsize firms, that are becoming even more aggressive globally. Midsize U.S. multinational companies may not have played the global game as long as their larger competitors, but many are proving re-

FIGURE 2-3
Possible Relationships with Other Departments

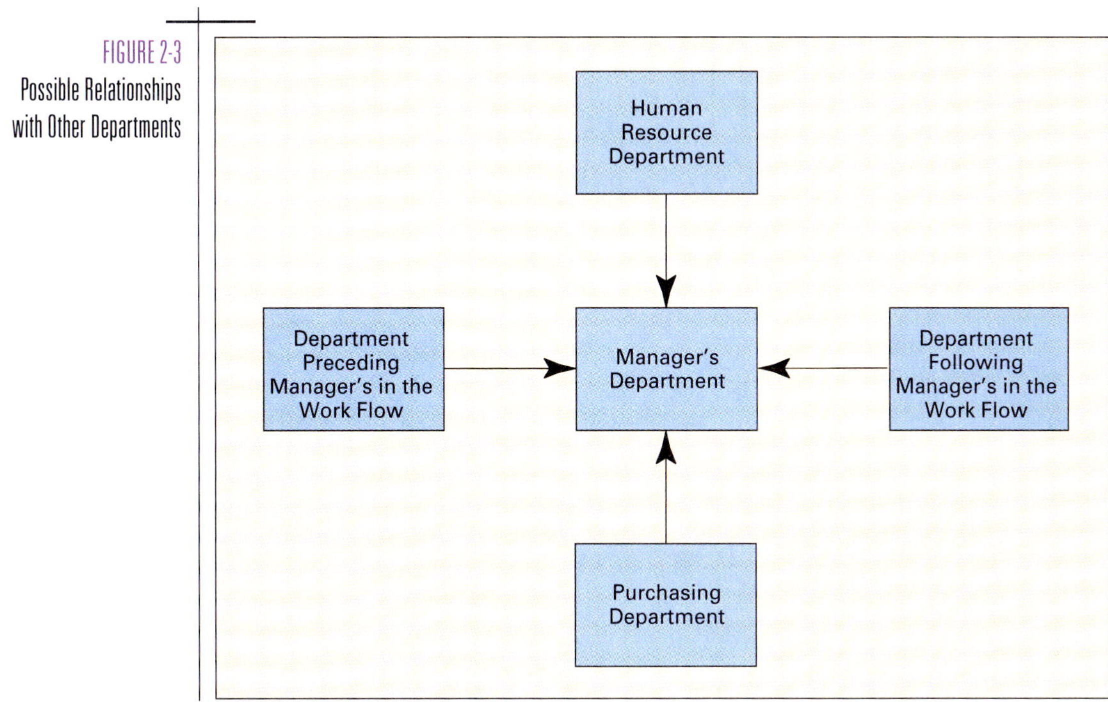

markably skilled, especially when it comes to the crucial task of creating efficient, responsive international and interactive workforces. They realize that human assets will play at least as large a role as advanced technology and economies of scale when it comes to competing in the global marketplace. According to a survey of 1,200 U.S. multinationals with annual sales of $1 billion or less, conducted by IBM and the human resources firm of Drake Beam Morin Inc., such companies are dealing with human asset problems in a unique way. These companies acknowledge that management compensation costs are rising faster outside the United States than inside, but still fall short of the total package required to establish a senior U.S. manager abroad, and, therefore, the companies try to fill senior positions abroad with locals,

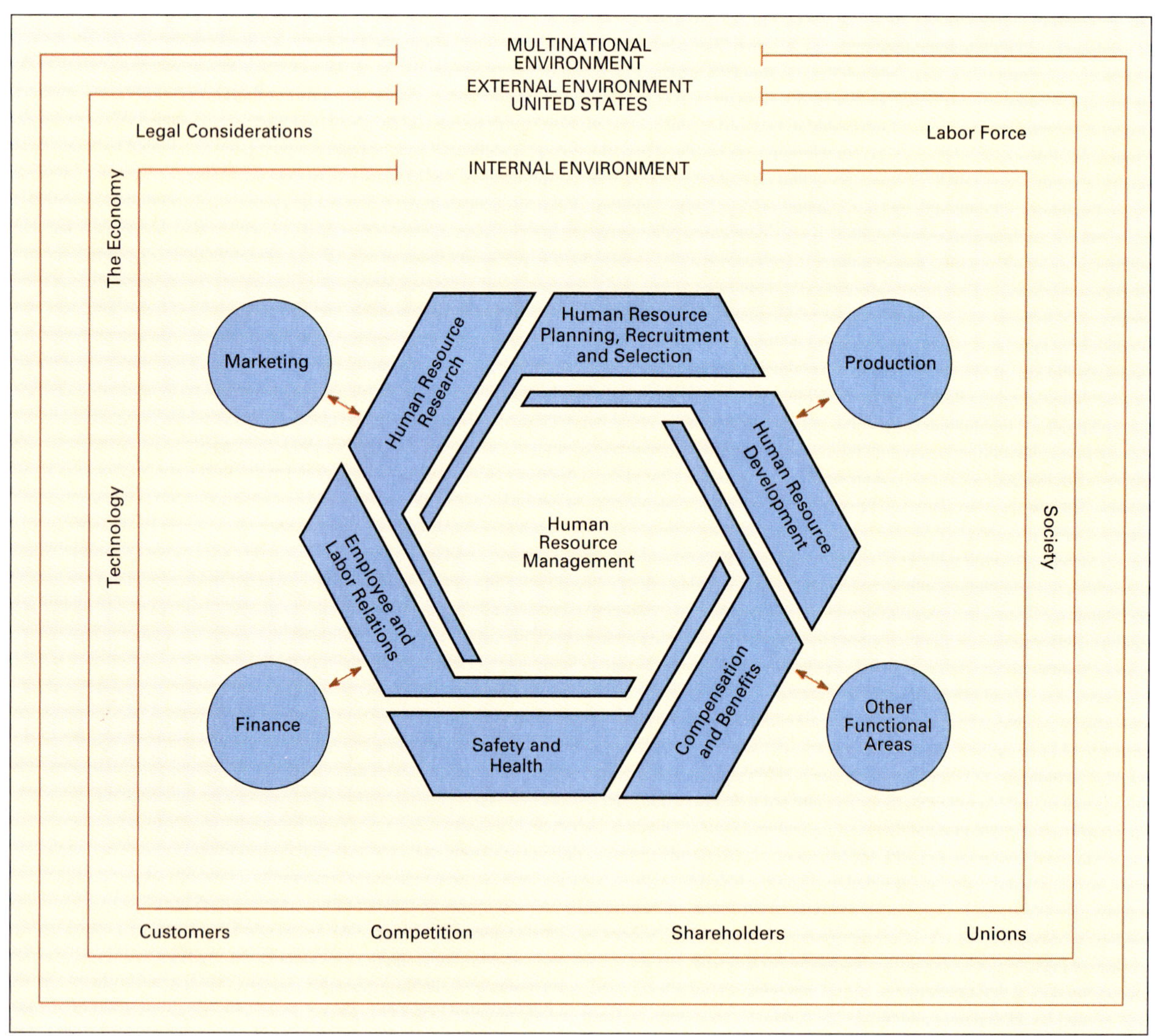

FIGURE 2-4 Human Resource Management in the Multinational Environment

importing U.S. experts only for such specific projects as technology transfer. This approach has proved quite successful without drawing heavily on domestic management talent.[36]

Earlier in this chapter our discussion focused primarily on environmental factors affecting organizations located and doing business only in the United States. The external environment confronting multinational enterprises is even more diverse and complex than that facing domestic firms. A **multinational corporation (MNC)** conducts a large part of its business outside the country in which it is headquartered and has a significant percentage of its physical facilities and employees in other countries. Thus, as illustrated in Figure 2-4, multinational operations add another environmental layer to human resource management. Although the basic human resource management tasks remain essentially the same, the manner in which they are accomplished may be altered substantially by the multinational's external environment. As previously mentioned, "A Global Perspective" is presented in each chapter to emphasize the importance of the multinational environment on human resource management.

Many interrelated factors affect human resource management. Effective HRM requires careful consideration of all environmental variables. The external environment affects a firm's human resources from inside. In addition, certain interrelationships complicate the management of human resources.

Factors in the external environment include the labor force, legal considerations, society, unions, shareholders, competition, customers, technology, and the economy. Each, separately or in combination with others, can impose constraints on the human resource manager's job.

The size of the labor force alone does not tell the entire employment story. The labor force now includes more working women, single parents, workers of color, and older persons. Many companies hire contingent or part-time workers, often for shared jobs. The use of temporary and leased employees is also increasing. Disabled employees are being included in the workforce in increasing numbers, and this trend may accelerate due to the passing of the Americans with Disabilities Act. Many new immigrants from developing areas, especially Southeast Asia and Latin America, continue to swell the U.S. labor force.

Society may also exert pressures on human resource management. Increasingly, firms must accomplish their purposes while meeting societal norms. A union is a group of employees who have joined together for the purpose of dealing with their employer. Unions are external factors because, essentially, they become a third party when dealing with the company. The owners of a corporation are called shareholders. Because shareholders have invested in the firm, they may challenge programs considered by management to be beneficial to the organization. Unless an organization is in the unusual position of monopolizing the market it serves, other firms will be producing similar goods or services. For a firm to succeed, grow, and prosper, it must be able to maintain a supply of competent employees.

Customers are those who actually use a firm's products and also are a part of the external environment. Because sales are crucial to the firm's survival, management must ensure that its employment practices and employees do not antagonize its customers.

Change is occurring at an ever increasing rate, and few firms operate today as they did even a decade ago. A major concern to those in HRM is the effect technological changes have had, and will have, on businesses.

In recent years, small and midsized companies have created 80 percent of the jobs. Every year thousands of individuals, motivated by a desire to be their own boss, to earn a better income, and to realize the American dream launch a new business venture.

The internal environment also exerts considerable pressure on human resource management. Internal factors include the firm's mission, policies, and corporate culture.

QUESTIONS FOR REVIEW

1. What is meant by the statement "The human resource manager's job is not accomplished in a vacuum"?
2. What factors make up the external environment of human resource management? Briefly describe each of these factors.
3. How is the composition of the U.S. labor force expected to change during the next decade?
4. What internal environment considerations exert pressure on the human resource manager?
5. How could changes in an organizational policy affect the human resource professional's work? Give an example.
6. Define *corporate culture.* What effect could it have on human resource management?

HRM SIMULATION

In any organization, it is important decisions be made based upon the best available information. The same is true with this simulation. Each decision period your team will have the opportunity to purchase industry research that will aid you in the decision-making process. The surveys available are industry average quality, morale, grievances, and absenteeism; industry average and local comparable wage rates; average industry training, safety, and quality budgets; and the number of firms with employee participation programs.

ABC VIDEO CASE

THE GRAYING OF AMERICA TAPE 2, NUMBER 4

The country's workforce is aging with a median age of 34.6 in 1980, 36.2 in 1989, and a projected 39.2 in the year 2000. Older executives are, however, finding their age to be a detriment. Such a detriment that they are starting over in new fields. Many are reworking their resume to leave off their executive experience.

The EEOC states that Age Discrimination is the fastest growing category it enforces. According to some economists, many companies feel that they are losing money by having an older workforce. Some feel that a 50-year-old executive is standing in the way of a young rising executive. Suits for discrimination charges can result in high verdict awards.

HRM INCIDENT 1

—A JAPANESE VIEW OF THE TRADE IMBALANCE

Throughout the mid-1980s, the U.S. trade deficit with Japan worsened. The Japanese share of American markets steadily increased, especially in automobiles and electronics. But very few products or services flowed the other way. The steadily growing stock of U.S. dollars in Japanese hands was used to buy up an increasing number of shares of U.S. companies. Labor unions and politicians complained about the loss of American jobs. Citizens expressed fear that the Japanese would come to own too much of American industry.

Corporations complained they were shut out of a potentially profitable foreign market.

The United States accused the Japanese of *dumping* products (that is, selling items in the United States for less than the cost of production). Another complaint frequently heard was that the Japanese government erected every conceivable trade barrier to keep American products out of Japan while American markets were essentially open to Japanese products.

But George Tanaka, senior vice president of Toyonoka Electronics, said that the problems were Americans' own fault. Tanaka described what he saw as the *real* source of U.S. trade balance problems.

"In a nutshell, in Japan we treat customers as God and you only say, 'The customer is king.' Let me explain. Toyonoka sells microwave ovens in the United States. I have been trying for over a year to find an American company to make some of the parts we need. We want to have the parts shipped to Japan for installation in United States-bound ovens. That would improve your trade balance. It would also allow us to take advantage of present favorable exchange rates.

"But I cannot find anyone who will produce the quality we need to stay competitive. American managers tell me, 'This is as good as we can do. You will have to change your operation to make the parts work.' In Japan, of course, suppliers value contracts like this and do all they can to meet our specifications. I am under a great deal of pressure to buy American. But American firms just do not seem to care about our needs.

"The same kind of attitude surfaces when I ask about shipping schedules. In our factories, we practice 'just in time' inventory control. Japanese suppliers deliver the parts we need just when we need them—and in small quantities. I know United States companies have to ship long distances. So we are willing to accept larger shipments and be somewhat flexible about delivery dates. But no American firm I have talked to will guarantee even the week of delivery. They say there are too many variables involved—strikes, raw materials, shortages, shipping problems. In Japan, a supplier would not ask me to worry about those things. I am the customer.

"The language also presents a problem. United States firms will not bother to use Japanese. They refuse to even print installation instructions and invoices in any language but English. This is especially grating since we take the time to learn even the American dialect of English. Can any American imagine buying a Toyonoka stereo or a Mazda automobile with the owner's manual written in Japanese? We take care of those problems because Americans are our valued customers."

Mr. Tanaka went on to reemphasize that American companies could sell as much in Japan as Japan sells in the United States if they gave Japanese customers proper regard.

Questions

1. Does Mr. Tanaka's "ugly American" argument have some validity?
2. What are the external environmental factors that both Japanese and U.S. companies encounter?

—HUMAN RESOURCE MANAGEMENT AT NUCOR STEEL

As steel producers went during the 1980s, Nucor Steel was a high flyer. While giants such as USX Corporation (formerly U. S. Steel) and Bethlehem Steel suffered huge losses in the early 1980s, Nucor Steel stayed prosperous. More than 100,000 steelworkers remained out of work in 1987, but Nucor Steel had not laid off a single hourly employee. Near the end of the decade, Nucor Steel stock sold at nineteen times earnings, compared to eleven for USX Corporation, five for Bethlehem Steel, and eight for Armco.

Things were not always so rosy for this relatively small—if $1 billion in sales can be called small—steel producer. Nucor Steel started off during the Great Depression as Reo Motors, Inc., a spinoff from the R. E. Olds Company. In 1938, the company filed for reorganization under the bankruptcy laws. It was briefly revived by World War II and then lingered until 1954, when liquidation seemed to have ended its suffering.

The only remnant that survived was Nuclear Corporation of America, the shares of which had been distributed to the former shareholders of Reo Motors. Nuclear Corporation of America was a hodgepodge of small, unrelated businesses, one of which was a steel bar joist maker. Bar joists are light steel beams made of angle iron and rods; they are used mainly to support elevated floors and roofs in commercial buildings.

Nuclear Corporation of America struggled along until 1965, posting a $2.2 million loss in that year alone. In the depths of Nuclear Corporation of America's despair, Kenneth Iverson took over as president and chief executive officer. Things began to change. By 1971, sales were $64.8 million and profits $2.7 million, healthy in comparison with the past. By 1980, sales had climbed to $482.4 million. Profits had increased even more markedly to $45.1 million. When the recession of the early 1980s decimated the rest of the steel industry, Nucor barely flinched. And the company remained continuously profitable through the last half of the decade.

What accounts for the success of Nucor while the rest of the steel industry stagnated? Opinions differ, but there are a number of possibilities. First, the company produces a narrow product line, using modern and highly efficient mini mills to melt scrap steel and shape it into angles, channels, and bars. Large, integrated producers, such as those mentioned earlier, mine iron ore and try to make every kind of steel plate and shape.

Probably the most significant single factor in Nucor's success is the productivity of its workforce. Nucor located its mini mills in rural areas where the work ethic was strong and there was little pro-union sentiment. This facilitated the company's use of certain innovative personnel policies designed to enhance productivity.

Iverson said, "Two things are very important to most people: What am I going to be paid, and am I going to have a job tomorrow?" Two fundamental Nucor policies grew out of this line of thinking. First, compensation is based on individual and group productivity and company profitability. Second, Nucor does not lay off hourly employees. Nucor also emphasizes communication with employees by having only three layers of management.

Questions

1. Evaluate the human resource management policies at Nucor Steel.
2. What are the environmental factors that affect human resource management at Nucor Steel?

DEVELOPING HRM SKILLS

AN EXPERIENTIAL EXERCISE

This is an exercise involving Jesse Heard, the human resource manager at Parma Cycle Company; Gene Wilson, the corporate planner; and Edmont Fitzgerald, the controller. Parma Cycle Company is one of only three companies in the United States that actually manufactures complete bicycles. Most of Parma Cycle Company's competitors import parts from other countries and simply assemble bicycles here. Parma Cycle Company currently employs about 800 workers at wages well above the average wage levels in the area. Most of these workers are machine operators and assemblers. Parma Cycle Company is experiencing severe difficulties competing with less expensive bicycles, and the time has come for Parma to lower its costs.

Jesse Heard, the human resource manager, is faced with a dilemma. He feels obligated to find the best quality labor at the best available price, but he is also concerned about the workers, some of whom have been with Parma Cycle Company for many years. Even though the highly favorable labor market allows replacement of many of these workers with others at lower pay, he hesitates to do so. Yesterday Jesse received an angry call from the president, Mr. Burgess, who told him to meet with the corporate planner and the controller to come up with a unified recommendation for taking advantage of the improved labor market.

Gene Wilson never really had much power at Parma Cycle Company, although his title, corporate planner, sounds impressive enough. Primarily, he maintains a chart room and keeps track of various trends. He basically agrees that Parma Cycle Company is headed downhill because of depressed markets and an inability on the part of company managers to decrease unit costs. In his opinion, the most important asset Parma Cycle Company has is a trained and loyal workforce. While many of the workers could be replaced with lower paid workers, he is afraid this would destroy the team spirit that now exists at Parma. He believes workers are more likely than ever to respond to financial incentives, such as some kind of piece rate program or bonus system.

Edmont Fitzgerald, the controller, is an Ohio State University graduate in finance, who believes that, above all, the corporation is an economic entity. He thinks market forces will take care of those workers who really wish to contribute to the economy. He believes in purchasing all resources, including labor, at the lowest possible price. He views the current situation as an opportunity to decrease costs radically. The union is weak, jobs are scarce, and there is a surplus of skilled workers in the area.

Three students will serve as the Parma Cycle Company's management: one as Jesse Heard, the human resource manager; one as Gene Wilson, the corporate planner; and one as Edmont Fitzgerald, the controller. All students not playing roles in the exercise should carefully observe the behavior of its participants. Your instructor will provide the participants with the additional information they will need.

NOTES

1. Kenneth E. Goodpaster and John B. Matthews, Jr., "Can a Corporation Have a Conscience?" *Harvard Business Review* 60 (January-February 1982): 132–41.

2. Robert J. Samuelson, "R.I.P.: The Good Corporation," *Newsweek* 122 (July 5, 1993): 41.

3. Aaron Bernstein, "Why America Needs Unions But Not the Kind It Has Now," *Business Week* (May 23, 1994): 70.

4. Michael Schroeder and Joseph Weber, "Is Merck Ready for Marty Wygod?" *Business Week* (October 4, 1993): 80–84.

5. Eric G. Flamholtz, Yvonne Randle, and Sonja Sack mann, "Personnel Management: The Tenor of Today," *Personnel Journal* 66 (June 1987): 64.

6. Marilyn Joyce, "Ergonomics Will Take Center Stage During '90s and Into New Century," *Occupational Health and Safety* 60 (January 1991): 31.

7. Joseph Spiers, "Behind the Job Worries, Business Keeps Plodding Along," *Fortune* 128 (August 9, 1993): 19.

8. Patricia Sellers, "The Best Cities for Business," *Fortune* 122 (October 22, 1990): 49.

9. Sinclair E. Hugh, "Observations from the Witness Stand," *HRMagazine* 39 (August 1994): 176.

10. Stephenie Overman, "Managing the Diverse Workforce," *HRMagazine* 36 (April 1991): 32.

11. Alice Cuneo, "Diverse By Design," *Business Week* (Reinventing America 1992): 72.

12. Lee Gardenswartz and Anita Rowe, *Managing Diversity* (San Diego: Business One Irwin/Pfeiffer & Company, 1993): 57–97; Mahalingham Subbiah, "Adding a New Dimension to the Teaching of Audience Analysis: Cultural Awareness," *IEEE Transactions on Professional Communication* 35 (March 1992); Marcus Mabry, "Pin a Label on a Manager—and Watch What Happened," *Newsweek* 14 (May 1990): 43.

13. Amanda Troy Segal and Wendy Zeller, "Corporate Women," *Business Week* (June 8, 1992): 74.

14. "More Women Are Executive VPs," *Fortune* 128 (July 12, 1993): 16.

15. Charlene Marmer Solomon, "Work/Family's Failing Grade: Why Today's Initiatives Aren't Enough," *Personnel Journal* 73 (May 1994): 72.

16. Amanda Troy Segal and Wendy Zellner, "Corporate Women," 74–78.

17. Dan Cordtz, "Hire Me, Hire My Family," *Finance World* 159 (September 18, 1990): 77.

18. Ella Bell, "The Bicultural Life Experience of Career Oriented Black Women," *Journal of Organizational Behavior* 11 (November 1990): 459–478.

19. Joan L. Kelly, "Employers Must Recognize That Older People Want to Work," *Personnel Journal* 69 (January 1990): 44.

20. Anthony J. Buonocore, "Older and Wiser: Mature Employees and Career Guidance," *Management Review* 81 (September 1992): 54.

21. Jaclyn Fierman, "The Contingency Workforce," *Fortune* 129 (January 24, 1994): 30.

22. John Ross, "Effective Ways to Hire Contingent Personnel," *HRMagazine* 36 (February 1991): 53.

23. Susan Goff Condon, "Hiring the Handicapped Confronts Cultural Uneasiness," *Personnel Journal* 66 (April 1987): 68.

24. Ibid.

25. Michael J. Mandel, "The Immigrants," *Business Week* (July 13, 1992): 114.

26. Larry Light, "The Job Engine Needs Fuel," *Business Week* (March 1, 1993): 78.

27. "A Surprising Finding on New-Business Mortality Rates," *Business Week* (June 14, 1993): 22.

28. Louis S. Richman, "Jobs That Are Growing and Slowing," *Fortune* 128 (July 12, 1993): 53.

29. "A Surprising Finding on New-Business Mortality Rates," *Business Week* (June 14, 1993): 22.

30. R. Wayne Mondy and Shane R. Premeaux, *Management: Concepts, Practices, and Skills,* 6th ed. (Boston: Allyn & Bacon, Inc., 1993): 450.

31. Stephanie Lawrence, "Voices of HR Experience," *Personnel Journal* 68 (April 1989): 71–72.

32. Judith H. Dobrzynski, Michael Schroeder, Gregory L. Miles, and Joseph Weber, "Taking Charge," *Business Week* (July 3, 1989): 66–71.

33. Michael J. Mandel, Wendy Zeller, and Robert Hof, "Jobs, Jobs," *Business Week* (February 22, 1993): 70.

34. Phillip R. Harris, "Employees Abroad: Maintain the Corporate Connection," *Personnel Journal* 65 (August 1986): 108.

35. Ellen Brandt, "Global HR," *Personnel Journal* 70 (March 1991): 38–39.

36. Lori Ioannou, "Human Resources Special Report: It's a Small Work After All," *International Business* (February 1994): 82–88.

CHAPTER 3

Equal Employment Opportunity and Affirmative Action

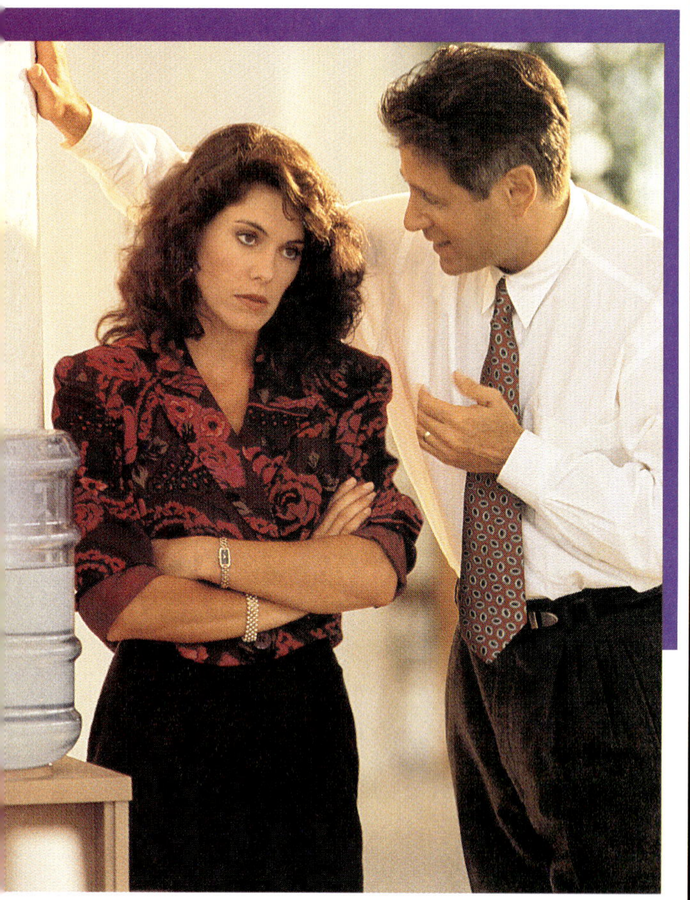

KEY TERMS

CHAPTER OBJECTIVES

1. Explain the major laws affecting equal employment opportunity.
2. Explain Presidential Executive Orders 11246 and 11375.
3. Identify and briefly describe some of the major Supreme Court decisions that have had an impact on equal employment opportunity.
4. Explain the purpose of the Equal Employment Opportunity Commission.
5. Describe the Uniform Guidelines on Employee Selection Procedures and the additional guidelines that have been adopted.
6. Describe affirmative action programs.

"I agree with you Phyllis," said Art Kurth, supervisor of the maintenance division of Allied Chemical. "Mary Martin is by far the best qualified to fill that vacant position in my department. She has done similar work at Olin for seven years and comes highly recommended. I really want to hire her, but do you think a woman could survive with that crew? They might not work with her, and you know how important cooperation is in that job. Remember what happened when we hired that woman a couple of years ago. She lasted a week before she walked out crying and didn't return."

Phyllis Jordon, human resource manager of Allied, was visibly upset when she heard Art's comments. Ten years ago when she joined Allied, she might have expected something like that, but not now. Allied has an aggressive nondiscrimination policy. "Listen, Art," she said, "I still recommend that you hire her. I know that you can find a way to see that she fits in. From all I can gather, she is a top-notch worker, and Allied is lucky to have an applicant of that quality. I'll help you make this work."

In this chapter, we provide an overview of the major equal employment opportunity legislation that has had an impact on human resource management. We first discuss the significant equal employment opportunity laws affecting human resource management. Then, we describe the importance of Presidential Executive Orders 11246 and 11375. Next, we review significant Supreme Court decisions and describe the Equal Employment Opportunity Commission. Then, we discuss the Uniform Guidelines on Employee Selection Procedures and address the issue of adverse impact. We devote the remainder of the chapter to affirmative action programs.

EQUAL EMPLOYMENT OPPORTUNITY: AN OVERVIEW

The concept of equal employment opportunity has undergone much modification and fine-tuning since the passage of the Civil Rights Act of 1964. Congress has passed numerous amendments to that act and has passed other legislation, as oversights in the initial act surfaced. Major Supreme Court decisions interpreting the provisions of the act have also been handed down. Executive orders were signed into law that further strengthened equal employment opportunity. Now nearly three decades have passed, and equal employment opportunity has become a part of the workplace.

Although continuing efforts are required, equal employment opportunity has come a long way since the early 1960s. Today the majority of businesses do attempt to make employment decisions based on who is the best qualified, as opposed to whether an individual is of a certain gender, race, religion, color, national origin, or age. By and large, the laws, the Supreme Court decisions, and the executive orders have provided organizations—both public and private—the opportunity to tap the abilities of a workforce that was largely underutilized before the mid-1960s.

LAWS AFFECTING EQUAL EMPLOYMENT OPPORTUNITY

Numerous national laws have been passed that have had an impact on equal employment opportunity. The passage of these laws reflects society's attitude toward the changes that should be made to give everyone an equal opportunity for employment. We briefly describe the most significant of these laws in the following sections.

Civil Rights Acts of 1866 and 1871

The Civil Rights Act of 1866 is based on the Thirteenth Amendment to the Constitution and prohibits racial discrimination in the making and enforcement of contracts, which could include hiring and promotion decisions. Private employers, unions, and employment agencies are all covered under this act. The 1871 act is based on the Fourteenth Amendment and prohibits deprivation of equal employment rights under state laws. State and local governments are included. There is virtually no effective statute of limitations on filing charges under these acts.[1]

Title VII of the Civil Rights Act of 1964—Amended 1972

One law that has greatly influenced human resource management is Title VII of the 1964 Civil Rights Act, as amended by the Equal Employment Opportunity Act of 1972. This legislation prohibits discrimination based on race, color, sex, religion, or national origin. Title VII covers employers engaged in an industry affecting interstate commerce with fifteen or more employees for at least twenty calendar weeks in the year in which a charge is filed, or the year preceding the filing of a charge. Included in the definition of employers are state and local governments, schools, colleges, unions, and employment agencies. The act created the Equal Employment Opportunity Commission (EEOC), which is responsible for its enforcement.

Age Discrimination in Employment Act of 1967—Amended in 1978 and 1986

As originally enacted, the Age Discrimination in Employment Act (ADEA) prohibited employers from discriminating against individuals who were forty to sixty-five years old. The 1978 amendment provided protection for individuals who were at least forty, but less than seventy years old. A 1986 amendment made employer discrimination against anyone over forty years old illegal. The latest amendment not only gives older employees the option to continue working past seventy, but the health care provision of the amendment also provides them with an additional incentive to continue to do so.[2] The act pertains to employers with twenty or more employees for twenty or more calendar weeks (either in the current or preceding calendar year); unions of twenty-five or more members; employment agencies; and federal, state, and local government sub-units. Administration of the act was transferred from the U.S. Department of Labor to the EEOC in 1979.

Enforcement begins when a charge is filed, but the EEOC can review compliance even if no charge is filed. The Age Discrimination in Employment Act differs from Title VII of the Civil Rights Act in that it provides for a trial by jury and carries a possible criminal penalty. The trial by jury provision is important because juries may have great sympathy for older people who may have been discriminated against. The criminal penalty provision means a person may receive more than lost wages if discrimination is proved. The 1978 amendment also makes class action suits possible.

The Older Workers Benefit Protection Act (OWBPA), an amendment to the Age Discrimination in Employment Act, was signed into law on October 16, 1990.[3] The amendment overturned the Supreme Court's decision in *Public Employees Retirement System of Ohio v Betts* and adopted an equal benefit or equal cost philosophy. This act prohibits discrimination in the administration of benefits on the basis of age, but also permits early retirement incentive plans as long as they are voluntary.[4] The act also establishes wrongful termination waiver requirements as a means of protecting older employees by ensuring that waiver acceptance was made by fully informed and willful personnel.[5]

Rehabilitation Act of 1973

The Rehabilitation Act covers certain government contractors and subcontractors and organizations that receive federal grants in excess of $2,500. Individuals are considered disabled if they have a physical or mental impairment that substantially limits one or more major life activities or if they have a record of such impairment. If a contract or subcontract exceeds $50,000 or if the contractor has fifty or more employees, an affirmative action program must be prepared. In it, the contractor must specify reasonable steps are being taken to hire and promote disabled persons. The Office of Federal Contract Compliance Programs (OFCCP) administers the act.

Pregnancy Discrimination Act of 1978

Passed as an amendment to Title VII of the Civil Rights Act, the Pregnancy Discrimination Act prohibits discrimination in employment based on pregnancy, childbirth, or related medical conditions. The basic principle of the act is women affected by pregnancy, and related conditions, must be treated the same as other applicants and employees on the basis of their ability or inability to work. A woman is, therefore, protected against such practices as being fired or refused a job or promotion merely because she is pregnant or has had an abortion. She usually cannot be forced to take a leave of absence as long as she can work. If other employees on disability leave are entitled to return to their jobs when they are able to work again, so too are women who have been unable to work because of pregnancy.

The same principle applies in the benefits area, including disability benefits, sick leave, and health insurance. A woman unable to work for pregnancy-related reasons is entitled to disability benefits or sick leave on the same basis as employees unable to work for medical reasons. Also, any health insurance provided must cover expenses for pregnancy-related conditions on the same basis as expenses for other medical conditions. However, health insurance for expenses arising from an abortion is not required except where the life of the mother would be endangered if the fetus were carried to term or where medical complications have arisen from an abortion.

In a class action suit originally filed in 1978 but settled in July 1991, American Telephone & Telegraph Company (AT&T) agreed to settle a pregnancy discrimination suit with the EEOC for $66 million. This suit was the largest cash recovery in the agency's history and involved more than 13,000 present and former female AT&T workers. The 1978 suit charged that Western Electric required pregnant workers to leave their jobs at the end of their sixth month of pregnancy, denied them seniority credit, and refused to guarantee them a job when they returned.[6]

Immigration Reform and Control Act of 1986

The Immigration Reform and Control Act (IRCA) established criminal and civil sanctions against employers who knowingly hire an unauthorized alien. The act further makes hiring anyone without verifying employment authorization and identity unlawful. Employers who unlawfully hire an illegal alien will be subject to fines of $250-$2,000 per worker for the first offense; $2,000-$5,000 for the second offense; and $3,000-$10,000 for the third offense. In addition, employers who fail to comply with the record-keeping provisions of the law are subject to a penalty of $100-$1,000 for each individual they fail to document even if the individual is legally entitled to be employed. Moreover, when dealing with the national origin provision of the Civil Rights Act, IRCA reduces the threshold coverage from fifteen to four employees. The effect of this extension of the 1964 law will be to curtail hiring actions of some businesses. They may choose to hire only U.S. citizens and, thereby, avoid any potential violation of IRCA. However, many foreign nationals are in this country legally (many who are legal immigrants awaiting citizenship); refusing to hire them would violate their civil rights.[7]

The Americans with Disabilities Act (ADA)

The Americans with Disabilities Act (ADA), passed in 1990, prohibits discrimination against *qualified individuals* with *disabilities.* Persons discriminated against because they have a known association or relationship with a disabled individual also are protected. The ADA defines an *individual with a disability* as a person who has, or is regarded as having, a physical or mental impairment that substantially limits one or more major life activities, and has a record of such an impairment, or is regarded as having such an impairment. The ADA prohibits discrimination in all employment practices, including job application procedures, hiring, firing, advancement, compensation, training, and other terms, conditions, and privileges of employment. It applies to recruitment, advertising, tenure, layoff, leave, fringe benefits, and all other employment-related activities.

The employment provisions apply to private employers, state and local governments, employment agencies, and labor unions. Employers with twenty-five or more employees were covered beginning in July 1992. Employers with fifteen or more employees were covered beginning July 26, 1994.[8] The full impact of this new law is yet to be fully determined. For example, some believe obesity may emerge as a lifestyle that is protected under the act.[9] In fact, a lower court ruling in December of 1993 stated that *uncontrollable obesity* is protected under ADA. Also, legislative history suggests Congress intended the act to protect persons with AIDS and the HIV virus.

The Equal Employment Opportunity Commission (EEOC) issued new guidelines on May 19, 1994 on preemployment inquiries and tests regarding disabilities that clarify provisions in the Americans with Disabilities Act of 1990 (ADA) that prohibit inquiries and medical examinations intended to gain information about applicants' disabilities before a conditional job offer. The guiding principle is to ask only about potential employees' ability to do the job, and not about their disabilities. Lawful inquiries include those regarding performance of specific functions or possession of training, while illegal inquiries include those that ascertain previous medical conditions or extent of prior drug use.[10]

It is quite interesting to note even as new U.S. laws, such as ADA and the Civil Rights Act of 1991, are generating a growing number of employment-related claims, overseas claims are increasing rapidly. In the United

Kingdom, Europe, and Japan, the court systems are becoming more accessible, and the number of employment related claims is increasing rapidly. According to Theodore Boundas of Peterson and Ross, the new laws written to govern the European Economic Community trading pact will greatly increase the number of employment-related claims filed annually.[11]

Civil Rights Act of 1991

The Civil Rights Act of 1991 amended the Civil Rights Act of 1964 and had the following purposes:

1. To provide appropriate remedies for intentional discrimination and unlawful harassment in the workplace.
2. To codify the concepts of *business necessity* and *job related* pronounced by the Supreme Court in *Griggs v Duke Power Co.,* and in the other Supreme Court decisions prior to *Wards Cove Packing Co., Inc. v Antonio.*
3. To confirm statutory authority and provide statutory guidelines for the adjudication of disparate impacts under Title VII of the Civil Rights Act of 1964.
4. To respond to recent decisions of the Supreme Court by expanding the scope of relevant civil rights statutes in order to provide adequate protection to victims of discrimination.

Under this act, a complaining party may recover punitive damages if the complaining party demonstrates the company engaged in a discriminatory practice with malice or with reckless indifference to the law. However, the following limits, based on the number of people employed by the company, were placed on the amount of the award:

- between 15 and 100 employees—$50,000
- between 101 and 200 employees—$100,000
- between 201 and 500 employees—$200,000
- more than 500 employees—$300,000

In each case, employees must be with the firm for twenty or more calendar weeks in the current or preceding calendar year.

With regard to burden of proof in disparate impact cases, an unlawful employment practice passed on disparate impact is established under this title only if a complaining party demonstrates a respondent uses a particular employment practice that causes a disparate impact on the basis of race, color, religion, sex, or national origin, and the company fails to demonstrate the challenged practice is job related for the position in question and consistent with business necessity. The act also extends the coverage of the Civil Rights Act of 1964 to extraterritorial employment. However, the act does not apply to U.S. companies operating in another country if it would violate the law of the foreign country. Furthermore, the act reverses the following Supreme Court decisions: *Patterson v McLean Credit Union, Martin v Wilks,* and *Wards Cove Packing Co., Inc. v Antonio.* However, in a recent Supreme Court decision, it was ruled that the act does not apply to the cases that were pending when the act took effect.[12]

The act mandates the establishment of the Equal Employment Opportunity Commission's Technical Assistance Training Institute (TATI) and enhances Title VII's provisions regarding education and outreach. The TATI provides technical assistance and training regarding the laws and regulations enforced by the commission. The commission is charged with carrying out educational and outreach activities (including dissemination of information in languages other than English) targeted to individuals who historically have been victims of employment discrimination and have not been equitably served by the commission. The act also extends the nondiscrimination principles to Congress and other government agencies, such as the General Accounting Office and the Government Printing Office.

Also included in the Civil Rights Act of 1991 is the Glass Ceiling Act of 1991. The purpose of this act is to establish a Glass Ceiling commission to study the manner in which businesses fill management and decision making positions, the developmental and skill enhancing practices used to foster the necessary qualifications for advancement to such positions, and the compensation programs and reward structures currently utilized in the workplace. It also established an annual award for excellence in promoting a more diverse skilled workforce at the management and decision making levels in business.

Glass Ceiling

A phrase that has been used in recent years is the **glass ceiling**, meaning the invisible barrier in organizations that prevents many women and minorities from achieving top level management positions. Companies have discovered the courts are being forceful in eliminating such barriers. In one instance, a highly rated female supervisor was denied a promotion because her boss said it would be easier for employees to work with a man who was their *chum*. The employer reasoned that when it came to working long hours, the staff would work better with the male worker who was promoted. The courts disagreed and called this action unlawful discrimination.[13]

Such situations may be less numerous in the future. As we mentioned in Chapter 2, half of today's entry level managers are women, which is up from 15 percent fifteen years ago.[14] Because of the critical mass of talent, many believe the 1990s will be the decade that women progress to upper level management. In fact, in a recent survey of 400 top female executives, it was found that the percentage of women who hold the title of executive vice president more than doubled over the past decade, from 4 percent to 8.7 percent.[15]

State and Local Laws

Numerous state and local laws also affect equal employment opportunity. A number of states and some cities have passed fair employment practice laws prohibiting discrimination on the basis of race, color, religion, gender, or national origin. Even prior to federal legislation, several states had antidiscrimination legislation relating to age and gender. For instance, New York protected individuals between the ages of eighteen and sixty-five prior to the 1978 and 1986 ADEA amendments, and California had no upper limit on protected age. However, when EEOC regulations conflict with state or local civil rights regulations, the legislation more favorable to women and minorities applies.

EXECUTIVE ORDER 11246, AS AMENDED BY EXECUTIVE ORDER 11375

An **executive order (EO)** is a directive issued by the president and has the force and effect of laws enacted by Congress. In 1965, President Lyndon B. Johnson signed EO 11246. This EO makes it the policy of the U.S. government to provide equal opportunity in federal employment for all qualified persons. It prohibits discrimination in employment because of race, creed, color, or national origin. The EO also requires promoting the full realization of equal employment opportunity through a positive, continuing program in each executive department and agency. The policy of equal opportunity applies to every aspect of federal employment policy and practice.

A major provision of EO 11246 requires adherence to a policy of nondiscrimination in employment as a condition for the approval of a grant, contract, loan, insurance, or guarantee. Every executive department and agency that administers a program involving federal financial assistance must include such language in its contracts. Contractors must agree not to discriminate in employment because of race, creed, color, or national origin during performance of a contract.

Affirmative action, stipulated by EO 11246, requires employers to take positive steps to ensure employment of applicants and treatment of employees during employment without regard to race, creed, color, or national origin. Human resource practices covered relate to employment, upgrading, demotion, transfer, recruitment or recruitment advertising, layoffs or termination, rates of pay or other forms of compensation, and selection for training, including apprenticeships. Employers are required to post notices to this effect in conspicuous places in the workplace. In the event of contractor noncompliance, contracts can be canceled, terminated, or suspended in whole or in part, and the contractor may be declared ineligible for future government contracts. In 1968, EO 11246 was amended by EO 11375, which changed the word *creed* to *religion* and added sex discrimination to the other prohibited items. These EOs are enforced by the Department of Labor through the Office of Federal Contract Compliance Programs (OFCCP).

SIGNIFICANT U.S. SUPREME COURT DECISIONS

Knowledge of the law is obviously important for human resource managers. However, they must be aware of and understand much more than the words in the law itself. The manner in which the courts interpret the law is also vitally important. And interpretation continuously changes even though the law may not have been amended. Discussions of some of the more significant U.S. Supreme Court decisions affecting equal employment opportunity follow.

Griggs v Duke Power Company

A major decision affecting the field of human resource management was rendered on March 8, 1971. A group of black employees at Duke Power Company had charged job discrimination under Title VII of the Civil Rights Act of 1964. Prior to Title VII, the Duke Power Company had two workforces, separated by race. After passage of the act, the company required applicants to have a high school diploma and pass a paper and pencil test to qualify for certain jobs. The plaintiff was able to demonstrate that, in the relevant labor market, 34 percent of the white males but only 12 percent of the black males had a high school education. The plaintiff was also able to show people already in those jobs were performing successfully even though they did not have high school diplomas. No business necessity could be shown for this educational requirement.

In an 8-0 vote, the Supreme Court ruled against Duke Power Company and stated, "If an employment practice which operates to exclude Negroes cannot be shown to be related to job performance, the practice is prohibited." A major implication of the decision is when human resource management practices eliminate substantial numbers of minority or women applicants, the burden of proof is on the employer to show that the practice is job related. This court decision significantly affected the human resource practices of many firms.

Albermarle Paper Company v Moody

In August 1966, a class action suit was brought against Albermarle Paper Company and the plant employees' labor union. A permanent injunction was requested against any policy, practice, custom, or usage at the plant that violated Title VII. In 1975, the Supreme Court in *Albermarle Paper Co. v Moody* reaffirmed the idea that any test used in the selection process, or in promotion decisions, must be validated if it is found its use has had an adverse impact on women and minorities. The employer has the burden of proof for showing the test is valid. Subsequently, the employer must show that any selection or promotion device actually measures what it is supposed to measure.

Phillips v Martin Marietta Corporation

In this 1971 case, the court ruled that the company had discriminated against a woman because she had young children. The company had a rule prohibiting the hiring of women with school-age children. The company argued that it did not preclude all women from job consideration—only those women with school-age children. Martin Marietta contended that this was a business requirement. The argument was obviously based on stereotypes and was rejected. A major implication of this decision is a firm cannot impose standards for employment only on women. For example, a firm cannot reject divorced women if it does not also reject divorced men. Neither application forms nor interviews should contain questions for women that do not also apply to men.

Weber v Kaiser Aluminum and Chemical Corporation

In 1974, the United Steelworkers of America (USWA) and Kaiser Aluminum and Chemical Corporation entered into a master collective bargaining agreement covering terms and conditions of employment at fifteen Kaiser plants.

HRM IN ACTION

—AN EQUAL EMPLOYMENT DILEMMA

You are the general manager of a great group of people, but you would rather be doing anything else. Today you must antagonize your friend Fred, who is the most successful dock foreman you have. You realize Fred will not understand when you tell him he needs to consider hiring qualified minorities and women. You know Fred believes he best understands who he needs to hire to get the job done. Fred has stated many times, "On the docks, we don't shuffle paper, we do real work, and it takes real men to do the work." According to Fred, "My men are the best dock workers on the pier. They have always exceeded the tonnage moved by any other group, and that is because they work well together. Change the makeup of the work group, and the productivity of the group will be severely damaged."

What would you do?

The agreement contained an affirmative action plan designed to eliminate conspicuous racial imbalances in Kaiser's then almost exclusively white craft workforce. Black craft hiring goals equal to the percentage of blacks in the respective local labor forces were set for each Kaiser plant. To enable the plants to meet these goals, on-the-job training programs were established to teach unskilled production workers—black and white—the skills necessary to become craft workers. The plan reserved 50 percent of the openings in the newly created in-plant training programs for black employees.

In 1974, only 1.83 percent (5 out of 273) of the skilled craft workers at the Gramercy, Louisiana, plant were black, even though the labor force in the Gramercy area was approximately 39 percent black. Thirteen craft trainees, of whom seven were black and six were white, were selected from Gramercy's production workforce. The most junior black selected for the program had less seniority than several white production workers whose bids for admission were rejected. Brian Weber subsequently instituted a class action suit alleging that the action by Kaiser and USWA discriminated against him and other similarly situated white employees in violation of Title VII. Although the lower courts ruled that Kaiser's actions were illegal because they fostered reverse discrimination, the Supreme Court reversed that decision, stating that Title VII does not prohibit race-conscious affirmative action plans. Since the affirmative action plan was voluntarily agreed to by the company and the union, it did not violate Title VII.

Dothard v Rawlingson

At the time Rawlingson applied for a position as a correctional counselor trainee, she was a twenty-two year old college graduate whose major course of study had been correctional psychology. She was refused employment because she failed to meet the minimum height and weight requirements. In this 1977 case, the Supreme Court upheld the U.S. District Court's decision that Alabama's statutory minimum height requirement of five feet two inches and minimum weight requirement of 120 pounds for the position of correctional counselor had a discriminatory impact on women applicants. The contention was that minimum height and weight requirements for the position of correctional counselor were job related. However, the Court stated this argument does not rebut *prima facie* evidence showing these requirements have a discriminatory impact on women, whereas no evidence was produced correlating these requirements with a requisite amount of strength thought essential to good performance. The impact of the decision was height and weight requirements must be job related.

University of California Regents v Bakke

This Supreme Court decision involved the first major test concerning reverse discrimination. The University of California had reserved sixteen places in each beginning medical school class for minority persons. Allen Bakke, a white man, was denied admission even though he scored higher on the admission criteria than some minority applicants who were admitted. The Supreme Court ruled 5-4 in Bakke's favor. As a result, Bakke was admitted to the university and later received his degree. But, at the same time, the Court reaffirmed that race may be taken into account in admission decisions.

American Tobacco Company v Patterson

This 1982 Supreme Court decision allows seniority and promotion systems established since Title VII to stand although they unintentionally hurt minority workers. Under *Griggs v Duke Power Co.*, a *prima facie* violation of Title VII may be established by policies or practices that are neutral on their face and in intent, but that nonetheless discriminate against a particular group. A seniority system would fall under the *Griggs* rationale if it were not for Section 703(h) of the Civil Rights Act, which provides:

> Notwithstanding any other provision of this subchapter, it shall not be an unlawful employment practice for an employer to apply standards of compensation, or different terms, conditions, or privileges of employment pursuant to a bona fide seniority or merit system . . . provided that such differences are not the result of an intention to discriminate because of race, color, religion, sex, or national origin, nor shall it be an unlawful employment practice for an employer to give and to act upon the results of any professionally developed ability test provided that such test, its administration or action upon the results is not designed, intended or used to discriminate because of race, color, religion, sex, or national origin. . . .

Thus, the Court ruled that a seniority system adopted after Title VII may stand even though it has an unintended discriminatory impact.

Meritor Savings Bank v Vinson

The first sexual harassment case to reach the U.S. Supreme Court was the June 1986 case, *Meritor Savings Bank v Vinson*. In ruling for the plaintiff, one of the outcomes from the case was that Title VII was ruled to be not limited to discrimination having only economic or tangible effects. The plaintiff in this case had obtained two promotions based on merit even though sexual harassment was involved. The Court also ruled on whether an employee's voluntary participation in sexual acts with a manager constitutes a valid defense for an employer to a Title VII complaint. Here, they said that the appropriate test is whether the sexual activity was *unwelcomed,* not whether the employee voluntarily engaged in sexual activity with her manager.[16]

City of Richmond v J.A. Croson Co.

The City of Richmond adopted a Minority Business Utilization Plan requiring prime contractors awarded city construction contracts to subcontract at least 30 percent of the dollar amount of each contract to one or more Minority Business Enterprises (MBEs), which the plan defined to include a business from anywhere in the country at least 51 percent of which is owned and controlled by black, Spanish-speaking, Oriental, Native American, Eskimo, or Aleut citizens. After J. A. Croson Co. was denied a waiver and lost its contract, it brought suit alleging that the plan was unconstitutional under the Fourteenth Amendment's Equal Protection Clause. On January 23, 1989, the Supreme Court affirmed a Court of Appeals ruling that the city's plan was not justified by a compelling governmental interest because the record revealed no prior discrimination by the city itself in awarding contracts, and the 30 percent set-aside was not narrowly tailored to accomplish a remedial purpose. The decision forced thirty-six states and many cities and counties to review their programs.

Adarand Constructors v Pena

In a 5-4 opinion, the U.S. Supreme Court on June 12, 1995, criticized the moral justification for affirmative action, saying that race-conscious programs can amount to unconstitutional reverse discrimination and even harm those they seek to advance. The Adarand case concerned a Department of Transportation policy that gave contractors a bonus if they hired minority subcontractors. A white contractor challenged the policy in court after losing a contract to build guardrails despite offering the lowest bid. A federal appeals court upheld the program as within the proper bounds of affirmative action. The Supreme Court decision did not uphold or reject that ruling, but instead sent the case back for further review under new, tougher rules. As a result, the ruling seemed to invite legal challenges to other federal affirmative action programs.

EQUAL EMPLOYMENT OPPORTUNITY COMMISSION

As we mentioned previously, Title VII of the Civil Rights Act, as amended, created the Equal Employment Opportunity Commission (EEOC). Under Title VII, filing a discrimination charge initiates EEOC action. Charges may be filed by one of the presidentially

FIGURE 3-1
EEOC Procedure Once a Charge Is Filed

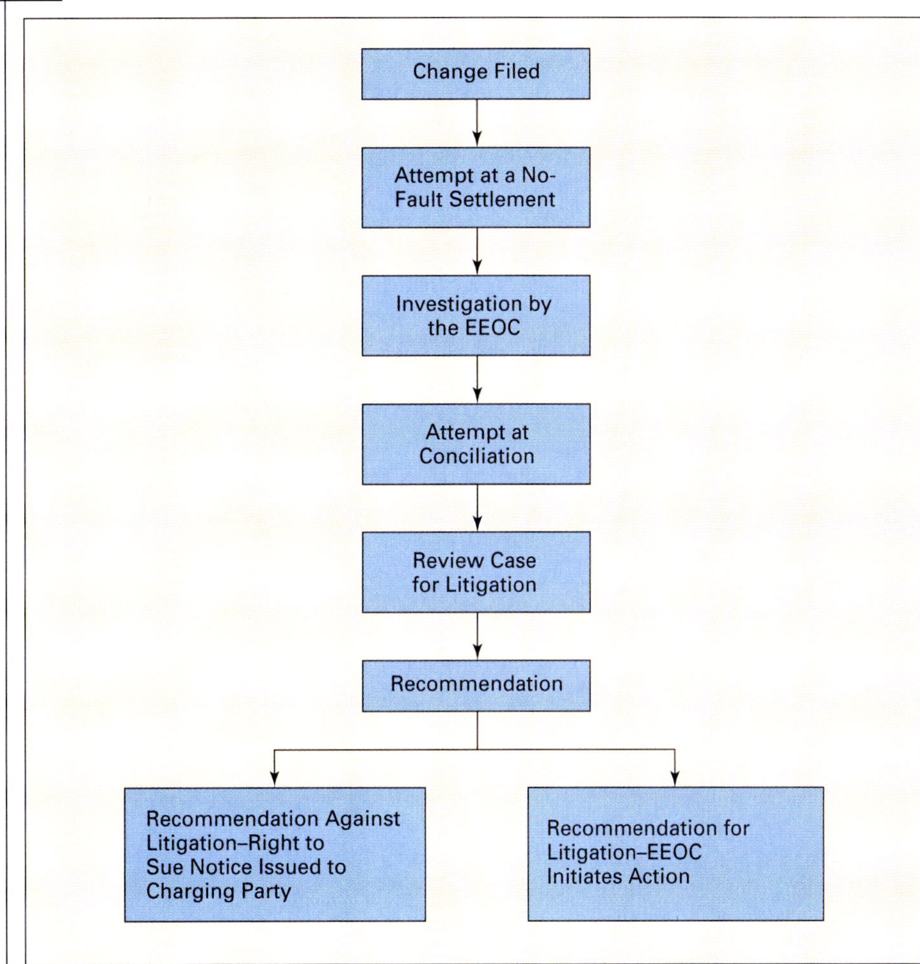

appointed EEOC commissioners, by any aggrieved person, or by anyone acting on behalf of an aggrieved person. Charges must be filed within 180 days of the alleged act. However, the time is extended to 300 days if a state or local agency is involved in the case.

As you can see in Figure 3-1, when a charge is filed, the EEOC typically proceeds in this manner. First, an attempt at no-fault settlement is made. Essentially, the organization charged with the violation is invited to settle the case with no admission of guilt. Most charges are settled at this stage.

Failing settlement, the EEOC investigates the charges. Once the employer is notified an investigation will take place, no records relating to the charge may be destroyed. During the investigative process, the employer is permitted to present a position statement. After the investigation has been completed, the district director of the EEOC will issue a *probable cause* or a *no probable cause* statement.

The next step involves attempted conciliation. In the event this effort fails, the case will be reviewed for litigation potential. Some of the factors determining whether the EEOC will pursue litigation are (1) the number of people affected by the alleged practice; (2) the amount of money involved in the charge; (3) other charges against the employer; and (4) the type of charge. Recommendations for litigation are then passed on to the general counsel of the EEOC. If the recommendation is against litigation, a right to sue notice will be issued to the charging party.

It is important to note that the Civil Rights Act of 1964 prohibits retaliation against employees who have opposed an illegal employment practice. The act also protects those who have testified, assisted, or participated in the investigation of discrimination.

There are certain exceptions to the coverage of Title VII. These exceptions include (1) religious institutions, with respect to the employment of persons of a specific religion in any of the institution's activities; (2) aliens; and (3) members of the Communist Party. Noncitizens are not protected from discrimination because of their lack of citizenship. However, they are protected from discrimination because of their national origin. Even with these exceptions, the impact of the law has been felt by virtually every organization.

UNIFORM GUIDELINES ON EMPLOYEE SELECTION PROCEDURES

Prior to 1978, employers were faced with complying with several different selection guidelines. In 1978, the *Uniform Guidelines on Employee Selection Procedures* were adopted by the Equal Employment Opportunity Commission, the Civil Service Commission, the Department of Justice, and the Department of Labor. These *Guidelines* cover several federal equal employment opportunity statutes and executive orders (EO) including Title VII of the Civil Rights Act, EO 11246, and the Equal Pay Act. They do not apply to the Age Discrimination in Employment Act or the Rehabilitation Act.

The *Uniform Guidelines* provide a single set of principles that were designed to assist employers, labor organizations, employment agencies, and licensing and certification boards in complying with federal prohibitions against employment practices that discriminate on the basis of race, color, religion, gender, and national origin. The *Guidelines* provide a framework for making legal employment decisions about hiring, promotion, demotion, referral, retention, licensing and certification, the proper use of tests, and other selection procedures. Under the *Guidelines,* recruiting procedures are not considered selection procedures, and, therefore, are not covered.

Regarding selection procedures, the *Guidelines* state that a test is:

> Any measure, combination of measures, or procedures used as a basis for any employment decision. Selection procedures include the full range of assessment techniques from traditional paper and pencil tests, performance tests, testing programs or probationary periods and physical, education, and work experience requirement through informal or casual interviews and unscored application forms.

Using this definition, virtually any instrument or procedure used in the selection decision is considered a test.

The Concept of Adverse Impact

Prior to the issuance of the *Uniform Guidelines on Employee Selection Procedures* in 1978, the only way to prove job relatedness was to validate each test. The

Guidelines do not require validation in all cases. Essentially, it is required only in instances where the test or other selection device produces an adverse impact on a minority group. Under the *Guidelines,* adverse impact has been defined in terms of selection rates, the selection rate being the number of applicants hired or promoted, divided by the total number of applicants.[17] **Adverse impact**, a concept established by the *Uniform Guidelines,* occurs if women and minorities are not hired at the rate of at least 80 percent of the best achieving group. This has also been called the four-fifths rule, which is actually a guideline subject to interpretation by the EEOC. The groups identified for analysis under the guidelines are (1) blacks, (2) Native Americans (including Alaskan natives), (3) Asians, (4) Hispanics, (5) women, and (6) men.

The following formula is used to compute adverse impact for hiring:

$$\frac{\text{Success rate for women and minority applicants}}{\text{Success rate for best achieving group applicants}} = \text{Determination of adverse impact}$$

The success rate for women and minority applicants is determined by dividing the number of members of a specific group *employed* in a period by the number of women and minority *applicants* in a period. The success rate of best achieving group applicants is determined by dividing the number of people in the best achieving group *employed* by the number of the best achieving group *applicants* in a period.

Using the formula, let us determine whether there has been an adverse impact in the following case. During 1992, 400 people were hired for a particular job. Of the total, 300 were white and 100 were black. There were 1,500 applicants for these jobs, of whom 1,000 were white and 500 were black. Using the adverse formula, we have:

$$\frac{100/500}{300/1{,}000} \; \frac{= 0.2}{= 0.3} = 66.67\%$$

We conclude that adverse impact exists.

Evidence of adverse impact involves more than the total number of minority workers *employed.* Also considered are the total number of qualified *applicants.* For instance, assume that 300 blacks and 300 whites were hired. But there were 1,500 black applicants and 1,000 white applicants. Putting these figures into the adverse impact formula, we conclude that adverse impact still exists:

$$\frac{300/1{,}500}{300/1{,}000} \; \frac{= 0.2}{= 0.3} = 66.67\%$$

Thus, it is clear firms must also monitor their recruitment efforts very carefully. Obviously, firms should attempt to recruit qualified individuals because once in the applicant pool, they will be used in computing adverse impact.

Assuming adverse impact is shown, employers have two avenues available to them if they still desire to use a particular standard. First, the employer may validate a selection device by showing it is indeed a predictor of success. If the device has proved to be a predictor of job performance, business necessity has been established. If the firm's selection device has not been validated, business necessity may be demonstrated in another manner: The employer can show a strong relationship between the selection device and job performance, and that if it did not use this procedure, the firm's training costs would become prohibitive.

The second avenue available to employers should adverse impact be shown is the *bona fide occupational qualification* (BFOQ) defense. The BFOQ defense means that only one group is capable of performing the job successfully. As you might expect, the BFOQ defense has been narrowly interpreted by courts because it almost always relates to sex discrimination. For instance, courts have rejected the concept that because most women cannot lift fifty pounds all women would be eliminated from consideration for a job requiring heavy lifting.

Creators of the *Guidelines* adopted the bottom-line approach in assessing whether a firm's employment practices are discriminatory. For example, if a number of separate procedures is used in making a selection decision, the enforcement agencies will focus on the end result of these procedures to determine whether adverse impact has occurred. Essentially, the EEOC is concerned more with what is occurring than how it occurred. They admit discriminatory employment practices that cannot be validated may exist. However, the net effect, or the bottom line, of the selection procedures is the focus of their attention.

ADDITIONAL GUIDELINES

Since the *Uniform Guidelines* were published in 1978, they have been modified several times. Some of these changes reflect Supreme Court decisions; others clarify implementation procedures. Three major changes—*Interpretative Guidelines on Sexual Harassment, Guidelines on Discrimination Because of National Origin,* and *Guidelines on Discrimination Because of Religion*—merit additional discussion.

Interpretative Guidelines on Sexual Harassment

In one survey, 42 percent of the women and 15 percent of the men reported that they had been sexually harassed on the job.[18] Perhaps because of the publicity caused by the Navy's Tailhook incident and the testimony of Anita Hill and Clarence Thomas, one of the most fervently pursued civil rights issues today relates to sexual harassment.[19] In fact, from 1990 to 1993, the number of sexual harassment complaints filed with the Equal Employment Opportunity Commission has nearly doubled from 6,100 to 12,500.[20] As we previously mentioned, Title VII of the Civil Rights Act generally prohibits discrimination in employment on the basis of gender. The EEOC has also issued interpretative guidelines stating that employers have an affirmative duty to maintain a workplace free from sexual harassment. The OFCCP has also issued similar guidelines. Managers in both for-profit and not-for-profit organizations should be particularly alert to the issue of sexual harassment. The EEOC issued the guidelines because of the belief that sexual harassment continued to be a widespread problem. Table 3-1 contains the EEOC's definition of sexual harassment.

The EEOC has issued interpretative guidelines stating that employers have an affirmative duty to maintain a workplace free from sexual harassment.

According to these guidelines, employers are totally liable for the acts of their supervisors, regardless of whether the employer is aware of the sexual harassment act. Where coworkers are concerned, the employer is responsible for such acts if the employer knew, or should have known, about them. The employer is not responsible when it can show that it took immediate and appropriate corrective action on learning of the problem.

Another important aspect of these guidelines is that employers may be liable for acts committed by nonemployees in the workplace if the employer knew, or should have known, of the conduct and failed to take appropriate action. Firms are responsible for developing programs to prevent sexual harassment in the workplace. They must also investigate all formal and infor-

TABLE 3-1
EEOC Definition of Sexual Harassment

Unwelcome sexual advances, requests for sexual favors, and verbal or physical conduct of a sexual nature that occur under any of the following situations:

1. When submission to such contact is made either explicitly or implicitly a term or condition of an individual's employment.
2. When submission to or rejection of such contact by an individual is used as the basis for employment decisions affecting such individual.
3. When such conduct has the purpose or effect of unreasonably interfering with an individual's work performance or creating an intimidating, hostile, or offensive working environment.

mal complaints alleging sexual harassment. After investigating, a firm must take immediate and appropriate action to correct the situation.[21] Failure to do so constitutes a violation of Title VII, as interpreted by the EEOC.[22] To prevail in court, companies must have clear procedures for handling sexual harassment complaints. Typically, employers choose an impartial ombudsperson, usually in the human resources department, to hear and investigate charges before lawyers get involved. If the sexual harassment complaint appears legitimate, the company must take *immediate* and *appropriate action* as established in the pivotal 1986 case, *Hunter v Allis-Chalmers*.[23] An impartial ombudsperson is essential for the resolution of these types of organizational problems.

The improper exercise of power is inappropriate and often costly. Sexual harassment is an improper exercise of power, and it is a costly abuse of power. Research by Freada Klein Associates, a workplace-diversity consulting firm, shows that 90 percent of Fortune 500 companies have dealt with power abuses which resulted in sexual harassment complaints. Klein estimates that this abuse of power costs the average large corporation $6.7 million a year.[24]

There have been numerous sexual harassment court cases. In *Miller v Bank of America,* a U.S. Circuit Court of Appeals held an employer liable for the sexually harassing acts of its supervisors, even though the company had a policy prohibiting such conduct and even though the victim did not formally notify the employer of the problem. Another U.S. Circuit Court of Appeals ruled that sexual harassment, in and of itself, is a violation of Title VII. The court ruled the law does not require the victim to prove she or he resisted harassment and was penalized for that resistance. As previously mentioned, the first sexual harassment case to reach the U.S. Supreme Court was the June 1986 case of *Meritor Savings Bank v Vinson*. In the Vinson decision, the Supreme Court recognized for the first time Title VII could be used for offensive environment claims.[25] However, only recently has a hostile environment been defined as a workplace atmosphere or behavior that a *reasonable woman* would find offensive.[26]

Guidelines on Discrimination Because of National Origin

The EEOC broadly defined discrimination on the basis of national origin as the denial of equal employment opportunity because of an individual's ancestors or place of birth or because an individual has the physical, cultural, or linguistic characteristics of a national origin group. Because height or weight requirements tend to exclude individuals on the basis of national origin, firms are expected to evaluate their selection procedures for adverse impact, regardless of whether the total selection process has an adverse impact based on national origin. Height and weight requirements are, therefore, exceptions to the bottom-line concept. As Table 3-2 shows, the EEOC has identified certain selection procedures that may be discriminatory.

Harassment on the basis of national origin is a violation of Title VII. Employers have an affirmative duty to maintain a working environment free from such harassment. Ethnic slurs and other verbal or physical conduct relating to an individual's national origin constitute harassment when this

TABLE 3-2
Selection Procedures That May Be Discriminatory with Regard to National Origin

1. Fluency in English requirements: One questionable practice involves denying employment opportunities because of an individual's foreign accent or inability to communicate well in English. When this practice is continually followed, the Commission will presume that such a rule violates Title VII and will closely study it. However, a firm may require that employees speak only in English at certain times if business necessity can be shown.[27]
2. Training or education requirements: Denying employment opportunities to an individual because of his or her foreign training or education, or practices that require an individual to be foreign trained or educated may be discriminatory.

conduct (1) has the purpose or effect of creating an intimidating, hostile, or offensive working environment; (2) has the purpose or effect of unreasonably interfering with an individual's work performance; or (3) otherwise adversely affects an individual's employment opportunity.

Guidelines on Discrimination Because of Religion

Employers have an obligation to accommodate religious practices unless they can demonstrate a resulting hardship. The most common claims filed under the religious accommodation provisions involve either employees objecting to Sabbath employment or to membership in or financial support of labor unions.[28] Consideration is given to identifiable costs in relation to the size and operating costs of the employer and the number of individuals who actually need the accommodation. These guidelines recognize that regular payment of premium wages constitutes undue hardship, whereas these payments on an infrequent or temporary basis do not. Undue hardship would also exist if an accommodation required a firm to vary from its bona fide seniority system.

These guidelines identify several means of accommodating religious practices that prohibit working on certain days. Some of the methods suggested included voluntary substitutes, flexible scheduling, lateral transfer, and change of job assignments. Some collective bargaining agreements include a provision that each employee must join the union or pay the union a sum equivalent to dues. When an employee's religious beliefs prevent compliance, the union should accommodate the employee by permitting that person to make an equivalent donation to a charitable organization.

AFFIRMATIVE ACTION PROGRAMS

An **affirmative action program (AAP)** is an approach certain organizations with government contracts develop to demonstrate workers are employed in proportion to their representation in the firm's relevant labor market. The need for affirmative action programs was created by EO 11246, as amended by EO 11375, and place enforcement with the OFCCP. An affirmative action program may be voluntarily implemented by an organization. In such an event, goals are established and action is taken to hire and move minorities and women upward in the organization. In other situations, an AAP may be mandated by the OFCCP. The degree of control the OFCCP will impose depends on the size of the contract. Contracts of $10,000 or less are not covered. The first level of control involves contracts that exceed $10,000 but are less than $50,000. These contractors are governed by the equal opportunity clause, as shown in Table 3-3.

The second level of control occurs if the contractor (1) has fifty or more employees; (2) has a contract of $50,000 or more; (3) has contracts that in any twelve month period total $50,000 or more or reasonably may be expected to total $50,000 or more; or (4) is a financial institution that serves as a depository for government funds in any amount, acts as an issuing or redeeming agent for U.S. savings bonds and savings notes in any amount, or subscribes to federal deposit or share insurance. Contractors meeting these criteria must develop a written affirmative action program for each of its establishments and file an annual EEO-1 report (see Figure 3-2). The affirmative action program is the major focus of EO 11246. It requires specific steps to guarantee equal employment opportunity. Prerequisite to development of a satisfactory AAP is identification and analysis of problem areas inherent in the employment of minorities and women and an evaluation of opportunities for utilizing minority and women employees.

The third level of control on contractors is in effect when contracts exceed $1 million. All previously stated requirements must be met, and in addition, the OFCCP is authorized to conduct preaward compliance reviews. The purpose of a compliance review is to determine whether the contractor is maintaining nondiscriminatory hiring and employment practices. The review also ensures the contractor is utilizing affirmative action to guarantee that applicants are employed, placed, trained, upgraded, promoted, terminated, and otherwise treated fairly without regard to race, color, religion, gender, national origin, veteran status, or disability during employment. In determining whether to conduct a preaward review, the OFCCP may consider, for example, the items presented in Table 3-4.

If an investigation indicates a violation, the OFCCP first tries to secure compliance through persuasion. If persuasion fails to resolve the issue, the OFCCP serves a notice to show cause or a notice of violation. A show cause notice contains a list of the violations, a statement of how the OFCCP proposes that corrections be made, a request for a written response to the findings, and a suggested date for a conciliation conference. The firm usually has thirty days to respond. Successful conciliation results in a written contract between the OFCCP and the contractor. In a conciliation agreement, the contractor agrees to take specific steps to remedy noncompliance with an EO. Firms that do not correct violations can be passed over in the awarding of future contracts.

The procedures for developing affirmative action plans were published in the *Federal Register* of December 4, 1974. These regulations are referred to as Revised Order No. 4. The OFCCP guide for compliance officers, outlining what to cover in a compliance review, is known as Order No. 14.

The OFCCP is very specific about what should be included in an affirmative action program. A policy statement has to be developed that reflects the CEO's attitude regarding equal employment opportunity, assigns overall responsibility for preparing and implementing the affirmative action program,

TABLE 3-3
Equal Opportunity Clause—Government Contracts

1. The contractor will not discriminate against any employee or applicant for employment because of race, color, religion, sex, or national origin. The contractors will take affirmative action to ensure that applicants are employed, and that employees are treated during employment, without regard to their race, color, religion, sex, or national origin. Such action shall include, but not be limited to the following: employment, upgrading, demotions, or transfer; recruitment or recruitment advertising, layoff or termination; rates of pay or other forms of compensation; and selection for training, including apprenticeship. The contractor agrees to post in conspicuous places, available to employees and applicants for employment, notices to be provided by the contracting officer setting forth the provisions for this nondiscrimination clause.
2. The contractor will in all solicitations or advertisements for employees placed by or on behalf of the contractor, state that all qualified applicants will receive consideration for employment without regard to race, color, religion, sex, or national origin.
3. The contractor will send to each labor union or representative of workers with which he or she has a collective bargaining agreement or other contract or understanding, a notice to be provided by the agency contracting officer, advising the labor union or workers' representative of the contractor's commitments under section 202 of Executive Order 11246 of September 24, 1965, and shall post copies of the notice in conspicuous places available to employees and applicants for employment.
4. The contractor will comply with all provisions of Executive Order 11246 of September 24, 1965, and the rules, regulations, and relevant orders of the Secretary of Labor.
5. The contractor will furnish all information and reports required by Executive Order 11246 of September 24, 1965, and by the rules, regulations, and orders of the Secretary of Labor, or pursuant thereto, and will permit access to his or her books, records, and accounts by the contracting agency and the Secretary of Labor for purposes of investigation to ascertain compliance with such rules, regulations, and orders.
6. In the event of the contractor's noncompliance with the nondiscrimination clauses of this contract or with any of such rules, regulations, or orders, this contract may be canceled, terminated, or suspended in whole or in part and the contractor may be declared ineligible for further Government contracts in accordance with procedures authorized in Executive Order 11246 of September 24, 1965, or by rule, regulation, or order of the Secretary of State, or as otherwise provided by law.
7. The contractor will include the provisions of paragraphs (1) through (7) in every subcontract or purchase order unless exempted by rules, regulations, or orders of the Secretary of Labor issued pursuant to section 204 of Executive Order 12146 of September 24, 1965, so that such provisions will be binding upon each subcontractor or vendor. The contractor will take such action with respect to any subcontract or purchase order as may be directed by the Secretary of Labor as a means of enforcing such provisions including sanctions for noncompliance: Provided, however, that in the event the contractor becomes involved in, or is threatened with litigation with a subcontractor or vendor as a result of such direction, the contractor may request the United States to enter into such litigation to protect the interests of the United States.

Source: Federal Register, 45, no. 251 (Tuesday, December 30, 1980): 86230.

Joint Reporting Committee

- Equal Employment Opportunity Commission
- Office of Federal Contract Compliance Programs (Labor)

EQUAL EMPLOYMENT OPPORTUNITY

EMPLOYER INFORMATION REPORT EEO–1

Standard Form 100
(Rev. 5–84)
O.M.B. No. 3046–0007
EXPIRES 3/31/85
100–211

Section A—TYPE OF REPORT
Refer to instructions for number and types of reports to be filed.

1. Indicate by marking in the appropriate box the type of reporting unit for which this copy of the form is submitted (MARK ONLY ONE BOX).

(1) ☐ Single-establishment Employer Report

Multi-establishment Employer:
(2) ☐ Consolidated Report (Required)
(3) ☐ Headquarters Unit Report (Required)
(4) ☐ Individual Establishment Report (submit one for each establishment with 50 or more employees)
(5) ☐ Special Report

2. Total number of reports being filed by this Company (Answer on Consolidated Report only) ______

Section B—COMPANY IDENTIFICATION *(To be answered by all employers)* — OFFICE USE ONLY

1. Parent Company
   a. Name of parent company (owns or controls establishment in Item 2) omit if same as label — a.

Name of receiving office				Address (Number and street)	b.
City or town	County	State	ZIP code	b. Employer Identification No.	

OFFICE USE ONLY

2. Establishment for which this report is filed. (Omit if same as label)
   a. Name of establishment — c.

Address (Number and street)	City or town	County	State	ZIP code	d.
b. Employer Identification No.		(Omit if same as label)			e.

Section C—EMPLOYERS WHO ARE REQUIRED TO FILE *(To be answered by all employers)*

☐ Yes ☐ No 1. Does the entire company have at least 100 employees in the payroll period for which you are reporting?

☐ Yes ☐ No 2. Is your company affiliated through common ownership and/or centralized management with other entities in an enterprise with a total employment of 100 or more?

☐ Yes ☐ No 3. Does the company or any of its establishments (a) have 50 or more employees AND (b) is not exempt as provided by 41 CFR 60–1.5, AND either (1) is a prime government contractor or first-tier subcontractor, and has a contract, subcontract, or purchase order amounting to $50,000 or more, or (2) serves as a depository of Government funds in any amount or is a financial institution which is an issuing and paying agent for U.S. Savings Bonds and Savings Notes?
If the response to question C–3 is yes, please enter your Dun and Bradstreet identification number (if you have one): ☐☐☐☐☐☐☐☐☐

☐ Yes ☐ No 4. Does the company receive financial assistance from the Small Business Administration (SBA)?

NOTE: If the answer is yes to questions 1, 2, or 3, complete the entire form, otherwise skip to Section G.

NSN 7540–00–180–6384

FIGURE 3-2 Equal Employment Opportunity Employer Information Report (EEO-1)

and provides for reporting and monitoring procedures. The policy should state that the firm intends to recruit, hire, train, and promote persons in all job titles without regard to race, color, religion, gender, or national origin, except where gender is a *bona fide organizational qualification* (BFOQ). The policy

SF 100 Page 2

Section D—EMPLOYMENT DATA

Employment at this establishment—Report all permanent full-time or part-time employees including apprentices and on-the-job trainees unless specifically excluded as set forth in the instructions. Enter the appropriate figures on all lines and in all columns. Blank spaces will be considered as zeros.

JOB CATEGORIES	NUMBER OF EMPLOYEES										
		MALE					FEMALE				
	OVERALL TOTALS (SUM OF COL. B THRU K) A	WHITE (NOT OF HISPANIC ORIGIN) B	BLACK (NOT OF HISPANIC ORIGIN) C	HISPANIC D	ASIAN OR PACIFIC ISLANDER E	AMERICAN INDIAN OR ALASKAN NATIVE F	WHITE (NOT OF HISPANIC ORIGIN) G	BLACK (NOT OF HISPANIC ORIGIN) H	HISPANIC I	ASIAN OR PACIFIC ISLANDER J	AMERICAN INDIAN OR ALASKAN NATIVE K
Officials and Managers 1											
Professionals 2											
Technicians 3											
Sales Workers 4											
Office and Clerical 5											
Craft Workers (Skilled) 6											
Operatives (Semi-Skilled) 7											
Laborers (Unskilled) 8											
Service Workers 9											
TOTAL 10											
Total employment reported in previous EEO–1 report 11											
(The trainees below should also be included in the figures for the appropriate occupational categories above)											
Formal On-the-Job trainees — White collar 12											
Formal On-the-Job trainees — Production 13											

NOTE: Omit questions 1 and 2 on the Consolidated Report.

1. Date(s) of payroll period used:

2. Does this establishment employ apprentices?
1 ☐ Yes 2 ☐ No

Section E—ESTABLISHMENT INFORMATION *(Omit on the Consolidated Report)*

1. Is the location of the establishment the same as that reported last year?
1 ☐ Yes 2 ☐ No 3 ☐ No report last year

2. Is the major business activity at this establishment the same as that reported last year?
1 ☐ Yes 2 ☐ No 3 ☐ No report last year

OFFICE USE ONLY

3. What is the major activity of this establishment? (Be specific, i.e., manufacturing steel castings, retail grocer, wholesale plumbing supplies, title insurance, etc. Include the specific type of product or type of service provided as well as the principal business or industrial activity.)

Section F—REMARKS

Use this item to give any identification data appearing on last report which differs from that given above, explain major changes in composition or reporting units and other pertinent information.

Section G—CERTIFICATION *(See Instructions G)*

Check one
1 ☐ All reports are accurate and were prepared in accordance with the instructions (check on consolidated only)
2 ☐ This report is accurate and was prepared in accordance with the instructions.

Name of Certifying Official	Title	Signature			Date
Name of person to contact regarding this report (Type or print)	Address (number and street)				
Title	City and State	ZIP code	Telephone Area Code	Number	Extension

All reports and information obtained from individual reports will be kept confidential as required by Section 709(e) of Title VII
WILLFULLY FALSE STATEMENTS ON THIS REPORT ARE PUNISHABLE BY LAW, U.S. CODE, TITLE 18, SECTION 1001

FIGURE 3-2 (continued) Equal Employment Opportunity Employer Information Report (EEO-1)

should guarantee that all human resource actions involving such areas as compensation, benefits, transfers, layoffs, return from layoffs, company-sponsored training, education, tuition assistance, and social and recreational programs will be administered without regard to race, color, religion, gender, or

TABLE 3-4

Factors That the OFCCP May Consider in Conducting a Preaward Review

1. The past EEO performance of the contractor, including its current EEO profile and indications of underutilization.
2. The volume and nature of complaints filed by employees or applicants against the contractor.
3. Whether the contractor is in a growth industry.
4. The level of employment or promotional opportunities resulting from the expansion of, or turnover in, the contractor's workforce.
5. The employment opportunities likely to result from the contract in issue.
6. Whether resources are available to conduct the review.

national origin. Revised Order No. 4 is quite specific with regard to dissemination of a firm's EEO policy, both internally and externally. An executive should be appointed to manage the firm's equal employment opportunity program. This person should be given the necessary support by top management to accomplish the assignment. Revised Order No. 4 specifies the minimum level of responsibility associated with the task of EEO manager.

An acceptable AAP must include an analysis of deficiencies in the utilization of minority groups and women. The first step in conducting a utilization analysis is to make a workforce analysis.

The second step involves an analysis of all major job groups. An explanation of the situation is required if minorities or women are currently being underutilized. A job group is defined as one or more jobs having similar content, wage rates, and opportunities. Underutilization is defined as having fewer minorities or women in a particular job group than would reasonably be expected by their availability. The utilization analysis is important because the calculations determine whether underutilization exists. For example, if the utilization analysis shows that the availability of blacks for a certain job group is 30 percent, the organization should have at least 30 percent black employment in that group. If actual employment is less than 30 percent, underutilization exists, and the firm should set a goal of 30 percent black employment for that job group.

The primary focus of any affirmative action program is on goals and timetables: The issue is how many, by when. Goals and timetables developed by a firm should cover its entire affirmative action program, including correction of deficiencies. These goals and timetables should be attainable; that is, they should be based on results that the firm, making good faith efforts, could reasonably expect to achieve.

Both human resource managers and line managers should be involved in the goal setting process. Goals should be significant and measurable, as well as attainable. Two types of goals must be established regarding underutilization: annual and ultimate. The annual goal is to move toward elimination of underutilization, whereas the ultimate goal is to correct all underutilization. Goals should be specific in terms of planned results, with timetables for completion. However, goals should not establish inflexible quotas that must be met. Rather, they should be targets that are reasonably attainable.

Employers should also conduct a detailed analysis of job descriptions to ensure that they accurately reflect job content. In addition, job specifications should be validated, with special attention given to academic, experience, and skills requirements. If a job specification screens out a disproportionate number of minorities or women, the requirements must be professionally validated in relation to job performance. Thus, a comprehensive job analysis program is required.

When an opening occurs, everyone involved in human resource recruiting, screening, selection, and promotion should be aware of the opening. In addition, the firm should evaluate the entire selection process to ensure freedom from bias. And individuals involved in the process should be carefully selected and trained in order to minimize bias in all human resource actions.

Firms should observe the requirements of the *Uniform Guidelines.* Selection techniques other than paper and pencil tests can also be used improperly and thus discriminate against minorities and women. Such techniques include unscored interviews, unscored or casual application forms, use of arrest records and credit checks, and consideration of marital status, dependency, and minor children. Where data suggest discrimination or unfair exclusion of minorities and women exists, the firm should analyze its unscored procedures and eliminate them if they are not objective and valid. Some techniques that can be used to improve recruitment and increase the flow of minority and women applicants are shown in Table 3-5.

TABLE 3-5
Techniques to Improve Recruitment of Minorities and Women

- Identify referral organizations for minorities and women.
- Hold formal briefing sessions with representatives of referral organizations.
- Encourage minority and women employees to refer applicants to the firm.
- Include minorities and women on the Personnel Relations staff.
- Permit minorities and women to participate in Career Days, Youth Motivation Programs, and related activities in their community.
- Actively participate in job fairs and give company representatives the authority to make on-the-spot-commitments.
- Actively recruit at schools having predominant minority or female enrollments.
- Use special efforts to reach minorities and women during school recruitment drives.
- Undertake special employment programs whenever possible for women and minorities. These might include technical and nontechnical co-op programs, after school and/or work-study jobs, summer jobs for underprivileged, summer work-study programs, and motivation, training, and employment programs for the hardcore unemployed.
- Pictorially present minorities and women in recruiting brochures.
- Include the minority news media and women's interest media when expending help wanted advertising.

Source: Federal Register, 45, no. 251 (Tuesday, December 30, 1980): 86243.

As previously discussed in the *Adarand Constructors v Pena* Supreme Court decision, affirmative action programs are presently receiving court challenges. As a result of this case, the future of affirmative action is yet to be determined.

A GLOBAL PERSPECTIVE

When operating in the multinational environment, U.S. based firms often find their human resource policies to be in conflict with the laws and accepted norms of the host country. For instance, the influence of Title VII of the Civil Rights Act of 1964, as amended, has been felt by virtually all firms operating in the United States. But most countries in the world do not have laws prohibiting discrimination. In fact, some countries practice overt discrimination against certain groups whose members would be protected if they were employed in the United States.

In 1991, the Supreme Court ruled that when Congress passed the Civil Rights Act of 1964, it did not want the statute to apply outside the United States. Specifically, in *Boureslan v Aramco* (1991), the U.S. Supreme Court held that Title VII of the Civil Rights Act of 1964 did not have extraterritorial application. Extraterritoriality refers to the operation of laws upon individuals who are beyond the geographical limits of the enacting state or nation but are still amenable to its laws. Scholarly analysis of the intended reach of Title VII based on the language of the statute and interpreted in light of its history policy universally supported extraterritorial application. However, the Court rejected the argument that the Title VII definitions of 'employer' and 'commerce' established congressional intent to regulate the conduct of U.S. employers operating overseas. The majority focused on the failure of the statute, on its face, to distinguish between American employers and foreign employers of U.S. citizens working abroad.[29]

As businesses scramble to stay competitive and international market barriers crumble, large and small companies are looking to expand their opportunities abroad. As a result, human resource professionals must learn to deal with varied employment laws as well as language and cultural differences. Human resource professionals should investigate potential recruits more thoroughly when hiring international employees. Designing compensation and benefits packages for expatriates and local nationals can be difficult. Human resource professionals should work closely with an international labor attorney to ensure the legality of the various packages. A successful international operation also requires a sound organizational structure. Staying in close contact with employees across time zones is probably the most important factor to successful international management. The human resource managers who communicate most effectively with overseas employees are the ones who take the time to understand their culture.[30]

SUMMARY

The concept of equal employment opportunity has evolved considerably since passage of the Civil Rights Act of 1964. Numerous amendments, and even other acts, have been passed when voids were found in the initial act. Major Supreme Court decisions have interpreted the provisions of these statutes. Presidential executive orders further strengthened the quest for equal employment opportunity.

The Civil Rights Acts of 1866 and 1871, based on the Thirteenth and Fourteenth Amendments to the Constitution, represented early efforts to outlaw discrimination in the workplace. Title VII of the Civil Rights Act of 1964, as amended by the Equal Employment Opportunity Act of 1972, has had a major impact on HRM. These laws prohibit discrimination based on race, color, sex, religion, or national origin. The Age Discrimination in Employment Act (ADEA), as amended, prohibits employers from discriminating against individuals because of age. The Rehabilitation Act covers certain government contractors and subcontractors, and organizations that receive federal grants in excess of $2,500. Passed as an amendment to Title VII of the Civil Rights Act, the Pregnancy Discrimination Act prohibits discrimination in employment based on pregnancy, childbirth, or related medical conditions. The Immigration Reform and Control Act of 1986 established criminal and civil sanctions against employers who knowingly hire an illegal immigrant, and made it unlawful to hire anyone without verifying employment authorization and identity. The Americans with Disabilities Act prohibits discrimination against qualified individuals with disabilities. The Civil Rights Act of 1991 amended the Civil Rights Act of 1964 and expanded the scope of relevant civil rights statutes.

Presidential executive orders (EOs) apply to governmental agencies and have the force and effect of laws enacted by Congress. In 1965, EO 11246 made it federal policy to provide equal opportunity in federal employment for all qualified persons. It not only prohibits discrimination in employment, but it also requires promoting the full realization of equal employment opportunity through a positive, continuing program in each executive department and agency.

The manner in which the courts interpret the law is vitally important. Important Supreme Court decisions related to equal employment opportunity and affirmative action include: *Albermarle Paper Co. v Moody, Washington v Davis, Griggs v Duke Power Co., Phillips v Martin Marietta Corporation, Espinoza v Farah Manufacturing Co., Weber v Kaiser Aluminum and Chemical Corporation, Dothard v Rawlingson, University of California Regents v Bakke, American Tobacco Co. v Patterson, Adarand Constructors v Pena, Meritor Savings Bank v Vinson,* and *City of Richmond v J. A. Croson Co.*

The *Uniform Guidelines on Employee Selection Procedures* provide a single set of principles designed to assist employers, labor organizations, employment agencies, and licensing and certification boards in complying with federal prohibitions against discriminatory employment practices. Adverse impact occurs when members of protected groups receive unequal consideration for employment. Three major changes in the *Uniform Guidelines* were the *Interpretative Guidelines on Sexual Harassment, Guidelines on Discrimination Because of National Origin*, and *Guidelines on Discrimination Because of Religion.* An affirmative action program (AAP) is developed by an organization to demonstrate women and minorities are employed in proportion to their representation in the firm's labor market.

QUESTIONS FOR REVIEW

1. Briefly describe the following laws: (a) Title VII of the Civil Rights Act of 1964, as amended in 1972; (b) Age Discrimination in Employment Act of 1967, as amended in 1978 and 1986; (c) Rehabilitation Act of 1973; (d) Pregnancy Discrimination Act of 1978; (e) Immigration Reform and Control Act of 1986; (f) the Americans with Disabilities Act; and (g) the Civil Rights Act of 1991.
2. What is a presidential executive order (EO)? Describe the major provisions of EO 11246, as amended by EO 11375.
3. What is the purpose of the Office of Federal Contract Compliance Programs?
4. Discuss the significant U.S. Supreme Court decisions that have had an impact on equal employment opportunity.
5. What is the purpose of the *Uniform Guidelines on Employee Selection Procedures*?
6. Distinguish between adverse impact and affirmative action programs.
7. How does the Equal Employment Opportunity Commission (EEOC) define sexual harassment?

HRM SIMULATION

One of the key elements of this simulation relates to affirmative action. The firm currently has fewer female and minority workers than the local working population. Hiring has been generally done on a "walk-in" basis, and there is no formal plan to increase the number of women and minorities in the firm. Although there is no litigation concerning this unbalanced workforce at the present time, your team has been directed by the CEO to begin integrating the workforce.

ABC VIDEO CASE

SEXUAL HARASSMENT IN THE FBI
TAPE 1, NUMBER 7

The traditional FBI agent has long had to live up to the macho image. Since the days of J. Edgar Hoover the attitude has been that women are not capable of doing the job. Since the first female agent was hired in 1972, there have been more than 1,000 women agents hired. Allegations of sexual harassment have been quashed in an effort to keep the bureau's image untarnished.

Decorated FBI agent Suzane Doucette called a press conference to make public her allegations of sexual harassment in the FBI. After complaining of a sexual assault by her supervisor, Doucette stated that she was put on administrative leave without pay. According to an internal FBI survey, 13 percent of the women agents admit to being sexually harassed, but only 10 percent say they reported it. Journalist Ronald Kessler stated that, "The real . . . problem is that in the FBI, ever since the Hoover days, image has been all. And anybody who tarnishes that image is felt to be disloyal, and so female agents who report discrimination or who report harassment are very often retaliated against."

HRM INCIDENT 1

—SO, WHAT'S AFFIRMATIVE ACTION?

Supreme Construction Company began as a small commercial builder located in Baytown, Texas. Until the 1980s, Alex Boyd, Supreme's founder, concentrated his efforts on small, freestanding shops and offices. Up to that time, Alex never employed more than fifteen people.

In 1982, Alex's son Michael graduated from college with a degree in construction and immediately joined the company full time. Michael had worked on a variety of Supreme jobs while in school, and Alex felt his son was really cut out for the construction business. Michael was given increasing responsibility, and the company continued its success although with a few more projects—and a few more employees—than before. In 1986, Mike approached his father with a proposition: "Let's get into some of the bigger projects now. We have the capital to expand, and I really believe we can do it." Alex approved, and Supreme began doing small shopping centers and multistory office buildings in addition to its traditional specialization. Soon employment had grown to seventy-five employees.

In 1989, the National Aeronautics and Space Administration (NASA) released construction specifications for two aircraft hangars to be built southeast of Houston. Although Supreme had never done any construction work for the government, Michael and Alex considered the job within the company's capabilities. Michael worked up the $582,000 bid and submitted it to the NASA procurement office.

Several weeks later the bids were opened. Supreme had the low bid. However, the acceptance letter was contingent on submission of a satisfactory affirmative action program.

Questions

1. Explain why Supreme must submit an affirmative action program.
2. Generally, what should the program be designed to accomplish?

HRM INCIDENT 2

WHO SHOULD I RECOMMEND?

Leroy Hasty was faced with a dilemma. He supervised twelve process technicians at the Indestro Chemical plant in El Dorado, Arkansas, but was being transferred to a new job. The production manager, Jack Richards, had just asked Leroy to nominate one of his subordinates as a replacement. Two possible choices immediately came to mind, Carlos Chavez and James Mitchell.

Carlos was a very capable worker. He was twenty-four years old and married, and he had earned his bachelor's degree in management by attending night school. His heritage was Mexican-American. He had done an excellent job on every assignment Leroy had given him. He had all the qualifications Leroy believed a good supervisor should have, including solid technical expertise. Leroy considered Carlos punctual, diligent, mature, and intelligent. A serious sort, Carlos often came to work early and stayed late and seemed to spend most of his spare time with his family.

James was a twenty-five year old high school graduate. He was single, and Hasty knew he often went hunting or partying with several of the other technicians. Like most of his fellow workers, James was a WASP (white Anglo-Saxon Protestant). He was a hard worker and was liked and respected by the others, including Carlos. On the basis of objective factors, Leroy believed James ran second to Carlos although the call was a close one.

But then there was the race issue. Several times Leroy had heard fellow workers refer to Carlos as a *spic* and *wetback*. Leroy believed some of the workers would prefer to have James as a supervisor, purely because of his national origin. In fact, he thought one or two of them might resist Carlos's authority to try to make him look bad. And if productivity in the section fell off because of administrative problems, Leroy knew his own record with the company might be tarnished.

At that moment, the phone rang. It was Jack Richards. "Leroy," he said, "I need to see you. Could you come to my office in a few minutes?" As Leroy hung up the phone, he thought, "I know Jack is going to want to talk about my replacement."

Question

1. What decision would you recommend that Leroy make? Discuss.

DEVELOPING HRM SKILLS

AN EXPERIENTIAL EXERCISE

Many laws have been passed and court decisions rendered that affect the everyday actions of human resource managers. Past decisions may no longer apply. Human resource managers have a responsibility to ensure that actions affecting human resource management adhere to both the letter and the intent of the law. Unfortunately, not everyone may share this view, which is when problems occur. In this situation, the human resource manager and a dock foreman for New York-based Hoffa Loading and Storage Company are having a disagreement on the necessity of hiring women dock workers.

The human resource manager must talk to the dock foreman concerning future hiring practices. The dock foreman is aware that the firm follows the policy of affirmative action; however, he rejects virtually every woman that is sent over to the docks. On the rare occasion that he does hire a woman, she does not last very long. The human resource manager realizes that this hiring practice puts the dock foreman in a somewhat precarious position, but this is the way things have to be.

The dock foreman is quite disgruntled about the company's directive to hire women on the dock. He thinks that the human resource manager and the bosses upstairs do not understand that on the dock, men are needed—red-blooded American men. The foreman believes that his men are the best dock workers on the pier and wants to keep the situation as it is. They have always exceeded the tonnage moved by any other group, and they work very well together. Every worker pulls his own weight. He also believes that women are just going to mess things up and that the wives of his dock workers do not want their husbands working with women.

Certainly, a potential for conflict exists in this situation. Two individuals will participate in this exercise: one to serve as the human resource manager and the other to play the role of dock foreman. All students not playing a role should carefully observe the behavior of both participants. Your instructor will provide the participants with necessary additional information that they will need.

NOTES

1. Howard C. Lockwook, "Equal Employment Opportunities," in Dale Yoder and Herbert S. Heneman (eds.), *Staffing Policies and Strategies* (Washington, D.C.: Bureau of National Affairs, Inc., 1979): 4–252.

2. Michael R. Carrell and Frank E. Kuzmits, "Amended ADEA's Effects on HR Strategies Remain Dubious," *Personnel Journal* 66 (May 1987): 112.

3. Rory Judd Albert and Neal S. Schelberg, "Highlighting the OWBPA," *Pension World* 27 (January 1991): 40.

4. Robert J. Noble, Esq., "To Waiver or Not to Waiver is the Question of OWBPA," *Personnel* 68 (June 1991): 11.

5. Kate Colborn, "You Want Me to Sign What?" *EDN* 38 (March 11, 1993): 69.

6. John J. Keller, "AT&T Will Settle EEOC Lawsuit for $66 Million," *The Wall Street Journal* 88, no. 13 (July 18, 1991): B8.

7. Art L. Bethke, "The IRCA: What's an Employer to Do?" *Wisconsin Small Business Forum* 6 (Fall 1987): 26.

8. "The Americans with Disabilities Act: *Questions and Answers*" (Washington, D.C.: U.S. Government Printing Office, 1991): 11.

9. Christine D. Keen, "Lifestyle Disabilities Could Become a Civil Rights Frontier," *HRNews* 9 (October 1990): 7.

10. Betty Southard Murphy, Wayne E. Barlow, and D. Diane Hatch, "Manager's Newsfront," *Personnel Journal* 73 (August 1994): 26 (3).

11. Brian Cox, "D&O Liability Risks Growing with Economy's Globalization," *National Underwriters* (November 22, 1993): 2, 20.

12. Robert L. Brady, "A Win for Employers: Civil Rights Act is Not Retroactive," *Legal Insights* 71 (August 1994): 19.

13. Jack Raisner, "When Workplace Relationships Cause Discrimination," *HRMagazine* 36 (January 1991): 75.

14. Amanda Troy Segal and Wendy Zeller, "Corporate Women," *Business Week* (June 8, 1992): 74.

15. "More Women Are Executive VPs," *Fortune* 128 (July 12, 1993): 16.

16. Frederick L. Sullivan, "Sexual Harassment: The Supreme Court's Ruling," *Personnel* 63 (December 1986): 37–38.

17. David E. Robertson, "New Directions in EEO Guidelines," *Personnel Journal* 57 (July 1978): 361.

18. Kelly Flynn, "Preventive Medicine for Sexual Harassment," *Personnel* 68 (March 1991): 17.

19. Michele Galen et al., "Ending Sexual Harassment: Business is Getting the Message," *Business Week* (March 18, 1991): 98.

20. Judith Waldrop, "Sex, Laws, Video Training," *American Demographics* 16 (April 1994): 14.

21. Robert K. McCalla, "Stopping Sexual Harassment Before It Begins," *Management Review* 80 (April 1991): 44.

22. Ibid.

23. Anne B. Fisher, "Sexual Harassment: What to Do," *Fortune* 128 (August 23, 1993): 84–88.

24. Ibid.

25. Stacey J. Garvin, "Employer Liability for Sexual Harassment," *HRMagazine* 36 (June 1991): 107.

26. Amanda Troy Segal, "Sexual Harassment: The Age of Anxiety," *Business Week* (July 6, 1992): 16.

27. In 1994, the Supreme Court voted 7-2 to refuse to hear arguments that the company discriminated illegally against Spanish-speaking employees by imposing the English-only rule. Although the court order was not a decision and set no legal precedent, it did leave intact a federal appeals court ruling that remains binding law in nine western states. Because English-only rules are increasingly common nationwide, it is likely that the issue will return to the high court someday.

28. Stephenie Overman, "Good Faith Is the Answer," *HRMagazine* 39 (January 1994): 76.

29. Janice R. Franke and Maria Whittaker, "The Extraterritoriality Issue," *American Business Law Journal* (May 1992): 143–168.

30. Stephenie Overman, "You Don't Have to be a Big Fish to Swim in International Waters," *HRMagazine* (September 1993): 46–49.

CHAPTER 4

Job Analysis

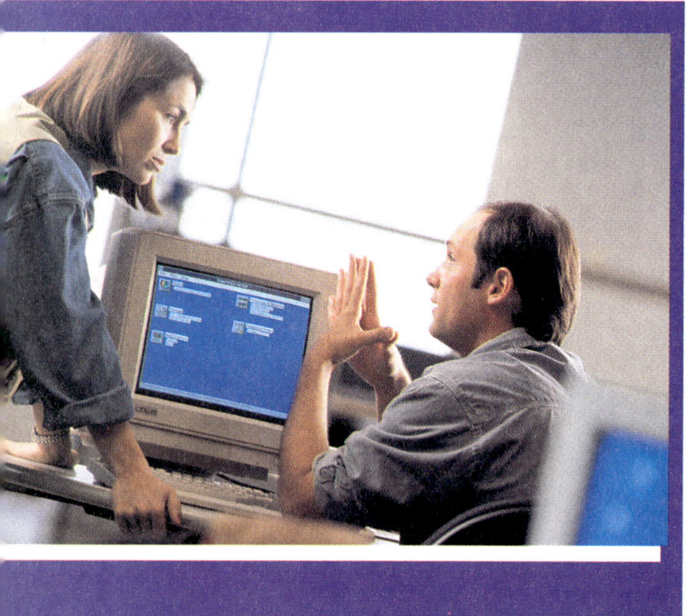

KEY TERMS

Job 92
Position 92
Job analysis 92
Job description 93
Job specification 93
Job Analysis Schedule (JAS) 102
Functional Job Analysis (FJA) 103
Position Analysis Questionnaire (PAQ) 107
Management Position Description Questionnaire (MPDQ) 107
Guidelines Oriented Job Analysis (GOJA) 108
Occupational Measurement System (OMS) 108
Reengineering 111
Job design 111
Job enrichment 112
Job enlargement 112
Employee-centered work redesign 113

CHAPTER OBJECTIVES

1. Define job analysis, describe why job analysis is the basic human resource tool, and explain the reasons for conducting job analysis.
2. State the types of information required for job analysis, describe the various job analysis methods, and explain the means of conducting job analysis.
3. Explain the components of a well-designed job description and job specification.
4. Describe the newer methods available for conducting job analysis and describe how job analysis helps to satisfy various legal requirements.
5. Explain reengineering and job design.

"Mary, I'm having trouble figuring out what kind of machine operators you need," said John Anderson, the human resource director at Gulf Machineries. "I've sent four people for you to interview who seemed to meet the requirements outlined in the job description. You rejected all of them."

"To heck with the job description," replied Mary. "What I'm concerned with is finding someone who can do the job. And, the people you sent me couldn't do the job. Besides, I've never even seen the job description."

John took a copy of the job description to Mary and went over it point by point. They discovered that either the job description never fit the job or the job had changed a great deal since it was written. For example, the job description specified experience on an older model drill press while the one in use is a new digital machine. Workers had to be more mathematically oriented to use the new machine effectively.

After hearing Mary describe the qualifications needed for the machine operator's job and explain the duties the operators perform, John said, "I think that we can now write an accurate description of the job, and using it as a guide, we can find the right kind of people. Let's work more closely, so this kind of situation won't happen again."

The situation just described reflects a very common problem in human resource management: The job description did not adequately define the duties and skills needed to perform the job. Therefore, it became virtually impossible for John Anderson, the human resource director, to locate people with the required skills. Job analysis was critically needed to resolve the problem. As we stress throughout the remainder of this book, job analysis is the most basic function of human resource management.

We begin the chapter by defining job analysis, describing its importance to all human resource functions and explaining the reasons for conducting job analysis. Next, we review the types of information required for job analysis, discuss job analysis methods, and explain the means of conducting job analysis. Then, we explain the use of job analysis data in preparing job descriptions and job specifications. We describe newer methods for conducting job analysis and the ways job analysis helps to satisfy various legal requirements. We end the chapter by explaining reengineering and job design.

JOB ANALYSIS: A BASIC HUMAN RESOURCE TOOL

A **job** consists of a group of tasks that must be performed for an organization to achieve its goals. A job may require the services of one person, such as that of president, or the services of seventy-five, as might be the case with data entry operators in a large firm.

In a work group consisting of a supervisor, two senior clerks, and four word processing operators, there are three jobs and seven positions. A **position** is the collection of tasks and responsibilities performed by one person; there is a position for every individual in an organization. For instance, a small company might have twenty-five jobs for its seventy-five employees, whereas in a large company 2,000 jobs may exist for 50,000 employees. In some firms, as few as ten jobs constitute 90 percent of a workforce.

Job analysis is the systematic process of determining the skills, duties, and knowledge required for performing jobs in an organization.[1] It is an essential and pervasive human resource technique. The purpose of job analysis is to obtain answers to six important questions:

1. What physical and mental tasks does the worker accomplish?
2. When is the job to be completed?
3. Where is the job to be accomplished?
4. How does the worker do the job?
5. Why is the job done?
6. What qualifications are needed to perform the job?

Job analysis provides a summary of a job's duties and responsibilities, its relationship to other jobs, the knowledge and skills required, and working conditions under which it is performed. Job facts are gathered, analyzed, and recorded as the job exists, not as the job should exist. The latter function is most often assigned to industrial engineers, methods analysts, or others. Job analysis is conducted after the job has been designed, the worker has been trained, and the job is being performed.

Job analysis is performed on three occasions. First, it is done when the organization is founded, and a job analysis program is initiated for the first time. Second, it is performed when new jobs are created. Third, it is used when jobs are changed significantly as a result of new technologies, methods, procedures, or systems. Job analysis is mostly performed because of changes in the nature of jobs. Job analysis information is used to prepare both job descriptions and job specifications.

The **job description** is a document that provides information regarding the tasks, duties, and responsibilities of the job. The minimum acceptable qualifications a person should possess in order to perform a particular job are contained in the **job specification**. We discuss both types of documents in greater detail later in the chapter.

REASONS FOR CONDUCTING JOB ANALYSIS

In this rapidly changing work environment, the need for a sound job analysis system is extremely critical. New jobs are being created, and old jobs are being redesigned. Referring to a job analysis that was conducted only a few years ago may provide inaccurate data. Essentially, job analysis helps organizations address the fact that change is taking place.[2] As Figure 4-1 shows, data derived from job analysis have an impact on virtually every aspect of human resource management. A major use of job analysis data is in the area of human resource planning. Merely knowing that a firm will need 1,000 new employees to produce goods or services to satisfy sales demand is insufficient. Each job requires different knowledge, skills, and ability levels. Obviously, effective human resource planning must take these job requirements into consideration.

Employee recruitment and selection would be haphazard if the recruiter did not know the qualifications needed to perform the job. Lacking up-to-date job descriptions and specifications, employees would have to be recruited and selected for a job without clear guidelines, and this practice could have disastrous consequences. Such a practice is virtually unheard of when firms procure raw materials, supplies, or equipment. For example, even when ordering a copying machine, the purchasing department normally develops precise specifications. Surely, the same logic should apply when searching for a firm's most valuable asset!

Also, job specification information often proves beneficial in identifying human resource development needs. If the specification suggests the job requires a particular knowledge, skill, or ability—and the person filling the position does not possess all the qualifications required—training and/or development is probably in order. It should be directed at assisting workers in performing duties specified in their present job descriptions or preparing them for promotion to higher level jobs. With regard to performance appraisal, employees should be evaluated in terms of how well they accomplish the duties specified in their job descriptions. A manager who evaluates an employee on factors not included in the job description is left wide open to allegations of discrimination.

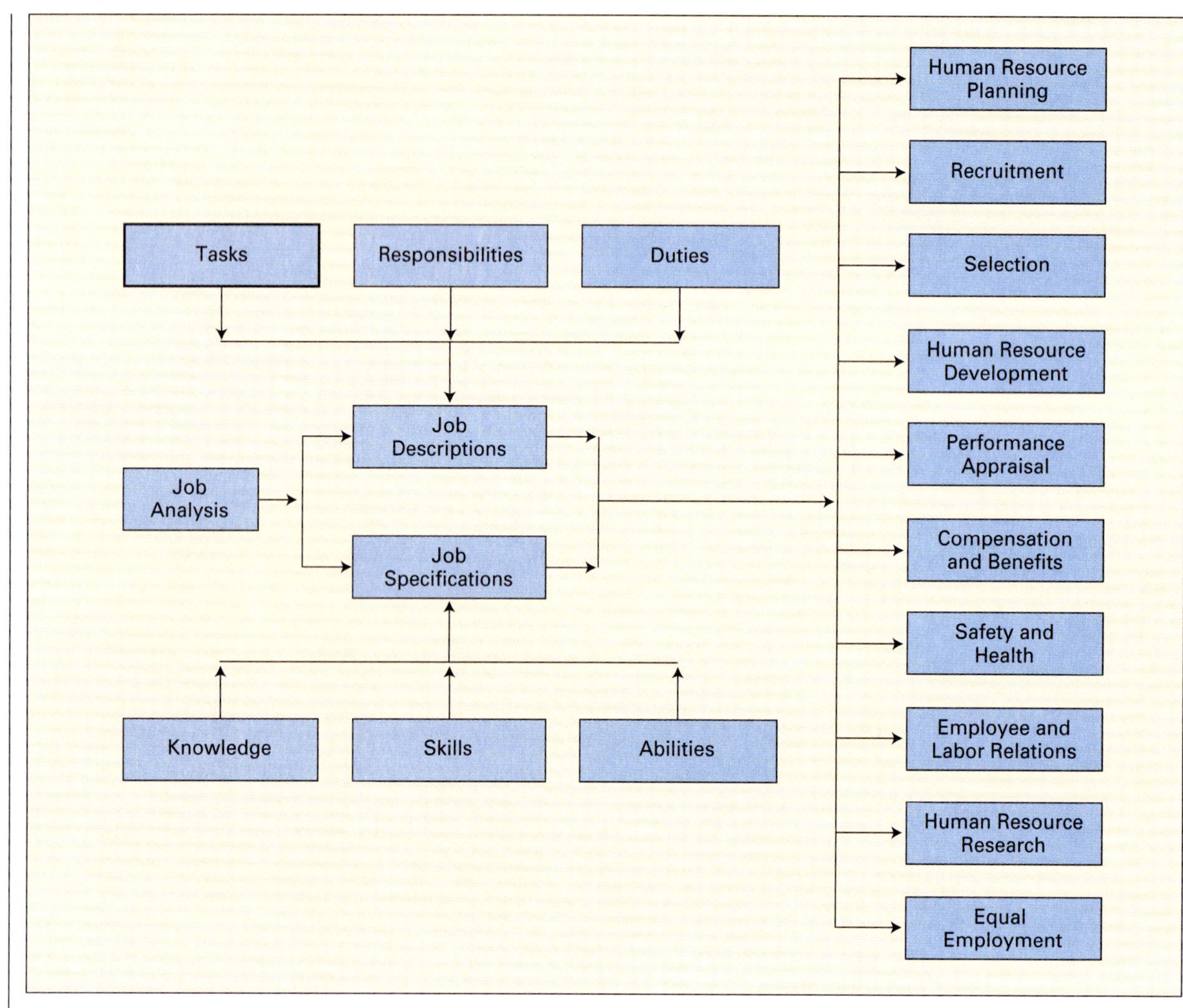

FIGURE 4-1 Job Analysis: The Most Basic Human Resource Management Tool

In the area of compensation, the relative value of a particular job to the company must be known before a dollar value can be placed on it. Relatively speaking, the more significant its duties and responsibilities, the more the job is worth. Jobs requiring greater knowledge, skills, and abilities should be worth more to the firm. For example, the relative value of a job calling for a master's degree normally would be higher than that of a job requiring only a high school diploma.

Information derived from job analysis is also valuable in identifying safety and health considerations. For example, employers are required to state whether a job is hazardous. The job description/specification should reflect this requirement. In addition, in certain hazardous jobs, workers may need specific information about the hazards in order to perform the jobs safely.

Job analysis information is also important to employee and labor relations. When employees are considered for promotion, transfer, or demotion, the job description provides a standard for comparison of talent. Regardless of whether the firm is unionized, information obtained through job analysis can often lead to more objective human resource decisions.

When human resource research is undertaken, job analysis information provides the researcher with a starting point. For example, if the human resource manager is trying to identify factors that distinguish successful employees from mediocre employees, the researcher needs to study only those employees who have similar job descriptions/specifications.

Finally, having properly accomplished job analysis is particularly important for supporting the legality of employment practices. Job analysis data are needed to defend, for example, decisions involving promotion, transfers, and demotions.

Thus far, we have described job analysis as it pertains to specific HRM functions. However, in practice these functions are interrelated. In fact, job analysis provides the basis for tying the functional areas together and the foundation for developing a sound human resource program.

TYPES OF JOB ANALYSIS INFORMATION

Considerable information is needed for successful accomplishment of job analysis. The job analyst identifies the job's actual duties and responsibilities and gathers the other types of data shown in Table 4-1. Note that work activities, worker-oriented activities, and the types of machines, tools, equipment, and work aids used in the job are important. This information is used later to help determine the job skills needed. In addition, the job analyst looks at job-related tangibles and intangibles, such as the knowledge needed, the materials processed, and the goods made or services performed.

Some job analysis systems identify job standards. Work measurement studies may be needed to determine, for example, how long it takes to perform a task. With regard to job content, the analyst studies the work schedule, financial and nonfinancial incentives, and physical working conditions. Since jobs are often performed in conjunction with others, organizational and social contexts are also noted. And, finally, specific education, training, and work experience pertinent to the job are identified.

JOB ANALYSIS METHODS

Job analysis has traditionally been conducted in a number of different ways because organizational needs and resources for conducting job analysis differ.[3] Selection of a specific method should be based on the ways in which the information is to be used (job evaluation, pay increases, development, and so on) and the approach that is most feasible for a particular organization. We describe the most common methods of job analysis in the following sections.

Questionnaires

Questionnaires are typically quick and economical to use. The job analyst may administer a structured questionnaire to employees, who identify the tasks they perform. However, in some cases, employees may lack verbal skills, which makes this method less useful. Also, some employees may tend

TABLE 4-1
Types of Data Collected in Job Analysis

SUMMARY OF TYPES OF DATA COLLECTED THROUGH JOB ANALYSIS*

1. **Work activities**
   a. Work activities and processes.
   b. Activity records (in film form, for example).
   c. Procedures used.
   d. Personal responsibility.
2. **Worker-oriented activities**
   a. Human behaviors, such as physical actions and communicating on the job.
   b. Elemental motions for methods analysis.
   c. Personal job demands, such as energy expenditure.
3. **Machines, tools, equipment, and work aids used**
4. **Job-related tangibles and intangibles**
   a. Knowledge dealt with or applied (as in accounting).
   b. Materials processed.
   c. Products made or services performed.
5. **Work performance†**
   a. Error analysis.
   b. Work standards.
   c. Work measurements, such as time taken for a task.
6. **Job context**
   a. Work schedule.
   b. Financial and nonfinancial incentives.
   c. Physical working conditions.
   d. Organizational and social contexts.
7. **Personal requirements for the job**
   a. Personal attributes such as personality and interests.
   b. Education and training required.
   c. Work experience.

*This information can be in the form of qualitative, verbal, narrative descriptions or quantitative measurements of each item, such as error rates per unit of time or noise level.
†All job analysis systems do not develop the work performance aspects.
Source: Reprinted by permission of Marvin D. Dunnette.

to exaggerate the significance of their tasks, suggesting more responsibility than actually exists.

A portion of a job analysis questionnaire used by First Interstate Bancorp is presented in Figure 4-2. Although the entire questionnaire consists of six sections, only Section III, Position Skills and Knowledge, is shown.

Observation

When using the observation method, the job analyst usually watches the worker perform job tasks and records his or her observations. This method is

Job Analysis Questionnaire

First Interstate Bancorp

Name ____________________

Position Title ____________________

Affiliate ____________________

Division/Group/Unit ____________________

City and State ____________________

Immediate Manager ____________________

General Instructions

This questionnaire is designed to provide information about your current position. It is ***not*** intended to measure your performance or productivity. It is a tool for analyzing and describing your job.

The questionnaire consists of six sections.

- ***Section I*** deals with the tasks and activities that comprise your job.
- ***Section II*** asks you to compare various job dimensions, which are groupings of similar tasks.
- ***Section III*** covers the skills and knowledge required to perform the tasks and activities of your position.
- ***Section IV*** identifies specific scope measures of your position.
- ***Section V*** focuses on individual factors that you may bring to your job.
- ***Section VI*** includes additional factors which may have an impact on your position.

Because this questionnaire covers a broad range of affiliates and jobs, a number of the questions may not apply to your position. However, ***if you perform tasks that are not covered by the questionnaire, space has been provided for you to write them in.*** Whether you perform a large number of tasks or only a few is not important. What is essential is that you respond to ***all*** of the questions (for example, you may perform certain financial management tasks, although you are in a marketing function), and in a manner which best describes your position as it is typically performed by you.

In responding to the questions, please use the following definitions:

- ***affiliate*** refers to an individual bank (e.g., First Interstate Bank of Arizona) or a nonbank subsidiary (e.g., First Interstate Services Company).
- ***customer*** means any individual or group, inside or outside the company, with which you deal on a client or customer basis. For example, an affiliate bank can be a customer for the data processing unit, a small business can be a customer for the venture capital group, and an individual or a corporation can be a customer for a bank.
- ***unit*** is the organizational group in which you report or for which you have responsibility. This could be a functional group, a department, or a division of a company. For example, for a Cashier position, the unit might be the Cashier's Department; for a VP Operations, the unit might be the Operations Department; for a VP Administration, the unit might be the Administration Division; or for a Chief Executive Officer, the unit would be the entire bank.

The questionnaires will be returned directly to Towers, Perrin, Forster & Crosby (TPF&C), so all responses on this form will remain confidential. However, to ensure that the information about your position is accurate and consistent, you and your immediate manager will review the results of TPF&C's analysis of the questionnaire.

Please follow the specific instructions at the beginning of each section. Read each section in full before attempting to complete it so that you can respond as accurately as possible.

Thank you for your efforts in participating in this study.

FIGURE 4-2 A Job Analysis Questionnaire

Source: Used with the permission of First Interstate Bancorp.

For every statement
- If a task is not part of your job, mark X in the first box
- If a task is a part of your job, rate

Relative Time Spent	*Relative Importance*
1 = Very small amount	A Unimportant
2 = Small amount	B Minor importance
3 = Moderate amount	C Important
4 = Large amount	D Very important
5 = Very large amount	E Crucial

A. Planning

	Not part of the job	Relative time spent	Relative importance
1 Develops business planning activities			
2 Directs business planning activities			
3 Develops annual unit goals and objectives			
4 Approves annual unit goals and objectives			
5 Develops longer-range strategic goals			
6 Approves longer-range strategic goals			
7 Develops specific strategy and action plans for unit			
8 Approves specific strategy and action plans for unit			
9 Reviews, approves, and monitors business plans			
10 Prepares profit plans and updates			
11 Approves profit plans and updates			
12 Prepares operating budgets			
13 Approves operating budgets			
14 Approves requests for nonbudgeted items			
15 Develops plans to improve administrative efficiency			
16 Approves plans to improve administrative efficiency			
17 Integrates the plans of other organizational units			
18 Coordinates with other units to meet predetermined schedules			
19 Proposes new or customized programs, services, products and research			
20 Approves new or customized programs, services, products and research			
21 Identifies impact of external conditions on unit			
22 Coordinates units in the development of plans and programs			
23 Monitors progress of specific projects			
24 Recommends revisions to the unit organizational structure			
25 Approves revisions to the unit organizational structure			
26 Evaluates and recommends approval of affiliate facility projects			
27 Recommends potential mergers, acquisitions or relocations			
28 Approves potential mergers, acquisitions or relocations			
29 *Other* please list task(s) and check boxes			
a ______			
b ______			
c ______			

From the above list of Planning tasks, please mark the numbers of the three most important tasks in rank order

1 ______

2 ______

3 ______

B. Policies and Procedures

	Not part of the job	Relative time spent	Relative importance
30 Formulates and recommends policies or procedures for others to follow			
31 Approves policies or procedures for others to follow			
32 Reviews agreements or documentation for compliance with appropriate policies and standards			
33 Directs the establishment of review or control procedures			
34 Evaluates operating policies or procedures against desired objectives			
35 Develops or maintains standards for service			
36 Develops quality control programs and procedures			
37 Approves quality control programs and procedures			
38 Formulates or recommends pricing policies			
39 Approves pricing policies			
40 Develops methods and procedures to evaluate business strategies			
41 Establishes planning guidelines and procedures			
42 Directs creation, handling and disposition of official records			
43 Directs safeguarding of records and documents			
44 Approves procedures for automating existing manual systems			
45 *Other* please list task(s) and check boxes			
a ______			
b ______			
c ______			

From the above list of Policies and Procedures tasks, please mark the numbers of the three most important tasks in rank order

1 ______

2 ______

3 ______

Section III. Position Skills and Knowledge

This section focuses on the type and depth of skills and knowledge that are 1) required to perform your job, and 2) that you may possess.

For each of the skills listed, you are asked to rate two items: the ***level required*** and the ***level you possess.*** In the appropriate boxes, write the number that best describes the skill or knowledge level, according to the following scale:

0 = Job neither requires nor do I possess skill/knowledge.
1 = Familiarity with skill/knowledge.
2 = General working skill/knowledge.
3 = Advanced skill/knowledge.
4 = Unique expertise in skill/knowledge.

In the first column, identify the ***level of skill/knowledge required*** to successfully perform your present job.

In the second column of boxes, identify the ***level of skill/knowledge*** that ***you possess,*** regardless of whether the job requires it.

The third column identifies sources of skills and knowledge. To indicate where you acquired each skill or knowledge that is required for the performance of your current position, identify up to, but no more than, two sources. Mark 1 in the column that represents the primary source. Mark 2 in the column that represents the secondary source.

A. Planning, Policies, Procedures

	Level required for position	Level you possess	On-the-job training	College/university	Formal banking program	Internal training program	External training program
1 Organization design							
2 Short-term planning (setting budgets, goals, etc.)							
3 Strategic planning							
4 Pricing fee structuring							

B. Business Development / Marketing

	Level required for position	Level you possess	On-the-job training	College/university	Formal banking program	Internal training program	External training program
5 Market research (identifying markets, competitive analyses and evaluation)							
6 Market analysis (client needs, trends, strategies, etc.)							
7 Marketing tools (advertising, promotional campaigns, etc.)							
8 Products/services (bank unit services, systems, etc.)							
9 Marketing/sales							

C. Customer Relations

	Level required for position	Level you possess	On-the-job training	College/university	Formal banking program	Internal training program	External training program
10 Customer industry (objectives, economics, trends, etc.)							
11 Customer counsel/problem solving							
12 Account management							
13 Profit analysis							

FIGURE 4-2 (continued) A Job Analysis Questionnaire

used primarily to gather information on jobs emphasizing manual skills, such as those of a machine operator. It can also help the analyst identify interrelationships between physical and mental tasks. However, observation alone is usually an insufficient means of conducting job analysis, particularly when mental skills are dominant in a job. For instance, observing a financial analyst at work would not reveal much about the requirements of the job.

Interviews

An understanding of the job may also be gained through interviewing both the employee and the supervisor. Usually, the job analyst interviews the employee first, helping the worker describe the duties performed. Then, the analyst normally contacts the supervisor to get additional information, to check the accuracy of the information obtained from the worker, and to clarify certain points.

Employee Recording

In some instances, job analysis information is gathered by having the employees describe their daily work activities in a diary or log. Again, the problem of employees exaggerating their job importance may have to be overcome. However, valuable understanding of highly specialized jobs, such as a recreation therapist, may be obtained in this way.

Combination of Methods

Usually, an analyst does not use one job analysis method exclusively. A combination of methods is often more appropriate. For instance, in analyzing clerical and administrative jobs, the analyst might use questionnaires supported by interviews and limited observation. In studying production jobs, interviews supplemented by extensive work observation may provide the necessary data. Basically, the analyst should employ the combination of techniques needed to conduct an effective job analysis.

CONDUCTING JOB ANALYSIS

The person who conducts job analysis is interested in gathering data on what is involved in performing a particular job. The people who participate in job analysis should include, at a minimum, the employee and the employee's immediate supervisor. Large organizations may have one or more job analysts, but in small organizations, line supervisors may be responsible for job analysis. Organizations that lack the technical expertise often use outside consultants to perform job analysis. Before conducting a job analysis, the analyst learns as much as possible about the job by reviewing organizational charts and talking with individuals acquainted with the job to be studied. Before beginning, the supervisor should introduce the analyst to the employees and explain the purpose of the job analysis. Although employee attitudes about the job are beyond the job analyst's control, the analyst must attempt to develop mutual trust and confidence with those whose jobs are being analyzed. Failure in this area will detract from an otherwise technically sound job analysis. Upon completion of job analysis, two basic human resource documents—job descriptions and job specifications—can be prepared.

JOB DESCRIPTION

Information obtained through job analysis is crucial to the development of job descriptions. Recall that we previously defined the job description as a document that states the tasks, duties, and responsibilities of the job. Job descriptions should be both relevant and accurate.[4] They should provide concise statements of what employees are expected to do on the job and indicate exactly what employees do, how they do it, and the conditions under which the duties are performed.[5] Job description takes on an even greater importance under the Americans with Disabilities Act (ADA) because the description of essential job functions may be critical to a defense regarding reasonable accommodation.

Among the items frequently included in a job description are:

- major duties performed
- percentage of time devoted to each duty
- performance standards to be achieved
- working conditions and possible hazards
- number of employees performing the job and to whom they report
- the machines and equipment used on the job

The contents of the job description vary somewhat with the purpose for which it will be used. Let us consider the sections most commonly included in a job description.

Job Identification

The job identification section includes the job title, the department, the reporting relationship, and a job number or code. A good title will closely approximate the nature of the work content and will distinguish that job from others. Unfortunately, job titles are often misleading. An *executive secretary* in one organization may be little more than a highly paid clerk, whereas a person with the same title in another firm may practically run the company. For instance, one former student's first job after graduation was with a major tire and rubber company as an *assistant district service manager*. Because the primary duties of the job were to unload tires from trucks, check the tread wear, and stack the tires in boxcars, a more appropriate title would probably have been *tire checker and stacker.*

One information source that assists in standardizing job titles is the *Dictionary of Occupational Titles (DOT)*.[6] The *DOT* includes standardized and comprehensive descriptions of job duties and related information for more than 200,000 occupations. Such standardization permits employers in different industries and parts of the country to match more accurately job requirements with worker skills.

An example of a *DOT* definition—for a *branch manager,* occupational code 183.137-010—is provided in Figure 4-3. The first digit of the code identifies one of the following major occupations:

0/1 Professional, technical, and managerial
2 Clerical and sales
3 Service

4 Farming, fishing, forestry, and related
5 Processing
6 Machine trade
7 Bench work
8 Structural work
9 Miscellaneous

For the branch manager, the major classification would be *managerial* occupations. Thus, this example has a code *1*.

The next two digits represent breakdowns of the general occupation category.

Digits four through six describe the job's relationship to data, people, and things. For the branch manager, a code *1* for data would be *coordinating,* a code *3* for people would be *supervising,* and a code *7* for things would be *handling*.

The final three digits indicate the alphabetical order of titles within the six-digit code group. These codes assist in distinguishing a specific occupation from other similar ones. The alphabetical order for *branch manager* is indicated by the digits 010.

Date of the Job Analysis

The job analysis date is placed on the job description to aid in identifying job changes that would make the description obsolete. Some firms have found it useful to place an expiration date on the document. This practice

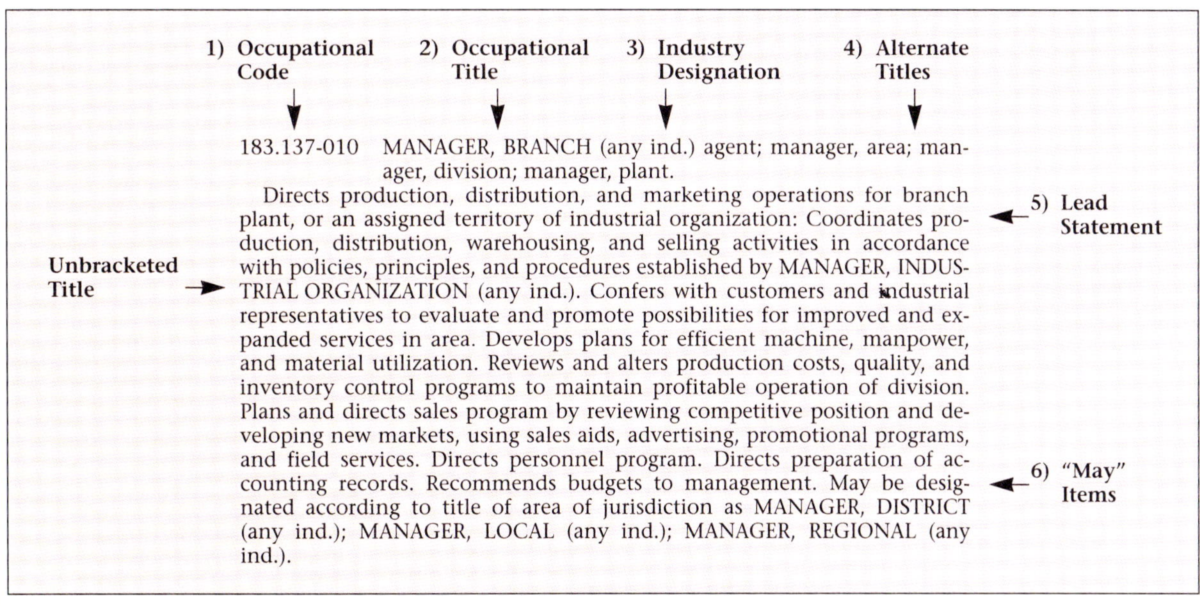

FIGURE 4-3 The Parts of the Dictionary of Occupational Titles Definition

Source: U.S. Department of Labor, *Dictionary of Occupational Titles*.

ensures periodic review of job content and minimizes the number of obsolete job descriptions.

Job Summary

The job summary provides a concise overview of the job. It is generally a short paragraph that states job content.

Duties Performed

The body of the job description delineates the major duties performed. Usually, one sentence beginning with an action verb such as *receives, performs, establishes,* or *assembles,* adequately explains each duty.

JOB SPECIFICATION

Recall that we defined job specification as a document containing the minimum acceptable qualifications that a person should possess in order to perform a particular job. Items typically included in the job specification are educational requirements, experience, personality traits, and physical abilities. In practice, job specifications are often included as a major section of job descriptions.

Figure 4-4 is an actual job description provided by General Mills, Inc. As you can see, the qualifications needed for the job of *Secretary II* include data entering at least sixty words per minute and demonstrated proficiency in English grammar, punctuation, spelling, and proper word usage. This type of information is extremely valuable in the recruitment and selection process.

After jobs have been analyzed and the descriptions written, the results should be reviewed with the supervisor and the worker to ensure they are accurate, clear, and understandable. The courtesy of reviewing results with employees also helps to gain their acceptance. Because the job description and job specification are often combined into one form, we use the term job description in this book to include both documents.

OTHER JOB ANALYSIS METHODS

Over the years attempts have been made to provide more systematic methods of conducting job analysis. We describe several of these approaches next.

U.S. Department of Labor Job Analysis Schedule

The U.S. Department of Labor established a method of systematically studying jobs and occupations called the **job analysis schedule (JAS)**. Its basic content is shown in Figure 4-5. When the JAS method is used, information is gathered by a trained analyst.

A major component of the JAS is the Work Performed Ratings section. Here, what workers do in performing a job with regard to data (D), people (P), and things (T) is evaluated. Subdivisions of these three categories are shown in Table 4-2. Each is viewed as a hierarchy of functions, with the higher in the category being more difficult. The codes in the Worker Functions section represent the highest level of involvement in each of the three categories.

POSITION TITLE				POSITION NUMBER
				217
SECRETARY II				APPROVAL
				RHS
DIVISION OR STAFF DEPARTMENT	LOCATION	REPORTS TO		EFFECTIVE DATE
All	All			May 1995
DEPARTMENT OR ACTIVITY	SECTION	POINTS	GRADE	REVISES
		165	6	

JOB SUMMARY
Performs clerical and administrative duties for a manager and often one or more staff members of a major function.

NATURE OF WORK
Performs a wide variety of office duties including most of the following:

a. Data entry of correspondence, reports, manuscripts, graphs, charts, etc., from notes, dictating machine, and/or hand written drafts proficiently and with minimum direction and instructions.
b. Receiving telephone calls and visitors skillfully and handling incoming mail efficiently.
c. Originating routine correspondence and handling inquiries, and routing non-routine inquiries and correspondence to proper persons.
d. Establishing and maintaining department files and records.
e. Assuming responsibility for arranging appointments and meetings, screening calls, and handling personal and confidential matters for superior.
f. Assembling, organizing, processing, and evaluating data and reports; operating office machines needed for accomplishing this.
g. Performing administrative duties and special projects as directed, such as collecting and compiling general reference materials and information pertaining to company, division, or department practices and procedures.

Works independently, receiving a minimum of supervision and guidance on established office procedures. Relieves supervisor of minor administrative details. May have some light work direction over others in department. Structure is light and most work is not checked.

QUALIFICATIONS
High school education or its equivalent plus three years of clerical experience, including one year with the Company, and a word processing skill of at least 60 WPM. Demonstrated proficiency in English grammar, punctuation, spelling, and proper word usage. Must be able to anticipate problems and use sound judgment and tact in handling confidential matters, screening telephone calls and visitors, and scheduling superior's time. Must have the ability to acquire a thorough knowledge of the organization's policies, procedures, and personnel in order to relieve superior of specified administrative duties. A basic figure aptitude and/or a working knowledge of certain word processing packages may be necessary depending on the specific job.

FIGURE 4-4 A Job Description

Source: Used with the permission of General Mills, Inc.

The JAS component Worker Traits Ratings relates primarily to job requirement data. The topics General Education Designation (GED), Specific Vocational Preparation (SVP), Aptitudes, Temperaments, Interests, Physical Demands, and Environmental Conditions are included. The Description of Tasks section (item 15) provides a specific description of the work performed. Both routine tasks and occasionally performed tasks are included.

Functional Job Analysis

Functional job analysis (FJA) is a comprehensive job analysis approach that concentrates on the interactions among the work, the worker, and the organization. This approach is a modification of the job analysis schedule. It is a worker-oriented method of describing jobs that identify what a person actually does rather than his or her responsibilities.[7] The fundamental elements of FJA follow:

FIGURE 4-5
A U.S. Department of Labor Job Analysis Schedule

JOB ANALYSIS SCHEDULE

1. Estab. Job Title DOUGH MIXER

2. Ind. Assign. (bake. prod.)

3. SIC Code(s) and Title(s) 2051 Bread and other bakery products

Code 520.782
DOT Title
Oper. Control p. 435
WTA Group
Ind. Desig.

4. JOB SUMMARY:

Operates mixing machine to mix ingredients for straight and sponge (yeast) doughs according to established formulas, directs other workers in fermentation of dough, and cuts dough into pieces with hand cutter.

5. WORK PERFORMED RATINGS:

Worker Functions

D	P	(T)
Data	People	Things
5	6	2

Work Field 148 - Cooking, Food Preparing

M.P.S.M.S. 384 - Bakery Products

6. WORKER TRAITS RATINGS:

GED	1	(2)	3	4	5	6				
SVP	1	2	3	(4)	5	6	7	8	9	
Aptitudes	G 3	V 3	N 3	S 3	P 3	Q 4	K 3	F 3	M 3	E 4 C 4
Temperaments	D	F	I	J	(M)	P	R	S	(T)	V
Interests	(1a)	1b	2a	2b	3a	3b	4a	(4b)	5a	(5b)
Phys. Demands	S	L	M	(H)	V	2	(3)	(4)	5	(6)
Environ. Cond.	(I)	O	B	2	3	4	(5)	6	7	

7. General Education

a. Elementary 6 High School ____ Courses ____

b. College None Courses ____

8. Vocational Preparation

a. College None Courses ____

b. Vocational Education None Courses ____

c. Apprenticeship None

d. Inplant Training None

e. On-the-Job Training Six Months

f. Performance on Other Jobs DOUGH-MIXER HELPER - One Year

Source: U.S. Department of Labor, Manpower Administration, *Handbook for Analyzing Jobs* (Washington, D.C.: U.S. Government Printing Office, 1972): 42–45.

FIGURE 4-5 (continued)
A U.S. Department of Labor Job Analysis Schedule

9. Experience One Year as DOUGH-MIXER HELPER

10. Orientation Four Hours

11. Licenses, etc. Food Handlers Certificate Issued by the Health Department

12. Relation to Other Jobs and Workers

Promotion: From DOUGH-MIXER HELPER To BAKER

Transfers: From None To None

Supervision Received By BAKER

Supervision Given DOUGH-MIXER HELPER

13. Machines, Tools, Equipment, and Work Aids - Dough-mixing machine; balance scales; hand scoops; measuring vessels; portable dough troughs.

14. Materials and Products

Bread dough

15. Description of Tasks:

1. Dumps ingredients into mixing machine: Examines production schedule to determine type of bread to be produced, such as rye, whole wheat, or white. Refers to formula card for quantities and types of ingredients required, such as flour, water, milk, vitamin solutions, and shortening. Weighs out, measures, and dumps ingredients into mixing machine. (20%)
2. Operates mixing machine: Turns valves and other hand controls to set mixing time according to type of dough being mixed. Presses button to start agitator blades in machine. Observes gauges and dials on equipment continuously to verify temperature of dough and mixing time. Feels dough for desired consistency. Adds water or flour to mix measuring vessels and adjusts mixing time and controls to obtain desired elasticity in mix. (55%)
3. Directs other workers in fermentation of dough: Prepares fermentation schedule according to type of dough being raised. Sprays portable dough *Trough* with lubricant to prevent adherence of mixed dough to trough. Directs DOUGH-MIXER HELPER in positioning trough beneath door of mixer to catch dough when mixing cycle is complete. Pushes or directs other workers to push troughs of dough into fermentation room. (10%)
4. Cuts dough: Dumps fermented dough onto worktable. Manually kneads dough to eliminate gases formed by yeast. Cuts dough into pieces with hand cutter. Places cut dough on proofing rack and covers with cloth. (10%)
5. Performs miscellaneous duties: Records on work sheet number of batches mixed during work shift. Informs BAKE SHOP FOREMAN when repairs or major adjustments are required for machines and equipment. (5%)

16. Definition of Terms

Trough - A long, narrow, opened vessel used for kneading or washing ingredients

17. General Comments

None

18. Analyst Jane Smith Date 3/21/95 Editor John Riley Date 3/30/95

Reviewed By Alexandra Purcey Title, Org. Foreman, Bake Shop

1. A major distinction is made between what gets done and what workers do to get things done. It is more important in job analysis to know the latter. For instance, a word processing operator does not just keep the system running; a number of tasks must be performed in accomplishing the job.
2. Each job is concerned with data, people, and things.
3. Workers function in unique ways as they relate to data, people, and things.
4. Each job requires the worker to relate to data, people, and things in some way.
5. Only a few definite and identifiable functions are involved with data, people, and things (refer again to Table 4-2).
6. These functions proceed from the simple to the complex. The least complex form of data would be comparing, and the most complex would be synthesizing. In addition, the assumption is that if an upper-level function is required, all the lower-level functions are also required.
7. The three hierarchies for data, people, and things provide two measures for a job. First, there is a measure of relative complexity in relation to data, people, and things—in essence, the amount of interrelationship among the three functions. Second, there is a measure of proportional involvement for each function. For instance, 50 percent of a person's time may be spent in analyzing, 30 percent in supervising, and 20 percent in operating.[8]

One study determined FJA was a useful technique for defining the work of heavy-equipment operators. Therefore, the knowledge, skills, and abilities required for the job could be easily communicated to the courts and the public.[9]

TABLE 4-2
Worker Function Scale for Job Analysis Schedule

DATA (4TH DIGIT)	PEOPLE (5TH DIGIT)	THINGS (6TH DIGIT)
0 Synthesizing	0 Monitoring	0 Setting-up
1 Coordinating	1 Negotiating	1 Precision working
2 Analyzing	2 Instructing	2 Operating—controlling
3 Compiling	3 Supervising	3 Driving—operating
4 Computing	4 Diverting	4 Manipulating
5 Copying	5 Persuading	5 Tending
6 Comparing	6 Speaking—signaling	6 Feeding—offbearing
7 No significant relationship	7 Serving	7 Handling
8 No significant relationship	8 No significant relationship	8 No significant relationship

Source: U.S. Department of Labor, *Dictionary of Occupational Titles.*

HRM IN ACTION

—NEEDED: A GOOD JOB DESCRIPTION

"I can't determine what kind of computer programmer you need, Alex," said Bob Sanders, the human resource director. "Every applicant I sent down was proficient in FORTRAN, just like the job description stated." "Get real, Bob," replied Alex. "We haven't required FORTRAN in ten years. The person I need has to be up-to-date on the latest software. None of those people you sent me were qualified."

How would you respond?

Position Analysis Questionnaire

The **Position Analysis Questionnaire (PAQ)** is a structured job analysis questionnaire that uses a checklist approach to identify job elements. Some 194 job descriptors relate to job-oriented elements. Advocates of the PAQ believe its ability to identify job elements, behaviors required of job incumbents, and other job characteristics make this procedure applicable to analysis of virtually any type of job. Each job descriptor is evaluated on a specified scale such as extent of use, amount of time, importance of job, possibility of occurrence, and applicability.

With the aid of a computer program, each job being studied is scored relative to the thirty-two job dimensions. The score derived represents a profile of the job, which can be compared with standard profiles to group the job into known job families; that is, jobs of a similar nature. In essence, the PAQ identifies significant job behaviors and classified jobs. Using the PAQ, job descriptions can be based on the relative importance and emphasis placed on various job elements.

The PAQ is completed by an employee or employees familiar with the job being studied—typically an experienced job incumbent or the immediate supervisor. The profiles and job descriptions are then prepared by a job analyst.[10]

Management Position Description Questionnaire

The **Management Position Description Questionnaire (MPDQ)** is a method of job analysis designed for management positions and uses a checklist to analyze jobs. It contains 208 items that are related to the concerns and responsibilities of managers.[11] These 208 items have been reduced to thirteen primary job factors:

1. Product, market, and financial planning
2. Coordination of other organizational units and workers
3. Internal business control
4. Products and service responsibility
5. Public and customer relations
6. Advanced consulting

7. Autonomy of action
8. Approval of financial commitment
9. Staff service
10. Supervision
11. Complexity and stress
12. Advanced financial responsibility
13. Broad human resources responsibility

The MPDQ has been used to determine the training needs of individuals who are slated to move into managerial positions. It has also been used to evaluate and set compensation rates for managerial jobs and to assign the jobs to job families.

Guidelines Oriented Job Analysis

The **Guidelines Oriented Job Analysis (GOJA)** responds to the growing amount of legislation affecting staffing and involves a step-by-step procedure for describing the work of a particular job classification.[12] It is also used for developing selection tools, such as application forms, and for documenting compliance with various legal requirements.

There are three versions of GOJA. The original method, *full GOJA,* is very detailed and requires approximately twenty hours to analyze a job completely. Its use is most appropriate when there is a high probability of discrimination suits. Next, *brief GOJA* was developed after the *Uniform Guidelines* were published in order to reduce the amount of time required to complete a job analysis. To reduce the amount of time required still further, a third version, *simplified GOJA,* was developed. Only about two to four hours are required to complete this job analysis form. The GOJA obtains the following types of information: (1) machines, tools and equipment; (2) supervision; (3) contacts; (4) duties; (5) knowledge, skills, and abilities; (6) physical and other requirements; and (7) differentiating requirements.

Occupational Measurement System[13]

Because of the many technological advances presently taking place, new and innovative job analysis methods are being developed.[14] The **Occupational Measurement System (OMS)** enables organizations to collect, store, and analyze information pertinent to human resources by means of a computer database. The computer provides fast turnaround and more accurate job analysis, job descriptions, and evaluations. The computer also makes feasible the use of multiple regression statistical techniques that increase objectivity and, hence, responsiveness to potential discrimination claims.

The OMS is designed to work with task-based information. Task-based job evaluation uses structured job analysis questionnaires covering work performed within the organization as the basic input document. The questionnaires are developed from a number of different sources, including a database of industry job tasks, the organization's job descriptions, and job experts within the firm's workforce. The system includes a booklet with instructions and general information. The questionnaire contains items specifically tailored to the category of positions covered. Responses are given in data entry or optical scanning format. Sample items from a questionnaire are shown in Figure 4-6.

For Every Statement:

- If a task is part of your job, mark X in the first box.
- If you PERFORM and/or SUPERVISE a task, rate it using the adjacent RELATIVE TIME SPENT scale:

1 = An extremely small amount of time.
2 = Between levels 1 and 3.
3 = A small amount of time.
4 = Between levels 3 and 5.
5 = A moderate amount ot time.
6 = Between levels 5 and 7.
7 = A large amount of time.
8 = Between levels 7 and 9.
9 = An extremely large amount of time.

Relative time spent SUPERVISING
Relative time spent PERFORMING
Part of job

CREDIT ADMINISTRATION

1. Works with officers on national accounts to solve credit problems.
2. Responds to inquiries from branches regarding consumer regulations.
3. Establishes goals for delinquency ratios, charge-offs and recoveries.
4. Maintains annual forecasts for nonaccrual loans and other nonperforming assets.
5. Develops loan policy and procedures.
6. Recommends loan policy and procedures.
7. Maintains annual forecasts of commercial, consumer and real estate loan losses.
8. Prepares reports on branch compliance with consumer regulations.
9. Recommends interest rates for loans.

Relative time spent SUPERVISING
Relative time spent PERFORMING
Part of job

10. Reviews periodicals for changes to consumer protection laws.
11. Reviews analysis reports and financial statement spreads.
12. Performs commercial credit investigations.
13. Prepares credit memos.
14. Prepares loan write-ups.
15. Assembles and interprets debtor credit information.
16. Surveys collateral status for credit extension on potential and current customers.
17. Contacts credit agencies to secure credit reports and special services.

FIGURE 4-6 A Job Analysis Questionnaire

Source: Used with the permission of First Interstate Bancorp.

The OMS is an integrated computer software system specifically designed to process, analyze, and display task-based information. The following are a few of the reports generated by OMS:

1. A functional and a detailed task-level job description. The job descriptions contain the functions performed by each employee, job, or job classification; the specific tasks covered by those functions; and the amount of time spent on the functions and tasks.
2. Skill and knowledge levels required to perform a function or a job, the skills and knowledge levels possessed by the workers, and the differences between the two, if any, along with identified training needs.
3. Costs of production, both in terms of performance and supervision.

JOB ANALYSIS AND THE LAW

Effective job analysis is essential to sound human resource management as an organization recruits, selects, and promotes employees. In particular, HRM has focused on job analysis because selection methods need to be clearly job related.[15] Legislation requiring thorough job analysis includes the following acts:

Fair Labor Standards Act: Employees are categorized as exempt or nonexempt, and job analysis is basic to this determination. Nonexempt workers must be paid time and a half when they work more than forty hours per week. Overtime pay is not required for exempt employees.

Equal Pay Act: In the past (and to some extent today), men were often paid higher salaries than women even though they performed essentially the same job. If jobs are not substantially different, similar pay must be provided. When pay differences exist, job descriptions can be used to show whether jobs are substantially equal in terms of skill, effort, responsibility, or working conditions.

Civil Rights Act: As with the Equal Pay Act, job descriptions may provide the basis for adequate defenses against unfair discrimination charges in initial selection, promotion, and all other areas of human resource administration. When job analysis is not performed, defending certain qualifications established for the job is usually difficult. For instance, stating a high school diploma is required without having determined its necessity through job analysis leaves the firm open to possible discrimination charges.

Occupational Safety and Health Act: Job descriptions are required to specify "elements of the job that endanger health, or are considered unsatisfactory or distasteful by the majority of the population." Showing the job description to the employee in advance is a good defense.

REENGINEERING

When business problems occur, workers are often blamed even though the real obstacle lies in process design. Unfortunately, many managers believe the manner in which an operation is accomplished is fixed. Rather than looking for process problems, managers often focus on worker deficiencies, at least initially. This is true even though the design of the process may be causing problems. If process is the problem, it can often be reengineered for a substantial improvement in productivity, as Procter & Gamble (P&G) discovered.

Reengineering essentially involves the firm rethinking and redesigning their business system to become more competitive. P&G Chairman Edwin L. Artzt has been preaching a strategy of good value since 1991 and has since launched sweeping changes in the way the company markets its products. P&G has gone far beyond just a strategy change. It is now involved in a far ranging self-appraisal aimed at streamlining its organization. P&G must be streamlined because a decade of acquisition and foreign expansion has resulted in an unwieldy organization with costs out of control. Overhead has risen 2 percent in only three years. P&G's solution to the problem is to "bottom-up reengineer" to cut costs in sales, research, and administration. Ten teams are determining how to streamline the company. Basically, at P&G "You've got people checking people," to determine who to cut, how many to cut, and how to improve the basic areas of sales, research, and administration. The key to this reengineering effort is that real contributors will remain at P&G. According to Artzt, "Real contributors don't have to worry (about these cuts)." One place where cuts are a must is in the area of overlapping staffs in the U.S., where bureaucracy is thickest. P&G has been trying to boost performance for years in the areas of marketing, sales, and logistics, but with only limited success. Artzt believes that reengineering is the answer.[16]

Reengineering is "the fundamental rethinking and radical redesign of business processes to achieve dramatic improvements in critical, contemporary measures of performance, such as cost, quality, service, and speed."[17] Reengineering emphasizes the radical redesign of work in which companies organize around process instead of by functional departments. It is not incremental changes that are desired, but radical changes which alter entire operations with the stroke of pens. Essentially, the firm must rethink and redesign its business system. Reengineering focuses on the overall aspects of job designs, organizational structures, and management systems. It stresses work should be organized around outcomes as opposed to tasks or functions. Reengineering should never be confused with restructuring (discussed in Chapter 5), even though a workforce reduction may result.[18]

The reengineering approach championed by consultant Michael Hammer, president of Hammer & Company in Cambridge, Massachusetts, has impressed some experts so much they believe it will displace Total Quality Management (TQM) at many companies.[19] In a recent survey of senior executives, reengineering comprised a major focus of the agenda of most corporate plans.[20] Some firms, such as Eastman Kodak Company and American Express, have gone so far as to appoint senior officers for reengineering.

In the language of reengineering, a term that is often used is *process manager.* As opposed to being a functional manager, such as a production manager, a marketing manager, a finance manager, and so forth, a process manager is responsible for accomplishing all operations associated with a specific process. The concept is similar in nature to the matrix organization.

JOB DESIGN

The previous section focused on processes and the concept of reengineering, which requires a certain degree of job design or redesign. In fact, many organizations do not need to reengineer, but rather need job design changes. **Job design** is the process of determining the specific tasks to be performed, the methods used in performing these tasks,

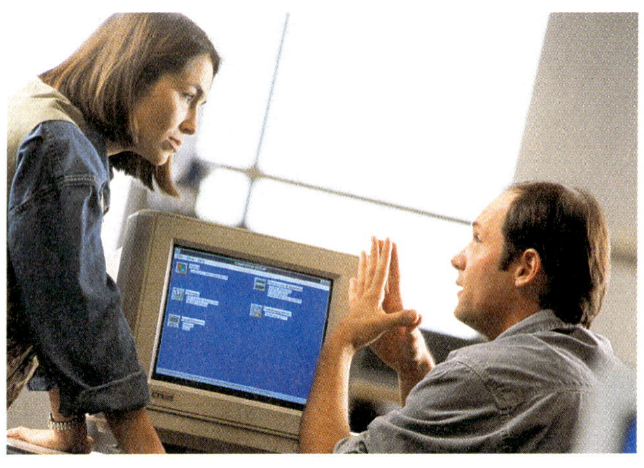

Jobs often need to be analyzed to determine if changes need to be made to improve productivity.

and how the job relates to other work in the organization. Several concepts related to job design, including job enrichment, job enlargement, and employee-centered work redesign, will be discussed next.

Job Enrichment

In the past two decades, there has been considerable interest in and application of job enrichment in a wide variety of organizations. Strongly advocated by Frederick Herzberg, **job enrichment** is basic changes in the content and level of responsibility of a job so as to provide greater challenge to the worker. Job enrichment provides a vertical expansion of responsibilities. The worker has the opportunity to derive a feeling of achievement, recognition, responsibility, and personal growth in performing the job. Although job enrichment programs do not always achieve positive results, they have often brought about improvements in job performance and in the level of satisfaction of workers in many organizations.

According to Herzberg, five principles should be followed when implementing job enrichment:

1. *Increasing job demands.* The job should be changed in such a way as to increase the level of difficulty and responsibility.
2. *Increasing the worker's accountability.* More individual control and authority over the work should be allowed while the manager retains ultimate accountability.
3. *Providing work scheduling freedom.* Within limits, individual workers should be allowed to schedule their own work.
4. *Providing feedback.* Timely periodic reports on performance should be made directly to workers rather than to their supervisors.
5. *Providing new learning experiences.* Work situations should encourage opportunities for new experiences and personal growth.[21]

Job Enlargement

Many people have attempted to differentiate between job enrichment and job enlargement. **Job enlargement** involves changes in the scope of a job so as to provide greater variety to the worker. Job enlargement is said to provide a horizontal expansion of duties. For example, instead of knowing how to operate only one machine, a person is taught to operate two or even three, but no higher level of responsibility is provided. On the other hand, job enrichment entails providing a person with additional responsibilities. There may be other tasks to perform, but responsibility is given with the tasks. For instance, the worker may be given the responsibility of scheduling the three machines. Increased responsibility means providing the worker with increased freedom to do the job, including making decisions and exercising more self-control over work.

Employee-Centered Work Redesign[22]

A concept designed to link the mission of the company with the job satisfaction needs of employees is **employee-centered work redesign**. Employees are encouraged to become involved in redesigning their work to benefit both the organization and themselves. Workers can propose changes in their job design to make their jobs more satisfying, but they must also show how these changes better accomplish the goals of the entire unit. With this approach, the contribution of each employee is recognized, while at the same time the focus remains on effective accomplishment of the organizational mission.

A GLOBAL PERSPECTIVE

Redesigning the way jobs are done is a strategy to increase global quality and productivity. One example of the positive impact of job redesign is the General Motors–Toyota NUMMI joint venture in Fremont, California. Before the NUMMI joint venture, General Motors's Fremont plant had one of the worst records in the company for poor labor relations and defective production. The plant was a typical assembly line operation in which workers and supervisors tried to push as many parts as possible down the line and let quality control inspectors discover the defects at the end of the line.[23]

Four years after the joint venture started, its productivity and quality levels rivaled Japan's best and exceeded anything in the U.S. automobile industry. The question arises as to what caused these changes. It cannot be the workers since they are still members of the United Auto Workers (UAW), and they are paid union scale wages and benefits. Nor did the change spring from the introduction of advanced robotics. It occurred because of a revolutionary team production system run by the workers themselves. Each worker is responsible for quality control and for ensuring no car moves on to the next station unless every job already completed is perfect. The system was worked out between the plant's Japanese and U.S. managers and the UAW members on the assembly line.[24] The key to this success did not lie in technology, workforce composition, specific management practices, or absence of collective bargaining. Rather, the key came in the higher expectations the Japanese managers held for their workers compared to U.S. workers. High expectations engender delegation, participation, and a sense of trust, all reciprocated with high performance.[25]

Conflict is common in international alliances, especially when they involve high technology companies and human egos. NUMMI's lessons for these alliances are simple ones: (1) involve all parties in the effort to redesign jobs; (2) be willing to listen and be receptive to new ideas; and (3) learn from each other's strengths and weaknesses.[26] At NUMMI, where the welding and assembling of GEO Prisms and Toyota Corollas take place, production processes are dynamic, based largely on teamwork and the Toyota Production System. In addition, there are only two job classifications at NUMMI: production workers and general maintenance and tool and die workers. This is highly unusual for a U.S. automobile assembly plant and even rarer for a unionized U.S. plant. Elimination of artificial lines drawn around functions enables teamwork to excel. This allows frequent job rotation, eliminating mind-dulling repetition and redundancy and requiring large doses of training and cross-training. A full 100 percent of the workforce at NUMMI receives training, and all associates effect process change. Both internal processes and external, vendor-related processes are open for review. Staffing and sourcing decisions are made by teams, and human resource managers are continually trying to reinvent the job to match the performance goals of the organization.[27]

SUMMARY

A job consists of a group of tasks that must be performed for an organization to achieve its goals. The systematic process of determining the duties and skills required for performing the organization's jobs is referred to as job analysis.

Job analysis information is used to prepare both job descriptions and job specifications. A job description specifies the tasks, duties, and responsibilities associated with a job. A job specification states the knowledge, skills, and abilities a person must possess in order to perform the job.

Job analysis may be conducted in several different ways. When using questionnaires, the job analyst has employees identify the tasks they perform in accomplishing the job. The job analyst actually watches the employee work and records observations when using the observation method. The job analyst may also gain an understanding of the job by interviewing both the employee and the supervisor. In some instances, job analysis information is gathered by having employees describe their daily work activities in a diary or log. Finally, the analyst may use a combination of any of these methods.

The sections most commonly used in a job description are (1) job identification, (2) date of the job analysis, (3) job summary, and (4) duties performed. Some of the items often included in the job specification section are requirements for education, experience, personality traits, and physical abilities.

In recent years, attempts have been made to provide more systematic methods for conducting job analysis. These newer approaches include (1) U.S. Department of Labor Job Analysis Schedule (JAS), (2) Functional Job Analysis (FJA), (3) Position Analysis Questionnaire (PAQ), (4) Management Position Description Questionnaire (MPDQ), (5) Guidelines Oriented Job Analysis (GOJA), and (6) Occupational Measurement System (OMS). Job analysis has become a focus of HRM because selection methods need to be job related.

Reengineering essentially involves the firm rethinking and redesigning their business system to become more competitive. Reengineering is the fundamental rethinking and radical redesign of business processes to achieve dramatic improvements in critical, contemporary measures of performance, such as cost, quality, service, and speed.

Job design is the process of determining the specific tasks to be performed, the methods used in performing these tasks, and how the job relates to other work in the organization. Job enrichment refers to basic changes in the content and level of responsibility of a job to provide a greater challenge to the worker. Job enlargement involves changes in the scope of a job to provide greater variety to the worker.

QUESTIONS FOR REVIEW

1. What is the distinction between a job and a position? Define job analysis.
2. Discuss what is meant by the statement, "Job analysis is the most basic human resource management tool."
3. Describe the traditional methods used to conduct job analysis.
4. List and briefly describe the types of data that are typically gathered when conducting job analysis.
5. What are the basic components of a job description? Briefly describe each.
6. What are the items typically included in a job specification?
7. Briefly describe each of the following: (a) U.S. Department of Labor Job Analysis Schedule (JAS); (b) Functional Job Analysis (FJA); (c) Position Analysis Questionnaire (PAQ); (d) Management Position Description Questionnaire (MPDQ); (e) Guidelines Oriented Job Analysis (GOJA); (f) Occupational Measurement System (OMS).
8. Describe how effective job analysis can be used to satisfy each of the following statutes: (a) Fair Labor Standards Act; (b) Equal Pay Act; (c) Civil Rights Act; and (d) Occupational Safety and Health Act.
9. Distinguish among reengineering, job design, job enrichment, and job enlargement.

HRM SIMULATION

Incident A in the *Simulation Players Manual* involves an opportunity to conduct job analysis. Your team has been investigating the various methods and costs of doing a job analysis for your organization. Any job analysis program would include writing a job description for each job in the organization. You have discovered that job descriptions have many uses, such as recruitment, interviewing, orientation, training, job evaluation, wage compensation survey, performance appraisal, and outplacement. Since your organization does not have the personnel or in-house expertise to do the work, your team has received bids from various firms. Your team is charged with the responsibility of choosing the best qualified and reasonably priced firm from a list of proposals.

ABC VIDEO CASE

MAKING IT IN A NONTRADITIONAL WORLD TAPE 1, NUMBER 6

One of the last bastions of male worker dominance is the construction industry. Less than 3 percent of the jobs are held by women—a figure that has not changed since 1980. This is the toughest battlefield for women fighting sex discrimination and sexual harassment.

In an effort to break down this barrier, Pacific Gas and Electric Company in California began a program called Fair Start. A preemployment training program, Fair Start will prepare women in this nontraditional field. Physical training, tool operation, and safety procedures are stressed along with group support meetings. The company also sponsored several committees made up of men and women in an effort to stop sexual harassment—one of the major reasons women have quit their jobs.

HRM INCIDENT 1

—WHO NEEDS JOB DESCRIPTIONS?

John Case, accounting supervisor, was clearly annoyed as he approached his boss, Gerald Jones. He began, "Gerald, this note you sent me says I have to update descriptions for all ten of the jobs in my department within the next two weeks."

"Well, what's the problem with that?" asked Gerald.

John explained, "This is a waste of time, especially since I have other deadlines. It will take at least thirty hours. We still have two weeks of work left on the internal audit reviews. You want me to push that back and work on job descriptions? No way.

"We haven't looked at these job descriptions in years. They will need a great deal of revision. And as soon as they get into the hands of the employees, I will get all kinds of flak."

"Why would you get flak for getting the job descriptions in order?" asked Gerald. John answered, "This whole thing is a can of worms. Just calling attention to the existence of job descriptions will give some people the idea they don't have to do things that aren't in the description. And if we write what the people in my division really do, some jobs will have to be upgraded and others downgraded, I'll bet. I just can't afford the morale problem and the confusion right now."

Gerald replied, "What do you suggest, John? I have been told just to get it done, and within two weeks." "I don't want to do it at all," said John, "But certainly not during the audit period. Can't you just go back up the line and get it put off until next month?"

Questions

1. What have John and Gerald forgotten to do prior to the creation of job descriptions? Why is that step important?
2. Evaluate John's statement, "Just calling attention to the existence of job descriptions will give some people the idea they don't have to do things that aren't in the description."

HRM INCIDENT 2

—A JOB WELL DONE

As Professor Sharpland toured the Plymouth Tube Company plant in Pontiac, New Jersey, he became more and more impressed with his young guide, Jim Murdoch. Jim was the assistant human resource director at Plymouth Tube and was primarily responsible for job analysis. An industrial engineer was assigned fulltime to the human resource department to assist Jim in job design. Professor Sharpland had been retained by the human resource director to study Plymouth Tube's job analysis system and to make recommendations for improvements. He had gone through the files of job descriptions in the human resource office with Jim and found them, in general, to be complete and directly related to the jobs performed.

One of the first stops on the tour was the office of the weld mill supervisor, a 10-foot by 10-foot room out on the factory floor with glass windows on all sides. As Jim approached, the supervisor, Roger Dishongh, was outside his office. "Hi, Jim," he said. "Hello, Roger," said Jim. "This is Professor Sharpland. Could we look at your job descriptions and chat with you for a moment?" "Sure, Jim," said Roger, opening the door. "Come on in and have a seat, and I'll get them out." From their vantage point, the men in the office could see the workers in the weld mill area. As they reviewed each job description, it was possible to observe every worker actually performing the work described. Roger Dishongh was familiar with each of the jobs. He was very knowledgeable about the job descriptions themselves, having contributed in preparing or revising each of them. "How are the job descriptions related to the performance evaluations here?" asked Professor Sharpland. "Well," answered Roger, "I only evaluate the workers on the items specified in the job descriptions, which were determined through careful job analysis. Limiting performance evaluations to those items encourages me to correct the job descriptions when something changes and they no longer accurately describe the job. Jim has conducted training sessions for all the supervisors so that we understand the relationships among job analysis, job descriptions, and performance evaluations. I think it's a pretty good system."

Jim and Professor Sharpland went on to several other areas of the plant and found similar situations. Jim seemed to have a good relationship with each of the supervisors as well as with the plant manager and the three midlevel managers they visited. As they headed back to the front office, Professor Sharpland was considering the comments he would soon make to the plant manager.

Questions

1. What desirable attributes of job analysis are evident at Plymouth Tube Company?
2. What kind of report do you think Professor Sharpland should present to the plant manager?
3. Describe the relationship that might exist between the industrial engineer and the assistant human resource director regarding job analysis.

DEVELOPING HRM SKILLS

AN EXPERIENTIAL EXERCISE

Developing and updating job descriptions is an integral part of the job of any human resource professional. Without properly designed job descriptions, performing necessary human resource management activities is extremely difficult. This exercise will permit you to gain a better appreciation of what is involved in preparing job descriptions. Job descriptions may vary even when the job analysis information is similar.

As senior human resource specialist at Pedal Cycle Company, you have been involved in job analysis planning for the new plant in Springfield, Missouri. Most of the job analysis data has been gathered, and now it is time to prepare specific job descriptions. You have been given a stack of job analysis information sheets and assigned the task of writing job descriptions based on this information. When the assistant human resource director, Ed Deal, handed you the data sheet, he said, "I'd like for you to do the first one, and then bring it to me and we'll go over it together."

The initial job description will be for the position of *Spot Welder. Work Activities* primarily involve welding parts together. All parts consist of thin steel pieces weighing less than two pounds. The preformed pieces to be welded together are taken from numbered bins surrounding the spot welder, placed in position on the machine, and welded. *Relationship With Other Workers* is fairly standard for a factory floor worker. Other machine operators running similar machines are within view, twenty to thirty feet away. The crane operator moves the parts bins to this work station and away as required, placing them wherever specified by the operator. There is little time for social interaction on the job. *Degree of Supervision* involved is fairly standard in this industry. The spot welder supervisor supervises twelve operators, all doing essentially the same job. Operators are expected to do their jobs with very little supervision, consulting the supervisor infrequently. *Records and Reports* are not generated as part of this job. *Skill and Dexterity Requirements* are marginal. In order to meet the standard times, the worker must be able to take two parts from separate bins, place them together in the correct position, and complete the part within 3.2 seconds. *Working Conditions* are not ideal; the work station is relatively crowded, the operator is required to wear safety goggles, ambient temperature varies from 50°F to 80°F in the summer. The noise level is about 60 decibels, safe but distracting, and the lighting is excellent.

Each participant will use the Pedal Cycle Company's *Job Description Form* and develop an appropriate job description. Several class members can participate in this exercise. Your instructor will provide the participants with additional information necessary to complete the exercise.

NOTES

1. R. Wayne Mondy, Robert M. Noe, and Robert E. Edwards, "What the Staffing Function Entails," *Personnel* 63 (April 1986): 55–58.

2. James P. Clifford, "Job Analysis: Why Do It, and How Should It Be Done?" *Public Personnel Management* 23 (Summer 1994): 324.

3. Ronald A. Ash and Edward L. Levine, "A Framework for Evaluating Job Analysis Methods," *Personnel* 57 (November-December 1980): 53–54.

4. Donald C. Busi, "The Job Description: More Than Bureaucratic Control," *Supervisory Management* 35 (October 1990): 5.

5. Hubert S. Field and Robert D. Gatewood, "Matching Talent with the Task: To Find the Right People, First Define the Jobs You Want Them to Do," *Personnel Administrator* 32 (April 1987): 113.

6. U.S. Department of Labor, *Dictionary of Occupational Titles,* 4th ed. (Washington, D.C.: U.S. Government Printing Office, 1977).

7. Felix M. Lopez, Gerald A. Kesselman, and Felix E. Lopez, "An Empirical Test of a Trait-Oriented Job Analysis Technique," *Personnel Psychology* 35 (August 1981): 480.

8. Ernest J. McCormick, "Job Information: Its Development and Application," in Dale Yoder and Herbert S. Heneman (eds.), *Staffing Policies and Strategies* (Washington, D.C.: The Bureau of National Affairs Inc., 1979): 54–58.

9. Howard C. Olson, Sidney A. Fine, David C. Myers, and Margarette C. Jennings, "The Use of Functional Job Analysis in Establishing Performance Standards for Heavy Equipment Operators," *Personnel Psychology* 34 (Summer 1981): 351.

10. Donald L. Caruth, Robert M. Noe III, and R. Wayne Mondy, *Staffing the Contemporary Organization* (New York: Praeger Publishers, 1990): 100.

11. W.W. Tornow and P.R. Pinto, "The Development of Management Job Taxonomy: A System for Describing, Classifying and Evaluating Executive Positions," *Journal of Applied Psychology* 11 (1976): 410–418.

12. Stephen E. Bemis, Ann Holt Belenky, and Dee Ann Soder, *Job Analysis: An Effective Management Tool* (Washington, D.C.: The Bureau of National Affairs, 1983): 42.

13. Information for this section was furnished by First Interstate Bancorp.

14. Kaye L. Aho, "Understanding the New Job-Analysis Technology," *Personnel* 66 (January 1989): 38.

15. Donald W. Myers, "The Impact of a Selected Provision in the Federal Guidelines on Job Analysis and Training," *Personnel Administrator* 26 (July 1981): 41–45.

16. Zachary Schiller, "A Nervous P&G Picks Up the Cost-Cutting Ax," *Business Week* (April 19, 1993): 28.

17. Michael Hammer and James Champy, *Reengineering the Corporation: A Manifesto for Business Revolution* (New York: HarperCollins Publishers, Inc., 1993): 32.

18. "The Malapropian 'R' Word," *Industry Forum* prepared by the American Management Association (September 1993): 1.

19. Otis Port, John Carey, Kevin Kelly, and Stephanie Anderson, "Quality: Small and Midsize Companies Seize the Challenge—Not a Moment Too Soon," *Business Week* (November 13, 1992): 72.

20. "The Malapropian 'R' Word," ibid.

21. Frederick Herzberg, "One More Time: How Do You Motivate Employees?" *Harvard Business Review* 65 (September-October 1987): 109–120.

22. Stephen L. Perlman, "Employees Redesign Their Jobs," *Personnel Journal* 69 (November 1990): 37–40.

23. Wayne F. Cascio and Manuel G. Serapio, Jr., "Human Resources Systems in an International Alliance: The Undoing of a Done Deal?" *Organizational Dynamics* 19 (Winter 1991): 68–69.

24. Ibid.

25. Thomas A. Mahoney and John R. Deckop, "Y'-Gotta Believe: Lessons from American- vs. Japanese-run U.S. Factories," *Organizational Dynamics* 21 (Spring 1993): 27–38.

26. Ibid.

27. Robin Yale Bergstrom, "NUMMI: Engineering the Process," *Production* (June 1993): 58–60.

CHAPTER 5

Human Resource Planning

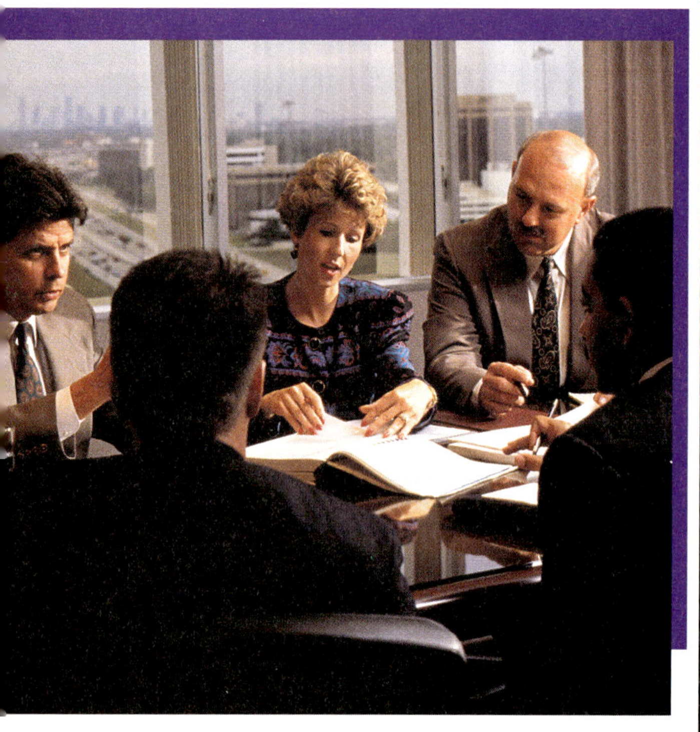

KEY TERMS

CHAPTER OBJECTIVES

1. Explain the human resource planning process and define the basic terms used in forecasting.
2. Describe some human resource forecasting techniques and explain how human resource requirements are forecasted.
3. Explain how human resource availability is forecasted and state what a firm can do when a surplus of workers exists.
4. Describe the concept of downsizing.
5. Describe the importance of a human resource information system.

Mark Swann, the marketing director for Sharpco Manufacturing, commented at the weekly executive directors' meeting, "I have good news. We can get the large contract with Medord Corporation. All we have to do is complete the project in one year instead of two. I told them we could do it."

Linda Crane, vice-president of human resources, brought everyone back to reality by asserting, "As I understand it, our present workers do not have the expertise required to produce the quality that Medord's particular specifications require. Under the two-year project timetable, we planned to retrain our present workers gradually. With this new time schedule, we will have to go into the job market and recruit workers who are already experienced in this process. We may need to analyze this proposal further to see if that is really what we want to do. Human resource costs will rise considerably if we attempt to complete the project in one year instead of two. Sure, Mark, we can do it, but with these constraints, will the project be cost effective?"

In the above instance, Mark failed to take into account the importance of human resource planning in his projections. In today's fast-paced, competitive environment, failure to recognize the importance of human resource planning will often destroy an otherwise well thought-out plan.

Our overall purpose in this chapter is to explain the role and nature of human resource planning in organizations today. First, we define *human resource planning* and describe the human resource planning process. Then, we review the terminology of forecasting and examine some human resource forecasting techniques. Next, we discuss forecasting human resource requirements and availability, and then examine action to be taken when a firm has a surplus of workers. After this, the concept of downsizing is described, followed by an example of effective human resource planning. We devote the final sections of the chapter to a discussion of human resource information systems.

THE HUMAN RESOURCE PLANNING PROCESS

Human resource planning (HRP) is the process of systematically reviewing human resource requirements to ensure that the required number of employees, with the required skills, are available when they are needed.[1] Human resource planning is vitally important because the main challenge for implementing overseas strategies relates to human resources issues, specifically stabilizing the workforce to facilitate implementation of corporate strategies.[2] Human resource planning involves matching the internal and external supply of people with job openings anticipated in the organization over a specified period of time. However, there is a growing mismatch between emerging jobs and qualified people available to fill them. The labor pool is changing as U.S. companies try to cope with rapid technological change and increasing globalization of the economy. The adequacy of the labor pool is vital to the success of the global organization. To develop global employees properly it is imperative that human resource managers provide individual technological training and cross-cultural training, and help broaden employee perspectives and relationships so that they can effectively deal with organizational changes.[3] As previously mentioned, human resource planning is increasingly being recognized as an important activity.

There is a growing realization among professional managers of the importance of including human resource management in the strategic planning process.

The human resource planning process is illustrated in Figure 5-1. Note that strategic planning—which requires consideration of both the external and internal environment—precedes human resource planning. **Strategic planning** is the process by which top management determines overall purposes and objectives and how they are to be achieved.[4] There is a growing real-

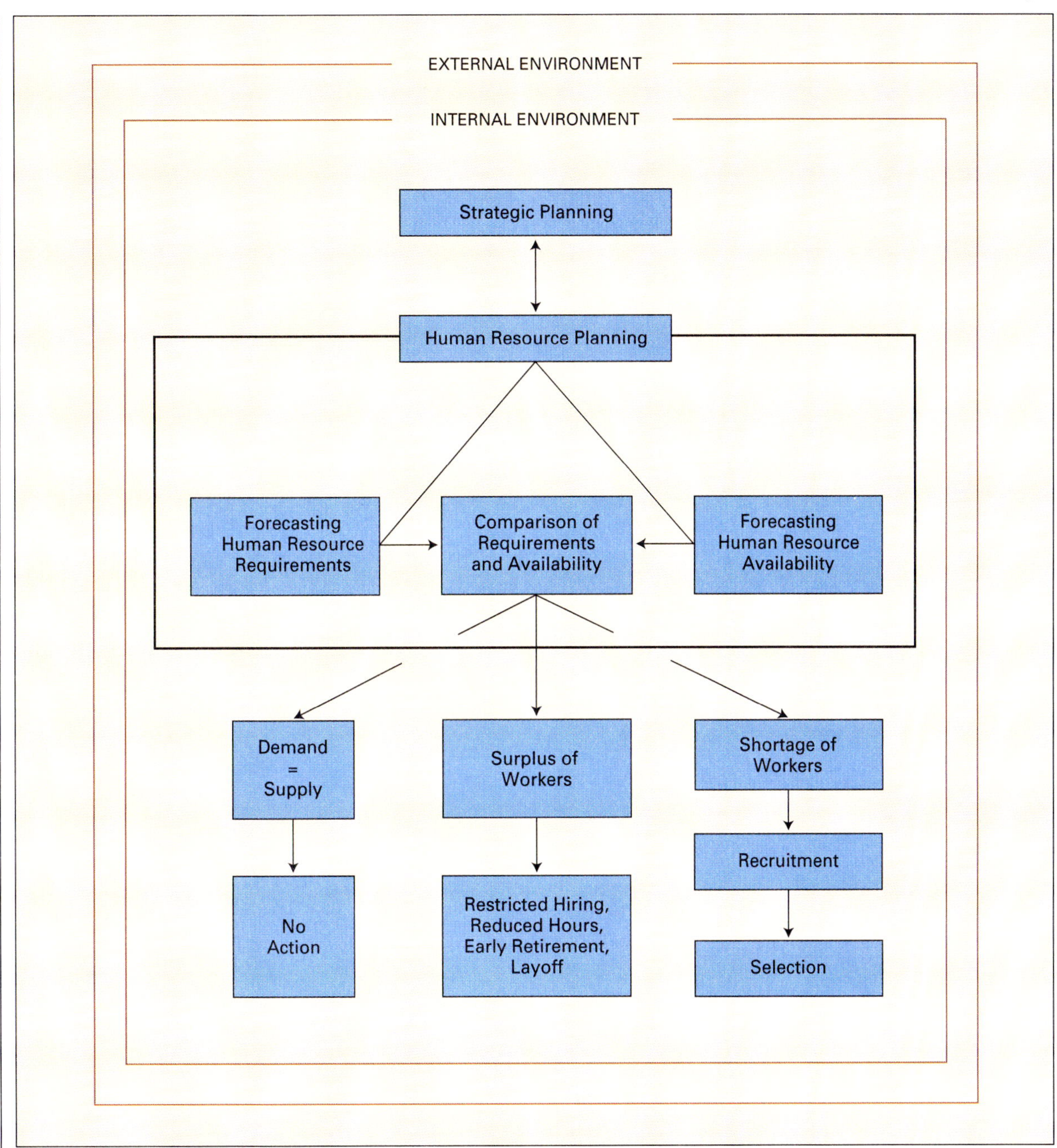

FIGURE 5-1 The Human Resource Planning Process

ization among professional managers of the importance of including human resource management in the strategic planning process. Essentially, human resource planning should be linked to organizational strategy.[5] In fact, in the 1990s, human resource planning will become an even more important aspect of strategic planning.

According to a recent survey of top-level executives, the best methods of improving quality and overall productivity are directly related to human resource issues. As may be seen in Figure 5-2, motivation, culture, and education were rated as the best methods for increasing productivity. Employees must be adequately motivated, they must be prepared to deal with the existing corporate culture, and they must be appropriately educated to cope with the challenges of their jobs. These and other human resource issues are the key for improving quality and productivity.[6] This fact reveals the absolute necessity for integrating HRM into a firm's strategic plans.

After an organization's strategic plans have been formulated, human resource planning can be undertaken. Strategic plans are reduced to specific quantitative and qualitative human resource plans. For example, note in Figure 5-1 that human resource planning has two components: requirements and availability. Forecasting human resource requirements involves determining the number and type of employees needed, by skill level and location. These projections will reflect various factors, such as production plans and changes in productivity. In order to forecast availability, the human resource manager looks to both internal sources (presently employed employees) and external sources (the labor market). When employee requirements and availability have been analyzed, the firm can determine whether it will have a surplus or a shortage of employees. Ways must be found to reduce the number of employees if a surplus is projected. Some of these methods include restricted hiring, reduced hours, early retirements, and layoffs. If a shortage is forecast, the firm must obtain the proper quantity and quality of workers from outside the organization. External recruitment and selection are required.

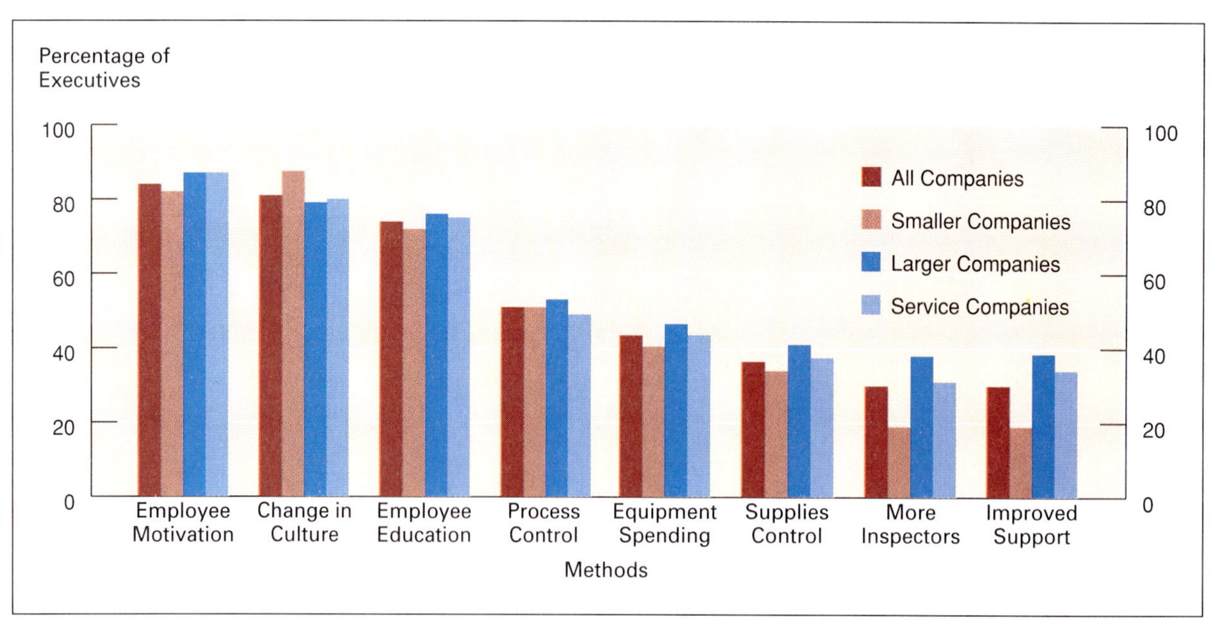

FIGURE 5-2 Most Effective Method for Improving Quality and Productivity

Source: Shetty, Y.K., et al., "Regaining Competitiveness Requires HR Solutions," *Personnel* 67 (July 1990): 12. Reprinted, by permission of the publisher, from *Personnel,* July/1990 © 1990. American Management Association, New York. All rights reserved.

HRM IN ACTION

—REPLACE OR NOT TO REPLACE

"Cynthia, what do you mean by saying that I'm going to have to justify my need for the typesetter's position? One of my ten employees in this job just quit, and I want a replacement now. We've had ten typesetters in my department for the thirteen years that I've been here, and probably a long time before that. If we've needed them in the past, certainly we will need them in the future." This is the beginning of a conversation between Richard Wiley, a first-line supervisor with Allen Industries, and Cynthia Larger, its human resource manager.

How should Cynthia respond?

Because conditions in the external and internal environments can change quickly, the human resource planning process must be continuous. Changing conditions could affect the entire organization, thereby requiring extensive modification of forecasts. Planning in general enables managers to anticipate and prepare for changing conditions, and HRP in particular allows flexibility in the area of human resource management. During the past ten years, various factors have caused some organizations to downsize (reduce the size of their workforces). Human resource planning allows workforce reductions with a minimum of disruption.

TERMINOLOGY OF FORECASTING

Four basic terms are used in forecasting. First, the **long-term trend** is a projection of demand for a firm's products, typically five years or more into the future. As Figure 5-3 shows, the hypothetical long-term trend is for increased sales, which are expected to double during the period shown. Early recognition of such a trend is crucial. A firm may not be able to fill the positions necessary to support such sales levels quickly if considerable training is required. Some employees may need extensive training and development before they are capable of taking on new or added responsibilities. Proper estimation of long-term trends, therefore, is essential for organizational success.

Second, **cyclical variations** are reasonably predictable movements about the trend line that occur over a period of more than a year. Cyclical variations may be caused by war, elections, changes in economic conditions and consumer demand, and societal pressures. These variations typically last between one and five years. Anticipating cyclical demand is important because of the potential for severe peaks and valleys. Extra people may be required to meet high cyclical demand, even though a stable long-term demand has been forecast. Conversely, although the long-term forecast may be upward, such conditions as a short-term recession may require a temporary workforce reduction.

Third, **seasonal variations** are reasonably predictable changes that occur during a period of a year. Seasonal variations follow cyclical variations

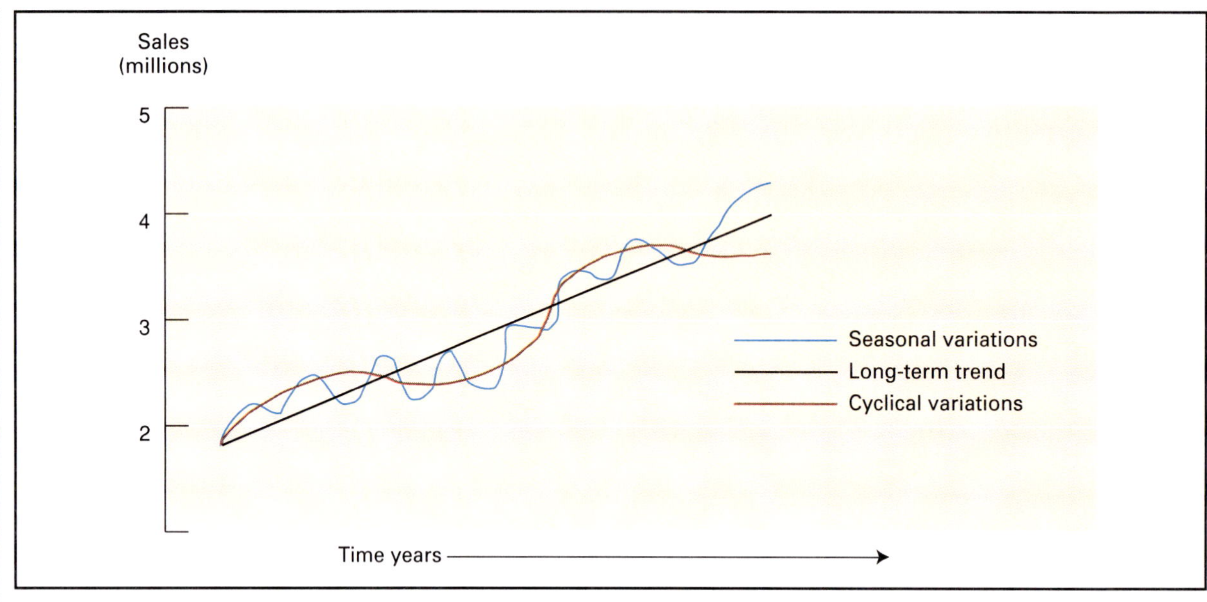

FIGURE 5-3 Forecasting Terminology Example

but may fluctuate drastically (see Figure 5-3). These variations occur within a twelve-month period and are of most immediate concern to many firms. Electric shavers are sold primarily during the Christmas holiday season, whereas motor boats are sold primarily in the spring. Seasonal demand can have a major impact on a firm as it attempts to stabilize its workforce and still meet production and inventory requirements.

Finally, **random variations** are changes without pattern. Even the most sophisticated forecasting techniques cannot anticipate such changes. Management must therefore anticipate and plan for long-term trends, cyclical variations, and seasonal variations—and be ready to deal with random variations.

HUMAN RESOURCE FORECASTING TECHNIQUES

Several techniques of forecasting human resource requirements and availability are currently used by those in the profession. Some of the techniques are qualitative in nature, and others are quantitative. Next, we describe several of the better known methods.

Zero-Base Forecasting

The **zero-base forecasting** approach uses the organization's current level of employment as the starting point for determining future staffing needs. Essentially the same procedure is used for human resource planning as for zero-base budgeting, whereby each budget must be rejustified each year. If an employee retires, is fired, or leaves the firm for any other reason, the position is not automatically filled. Instead, an analysis is made to determine whether the firm can justify filling it. Equal concern is shown for creating new positions when they appear to be needed. The key to zero-base forecasting is a thorough analysis of human resource needs.

Bottom-Up Approach

Some firms use what might be called the bottom-up approach to employment forecasting. It is based on the reasoning that the manager in each unit is most knowledgeable about employment requirements. In the **bottom-up approach**, each successive level in the organization—starting with the lowest—forecasts its requirements, ultimately providing an aggregate forecast of employees needed. Human resource forecasting is often most effective when managers periodically project their human resource needs, comparing their current and anticipated levels and giving the human resource department adequate lead time to explore internal and external sources.

Use of Predictor Variables

Another means of forecasting human resource requirements is to use past employment levels to predict future requirements. **Predictor variables** are factors known to have had an impact on employment levels. One of the most useful predictors of employment levels is sales volume. The relationship between demand and the number of employees needed is a positive one. As you can see in Figure 5-4, a firm's sales volume is depicted on the horizontal axis, and the number of employees actually required is shown on the vertical axis. In this illustration, as sales increase, so does the number of employees. Using such a method, managers can approximate the number of employees required at different demand levels.

With the increased use of computers and statistical software packages, human resource managers have at their disposal an important forecasting tool: regression analysis. **Regression analysis** is used to predict one item (known as the *dependent variable*) through knowledge of other items (known as the *independent variables*). When there is one dependent variable and one independent variable, the process is called *simple linear regression*. When

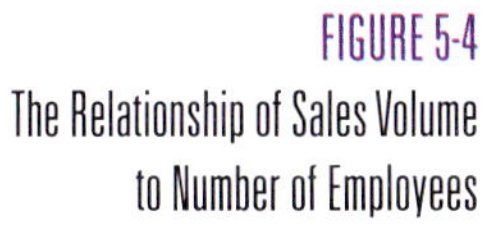
FIGURE 5-4
The Relationship of Sales Volume to Number of Employees

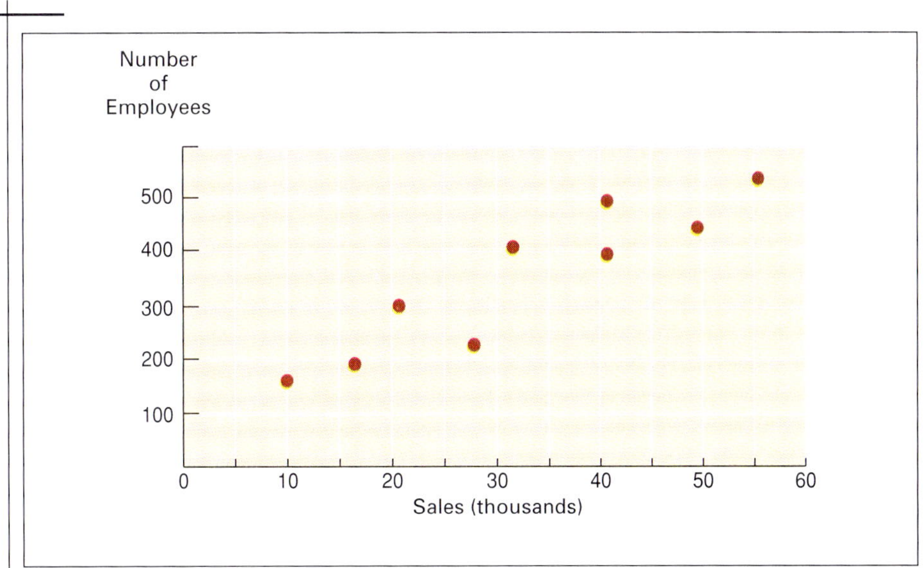

there is more than one independent variable, the technique is called *multiple regression*.

Regression is often used because of the direct relationship between demand for a firm's goods and/or services and employment levels. However, in most instances, the employment level is determined by several independent variables, and multiple regression is required. Instead of predicting employment levels solely on the basis of sales, an analyst might also use other variables, such as productivity of the workforce. Multiple regression often produces results superior to those obtained from simple linear regression because it recognizes that a variety of factors may influence future employment levels.

Simulation

Simulation is a technique for experimenting with a real-world situation through a mathematical model representing that situation. A model is an abstraction of the real world. Thus, a simulation model is an attempt to represent a real-world situation through mathematical logic in order to predict what will occur. Simulation assists the human resource manager by permitting the asking of many "what if" questions without having to make a decision resulting in real-world consequences.

In human resource management, a simulation model might be developed to represent the interrelationships among employment levels and many other variables. The manager could then ask "what if" questions such as:

- What would happen if we put 10 percent of the present workforce on overtime?
- What would happen if the plant utilized two shifts? Three shifts?

The purpose of the model is to permit the human resource manager to gain considerable insight into a particular problem before making an actual decision.

FORECASTING HUMAN RESOURCE REQUIREMENTS

A **requirements forecast** is an estimate of the numbers and kinds of employees the organization will need at future dates in order to realize its stated goals. Before human resource requirements can be projected, demand for the firm's goods or services must first be forecast. This forecast is then converted into people requirements for the activities required to meet this demand. For a firm that manufactures personal computers, activities might be stated in terms of the number of units to be produced, the number of sales calls to be made, the number of vouchers to be processed, or a variety of other activities. For example, manufacturing 1,000 personal computers each week might require 10,000 hours of work by assemblers during a forty-hour week. Dividing the 10,000 hours by the forty hours in the workweek gives 250 assembly workers needed. Similar calculations are performed for the other jobs needed to produce and market the personal computers.

FORECASTING HUMAN RESOURCE AVAILABILITY

Forecasting requirements provides managers with the means of estimating how many and what types of employees will be required. But there is another side to the coin, as this example illustrates:

> A large manufacturing firm on the West Coast was preparing to begin operations in a new plant. Analysts had already determined there was a large long-term demand for the new product. Financing was available, and equipment was in place. But production did not begin for two years! Management had made a critical mistake: It had studied the demand side of human resources but not the supply side. There were not enough qualified workers in the local labor market to operate the new plant. Workers had to receive extensive training before they could move into the newly created jobs.

Determining whether the firm will be able to secure employees with the necessary skills and from what sources is called an **availability forecast**. It helps the human resource manager to determine whether the needed employees may be obtained from within the company, from outside the organization, or from a combination of the two sources.

Internal Sources of Supply

Many of the workers that will be needed for future positions may already work for the firm. If the firm is small, management probably knows all the workers sufficiently well to match their skills and aspirations with the company's needs. If, for instance, the firm is creating a new sales position, it may be common knowledge that Mary Garcia, a five-year employee with the company, has both the skills and the desire to take over the new job. This unplanned process of matching people and positions may be sufficient for smaller firms. As organizations grow, however, the matching process becomes increasingly difficult. Both management and skills inventories are being used by human resource professionals and organizations that take human resources seriously.

Management Inventories. Managerial talent is an essential resource in every organization. Thus, firms maintain better data on the skills of managers than they do on those of nonmanagers. A **management inventory** contains detailed information about each manager and is used to identify individuals who have the potential to move into higher level positions. Essentially, this type of inventory provides information for replacement and promotion decisions. It would likely include data such as:

- work history and experience
- educational background
- assessment of strengths and weaknesses
- developmental needs
- promotion potential at present and with further development
- current job performance
- field of specialization
- job preferences
- geographic preferences
- career goals and aspirations

- anticipated retirement date
- personal history, including psychological assessments

Succession Planning. Because of the tremendous changes that will confront management in the 1990s, succession planning takes on more importance than perhaps ever before. In view of these expected changes, organizations need to develop a profile of the type of individuals who can effectively lead the organization both now and in the future.[7] Many companies are doing this; in a 1990 survey of over 400 boards of large U.S. companies, nearly three-quarters of the firms questioned had a succession plan.[8]

One of the outcomes of a management inventory is a succession plan. Detroit Edison calls its plan a Career Planning Inventory Organization Review Chart. As you can see in Figure 5-5, the chart shows a manager in the top box with immediate subordinates in the lower boxes. Information shown on the chart includes the following:

> *Position Box:* Shows the position title and the incumbent's name in each box. The symbol * preceding the name identifies incumbents who will retire between 1991 and 1996, indicating that short-range planning is required. The symbol ** preceding the name identifies incumbents who will retire between 1996 and 2002, indicating that long-range planning is required. If the word *open* appears in the box, the position is unfilled. If *future* appears, the position is anticipated but does not exist yet.
>
> *dev pgm:* Identifies the particular development program in which the employee participates.
>
> *retire:* Indicates the month and year of the employee's planned retirement.
>
> *est prom:* Indicates the employee's estimated potential for promotion.
>
> *lrp:* Indicates the employee's long-range career potential with the company.
>
> *ppc:* Indicates the incumbent's current organizational level.
>
> *3 Development Needs:* Describes three priority development needs that have been identified.
>
> *Potential Positions:* Shows the title of each position to which the incumbent is potentially promotable, along with codes that indicate an estimate of when the employee would be ready.
>
> *Possible Replacements:* Lists the names of up to ten possible replacements for the incumbent, with codes indicating when the replacements would be ready for promotion to this position.

Another example of an effective succession plan occurred recently at NCR when a senior vice president of finance retired. Following his departure, nine people moved up in the organization. At the end of the chain reaction, a young college student was hired as a financial analyst.[9]

The planned CEO succession at the new Chemical Bank, resulting from the merger between Chemical Banking Corporation and Manufacturers

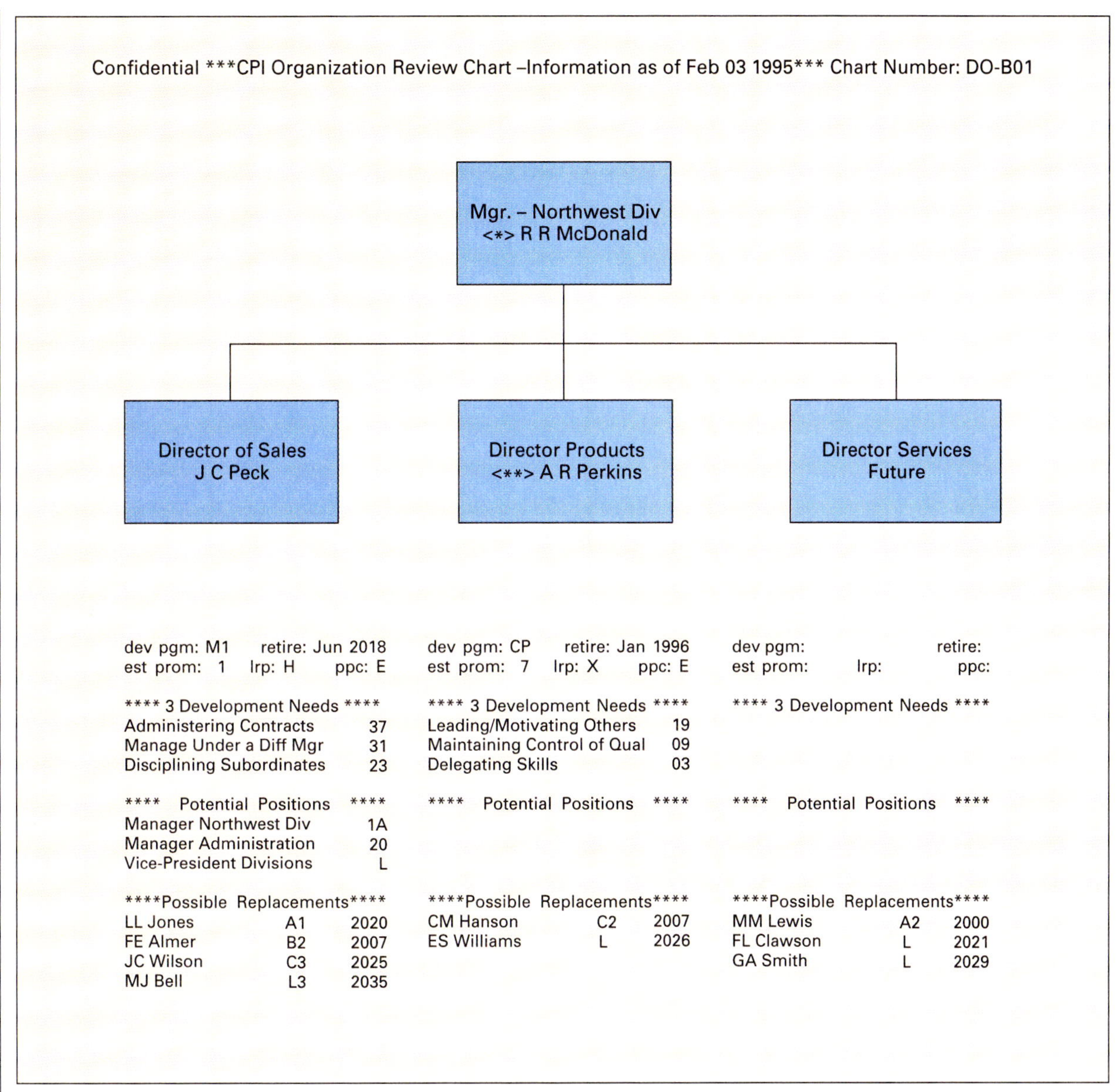

FIGURE 5-5 Career Planning Inventory Organization Review Chart

Hanover Corporation, will help assure management stability at the new company. At the time of the merger, CEO McGillicuddy planned to depart, and the succession plan was in place to assure a smooth transition and takeover by Walter V. Shipley. McGillicuddy would really liked to have stayed on, because he loved the people and what he was doing. However, he also believed that the succession was necessary. According to McGillicuddy, he felt even more strongly that he had had his time. With proper succession planning, McGillicuddy believes the best thing you can do is "put your hat on, say, 'Good luck, gang,' and go out and do something else."[10]

Skills Inventories. A **skills inventory** is information maintained on the availability and preparedness of nonmanagerial employees to move either into higher level positions or laterally in the organization. Although the process and the intent of the skills inventory are essentially the same as for a management inventory, the information differs somewhat. Generally included in a skills inventory are:

- background and biographical data
- work experience
- specific skills and knowledge
- licenses or certifications held
- in-house training programs completed
- previous performance appraisal evaluations
- career goals

A properly designed and updated skills inventory system permits management to readily identify employees with particular skills and match them as much as possible to the changing needs of the company.

External Supply

Unless a firm is experiencing declining demand, it will have to recruit some employees from outside the organization. However, finding and hiring new employees capable of performing immediately is usually quite difficult. The best source of supply varies by industry, firm, and geographic location. Some organizations find their best sources of potential employees are colleges and universities. Other companies get excellent results from vocational schools, competitors, or even unsolicited applications.

If the company has information revealing where its present employees were recruited, it can develop statistics and project the best sources. For instance, a firm may discover that graduates from a particular college or university adapt well to the firm's environment and culture. One large farm equipment manufacturer has achieved excellent success in recruiting from regional schools located in rural areas. Managers in this firm believe that since many students come from a farming environment, they can adapt more quickly to the firm's method of operation. Pepsi often recruits from second-tier schools because graduates of top business schools are seldom willing to start out in menial jobs.

Other firms may discover from past records that the majority of their more successful employees live no more than twenty miles from their place of work. This information may suggest concentrated recruiting efforts in that particular geographic area.

Forecasting can assist not only in identifying where potential employees may be found but also in predicting the type of individuals that will likely succeed in the organization. For example, a regional medical center—located far from any large metropolitan area—reviewed its employment files of registered nurses. It discovered that RNs born and raised in smaller towns adapted better to the medical center's small town environment than those who grew up in large metropolitan areas. After studying these statistics, management modified its recruiting efforts.[11]

Forecasting has many pitfalls, and examples of improper forecasting are numerous. Managers of one large convenience store chain, for instance, were disturbed by their unusually high employee turnover rate. When they analyzed their recruiting efforts, they discovered that the large majority of short-term employees had merely seen a sign in the store window announcing that a position was available. These individuals, often unemployed at the time, were highly transient. The recruitment method used tapped a source of supply that virtually guaranteed a high turnover rate. When the managers discovered this fact, they utilized new approaches, which significantly reduced turnover.

SURPLUS OF EMPLOYEES

When a comparison of requirements and availability indicates a worker surplus will result, restricted hiring, reduced hours, early retirements, and layoffs may be required to correct the situation. Downsizing, one cause of worker surpluses, will be discussed as a separate topic.

Restricted Hiring

When a firm implements a restricted hiring policy, it reduces the workforce by not replacing employees who leave. New workers are hired only when the overall performance of the organization may be affected. For instance, if a quality control department that consisted of four inspectors lost one to a competitor, this individual probably would not be replaced. However, if the firm lost all of its inspectors, it would probably replace at least some of them to ensure continued operation.

Reduced Hours

Reaction to declining demand can also be made by reducing the total number of hours worked. Instead of continuing a forty-hour week, management may decide to cut each employee's time to thirty hours. This cutback normally applies only to hourly employees because management and other professionals typically are salaried (not paid on an hourly basis).

Early Retirement

Early retirement of some present employees is another way to reduce the number of workers. Some employees will be delighted to retire, but others will be somewhat reluctant. The latter may be willing to accept early retirement if the total retirement package is made sufficiently attractive. A key point to remember is that because of the Age Discrimination in Employment Act, as amended, retirement can no longer be mandated by age.

Layoffs

At times, a firm has no choice but to lay off part of its workforce. A layoff is not the same as a firing, but it has the same basic effect—the worker is no longer employed. When the firm is unionized, layoff procedures are usually stated clearly in the labor-management agreement. Typically, workers with the least seniority are laid off first. If the organization is union free, it may base layoff on a combination of factors, such as seniority and productivity level. When managers and other professionals are laid off, the decision is likely to be based on ability, although internal politics may be a factor.

DOWNSIZING

Tied very closely to layoffs is **downsizing**, also known as restructuring and rightsizing. This is essentially the reverse of a company growing and suggests a one-time change in the organization and the number of people employed by it. Typically, both the organization and the number of people in the organization shrink. The trend among many companies in the 1980s and early 1990s was to cut staff and downsize.

Downsizing has certainly been the case in recent years with utility companies, which traditionally have been able to survive with rate increases when times got tough. When the price of coal or natural gas increased, the utility company usually got to pass the increase on to the consumer, reasoning that the increase was not their fault. But now, with utility companies investing in the unproven area of nuclear power generators, state regulators have begun to scrutinize their management actions more closely. If utility managers made bad decisions in this area, then it was an inappropriate management decision, not some external factor causing profitability problems. Commonwealth Edison made this mistake, for example, but it was not alone; Cincinnati Gas & Electric made similar management errors, and Houston Lighting & Power Company was also caught in the no rate increase pinch. Since regulators appear to be worried about ratepayer rebellion and recession, these and other utility companies have had no choice but to cut costs. Commonwealth Edison turned to restructuring and inevitable personnel cuts. Often restructuring is unsuccessful, but at Commonwealth Edison the individuals who are most responsible for such mistakes, managers, are the ones paying the price. Approximately 1,250 managers were cut, an additional 1,200 managers may be cut, and other jobs could be on the block. Cincinnati Gas & Electric announced that it would eliminate 800 jobs, and Houston Lighting & Power Company cut staff positions by 17 percent. Naturally, other changes are being made in all of these restructuring activities, but the one common thread that runs through all of them is that personnel cuts are inevitable.[12]

However, downsizing is often unsuccessful. The reason for this is that downsizings have not been able to solve the fundamental causes of the problems. Organizations have not developed an appropriate strategy for growth, but rather focused on reducing costs, which is merely a symptom of the problem. Downsizings at such firms as American Express, Westinghouse, and Sears Roebuck have not achieved the expected results.[13]

One result of downsizing is that many layers are often pulled out of an organization, making it more difficult for individuals to advance in the organization. In addition, often when one firm downsizes, others must follow if they are to be competitive. Thus, more and more individuals are finding themselves plateaued in the same job until they retire. To reinvigorate demoralized workers, some firms are providing additional training, lateral moves, short sabbaticals, and compensation based on a person's contribution, not his or her title.[14] Some firms are gaining enthusiasm from their employees by providing raises based on additional skills those employees acquire and use.

Historically, firms have downsized in difficult times and rehired when times got better. Today, with firms competing globally, managers are rethinking their automatic rehiring strategies. For instance, Arvin Industries, a manufacturer of automotive components, cut its workforce by 10 percent to just under 16,000, but the company had rebounded with profits estimated to grow at an annual rate of 20 percent through the 1990s. Even with enhanced business success, Arvin is not rehiring but instead trying to trim its staff further. According to Arvin's human resources director Ray Mack, "To remain globally competitive, we must continue to streamline operations and keep a tight rein on labor costs."[15]

HUMAN RESOURCE PLANNING: AN EXAMPLE

The human resource planning model presented in Figure 5-1 is a generalized one. Each firm must tailor human resource planning to fit its specific needs. Figure 5-6 shows the human resource planning process for Honeywell, Inc., which we will discuss in the following sections.

Organizational Goals

To be relevant, a human resource planning process should be clearly tied to the organization's strategic goals. It must rest on a solid foundation of information about sales forecasts, market trends, technological advances, and major changes in processes and productivity. Considerable effort should be devoted to securing reliable data on business trends and needs—in terms of quantity and quality of labor—as the basic input for human resource planning.

Human Resource Needs Forecast

A second element of the planning process is forecasting human resource needs based on business strategies, production plans, and the various indicators of change in technology and operating methods. Forecasting is usually accomplished by utilizing historical data and reliable ratios (such as indirect/direct labor) and adjusting them for productivity trends. The result of this forecast is a spreadsheet of employees in terms of numbers, mix, cost, new skills, job categories, and numbers and levels of managers needed to accomplish the organization's goals. Experience has shown that producing this forecast is the most challenging part of the planning process because it requires creative and highly participative approaches to dealing with business and technical uncertainties several years in the future.

Employee Information

A third element of the planning process is maintaining accurate information concerning the composition, assignments, and capabilities of the current workforce. This information includes job classifications, age, gender, minority status, organization level, rate of pay, and functions. Employee information may also include resume data, such as skills, education, training received, and career interests. Much of the data needed for human resource planning currently exists in other data systems (such as payroll, talent review, or professional development).

FIGURE 5-6
Elements of a Human Resource Plan

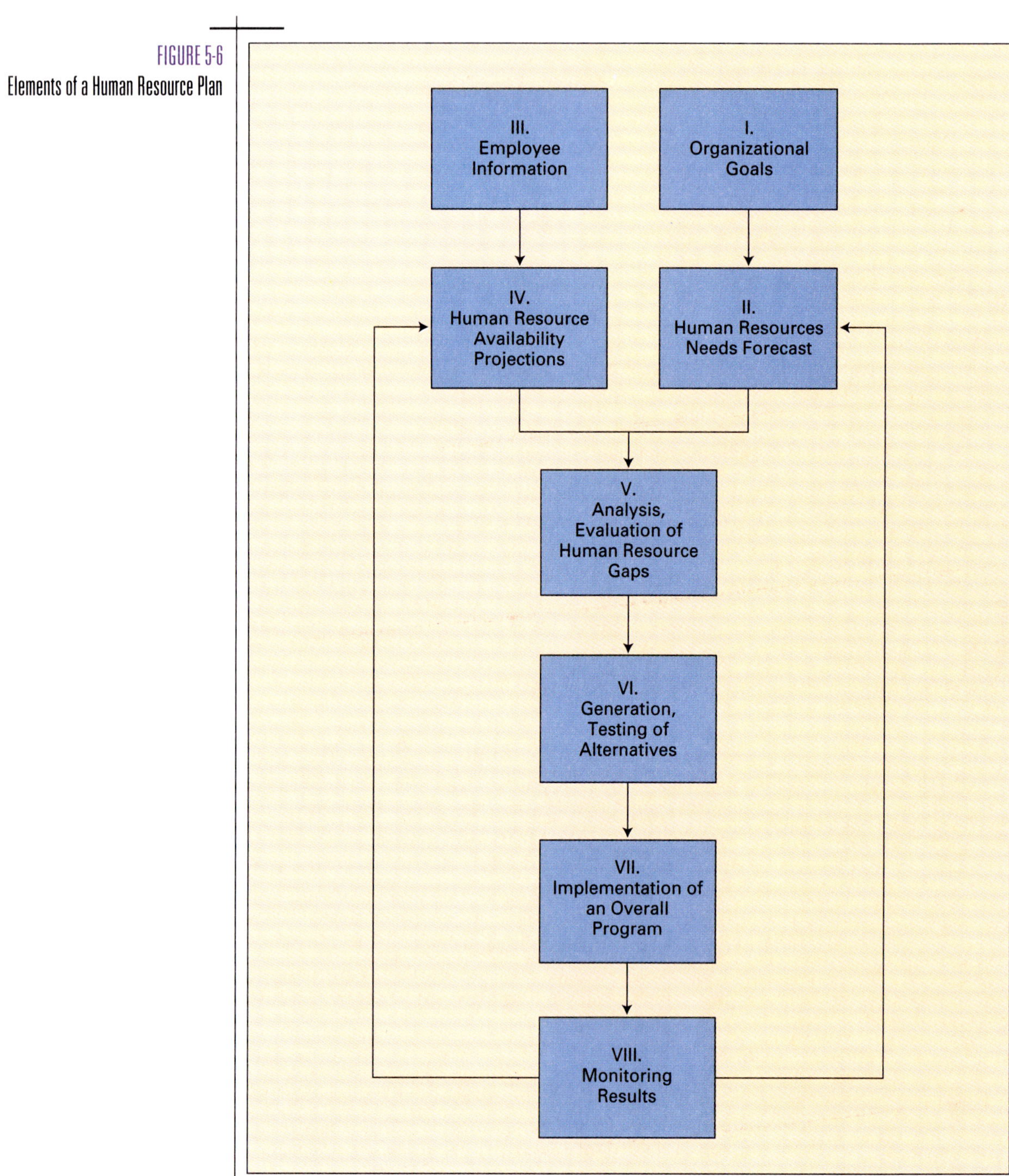

Source: Used with the permission of Honeywell, Inc.

Human Resource Availability Projections

The fourth element of the planning process is estimating which current employees could or will be available in the future. By projecting past data about the size, organization, and composition of the workforce and about turnover, aging, and hiring, availability at a specific future date can be estimated. The result is a picture of the organization's current human resources and how they can be expected to evolve over time in terms of turnover, retirement, obsolescence, promotability, and other relevant characteristics.

Analyzing and Evaluating Human Resource Gaps

The fifth element of the planning process is comparing what is needed with what is available in terms of numbers, mix, skills, and technologies. This comparison permits the human resource manager to determine gaps and evaluate where the most serious mismatches are likely to be. This type of analysis should help management address issues such as the following:

- Are imbalances developing between projected human resource requirements and availability?
- What is the effect of current productivity trends and pay rates on workforce levels and costs?
- Do turnover problems exist in certain jobs or age levels?
- Are there problems of career blockage and obsolescence?
- Are there sufficient high potential managers to fulfill future needs?
- Is there a shortage of any critical skills?

Such an analysis permits the development of long-range plans for recruiting, hiring, training, transferring, and retraining appropriate numbers and types of employees.

Generating and Testing Alternatives

The analysis of human resources should reveal much about a wide range of policies and practices, such as staffing plans, promotion practices and policies, EEO plans, organization design, training and development programs, salary planning, and career management. This phase of the process explores the implications of the analysis and generates alternatives to current practices and policies. Some of the more comprehensive human resource planning systems utilize modeling to simulate the types and organization of employees that would result from specific changes and employment strategies or policies. Testing of complex alternatives and anticipated consequences is usually performed on a computer model. However, manual systems should be utilized if computers are not available.

Implementing an Overall Human Resource Program

After the optimal alternative for addressing the organization's human resource issues has been chosen, it is translated into operational programs with specific plans, target dates, schedules, and resource commitments. The analytical steps described—from considering organizational goals to generating and testing alternatives—should shape an organization's staffing plan, EEO plan, human resource development activities, mobility plans, productivity programs, bargaining strategies, and compensation programs.

Monitoring Results

The final element in any human resource planning process is to provide a means for management to monitor results of the overall program. This step should address questions such as the following:

- How well is the plan working?
- Is the plan cost effective?
- What is the actual versus planned impact on the workforce?
- Where are the plan's weaknesses?
- What changes will be needed during the next planning cycle?

HUMAN RESOURCE INFORMATION SYSTEMS

A **human resource information system (HRIS)** is any organized approach for obtaining relevant and timely information on which to base human resource decisions. An effective HRIS is crucial to sound human resource decision making; it typically employs computers and other sophisticated technologies to process data that reflect day-to-day operations of a company, organized in the form of information to facilitate the decision-making process.

An HRIS should be designed to provide information that is:

- *Timely.* A manager must have access to up-to-date information.
- *Accurate.* A manager must be able to rely on the accuracy of the information provided.
- *Concise.* A manager can absorb only so much information at any one time.
- *Relevant.* A manager should receive only the information needed in a particular situation.
- *Complete.* A manager should receive complete, not partial, information.

The absence of even one of these characteristics reduces the effectiveness of an HRIS and complicates the decision-making process. Conversely, a system possessing all of these characteristics enhances the ease and accuracy of the decision-making process. An effective HRIS also produces several important reports and forecasts related to business operations.

Routine Reports. Business data summarized on a scheduled basis are referred to as routine reports. Weekly and monthly employment status reports may be sent to the general manager, whereas quarterly reports may be forwarded to top management.

Exception Reports. Exception reports highlight variations in operations that are serious enough to require management's attention. One type of exception report is the quality-exception report, completed when the number of product defects exceeds a predetermined maximum. The human resource manager may be interested in this type of information in order to identify additional training needs.

On-Demand Reports. An on-demand report provides information in response to a specific request. The number of engineers with five years' work experience who speak fluent Spanish is an example of an on-demand report that the human resource manager could request from the database.[16]

Forecasts. A forecast applies predictive models to specific situations. Managers need forecasts of the number and types of employees required to satisfy projected demand for the firm's product.

Creating the HRIS

Four steps need to be considered in designing an HRIS that will provide the types of output just discussed and also conform to the HRIS criteria presented. These steps are not separate and distinct—in fact, they overlap considerably. Development of an HRIS is not merely a matter of properly designing the system. Without a major commitment from top management, creating a smoothly functioning and operational HRIS is virtually impossible. However, following the four steps can result in a HRIS design that becomes quite an effective system if supported strongly by top management.

Study the Present System. In defining requirements or assessing the existing information system, three questions need to be answered: (1) What is wanted from the new system and what is the present flow of information? (2) How is the information used? (3) How valuable is this information to decision making?[17] A prime example of a flawed system was encountered by Art Simmons. Art was employed as a consultant to develop a human resource information system for a national forest products firm. In studying the firm's existing system, Art was amazed to discover a large amount of duplication and wasted effort. Some weekly reports were essentially useless for decision making. In addition, two employees had to work a total of eight hours to prepare one particular report. If the report was late, the vice president's secretary would send a strongly worded reprimand to the delinquent division chief. However, when the information arrived at headquarters, it was neatly filed and never used. Numerous questions regarding this practice finally revealed that about five years ago this type of information was requested as a one-time report. Preparation of the report had continued through the administrations of three vice presidents because no one thought to stop it.

Develop a Priority for Information and a Conceptual Design. Once the current information system is thoroughly understood, it is used to develop a priority for needed information. There is certain information a manager must have if proper decisions are to be made, but some items are merely nice to have but not critical to the manager's job performance. The HRIS design must ensure provision of high priority information; data lower on the priority list should be generated only if their benefits exceed the costs of producing them. The weekly report just described should not have had the priority it was accorded. Once the information needs are determined, a conceptual design of the human resource information system is developed.

To set priorities for information needs, individual managers should develop their own priority lists, and the lists should be streamlined into a single list for the entire organization. Certain departments may discover the information they identify as top priority will be far down on the organization's list. The needs of the entire organization must be the controlling factor.

Develop the New Information System. The organization-wide priority list should govern the design of the HRIS. Information judged not worth the cost should not be included. A system of required reports should be developed and diagrammed. The entire organization is treated as a unit to eliminate duplication of information.

Implement the Finalized HRIS. Once the formal model has been finalized, the new human resource information system is ready to be implemented. At this point, the system must be made operational. Space allocations are made, computer equipment is selected, and all structural aspects of implementation are finalized. Once these decisions are made, the training program must commence. Software is completed or purchased, and the organization's data are entered into the system. Human resource software is almost always the responsibility of the human resource department.[18]

After all of this is completed and final checks are made, the human resource information system is ready for implementation. Naturally, once the system is in place and functioning, it must be maintained to ensure that continuous *enhancements and changes to the system* are made to keep the system effective.[19]

An Illustrative HRIS

Historically, the accounting information system was the first to be established in a firm, and the human resource information system was often the last. Firms now realize that a properly developed HRIS can provide tremendous benefits to the organization.

Figure 5-7 presents an overview of the human resource information system designed for one organization. Utilizing numerous types of input data, the HRIS makes available many types of output data that have far-reaching human resource planning and operational value. The HRIS ties together all human resource information into a system. Data from various input sources are integrated to provide the needed output. Information needed in the firm's human resource decision-making process is readily available when the system is properly designed. For instance, many firms are now studying historical trends to determine the best means of securing qualified applicants. In addition, complying with statutes and government regulations would be extremely difficult were it not for the modern HRIS. As the human component of a firm gains greater importance, use of the HRIS is likely to expand in the future.

One firm that has pioneered the development of human resource information systems is Information Science Incorporated (InSci). Founded in

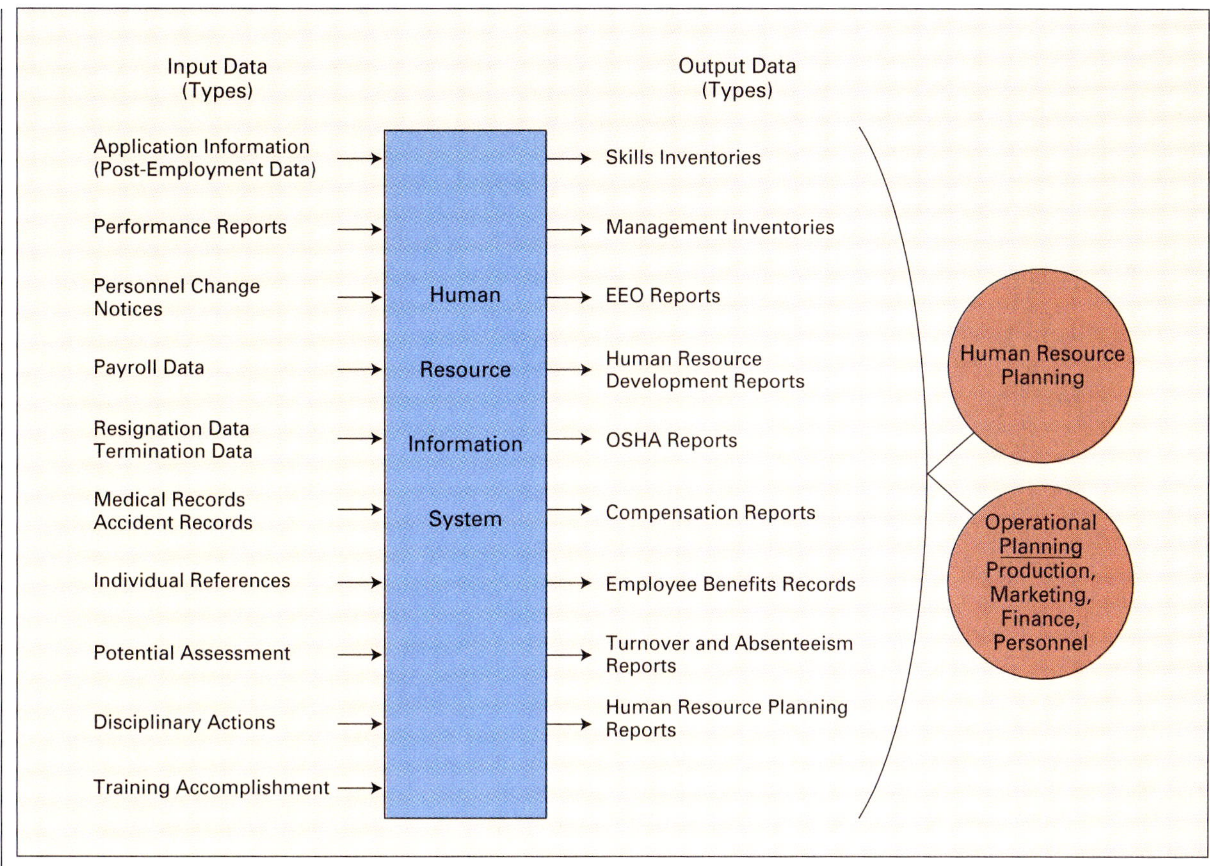

FIGURE 5-7 A Human Resource Information System

1965, InSci was the first company to engage in the commercial development of computer-based human resource information systems. InSci's comprehensive concept of human resource management consists of human resource, payroll, pension, health claim, flexible compensation, and decision support systems. Today, more than 1,000 organizations, including half of Fortune's top 100 and forty-five of the nation's largest banks, rely on InSci systems to help them manage their human resources effectively. One major advantage of the InSci system is its ability to provide management with information in the form required for planning.

A GLOBAL PERSPECTIVE

Developing an effective global human resource information system (HRIS) is virtually essential because of the complexity involved in managing a global labor force. A global HRIS is an organized approach for obtaining relevant and timely information on which to base human resource decisions. An ideal information system exists when users are supplied with all the information they need when they need it. Such a utopian situation has not yet arrived for most companies, especially those with global operations. To help offset less effective global human resource management information systems, companies are developing decision support systems that allow users to interact directly with a computer to get information quickly. A decision support system lets managers call up a menu of available programs. Normally, decision support systems are sophisticated database systems capable of retrieving, displaying, and processing information. Graphics, simulation, modeling, and quantitative analysis are also typically available through decision support systems.[20] Regardless of the nature of the information system, it is essential that information concerning the many relevant factors affecting human resources be available in a timely fashion to ensure that the best human resource decisions are made.

According to Ralph W. Stevens, vice president of personnel and employee relations for the Denver-based Hamilton Oil Corporation, human resource professionals in each location must be experts on local laws, customs, salary structures, and so on. It is, therefore, essential that these professionals have quality information. Through an effective HRIS, Hamilton Oil's human resource management approach is becoming much more integrated. Presently, Stevens shares information with his international counterparts by telephone, fax, and telex. All of Hamilton Oil's human resource managers are linked electronically with a PC-based network. This system allows the establishment of a database of human resource statistics and other relevant material.[21]

Other companies have developed ways to share human relations information. An organized approach for obtaining relevant and timely information on which to base global human resource decisions has become a top priority for Dow's chemical group. Dow's goal is to link electronically human resource managers worldwide, thereby providing greater access to international personnel records and other data. Presently, however, local laws and restrictions make establishing an effective HRIS very complicated.[22] 7-Eleven Japan has defined its business around information. According to Richard Rawlinson, managing director of a Tokyo consulting firm: "No other retailer in the world has defined its business so tightly around information. At the heart of the information system is a custom-made NEC personal computer in each store. The system tracks the buying habits of customers by sex and approximate age. It is an efficient system, with easy-to-follow graphics and coded keys. By adding a very powerful Hewlett-Packard system, 7-Eleven Japan can effectively staff stores, help manufacturers develop new products, and allow headquarters to monitor individual store sales as well as aggregate sales. The system is a model for what a global information system should be; it is timely, accurate, useful, and easy to use by all concerned.[23] Sharing information from a centralized database is essential for maximizing the efforts of human resource professionals.

SUMMARY

Human resource planning (HRP) is the process of systematically reviewing human resource requirements to ensure that the required number of employees, with the required skills, are available when they are needed.

Strategic planning is the determination of overall organizational purposes and goals and how they are to be achieved. Strategic plans affect every major department and activity, including human resources.

After strategic plans have been formulated, human resource planning can be undertaken. Human resource planning has two components: requirements and availability. Forecasting human resource requirements involves determining the number and type of employees needed, by skill level and location. In forecasting the availability of human resources, the organization looks to both internal sources (the present employees) and external sources (the labor market). After requirements and availability have been analyzed, management can determine whether there will likely be a surplus or shortage of employees in the future. Ways must be found to reduce the number of employees if a surplus of workers is projected; such methods include restricted hiring, reduced hours, early retirements, and layoffs. If a shortage is forecast, the firm must look outside the organization to recruit and select the proper quantity and quality of workers.

Four basic terms are used in forecasting. First, the long-term trend represents the expected demand for a firm's goods or services, typically five years or more into the future. Second, cyclical variation is a reasonably predictable movement about the trend line that occurs over a period of more than a year. Third, seasonal variations are reasonably predictable changes that occur during a period of a year. Finally, random variations are changes for which there are no patterns.

Several techniques of forecasting human resource requirements and availability are currently in use by human resource professionals. The zero-base forecasting approach uses the organization's current level of employment as the starting point for determining future staffing needs. The bottom-up approach is a forecasting method that progresses upward from lower organizational units ultimately to provide an aggregate forecast of employment needs for the organization. Another method is to use past employment levels as a predictor of future requirements. Regression analysis is used to predict one item (the dependent variable) through knowledge of other items (the independent variables). Simulation is a technique for testing alternatives on a mathematical model representing a real-world situation.

A management inventory contains information about each manager for use in identifying individuals having the potential to move into higher level positions. A skills inventory is information maintained on the availability and readiness of nonmanagerial employees to move into higher level or lateral positions. Downsizing, also known as restructuring and rightsizing, is essentially the reverse of a company growing and suggests a one-time change in the organization and the number of people employed by it.

A human resource information system (HRIS) is any organized approach for obtaining relevant and timely information on which to base human resource decisions. An HRIS allows the organization of data and outputs to facilitate the decision-making process.

QUESTIONS FOR REVIEW

1. Describe the human resource planning process.
2. Identify and define the basic terms used in demand forecasting.
3. Identify and briefly describe the methods used to forecast human resource needs.
4. Distinguish between forecasting human resource requirements and availability. Use definitions and examples.
5. What actions could a firm take if it had a worker surplus?
6. Distinguish between a management inventory and a skills inventory. What are the essential components of each?
7. Define and describe the purpose of downsizing.
8. What is the purpose of a human resource information system? What are the basic steps that should be considered in developing an HRIS?

HRM SIMULATION

Human resource planning and forecasting are key elements of this simulation. Your team will be furnished with the total number of operations/production employees needed each quarter and an estimate of how many employees may quit during the quarter. Your team will then need to hire and/or promote employees to fill jobs at all levels. If your team does not hire sufficient people, the firm will need to schedule overtime work to fill production quotas, and your team will be charged for this extra expense. Due to the nature of the work and wage rates that are lower than local rates, your organization has fairly high turnover when the simulation begins. First, you will need to develop a strategy to decrease this costly turnover rate.

ABC VIDEO CASE

PLANNING TO COPE WITH THE ADA
TAPE 1, NUMBER 5

Businesses across the nation are making plans to come to grips with the second phase of the Americans with Disabilities Act. The ADA states that any business with 15 or more employees may not discriminate against the disabled in hiring. The law will protect the estimated 14 million Americans of working age who are mentally or physically disabled. A concern is the lack of cost benefit analysis that is attached to most legislation passed by Congress. The law is intended to level the playing field by making it illegal for employers to discriminate against the disabled in hiring and promotion practices. The act also requires that "reasonable accommodations be made as long as they don't create an undue burden on the company involved."

As costs to accommodate the act rise, small business owners feel that those costs will be prohibitive, but the biggest worry for them is the vague wording of the law about hiring discrimination against the disabled. Some owners feel that damages of around $50,000 for even a very small business provides an incentive to sue. The EEOC has estimated that there will be approximately 10,000-12,000 cases filed in the first year.

HRM INCIDENT 1

—A DEGREE FOR METER READERS?

Judy Anderson was the personnel recruiter for South Illinois Electric Company (SIE), a small supplier of natural gas and electricity for Cairo, Illinois, and the surrounding area. The company had expanded rapidly during the last half of the 1980s, and this growth was expected to continue into the 1990s. In January 1989, SIE purchased the utilities system serving neighboring Mitchell County. This expansion concerned Judy. The company workforce had increased by 30 percent the previous year, and Judy had found it a struggle to recruit enough qualified job applicants. She knew that new expansion would intensify the problem.

Judy is particularly concerned about meter readers. The tasks required in meter reading are relatively simple. A person drives to homes served by the company, finds the gas or electric meter, and records its current reading. If the meter has been tampered with, it is reported. Otherwise, no decision-making of any consequence is associated with the job. The reader performs no calculations. The pay was $8.00 per hour, high for unskilled work in the area. Even so, Judy had been having considerable difficulty keeping the thirty-seven meter reader positions filled.

Judy was thinking about how to attract more job applicants when she received a call from the human resource director, Sam McCord. "Judy," Sam said, "I'm unhappy with the job specification calling for only a high school education for meter readers. In planning for the future, we need better educated people in the company. I've decided to change the education requirement for the meter reader job from a high school diploma to a college degree." "But, Mr. McCord," protested Judy, "the company is growing rapidly. If we are to have enough people to fill those jobs, we just can't insist on finding college applicants to perform such basic tasks. I don't see how we can meet our future needs for this job with such an unrealistic job qualification." Sam terminated the conversation abruptly by saying, "No, I don't agree. We need to upgrade all the people in our organization. This is just part of a general effort to do that. Anyway, I cleared this with the president before I decided to do it."

Questions

1. Should there be a minimum education requirement for the meter reader job? Discuss.
2. What is your opinion of Sam's effort to upgrade the people in the organization?
3. What legal ramifications, if any, should Sam have considered?

HRM INCIDENT 2

—A BUSY DAY

Dave Johnson, human resource manager for Eagle Aircraft, had just returned from a brief vacation in Cozumel, Mexico. Eagle is a Wichita, Kansas, manufacturer of small commercial aircraft. Eagle's workforce in 1989 totaled 236. Dave's friend Carl Edwards, vice president for marketing, stopped by to ask Dave to lunch, as he often did. In the course of their conversation, Carl asked Dave's opinion on the president's announcement concerning expansion. "What announcement?" was Dave's response.

Carl explained that there had been a special meeting of the executive council to announce a major expansion, involving a new plant to be built near St. Louis, Missouri. He continued, "Everyone at the meeting seemed to be completely behind the president. Joe Davis, the controller, stressed our independent financial position. The production manager had written a complete report on the equipment we are going to need, including availability and cost information. And I have been pushing for this expansion for some time. So I was ready. I think it will be good for you too, Dave. The president said he expects employment to double in the next year."

As Carl left, Rex Schearer, a production supervisor, arrived. "Dave," said Rex, "the production manager jumped on me Friday because maintenance doesn't have anybody qualified to work on the new digital lathe that's being installed." "He's right," Dave replied, "Maintenance sent me a requisition last week. We'd better get moving and see if we can find someone." Dave knew that it was going to be another busy Monday.

Questions

1. What should Dave do, if anything, about being kept in the dark regarding the expansion? Explain.
2. Discuss any additional problems highlighted by the case and suggest what should be done to solve them.

DEVELOPING HRM SKILLS

AN EXPERIENTIAL EXERCISE

This exercise is designed to give participants experience in dealing with some aspects of planning that a typical human resource manager faces. Students will also be exposed to some of the activities that human resource managers confront on a daily basis. The old axiom "plan your work and work your plan" will probably have new meaning after this exercise.

You are the human resource manager at a large canning plant. Your plant produces several lines of canned food products that are shipped to wholesale distributors nationwide. You are responsible for the human resource activities at the plant.

It is Monday morning, August 30. You have just returned from a week-long corporate executives' meeting at the home office. The meeting was attended by the human resource managers from each of the company's plants. You returned with notes from the meeting and other materials concerning the company's goals and plans for the next six months. When you arrive at your office (an hour early), you find your in basket full of notes, messages, and other correspondence.

The material provided to participants represents your notes and information from the meeting, as well as what was in your in basket. You must go through these items and be prepared for the meeting the plant manager has scheduled for 8:00 a.m. It is now 7:30 a.m. Remember, you need to deal with some items immediately, some later today, and some tomorrow or later in the week. You will need to sort, prioritize, and set up your plan of activities. Do the following for each item:

1. Note when it is to be handled.
2. Note who is to handle it, if not yourself.
3. Note what is to be done or who is to be informed.
4. If a meeting is to be called, set up an agenda.
5. If a memo or notice is to be sent out, write it.

Your instructor will provide you with additional information necessary to participate.

NOTES

1. R. Wayne Mondy, Robert M. Noe, and Robert E. Edwards, "What the Staffing Function Entails," *Personnel* 63 (April 1986): 55–56.

2. David M. Schweiger, Ernst N. Csiszar, and Nancy K. Napier, "Implementing International Mergers and Acquisitions," *Human Resource Planning* (December 1993): 53–70.

3. Paul A. Evans, "Management Development As Glue Technology," *Human Resources Planning* (December 1992): 85–106.

4. R. Wayne Mondy and Shane R. Premeaux, *Management: Concepts, Practices, and Skills,* 6th edition (Boston: Allyn & Bacon, 1993): 164.

5. Lincoln Akin Norton, "Link HR to Corporate Strategy," *Personnel Journal* 70 (April 1991): 75.

6. Y.K. Shetty and Paul F. Buller, "Regaining Competitiveness Requires HR Solutions," *Personnel* 67 (July 1990): 8–12.

7. James E. McElwain, "Succession Plans Designed to Manage Change," *HRMagazine* 36 (February 1991): 67.

8. "Heirs and Races," *The Economist* 318 (March 9, 1991): 69.

9. Ibid.

10. Kelley Holland, "Why the Chemistry is Right at Chemical," *Business Week* (June 7, 1993): 90–93.

11. R. Wayne Mondy and Harry N. Mills, "Choice Not Chance in Nurse Selection," *Supervisor Nurse* 9 (November 1978): 35–39.

12. Kevin Kelly, "Why Commonwealth Edison Is Feeling the Heat," *Business Week* (August 17, 1992): 59.

13. Elizabeth Lesly and Larry Light, "When Layoffs Alone Don't Turn the Tide," *Business Week* (December 7, 1992): 100–101.

14. Jaclyn Fierman, "Beating the Midlife Career Crisis," *Fortune* 128 (September 6, 1993): 53.

15. Louis S. Richman, "When Will the Layoffs End?" *Fortune* 128 (September 20, 1993): 54.

16. Janet Bensu, "Use Your Data Base in New Ways," *HRMagazine* 35 (March 1990): 33–34.

17. Timothy R. Adams, "Buying Software Without the Glitches," *HRMagazine* 35 (January 1990): 40–42.

18. Timothy V. Welo, "HR Computer Study: Who Buys? What? How? and Why?" *Personnel* 67 (February 1990): 36–94.

19. Henry C. Benham, R. Leon Price, and Jennifer L. Wagner, "Comparison of Structured Development Methodologies," *Information Executive* 2 (Spring 1989): 19.

20. Gale Eisenstodt, "Information Power," *Forbes* 151 (June 21, 1993): 44–45.

21. Ellen Brandt, "Global HR," *Personnel Journal* 70 (March 1991): 38–39.

22. Ibid., 42.

23. Gale Eisenstodt, "Information Power," ibid.

CHAPTER 6

Recruitment

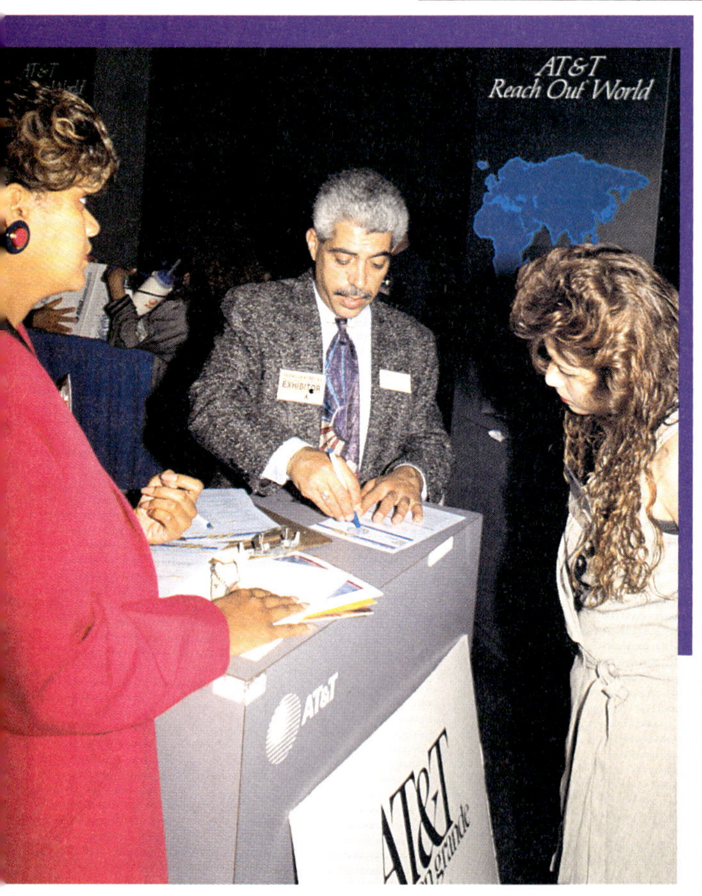

KEY TERMS

CHAPTER OBJECTIVES

1. Describe the recruitment process and identify actions that a firm might consider before resorting to outside recruitment.
2. Describe the external and internal factors that can influence the recruitment process and explain internal recruitment methods.
3. Identify the various sources and methods available to an organization for external recruiting.
4. State what should be done to ensure that recruitment efforts meet legal requirements.

Dorothy Bryant, recruiting supervisor for International Manufacturing Company, had been promoted to her position after several years as a group leader in the production department. One of Dorothy's first assignments was to recruit two software design engineers for International. After considering various recruitment alternatives, Dorothy placed the following ad in a local newspaper with a circulation in excess of 1,000,000:

EMPLOYMENT OPPORTUNITY
FOR SOFTWARE DESIGN ENGINEERS
2 positions available for software design engineers desiring career in growth industry.
Prefer recent college graduates with good appearance.
Apply Today! Send your resume,
in confidence, to: D.A. Bryant
International Manufacturing Co., P.O. Box 1515
Alexandria, VA 22314

More than 300 applications were received in the first week, and Dorothy was elated. However, when she reviewed the applicants, it appeared that few people possessed the desired qualifications for the job.

Dorothy learned, the hard way, the importance of proper recruiting practices. She obviously failed to include specific job requirements in her newspaper ad. As a result, an excessive number of unqualified persons applied. Also, the road is paved for a potential legal problem because Dorothy uses a subjective criterion, "good appearance," which may not be job related. In addition, stating a preference for a "recent college graduate" may also prove to be ill-advised because of the age implication. Adding further to Dorothy's dilemma is the potential liability her ad creates for the firm by implying a "career" for employees. Her corporate attorney will probably advise her to avoid any semblance of creating an implied contract for a candidate who is hired. The individual may later be discharged and could then sue the company for breach of contract. Dorothy has found that preparing an effective, legally sound recruitment ad isn't as simple as it once was.

Determining appropriate means to encourage qualified candidates to apply for employment is extremely important. Tapping appropriate sources of applicants and utilizing suitable recruitment methods are essential to maximizing recruiting efficiency and effectiveness. We begin this chapter by describing the recruitment process and alternatives to recruitment. Next, we describe the external and internal environments of recruitment. Then, we present methods used in external and internal recruitment, and discuss how methods should be tailored to sources. Finally, we cover recruiting efforts under the law.

THE RECRUITMENT PROCESS

Recruitment is the process of attracting individuals on a timely basis, in sufficient numbers, and with appropriate qualifications, and encouraging them to apply for jobs with an organization.[1] Applicants with qualifications most closely related to job specifications may then be selected. How many times do we hear CEOs state, "Our most important assets are human"? While this has probably always been true, an increasing number of people in organizations are beginning to believe it. Hiring the best people available has never been more critical than today. Furthermore, hiring decisions can be no better than the alternatives presented through recruitment efforts.

In most medium-sized and large organizations, the human resource department is responsible for the recruitment process. In small firms, recruitment is likely handled by individual managers. Regardless of who is responsible, recruitment is an essential function of every firm.

As you can see in Figure 6-1, when human resource planning indicates a need for employees, the firm may evaluate alternative ways to meet this demand through the recruitment process. When other alternatives are not appropriate, the recruitment process starts. Frequently, recruitment begins when a manager initiates an employee requisition. The **employee requisition** is a document that specifies job title, department, the date the employee is needed for work, and other details (see Figure 6-2). With this information, the human resource manager can refer to the appropriate job description to determine the qualifications the person to be recruited needs. At times, firms continue to recruit even when they have no vacancies. This practice permits them to main-

FIGURE 6-1
The Recruitment Process

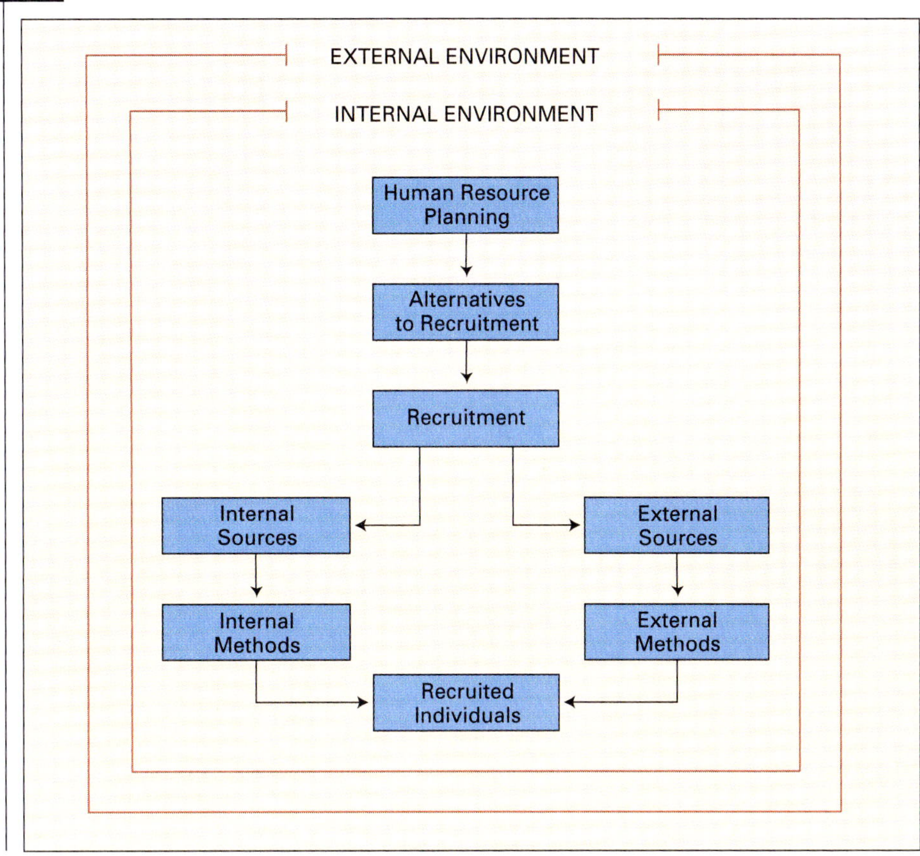

tain recruitment contacts and to identify exceptional candidates for future employment.

The next step in the recruitment process is to determine whether qualified employees are available within the firm (the internal source) or must be recruited from external sources, such as colleges, universities, and other organizations. Because of the high cost of recruiting, organizations need to utilize the most productive recruitment sources and methods available. With the even greater cost of global recruiting, progressive human resource managers are keeping records of recruitment, selection, development, deployment, and retention costs to make credible decisions regarding which types of HR activities are most cost effective in relation to results. Such hands-on global human resource management will develop a means of measurement that provides the best qualified and developed employee for every HR dollar spent.[2]

Recruitment sources are the places where qualified individuals can be found. **Recruitment methods** are the specific means by which potential employees can be attracted to the firm. When the sources of potential employees have been identified, appropriate methods for either internal or external recruitment are used to accomplish recruitment objectives.

FIGURE 6-2
An Employee Requisition

JOB NUMBER	JOB TITLE	DATE OF JOB VACANCY	DATE REPLACEMENT NEEDED
PLEASE CHECK	☐ Permanent	☐ Temporary	☐ Part-Time
	☐ Exempt	☐ Nonexempt	If Nonexempt, Enter Job Class
REASON FOR REQUEST: What management or employee action(s) caused the opening?			
BRIEF DESCRIPTION OF MINIMUM QUALIFICATIONS FOR THE JOB CANDIDATES:			
BRIEF DESCRIPTION OF JOB DUTIES:			
LOCATION NAME			
DATE	MANAGER'S SIGNATURE		

Companies may discover that some recruitment sources and methods are superior to others for locating and attracting potential executive talent. For instance, one large equipment manufacturer determined that medium-sized, state-supported colleges and universities located in rural areas were good sources of potential managers. Other firms may arrive at different conclusions. Thus, in order to maximize recruiting effectiveness, utilizing recruitment sources and methods tailored to a specific organization's needs is vitally important.

ALTERNATIVES TO RECRUITMENT

Even when human resource planning indicates a need for additional or replacement employees, a firm may decide against jumping into recruitment efforts immediately. Recruitment and selection costs, although they decline somewhat in a buyer's market, are still high. Often included in the calculation are costs of the search process, interviewing, agency fee payment, and relocation and processing of the new employee. Although selection decisions are not irreversible, once employees are placed on the payroll, they may be difficult to remove, even if their performance is marginal. Therefore, a firm should consider its alternatives carefully before engaging in recruitment. Alternatives to recruitment commonly include overtime, subcontracting, contingent workers, and employee leasing.

Overtime

Perhaps the most commonly used method of meeting short-term fluctuations in work volume is through the use of overtime. Overtime may help both the employer and the employee. The employer benefits by avoiding recruitment, selection, and training costs. The employee's gain stems from a higher rate of pay.

Along with the obvious advantages of using overtime are potential problems. Many managers believe that when they work employees for unusually long periods of time, the company pays more and receives less in return. Employees may become fatigued and lack the energy to perform at a normal rate, especially when excessive overtime is required.

Two additional potential problems are related to the use of prolonged overtime. Employees may, consciously or not, pace themselves so that overtime will be assured. They may also become accustomed to the added income resulting from overtime pay. Employees may even elevate their standard of living to the level permitted by this additional income. Then, when overtime is no longer required and the paycheck shrinks, employees may become disgruntled.

Subcontracting

Even though a long-term increase in demand for its goods or services is anticipated, an organization may still decide against further hiring. Instead, the firm may choose to subcontract the work to another organization. This approach has particular appeal when the subcontractor actually has greater expertise in producing certain goods or services. Such an arrangement often benefits both parties.

Contingent Workers

As described in Chapter 2, contingent workers—also known as part-timers, temporaries, and independent contractors—comprise the fastest growing segment of the U.S. economy. Most contingent workers are women. Only half of the new jobs created in 1992 were full-time jobs, and the number of contingent workers has grown three times faster than the workforce as a whole. Manpower, Inc., the largest temporary agency in the United States, is now the nation's largest private employer, with about 560,000 employees in 1993.[3]

What accounts for the rapid growth of jobs for these workers? The total cost of a permanent employee is generally estimated at 30 to 40 percent above gross pay, which does not include, among other things, the costs of recruitment. To avoid some of these costs and to maintain flexibility as workloads vary, many organizations utilize part-time or temporary employees. Temporary help companies assist their clients by furnishing the means for handling excess or special workloads. These companies assign their own employees to their customers and fulfill all the obligations normally associated with an employer. The expenses of recruitment, absenteeism and turnover, and employee benefits are avoided.

During periods of downsizing, contingent workers are the human equivalents of just-in-time inventory. These disposable workers permit maximum flexibility for the employer and lower labor costs. The huge unanswered question is whether this approach to staffing is healthy for our society in the long run. However, for the shorter term, the advantages obtained through contingent workers may be essential for success or even survival of many companies.

Employee Leasing[4]

An alternative to recruitment that is growing in popularity is employee leasing. Using this approach, a firm formally terminates some or most of its employees. A leasing company then hires them, usually at the same salary, and leases them back to the former employer, who becomes the client. The employees continue to work as before, with the client supervising their activities. The leasing company, however, assumes all responsibilities associated with being the employer.

A primary advantage of employee leasing to the client is being free from human resource administration, including the maintenance of a benefits program. Another advantage of employee leasing is that it provides a way of avoiding union-organizing activities or the requirement to recognize and bargain with an existing union. If the leasing company does not qualify as an "employer" under the National Labor Relations Act, employee leasing permits a firm to escape any requirement to recognize a representative of leased workers.

Advantages of leasing also accrue to the employees. Since leasing companies provide workers for many companies, they often enjoy economies of scale that permit them to offer excellent, low-cost benefit programs. In addition, there are often greater opportunities for job mobility. Since some leasing firms operate throughout the nation, if one employed spouse is relocated in a dual career family, the leasing company may offer the other a job in the new location, too. Also, if a client organization suffers a downturn in business, the leasing company can transfer employees to another client, avoiding both layoffs and losses of seniority.

A potential disadvantage to the client is that employee loyalty may be eroded since workers receive pay and benefits from the leasing company. Regardless of any shortcomings, use of employee leasing is growing. Currently, about 75,000 employees are being leased. It is estimated that 20 percent of the 4.4 million businesses in the United States with less than 35 employees will be attracted to employee leasing, resulting in 10 million leased employees by the year 2000. Larger companies have also begun using employee leasing to a greater extent; it provides them with a body of well-trained, long-term employees that can expand or contract as business conditions dictate.[5]

EXTERNAL ENVIRONMENT OF RECRUITMENT

As with the other human resource functions, the recruitment process does not take place in a vacuum. Factors external to the organization can significantly affect the firm's recruitment efforts. Of particular importance is the demand for and supply of specific skills in the labor market. If demand for a particular skill is high relative to supply, an extraordinary recruiting effort may be required.

When the unemployment rate in an organization's labor market is high, the firm's recruitment process may be simplified. The number of unsolicited applicants is usually greater, and the increased size of the labor pool provides a better opportunity for attracting qualified applicants. Conversely, as the unemployment rate drops, recruitment efforts must be increased and new sources explored.

Local labor market conditions are of primary importance in recruitment for most nonmanagerial, many supervisory, and even some middle-management positions. However, recruitment for executive and professional positions often extends to national or international markets. Although the recruiter's day-to-day activities provide a feel for the labor market, accurate employment data—found in professional journals and U.S. Department of Labor reports—is essential.

Legal considerations also play a significant role in recruitment practices in the United States. The individual and the employer first make contact during the recruitment process. Therefore, nondiscriminatory practices at this stage are absolutely essential. We discuss this topic later in this chapter.

The firm's corporate image is another important factor that affects recruitment. If employees believe their employer deals with them fairly, the positive word-of-mouth support they provide is of great value to the firm. It assists in establishing credibility with prospective employees. Good reputations earned in this manner can result in more and better qualified applicants seeking employment with the firm. Prospective employees are more inclined to respond positively to the organization's recruitment efforts if the firm is praised by employees. The firm with a positive public image is one believed to be a "good place to work," and its recruitment efforts are greatly enhanced.

INTERNAL ENVIRONMENT OF RECRUITMENT

Although the labor market and the government exert powerful external influences, the organization's own practices and policies also affect recruitment. Global and domestic firms that want to succeed in the future at recruiting and retaining talented employees must create a supportive internal environment, one in which people can bring their whole selves to the company and contribute to their full potential. PepsiCo believes that this is the best route to long-term global success.[6]

A major internal factor that can greatly aid recruitment is human resource planning. In most cases, a firm cannot attract prospective employees in sufficient numbers and with the required skills overnight. Examining alternative sources of recruits and determining the most productive methods for obtaining them takes time. After identifying the best alternatives, the human resource manager can make appropriate recruitment plans.

An organization's promotion policy can also have a significant impact on recruitment. Basically, an organization can stress a policy of promotion from within its own ranks or a policy of filling positions from outside the organization. Depending on the circumstances, either approach may have merit.

Promotion from within (PFW) is the policy of filling vacancies above entry-level positions with current employees. When an organization emphasizes promotion from within, its workers have an incentive to strive for advancement. When employees see coworkers being promoted, they become more aware of their own opportunities. Motivation provided by this practice often improves employee morale.

Another advantage of internal recruitment is that the organization is usually well aware of its employees' capabilities. An employee's job performance may not, by itself, be a reliable criterion for promotion. Nevertheless, many of the employee's personal and job-related qualities will be known. The employee has a track record, as opposed to being an "unknown quantity." Also, the company's investment in such an individual may yield a higher return. Still another positive factor is the employee's knowledge of the firm, its policies, and its people.

However, it is unlikely that a firm can (or would even desire to) adhere rigidly to a practice of promotion from within. The vice president of human resources for a major automobile manufacturer offers this advice: "A strictly applied 'PFW' policy eventually leads to inbreeding, a lack of cross-fertilization, and a lack of creativity. A good goal, in my opinion, is to fill 80 percent of openings above entry-level positions from within." Frequently, new blood is needed to provide new ideas and innovation that must take place for firms to remain competitive. In such cases, even organizations with promotion from within policies may opt to look outside the organization for new talent. In any event, a promotion policy that first considers insiders is great for employee morale and motivation and is often beneficial to the organization.

Policies related to the employment of relatives may also affect a firm's recruitment efforts. The content of such policies varies greatly, but it is not uncommon for companies to have antinepotism policies that discourage the employment of close relatives. This is especially true when related employees would be placed in the same department, under the same supervisor, or in supervisor-subordinate roles.

METHODS USED IN INTERNAL RECRUITMENT

Management should be able to identify current employees who are capable of filling positions as they become available. Helpful tools used for internal recruitment include management and skills inventories and job posting and bidding procedures. As we mentioned in Chapter 5, management and skills inventories permit organizations to determine whether current employees possess the qualifications for filling open positions. As a recruitment device, these inventories have proved to be extremely valuable to organizations when they are kept up-to-date. Inventories can be of tremendous value in locating talent internally and supporting the concept of promotion from within.

Job posting is a procedure for informing employees that job openings exist. **Job bidding** is a technique that permits employees who believe they possess the required qualifications to apply for a posted job. Table 6-1 shows the procedure a medium-sized firm might use. Larger firms often provide employees with a weekly list of job openings, for which any qualified employee is encouraged to apply.

The job posting and bidding procedure minimizes the complaint commonly heard in many companies that insiders never hear of a job opening until it has been filled. Implementation of a job posting and bidding system avoids this problem. It reflects an openness that most employees generally

TABLE 6-1
Job Posting and Bidding Procedure

RESPONSIBILITY	ACTION REQUIRED
Human resource assistant	1. Upon receiving a *Human Resource Requisition,* write a memo to each appropriate supervisor stating that a job vacancy exists. The memo should include a job title, job number, pay grade, salary range, a summary of the basic duties performed, and the qualifications required for the job (data to be taken from job description/specification).
	2. Ensure that a copy of this memo is posted on all company bulletin boards.
Supervisors	3. Make certain that every employee who might qualify for the position is made aware of the job opening.
Interested employees	4. Contact the human resource department.

value highly. In addition, this system can assist in college recruitment efforts. A firm that offers freedom of choice and encourages career growth has a distinct advantage over those firms that do not. However, a job posting and bidding system does have some negative features. An effective system requires the expenditure of considerable time and money. When bidders are unsuccessful, someone must explain to them why they were not chosen. If care has not been taken to ensure that the most qualified applicant is chosen, the system will lack credibility. Even successful implementation of such a system cannot completely eliminate complaints.

EXTERNAL SOURCES OF RECRUITMENT

At times, a firm must look beyond itself to find employees, particularly when expanding its workforce. The following needs require external recruitment: (1) to fill entry-level jobs; (2) to acquire skills not possessed by current employees; and (3) to obtain employees with different backgrounds to provide new ideas. As Figure 6-3 shows, even when promotions are made internally, entry-level jobs must be filled from the outside. Thus, after the president of a firm retires, a series of internal promotions is made. Ultimately, however, the firm has to recruit externally to fill the entry-level position of salary analyst. If the president's position had been filled from the outside, the chain-reaction of promotions from within would not have occurred. Depending on the qualifications desired, employees may be attracted from a number of outside sources.

High Schools and Vocational Schools

Organizations concerned with recruiting clerical and other entry-level operative employees often depend heavily on high schools and vocational schools. Many of these schools have outstanding training programs for specific occupational skills, such as home appliance repair and small engine mechanics. Some companies work with schools to ensure a constant supply of

FIGURE 6-3
Internal Promotion and External Recruitment

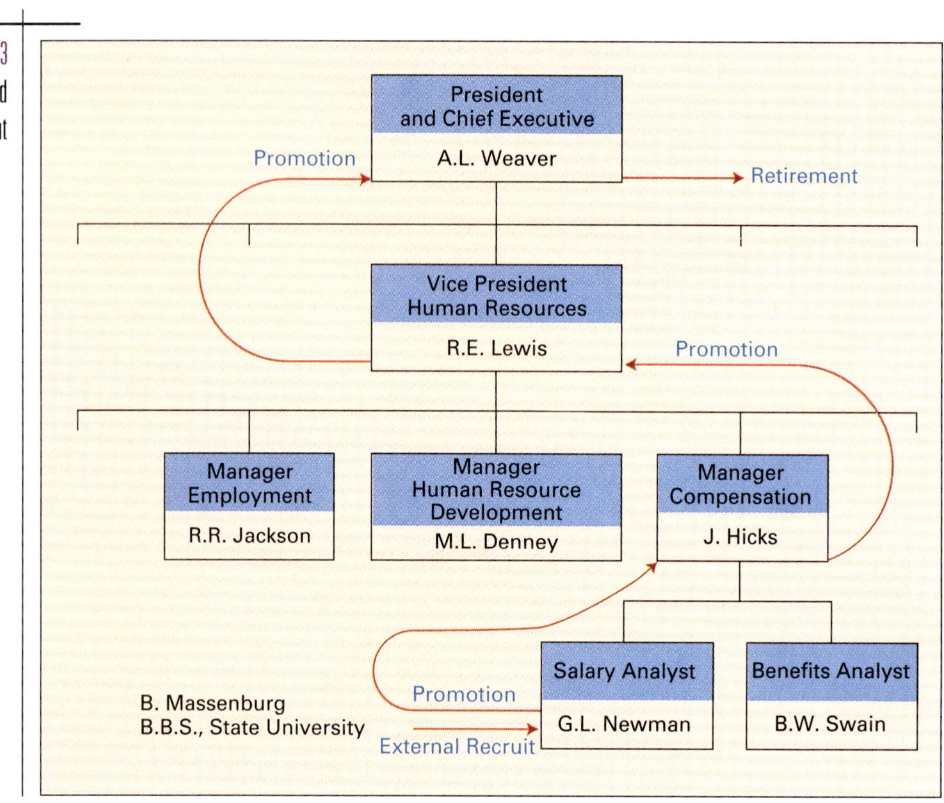

trained individuals with specific job skills. In some areas, companies even loan employees to schools to assist in the training programs.

Community Colleges

Many community colleges are sensitive to the specific employment needs in their local labor markets and graduate highly sought after students with marketable skills. Typically, community colleges have two-year programs designed for both a terminal education and preparation for a four-year university degree program. Many community colleges also have excellent mid-management programs combined with training for specific trades. In addition, career centers often provide a place for employers to contact students, thereby facilitating the recruitment process.

Colleges and Universities

Colleges and universities represent a major recruitment source for many organizations. Potential professional, technical, and management employees are typically found in these institutions. Firms commonly send recruiters to campuses to interview prospective employees, although cost reduction programs and labor market conditions have reduced this practice in recent years.

Placement directors, faculty, and administrators can be helpful to organizations in their search for recruits. Because on-campus recruitment is mutually beneficial, both employers and universities should take steps to develop and maintain close relationships. When a company establishes recruitment programs with educational institutions, it should continue those programs year after year to maintain an effective relationship with each school. It is important that the firm knows the school and that the school knows the firm.

Competitors and Other Firms

Competitors and other firms in the same industry or geographic area may be the most important source of recruits for positions in which recent experience is highly desired. The fact that approximately 5 percent of the working population, at any one time, is either actively seeking or receptive to a change of position emphasizes the importance of these sources. Furthermore, one of every three people—especially managers and professionals—changes jobs every five years.

Even organizations that have policies of promotion from within occasionally look elsewhere to fill important positions. Volkswagen drew the ire of General Motors when it hired José Ignacio Lopez de Arriortua, head of GM's huge purchasing operation. Not only was GM fearful of Lopez divulging company trade secrets, but also it alleged that Volkswagen stepped up its efforts to raid other key GM executives. The chairman of Opel claimed that VW had targeted more than 40 managers at Opel and General Motors.[7] While the ethics of corporate raiding may be debatable, it is apparent that competitors and other firms do serve as external sources of recruitment for high quality talent.

Smaller firms, in particular, look for employees who have been trained by larger organizations with greater developmental resources. For instance, an optical firm believes that its own operation is not large enough to provide extensive training and development programs. Therefore, a person recruited by this firm for a significant management role is likely to have held at least two previous positions with a competitor.

The Unemployed

The unemployed often provide a valuable source of recruits. Qualified applicants join the unemployment rolls every day for various reasons. Companies may go out of business, cut back operations, or be merged with other firms, leaving qualified workers without jobs. Employees are also fired sometimes merely because of personality differences with their bosses. Not infrequently, employees become frustrated with their jobs and simply quit.

Older Individuals

Older workers, including those retired, may also comprise a valuable source of employees. Although these workers are often victims of negative stereotyping, the facts support the notion that older people can perform some jobs extremely well. When Kentucky Fried Chicken Corporation had difficulty recruiting younger workers, it turned to older individuals and those with disabilities. The results were dramatically reduced vacancies and turnover rates within six months. Management surveys indicate most employers have high opinions of their older workers; they value them for many reasons, including their knowledge, skills, work ethic, loyalty, and good basic literacy skills.[8]

Military Personnel

Operation Transition is a program begun to ease the largest downsizing of the armed services since the end of World War II. Hiring from this source may make sense to many employers because these individuals typically have a proven work history and are flexible, motivated, and drug free. Another common characteristic of veterans, especially appropriate for firms emphasizing total quality management, is their goal and team orientation.[9]

Employers registered with Operation Transition may place ads electronically on the transition bulletin board for either a two-week or six-month period. The ads are available the next day to prospects at more than 350 military installations throughout the world. Since skills possessed by veterans are wide ranging, this source of employees should not be overlooked.

Self-Employed Workers

Finally, the self-employed worker may also be a good potential recruit. Such individuals may constitute a source of applicants for any number of jobs requiring technical, professional, administrative, or entrepreneurial expertise within a firm.

EXTERNAL METHODS OF RECRUITMENT

By examining recruitment sources, a firm determines where potential job applicants are. It then seeks to attract these applicants by specific recruitment methods. Such methods as advertising, employment agencies, and employee referrals may be effective in attracting individuals with virtually every type of skill. Recruiters, special events, and internships are used primarily to attract students, especially those attending colleges and universities. Also, executive search firms and professional organizations are particularly helpful in the recruitment of managerial and professional employees.

Advertising

Advertising communicates the firm's employment needs to the public through media such as radio, newspapers, television, and industry publications. In determining the content of an advertising message, a firm must decide on the corporate image it wants to project. Obviously, the firm should give prospective employees an accurate picture of the job and the organization. At the same time, the firm should attempt to appeal to the self-interest of prospective employees, emphasizing the job's unique qualities. The ad must tell potential employees why they should be interested in that particular job and organization. The message should also indicate how an applicant is to respond: apply in person, apply by telephone, or submit a resume.

The firm's previous experience with various media should suggest the approach to be taken for specific types of jobs. The least expensive form of advertising that provides the broadest coverage is probably the newspaper ad. Many firms use help-wanted advertising. The greatest problem with this form of external recruitment is the large number of unqualified individuals who respond to such ads. This situation increases the likelihood of poor selection decisions.

Although no one bases a decision to change jobs on advertising, an ad creates awareness, generates interest, and encourages a prospect to seek more information about the firm and the job opportunities it provides. Examination of the Sunday edition of any major newspaper reveals the extensive use of advertising in recruiting practically every type of employee.

Certain media attract audiences that are more homogeneous in terms of employment skills, education, and orientation. Advertisements placed in such publications as *The Wall Street Journal* relate primarily to managerial, professional, and technical positions. The readers of these publications are generally individuals qualified for many of the positions advertised. Focusing on a specific labor market minimizes the likelihood of receiving marginally qualified or even totally unqualified applicants.

Virtually every professional group publishes a journal that is widely read by its members. Advertising for a human resource executive position in *HRMagazine*, for example, would hit the target market because it is read almost exclusively by human resource professionals. Trade journals are also widely utilized. The use of journals does, however, present some problems. For example, they lack scheduling flexibility, and their publishing deadlines may be weeks prior to the issue date. Since staffing needs cannot always be anticipated far in advance, the use of journals for recruitment obviously has limitations.

Recruitment advertisers assume that qualified prospects who read job ads in newspapers and professional and trade journals are sufficiently dissatisfied with their present jobs that they will pursue opportunities advertised. This is not always the case, especially for those qualified individuals not actively considering a job change. Therefore, in high demand situations, a firm needs to consider all available media resources.

Other media that can be used include radio, billboards, television, and the Internet. Most of these methods are likely to be more expensive than newspapers or journals, but they have been used with success in specific situations. For instance, a regional medical center used billboards successfully to attract registered nurses. One large manufacturing firm achieved considerable success in advertising for production trainees by means of spot ads on the radio. A large electronics firm used television to attract experienced engineers when it opened a new facility and needed more engineers immediately. Thus, in situations where hiring needs are urgent, television and radio may provide good results; although by themselves, they may not be sufficient. Broadcast messages can alert people to the fact that an organization is seeking recruits. They are, however, limited in the amount of information they can transmit. Advertising jobs on the Internet does not have such a limitation. Although it is a relatively new approach, this medium offers great potential as an advertising channel.

Employment Agencies—Private and Public

An **employment agency** is an organization that helps firms recruit employees and, at the same time, aids individuals in their attempts to locate jobs. These agencies perform many recruitment and selection functions that have proven quite beneficial to many organizations.

Private employment agencies are utilized by firms for virtually every type of position. However, they are best known for recruiting white-collar employees. Although some parts of the industry have a bad reputation, a number of highly reputable employment agencies have operated successfully for decades. Difficulties that occasionally occur stem from a lack of industry standards. The quality of a particular agency depends on the professionalism of its management. Even though problems may exist, private employment agencies offer an important service in bringing qualified applicants and open positions together. They should not be overlooked by either the organization or the job applicant. Individuals are often turned off by the one-time fees that agencies charge, although these are frequently paid by the employer.

The public employment agencies operated by each state receive overall policy direction from the U.S. Employment Service. Public employment agencies are best known for recruiting and placing individuals in operative jobs, but they have become increasingly involved in matching people with technical, professional, and managerial positions. Some public agencies utilize computerized job matching systems to aid in the recruitment process. Public employment agencies provide their services without charge to either the employer or the prospective employee.

Recruiters

The most common use of recruiters is with technical and vocational schools, community colleges, colleges, and universities. The key contact for recruiters on college and university campuses is often the director of student placement. This administrator is in an excellent position to arrange interviews with students possessing the qualifications desired by the firm. Placement services help organizations utilize their recruiters efficiently. Qualified candidates are identified, interviews are scheduled, and suitable rooms are provided for interviews.

The company recruiter plays a vital role in attracting applicants. The interviewee often perceives the recruiter's actions as a reflection of the character of the firm. If the recruiter is dull, the interviewee may think the company dull; if the recruiter is apathetic, discourteous, or vulgar, the interviewee may well attribute all these negative characteristics to the firm. Recruiters must always be aware of the image they present at the screening interview because it makes a lasting impression.

Recruiters determine which individuals possess the best qualifications and therefore should be encouraged to continue their interest in the firm. In making this determination, the recruiter becomes involved with the interviewee in two-way communication about the company, its products, its general organizational structure, its policies, its compensation and benefits program, and the position to be filled. The recruiter will also ask the prospect numerous job related questions, which may include those involving grades, extracurricular activities, and employment while attending school.

Considering the importance of the occasion, the interview is often short—about thirty minutes on average. Recruiters may spend more than half this time discussing the student's high school and college education, eliciting information about knowledge and skills required by the job. This information may include:[10]

Information Sought	Topics
intelligence and aptitude	grades amount of effort to achieve grades college board scores
motivation	effort spent on academic work
judgment and maturity	decisions involving choice of college and major field
analytical power	reasons for subject preferences
leadership and ability to get along with people	participation in extracurricular activities

Responding to criticism from the business community, many business schools have revised the curricula in recent years to add or place increased emphasis on such topics as communication, values, negotiation, international competitiveness, quality management, leadership, creativity, ethics, team building, and cross-cultural understanding. Questions focusing on these areas may also be asked in campus interviews.[11]

An applicant should definitely prepare for the recruitment interview. To make a good impression, the prospect must do some homework on the company. The school's placement service often has literature that describes the organization and its operations in general terms. In addition, library research may yield information about the company's sales volume, number of employees, products, and so on. Prospects armed with facts such as these can confidently engage the recruiter in conversation and ask relevant questions. Other things being equal, an informed prospect has a competitive advantage.

Resume databases, discussed later in this chapter, have already begun to shape the way college recruitment is approached. By using a database system, recruiters can receive copies of students' resumes before they visit the campus. It makes college recruitment much more effective. Schools offering the most promising prospects can be determined, as well as the specific students the recruiter wishes to interview.[12]

Special Events

Holding **special events** is a recruiting method that involves an effort on the part of a single employer, or group of employers, to attract a large number of applicants for interviews. Job fairs, for example, are designed to bring together applicants and representatives of various companies. One convention held exclusively for women attracted 90 firms and about 4,000 prospects from 16 states. From an employer's viewpoint, a primary advantage of job fairs is the opportunity to meet a large number of candidates in a short time—usually one or two days. More than a dozen commercial firms operate job fairs, but government agencies, charitable organizations, and business alliances also frequently sponsor them. As a recruitment method, job fairs offer the potential for a much lower cost per hire than traditional approaches.

Internships

An **internship** is a special form of recruiting that involves placing a student in a temporary job. In this arrangement, there is no obligation by the company to

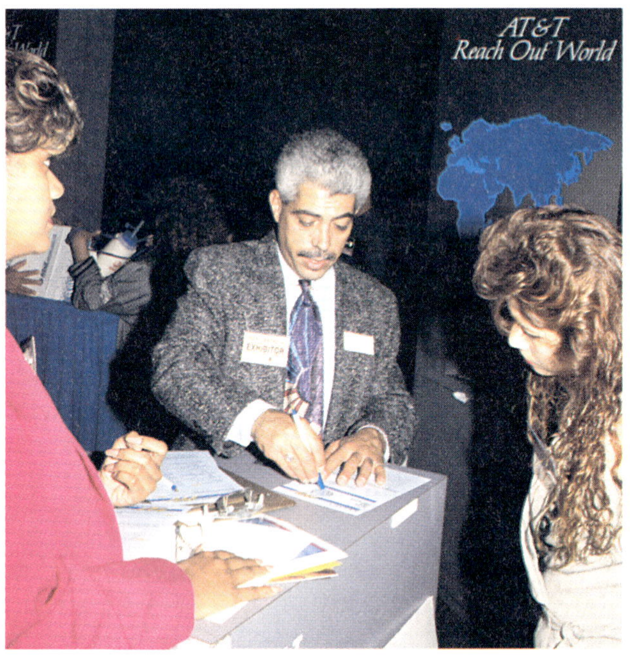

Job fairs are designed to bring together applicants and representatives of various companies.

hire the student permanently or by the student to accept a permanent position with the firm following graduation. An internship typically involves a temporary job for the summer months or a part-time job during the school year. In many instances, students alternate their schedules by working full-time one semester and becoming full-time students the next. During the internship, the student gets to view business practices firsthand. At the same time, the intern contributes to the firm by performing needed tasks. Through this relationship, a student can determine whether a company would be a desirable employer. Similarly, having a relatively lengthy period of time to observe the student's job performance, the firm can make a better judgment regarding the person's qualifications. In addition to other benefits, internships provide opportunities for students to bridge the gap from business theory to practice.

Internships have also proved useful in moving minorities into the workforce. Bob Edwards, senior vice president for Drake Beam Morin, Inc., describes a program he helped implement for a former employer:

> The successful integration of our office workforce after the Civil Rights legislation in 1964 required innovative approaches to selection as well as placement of minorities. The business leaders in the city were not yet confident that an acceptable solution could be found to answer the critics of integration or those advocates who did not want to weaken their companies' performance by active compliance.
>
> We elected to deal with this important issue by strengthening our high school internship program. Business-minded students in this program were provided full-time summer jobs in our home office prior to their senior year and were moved to part-time jobs through their final school term.
>
> Our approach provided:
>
> 1. Summer employment to a predominantly minority population.
> 2. Part-time employment, without giving any employment test, to high school students that more accurately reflected the demands of an adult work environment.
> 3. Maximum discretion for the student, as the company required no commitment beyond the school term.
> 4. Maximum discretion for the company, as full-time employment could be offered to those students who performed well on the internship jobs.
> 5. Up-to-date information for high school teachers and administrators on industry needs and hard data to motivate student development.

> In summary, we integrated our workforce with performers and minimized management reluctance to enter an unknown and, in some situations, a feared adventure with a population whose background was different from their own. Our success with this approach was evidenced by the size of our employee minority population and their presence at all levels of responsibility.

Local communities also view favorably firms that offer internships. Internships serve as an effective public relations tool that provides visibility for the company name. Allstate Insurance Company has carried the concept of internships one step further. Ken Marques, employment director for the firm, believes that internships can also serve as a strategic retention tool. He has set a goal to hire 60 percent of his company's 1995 entry-level staff from its internship program. He calls the program "the ten week interview" and states that his firm prefers to have its turnover up front, by eliminating the mismatches, rather than two years later.[13]

Executive Search Firms

Executive search firms may be used by organizations in their recruitment efforts to locate experienced professionals and executives when other sources prove inadequate. **Executive search firms** are organizations that seek the most qualified executive available for a specific position. They are generally retained by the companies needing specific types of individuals.

Executive search is a rapidly growing industry with estimated revenue reaching $2.5 billion annually. More than 4 million potential candidates are contacted in order to place 80,000 executives.[14] The executive search industry has evolved from a basic recruitment service to a highly sophisticated profession serving a greatly expanded role. Search firms now assist organizations in determining their human resource needs, establishing compensation packages, and revising organizational structures.

Most executive search firms differ from employment agencies and job advisory consultants in that they do not work for individuals. *Retainer search firms* work for corporations and governmental agencies, which pay the fees; they are paid for each search regardless of whether a suitable candidate is recruited. These search firms normally develop a close relationship with their clients. They acquire an intimate knowledge of the organization, its culture, its goals, its structure, and the position to be filled. Retainer firms typically recruit executives for middle and upper level management positions or senior technical positions calling for salaries of more than $60,000. *Contingency search firms*, which grew out of the employment agency industry, focus on lower and mid-management positions, as well as some technical positions with salaries from $30,000 to $70,000. Unlike retainer search firms, these organizations are paid only when a candidate is accepted.[15]

An executive search firm's representatives often visit the client's offices and interview the company's management. This enables them to gain a clear understanding of the company's goals and the job qualifications required. After obtaining this information, they contact and interview potential candidates, check references, and refer the best qualified person to the client for the selection decision. Search firms maintain databases of resumes that are used during this process. Other sources used include networking contacts, files from previous searches, specialized directories, personal calls, previous clients, colleagues and unsolicited resumes.[16] The search firm's fee is generally a percentage of the individual's compensation for the first year. Expenses, as well as the fee, are paid by the client.

The relationship between a client company and a search firm should be based on mutual trust and understanding. Both parties gain most from their relationship when they interact often and maintain good communication.[17] In order to be successful, the search firm must understand in detail the nature of the client's operations, the responsibilities of the position being filled, and the client's corporate culture. Similarly, the client must understand the search process, work with the consultant, and provide continuous, honest feedback.

Professional Associations

Finance, marketing, accounting, and human resource professional associations provide recruitment and placement services for their members. The Society for Human Resource Management, for example, operates a job referral service for members seeking new positions and employers with positions to fill.

Employee Referrals

Many organizations have found that their employees can assist in the recruitment process. Employees often actively solicit applications from their friends and associates. In some organizations, especially where certain skills are scarce, this approach has proven quite effective. For example, at NEC Technologies, hires from employee referrals have risen from 15 percent to 52 percent in the past few years. This firm has found that as referrals have become their primary recruitment and retention approach, the costs previously incurred from advertising and using placement agencies have been significantly reduced. With a goal not only to attract employees but also to retain them, NEC has found that this recruitment method results in effective employee/employer bonding.[18]

Unsolicited Walk-in Applicants

If an organization has the reputation of being a good place to work, it may be able to attract qualified prospects even without extensive recruitment efforts. Acting on their own initiative, well-qualified workers may seek out a specific company to apply for a job. Unsolicited applicants who apply because they are favorably impressed with the firm's reputation often prove to be valuable employees.

Recruitment Databases/Automated Applicant Tracking Systems

Computers have greatly facilitated many HRM functions, a trend that is sure to accelerate. The size of databases operated by several independent networks continues to grow as some firms downsize and others become more aware of what computers can do. One such firm permits employers to advertise job listings on-line to PRODIGY subscribers or to access a resume database. Others offer resume banks of individuals at all career levels in a wide variety of fields.[19] Central databases can be accessed by corporate clients using their own PCs. When a candidate's background matches an open position, the client may obtain a copy of the resume to review. The process of matching candidates with positions dramatically reduces paperwork costs. For example, it typically costs $1,000 to conduct a job search through one national database firm. An executive search firm, on the other hand, may charge as much as $30,000 to hire a $90,000 per year executive. The cost and time efficiency of databases may make some recruiting methods obsolete, although they will not completely replace currently used systems. For example, searches for CEOs will always be politically sensitive and require special handling.[20]

Internal databases make automated applicant tracking systems possible. In an automated system, information can be drawn from a firm's database to produce fast and accurate requisitions. Next, applicant information can be accessed from the database. In seconds, the few individuals who meet specific selection criteria can be identified from a group of many applicants. The selection procedure, discussed in the next chapter, can also be facilitated. With a few simple keystrokes, managers can get a detailed picture of each candidate's background.

An automated tracking system streamlines the recruitment process and permits managers to spend more time finding high quality candidates. A firm gains a sophisticated means of handling all steps of the process, from generating routine correspondence to tracking requisitions and scheduling interviews. Such a system provides detailed documentation of hiring practices and is a tremendous help in meeting EEO guidelines.[21]

TAILORING RECRUITMENT METHODS TO SOURCES

Because every organization is unique in many ways, the types and qualifications of workers needed to fill positions vary greatly. Thus, successful recruitment must be tailored to the needs of each firm. In addition, recruitment sources and methods often vary according to the type of position being filled.

Figure 6-4 shows a matrix that depicts methods and sources of recruitment for a data processing manager. A human resource professional must first identify the source (where prospective employees are) before choosing the methods (how to get them). Suppose, for example, that a large firm has an immediate need for an accounting manager with a minimum of five years' experience, and no one within the firm has these qualifications. It is most likely that such an individual is employed by another firm, very possibly a competitor, or is self-employed. The recruiter must then choose the method (or methods) of recruitment that offers the best opportunity for attracting qualified candidates. Perhaps the job can be advertised in the classified sections of *The Wall Street Journal, National Employment Weekly,* or *The CPA Journal*. Or an executive search firm may be used to locate a qualified person. In addition, the recruiter may attend meetings of professional accounting associations. Using one or more of these methods will likely yield a pool of qualified applicants.

Suppose, for example, that a firm needs twenty entry-level machine operators, whom the firm is willing to train. High schools and vocational

FIGURE 6-4
Methods and Sources of Recruitment for a Data Processing Manager

EXTERNAL METHODS OF RECRUITING

SOURCES	Advertising	Private employment agencies	Public employment agencies	Recruiters	Special events	Internships	Executive search firms	Unsolicited applications	Professional associations	Employee referrals	Unsolicited applicants	Automated Applicant Tracking System	Resume Databases
High schools													
Vocational schools													
Community colleges													
Colleges and universities													
Competitors and other firms	X	X					X		X				
Unemployed													
Self-employed													

schools would probably be good recruitment sources. Methods of recruitment might include newspaper ads, public employment agencies, sending recruiters to vocational schools, and employee referrals.

The specific recruitment methods used will be affected by external environmental factors, including market supply and job requirements. Each organization should maintain employment records and conduct its own research in order to determine which recruitment sources and methods are most appropriate under various circumstances. For the most prevalent recruiting sources and methods by various job categories, see Figure 6-5.

RECRUITMENT UNDER THE LAW

In spite of equal opportunity laws, human resource practices that have an unequal impact on women and minorities are deeply embedded in some organizations. A traditional recruitment method, such as employee referrals, may perpetuate the effects of past discrimination even after other discriminatory practices have been discontinued. The result, though not necessarily conscious, is a continuation of what has been labeled systemic discrimination.[22] Courts have found that some employment practices, regardless of intent, have resulted in discrimination against women and minorities. In addition, gender stereotypes may contribute to beliefs that members of one sex either do not prefer, or perform less well in, certain jobs compared to members of the other sex. To offset the

FIGURE 6-5
Most Prevalent Recruiting Source Method by Job Category

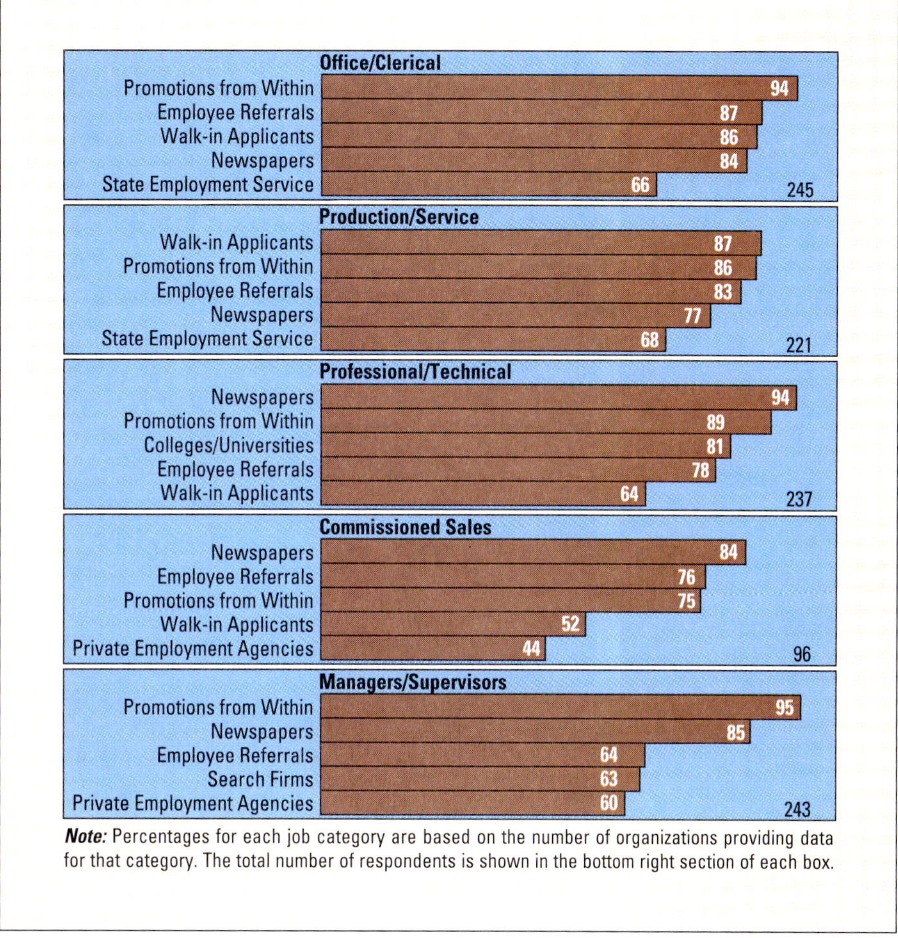

Source: The Bureau of National Affairs Inc.'s *Personnel Management*, BNA Policy and Practice Series cited in K. Michele Kacmar, "Look at Who's Talking," *HRMagazine* 38 (February 1993): 57.

effects of past discrimination in employment, firms may need to use new recruitment approaches.

As we discussed in Chapter 3, equal employment opportunity, as provided by federal legislation, prohibits considering such characteristics as race, gender, and disabilities in employment decisions. In other words, these attributes are not to be a factor when decisions such as firing, promoting, and discharging employees are made. On the other hand, affirmative action may be mandated by executive order or court order. In this case, special provisions must be made to recruit, train, retain, and promote members of protected groups, such as women and minorities. If affirmative action remains a viable concept in our society, such factors as race and gender will continue to be considered in certain employment decisions.[23]

Some groups are opposed to the concept of affirmative action and may even charge that it results in so-called *reverse discrimination*. There is another

HRM IN ACTION

—ONLY ABLE BODIED MEN?

Mark Smith and Debra Coffee, two executives from competing firms, met at their annual professional conference. They were discussing the effect of recent civil rights legislation on their firms. Mark said, "I don't think we will have any difficulty at our company. We don't employ any disabled people, but then all our production jobs require able bodied men."

"Have you considered making reasonable accommodations for applicants with disabilities?" Debra asked. After thinking a moment, Mark replied, "I don't believe so, Debra. You see, our executive group is very pleased with the productivity in our plant. I really don't think they want to fix something that isn't broke."

As a human resource professional,
how would you respond?

side to the story, however. Because of past unequal opportunity, women, minorities, and individuals with disabilities may not respond to traditional recruitment methods. These groups may be omitted altogether from the typical recruitment process unless specific action is taken to attract them. If this action is not taken, there is a question whether they will ever be adequately represented in the workforce. Therefore, any organization that adopts affirmative action (either voluntarily or by mandate) must implement recruitment and other employment programs that assure women, minorities, and those with disabilities will be included in decision-making processes. Otherwise, organizations will overlook a great deal of much needed talent.

Analysis of Recruitment Procedures

To ensure that its recruitment program is nondiscriminatory, a firm must analyze its recruitment procedures. For example, it might be wise to reconsider the use of employee referral or unsolicited applicants as primary recruitment methods. These actions may perpetuate the composition of the organization's workforce. In cases where minorities and women are not well represented at all levels, the courts have ruled that reliance on these particular practices is discriminatory.

In identifying sources of continuing discrimination, it is helpful to develop a record of applicant flow. In fact, this record may be mandatory if the firm has been found guilty of discrimination or operates under an affirmative action program. An applicant flow record includes personal and job-related data concerning each applicant. It indicates whether a job offer was extended and, if no such offer was made, an explanation of the decision. Such records enable the organization to analyze its recruitment and selection practices and take corrective action when necessary.

Utilization of Minorities, Women, and Individuals with Disabilities

Recruiters should be trained in the use of objective, job-related standards because they occupy a unique position in terms of encouraging or discouraging minorities, women, and the disabled to apply for jobs. Qualified members of these groups may be utilized effectively in key recruitment activities, such as visiting schools and colleges and participating in career days. They are also in an excellent position to provide valuable input for recruitment planning and can effectively serve as referral sources. Pictures of minority, women, and disabled employees in help-wanted advertisements and company brochures give credibility to the message, "We are an equal opportunity employer."

Advertising

With few exceptions, jobs must be open to all individuals. Therefore, gender-segregated ads, for example, must not be used unless gender is a bona fide occupational qualification (BFOQ). The BFOQ exception provided in Title VII of the Civil Rights Act requires that qualifications be job related. This definition is narrowly interpreted by EEOC and the courts. The burden of proof is on the employer to establish that the requirements are essential for successful performance of the job. Other advertising practices designed to provide equal opportunity include:

1. Ensuring that the content of advertisements does not indicate preference for any race, gender, or age or that these factors are a qualification for the job.
2. Utilizing media that are directed toward minorities, such as appropriate radio stations.
3. Emphasizing the intent to recruit without regard to race, gender, or disabled status by including the phrase *EEO/AA/ADA*, Equal Employment Opportunity, Affirmative Action, and American With Disabilities in job ads (see Figure 6-6).

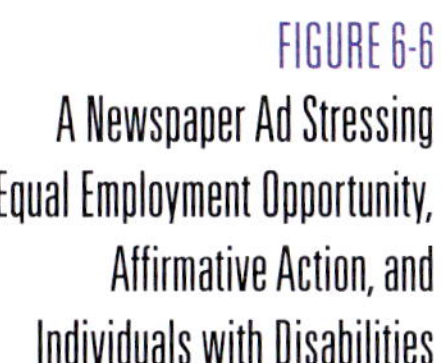

FIGURE 6-6 A Newspaper Ad Stressing Equal Employment Opportunity, Affirmative Action, and Individuals with Disabilities

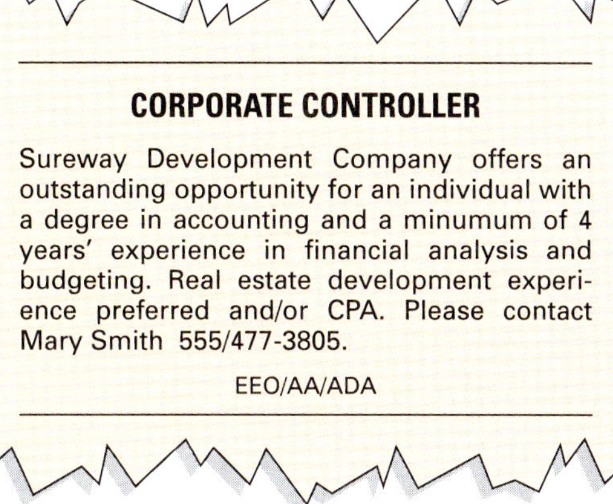

CORPORATE CONTROLLER
Sureway Development Company offers an outstanding opportunity for an individual with a degree in accounting and a minumum of 4 years' experience in financial analysis and budgeting. Real estate development experience preferred and/or CPA. Please contact Mary Smith 555/477-3805.
EEO/AA/ADA

Employment Agencies

An organization should emphasize its nondiscriminatory recruitment practices when utilizing employment agencies. Even when private agencies, which are also covered under Title VII, are retained, jobs at all levels should be listed with the state employment service. These agencies can provide valuable assistance to organizations seeking to fulfill affirmative action goals. In addition, agencies and consultant firms that specialize in minority and women applicants should be contacted.

Other Suggested Affirmative Recruitment Approaches

Personal contact should be made with counselors and administrators at high schools, vocational schools, and colleges with large minority and/or female enrollments. Counselors and administrators should be made aware that the organization is actively seeking minorities, women, and disabled individuals for jobs that they have not traditionally held. Also, counselors and administrators should be familiar with the types of jobs available and the training and education needed to perform these jobs. The possibilities for developing internships and summer employment should be carefully investigated. Firms should develop contact with minority, women's, and other community organizations. These organizations include the National Association for the Advancement of Colored People (NAACP), the League of United Latin American Citizens, the National Urban League, the American Association of University Women, the Federation of Business and Professional Women's Talent Bank, the National Council of Negro Women, and the Veterans Administration. The EEOC's regional offices will assist employers in locating appropriate local agencies.

A GLOBAL PERSPECTIVE

Recruitment worldwide is no less vital than it is in the United States. No firm anywhere on the planet is able to avoid the pressures of increasing competition. And competition in the labor market is just as intense as it is in the product market. Recall Volkswagen's raiding of General Motors' executives. Raiding has long been a practice within our own borders. Because of the scarcity of top talent, we can expect more of the same to occur globally.

Many of the recruitment methods used in the United States are also common practice in other countries. Even some alternatives to recruitment are identical. The use of temporary help, for instance, is not foreign in Europe.[24] In fact, in Western Europe, the temporary help industry is about 50 percent larger than in the United States. While language is not a major problem, different cultures and employment laws vary from country to country. Operations in the United Kingdom are much the same as in the United States. In other parts of Europe, however, hiring temporary help is much more highly regulated. In France, for example, the law requires that temporary employees be paid the same rate as full-time employees in addition to a premium. Germany is also highly regulated, with temporary workers being considered permanent employees of the temporary company that employs them. Since younger workers in Japan are not as tied to their employers as their parents were, the door for temporary employment firms is open. Japanese laws, however, are new and relatively inflexible; for instance, they specify the kinds of work permitted by a temporary worker, and permission must be granted for any changes.[25]

The most formidable task facing many multinational firms in the United Kingdom is the recruitment and development of a cadre of managers and executives who understand and can operate effectively in the global market environment. Many companies are attempting to identify managers of high potential at an early stage in their careers and then give them international experience as soon as possible. There is also an increase in external recruitment to fill management positions abroad. Another strategy is to sell the company more effectively to graduates through various types of marketing designed to highlight the international nature of the company's activities. Unfortunately, there is an unwillingness to recruit and develop women as international managers. This is of particular concern because recent research suggests that women are more sensitive to cultural differences and are, therefore, more able to work effectively with managers from other countries. It is essential that human resource managers do not ignore any portion of the labor pool, or they will not be able to recruit effectively worldwide.[26]

SUMMARY

Recruitment is the process of attracting individuals on a timely basis, in sufficient numbers, and with appropriate qualifications, and encouraging them to apply for jobs with an organization. When human resource planning indicates a need for employees, a firm should first evaluate alternatives to hiring additional workers. Common alternatives to recruitment include overtime, subcontracting, contingent workers, and employee leasing.

When these other alternatives do not meet the demand, the recruitment process starts. Frequently, recruitment begins when a manager initiates an employee requisition. The next step is to determine whether qualified employees are available within the firm (the internal source) or must be recruited externally from sources such as colleges, universities, and other organizations. Recruitment sources are places where qualified individuals can be found. Recruitment methods are the specific means by which potential employees are attracted to the firm. After identifying the sources of potential employees, the human resource manager chooses the appropriate methods for internal and/or external recruitment.

External factors can significantly affect a firm's recruitment efforts. Of particular importance is the demand for, and supply of, specific skills in the labor market. If demand for a particular skill is high relative to supply, an extraordinary recruitment effort may be required. When the unemployment rate in the firm's labor market is high, its recruitment process may be simplified. Legal considerations and the firm's corporate image also play significant roles in recruitment practices in the United States.

An organization's promotion policy can also have a significant impact on recruitment. Basically, an organization can utilize two promotion approaches: a policy of promotion from within or a policy of filling positions from outside the organization. Depending on the circumstances, each approach may have merit.

Tools used for internal recruitment include management and skill inventories and job posting and bidding procedures. Management and skills inventories indicate whether current employees possess the qualifications needed for promotion. Job posting informs employees of job openings, while job bidding permits employees who believe they possess the required qualifications to apply for a posted job.

Candidates for jobs may be attracted from various outside sources. Firms often depend heavily on high schools and vocational schools when recruiting clerical and other entry-level operative employees. Many community colleges are sensitive to specific employment needs in local labor markets and graduate highly sought after students. Colleges and universities represent a major source of recruitment for many organizations. Competitors and other firms in the same geographic area or industry may be the most important source of recruits for positions in which recent experience is highly desired. The unemployed, the self-employed, older individuals, and military personnel may also be good sources of recruits.

Recruitment methods such as advertising, employment agencies, and employee referrals may be effective in attracting individuals with virtually every type of skill. Recruiters, special events, and internships are used primarily to attract college and university students. Also, executive search firms and professional organizations are particularly useful in the recruitment of managerial and professional employees.

In spite of equal opportunity laws, certain human resource practices that have an unequal impact on women, minorities, and disabled individuals are deeply embedded in some organizations. To ensure that its recruitment program is nondiscriminatory, a firm must analyze its recruitment procedures.

QUESTIONS FOR REVIEW

1. Describe the basic components of the recruitment process.
2. What are some actions that can be taken prior to engaging in recruitment?
3. List and discuss the various external and internal factors that may affect recruitment.
4. What is meant by the term *internal recruitment*? Describe the advantages and disadvantages of internal recruitment.
5. Describe the methods commonly used in internal recruitment. Briefly define each.
6. Discuss the reasons for an external recruitment program.
7. Distinguish between sources and methods of external recruitment. Identify various sources and methods of external recruitment.
8. Explain the difference between an executive search firm and an employment agency.
9. How can a firm improve its recruiting efforts under the law?

HRM SIMULATION

Incident C in the *Simulation Players Manual* involves recruiting for temporary positions. Your organization has been instructed by a customer (or client) to augment your product (or service) for the next quarter's production. No additional units are to be produced, but you need to do the work to the customer/client's specific instructions. This will require the addition of 50 employees for only one quarter. Your team must recommend which recruitment method should be used to handle this temporary situation.

ABC VIDEO CASE

MAKING IT BETTER TAPE 1, NUMBER 12

In the inner city atmosphere of West Philadelphia, Presbyterian Medical Center was not able to get the trained staff it needed through the usual recruitment methods. Since nurses were in demand everywhere, applicants would choose to accept those positions where the living conditions were better. Knowing that there were healthy, able people already living in the area, Presbyterian Medical Center started a school to train those individuals in the field of practical nursing. The school actively recruited those in the neighborhood with a high school education and a strong desire to care for others. Tutoring was given to those students who needed it, and flexible scheduling of classes was available for those who needed to continue working. Scholarships were given to those students with extraordinary need. The program has been deemed a success, as evidenced by the 46 graduates on Presbyterian's staff who will be making approximately $25,000 per year. The program also has inspired one student to become a registered nurse. This inner city medical center has truly done what hospitals are supposed to do—make people better.

HRM INCIDENT 1

—RIGHT IDEA, WRONG SONG

Robert Key is human resource manager at Epler Manufacturing Company in Greenfield, Wisconsin. He was considering the need to recruit qualified blacks for Epler when Betty Alexander walked into his office. "Got a minute?" asked Betty. "I need to talk to you about the recruiting trip to Michigan State next week." "Sure," Robert replied, "but first I need your advice about something. How can we get more blacks to apply for work here? We're running ads on WBEZ radio along with the classified ads in the *Tribune*. I think you and John have made recruiting trips to every community college within 200 miles. We've encouraged employee referral, too, and I still think that's our most reliable source of new workers. But we just aren't getting any black applicants."

From the president on down, the management at Epler claimed commitment to equal employment opportunity. According to Robert, the commitment went much deeper than posting the usual placards and filing an *affirmative action program* with the federal government. However, the percentage of black employees at Epler remained at only 5 percent, while the surrounding community was 11 percent black. Epler paid competitive wages and had a good training program.

Epler had a particular need for machine operator trainees. The machines were not difficult to operate, and no educational requirement was necessary for the job. There were also several clerical and management trainee positions open.

Question

1. Evaluate the current recruitment effort. How could Robert better the firm's goal of equal employment?

HRM INCIDENT 2

—A DILEMMA

As the human resource director for KBH Stores in St. Louis, Missouri, Virginia Stutes knew she had her work cut out for her. Company management was moving forward on a goal of opening ten new stores in twelve months. KBH already employed 480 people in thirty-five stores, in addition to the headquarters staff of thirty-one. Virginia knew that staffing the ten new stores would require recruiting about 150 more people. She felt that her own small office was inadequately funded and staffed to handle this task. She sat at her desk, mulling over how to present a recommendation for her own staffing needs.

One of Virginia's concerns was broaching the subject with her boss because she had not officially been told of the expansion plans. Virginia had learned about them through the office grapevine. While she did not like being kept in the dark, she was not surprised that she hadn't been told. Glenn Sullivan, the president of KBH, was noted for his autocratic leadership style. Virginia had been warned early on that

Glenn told subordinates only what he wanted them to know and that he expected everyone who worked for him to follow orders without question. He was not an unkind person, though, and Virginia had always gotten along with him well enough. She had never confronted Mr. Sullivan about anything, so it was with some concern that she approached him in his office later that day.

"Mr. Sullivan," she began, "I hear that we are going to be opening ten new stores next year."

"That's right, Virginia," said Mr. Sullivan. "We've already arranged the credit lines and picked out several of the sites."

"What about staffing?" asked Virginia.

"Well, I assume you will take care of that, Virginia, when we get to that point."

"What about my own staff?" asked Virginia. "I think I am going to need at least three or four more people. And we are already crowded for space. So I hope you plan to expand the human resource office."

"Not really," said Mr. Sullivan, "The new demands on the human resource staff will be temporary. It wouldn't be cost effective to hire and train additions to your staff that will only be cut the next year. I am counting on you to plan the expansion staffing within our current proposed budget allowances for the human resource office. It may require some reallocation, but I am sure you can handle that."

Questions

1. What recruiting sources and methods should Virginia use? Explain.
2. Describe the elements of the internal environment that the case highlights. How does each affect Virginia?

DEVELOPING HRM SKILLS

AN EXPERIENTIAL EXERCISE

Human resource managers have the responsibility of preparing job descriptions. From these job descriptions, profiles of the types of individuals needed to fill various positions in the firm can be developed and recruitment efforts can be designed. The human resource manager must determine where the best applicants are located (recruitment sources) and how to entice them to join the organization (recruitment methods). This exercise is designed to provide an understanding of the relationship between recruitment sources and methods.

Each participant will identify both recruitment sources and methods for the job description. The job description is for a *Human Resource Assistant,* who reports to the Manager of Employee Relations and Recruitment in the human resource department. The *accountability objective* for the position is fairly standard: to perform employment activities for the off-site claims division in order to staff the organization with proficient, suitable personnel and provide effective administration of human resource policies and procedures. The successful applicant will have a four-year college degree, preferably in business administration, but needs little or no experience because the candidate selected for the position will be placed in a six-month training program before assuming these duties and functions. The span of control is limited to two people, one clerk and one secretary. The primary duties of the incumbent include the recruitment and interviewing of applicants for employment, as well as the performance of the basic employment functions, which include: screening, recruiting, and interviewing candidates (clerical, technical, and professional); devising recruiting ads; performing reference checks; and administering standard skills tests where applicable.

The incumbent will function independently as a counseling source and is expected to create an atmosphere of impartiality and equity; in addition, he or she will probably choose the appropriate method of communicating information to personnel. The incumbent may also assess training needs for on-site personnel. In order to make personnel recommendations, the incumbent must be capable of maintaining an updated knowledge of all areas of human resources, a knowledge base of the external environment, and an awareness of the internal climate. Knowledge of the employment marketplace, as well as hiring practices and legal considerations, is required. Excellent interpersonal skills and the ability to establish rapport are also essential.

Participants will attempt to determine the most appropriate recruitment sources and methods for the job description that will be given to them. Your instructor will provide the participants with additional information necessary to complete the exercise.

NOTES

1. R. Wayne Mondy, Robert M. Noe, and Robert E. Edwards, "What the Staffing Function Entails," *Personnel* 63 (April 1986): 54–58.

2. Gary M. Wederspahn, "Costing Failures in Expatriate Human Resources Management," *Human Resource Planning* 15 (September 1992): 27–35.

3. Ann Crittenden, "Temporary Solutions," *Working Woman* 19 (February 1994): 32.

4. Paul N. Keaton and Janine Anderson, "Leasing Offers Benefits to Both Sides," *HRMagazine* 35 (July 1990): 5.

5. John Ross, "Effective Ways to Hire Contingent Personnel," *HRMagazine* 36 (February 1991): 53.

6. Don McNerney, "Competitive Advantage: Diverse Customers and Stakeholders," *HR Focus* 71 (January 1994): 9–10.

7. John Templeton and David Woodruff, "The Aftershock from the Lopez Affair," *Business Week* (April 19, 1993): 31.

8. Stephenie Overman, "Myths Hinder Hiring of Older Workers," *HRMagazine* 38 (June 1993): 51.

9. Stephenie Overman, "Heroes for Hire," *HRMagazine* 38 (December 1993): 61–62.

10. Richard A. Fear, *The Evaluation Interview,* 3rd edition (New York: McGraw-Hill, 1984): 74–75.

11. Thomas L. Watkins, "What Do You Want from Us?" *Across the Board* 30 (June 1993): 11.

12. Bill Leonard, "Resume Databases to Dominate Field," *HRMagazine* 30 (April 1993): 59–60.

13. Mary E. Scott, "Internships Add Value to College Recruitment," *Personnel Journal* 71 (April 1992): 25.

14. Howard S. Freedman, *How to Get a Headhunter to Call* (New York: John Wiley & Sons, 1989): 60.

15. Ibid., 56.

16. Ibid., 57.

17. Paul DiMarchi, "The Two Faces of Search Firms," *Financial Executive* 10 (January-February 1994): 53.

18. Albert H. McCarthy, "The Human Touch Helps Recruit Quality Workers," *Personnel Journal* 70 (November 1991): 68.

19. "HR Agenda: Recruitment/Hiring Practices," *HRMagazine* 37 (February 1992): 54.

20. Ibid., 60.

21. Peg Anthony, "Track Applicants, Track Costs," *Personnel Journal* 69 (April 1990): 75–81.

22. Gary N. Powell, "The Effects of Sex and Gender on Recruitment," *Academy of Management Review* 12 (October 1987): 7.

23. Gerard P. Panaro, *Employment Law Manual* (Boston: Warren, Gorham & Lamont, 1990): 5–2–5.

24. Stephenie Overman, "Temporary Services Go Global," *HRMagazine* 38 (August 1993): 72.

25. Ibid., 72–74.

26. Hugh Scullion, "Attracting Management Globetrotters," *Personnel Management* 24 (January 1992): 28–32.

CHAPTER 7

Selection

KEY TERMS

CHAPTER OBJECTIVES

1. Define selection, explain how environmental factors affect the selection process, and describe the selection process.
2. Describe the importance of the preliminary interview and the review of the application for employment in the selection process.
3. State the role of tests and the importance of interviewing in the selection process.
4. State why reference checks and background investigations are conducted, describe the reasons for preemployment physical examinations, and explain the considerations related to acceptance or rejection of job applicants.
5. Describe staffing in the multinational environment.

Bill Jenkins is the printing shop owner/manager of Quality Printing Company. Because of an increase in business, shop employees have been working overtime for almost a month. Last week Bill put an ad in the newspaper to hire a printer. Three people applied for the job. Bill considered only one of them, Mark Ketchell, to be qualified. Bill called Mark's previous employer in Detroit, who responded, "Mark is a diligent, hardworking person. He is as honest as the day is long. He knows his trade, too." Bill also learned that Mark had left Detroit after he was divorced a few months ago and that his work had deteriorated slightly prior to the divorce. The next day Bill asked Mark to operate one of the printing presses. Mark did so competently, and Bill immediately decided to hire him.

Mary Howard is the shipping supervisor for McCarty-Holman Warehouse, a major food distributor. One of Mary's truck drivers just quit. She spoke to the human resource manager, Tom Sullivan, who said that he would begin the search right away. The next day an ad appeared in the local paper for the position. Tom considered three of the fifteen applicants to be qualified and called them in for an initial interview. The following morning Tom called Mary and said, "I have three drivers who look like they can do the job. When do you want me to set up an interview for you with them? I guess you'll want to give them a driving test at that time." Mary interviewed the three drivers and gave them each a driving test and then called Tom to tell him her choice. The next day the new driver reported to Mary for work.

These incidents provide only a brief look at the all-important selection process. In the first case, Bill, as owner/manager of a small printing shop, handled the entire selection process himself. In the second case, Tom, the human resource manager, was heavily involved in the selection process, but Mary, the shipping supervisor, made the actual decision. However, knowledge of the selection process was important in both situations.

We begin the chapter with a discussion of the selection process and the environmental factors that affect it. Then, we describe the preliminary interview and review of the application for employment and resume. Next, we cover administration of selection tests, validity studies, cutoff scores, and types of employment tests. In the ensuing sections, we present the employment interview and methods of interviewing. We follow those topics with a discussion of reference checks, background investigation, negligent hiring and retention, and polygraph tests. We then describe factors related to the selection decision, physical examination, and acceptance or rejection of job applicants. The final section relates to staffing in the multinational environment.

THE SIGNIFICANCE OF EMPLOYEE SELECTION

Whereas recruitment encourages individuals to seek employment with a firm, the purpose of the selection process is to identify and employ the best qualified individuals for specific positions. **Selection** is the process of choosing from a group of applicants the individual best suited for a particular position. As you might expect, a firm's recruitment efforts have a significant impact on the quality of the selection decision. The organization may be forced to employ marginally acceptable workers if recruitment efforts result in only a few qualified applicants.

Most managers admit that employee selection is one of their most difficult, and most important, business decisions.[1] As Peter Drucker has stated, "No other decisions are so long lasting in their consequences or so difficult to unmake. And yet, by and large, executives make poor promotion and staffing decisions. By all accounts, their batting average is no better than .333: At most, one-third of such decisions turn out right; one-third are minimally effective, and one-third are outright failures."[2] However, if a firm hires too many mediocre or poor performers, it cannot be successful long even if it has perfect plans, a sound organizational structure, and finely tuned control systems. These organizational factors are not self-actuating. Competent people must be available to ensure that organizational goals are attained.

The U.S. Labor Department estimates that the average cost of hiring one worker is $40,000. When you add the hidden costs, such as loss of productivity and overtime for the remaining staff, the cost of replacing a key employee approaches two times his or her annual salary.[3] Another estimate of the entire process has been valued as high as $500,000 per hire. While this figure may appear to be excessive, it is important to consider the productivity difference between high and low performers. This differential has been estimated to be as high as 3 to 1.[4] A firm that selects qualified employees can reap substantial benefits, which may be repeated every year the employee is on the payroll.

The selection process affects, and is also affected by, the other human resource functions. For instance, if the selection process only provides the firm with marginally qualified workers, the organization may have to intensify its training efforts. If the compensation package is inferior to those provided by the firm's competition, attracting the best qualified applicants may be difficult or impossible.

The goal of the selection process is to properly match people with jobs. If individuals are overqualified, underqualified, or for any reason do not *fit* either the job or organization, they will probably leave the firm. In fact, about 40 percent of all U.S. workers have been in their jobs for less than two years. Half of those in their first year will leave or be fired during the next year.[5]

While some turnover may be positive for an organization, it can become extremely expensive. A high turnover rate makes it almost impossible to achieve superior performance. For example, product research and development is delayed, manufacturing loses efficiency, and marketing penetration is slowed. These hidden consequences of turnover, not the visible costs of recruitment, relocation, and training, constitute the major costs. Two studies conducted almost a decade apart indicate that such expenses, although they are rarely measured, account for 80 percent or more of turnover costs.[6]

As we emphasized in Chapter 4, job analysis provides data for preparing job descriptions and specifications, which in turn is essential for making good selection decisions. However, a real problem exists when selection criteria are different from what is actually required by the job. Therefore, human resource managers must continually update job descriptions and specifications to ensure only properly qualified employees are recruited and subjected to the selection process.

ENVIRONMENTAL FACTORS AFFECTING THE SELECTION PROCESS

A permanent, standardized screening process could greatly simplify the selection process. However, development of such a process—even if it were possible and desirable—would not eliminate deviations to meet the unique needs of particular situations. As one human resource manager expressed it, "The only thing certain is that exceptions will be made." And exceptions are often made in response to the following environmental factors.

Legal Considerations

As we described in Chapter 3, legislation, executive orders, and court decisions have a major impact on human resource management. It is imperative human resource managers have extensive knowledge of the legal aspects of selection including awareness of the selection criteria to avoid. Table 7-1 identifies criteria that should be carefully avoided because of their discriminatory potential.

Speed of Decision Making

The time available to make the selection decision can also have a major effect on the selection process. Suppose, for instance, that the production manager for a manufacturing firm comes to the human resource manager's office and says, "My only quality control inspectors just had a fight and both resigned. I can't operate until those positions are filled." Speed is crucial in this instance, and two interviews, a few telephone calls, and a prayer may constitute the entire selection process. On the other hand, selecting a chief executive officer may take an entire year, with considerable attention being devoted to careful study of resumes, intensive reference checking, and hours of interviews. Closely followed selection policies and procedures provide greater protection against legal problems. However, there are times when the pressure of business will dictate that exceptions be made.

Organizational Hierarchy

Different approaches to selection are generally taken for filling positions at different levels in the organization. For instance, consider the differences in hiring a top level executive and a person to fill a clerical position. Extensive background checks and interviewing would be conducted to verify the experience and capabilities of the applicant for the executive position. On the other hand, an applicant for a clerical position would most likely take only a word processing test and perhaps have a short employment interview.

Applicant Pool

The number of applicants for a particular job can also affect the selection process. The process can be truly selective only if there are several qualified applicants for a particular position. However, only a few applicants with highly demanded skills may be available. The selection process then becomes a matter of choosing whomever is at hand. Expansion and contraction of the labor market also exert considerable influence on availability and, thus, the selection process.

The number of people hired for a particular job compared to the individuals in the applicant pool is often expressed as a **selection ratio**, or

$$\text{Selection Ratio} = \frac{\text{Number of persons hired to fill a particular job}}{\text{Number of available applicants}}$$

A selection ratio of 1.00 indicates that there is only one applicant for each position. Having an effective selection process is difficult if this situation exists. People who might otherwise be rejected are often hired. The lower the ratio falls below 1.00, the more alternatives the manager has in making a selection decision. For example, a selection ratio of 0.10 indicates that there are ten applicants for each position.

Type of Organization

The sector of the economy in which individuals are to be employed—private, governmental, or not-for-profit—can also affect the selection process. A business in the private sector is heavily profit oriented. Prospective employees are screened with regard to how they can help achieve profit goals. Consideration of the total individual, including personality factors that are job related, is involved in the selection of future employees for this sector.

TABLE 7-1
Hiring Criteria and Standards to Avoid

Gender

Hiring persons based on whether they are men or women is unlawful. The only exception is a case in which gender is a bona fide occupational qualification (BFOQ). However, the use of BFOQs has been narrowly interpreted by EEOC and the courts. The specification of a man versus a woman must be made in view of whether gender is absolutely job related. For example, if the job in question is for an attendant for a women's restroom, gender can legitimately be specified.

Presuming that a particular job is physically too demanding for a woman to perform is also ill-advised. Instead, women applicants should be given the opportunity to prove that they can perform the job. For example, if a job requires frequent lifting of a fifty-pound object, an employer may require applicants to demonstrate that they—both men and women—can regularly lift the required weight.

National Origin

Information regarding an applicant's national origin should not be sought. In addition, other data that might be used to determine national origin should not be requested. Questions regarding an applicant's place of birth and the place of birth of parents, grandparents, or spouse fall into this category.

Marital Status

This is a difficult selection standard to defend and should be avoided. Although asking marital status is not by itself illegal under federal law, the standard has often been applied differently to women than to men.

Disabilities

The passage of the Americans with Disabilities Act (ADA) will cause large and small firms to reevaluate their hiring practices as well as their physical workplaces. Virtually all employers must provide equal employment opportunities to disabled persons who are qualified. This may include making reasonable accommodations for them.

Religion

Discrimination based on religious beliefs is generally unlawful. The only exception is when the employer is a religious corporation, association, educational institution, or society. Questions regarding the applicant's religious denomination, religious affiliation, church, parish, or religious holidays observed are generally ill-advised. Another form of discrimination occurs when individuals' religious beliefs cause them to be away from work before sundown, on Saturdays, or at other times. When this occurs, these practices should be reasonably accommodated unless undue hardships are imposed on the employer.

Race

Race is very rarely a legal employment requirement. Therefore selection decisions should be made without regard to this factor.

Age

Questions asked about an applicant's age or date of birth may be ill-advised in light of the Age Discrimination in Employment Act as amended. However, a firm may ask for age information to comply with the child labor law. For example, the question could be asked, "Are you under the age of 18?" With this exception, an applicant should not be asked his or her age or date of birth. Also, questions about the ages of children, if any, could be potentially discriminatory because a close approximation of the applicant's age often is obtained through knowledge of the ages of the children.

TABLE 7-1 (continued)
Hiring Criteria and Standards to Avoid

Pregnancy

Discrimination in employment based on pregnancy, childbirth, or complications arising from either is illegal. Questions regarding a women's family and childbearing plans should not be asked. Similarly, questions relating to family plans, birth control techniques, and the like may be viewed as discriminatory because they are not also asked of men.

Physical Requirements

Specifications that set a minimum height or weight should be used only when these characteristics are necessary for performing a particular job. Hispanics, Asians, and Pacific Islanders are generally shorter and smaller than others, and women are generally smaller than men. Therefore, nonjob-related physical requirements would tend to reject a disproportionate number of individuals in certain groups.

Standards relating to the ability to lift a certain amount of weight also should not be used unless they are clearly job related. At times, it may be feasible for the employer to redesign the job to overcome a weight-lifting requirement.

Credit Record

An individual's poor credit rating has been found to be an improper standard for rejecting applicants for cases in which this has a disproportionate negative effect on women and minorities. Members of certain groups are more likely to have credit problems than others. Therefore, the standard should not be used unless the employer has a business necessity for obtaining the information. Inquiries about charge accounts, credit references, and home or car ownership should not be made unless they are job related.

Background of Spouse

Basing employment decisions on the background of a spouse is very difficult, if not impossible, to support. Some employers believe that they need to know what the spouse does for a living in making selection decisions. Merely asking this type of question may be interpreted as sex discrimination. In certain instances, women have been turned down for employment because the employer believed that a woman with a working husband would be denying an unemployed man the opportunity for a job.

Care of Children

Employers have, at times, denied employment to women who have non-school-age children. If this standard is imposed on women and not on men, it amounts to sex discrimination. While it may be true that some women find it difficult to work and take care of children at the same time, the same can be said for men. A person should be evaluated on his or her ability to perform a particular job. The U.S. Supreme Court has clearly decided this issue.

Arrest Record

In our system of justice, an arrest is not an indication of guilt. Standards related to arrest records have been found to constitute race or national origin discrimination because the arrest rate for minority group members tends to be higher than that for nonminorities. Therefore, this selection criterion can rarely be used as a justification for rejecting applicants from certain minority groups.

TABLE 7-1 (continued)
Hiring Criteria and Standards to Avoid

Conviction Record

Unlike an arrest record, a conviction record is an indication of guilt. Even though some minorities have a greater conviction rate than nonminorities, this standard may be used if it is job related. It would be quite acceptable to reject a job applicant who had been convicted of robbery if the job required handling of large sums of money. On the other hand, it would be difficult to justify rejecting an applicant for a laborer job if that individual had only been convicted for failure to pay alimony.

Work Experience Requirements

Experience requirements should be reviewed to ensure that they are actually job related. Many women and minorities have not been in the labor force long enough to gain extensive work experience. Requiring that a person have, for example, ten years' work experience may tend to eliminate a large portion of women and minorities and would be discriminatory if this experience is not actually needed to perform the job.

Garnishment Record

As with arrest and conviction records, members of certain minority groups have had their wages garnished more than nonminorities. Therefore, if knowledge of this information cannot be shown to be job related, it should not be used as an employment standard.

Dress and Appearance

Employers have the right to establish standards relating to dress and appearance. This is especially true in situations in which the applicant is dealing directly with the public. Requiring hair to be a certain length has been found by the courts to be nondiscriminatory except when standards have varied by gender. Care should be taken when rejecting applicants strictly on their appearance. A person's appearance may be related to a special dress and style typical of a certain group.

Education Requirements

Nonjob-related educational standards should not be used because of their potential for discrimination. For example, the ability to speak English should be required only if it is job related. A disproportionate number of certain minorities have not graduated from high school or college. Stating that a job requires a college degree when it could be accomplished effectively by a high school graduate can potentially be discriminatory.

Any educational standard may be difficult to defend. Therefore, it may be advisable to focus on the knowledge, skills, and abilities needed to perform the job.

Relatives Working for the Company (Antinepotism Rule)

Standards established about an applicant's relatives working for the company may be discriminatory if they result in reducing employment opportunities for women and members of minorities. Some firms have rules that prohibit hiring the spouse of a current employee. On the surface, this rule appears to affect men and women similarly. In reality, because men have normally been in the labor force longer, the rule reduces employment opportunities much more for women. Therefore, antinepotism rules should be avoided unless they can be shown to be a business necessity.

Government civil service systems typically identify qualified applicants through competitive examinations. Often a manager is allowed to select only from among the top three applicants for a position. A manager in this sector frequently does not have the prerogative to interview other applicants.

Individuals being considered for positions in not-for-profit organizations (such as the Boy and Girl Scouts, YMCA, or YWCA) confront still a different situation. The salary level may not be competitive with private and governmental organizations. Therefore, a person who fills one of these positions must not only be qualified but also dedicated to this type of work.

Probationary Period

Many firms use a probationary period which permits evaluating an employee's ability based on performance. This may be either a substitute for certain phases of the selection process or a check on the validity of the process. The rationale is that if an individual can successfully perform the job during the probationary period, other selection tools may not be needed. In any event, newly hired employees should be monitored to determine whether the hiring decision was a good one. Employees who voluntarily leave should have an exit interview to determine possible deficiencies in the selection process. The results of this interview should be shared with all managers who are involved in selecting employees.

Even though a firm may be unionized, a new employee typically is not protected by the union-management agreement until after a certain probationary period. This period is typically from sixty to ninety days. During that time, an employee may be terminated with little or no justification. When the probationary period is over, terminating a marginal employee may prove to be quite difficult. When a firm is unionized, it becomes especially important for the selection process to identify the most productive workers. Once they come under the union-management agreement, its terms must be followed in changing the status of a worker, and these terms may not include productivity.

THE SELECTION PROCESS

Figure 7-1 shows the selection process in general. It typically begins with the preliminary interview, after which obviously unqualified candidates are quickly rejected. Next, applicants complete the firm's application for employment. Then, they progress through a series of selection tests, the employment interview, and reference and background checks. The successful applicant receives a company physical examination. The individual is employed if results of the physical examination are satisfactory. Several external and internal factors impact the selection process, and the manager must take them into account in making selection decisions.

PRELIMINARY INTERVIEW

The selection process often begins with a preliminary interview. The basic purpose of this initial screening of applicants is to eliminate those who obviously do not meet the position's requirements. At this stage, the interviewer asks a few straightforward questions. For instance, a position may require considerable work experience. If the interview fails to reveal relevant experience, any further discussion wastes time for both the firm and the applicant regarding this particular position.

FIGURE 7-1
The Selection Process

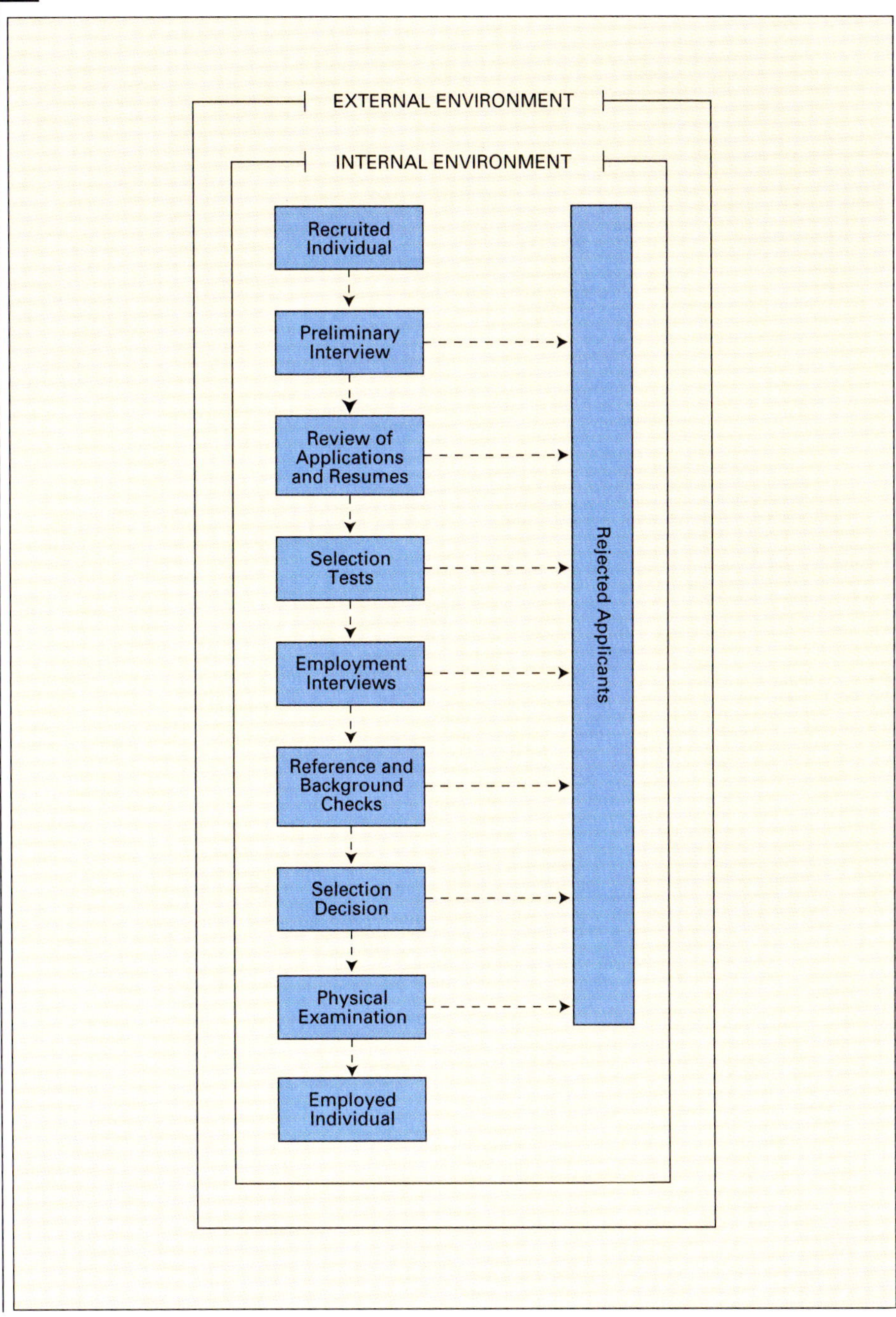

In addition to eliminating obviously unqualified job applicants quickly, a preliminary interview may produce other positive benefits for the firm. It is possible the position for which the applicant applied is not the only one available. A skilled interviewer will know about other vacancies in the firm and may be able to steer the prospective employee to another position. For instance, an applicant may obviously be unqualified to fill the advertised position of senior programming analyst but be well qualified to work as a computer operator. This type of interviewing not only builds goodwill for the firm but also can maximize recruitment and selection effectiveness.

REVIEW OF APPLICATIONS AND RESUMES

Another early step in the selection process may involve having the prospective employee complete an application for employment. The employer then evaluates it to see whether there is an apparent match between the individual and the position. A well-designed and properly used application form can be a real time-saver because essential information is included and presented in a standardized format. For these reasons, an application form can be used more effectively than resumes to reduce dozens of applicants to a few bona fide candidates.

The specific type of information requested on an application for employment may vary from firm to firm, and even by job type within an organization. An application form typically contains sections for name, address, telephone number, military service, education, and work history. Preprinted statements that are very important when the applicant signs the form include certification that everything on the form is true, and if not, the candidate can be released. When not prohibited by state law, the form should also state that the position is employment at will, and that the employer or the employee can terminate employment at any time for any reason or no reason. Finally, the form should contain a statement whereby the candidate gives permission to check the references.[7]

An employment application form must reflect not only the firm's informational needs but also EEO requirements. Yet, one recent study of 151 Fortune 500 firms found that more than 98 percent of the forms contained either items not necessary for personnel decisions or questionable with respect to Title VII. Another study of fifty national U.S. companies determined that forty-eight out of fifty forms contained inappropriate items. The most common problems related to questions about arrest records, physical handicaps, military background, and education.[8]

An example of a properly designed application form is provided in Figure 7-2. Potentially discriminatory questions inquiring about such factors as gender, race, age, and number of children living at home do not appear on the form.

The information contained in a completed application for employment is compared to the job description to determine whether a potential match exists between the firm's requirements and the applicant's qualifications. As you might expect, this comparison is often difficult. Applicants frequently attempt to present themselves in an exaggerated, somewhat unrealistic light. Comparing past duties and responsibilities with those needed for the job the applicant is seeking is not always easy.

Some companies now have terminals in their lobbies on which applicants can complete a job application form. A few human resource departments are setting up optical scanning programs that can handle the first-level screening of applications. These programs may also scan applications for other jobs that the applicants do not know they are qualified to fill. This comprehensive approach is not only more objective but also less expensive.[9]

Employment Application

An Equal Opportunity Employer

For use in Connecticut

It is the policy of the General Electric Comany to recruit, hire, train, compensate, promote and provide other conditions of employment without regard to a person's race, color, religion, national origin, sex, sexual orientation, age, disability, veteran status or other characteristic protected by law.

Print
Name ______ (Last) (First) (Middle) Date of Application ______
Address ______ (Number and Street)
______ (City) (State) (Zip Code)
Telephone ______ (Area Code/Number) Social Security No. ______

Job Interest

Position Desired ______
Wages or Salary Expected $ ______ Per Hr. ☐ Week ☐ Month ☐ (Please Check One)
Other Positions for Which You Are Qualified ______
Date Available for Employment ______ Were You Ever Employed by GE? Yes ☐ No ☐
If Yes, Where? ______ Dates ______ (From) (To)

Education and Training

Circle Highest Grade Completed in Each School Category

Grade School	High School	Tech School	College	Grad School
1 2 3 4 5 6 7 8	9 10 11 12	1 2	1 2 3 4	1 2 3 4

	Name	Location	Course/Degree	Class Standing
Grade School				
High School				
College				
Graduate School				

Apprentice, Business, Technical, Military or Vocational School ______
Other Training or Skills (Factory or Office Machines Operated, Special Courses, Military Training, etc.) ______

Other Job-Related Activities

List professional, trade, business or civic activities and offices held ______

FF-75C (8/93) Page 1 Please Turn Page

Employment History

Please read carefully before starting. List all employment starting with the **present** or **most recent** employer. Account for all periods, including unemployment and **service with the Armed Forces**. Also include relevant voluntary and/or part-time work experience. **Attach a copy of your resume to provide additional information.**

	Dates	Hourly Rate/Salary
Employer	From (Month) (Year)	Starting $ per
Address	To (Month) (Year)	Final $ per
	Describe Major Duties	
Job Title		
Department		
Supervisor	Reason for Leaving	

	Dates	Hourly Rate/Salary
Employer	From (Month) (Year)	Starting $ per
Address	To (Month) (Year)	Final $ per
	Describe Major Duties	
Job Title		
Department		
Supervisor	Reason for Leaving	

	Dates	Hourly Rate/Salary
Employer	From (Month) (Year)	Starting $ per
Address	To (Month) (Year)	Final $ per
	Describe Major Duties	
Job Title		
Department		
Supervisor	Reason for Leaving	

	Dates	Hourly Rate/Salary
Employer	From (Month) (Year)	Starting $ per
Address	To (Month) (Year)	Final $ per
	Describe Major Duties	
Job Title		
Department		
Supervisor	Reason for Leaving	

Interviewer's Comments:

Interviewed by: ______ Date: ______

Page 2 Continue on next page

FIGURE 7-2 An Application for Employment

Source: General Electric Company.

Personal Data

Print
Name ______________________________
Last First Middle

Address ______________________________
Number and Street

____
City State Zip Code

Telephone ______________ Social Security No. ______________
Area Code/Number

Is Your Age Under 18? .... Yes ☐ No ☐ (Please Check One)

Are You a Citizen of USA, Permanent Resident or Otherwise Legally Authorized to Work in the U.S.? Yes ☐ No ☐ (Please Check One)

Military

Were you in the U.S. Armed Forces? .... Yes ☐ No ☐ (Please Check One)

If yes, what branch? ______________

Date Entered ______________ Date of Discharge ______________

Final Rank ______________ Type of Discharge ______________

Military experience should have been included in Employment History section on Page 2

Convictions

Have you ever been convicted of a felony? .... Yes ☐ No ☐ (Please Check One)

Have you been convicted of a misdemeanor committed within the past five years, or were you imprisoned for a misdemeanor which occurred more than five years ago? .... Yes ☐ No ☐ (Please Check One)

If **Yes** to either of the above questions, please explain fully. **This information will not necessarily bar an applicant from employment.**

____

____

____

Additional Information

State any additional information you feel may be helpful to us in considering your application: ______________

____

____

____

____

____

____

Page 3

Please Turn Page

Employment Eligibility

The Immigration Reform and Control Act of 1986 prohibits the employment of unauthorized aliens, and employers are required to verify the employment eligibility of all new employees. An offer of employment with the Company will be made conditional based on your providing the documentation required by law as evidence of your personal identity and your authorization to work in the United States.

Any offer of employment is also conditioned upon the successful completion of a physical examination, which includes a drug screen.

Your Personal Commitment to Integrity

As a condition of employment, each new employee must sign a form acknowledging that all employees are required to comply with GE Policies and to report any concerns about possible violations.

Affirmative Action

Employment Notice to Special Disabled Veterans, Vietnam Era Veterans and Individuals with Physical or Mental Disabilities:

Government contractors are subject to Section 402 of the Vietnam Era Veterans Readjustment Act of 1974 which requires that they take affirmative action to employ and advance in employment qualified special disabled veterans and veterans of the Vietnam Era, and Section 503 of the Rehabilitation Act of 1973, as amended, which requires government contractors to take affirmative action to employ and advance in employment qualified individuals with disabilities.

Please check below if the description applies and the box to the right if you wish to be considered under the Affirmative Action Plan (AAP).

I am a	***And wish consideration under the AAP:***
☐ ***Vietnam Era Veteran*** *(An eligible veteran any part of whose active military, naval or air service was during the Vietnam Era.)*	☐
☐ ***Special Disabled Veteran*** *(A) A veteran who is entitled to compensation (or who, but for the receipt of military retired pay, would be entitled to compensation) under laws administered by the Department of Veterans' Affairs for a disability (i) rated at 30% or more, or (ii) rated at 10% or 20% in the case of a veteran who has been determined under Section 1506 of Title 38, U.S.C. to have a serious employment handicap;* ***or*** *(B) a person who was discharged or released from active duty because of a service connected disability.)*	☐
☐ ***Disabled Individual***	☐

Your response is voluntary and confidential and the information will be used only in accord with the laws above.

Employee Release and Privacy Statement *Please read this carefully before signing:*

I understand that the General Electric Company requires certain information about me to evaluate my qualifications for employment and to conduct its business if I become an employee. Therefore, I authorize the Company to investigate my past employment, educational credentials and other employee-related information. I agree to cooperate in such investigations, and release those parties supplying such information to the Company from all liability or responsibility with respect to information supplied.

I agree that the Company may use the information it obtains concerning me in the conduct of its business. I understand that such use may include disclosure outside the Company in those cases where its agents and contractors need such information to perform their functions, where the Company's legal interests and/or obligations are involved, or where there is a medical emergency involving me. I understand, however, that the company intends to protect the confidentiality of personal information it obtains concerning me. Consequently, personal information in Company record keeping systems, other than the fact and location of past or present Company employment, the dates of employment, or the job name or description of general duties, will not otherwise be disclosed outside the Company with a personal identifier without my consent. Further, the Company will require its agents and contractors to safeguard information disclosed to them by the Company.

I understand that any employment with the Company would not be for any fixed period of time and that, if employed, I may resign at any time for any reason or the Company may terminate my employment at any time for any reason in the absence of a specific written agreement to the contrary.

I understand that any false answers or statements made by me on this application or any supplement thereto or in connection with the above-mentioned investigations will be sufficient grounds for immediate discharge, if I am employed.

Applicant's Signature ______________ ***Date:*** ______________

Page 4

FIGURE 7-2 (continued) An Application for Employment

A **resume** is a common method applicants use to present background information. Even when resumes are not required by prospective employers, they are frequently submitted by job seekers. While there are no hard and fast rules for designing resumes, there are some general guidelines to follow depending upon the type and level of position sought. An example of a resume submitted by a recent college graduate for a position in a public accounting firm is shown in Figure 7-3. As you can see in this example, there is much *white space*, which makes it easier to read. The current and permanent ad-

FIGURE 7-3
Example of Resume for an Entry-Level Position

Henry Sanchez

Current Address:
1508 Westwood Dr.
New York, NY 20135
914/594-3869

Permanent Address:
4123 Pleasant Ave.
Spokane, WA 85036
509/876-5468

OBJECTIVE:	To obtain an entry-level position in a public accounting firm.
EDUCATION:	University of New York **Master of Business Administration, December 1994** **Bachelor of Science, Business Administration, May 1993** Concentration: Individual and Corporate Tax with emphasis on Management Information Systems GPA: 3.2 / 4.0
HONORS:	Honors in Accounting and Finance Full Academic Scholarship President of Summer Conference Program
ACCOMPLISHMENTS:	Conducted TQM seminars Successfully completed ISO-9002 courses Graduate Assistant to the Dean
EXPERIENCE: *November 1993* *Present*	**ASSISTANT ADMINISTRATOR** Touch of Class Foods Corporation Accounting Department ▪ Responsible for building A/P and A/R ledgers ▪ Originated a Responsive Invoice Program ▪ Prepared Corporate Tax Returns and all Schedules ▪ Oversaw intern program ▪ Initiated ISO-9002 Certifications in all areas of plant production
Summer 1991 *Spring 1992*	**PERSONAL ASSISTANT** Mr. Charles Brandon Park Board of Trustees ▪ Research and Development with City Sewer District ▪ Assisted with general accounting procedures ▪ Assisted with customer related issues ▪ Assisted with the allocation of public funds
COMPUTER SKILLS:	Microsoft Word, AmiPro, Word Perfect 5.1-6.0 Lotus 123, Microsoft Excel, Quadrapro Windows and Windows 95 Applications
AFFILIATIONS:	ISO-9002 Certified Consultant TQM National Association
REFERENCES:	Available upon request

dresses and telephone numbers of the applicant are prominently located. An *objective* statement is written to describe the type of opportunity desired. Since most recent graduates are being hired for their potential value to a firm, education is a vital factor at this stage of their careers, and this is shown next. Work experience, especially internships where students have worked in their degree field, follows and should be shown in reverse chronological order. Prospective employers spend little time reading resumes. Therefore, it is imperative that the document be concise. A typical college graduate's resume should not be longer than a page in length. The resume's appearance must be neat and typographical, and grammatical errors must be avoided. A single slip here can be a killer. If the resume is being prepared in response to an ad or knowledge of a specific job opening, the resume should reflect the skills and abilities of the applicant that apply to the open position. Use of personal computers makes it feasible to tailor resumes for specific purposes. In the few seconds recruiters spend with a resume, they strive to determine the extent to which the applicant's qualifications meet the requirements of the job.

The resume of an experienced professional should differ somewhat from that of a new graduate. For example, in lieu of an objective statement, a summary of several skills related to requirements of the open position is more appropriate. Although education may still be an important factor, the candidate's experience should take priority in the resume and appear next. Rather than focusing on responsibilities in each previously held position, the applicant should emphasize accomplishments. Self-improvement activities, rather than hobbies, should be included. While the recent graduate's resume should be no more than one page, this limitation does not apply to the experienced professional. Conciseness, however, is still a necessity.[10]

ADMINISTRATION OF SELECTION TESTS

Selection tests are often used to assist in assessing an applicant's qualifications and potential for success. The popularity of selection tests declined sharply following enactment of the Civil Rights Act and subsequent court decisions. For instance, in *Griggs v Duke Power Company*, the U.S. Supreme Court ruled that preemployment requirements, including tests, must be related to job performance. In *Albermarle Paper v Moody*, the Supreme Court ruled that any test used in the selection process or in promotion decisions must be validated if its use has had an adverse impact on women or minorities.

By curtailing test usage, some employers apparently felt that they would be immune from legal requirements for valid instruments. Clearly, however, all the tools used in making selection and other employment decisions are subject to the same validity requirements. Although many individuals distrust tests, they may well be the most valid instrument available. Recognition of this—and increased awareness of the interview's vulnerability—has led to a resurgence of test usage in the selection process.

Evidence suggests that the use of tests is widespread—more so in the public sector than in the private sector and in medium-sized and large companies than in small companies. Large organizations are likely to have trained specialists to run their testing programs. While it may be hard to believe, some large firms are even using gene testing to screen out applicants who may be vulnerable to debilitating diseases. While this legally dubious practice is not widespread, it does indicate some firms are keenly aware of the importance of employee selection and for using tests in this process.[11]

Advantages of Selection Tests

Selection testing is reemerging as a selection tool because it is the most reliable and accurate means of selecting candidates from a pool of applicants.[12] An extreme example of the contribution of effective selection tests to productivity was provided years ago by the Philadelphia Police Department. Labor savings in this 5,000 member organization from the use of cognitive ability tests to select officers was estimated to be $18 million for each year's hires.[13]

As with all selection procedures, it is important to identify the essential functions of each job and to determine the skills needed to perform them. Selection tests must be job related and must meet standards as outlined in the EEOC's *Uniform Guidelines on Employee Selection Procedures*.

Disadvantages of Selection Tests

Job performance is related primarily to an individual's ability and motivation to do the job. Selection tests may accurately predict an applicant's ability to perform the job, but they are less successful in indicating the extent to which the individual will want to perform it. For one reason or another, many employees with high potential never seem to reach it. The factors related to success on the job are so numerous and complex that selection may always be more of an art than a science.

Another potential problem, related primarily to personality tests and interest inventories, has to do with applicants' honesty. An applicant may be strongly motivated to respond to questions untruthfully or to provide answers that he or she believes the firm expects. To prevent this occurrence, some tests have built-in lie detection scales.

A common problem is test anxiety. Applicants often become quite anxious when confronting yet another hurdle that might eliminate them from consideration. The test administrator's reassuring manner and a well-organized testing operation should serve to reduce this threat. Actually, although a great deal of anxiety is detrimental to test performance, a slight amount is helpful.

The dual problems of hiring unqualified or less qualified candidates and rejecting qualified candidates will continue regardless of the procedures followed. Organizations can minimize such errors through the use of well-developed tests administered by competent professionals. Nevertheless, selection tests rarely, if ever, are perfect predictors. Using even the best test, errors will be made in predicting success. For this reason, tests alone should not be used in the selection process but rather in conjunction with other tools.

Characteristics of Properly Designed Selection Tests

Properly designed selection tests are standardized, objective, based on sound norms, reliable, and—of utmost importance—valid. We discuss the application of these concepts next.

Standardization. **Standardization** refers to the uniformity of the procedures and conditions related to administering tests. In order to compare the performance of several applicants on the same test, it is necessary for all to take the test under conditions that are as close to identical as possible. For example, the content of instructions provided and the time allowed must be the same, and the physical environment must be similar. If one person takes a test in a noisy room and another takes it in a quiet environment, differences in test results are likely. Differences in conditions may affect an applicant's performance. Even though test administration procedures may be specified by a test's developers, test administrators are responsible for ensuring standardized conditions.

Objectivity. **Objectivity** in testing is achieved when everyone scoring a test obtains the same results. Multiple-choice and true-false tests are said to be objective. The person taking the test either chooses the correct answer or does not. Scoring these tests is a highly mechanical process, which lends itself to machine grading.

Norms. A **norm** provides a frame of reference for comparing an applicant's performance with that of others. Specifically, a norm reflects the distribution of many scores obtained by people similar to the applicant being tested. The scores will tend to be distributed according to the normal probability curve presented in Figure 7-4. Standard deviations measure the amount of dispersion of the data. A normalized test will have approximately 68.3 percent of the scores within ±1 standard deviation from the mean. Individuals scoring in this range would be considered average. Individuals achieving scores outside the range of ±2 standard deviations would probably be highly unsuccessful or highly successful, based on the particular criteria used.

When a sufficient number of employees are performing the same or similar work, employers can standardize their own tests. Typically, this is not the case, and a national norm for a particular test must be used. A prospective employee takes the test, the score obtained is compared to the norm, and the significance of the test score is determined.

Reliability. **Reliability** is the extent to which a selection test provides consistent results. Reliability data reveal the degree of confidence that can be placed in a test. If a test has low reliability, its validity as a predictor will also be low. But the existence of reliability does not in itself guarantee validity.

To ensure its usefulness, the test's reliability must be verified. The **test-retest method** is a way of determining selection test reliability by giving the test twice to the same group of individuals and correlating the two sets of scores. A perfect positive correlation is +1.0. The closer the reliability coefficient is to perfection, the more consistent the results and the more reliable the test. Problems with this method for determining reliability include the cost of administering the test twice, employees recalling test questions, and the learning that may take place between tests.

Similar to the test-retest method, the **equivalent forms method** tests reliability by correlating the results of tests that are similar but not identical. This approach overcomes some of the difficulties encountered with the test-

FIGURE 7-4
A Normal Probability Curve

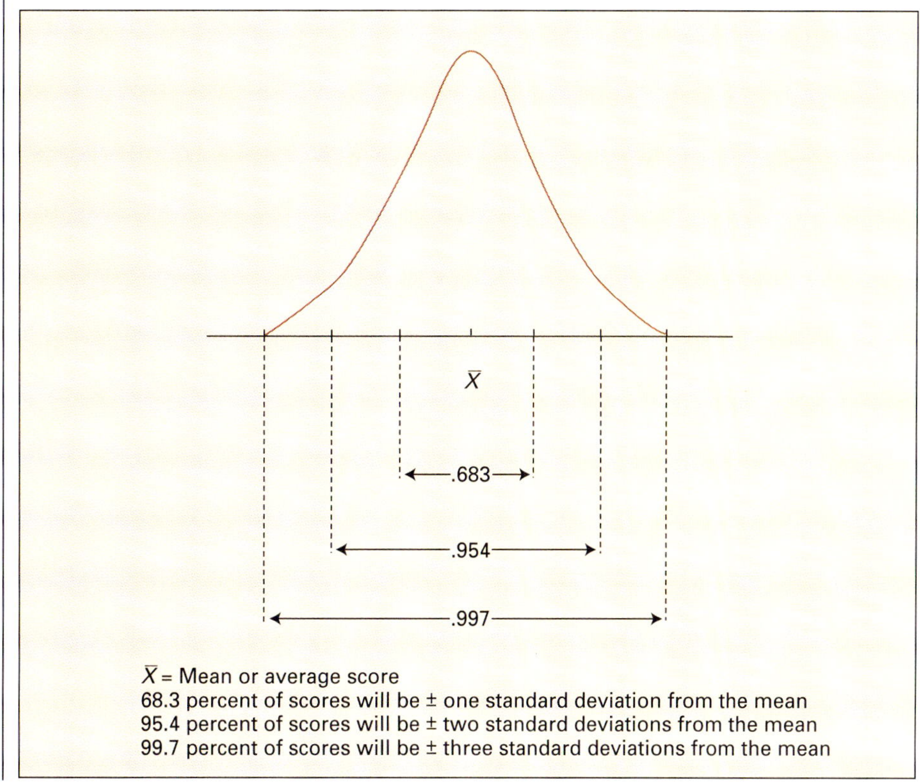

retest method, but developing two forms of a test can be expensive. To overcome this weakness somewhat, the split-halves method may be used. The **split-halves method** tests reliability by dividing the results of a test into two parts and then correlating the results of the two parts. The onetime administration of the test has the obvious advantage of minimizing costs. Also, there is no opportunity for learning or recall, which would distort the second score.

Validity. The basic requirement for a selection test is that it be valid. **Validity** is the extent to which a test measures what it purports to measure. If a test cannot indicate ability to perform the job, it has no value as a predictor. For this reason, validity has always been a proper concern of organizations that use tests. Because our society is committed to equal employment opportunity, greater emphasis has been given in recent years to the validation process.

Validity is commonly reported as a correlation coefficient, which summarizes the relationship between two variables. For example, these variables may be the score on a selection test and some measure of employee performance. A coefficient of 0 shows no relationship, while coefficients of either +1.0 or –1.0 indicate a perfect relationship, one positive and the other negative. Naturally, no test will be 100 percent accurate, yet organizations strive for the highest feasible coefficient. The cumulative body of previous research indicates that tests yield correlation coefficients of from .30 to .60, depending upon the test and the position.[14] If a test is designed to predict job performance, and validity studies of the test indicate a high correlation coefficient, most prospective employees who score high on the test will probably later prove to be high performers. As previously stated, the ability to select better qualified individuals will help increase the firm's productivity.

Employers are not required to validate their selection tests automatically. Generally speaking, validation is required only when the selection process as a whole results in an adverse impact on women or minorities. Validation of selection tests is expensive. However, an organization cannot know whether the test is actually measuring the qualities and abilities being sought without validation.

TYPES OF VALIDATION STUDIES

The *Uniform Guidelines* established three approaches that may be followed to validate selection tests: criterion-related validity, content validity, and construct validity.

Criterion-Related Validity

Criterion-related validity is determined by comparing the scores on selection tests to some aspect of job performance as determined, for example, by performance appraisal. Performance measures might include quantity and quality of work, turnover, and absenteeism. A close relationship between the score on the test and job performance suggests the test is valid.

There are two basic forms of criterion-related validity: concurrent and predictive validity. With **concurrent validity**, the test scores and the criterion data are obtained at essentially the same time. For instance, all currently employed telemarketers may be given a test. Company records contain current information about each employee's job performance. If the test is able to identify productive and less productive workers, one could say that it is valid. A potential problem in using this validation procedure results from changes that may have occurred within the work group. For example, the less productive workers may have been fired, and the more productive employees may have been promoted out of the group.

Predictive validity involves administering a test and later obtaining the criterion information. For instance, a test might be administered to all applicants but test results are not used in the selection decision; employees would be hired on the basis of other selection criteria. After employee performance has been observed over a period of time, the test results are analyzed to determine whether they differentiate the successful and less successful employees. Predictive validity is considered to be a technically sound procedure. However, because of the time and cost involved, its use is often not feasible.

Content Validity

Although statistical concepts are not involved, many human resource practitioners believe that content validity provides a sensible approach to validating a selection test. **Content validity** is a test validation method whereby a person performs certain tasks that are actually required by the job or completes a paper and pencil test that measures relevant job knowledge. Thorough job analysis and carefully prepared job descriptions are needed when this form of validation is used.

The classic example of the use of content validity is giving a typing test to an applicant whose primary job would be to type. In *Washington v Davis*, the U.S. Supreme Court supported content validity.

Construct Validity

Construct validity is a test validation method that determines whether a test measures certain traits or qualities that are important in performing the job. For instance, if the job requires a high degree of teamwork, as is increasingly the case in TQM-oriented firms, a test would be used to measure the applicant's ability to work effectively in teams. Traits or qualities such as teamwork, leadership, and planning or organization ability must first be carefully identified through job analysis.

CUTOFF SCORES

After a test has been shown to be valid, an appropriate cutoff score must be established. A **cutoff score** is the score below which an applicant will not be selected. Cutoff scores will vary over time because they are directly related to the selection ratio. The more individuals applying for a job, the more selective the firm can be and, therefore, the higher the cutoff scores can be. Cutoff scores should normally be set to reflect a reasonable expectation of acceptable proficiency.

An example of what would likely occur if a validated test was administered to prospective employees is shown in Figure 7-5. The firm's experience indicates that individuals who score 40 and above on the test will be successful. Those who score below 40 will be less successful. Note that test results do not precisely predict performance. A small number of individuals who scored below the cutoff score of 40 proved to be good workers. Also, some applicants scoring above 40 proved to be less successful. However, the test appears to be a reasonably good predictor of success. It is because of this gray area that test results should serve as only one of several criteria in the selection

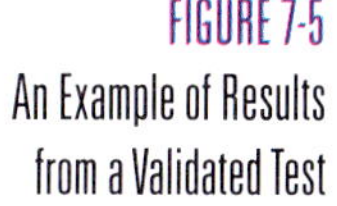
FIGURE 7-5
An Example of Results from a Validated Test

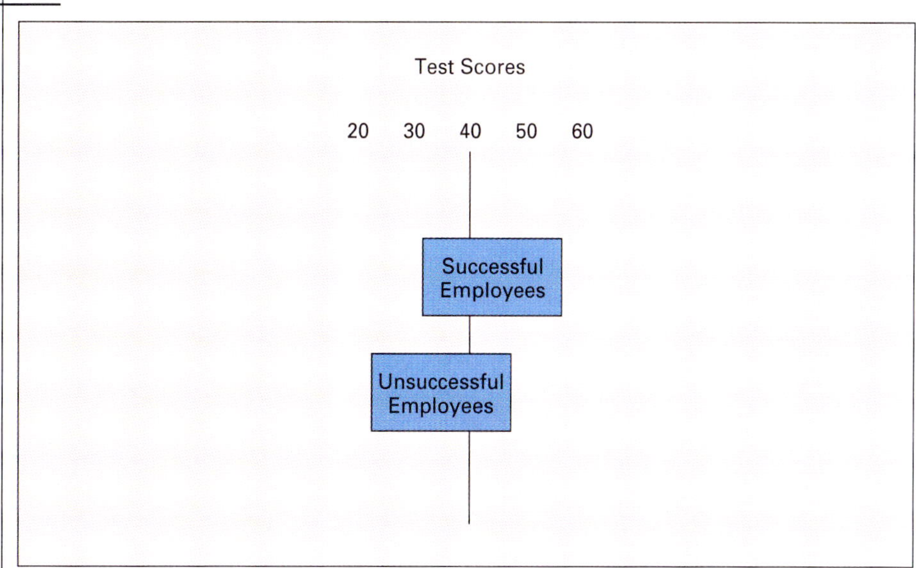

decision. The setting of a cutoff score to determine who will be screened out may have an adverse impact. If so, the *Uniform Guidelines* require an employer to justify the initial cutoff score used.

TYPES OF EMPLOYMENT TESTS

Individuals differ in characteristics related to job performance. These differences, which are measurable, relate to cognitive abilities, psychomotor abilities, job knowledge, work samples, vocational interests, personality, drugs, and AIDS. We discuss tests to measure these differences next.

Cognitive Aptitude Tests

Cognitive aptitude tests measure an individual's ability to learn, as well as to perform a job. This type of test is particularly appropriate for making a selection from a group of inexperienced candidates. Job-related abilities may be classified as verbal, numerical, perceptual speed, spatial, and reasoning.

Psychomotor Abilities Tests

Psychomotor abilities tests measure strength, coordination, and dexterity. The development of tests to determine these abilities has been accelerated by miniaturization in assembly operations. Much of this work is so delicate that magnifying lenses must be used, and the psychomotor abilities required to perform the tasks are critical. While standardized tests are not available to cover all these abilities, it is feasible to measure those that are involved in many routine production jobs and some office jobs. **Finger dexterity** is the ability to make precise, coordinated finger movements, such as those performed by an electronics assembler or a watchmaker. **Manual dexterity** involves the coordinated movements of both hands and arms, such as those required by large assembly jobs. **Wrist-finger speed** is the ability to make rapid wrist and finger movements, such as those required in inspector-packer and assembly operation jobs. **Aiming** is the ability to move the hands quickly and accurately from one spot to another, which is important in such jobs as electronics parts assembly.

Job Knowledge Tests

Job knowledge tests are designed to measure a candidate's knowledge of the duties of the position for which he or she is applying. Such tests are commercially available but may also be designed specifically for any job, based on the data derived from job analysis. While such tests frequently involve written responses, they may be administered orally. Regardless of the form, they contain key questions that serve to distinguish experienced, skilled workers from those with less experience or skill.

Job knowledge tests, based on job analysis information, must be designed specifically for unique jobs. When in-house specialists are not available, consultants are often utilized to design the tests.

Work-Sample Tests

Work-sample tests require an applicant to perform a task or set of tasks representative of the job. The evidence to date concerning these tests is that they produce high predictive validities, reduce adverse impact, and are more acceptable to applicants. Work sample tests are by definition job related, but they do present some problems. For example, heavy equipment may not easily be moved to a testing site, untrained applicants may injure themselves or damage expensive equipment, and the economy of group testing is not always feasible.

Vocational Interest Tests

Vocational interest tests indicate the occupation in which a person is most interested and is most likely to receive satisfaction from. These tests compare the individual's interests with those of successful employees in a specific job.

Interests appear to be stable over a long period of time and have been related to success in some fields. However, interests must not be confused with aptitudes or abilities. Tests for these characteristics should accompany the administration of an interest test. Moreover, answers to interest test questions can easily be faked. Although interest tests may possibly have some application in employee selection, their primary use has been in counseling and vocational guidance.

Personality Tests

As selection tools, personality tests have not been as useful as other types of tests. They are often characterized by low reliability and low validity. Because some personality tests emphasize subjective interpretation, the services of a qualified psychologist are required to administer them.

Drug Testing

Few issues generate more controversy today than drug testing. Proponents of drug testing programs contend that it is necessary to ensure workplace safety, security, and productivity. It is also viewed as an accurate measure of drug use and a means to deter it. Critics of drug testing argue just as vigorously that drug testing is an unjustifiable intrusion into private lives.[15]

While the controversy remains, along with legal questions, it appears that drug testing in the United States is alive and well. A recent survey of Fortune 500 companies found that 88 percent of the responding firms currently conduct drug testing of applicants as a condition of employment. Of the companies that did not conduct such tests, 80 percent indicate that they have plans to do so.[16] Two large drug testing companies estimate that 15 million Americans, or 13 percent of the workforce, are being required to give urine samples for annual testing. Between 5 and 8 percent of those tested by these firms are found to have drugs in their system. Of those testing positive, 40 to 50 percent have been using marijuana, 20 to 25 percent cocaine, and about 10 percent opiates, mainly codeine.[17]

In addition to concerns about privacy, some employers may worry that applicants denied employment may seek protection as a person with a disability under the Americans with Disabilities Act. The act, however, is actually supportive of testing when it is carefully performed. Persons engaging in the illegal use of drugs are excluded from the act's definition of the term *qualified individual with a disability*.[18] It is important to note, however, that persons who have successfully completed or who are participating in a supervised drug-rehabilitation program and who no longer engage in illegal drug use are not automatically excluded from this definition.[19]

Testing for Acquired Immune Deficiency Syndrome (AIDS)

Individuals with AIDS and those who test positive for the HIV virus are protected by both the Vocational Rehabilitation Act and the Americans with Disabilities Act. It is not common practice to test for these conditions unless the nature of the work creates a high potential for employee exposure to infected coworkers. Health care institutions, for example, may be able to show the business necessity for using this selection tool. We discuss AIDS further in Chapter 14.

THE EMPLOYMENT INTERVIEW

The **employment interview** is a goal-oriented conversation in which the interviewer and applicant exchange information. Historically, interviews have not been shown to be valid predictors of success on the job. Most interviews have correlation coefficients in the 0.00 to 0.30 range.[20] Nevertheless, they continue to be the primary method used to evaluate applicants, and they are utilized by virtually every company in the United States. As we discuss later in the chapter, progress has been made by some firms to improve the validity of interviews.

The employment interview is especially significant because the applicants who reach this stage are considered to be the most promising candidates. They have survived the preliminary interview and scored satisfactorily on selection tests. At this point, the candidates appear to be qualified, at least on paper. Every seasoned manager knows, however, that appearances can be quite misleading. Additional information is needed to indicate whether the individual is willing to work and can adapt to that particular organization.

Legal Implications of Interviewing

For a number of years following the enactment of the Civil Rights Act, many employers stopped using tests and relied even more heavily on the employ-

The interview helps to determine whether the individual is willing to work and can adapt to that particular organization.

ment interview as a selection tool. This change in practice was based on the false assumption that legal validity requirements applied only to tests. But the definition of a test in the *Uniform Guidelines* included "physical, education and work experience requirements from informal or casual interviews." Since the interview is clearly a test, it is subject to the same validity requirements as any other step in the selection process, should adverse impact be shown. For the interview, this constraint presents special difficulties. To begin with, few firms are willing to pay the cost of validating interviews. They can be validated only by a long-term follow-up—a method that requires collecting much data over a long period of time. However, significant evidence indicates that if two managers in a firm interview the same applicant at different times, the outcomes will differ. In fact, the interview is perhaps more vulnerable to charges of discrimination than any other tool used in the selection process. In most cases, there is little or no documentation of the questions asked or the answers received. The interviewer may tend to ask irrelevant questions that would never appear on an application form. Some interviewers are inclined to ask questions that are not job related and that reflect their personal biases. They probably reason that this practice wiil go uncriticized because there is no written or verbal record of the interview. Nevertheless, interviewing in this manner is risky and can lead to charges of discrimination. Since an interview is a test, all questions should be job related.

Interviewer Objectives of the Interview

The interviewer needs to achieve several basic objectives during the employment interview. It is important that at least the following objectives be successfully attained.

Create an Appropriate Environment. The interviewer should quickly establish rapport with the applicant. It is essential that the interviewer obtain accurate information from the candidate. Honest communication is more likely to take place in a climate of mutual trust and confidence.

Obtain Behavioral, Job-Related Information from the Applicant. The interview is a valuable method for obtaining additional job-related information about the applicant to complement the data provided by other selection tools. The interview permits clarification of certain points, the uncovering of additional information, and the elaboration of data needed to make a sound selection decision.

Provide Information About the Job and the Company. General information about the job, company policies, its products, and its services should be communicated to the applicant during the interview. This information should be presented in a realistic manner, not through rose-colored glasses.

Determining the Next Step. After the interview is concluded, the interviewer must determine whether the candidate is suitable for the open position. If the conclusion is positive, the process continues; if there appears to be no match, the candidate is eliminated from consideration.

Interviewee Objectives of the Interview

It is important to remember that interviewees also have objectives of the interview. These may be summarized as follows:[21]

- to be listened to and understood
- to have ample opportunity to present their qualifications
- to be treated fairly and with respect
- to gather information about the job and the company
- to make an informed decision concerning the desirability of the job

Content of the Interview

The specific content of employment interviews varies greatly by organization and the level of the job. However, the following general topics appear fairly consistently in employment interviews: technical competence (often revealed through academic achievement and occupational experience), personal qualities (such as interpersonal skills), and potential, which includes the candidate's career orientation.

Academic Achievement. In the absence of significant work experience, a person's academic background takes on greater importance. It should not be accepted at face value, however. The interviewer should try to discover any underlying factors related to academic performance. For example, a student who earned only a 2.28/4.0 GPA may turn out to be a very bright individual who, because of financial difficulties, might have worked virtually full time while still participating in a variety of activities. On the other hand, in different circumstances, a student who received a 3.8/4.0 GPA may not be a strong candidate for the position.

Occupational Experience. Exploring an individual's occupational experience requires determining the applicant's skills, abilities, and willingness to handle responsibility. Job titles in one organization may not reflect the same job content in another. Successful performance in one job does not guarantee success in another. At the same time, past performance does provide an indication of the employee's ability and willingness to work.

Personal Qualities. Personal qualities normally observed during the interview include physical appearance, speaking ability, vocabulary, poise, adaptability, and assertiveness. Even though he or she may have personal preferences, the interviewer must make every effort to keep nonjob-related personal biases out of the selection process.

Because of the legal ramifications, it is unwise to permit the applicant's personal characteristics to influence the selection decision, unless they are BFOQs. Physical appearance, for example, would likely be an occupational qualification if the job being filled is that of an actress who is to portray the early career of Julia Roberts. Speaking ability, vocabulary, and poise may be job-related qualifications if the job is that of a sportscaster. Assertiveness may be required for the successful performance of a credit collector's job.

Interpersonal Skills. To a degree, the interview may permit observing an applicant's interpersonal skills. However, the interviewer may be merely witnessing an Academy Award performance. Studies have indicated that candidates are often hired on the basis of their interviewing skills rather than their ability to perform the job. For this reason, the interviewer may need to ask questions regarding the applicant's interpersonal relationships with people in other social and civic situations. Most jobs are not performed in isolation and the need to interact is often essential. In fact, most failures in the workplace are not due to lack of technical ability, but rather to shortcomings in interpersonal competence. An individual may be a highly skilled worker. However, if he or she cannot work well with other employees, chances for success are slim. This is especially true in today's world with increasing emphasis being placed on the use of teams.

Career Orientation. Questions about a candidate's career objectives may help the interviewer determine whether the applicant's aspirations are realistic. The odds are rather great that a recent college graduate who expects to become a senior vice president within six months will become quickly dissatisfied.

In addition to determining an applicant's career goals, the interviewer should present an honest and accurate description of career prospects in the organization. Deception may well prove counterproductive if the applicant is hired and later becomes dissatisfied as the truth unfolds. The firm may lose a substantial investment in the form of recruitment, selection, and training.

Types of Interviews

Interviews may be classified as highly structured at one extreme and as having virtually no structure at the other. Since the interview is a test and must be shown to be valid if adverse impact is proven, structured interviews have emerged as the more legally defensible type. Not considering the legal ramifications, a hiring firm should only want a tool that is helpful in making selection decisions. Historically, interviews have been very poor in this regard. However, it is possible, with a structured interview using job-related questions, to obtain acceptable validity coefficients.

The Unstructured (Nondirective) Interview. In the **unstructured interview**, the interviewer asks probing, open-ended questions. This type of interview is comprehensive, and the interviewer encourages the applicant to do much of the talking. The nondirective interview is often more time-consuming than structured interviews and results in obtaining different information from different candidates. This adds to the potential legal woes of organizations using such an approach. Compounding the problem is the likelihood of ill-advised, potentially discriminatory information being discussed. The applicant who is being encouraged to pour his or her heart out may volunteer information that the interviewer does not need or want to know. Unsuccessful applicants subjected to this interviewing approach may later claim in court that the reason for his or her failure to get the job was based on the employer's use of this information.

The Structured (Directive or Patterned) Interview. The **structured interview** consists of a series of job-related questions that are consistently asked of each applicant for a particular job. Use of structured interviews increases reliability and accuracy by reducing the subjectivity and inconsistency of unstructured interviews.

Interviewers should follow a structured, systematic interview procedure in order to obtain the information necessary to evaluate the candidate fairly and objectively. The advantages of structure are diminished, however, if the interviewer asks each of the questions perfunctorily. This approach could easily result in an overly formal setting and severely impair the candidate's ability or desire to respond.

A structured job interview typically contains four types of questions. **Situational questions** pose a hypothetical job situation to determine what the applicant would do in that situation. **Job knowledge questions** probe the applicant's job-related knowledge; these questions may relate to basic educational skills or complex scientific or managerial skills. **Job-sample simulation questions** involve situations in which an applicant may be actually required to perform a sample task from the job. When this is not feasible, a simulation of critical job aspects may be utilized. Also, answering these types of questions may require physical activity.

Another type of question used in structured interviews deals with worker requirements. **Worker requirements questions** seek to determine the applicant's willingness to conform to the requirements of the job. For example, the interviewer may ask whether the applicant is willing to perform repetitive work or move to another city. The nature of these questions serves as a realistic job preview and may aid in self-selection.

A properly designed and patterned interview will contain only job-related questions. Each question should be asked for a specific purpose.

Behavior Description Interviewing. The **behavior description interview** is a structured interview that uses questions designed to probe the candidate's past behavior in specific situations. It avoids making judgments about applicants' personalities and avoids hypothetical and self-evaluative questions.[22] The situational behaviors are carefully selected for their relevance to job success. Questions are formed from the behaviors by asking applicants how they performed in the described situation. For example, a candidate for an engineering position might be asked, "Tell me about a time when you had to make an important decision without having all the information you needed." Benchmark answers derived from behaviors of successful employees are prepared for use in rating applicant responses.

Questions asked in behavior description interviewing are legally *safe* since they are job related. Equally important, since both questions and answers are related to successful job performance, they are more accurate in predicting whether applicants will be successful for the job they are hired to perform. Validity coefficients for behavior description interviewing have been shown to be several times higher than for traditional interviewing.[23] One caveat, however, is that the *correct* answer for evaluating responses may reflect behavior of the traditional white male employee. Women and minorities may not have the experiences in life that provide similar responses. Individuals from other cultures may experience similar problems. For example, the Japanese culture emphasizes fitting into a group and not sticking out. Being asked to describe how they best demonstrated their management skills in a certain situation could be embarrassing to them.[24]

METHODS OF INTERVIEWING

Interviews may be conducted in several ways. In a typical employment interview, the applicant meets one-on-one with an interviewer. As the interview may be a highly emotional occasion for the applicant, meeting alone with the interviewer is often less threatening.

Unlike a one-on-one interview, in a **group interview** several applicants interact in the presence of one or more company representatives. This approach, while not mutually exclusive of other interview types, may provide useful insights into the candidates' interpersonal competence as they engage in group discussion. Another advantage of this technique is that it saves time for busy professionals and executives.

In a **board interview**, one candidate is interviewed by several representatives of the firm. Although a thorough examination of the applicant is likely, the interviewee's anxiety level is often quite high. A vice president of industrial relations for an aircraft firm stated, "We use a three-person board to screen each applicant, asking a series of questions designed to ferret out the individual's attitudes toward former employers, jobs, etc. Then, a week later, we bring successful applicants and their spouses in for a family-night meeting with top management and their spouses, where we further screen them while discussing the company and employee benefits." Naturally, the amount of time devoted to a board interview will differ depending on the type and level of job.

Most interview sessions are designed to minimize stress on the part of the candidate. However, the **stress interview** intentionally creates anxiety to determine how an applicant will react to stress on the job. The interviewer deliberately makes the candidate uncomfortable by asking blunt and often discourteous questions. The purpose is to determine the applicant's tolerance for stress. Knowledge of this factor may be important if the job requires the ability to deal with a high level of stress. On the other hand, some human resource professionals believe that the stress interview is not only inconsiderate but is also ineffective. Proponents of this view feel that information exchange in a stressful environment is often distorted and misinterpreted. These critics maintain that the data obtained are not the type of information upon which to base a selection decision. In any event, it seems clear that the stress interview is not appropriate for the majority of situations.

Interview Planning

Interview planning is essential to effective employment interviews. The physical location of the interview should be both pleasant and private, providing for a minimum of interruptions. The interviewer should become familiar with the applicant's record by reviewing the data collected from other selection tools. In preparing for the interview, a job profile should be developed based on the job description. After job requirements have been listed, it is helpful to have an interview checklist that includes these hints:

- Compare an applicant's application and resume with the job requirements.
- Develop questions related to the qualities sought.
- Prepare a step-by-step scenario of how to present the position, company, division, and department.
- Determine how to ask for examples of past applicant behavior, not what future behavior might be.[25]

The Interviewer and the Interview Process

The interviewer should possess a pleasant personality, empathy, and the ability to listen and communicate effectively. He or she should have a through knowledge of the requirements for the job being filled and the applicant's qualifications as they relate to the job. In order to elicit needed information, the interviewer must create a climate that encourages the applicant to speak freely. However, the conversation should not become too casual. While engaging in friendly chitchat with candidates might be pleasant, in our litigious society, it may be the most dangerous thing an interviewer can do.

When the office manager at a Midwestern newspaper made friendly inquiries about a job applicant's children, he thought he was merely breaking the ice and setting the tone for an effective dialogue. A year later, however, he was the target of a lawsuit filed by the applicant who had not been selected. The applicant claimed to have been the victim of sexual discrimination because she had told the manager she had need of a day care facility when she went to work. She claimed that a man would not have been asked questions about his children.

To minimize the chances of lawsuits, employers should use structured interviews and ask the same questions of all applicants. It is also critical to record the applicant's responses. If a candidate begins volunteering personal information that is not job related, the interviewer should steer the conversation back on course. It might do well to begin the interview by tactfully stating, "This selection decision will be based strictly on qualifications. Let's not discuss topics such as religion, social activities, national origin, gender, or family situations. We are definitely interested in you, personally. However, these factors are not job related and will not be considered in our decision."[26] Table 7-2 shows potential problems that can threaten the success of employment interviews. These problems can be circumvented by a competent interviewer using a properly planned, structured interview format.

When the interviewer has obtained the necessary information and answered the applicant's questions, the interview should be concluded. At this point, the interviewer should tell the applicant that he or she will receive notification of the selection decision shortly. When this promise is broken, a positive relationship between the applicant and the organization may be destroyed.

TABLE 7-2
Potential Interviewing Problems

Inappropriate Questions

While there are no illegal questions, many are clearly inappropriate. When asked, the responses generated create a legal liability for the employer. The most basic interviewing rule is: "Ask only job-related questions!"

Premature Judgments

Research suggests that interviewers often make judgments about candidates in the first few minutes of the interview. When this occurs, a great deal of potentially valuable information is not considered.

Interviewer Domination

In successful interviews, relevant information must flow both ways. Therefore, interviewers must learn to be good listeners as well as suppliers of information.

Inconsistent Questions

If interviewers ask applicants essentially the same questions and in the same sequence, all the applicants are judged on the same basis. This enables better decisions to be made while decreasing the likelihood of discrimination charges.

Central Tendency

When interviewers rate virtually all candidates as average, they fail to differentiate between strong and weak candidates.

Halo Error

When interviewers permit only one or a few personal characteristics to influence their overall impression of candidates, the best applicant may not be selected.

Contrast Effects

An error in judgment may occur when, for example, an interviewer meets with several poorly qualified applicants and then confronts a mediocre candidate. By comparison, the last applicant may appear to be better qualified than he or she actually is.

Interviewer Bias

Interviewers must understand and acknowledge their own prejudices and learn to deal with them. The only valid bias for an interviewer is to favor the best-qualified candidate for the open position.

Lack of Training

When the cost of making poor selection decisions is considered, the expense of training employees in interviewing skills can be easily justified.

Behavior Sample

Even if an interviewer spent a week with an applicant, the sample of behavior might be too small to properly judge the candidate's qualifications. In addition, the candidate's behavior during an interview is seldom typical or natural.

Nonverbal Communication

Interviewers should make a conscious effort to view themselves as applicants do in order to avoid sending inappropriate or unintended nonverbal signals.

Realistic Job Previews[27]

Many applicants have unrealistic expectations about the prospective job and employer. This inaccurate perception, which may have negative consequences, is often encouraged by firms that present themselves in overly attractive terms. Too many interviewers paint false, rosy pictures of the job and company. This practice leads to mismatches of people and positions. The problem is further compounded when candidates also engage in exaggerating their own qualifications.[28] To correct this situation from the employer's side, a realistic job preview should be given to applicants early in the selection process and definitely before a job offer is made.

A **realistic job preview (RJP)** conveys job information to the applicant in an unbiased manner, including both positive and negative factors. An RJP conveys information about tasks the person would perform, behavior expected to *fit into* the organization and company policies and procedures. This approach helps applicants develop a more accurate perception of the job and the firm. Considerable research confirms the effectiveness of RJPs. Although applicants subjected to an RJP tend to accept job offers less often than those who are not, their productivity is virtually the same as candidates selected without one. The important results are that employees experiencing RJPs exhibit lower turnover and greater job satisfaction.[29] A comparison of the results of traditional preview procedures and realistic preview procedures is shown in Figure 7-6. Note that traditional procedures result in low job survival and dissatisfaction, whereas RJPs help to overcome these difficulties.

FIGURE 7-6
Typical Consequences of Job Procedures

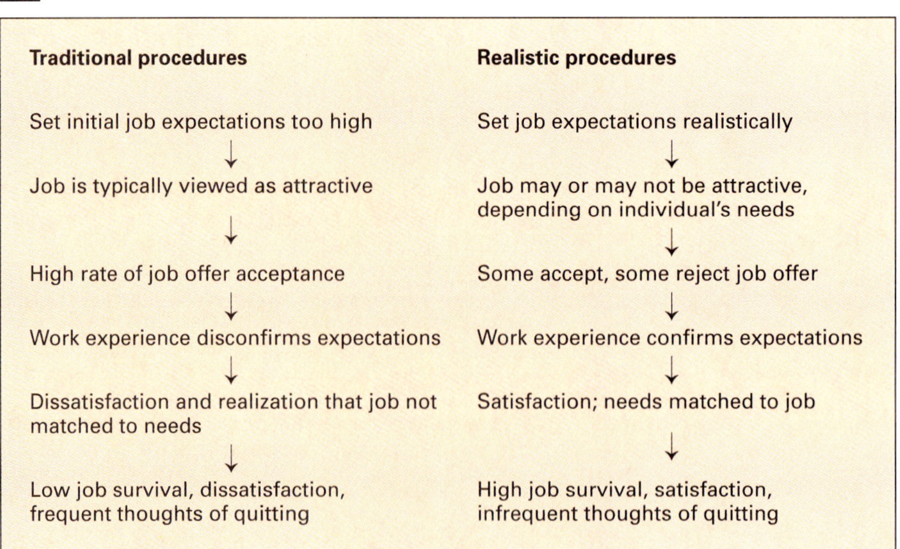

Traditional procedures
Set initial job expectations too high
Job is typically viewed as attractive
High rate of job offer acceptance
Work experience disconfirms expectations
Dissatisfaction and realization that job not matched to needs
Low job survival, dissatisfaction, frequent thoughts of quitting
Realistic procedures
Set job expectations realistically
Job may or may not be attractive, depending on individual's needs
Some accept, some reject job offer
Work experience confirms expectations
Satisfaction; needs matched to job
High job survival, satisfaction, infrequent thoughts of quitting

Source: Reprinted, by permission of the publisher, from "Tell It Like It Is at Realistic Job Previews," by John Wanous, *Personnel* 52 (July-August 1975): 54, © 1975. American Management Association, New York. All rights reserved.

PERSONAL REFERENCE CHECKS

Personal **reference checks** may provide additional insight into the information furnished by the applicant and allow verification of its accuracy. In fact, applicants are often required to submit the names of several references who can provide additional information about them. The basic flaw with this step in the selection process is that virtually every living person can name three or four individuals willing to make favorable statements about him or her. Furthermore, personal references are likely to focus on personal characteristics of the candidate. Objective job-related data are seldom gathered from these sources. For this reason, most organizations place more emphasis on investigations of previous employment.

BACKGROUND INVESTIGATIONS

Background investigations primarily seek data from references supplied by the applicant, including his or her previous employers. The intensity of background investigations depends on the level of responsibility inherent in the position to be filled. The employer faces several potential problems at this stage of the selection process. If a *reasonable* background investigation is not conducted, the employer may be legally liable for negligent hiring, or if the investigation reveals negative information about the applicant, invasion of privacy or defamation charges may be filed. A true *Catch 22* situation is created for employers.[30]

A related problem in obtaining information from previous employers is their general reluctance to reveal such data. The Privacy Act of 1974, although limited to the public sector, provides a major reason for this hesitancy. Employers and employees in the private sector have become very sensitive to the privacy issue. A study conducted by the National Consumers League in 1990 found that about 80 percent of the job seekers stated that the firms they wanted to join intruded into their private lives by asking inappropriate questions.[31] There have been instances in which applicants have sued and won court cases when it was proven that information supplied by previous employers was biased.

There are two schools of thought with regard to supplying information about former employees. One is "Don't tell them anything." The other is "Honesty is the best policy." The more conservative approach typically involves the employer providing only basic data, such as starting and termination dates and last job title. The *honesty* approach is based on the fact that most courts have recognized that you cannot be held liable for defamation of character unless it can be shown that the source intentionally lied about a former employee. Facts honestly given or opinions honestly held constitute a solid legal defense. When former employers are unwilling to give any information about a job applicant, both the potential employer and the applicant are disadvantaged. A red flag is quickly raised when a former employer refuses to talk about a onetime employee.[32]

Regardless of the difficulties encountered in background investigations, employing organizations have no choice but to engage in them. One compelling reason is that credential fraud has increased in recent years. Some 7 to 10 percent of job applicants are not what they present themselves to be. Some applicants are not even who they say they are. They may also exaggerate their skills, education, and experience when given the chance. One firm gave applicants a list of equipment and asked them to identify the items they were qualified to operate. A high percentage of the candidates indicated they could operate equipment that did not exist.[33]

In 1991, a medium-sized Greenville, North Carolina, business firm abruptly lost its controller. Needing to fill the position quickly, the firm hired an individual whose resume indicated he was a CPA, possessed B.A. and M.B.A. degrees, and had experience as a controller with a large firm. This candidate received a recommendation from a person known by an executive of the prospective employer's firm, and he was hired. After a few months, it became obvious that this person could not satisfactorily perform the work, and he was fired. Soon after, the replacement noticed something wrong with the firm's books. It seemed that his predecessor had embezzled $60,000 during the brief period of his employment. He was arrested and confessed to the crime. A quick, although belated, background check revealed no record of his degrees or his CPA credentials.[34]

Every prospect for employment should be asked to sign a comprehensive waiver that grants the employer permission to contact references. Such a waiver releases former employers, business references, and others from liability. The waiver can also authorize checks of court records and the verification of the applicant's educational history and other credentials.[35] To protect itself from charges of discrimination, the Voca Corporation, a $70 million company based in Columbus, Ohio, conducts background investigations only after making a job offer.[36] The results of all reference and background checks should be fully documented.

Small firms may not possess the staff to screen backgrounds of prospective employees thoroughly. Even large organizations may prefer to utilize the specialized services of professional screening firms. An alternative is presented by consultants who may electronically tap into public records, buy computerized records of credit reporting firms, and serve their clients effectively and efficiently. Some background checks may be performed within twenty-four hours for a few dollars per search.[37] Pinkerton Security and Investigation Services screens more than one million job applicants each year for its own operations and for its clients.[38]

Regardless of how they are accomplished, background investigations have become increasingly important in making sound selection decisions and avoiding charges of negligent hiring. The investigations may provide information critical to selection decisions since virtually every qualification an applicant lists can be verified.[39]

NEGLIGENT HIRING AND RETENTION

Negligent hiring has become a critical concern in the selection process. An employer can be held responsible for an employee's unlawful acts if it does not reasonably investigate applicants' backgrounds and then assigns potentially dangerous persons to positions where they can inflict harm. This liability exists for an employer even if the employee's actions are not job related. A firm should not go overboard with the investigation, however, because invasion of privacy is a possibility. Negligent retention, a related potential liability, involves keeping persons on the payroll whose records indicate strong potential for wrongdoing.

Employers are beginning to be held responsible for actions outside the scope of the employees' duties. For example, if an employer hired a manager of an apartment complex without investigating the person's background and the individual later assaulted a tenant, the employer could be held responsible for the action. Employers are required by law to provide employees a safe place to work. This duty has been extended to providing safe employees because the courts have reasoned that a dangerous worker is comparable to a defective machine.

Negligent hiring cases often involve awards in the hundreds of thousands of dollars. In addition, they are likely to be upheld on appeal. The primary consideration in negligent hiring is whether the risk of harm from a dangerous employee was reasonably foreseeable. The nature of the job also has a critical bearing on the employer's obligation. If the job gives employees access to homes or property (as in the case of meter readers, security guards, and exterminators), the hiring firm may be found to have an obligation to make a reasonable investigation into the person's background. Professions that involve an even higher degree of care include landlords, common carriers, workers in hospitals and other patient care facilities, and taxi drivers.[40]

A case in point is a Fort Worth, Texas, cab company. One of its drivers picked up a young mother and her daughters at a bus station and took them to a deserted area, where he raped and robbed the mother. The young woman sued the cab company and won a judgment of $4,500,000 for *negligent hiring*.[41] The Texas Supreme Court determined a reasonable background investigation would have made it quite clear that the cab driver should not have been hired. He had been previously convicted of robbery and forgery and, before that, had been arrested and charged for using a hammer to assault a woman. To avoid cases of this sort, employers should consider the type of interaction employees have with customers. Employers should also make reasonable background investigations and keep written records of the investigations.[42] A hiring organization cannot avoid the possibility of legal action. However, interviewing a minimum of three references is one of the surest ways to avoid a charge of negligent hiring.[43]

POLYGRAPH TESTS

For many years, another means used to verify background information has been the polygraph, or lie detector, test. One purpose of the polygraph was to confirm or refute the information contained in the application blank. However, the Employee Polygraph Protection Act of 1988 severely limited the use of polygraph tests in the private sector. It made it unlawful for any employer engaged in interstate commerce to use a polygraph test. However, the act does not apply to governmental employers, and there are limited exceptions for ongoing investigations and for drug security, drug theft, or drug diversion investigations.

THE SELECTION DECISION

After obtaining and evaluating information about the finalists in a job selection process, the manager must take the most critical step of all: Making the actual hiring decision. The other stages in the selection process have been used to narrow the number of candidates. The final choice will be made from among those still in the running after reference checks, selection tests, background investigations, and interview information have been evaluated. The individual with the best overall qualifications may not be hired. Rather, the person whose qualifications most closely conform to the requirements of the open position should be selected. If an organization is going to invest thousands of dollars to recruit, select, and train an employee, it is important for the manager to hire the most qualified available candidate for the position.

Human resource professionals are heavily involved in all phases leading up to the final employment decision. However, the person who normally makes the final selection is the manager who will be responsible for the performance of the new employee. In making this decision, the operating manager may or may not ask the advice of the human resource manager. The role of HRM in this process is to provide service and counsel to help the operating manager make the selection decision. The rationale for permitting the supervisor to make the final selection is simple: Managers should be allowed to select the individuals for whom they will be responsible.

In certain instances, however, the human resource manager serves in a strong advisory capacity. For example, if the organization is under pressure from the federal government to employ more women and minorities, a recommendation by the human resource manager may carry additional weight.

PHYSICAL EXAMINATION

After the decision has been made to extend a job offer, the next phase of the selection process involves a physical examination for the successful applicant. Typically, a job offer is contingent on the applicant's passing of this examination. The basic purpose of the physical examination is to determine whether an applicant is physically capable of performing the work. For instance, if the work is physically demanding and the examination clearly reveals a condition prohibiting the performance of required tasks, the individual will likely be rejected. In addition, the physical examination information may be used to determine whether certain physical capabilities differentiate successful from less successful employees.

Human resource managers must be aware of the legal liabilities related to physical examinations. The *Uniform Guidelines* state that these examinations should be used to reject applicants only when the results show that job performance would be adversely affected.

The Rehabilitation Act of 1973 and the Americans with Disabilities Act of 1990 do not prohibit employers from requiring physical examinations. However, they have encouraged employers considering hiring covered employees to examine carefully each job's physical requirements. The acts require employers to take affirmative action to hire qualified disabled persons who, with reasonable accommodation, can perform the essential components of a job.

ACCEPTANCE OF JOB APPLICANTS

Assuming that the physical examination fails to uncover any disqualifying medical problems, the applicant can be employed. The starting date normally is based on the wishes of both the firm and the individual. If currently employed by another firm, the individual customarily gives between two and four weeks' notice. Even after this notice, the individual may need some personal time to prepare for the new job. This transition time is particularly important if the new job requires a move

HRM IN ACTION

—FRIENDSHIP?

Julie Thompson, the production manager for Ampex Manufacturing, called her friend, Bill Alexander, in human resources, to ask a favor. "Bill, I have a friend I'd like you to consider for the new sales manager's position. I really like the fellow and would appreciate anything you could do."

"Tell me about the person," said Bill.

"He just graduated from State University with a degree in history, I believe. He has no real work experience, but I am sure he could learn quickly. His parents are real good friends of mine, and I sure would like to help him out."

How would you respond?

to another city. Thus, the amount of time before the individual can join the firm is often considerable—but necessary.

The firm may also want the individual to delay the date of employment. If, for example, the new employee's first assignment upon joining the firm is to attend a training school, the organization may request that the individual delay joining the firm until the school begins. This practice, which would only benefit the company, should not be abused, especially if an undue hardship would be placed on the individual.

REJECTION OF JOB APPLICANTS

Applicants may be rejected during any phase of the selection process. In this section, we focus on the applicants who for various reasons were not offered employment. When someone applies for a position, that person is essentially saying, "I think I am qualified for the job. Why don't you hire me?" Tension builds as the applicant progresses through the selection process. If the preliminary interview shows that the applicant clearly is not qualified, the ego damage is likely to be slight. The company may even be able to steer the individual to other jobs in the firm that better match his or her qualifications.

For most people, the employment interview is not one of the most enjoyable experiences. Taking a test that could affect an individual's career often causes hands to become moist and perspiration to break out on the forehead. Suffering through all this only to be told, "There does not appear to be a proper match between your qualifications and our needs" can be a painful experience. Most firms recognize this fact and attempt to let the individual down as easily as possible. But it is often difficult to tell people that they will not be hired.

When considerable time has been spent on the individual in the selection process, a company representative may sit down with the applicant and explain why another person was offered the job. But, increasingly, time constraints may force the firm to write a rejection letter. However, such a letter can still be personalized. A personal touch will often reduce the stigma of rejection and the chance that the applicant will feel negatively about the company. An impersonal letter is likely to have the opposite effect. The best an organization can do is to make selection decisions objectively. Hopefully, most individuals can, with time, accept the fact that they were not chosen.

STAFFING IN THE MULTINATIONAL ENVIRONMENT

When hiring for the global age, employers have a number of decisions to make. For example, should an expatriate workforce be utilized or should the firm rely on local talent? What qualities in individuals lead to success? In short, what does global talent look like? While there may be no single answer to this question, the characteristics of Mary Beth Robles may provide a clue:

> Mary Beth Robles has an office suite not unlike other American executives. However, the plaques on her wall are written in Portuguese, her coffee cup is filled with black espresso, and the speed dial on her phone lists numbers in Manila and Mexico City in addition to her headquarters in New York. As director of marketing for Colgate-Palmolive Co. in Brazil, the New York native is fluent in English, Spanish, and Portuguese. She also speaks a little French. She has lived in Madrid and Washington, D.C., and her assignments with the company include Mexico, Uruguay, and Atlanta.[44]

Regardless of the nature of their business, organizations need to locate a good *fit* for global operations. Global workers will also become increasingly mobile. They will be recruited, selected, and moved with less regard to national boundaries. At some point in the future, human resources will cross national borders as easily as computer chips and cars.[45]

Global staffing has been called the *Achilles heel of international business.* Inappropriate selections are often made, which negatively affect the multinational operation. Although specific failure rates vary by country and company, an estimated 25 percent of Americans selected for overseas assignments are obvious failures and return home prematurely. Approximately the same number are hidden failures or marginal performers.[46] Some firms have experienced a 60 to 90 percent failure rate in certain countries.[47]

After being carefully selected for the assignment and briefed on the new job and locale, employees based in the United States do business in familiar surroundings. However, the multinational environment is often unfamiliar, and doing business as it has always been done may be ineffective. The tasks of everyday living may also be very different and unnerving. Poor selection, coupled with the stress of living and working overseas, are documented contributors to mental breakdown, alcoholism, and divorce.

There are three primary reasons why U.S. workers sent overseas fail: (1) their families are misjudged, or are not even considered at the time of selection; (2) they are selected because of their domestic track records; or (3) they lack adequate cross-cultural training.[48] To overcome these obstacles, human resource managers should plan carefully to ensure that selectees possess certain basic characteristics. Obviously, they must be technically qualified to do the job. Unfortunately, however, U.S. firms seem to focus their selection efforts on the single criterion *technical competence* at the expense of other criteria. For example, few firms administer tests to determine the relational/cross-cultural/interpersonal skills of their selectees. Other contributing factors also needed are:

- a real desire to work in a foreign country
- spouses and families who have actively encouraged the person to work overseas
- cultural sensitivity and flexibility
- a sense for politics

Several surveys of overseas managers have revealed that the spouse's opinion and attitude should be considered the most important screening factor. Cultural sensitivity is also essential to avoid antagonizing host country nationals unnecessarily.

The selection process should measure and evaluate the candidate's expertise broadly. Psychological tests, stress tests, evaluations by the candidate's superiors, subordinates, peers, and acquaintances, and professional evaluations from licensed psychologists can all aid in ascertaining the candidate's current level of interpersonal and cross-cultural skills. The candidate's spouse and children should undergo modified versions of the selection process since the family members confront slightly different challenges overseas than do employees.

In selecting individuals for overseas assignments, management must recognize that no one style of leadership will be equally effective in all countries. People in various countries have widely divergent backgrounds, education, cultures, and religions—and live within a variety of social conditions and economic and political systems. Employees must consider all these factors because they can have a rather dramatic effect on the working environment of the person selected.

An appropriate management approach for the multinational corporation must be based on common sense and informed conjecture. It seems reasonable that a successful international manager should possess the following qualities, among others:

- a basic knowledge of history, particularly in countries of old and homogeneous cultures
- an understanding of the basic economic and sociological concepts of various countries
- an interest in the host country and a willingness to learn and use its language
- a respect for differing philosophical and ethical approaches to living

Basically, individuals transferred overseas should have a desire to function, as well as possible, in the host country's environment. In addition to employing the most suitable workforce, managers must also assemble a cost-effective workforce. As is indicated from the information in Figure 7-7, the most expensive employee except for those from Belgium is ordinarily a U.S.

FIGURE 7-7

Costs of Employing Local Nationals

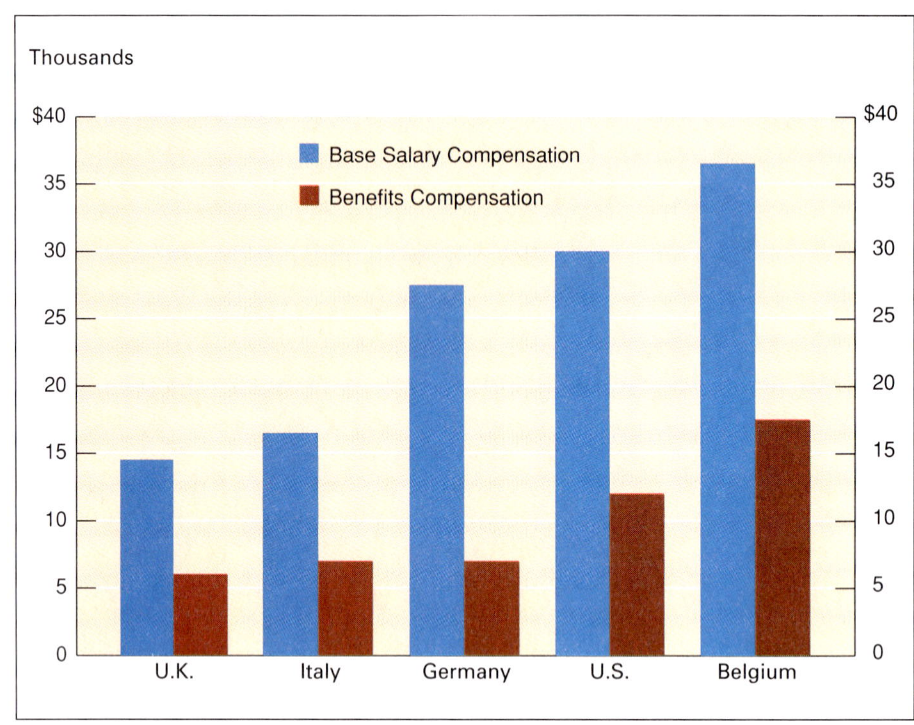

Source: Adapted from Neil B. Krupp, "Overseas Staffing for the New Europe," *Personnel* 67 (July 1990): 23. Reprinted, by permission of the publisher, from *Personnel*, July/1990 © 1990. American Management Association, New York. All rights reserved.

citizen, although the cost gap between U.S. citizens and U.S. foreign employees is narrowing.

To fully utilize a cost-benefit strategy, employers should hire local nationals whenever possible, concentrate on foreign service employees in low allowance and low tax cost locations (such as the United Kingdom), and minimize relocation cost by reshuffling overseas employees whenever possible. Some companies try to cut costs overseas by employing such strategies as hiring single employees rather than those with spouses or children. Although discriminating on the basis of marital status does not violate Title VII of the Civil Rights Act, it does violate some U.S. state laws.

The methods for selecting a cost-effective international staff will continue to evolve. Employers must constantly search for innovative methods for recruiting and selecting a qualified workforce. However, they must never focus on cost to the detriment of hiring appropriate candidates. Such an approach may result in employees who fail to perform satisfactorily. Failures are even more costly than any initial selection expense. One human resource professional estimates that the cost of a failed expatriate employee is three times the individual's salary, not including the price of lost productivity.[49]

A GLOBAL PERSPECTIVE

In the global job market, human resource managers are facing a growing mismatch between new jobs requiring higher level skills and the people available to fill them. In addition, many potential and highly skilled managers are overlooked because they are women. In the case of American multinationals, human resource management is becoming an even greater challenge because, according to the Commission on Workforce Quality and Labor Market Efficiency, "Unless government and business undertake a vast increase in their investment in human capital, U.S. companies will not be able to hire the types of workers they need to compete in international markets."[50] To compound the problem even more, managers affiliated with some companies—for example, General Motors (GM)—are learning the techniques for improving the quality of production but are not learning the management attitudes that make operations such as GM's joint venture with Toyota (NUMMI) successful.[51]

In addition, women managers are often overlooked for global assignments that further reduces the global labor pool and may result in less effective global managers. As with other assignments, the best-qualified person should get the assignment. The three aspects which have limited global assignments for women are the perception that women do not want to be international managers, that companies refuse to send women abroad, and that foreigners are prejudiced against women managers. According to a survey conducted by Nancy J. Adler, a McGill University professor, women do want overseas assignments as much as their male counterparts, but four times as many firms are reluctant to select women for international assignments. Finally, even though few overseas management assignments are currently given to women, 97 percent of the women who have had overseas assignments were successful. Even in Japan, a professional woman is viewed as a professional manager.[52]

Coping with human resource problems in the global environment is very complex. American human resource managers must find a way to educate, or reeducate, much of the American labor force to give the United States a competitive workforce; they must carefully review the human resource situation in host countries; and they must plan to cope with the limitations of the labor situation and take advantage of the strengths of the host countries' labor forces. Human resource professionals cannot afford to overlook qualified women for overseas assignments. Whether it will take more progressive attitudes toward managing the country's labor force, or a more progressive attitude about global women managers, or some other approach, effective human resource management is essential for success in the global environment.

SUMMARY

Selection is the process of choosing from a group of applicants those individuals best suited for a particular position. The selection process often begins with an initial screening of applicants to eliminate those who obviously do not meet the position's requirements. The next step may involve having the prospective employee complete an application for employment.

Selection tests are often used to help assess an applicant's qualifications and potential for success. Properly designed selection tests are standardized, objective, based on sound norms, reliable and—of utmost importance—valid. The *Uniform Guidelines* established three approaches to validation: criterion-related validity, content validity, and construct validity. After a test has been validated, an appropriate cutoff score must be established. An applicant scoring less than the cutoff score will be disqualified. Characteristics related to job performance, which are measurable, include cognitive aptitudes, psychomotor abilities, job knowledge, work samples, vocational interests, and personality. Some firms also test applicants for AIDS and for drug use.

The employment interview is a goal-oriented conversation in which the interviewer and applicant exchange information. Interviews may be conducted in several ways. In a group interview, several applicants interact with one or more company representatives. In a board interview, one candidate is interviewed by several company representatives. The stress interview intentionally creates anxiety to determine how an applicant will react in certain types of situations. A realistic job preview (RJP) conveys unbiased job information to the applicant.

Reference checks provide additional insight into the applicant and are used to verify the accuracy of the information provided. Often a background investigation of the applicant's past employment history is necessary.

Based on all the information obtained, the manager must take the critical step of making the actual hiring decision. After the decision has been made to extend a job offer, the successful candidate receives a physical examination. Typically, a job offer is contingent on the candidate's successful passing of the physical examination. Assuming that no disqualifying medical problems are discovered during the physical examination, the applicant can now be employed.

QUESTIONS FOR REVIEW

1. What basic steps are normally followed in the selection process?
2. Identify and describe the various factors outside the control of the human resource manager that could affect the selection process.
3. What would be the selection ratio if there were fifteen applicants to choose from and only one position to fill? Interpret the meaning of this selection ratio.
4. If a firm wants to use selection tests, how should the tests be used to avoid discriminatory practices?
5. What is the general purpose of the preliminary interview?
6. What types of questions should be asked on an application form?
7. What basic conditions should be met if selection tests are to be used in the screening process? Briefly describe each.
8. Briefly describe the objectives of the employment interview.
9. Define each of the following terms:
   a. *unstructured interview*
   b. *structured interview*
   c. *group interview*
   d. *board interview*
   e. *stress interview*
10. What is the purpose of reference checks and background investigations?
11. What are the reasons for administering a physical examination?

HRM SIMULATION

Your team will have to make a critical selection decision with Incident D in the *Simulation Players Manual*. Four applicants have applied for a Level 3 supervisor's job, and your team has been provided a job description. Your team will have a tough decision because all applicants have different strengths and weaknesses.

ABC VIDEO CASE

INTEGRITY TESTS TAPE 2, NUMBER 5

Millions of Americans applying for jobs are now being asked to take detailed written tests that go far beyond their education or experience. These tests are prepared to measure an applicant's honesty, emotional stability, and religious commitment. Some of the answers are invasive and often prove nothing. Employers are using written tests to probe the thoughts, morals, and values of their potential employees. Questions on sexual practices and family background are commonly asked.

American Civil Liberties Union representative Lewis Maltby says, "What goes on in the bedroom, or the bathroom, or someone's religious beliefs are none of the employers' business, and it is wrong for their employers to require someone to answer these sorts of questions. And it's even more wrong to deny someone a job based on the answers." In Washington, there is concern that these tests may be abusive, invasive, or unconstitutional. Congress will ultimately decide whether these tests will be banned, as the polygraph was.

HRM INCIDENT 1

BUSINESS FIRST!

As production manager for Thompson Manufacturing, Jack Stephens has the final authority to approve the hiring of any new supervisors who work for him. The human resource manager performs the initial screening of all prospective supervisors and then sends the most likely candidates to Jack for interviews.

One day recently, Jack received a call from Pete Peterson, the human resource manager: "Jack, I've just spoken to a young man who may be just who you're looking for to fill that final line supervisor position. He has some good work experience and it appears as if his head is screwed on straight. He's here right now and available if you could possibly see him." Jack hesitated a moment before answering, "Gee, Pete" he said, "I'm certainly busy today but I'll try to squeeze him in. Send him on down."

A moment later Allen Guthrie, the new applicant, arrived at Jack's office and introduced himself. "Come on in, Allen," said Jack. "I'll be right with you after I make a few phone calls." Fifteen minutes later Jack finished the calls and began talking with Allen. Jack was quite impressed. After a few minutes Jack's door opened, and a supervisor yelled, "We have a small problem on line number 1 and need your help." Jack stood up and said, "Excuse me a minute, Allen." Ten minutes later Jack returned, and the conversation continued for ten more minutes before a series of phone calls again interrupted them.

The same pattern of interruptions continued for the next hour. Finally, Allen looked at his watch and said, "I'm sorry, Mr. Stephens, but I have to pick up my wife." "Sure thing, Allen," Jack said as the phone rang again. "Call me later today."

Questions

1. What specific policies should a company follow to avoid interviews like this one?
2. Explain why Jack, not Pete, should make the selection decision.

HRM INCIDENT 2

—SHOULD WE INVESTIGATE?

Patsy Swain, district sales manager for Avco Electronics, was preparing to interview her first applicant, Ray Wyscup, for a sales representative position. She had advertised for an individual with detailed knowledge of computers and spreadsheet software in addition to at least five years' sales experience. "Hello Ray, I'm Pat Swain. I've looked at your resume and am anxious to talk to you about this job. You have a very impressive sales record." "It's nice to meet you, Pat. Your ad in the *Journal* certainly caught my attention. I would like to catch on with a firm offering such a promising career." "Glad you saw it Ray. We like to believe that our firm is unique and truly has something to offer top caliber people such as you. Why don't you begin this session by telling me all about yourself? We are a very close knit group here, and I would like to learn about you and your family." Ray appeared to be very relaxed and comfortable in Pat's presence. He began, "Well, you see, I'm a single parent with two preschool children. Since I'm only forty-one years old, I'm pretty well able to keep up with their various activities. Of course, you understand that one gets sick occasionally, and this causes me to take a few personal days off. But, I've always been able to handle it. This circumstance wouldn't affect my job performance." "Well, I'm sure it wouldn't. I also have some youngsters at home," Pat replied. "Would you now tell me about your last job with IBX?" Ray, feeling more confident than ever, began, "Well, Pat, I had a brief, but very successful stint with them. But I had rather you not contact them about me. You see, my regional manager and I had a personality conflict, and I'm afraid he might not tell a straight story." "I see," Pat said. "What about your position before that, your job with Uniserv?" "I did well there too," Ray stated. "But that outfit went belly up. I have no idea where any of those people are now." After the interview had continued for about an hour, Pat said, "Well, I guess that about wraps it up, Ray, unless you have questions for me?" "No," Ray responded, "I believe I understand the nature of the position, and I can assure you that I will do a great job for you." Pat smiled and nodded and the two shook hands as Ray departed.

Questions

1. Do you agree with the interview format provided by Patsy Swain? Explain.
2. How will Patsy handle a background investigation of Ray Wyscup?

DEVELOPING HRM SKILLS

AN EXPERIENTIAL EXERCISE

Selecting the best person to fill a vacant position is one of the most important tasks of human resource management. As all managers recognize, many factors must be considered in order to ensure proper selection. The selection decision you will be dealing with in this exercise is necessary because George Winston has just been promoted, and before he starts his new job, he must determine his replacement. George's firm is an affirmative action employer, and presently there are few women in management. George has some excellent employees to choose from, but there are many factors to consider before a decision can be made. The people upstairs made it perfectly clear that they expect George to select an individual who can perform as well as he did over the last six years. The people he worked with on the line made it clear that they want Sam. The women on the line have indicated, to everyone who will listen, that it is time for a female supervisor, in at least one division. But it is George's decision, and he must select the best person, regardless of any criticism he may receive.

Sam Philips, an employee of the company for the past eleven years, is one possible candidate. He wants this promotion, needs the higher pay, wants the respect and influence to be gained, and admires the nice office that George has now. Sam is recognized as one of the most technically capable individuals in the division. He is from the old school of thought: We get things done through discipline, and we don't put up with people allowing their personal problems to interfere with work.

Frieda Lott, an employee for seven years, is another candidate for the promotion. She wants the promotion primarily because she can do a good job and represent the women on the line. She was an excellent student in college and believes she can deal effectively with the personal problems of others. She is recognized as technically capable and has an undergraduate degree in management.

Fred Rubble, an employee of the company for six years, is the final candidate. He believes he should get the promotion primarily because he can do the best job. Fred is very capable but not quite as familiar with all the technical aspects of the job as Frieda or Sam. He has an associate degree in liberal arts, but he is taking business classes at night. Fred is also actively involved in the community and has held various civic offices.

Four individuals will have roles in this exercise: one to serve as George Winston, the current supervisor, and three to be the candidates for the promotion. Your instructor will provide the participants with additional information necessary to complete the exercise.

NOTES

1. Stephen L. Guinn, "Gain Competitive Advantage Through Employment Testing," *HR Focus* 70 (September 1993): 15.

2. Peter F. Drucker, "Getting Things Done: How to Make People Decisions," *Harvard Business Review* 63 (July-August 1985): 22.

3. Donald D. DeCamp, "Are You Hiring the Right People?" *Management Review* 81 (May 1992): 44.

4. Vandra L. Huber, Gregory B. Northcraft, and Margaret A. Neale, "Effects of Decision Strategy and Number of Openings on Employment Selection Decisions," *Organizational Behavior and Human Decisions Processes* 45 (April 1990): 276.

5. Louis S. Richman, "The Dark Side of Job Churn," *Fortune* 128 (August 9, 1993): 24.

6. J. Douglas Phillips, "The Price Tag on Turnover," *Personnel Journal* 69 (December 1990): 58–61.

7. Edwin N. Walley, "Successful Interviewing Techniques," *The CPA Journal* 63 (September 1993): 70.

8. Stephen J. Vodanovich and Rosemary H. Lowe, "They Ought to Know Better: The Incidence and Correlates of Inappropriate Application Blank Inquiries," *Public Personnel Management* 21 (Fall 1992): 363–364.

9. Jac Fitz-enz, "Getting—and Keeping—Good Employees," *Personnel* 67 (August 1990): 27.

10. Tom Smith, "Resume Help for the Experienced Candidate," *Planning Job Choices*: 1994, 37th edition (College Placement Council, Inc.: Bethlehem, PA, 1994): 40–41.

11. Michael P. Cronin, "Hiring: This is a Test," *Inc.* 15 (August 1993): 64.

12. Stephen L. Guinn, "Gain Competitive Advantage Through Employment Testing," ibid.

13. John E. Hunter and Frank L. Schmidt, "Ability Tests: Economic Benefits versus the Issue of Fairness," *Industrial Relations* 21 (Fall 1982): 293.

14. T. L. Brink, "A Discouraging Word Improves Your Interviews," *HRMagazine* 37 (December 1992): 49.

15. Robert M. Solomon and Sydney J. Usprich, "Employment Drug Testing," *Business Quarterly* 58 (Winter 1993): 73.

16. George R. Gray and Darrel R. Brown, "Issues in Drug Testing for the Private Sector," *HR Focus* 69 (November 1992): 15.

17. Joseph B. Treaster, "Testing Workers for Drugs Reduces Company Problems," *New York Times* (October 10, 1993): 42.

18. While current illegal drug users are excluded from the definition of "individual with a disability," in the Americans with Disabilities Act, persons disabled by alcoholism are specifically included.

19. Samuel J. Bresier and Roger D. Sommer, "Take Care in Administering Tests Under ADA," *HRMagazine* 37 (April 1992): 49–50.

20. T. L. Brink, "A Discouraging Word Improves Your Interviews," ibid.

21. *Selection Interviewing for the 1990s* (New York: DBM Publishing, A Division of Drake Beam Morin, Inc., 1993): 28.

22. Philip L. Roth and Jeffrey J. McMillan, "The Behavior Description Interview," *The CPA Journal* 63 (December 1993): 76.

23. Tom Janz, Lowell Hellervik, and David C. Gilmore, *Behavior Description Interviewing* (Boston, MA: Allyn & Bacon, Inc., 1986): 15.

24. K. Michele Kacmar, "Look at Who's Talking," *HRMagazine* 38 (February 1993): 56.

25. James M. Jenks and Brian L. P. Zevnik, "ABCs of Job Interviewing," *Harvard Business Review* 67 (July-August 1989): 38–39.

26. Phillip M. Perry, "Your Most Dangerous Legal Traps When Interviewing Job Applicants," *Editor & Publisher* 126 (February 27, 1993): 21–23.

27. John P. Wanous, "Tell It Like It Is at Realistic Job Previews," in Kendrith M. Rowland, Manual London, Gerald R. Ferris, and Jay L. Sherman (eds.), *Current Issues in Personnel Management* (Boston: Allyn & Bacon, 1980): 41–50.

28. T. L. Brink, "A Discouraging Word Improves Your Interviews," 52.

29. Michael W. Mercer, "Turnover: Reducing Costs," *Personnel* 65 (December 1988): 40–42.

30. Ann Marie Ryan and Marja Lasek, "Negligent Hiring and Defamation: Areas of Liability Related to Pre-employment Inquiries," *Personnel Psychology* 44 (Summer 1991): 293.

31. Arthur Bragg, "Checking References," *Sales and Marketing Management* 142 (November 1990): 68.

32. Paul W. Barada, "Check References with Care," *Nation's Business* 81 (May 1993): 54–55.

33. Stevan P. Payne, "A Closer Look at Hiring and Firing," *Security Management* 33 (June 1989): 50.

34. Michael P. Cronin, "Hiring: This is a Test," ibid.

35. Paul W. Barada, "Check References with Care," ibid.

36. Michael P. Cronin, "Hiring: This is a Test," ibid.

37. Eugene Carlson, "Business of Background Checking Comes to the Fore," *Wall Street Journal* (August 31, 1993): 82.

38. Bob Smith, "The Evolution of Pinkerton," *Management Review* 82 (September 1993): 56.

39. Kurt W. Decker, "The Rights and Wrongs of Screening," *Security Management* 34 (January 1990): 46.

40. James W. Fenton, Jr., "Negligent Hiring/Retention Adds to Human Resources Woes," *Personnel Journal* 69 (April 1990): 62; and Stephanie Overman, "A Delicate Balance Protects Everyone's Rights," *HRMagazine* 35 (November 1990): 36–39.

41. Caleb S. Atwood and James M. Neel, "New Lawsuits Expand Employer Liability," *HRMagazine* 35 (October 1990): 74.

42. Joseph W. Ambash, "Knowing Your Limits: How Far Can You Go When Checking an Applicant's Background?" *Management World* 19 (March/April 1990): 8–10.

43. Paul W. Barada, "Check References with Care," 56.

44. Charlene Marmer Solomon, "Staff Selection Impacts Global Success," *Personnel Journal* 73 (January 1994): 88.

45. Ibid.

46. Allen L. Hixon, "Why Corporations Make Haphazard Overseas Staffing Decisions," *Personnel Administrator* 31 (March 1986): 91.

47. Parbhu Guptara, "Searching the Organization for the Cross-Cultural Operators," *International Management* (August 1986): 39–40.

48. Allen L. Hixon, "Why Corporations Make Haphazard Overseas Staffing Decisions," ibid.

49. Mike Fergus, "Employees on the Move," *HRMagazine* 36 (May 1990): 45.

50. Stephen B. Wildstrom, "A Failing Grade for the American Workforce," *Business Week* (September 11, 1989): 22.

51. Dean Foust, "A Tough Look at General Motors," *Business Week* (September 11, 1989): 22.

52. Nancy J. Adler, "Women Managers in a Global Economy," *HRMagazine* 36 (September 1993): 52–55.

CHAPTER 8 Organization Change & Human Resource Development

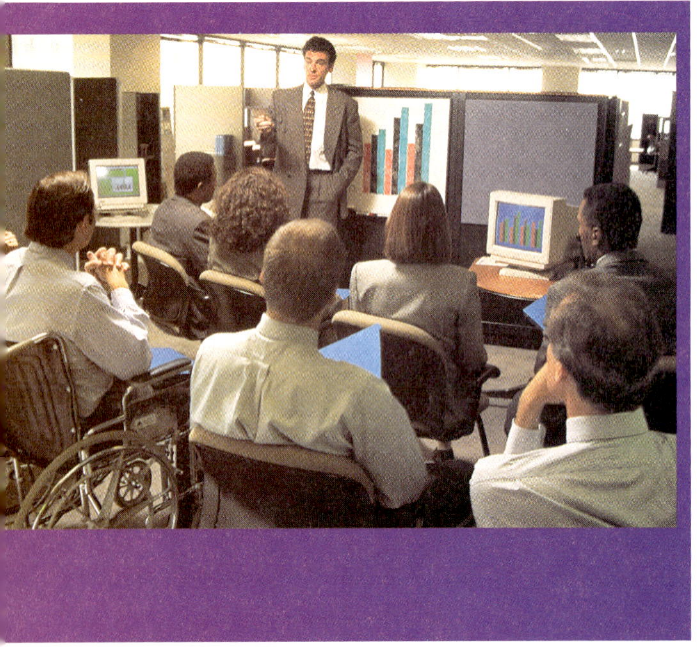

KEY TERMS

Human resource development (HRD) 230
Training 230
Development 230
Orientation 238
Management development 243
Coaching 246
Mentoring 246
Business games 246
Case study 246
Conference method 247
Behavior modeling 247
In-basket training 247
Role playing 248
Job rotation 248
Programmed instruction (PI) 248
Computer-based training 248
On-the-job training (OJT) 255
Apprenticeship training 256
Simulators 256
Vestibule training 257
Job Training Partnership Act (JTPA) 257
Media 258

CHAPTER OBJECTIVES

1. Describe organization change, and define and explain the scope of human resource development (HRD).
2. Describe the HRD process and explain factors influencing HRD.
3. Explain how HRD needs are determined and how HRD objectives are established, and describe the significance of employee orientation.
4. Describe management development, explain training methods for entry-level professional employees and for operative employees, and explain the Job Training Partnership Act.
5. Explain uses of various HRD methods, describe HRD media, and explain how HRD programs are implemented and how HRD programs are evaluated.

Marian Lillie, an experienced accountant, competently handled the administrative tasks for an automobile dealership for more than ten years. She was familiar with all aspects of the business. Two months ago the dealership was sold to a young man who had graduated from a prominent university in the Northeast. Soon after he assumed control of the firm, he automated every conceivable administrative function. Marian was not consulted at any point in the process. She was, however, presented with a procedures manual when the project was completed. Later she was overheard telling a coworker, "I know this new system is not going to work."

Howard Folz, a young college graduate with a major in MIS, was elated over a job offer from the region's largest employer. Upon arriving for his first day of work, his supervisor, Peggy Rodman, took him on a tour of the office and factory. He was shown all the facilities, the firm's cafeteria, and finally his own work station. Peggy's final remarks to him were, "We are delighted to have you with us, Howard. I will let you have your first assignment right after lunch. It's a simple system that involves two of our electronics groups utilizing fiber optics. I'll check with you in a few days to see how you're doing." As Peggy left his work area, Howard was aghast. He wondered if he had just received the only initial training he would get.

It is easy to imagine Marian Lillie's opposition to changes that she does not understand. Based on her last statement, she is not likely to support the changes, which were made without her consultation. Howard has a different, but equally serious problem. The college training he received in MIS was excellent, but he had learned very little about electronics, fiber optics, or the organization of his new employer.

We devote the first portion of this chapter to discussing organization change, to defining human resource development (HRD), and to describing the HRD process. Then, we describe factors that influence HRD. Next, we address elements of the HRD process, which include determining HRD needs, establishing objectives, conducting orientation, and selecting HRD methods. This section is followed by a discussion of management development, other training methods, and the Job Training Partnership Act. In the final portion of the chapter, we consider uses of various HRD methods, HRD media, and ways in which HRD programs are implemented and evaluated.

ORGANIZATION CHANGE

Change involves moving from one condition to another, and it will affect individuals, groups, and entire organizations. Tom Peters has stated, "I can give you modern examples of companies that took for instance a 4,000 person headquarters and trimmed it down to 200 people."[1] While this example is extreme, all organizations will experience change of some sort, and the rate at which change takes place is accelerating. The most prominent changes occurring today in business include the following:

- changes in organizational structure caused by mergers, acquisitions, rapid growth, and downsizing
- changes in technology and the way people work, resulting largely from computerization
- changes in human resources—a diverse workforce consisting of many groups

In today's world, change is the constant. Everyone is affected by it. As change agents, individuals involved with human resource development must understand the change sequence, the accompanying difficulties, and the ways to reduce resistance to change.

The Organization Change Sequence

Because of the impact of change on the organization and its employees, change should be undertaken only when a real need for it exists. Of course, circumstances in the internal or external environments may make change desirable or even necessary (see Figure 8-1). Basically, the impetus for change comes from a belief that the organization and its human resources can be more productive and successful after change occurs. However, if change is to be successfully implemented, it must be approached systematically. Some managers tend to feel, "We have always done it this way, so why argue with success?" However, a firm's past success guarantees neither future prosperity nor even survival.

Reducing resistance to change is crucial to success. At times, this may be extremely difficult because it usually requires shifts in attitudes. Although Marian Lillie may not overtly resist a change and risk losing her job, the new owner could have prepared her better to accept the change and work to make it successful. Many times resistance to change is substantial. However, if resistance to it can be reduced, or even eliminated, change can be implemented more effectively. Change may stem from an order or a suggestion, or it may be undertaken voluntarily. The change will be accomplished more satisfactorily if the person involved in it desires the change and believes it is needed. Bringing about a change in attitude requires trust and respect between the person attempting to implement the change and the individual(s) affected by the change.

FIGURE 8-1
The Organization Change Sequence

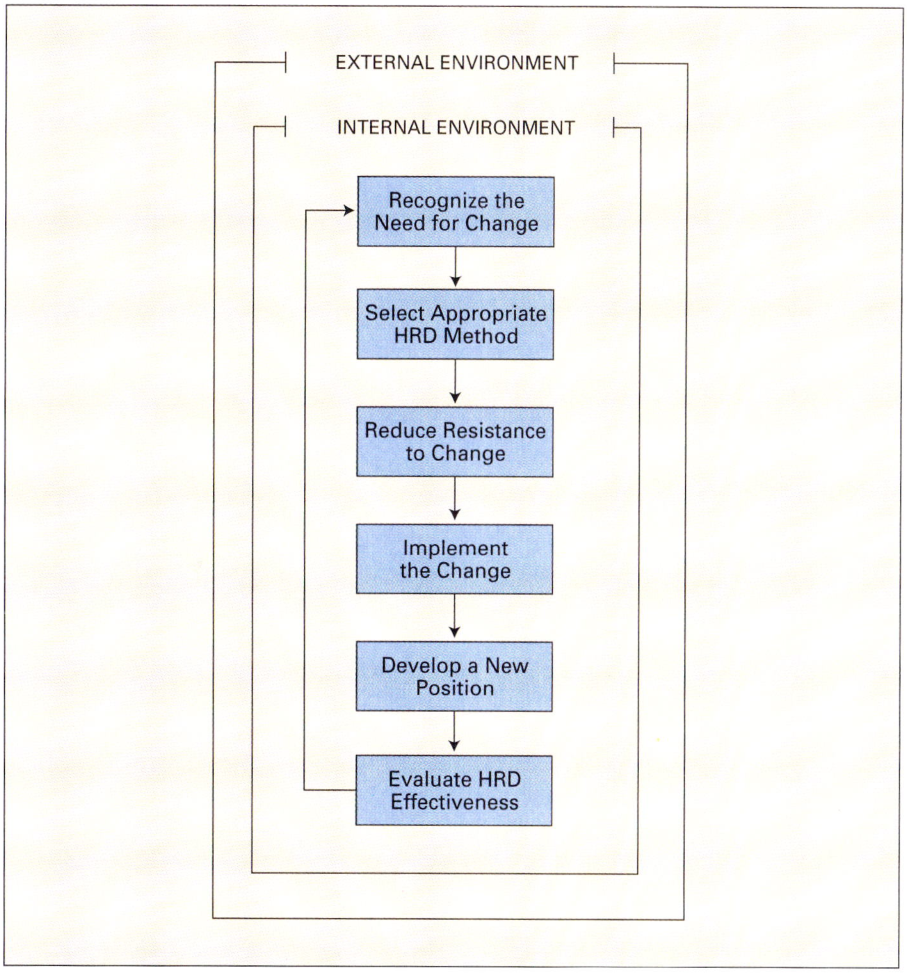

The change sequence does not end when a change is implemented. A new and flexible position capable of dealing with present requirements and adapting to further change must be developed. The final phase of the change sequence involves evaluating the effectiveness of the specific HRD method chosen. As mentioned previously, one primary measure of effectiveness is how the program affected the firm's *bottom line*. Human resource development is an ongoing process because both the organization's internal and external environments are dynamic and are always impinging upon the status quo.

Reasons for Resistance to Change

In business circles, employees' *natural* resistance to change has been discussed widely. Although change is often resisted, sometimes quite vigorously, such opposition is not innate. Rather, the resistance may be explained in terms of employee expectations and past experiences. Individuals may resist change when they feel it will deny satisfaction of their basic needs. For instance, one of the most frightening prospects for many people is the threat of being deprived of employment. At times, changes in methods and systems do downgrade and eliminate jobs. In a more positive vein, changes may also generate the need for greater skills. Yet, many employees believe they lack the flexibility to adjust. Because most adults derive their primary income from their work, they would be economically unable to obtain the basic necessities of life if they were unemployed. Therefore, it is easy to understand the threatening nature of change.

Many changes in organizations are perceived as disrupting established social groups. In fact, there may be an inordinate fear that change will disturb established friendships. Because numerous social needs are satisfied on the job, any threat to these relationships may be resisted.

The potential threat to a person's status in the organization may also be a powerful reason for resisting change. Many workers literally invest their lives in their jobs. They are likely to resist any change that they perceive as upsetting their standing in the organization or their sense of importance. For instance, master machinists, when faced with new automation in their firms, may fear that high-level skills will no longer be needed and that their prestige will be lowered. Regardless of the reasons individuals resist change, management must take action to minimize the loss of productivity associated with change. Productivity and accuracy generally do decline during periods of change. Instead of thinking about their work, employees are worrying about their survival or loss of status. They may be absent more, either because of illness or because they are looking for another job.

In summary, the prospect of change can conceivably threaten every level of human need. This feeling of being threatened often causes employees to resist change. The resistance is not *natural* but is based on reasons that are perceived as being quite logical.

Reducing Resistance to Change

In order for a firm to gain general acceptance of a needed change, management must be aware of ways to lessen resistance. Although negative attitudes cannot be overcome overnight, the following approaches can serve to increase employees' acceptance of change.

Building Trust and Confidence. The degree of employee trust and confidence in management relates directly to past experiences. If employees have suffered in the past as a result of change, they may reasonably attempt to avoid future changes. When management has misrepresented the effects of change, resistance tends to be even greater. For example, when faced with the prospect of having to reduce the workforce, management may assure employee layoffs will be based on individual performance. However, if previous layoffs appeared to be determined by seniority or favoritism, employees may not believe current actions will be any different.

Conversely, management builds trust by dealing with employees in an open and straightforward manner. Workers who are told they need additional training will accept the idea much more readily if they have confidence in management. The desired level of trust cannot be achieved quickly. Rather, it results from a long period of fair dealing by the firm's management.

Developing Open Communication. A great deal of information in organizations is treated as confidential when actually it is not. Information is often withheld from employees for a variety of reasons, including management's unwillingness to share it. Regardless of the reason, the practice of secrecy creates a climate of mistrust and fear. Any rumor of planned changes may then be blown out of proportion, with the firm's employees programmed to fear the worst.

By sharing information with employees, management can take a giant step toward developing open communications. Managers must recognize that subordinates have strong informational needs, and these needs should be met whenever possible.

Employee Participation. People such as Marian Lillie are more inclined to accept changes if they are given the opportunity to participate in the planning. For instance, suppose management determines a department's operating budget must be cut by 25 percent. The department's manager may more readily accept this change if permitted to help determine the extent of the cuts and where they should be made. Participation is also more effective when permitted in the early planning stages. Another caution regarding participation relates to the effect of the change on the individuals involved. If the change will have a negative impact—for example, if these individuals' jobs are in jeopardy—then management should not have them participate in their own demise.[2]

Generally speaking, participation can be helpful in minimizing resistance to change. In some cases resistance can be eliminated. In fact, developing a participative climate within which employees aggressively seek change is often possible. In order to achieve such an atmosphere, it is necessary to remove, or at least minimize, the employees' fears of being unable to satisfy their personal needs. Managers must be convinced that their own actions—not the employees' inherent nature—are most often responsible for attitudes toward change. Only then can the effectiveness of human resource development programs be maximized.

HUMAN RESOURCE DEVELOPMENT: DEFINITION AND SCOPE

Human resource development (HRD) is a planned, continuous effort by management to improve employee competency levels and organizational performance through training and development programs. In practice, HRD may be referred to as *training and development* (T&D) or simply training. However, a distinction is sometimes made between these two terms. **Training** is designed to permit learners to acquire knowledge and skills needed for their present jobs.[3] Showing a worker how to operate a lathe or a supervisor how to schedule daily production are examples of training. The recent growth in the need for training stems from the need to adapt to rapid environmental changes, improve the quality of products and services, and increase productivity to remain competitive. **Development** involves learning that looks beyond today and today's job; it has a more long-term focus.[4] It prepares employees to keep pace with the organization as it changes and grows. Developing human resources has become crucial with the rapid advances in technology. *High tech* has made the need for development quite apparent. As jobs grow increasingly complex and impersonal, the need for improved human relations within a firm also becomes increasingly significant. Largely because of this, training and development should be conducted on a continuous basis.

The connection between economic survival and productivity is obvious. Increased productivity—the primary purpose of HRD—is a strategic goal for many firms. In a recent year, it was estimated that more than 47 million people received some kind of formal training from their employers, a 15 percent increase over the previous year.[5] Budgeted training expenditures were estimated to exceed $48 billion.[6] It is important to note that *formal* training refers to training activity that is planned, structured, and occurs when people are called away from their desks. It does not include the amount of informal training that occurs on the job in the form of on-the-job training.[7] Continued growth in both forms of training appears to be a given. Most organizations invest in HRD because they believe that higher profits will result—which often happens. Training frequently improves workers' skills and boosts their motivation. This, in turn, leads to higher productivity and increased profitability.

Although training budgets are increasing in many firms, it should be noted that most firms do not offer any formal training. In fact, just 15,000 companies (0.5 percent of the total) account for 90 percent of the billions spent on training annually. In addition, most of the training efforts are directed toward executives and managers overlooking the majority of American workers who do not have college degrees. Notable exceptions are Motorola, Federal Express, and Corning. These firms have been cited for allocating more than 3 percent of their payroll for training. The president of Motorola stated, "When you buy a piece of equipment, you set aside a percentage for maintenance. Shouldn't you do the same for people?"[8]

Another major goal of HRD is to prevent obsolescence of skills at all levels in the company. Not only can effective HRD programs play a vital role in achieving this goal, they can also upgrade employees' skills to qualify them for promotion. The organization is responsible for helping employees upgrade their skills based on employee aptitudes and interests, in addition to meeting the needs of the company. Human resource development costs should be accepted for what they are—an investment in human resources.

THE HUMAN RESOURCE DEVELOPMENT PROCESS

Major adjustments in the external and internal environments necessitate corporate change. The general human resource development process that helps facilitate change is shown in Figure 8-2.

FIGURE 8-2
The Human Resource Development Process

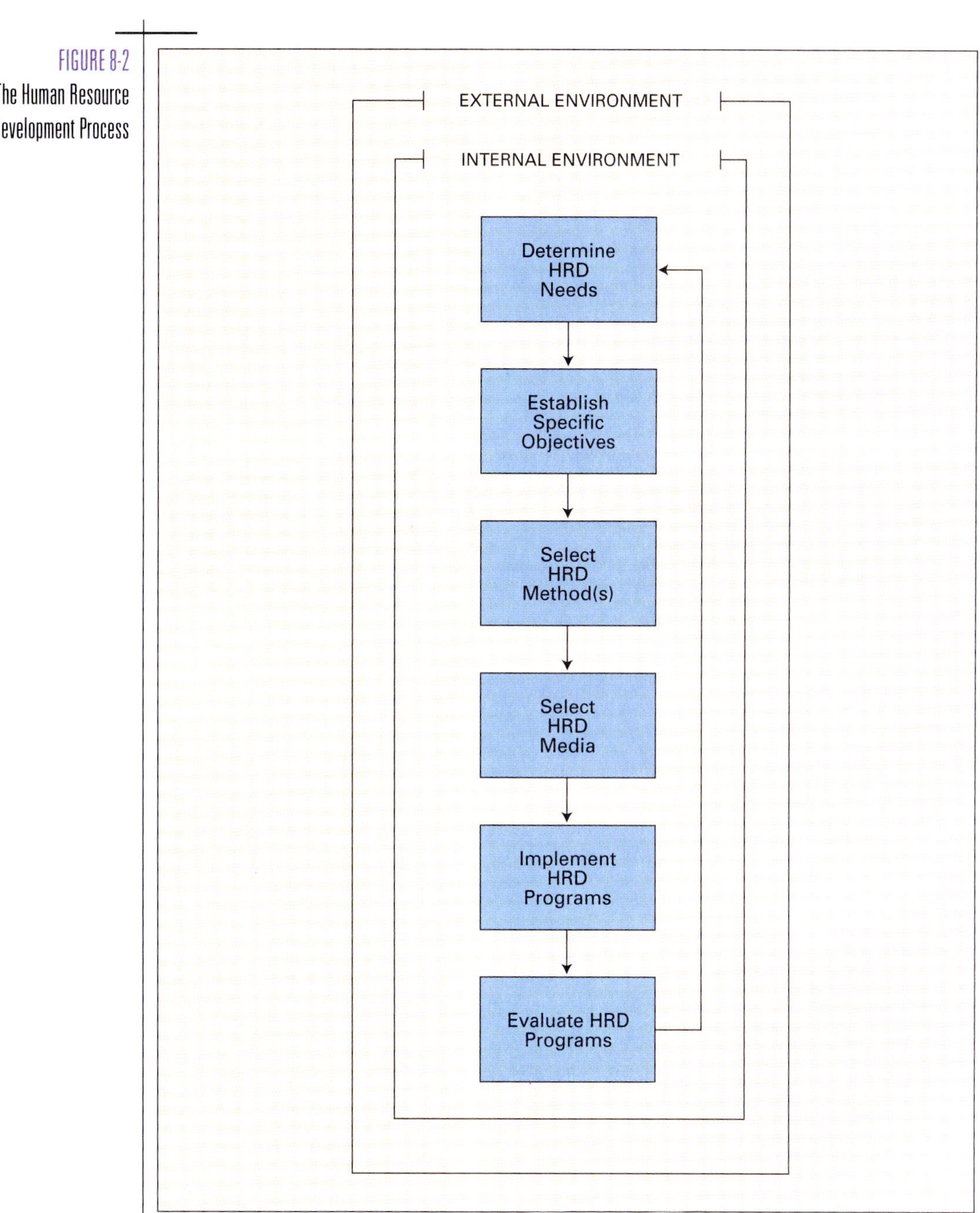

Once the need for change is recognized, the process of determining training and development needs begins. Essentially, two questions must be asked: "What are our training needs?" and "What do we want to accomplish through our HRD efforts?" The objectives might be quite narrow if limited to the supervisory ability of a manager. Or they might be broad enough to include improving the management skills of all first-line supervisors.

After stating the process objectives, management can determine the appropriate methods for accomplishing them. Various methods and media are available; the selection depends on the nature of HRD goals. Naturally, HRD must be continuously evaluated in order to facilitate change properly and accomplish organizational objectives.

Increasingly, training departments are being considered as profit centers rather than overhead. A training department that is evaluated on results achieved must function like a profit center. This requires continuous evaluation.

FACTORS INFLUENCING HUMAN RESOURCE DEVELOPMENT

Several of the most important factors that influence human resource development are shown in Figure 8-3. How these factors are addressed often determines whether a firm achieves its HRD objectives.

First and foremost, training and development programs must have top management's full support. This support must be real— not merely lip service—and it should be communicated to the entire organization. True support becomes evident when executives provide the resources needed for the HRD function. The support is further strengthened when top executives

FIGURE 8-3
Factors Influencing Human Resource Development

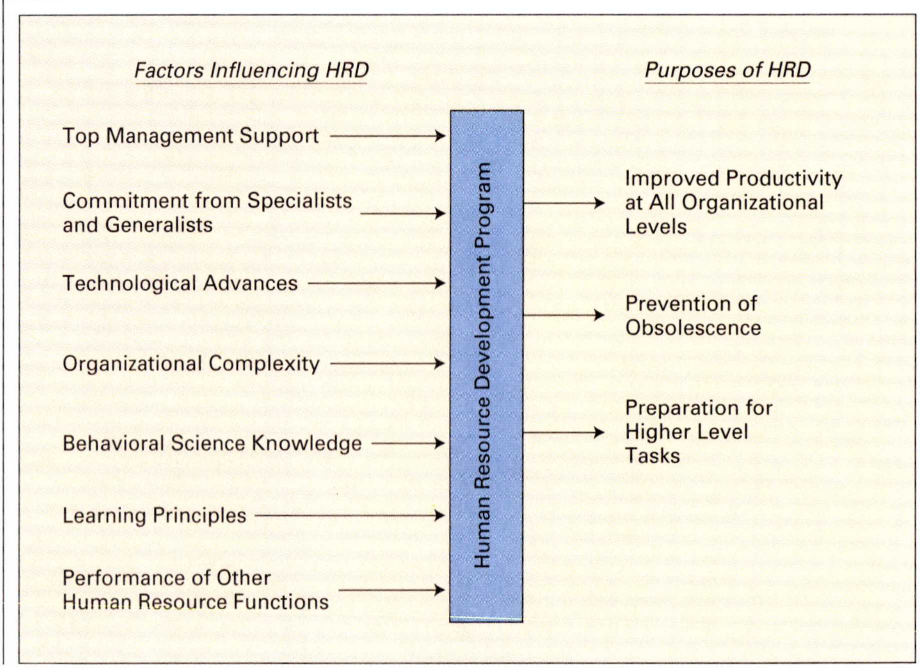

TABLE 8-1
Today's Role of the Human Resource Development Manager

EXECUTIVE	COMMENTS
Senior Advisor, Personnel Development, Chevron Corporation	Principal role is to be a consultant to managers to help identify: (1) operating problems or potential problems; (2) scenarios or alternative courses of action to solve these problems or prevent them from occurring; and (3) feedback processes to see that on-job results are consistent with stated management goals.
Director of Personnel Fotomat Corporation	The role varies greatly, depending on the industry and the individual in the job. My perception is that the role is becoming more important and is expanding into nontraditional training and development functions.
District Manager, Training, Ohio Bell Telephone Company	The role of the training/development manager is a staff function that must prove to the line organization and users that the services provided are job relevant, and will improve productivity, lower costs, and increase profits.
Manager, Employee Development and Planning, The Upjohn Company	Plan, develop, and administer programs that meet the needs of line managers in assisting their people to obtain the knowledge and skills they need to perform their present jobs satisfactorily; prepare employees for future jobs in the company; and assist them in achieving their personal goals.

actually take part in the training. These actions tend to convince employees of the true importance of HRD programs.

In addition, other managers, both generalists and HRD specialists, should be committed to and involved in the HRD process. Views of several practitioners concerning the HRD manager's role are presented in Table 8-1. Some important conclusions regarding the HRD manager's responsibilities can be drawn from these comments.

The HRD manager operates essentially in a staff, or advisory, capacity. According to one prominent director of corporate management development, "The primary responsibility for training and development lies with line managers, from the president and chairman of the board on down. HRD management merely provides the technical expertise, plus blood, sweat, and tears."

In order to ensure effective programs, managers must be convinced that there will be a tangible payoff if resources are committed to this effort. M. Farooq Kathwari, chairman, president, and CEO of Ethan Allen Interiors Inc., believes that training is his company's *secret weapon*. He feels it has given the firm a competitive edge in the industry and contributes to its successful sales and earnings.[9]

Some form of cost-benefit analysis should be made prior to implementing any HRD program. The program should be job related, improve productivity, lower costs, and increase profits. A major role of the HRD manager is to assist people in obtaining the knowledge and skills they need for present and future jobs and to assist them in attaining personal goals. Learning is a self-determined activity, and all development is self-development. The HRD manager explains the type of training available, shows how it can be accomplished, and provides encouragement to ensure its successful accomplishment.

In recent years, the increasingly rapid changes in products, systems, and methods have had a significant impact on job requirements. Thus, employees face the need to upgrade their skills constantly and to develop an attitude that permits them not only to adapt to change, but also to accept and even seek it.

Many organizations have changed dramatically as a result of downsizing, technological innovations, and customer demands for new and better products and services. The result is often that more work must be accomplished by fewer people. Employees must not only do more work, but they must perform work at a more complex level. Supervisors and operative employees performing in self-directed teams are taking up much of the slack from dwindling middle management ranks. All these changes translate into a greater need for training and development.

During the past several decades, a vast amount of new knowledge has emerged from the behavioral sciences. Much of it relates directly to human resource management. Today's managers must be aware of this knowledge and be capable of utilizing it. The HRD function faces a substantial task in keeping pace with behavioral science developments and informing others in the organization about them.

Human resource development specialists must know more than the topic to be presented in a training program. They must also have some understanding of basic learning principles. The purpose of training is to change employee behavior, and information must be learned if change is to occur. Although much remains to be discovered about the learning process, several generalizations may be helpful in understanding this phenomenon. Some general concepts—fundamentals related to learning—are shown in Table 8-2.

Most of these concepts relate to the management and development of human resources. For example, behavior that is rewarded (reinforced) is more likely to recur. In applying this thought to managing people, management should strive to ensure that the firm rewards the behaviors it desires. If the firm wants greater productivity from its employees, then productivity must be rewarded. As will be discussed in Chapter 12, important forms of compensation exist other than those financial. For example, participants in HRD programs should be praised for their accomplishments to provide desired feedback and encourage continual learning.

From the human resource manager's viewpoint, successful accomplishment of other human resource functions can have a significant impact on HRD. For instance, if recruitment and selection efforts attract marginally qualified workers, a more extensive HRD program may be needed to train entry-level workers. Training and development efforts may also be influenced by the firm's compensation package. A firm with a competitive program may find it easier to attract qualified workers, which substantially influences the type of training required. Also, a competitive compensation plan may help lower the turnover rate, thereby minimizing the need to train new workers continuously.

TABLE 8-2
General Learning Concepts

- Behavior that is rewarded (reinforced) is more likely to recur.
- This reinforcement, to be most effective, must immediately follow the desired behavior and be clearly connected with that behavior.
- Mere repetition, without reinforcement, is an ineffective approach to learning.
- Threats and punishment have variable and uncertain effects on learning. Punishment may disturb the learning process.
- The sense of satisfaction that stems from achievement is the type of reward that has the greatest transfer value to other situations.
- The value of an external reward depends on who dispenses the reward. If the reward giver is highly respected, the extrinsic reward may be of great value; if not, it may be without value.
- Learners progress in an area of learning only as far as they need to in order to achieve their purposes.
- Individuals are more likely to be enthusiastic about a learning situation if they themselves have participated in the planning of the project.
- Autocratic leadership has been found to make members more dependent on the leader and to generate resentment in the group.
- Overstrict discipline tends to be associated with greater conformity, anxiety, shyness, and acquiescence; greater permissiveness is associated with more initiative and creativity.
- Many people experience so much criticism, failure, and discouragement that their self-confidence, level of aspiration, and sense of worth are damaged.
- When people experience too much frustration, their behavior ceases to be integrated, purposeful, and rational.
- People who have met with little success and continual failure are not apt to be in the mood to learn.
- Individuals tend to think best whenever they encounter an obstacle or intellectual challenge that is of interest to them.
- The best way to help people form a general concept is to present an idea in numerous and varied situations.
- Learning from reading is aided more by time spent recalling what has been read than by rereading.
- Individuals remember new information that confirms their previous attitudes better than they remember new information that does not confirm their previous attitudes.
- What is learned is more likely to be available for use if it is learned in a situation much like that in which it is to be used, and immediately preceding the time when it is needed.
- The best time to learn is when the learning can be useful. Motivation is then at its strongest peak.

A firm's employee relations efforts can also influence the HRD program. Workers want to feel that the company is interested in them. One way to express this interest is through management's support of HRD. The HRD process can also train managers to deal more effectively with employees and their problems. Managers can be taught to treat employees as individuals and not merely as numbers.

The emphasis a firm places on its employees' health and safety can also affect the HRD process. Heavy emphasis in this area can pave the way for extensive training programs throughout the organization. Providing a healthy and safe work environment can benefit all other human resource functions as the firm gains a reputation as a rewarding place to work.

DETERMINING HUMAN RESOURCE DEVELOPMENT NEEDS

In order to compete effectively, firms must keep their employees well trained. The question is often, "What type of training is needed?" A study conducted by the Olsten Corporation found that for three levels of employees (management, support staff, and professional/technical employees), the skills most needed were basic computer, written communications, listening, and interpersonal communications.[10] A summary of the results of this study is shown in Table 8-3.

The first step in the HRD process is to determine specific training and development needs. In today's highly competitive business environment, undertaking programs simply because *other firms are doing it* is asking for trouble. Rather, a systematic approach to addressing bona fide needs must be undertaken.

TABLE 8-3

Skill Needs by Employee Level (Percent of Companies Responding)

TYPE OF SKILL	SUPPORT STAFF	PROFESSIONAL/ TECHNICAL	MANAGEMENT
Basic computer	63%	50%	65%
Written communications	65%	58%	52%
Listening	60%	58%	69%
Interpersonal communications	62%	63%	67%
Organizational	50%	53%	50%
Customer service	61%	50%	39%
Quality awareness	55%	50%	48%
Analytical	42%	38%	33%
Cross-cultural communications	47%	47%	54%
Sales/marketing	27%	34%	32%
Basic math	43%	14%	9%
Reading comprehension	42%	19%	12%

Source: "Skills for Success," *The Olsten Forum™ on Human Resource Issues and Trends,* The Olsten Corporation, Fall 1994, p. 7.

Three types of analysis are required in order to determine an organization's HRD needs: organization analysis, task analysis, and person analysis.[11] In this context, *organization analysis* examines the entire firm to determine where training and development should be conducted. The firm's strategic goals and plans should be studied along with the results of human resource planning.

In conducting *task analysis*, two primary factors should be determined: importance and proficiency. Importance relates to the relevance of specific tasks and behaviors in a particular job and the frequency with which they are performed. Proficiency is the employees' competence in performing these tasks. Job descriptions, performance appraisals, and interviews or surveys of supervisors and job incumbents should provide the data needed.[12]

Person analysis, which focuses on the individual employee, deals with two questions: "Who needs to be trained?" and "What kind of training is needed?" The first step in a person analysis is to compare employee performance with established standards. If the person's work is acceptable, training may not be needed. However, if the employee's performance is below standard, further investigation will be needed to identify the specific knowledge and skills required for satisfactory job performance.[13]

Tests, role playing, and assessment centers may also be helpful in conducting person analysis. The results of career planning programs may prove to be quite revealing as well.

ESTABLISHING HUMAN RESOURCE DEVELOPMENT OBJECTIVES

Clear and concise objectives must be formulated for HRD. Without them, designing meaningful HRD programs would not be possible. Worthwhile evaluation of a program's effectiveness would also be difficult at best. The following statement of purposes and objectives is from a segment of a training program designed by the Chevron Corporation.

Employment Compliance

Purpose. To provide supervisor with:

1. Knowledge and value of consistent human resource practices.
2. The intent of EEO legal requirements.
3. The skills to apply them.

Objectives. Be able to:

1. Cite the supervisory areas affected by EEO laws on discrimination.
2. Identify acceptable and nonacceptable actions, according to EEO laws.
3. State how to get help on EEO and Affirmative Action matters.
4. Describe why we have discipline and grievance procedures.
5. Describe our discipline and grievance procedures, including who is covered.

As you can see, the purpose is clearly established first. Managers would have little difficulty in determining whether this is the type of training a subordinate needs. The specific learning objectives leave little doubt of what should be learned from the training. Action words, such as *cite*, *identify*, *state*, and *describe*, are used to disclose the specific content of the program. With these types of objectives, the HRD specialist may determine whether a person has obtained the necessary knowledge. For instance, a trainee either can or cannot state how to get help on EEO and Affirmative Action matters.

ORIENTATION

The initial HRD effort designed for employees is orientation. **Orientation** is the guided adjustment of new employees to the company, the job, and the work group. It is a common type of formal training in U.S. organizations. While many typical HRD methods are not used for orientation for new employees, some firms have developed sophisticated approaches. For example, Federal Express, a recent Malcolm Baldrige National Quality Award winner, uses computer-based training for orienting new employees. Specifically, laser disks (discussed later in this chapter) provide a two-hour program that offers detailed information on the corporate culture, benefits, policies, and procedures. It also outlines the company's organizational structure and features a video message from the chief executive officer.[14] Comprehensive orientation makes many of the other tasks associated with human resource management easier.

In an orientation program, requirements for promotion will likely be explained. Rules, the infraction of which may lead to potential disciplinary action, will be stated. The mechanics of promotion, demotion, transfer, resignation, discharge, layoff, and retirement should be spelled out in policy handbooks and given to each new employee. Also, a summary of employee benefits is often provided.

To perform effectively, new employees need information that permits them to do their jobs and information that will help them understand their coworkers' behavioral patterns. In this regard, peers have been found to serve as excellent information agents. There are several reasons for peers' success in performing this function. For one thing they are accessible to newcomers and often more available than the boss. Peers also tend to have a high degree of empathy for new people. In addition, they have the organizational experience and technical expertise to which new employees need access.

Disney's orientation begins in the selection interview. At this time, prospective employees are given a realistic view of working for the organization, as in a realistic job preview discussed in the previous chapter. The emphasis is on ensuring that employees understand that a Disney job is not all glamour but also hard work. At Disney University, all new *cast members*, as employees are called, attend a two-day seminar that focuses on corporate traditions and values and also provides generic skills necessary for job performance. The skills emphasized relate mainly to basic information giving and customer relations. Disney's approach to orientation is so impressive that people from other well-known American businesses attend seminars conducted for outsiders to learn how to apply Disney's orientation techniques to their own firms.[15]

Orientation is often the joint responsibility of the training staff and the line supervisor. The new hire is primarily concerned about the job and his or her supervisor. When anxiety about these factors is reduced, the corporate message can be communicated more effectively.

Successful orientation programs also tend to have a high degree of senior management involvement both in developing the program and implementing it. Actually, for any type of program to be successful, top management support is essential.

Purposes of Orientation

A new employee's first few days on the job may be spent in orientation. However, some firms feel that learning is more effective if spread out over a period of time. For example, Web Industries' program is delivered in a system of 20 one-hour sessions over a period of four weeks.[16]

Micron Technology, a computer chip manufacturing firm in Boise, Idaho, has a program to emphasize its multicultural environment. A course was developed which involves two and a half hour sessions for thirty participants who meet once a week for six weeks. The program includes these topics:

- joining the company team
- participating in groups
- gaining responsibility
- planning employee development
- resolving workplace issues
- dealing with change

Micron's program is titled *Reaching High Performance*. Company executives believe that the program guides new employees through the corporate culture and trains them to become valued members of the company team.[17]

Orientation programs are designed basically for new employees. A high percentage of an organization's workforce is new not only to the job, but also to the job market. These new workers include a large number of late entries or reentries of women, men and women who were self-employed, recent graduates, and people who have made radical career changes. Many of these individuals are inexperienced and have anxieties about entering the organization. An effective orientation program can do much to reduce these anxieties. Orientation has three primary purposes, which will be discussed next.

Easing the New Employee's Adjustment to the Organization

Orientation helps the new employee adjust to the organization, both formally and informally. Formally, the organization wants the employee to become productive as rapidly as possible. In order to facilitate this process, the employee needs to know specifically what the job involves. Explanations concerning the job by the supervisor can do much to speed this process.

Many of the benefits of orientation relate to the informal organization. New employees are not automatically greeted with open arms. There may be a certain amount of hazing and kidding. In order to reduce the anxiety that new employees experience, attempts should be made to integrate the person into the informal organization. Many years ago Texas Instruments conducted research that clearly revealed the importance of this purpose. The experimental design included randomly assigning new employees to one of two training groups—either the traditional orientation program or the experimental group's *socialization program*. The latter group covered such subjects as career management, the importance of politics, picking the right boss, and the importance of being at the right place at the right time. At the end of two years, the learning rates of the two groups were compared. Employees in the socialization program proved to be significantly superior on all measures to those in the traditional group. The most dramatic finding was the impact on turnover among professionals, such as engineers and computer specialists. The turnover rate for those who had completed the socialization program was 40 percent lower than for those in the traditional group.[18]

New employees characteristically have enthusiasm, creativity, and commitment. Much of this can be lost through an inept orientation program that fails to integrate new hires into the work group. On the other hand, an effective program enhances the employment relationship and provides the foundation for employee motivation, commitment, and productivity.

Providing Information Concerning Tasks and Performance Expectations

Another purpose of orientation is to provide specific information about task and performance expectations. Employees want and need to know precisely what is expected of them. Thus, new employees should be informed of the standards that they must meet in order to qualify for pay raises, and the criteria for promotion. Rules of the company and of the particular department to which the individual is assigned should also be explained.

Reinforcing a Favorable Impression

A final purpose of orientation is to maintain a favorable impression on new employees of the organization and its work. The orientation process can do much to allay fears new employees may have about whether they made a sound employment decision.

STAGES IN EFFECTIVE ORIENTATION

There are essentially three different stages in an effective orientation program.[19] During the first stage, general information about the organization is provided. Matters that relate to all employees, such as a company overview, review of company policies and procedures, and salary, are presented, usually by members of the HR department. A checklist for new employees is often used to ensure that certain information is provided to the new hire. One such checklist is shown in Figure 8-4. It is also helpful for the new employee to know how his or her department fits into the overall scheme of the company's operations. Orientation programs should also provide information about how the products or the services of the company benefit society as a whole.

The employee's immediate supervisor usually is responsible for the second stage of orientation. In some instances, the supervisor may delegate this task to a senior employee in the department. Topics and events covered include an overview of the department, job requirements, safety, a tour of the department, a question and answer session, and introductions to other employees. The supervisor should clearly explain performance expectations and specific work rules at this point. It is also important for the supervisor to ease the new hire into social acceptance by the work group as quickly as possible.

NEW EMPLOYEE CHECKLIST

NAME ______________________ EMPLOYMENT DATE ______________

POSITION TITLE ______________________ DEPARTMENT ______________

PAY GRADE ________ APPOINTMENT TYPE: PT___ FT___ SUPERVISOR ______________

PROBATIONARY PERIOD ENDS ______________________

FIVE MONTH PERFORMANCE APPRAISAL DUE ______________________

INFORMATION PROVIDED:

____ Orientation packet	By: ______________	Date ______________
____ I.D. card	By: ______________	Date ______________
____ Staff handbook	By: ______________	Date ______________
____ Grievance guide	By: ______________	Date ______________
____ Retirement information	By: ______________	Date ______________
____ Life insurance	By: ______________	Date ______________
____ Disability insurance	By: ______________	Date ______________
____ Health insurance	By: ______________	Date ______________

I have received the information checked above, understand my employment status, and have been fully informed about my insurance options and benefits.

I have chosen not to enroll in HEALTH, LIFE, DISABILITY insurance. (Circle those you are not enrolling in.)

____
Employee Signature Date

____
Human Resource Representative Date

Effective Date ______________

FIGURE 8-4 Checklist for New Employees

The third stage involves evaluation and follow-up, which are conducted by the human resource department in conjunction with the immediate supervisor. The new employee does not go through the orientation program simply to be forgotten. During the first week or so, the supervisor works with the new employee to clarify information and to make sure of integration into the work group. Human resource professionals assist supervisors to ensure that this vital third step is accomplished.

TRAINING THE SUPERVISOR

One of the most vital aspects of an orientation program is training supervisors to conduct orientation properly. Human resource professionals can provide the new hire with organizational information, but it is the supervisor who must successfully integrate the employee into the work setting.

The supervisor should first express confidence that new employees are going to do well on the job. New hires often begin work not fully convinced that they are capable of doing the job. Supervisors need to reassure these individuals that the company would not have hired them if it did not believe that they could do the job.

Second, supervisors need to explain both the good and the bad points of the job. During the orientation period, managers often spend most of their time emphasizing the positive aspects of the job, leaving the new employees to learn of the negative features on their own. Studies have verified that good employee understanding of the job lowers turnover rates. Ideally, new employees will have received a realistic job preview and will not face any unpleasant surprises at this time.

Third, the supervisor should inform the new hire of what he or she likes and dislikes in job performance. Every supervisor has particular preferences—usually small things that they react to favorably or unfavorably. Knowing these preferences, employees can more easily adapt to a particular work situation. For example, a supervisor who is a stickler for neatness should communicate this fact to new hires.

Fourth, the supervisor should describe both the standards set by the company and any unique customs of the employee's particular work group. All company rules, especially those pertaining to the new hire's section, should also be explained.

Finally, the supervisor should introduce the new employee to members of the work group. Any informal group leader should be identified. Here again, an attempt should be made to minimize the number of surprises that the employee will encounter. Starting off on the wrong foot with leaders of the informal organization can hurt the new employee's chances for quick acceptance. In jobs that require considerable interaction among group members, group acceptance is especially important.

REORIENTATION

While orientation programs are typically conducted for new employees, programs designed for employees who have been on the payroll for a longer period may also be needed. As organizations change, different management styles may develop, communication methods may be altered, and the structure of the organization itself may, and typically does, take on a new form. Even the corporate culture may evolve into something different over time. Any of these changes may warrant reorientation. Without it, employees may find themselves in organizations that they do not even recognize.

SELECTING HUMAN RESOURCE DEVELOPMENT METHODS

When a person is working on a car, some tools are more helpful in doing certain tasks than others. The same logic applies when considering various HRD methods. Note the diverse methods shown in Table 8-4. Some methods apply strictly to managers and entry-level professionals, others to operative employees, and several are used in the training and development of both managers and operative employees. Methods that apply to both management and operative employees are discussed under the heading of management development.

Again referring to Table 8-4, note that HRD methods are used both on and off the job. Often it is not feasible to learn while doing. Thus, although a large portion of training and development takes place on the job, many HRD programs occur away from the work setting.

MANAGEMENT DEVELOPMENT

A firm's future lies primarily in the hands of its management. This group performs certain functions that are essential to the organization's survival and prosperity. Managers must make the right choice in most of the numerous decisions they make. Otherwise, the firm will not grow and may even fail. One unnerving statistic is that between six or seven of every ten American managers have significant shortcomings in the managerial abilities.[20] For these reasons, it is imperative managers keep up with the latest developments in their respective fields and—at the same time—manage an ever changing workforce operating in a dynamic environment. Thus, many organizations emphasize training and development programs for managers. **Management development** consists of all learning experiences resulting in an upgrading of skills and knowledge required in current and future managerial positions. While critical knowledge and skills are provided by organizations in development programs, the process also requires

TABLE 8-4 Human Resource Development Methods

	UTILIZED FOR			CONDUCTED	
METHOD	Managers and Entry-Level Professionals	Operative Employees	Both	On the Job	Off the Job
Coaching/mentoring			X	X	
Business games	X				X
Case study	X				X
Conference method	X				X
Behavior modeling	X				X
In-basket training	X				X
Internships	X			X	
Role playing	X				X
Job rotation			X	X	
Programmed instruction			X		X
Computer-based training			X		X
Classroom lecture			X		X
On-the-job training (OJT)		X		X	
Apprenticeship training		X		X	
Simulators		X			X
Vestibule training		X			X

It is imperative that managers keep up with the latest developments in their respective fields and—at the same time—manage an ever changing workforce operating in a dynamic environment.

personal commitment of the individual manager. In fact, taking responsibility for one's own development may be the most important aspect.[21]

First-line supervisors, middle managers, and executives may all be expected to participate in management development programs. These programs are offered in-house or by professional organizations, colleges, and universities. In-house programs are planned and presented by a firm's HRD specialists from the human resource department. Line managers are also frequently utilized to conduct segments of a program.

Professional organizations, colleges, and universities are additional sources of management development programs. Organizations, such as the Society for Human Resource Management and the American Management Association, conduct conferences and seminars in a number of specialties. Numerous colleges and universities also provide management training and development programs. At times, colleges and universities possess expertise not available within business organizations. In some cases, academicians and management practitioners can advantageously present HRD programs jointly. A recent survey revealed the most frequently mentioned reasons to conduct management training outside the company:

- an outside perspective
- new viewpoints
- possibility of taking executives out of the work environment
- exposure to faculty experts and research
- broader vision

The most frequently mentioned reasons for keeping management training inside the company are listed below:

- training that is more specific to needs
- lower costs
- less time
- consistent, relevant material
- more control of content and faculty
- helps develop organizational culture and teamwork[22]

Basically, companies have various training and development options. A recent survey of organizations with 100 or more employees revealed numerous types of training currently being used. These data are shown in Table 8-5. As you can see, management skills/development was the most popular type of training, followed by basic computer skills, communication skills, and supervisory skills. Management skills/development training was provided by 91 percent of the responding firms. Twelve percent provided this type of training solely in-house, and 18 percent used outside sources, such as universities and consultants. Sixty-one percent of the firms used both in-house and outside trainers for their management skills development.[23]

Regardless of whether programs are presented in-house or by an outside source, a number of methods are utilized in imparting knowledge to managers. We discuss these methods next.

TABLE 8-5
General Types of Training

TYPES OF TRAINING	% PROVIDING[1]	IN-HOUSE ONLY (%)[2]	OUTSIDE ONLY (%)[3]	BOTH (%)[4]
Management Skills/ Development	91	12	18	61
Basic Computer Skills	90	21	14	55
Communication Skills	87	21	12	53
Supervisory Skills	86	18	12	56
Technical Skills/ Knowledge	82	22	6	54
New Methods/ Procedures	80	38	5	37
Executive Development	77	8	26	44
Customer Relations/ Services	76	25	9	41
Personal Growth	73	14	15	45
Clerical/ Secretarial Skills	73	23	18	32
Employee/Labor Relations	67	23	12	31
Customer Education	65	28	5	31
Wellness	63	21	15	28
Sales Skills	56	15	11	30
Remedial/Basic Education	48	11	21	15

Of all organizations with 100 or more employees . . .
[1]Percent that provide each type of training.
[2]Percent that say all training of this type is designed and delivered by in-house staff.
[3]Percent that say all training of this type is designed and delivered by outside consultants or suppliers.
[4]Percent that say training of this type is designed and delivered by a combination of in-house staff and outside suppliers.
Source: Paul Froiland, "Who's Getting Trained?" *Training* (October 1993): 60.

Coaching and Mentoring

Coaching is an on-the-job approach to management development in which the manager is given an opportunity to teach on a one-to-one basis. Some firms create *assistant to* positions for this purpose. An individual placed in this type of staff position becomes an understudy to his or her boss. In addition to having the opportunity to observe, the subordinate will also be assigned significant tasks requiring decision-making skills. To be productive, coach-counselor managers must have a thorough knowledge of the job and how it relates to the firm's goals. They should also have a strong desire to share information with the understudy and be willing to take the time—which can be considerable—for this endeavor. The relationship between the supervisor and subordinate must be based on mutual trust and confidence for this approach to be effective.

Mentoring is an on-the-job approach to management development in which the trainee is given the opportunity to learn on a one-to-one basis from more experienced organizational members. The mentor is usually an older, experienced executive who serves as a host, friend, confidant, and advisor to a new firm member. The mentor is located anywhere in the organization. The relationship may be formally planned, or it may develop informally. The concept of mentoring has some prestigious advocates, such as Ortho Pharmaceutical Corporation, Bell Labs, AT&T, and the Internal Revenue Service. Mentoring has received considerable attention, most of which has emphasized its advantages. There have even been suggestions that mentoring is necessary to *make it to the top*.

For mentoring to work, the parties' interests must be compatible, and they must understand each other's psyches. Getting teachers and students together can obviously have advantages. In a mentoring relationship, this combination has the potential for positive results.[24]

Business Games

Simulations that represent actual business situations are referred to as **business games**. These simulations attempt to duplicate selected factors in a particular situation, which are then manipulated by the participants. Business games involve two or more hypothetical organizations competing in a given product market. The participants are assigned roles, such as president, controller, and marketing vice president. They make decisions affecting price levels, production volumes, and inventory levels. Their decisions are manipulated by a computer program, with the results simulating those of an actual business situation. Participants are able to see how their decisions affect other groups and vice versa. The best part about this type of learning is that if a decision is made that costs the company $1 million, no one gets fired, and still the business lesson is learned.

Case Study

The **case study** is a training method that utilizes simulated business problems for trainees to solve. The individual is expected to study the information given in the case and make decisions based on the situation. If the student is provided a case involving an actual company, he or she would be expected to research the firm to gain a better appreciation of its financial condition and environment. Typically, the case study method is used in the classroom with an instructor who serves as a facilitator.

Conference Method

The **conference method**, or discussion method, is a widely used instructional approach that brings together individuals with common interests to discuss and attempt to solve problems. Often the leader of the group is the supervisor. The group leader's role is to keep the discussion on course and avoid the tendency of some individuals to get off the subject. As problems are discussed, the leader listens and permits group members to solve their own problems. Individuals engaged in the conference method, although in training, work to solve actual problems that they face in their everyday activities.

Behavior Modeling

Behavior modeling has long been a successful training method that utilizes live demonstrations or videotapes to illustrate effective interpersonal skills and how managers function in various situations. The trainees observe the model's actions. Behavior modeling has been used successfully to train supervisors in such tasks as conducting performance appraisal reviews, correcting unacceptable performance, delegating work, improving safety habits, handling discrimination complaints, overcoming resistance to change, orienting new employees, and mediating between conflicting individuals or groups.[25]

As an example, a supervisor may act out his or her role in disciplining an employee who has been consistently late in reporting to work. Since the situations presented are typical of the firm's problems, the participants are able to relate the behavior to their own jobs. The concept of behavior modeling has been around for a long time. For example, most linguists agree that learning language is imitative. Consider for a moment how most of us learn to drive a car, hit a golf ball, or mow the lawn. We probably learned by observing others doing these activities.

In-Basket Training

In-basket training is a simulation in which the participant is given a number of business papers, such as memoranda, reports, and telephone messages, that would typically cross a manager's desk. The papers, presented in no particular order, call for actions ranging from urgent to routine handling. The participant is required to act on the information contained in these papers. In this training method, assigning a priority to each particular situation precedes making decisions called for in each situation.

Internships

As we mentioned in Chapter 6, an internship program is a recruitment method whereby university students divide their time between attending classes and working for an organization. Internships can also serve as an effective training method.

From the employer's viewpoint, an internship provides an excellent means of viewing a potential permanent employee at work. Internships also provide advantages for students. The experience they obtain through working enables them to integrate theory learned in the classroom with the practice of management. At the same time, the interns' experience will help them determine whether a particular type of firm and job appeals to them.

Role Playing

In **role playing**, participants are required to respond to specific problems they may actually encounter in their jobs. Rather than hearing about how a problem might be handled, or even discussing it, they learn by doing. Role playing is often used in management development. It may be effectively utilized to teach such skills as interviewing, grievance handling, performance appraisal, conference leadership, team problem solving, effective communication, and analyzing leadership styles. The Developing HRM Skills section at the end of each chapter is a role playing exercise that demonstrates the benefits of this training approach.

Job Rotation

Job rotation involves moving employees from one job to another to broaden their experience. This breadth of knowledge is often needed for performing higher level tasks. Rotational training programs help new employees understand the variety of jobs within their fields. However, there are some potential problems. The new hires may have such short assignments that they feel more like visitors in the department rather than a part of the workforce. Since they often do not develop a high level of proficiency, the new hires can lower the overall productivity of the work group. In addition, employees who observe or have to work with an individual rotating through their department may resent a *fast-track* employee who may in time become their boss.

Programmed Instruction

A teaching method that provides instruction without the intervention of an instructor is called **programmed instruction (PI)**. In PI, information is broken down into small portions (frames). The learner reads each frame in sequence and responds to questions, receiving immediate feedback on response accuracy. If correct, the learner proceeds to the next frame. If not, the learner repeats the frame. Primary features of this approach are immediate reinforcement and the ability of learners to proceed at their own pace. Programmed instruction material may be presented in a book or by more sophisticated means, such as computers.

Computer-Based Training

Computer-based training takes advantage of the speed, memory, and data manipulation capabilities of the computer for greater flexibility. The increased speed of presentation and less dependence on an instructor are advantages of this training approach. Instruction can be provided either in a central location or a satellite office. On the down side, some students object to the absence of a human facilitator. Another disadvantage is the cost of hardware and software. However, with enough trainees, the cost may quickly reach an acceptable level.

In using computers for training, the world of interactive technology is fast becoming a reality. U.S. firms are investing billions of dollars a year in this training approach. Laser disks, CD-ROM, interactive-voice systems, and other devices are revolutionizing the way training and development programs are delivered. (See Table 8-6 for a summary of interactive devices.) One executive has stated, "It allows a human resources department to provide on-demand information that can be updated constantly and distributed nationally or globally."[26]

Computer-based training is clearly more than a fad. In fact, more than 80 percent of large organizations use computers in training.[27] One market research and consulting firm predicts that American companies will increase their investment in multimedia training almost tenfold during the mid-1990s. Much of that investment is expected to be in CD-ROM, which has the ability to deliver information in an interactive form. Holiday Inn Worldwide is investing $60 million in such a system that will put multimedia training stations in the chain's 1600 hotels in Canada, Latin America, and the United States.[28] Programs such as these may provide increased retention rates and less cost. Studies have indicated that laser disc instruction takes 30 percent less time to achieve learning objectives than traditional classroom training. A 1988 study conducted at General Motors indicated that students trained using interactive learning programs scored an average of 83 percent on a final exam compared with an average of 63 percent for classroom students. Still other studies have suggested that cost savings of 50 percent or more can be achieved.[29]

Distance Learning and Videoconferencing

For the past decade, a number of firms in the United States have used videoconferencing and satellite classrooms for training. This approach to training is now going interactive and appears to offer the flexibility and spontaneity of a traditional classroom. At an IBM subsidiary, for example, highly sophisticated programs are offered over a satellite based network. At each of the 44 sites in the system, a 25-inch monitor is used on a desk equipped with a student response unit. These units allow interconnection with other classrooms and the instructor. The student response unit has a voice activated microphone, question and question-cancel buttons, and keypads that allow students to answer questions from the instructor. Other firms such as AT&T, DuPont, Ford, General Electric, Mobil Oil, Sears, and Wal-Mart also use this type of service. A great deal of training is beginning to take place using this technology, offering the prospect of increasing the number of trainees and at the same time saving a lot of money for the company.[30]

Multinational companies, in particular, can benefit from this new technology. With far flung operations, travel expenses are getting more and more out of hand. Distance learning, videoconferencing, and similar technology can be used to increase access to training, ensure consistency of instruction, and reduce the cost of delivering training and development programs. While

TABLE 8-6 Interactive Technology at a Glance

CD-ROM	
Technology	Uses a laser to read up to 600 megabytes of text, graphics, audio and video off a 4½ inch aluminum disc. Works in conjunction with either a PC (DOS or Windows) or a Macintosh.
Cost	$300-$700 per unit; approximately $4,500 for a complete station. Off-the-shelf software generally runs $75-$1,500 per program; custom programs can cost $2,000-$10,000 to produce.
Advantages	Excellent for combining text and graphics on the same screen. Can be installed internally to save space. Thousands of off-the-shelf programs and applications available, including many reference guides.
Disadvantages	Video quality not up to par with laser discs. Not capable of displaying video full screen.
Comments	Useful for most training situations.
Satellite Instruction	
Technology	Uses a satellite to link various locations into a single classroom.
Cost	Highly variable, depending on the set-up. Conventional classroom training generally ranges from $150-$300 per day per student; other programs can cost $8,000-$10,000 per location for a single day.
Advantages	Provides an efficient way to train large numbers of people in a consistent way without investing large sums to fly them into a corporate training center. For incentive-based programs can make learning entertaining and fun.
Disadvantages	Requires a relatively large investment that may be suitable only for large companies. Individuals sometimes think that systems are unwieldy and inflexible.
Comments	Becoming more popular. New wrinkles offer intriguing possibilities.
CD-I	
Technology	Stand-alone unit uses a laser to read up to 72 minutes of video and data from a 4½ inch disc to a monitor.
Cost	$500-$600 per unit; $400-$1,200 for an accompanying monitor. Kiosk configuration can run $200-$10,000.
Advantages	Interactive video without a computer. Portability makes it ideal for remote training and recruiting.
Disadvantages	Can't store data on how system is being used; can't administer tests or track scores.
Comments	More sophisticated than a VCR; less sophisticated than CD-ROM or laser disc.

Source: Samuel Greengard, "How Technology Is Advancing HR," *Personnel Journal* (September 1993): 82–83.

the heaviest users to date have been universities, a recent study indicated that about ten percent of U.S. organizations, with more than 100 employees, used videoconferencing for some type of training.[31]

Classroom Lecture

Although lacking the glitz of newer approaches, the classroom lecture continues to be effective for certain types of employee training. A great advantage is that the lecturer may convey a great deal of information in a relatively short period of time. The effectiveness of lectures can be improved

TABLE 8-6 (continued) Interactive Technology at a Glance

Interactive-Voice Technology	
Technology	Uses a program installed on a conventional PC to create an automated phone-response system.
Cost	$10,000-$75,000
Advantages	Can be produced internally or purchased from outside firm. System can be updated, and new recordings added with relative ease. Frees HR staff to handle other projects; can slash printing costs for producing benefits booklets and job-opening notices.
Disadvantages	Poorly designed or overly complicated system can create headaches for those trying to use it. System must be thoroughly tested so as not to provide inaccurate information.
Comments	Quickly growing in popularity as a way to provide information on benefits and accounts; and as a way to post job openings electronically.
Laser Disc	
Technology	Uses a laser to read one hour of video (two hours at a lower resolution) from a 10-inch disc. Picture can be displayed on a TV monitor or computer.
Cost	$300-$1,000 per unit; approximately $4,500-$5,000 for a complete station. Off-the-shelf software runs $1,000-$15,000; custom software can run as high as $300,000.
Advantages	Highest-quality video of any disc-based medium; also capable of producing digital audio. Can be used as a basic video data base with a bar-code reader or controller; or as part of a sophisticated computing system when interfaced to a PC or Macintosh.
Disadvantages	Bulky discs; can't be used for as many applications as CD-ROM; requires a special video card (DVI) inside the computer.
Comments	Has become the media of preference for interactive training because of high-quality video and sound.

when groups are small enough to permit discussion, when the lecturer is able to capture the imagination of the class, and when audiovisual equipment is used in a timely and appropriate manner.

EXECUTIVE AND MANAGEMENT DEVELOPMENT AT IBM

At IBM, formal executive and management development programs are conducted for various organizational levels. These programs vary from three-day sessions for recently appointed managers to two-week programs designed for newly named executives having worldwide responsibilities. Specifically, the following programs are provided: New Manager Training—U. S. Policy and Practices; New Manager School—IBM Leadership Program; IBM Business Management Institute; and IBM Global Executive Program.

New Manager Training—U. S. Policy and Practices is provided for newly appointed managers at various locations. This three-day program's purpose is to develop an understanding of IBM's basic management policies, practices, and skills. It focuses on performance management, compensation, diversity, career development, and management of individuals.

New Manager School—IBM Leadership Program is designed for all individuals appointed to the initial level of management responsibility. The three-and-a-half-day school normally begins within 60 to 90 days after the appointment and is held at the Central Headquarters Management Development Center in Armonk, New York.

IBM Business Management Institute is an eight-day program held worldwide. It is for individuals newly appointed to responsibility for an organization having significant impact on IBM's success in the marketplace. The program focuses on profitability and customer satisfaction. Case studies and business simulation models are utilized to work on actual IBM business problems.

IBM Global Executive Program is for newly named executives with worldwide responsibilities. This two-week program is conducted in New York and La Hulpe, Belgium. The program focuses on building global perspectives, fostering performance and change, and leveraging IBM's capabilities. A significant part of the program is addressing a strategic business issue, including the presentation of results to the sponsoring senior executive.

SUPERVISORY MANAGEMENT TRAINING PROGRAMS: AN ILLUSTRATION

Some firms also conduct supervisory training programs. They consider such training to be necessary for their first-line managers to perform to their maximum potential. An overview of a supervisory training program developed by the Chevron Corporation for its first-line managers is shown in Figure 8-5. This program is designed to provide new supervisors with the skills and knowledge they need to manage people effectively. The training program is also available to supervisors with long-term service to update their knowledge. The program has three phases: presession activities; a five-day live, live-in session; and postsession activities.

Several weeks prior to the live-in session, participants are asked to engage in the following activities, which will prepare them for involvement in the program:

1. Identify productive and nonproductive activities.
2. Discuss the basic elements of their jobs with their bosses.
3. Select a major opportunity or problem that both the participant and the boss are committed to deal with. (This becomes an action plan.)
4. Send a sample of an employee evaluation to the training program coordinator.

The five-day, live-in session comprises the heart of the program. It begins on a Sunday night with a social get-together, dinner, and business meeting. Participants are asked to tell briefly about their jobs and discuss their action plans. A top-management representative meets with the group during this initial meeting to discuss the role of the supervisor, the purpose of the program, and expected on-the-job results.

During this main session, a number of support subjects and key course subjects are presented. At the same time, information is provided concerning laws and company policies and practices. Brief descriptions of the purposes of support subjects and key course subjects are presented in Table 8-7. Action plan projects are worked with during the program evaluation phase, and the results are used to measure the program's value.

Presession Activities	Five-Day, Live-in Session Activities			Postsession Activities
	Support subjects	Key course subjects	Program evaluation	
Time Analysis	Why We Are Here	Performance Planning and Review	Formulate an Action Plan Project	Approval and Implementation of an Action Plan Project
Work Analysis	Analyzing Performance Problems	Documentation Skills		
Performance Planning Discussion	Training	Employee Ranking	Rank Session's Topics	Possible Performance Planning and Review Discussions
Selecting an Action Plan Project	Special Health Services	Salary Administration	Evaluate Program	Follow-up Questionnaire to Participant and Boss
Writing a Performance Evaluation	Time Management Employment Compliance	Employee Development		
Interview with Coordinator				
Time:	*Time:*	*Time:*	*Time:*	*Time:*
Completed Prior to Start of Program	1 1/2 days →	2 1/2 days →	1 day →	2–4 months after program →

FIGURE 8-5 An Overview of Chevron Corporation's Supervisory Training Program

Source: Used with the permission of the Chevron Corporation.

The postsession phase of the program consists of implementing the action plans. Further attempts are also made to relate the program's impact to the supervisor's job performance. At this point, training needs that are not being met are emphasized. Appropriate changes are made to ensure that the training program continues to have practical value to both the employee and the company.

TRAINING METHODS FOR ENTRY-LEVEL PROFESSIONAL EMPLOYEES

Firms have a special interest in college-trained employees hired for entry-level professional positions, including management trainees. Of all the technologies affecting management in today's business world, information management is experiencing the most rapid change. This fast-paced development is expected to continue well into the future. To prepare enterprising minds for this challenge, General

TABLE 8-7
Chevron Corporation's Supervisory Training Program's Purposes for a Five-Day, Live-in Session

SUPPORT SUBJECTS Why We Are Here	KEY COURSE SUBJECTS Performance Planning and Review
To orient participants with top management views of the role of a supervisor, the purpose of this program, and what on-job results are expected to occur. **Analyzing Performance Problems** To provide supervisors with the skills necessary to analyze a performance discrepancy so that they can determine the best solution. **Training** To provide supervisors with the skill and knowledge to effectively train others. **Special Health Services** To provide supervisors with an expanded awareness of their responsibilities in the area of Special Health Services and with information and skills to deal with the troubled employee. **Time Management** To provide skills in how to better manage and use time. **Employment Compliance** To teach supervisors the value of consistent personnel practices and the skills to apply them, as well as the intent of EEO legal requirements.	To increase supervisory productivity and efficiency by creating better: ■ Communications ■ Understanding of the job ■ Planning and allocation of time ■ Data for evaluating employees' work performance **Documentation Skills** To improve writing skills of supervisors in order that they may better manage their human resources. **Employee Ranking** To provide supervisors with the skill and knowledge needed to objectively evaluate employee performance on the job. **Salary Administration** To review the basics of salary administration so that supervisors can provide meaningful inputs to higher management and provide feedback to employees about salary decisions. **Employee Development** To assist supervisors in their role of developing employees both within their current jobs and for future jobs as appropriate.

Source: Used with the permission of the Chevron Corporation.

Electric (GE) conducts the Information Management Leadership Program (IMLP). This is a two-year program combining rotational work assignments with graduate-level seminars. It prepares employees to design, program, and implement integrated computerized and manual information systems.

General Electric's IMLP emphasizes challenging work assignments in such areas as programming, systems analysis and design, computer center operation, project management, and functional work. The length of these assignments varies, and individual progress is determined by employee performance and demonstrated potential.

A candidate for IMLP will most likely have a degree in computer science, information systems, or engineering. However, a strong interest in technical applications must be balanced with business acumen. Therefore, individuals possessing degrees in business or liberal arts with a minor in computer science will be considered if other criteria are met. Given GE's diverse businesses and unique needs, a wide range of candidates are considered for the IMLP. Candidates' overall qualifications are considered, including their course curricula, academic records, leadership in extracurricular activities, and work experience.

Other training programs for college graduates may have more or less structure than General Electric's IMLP. However, most of them also emphasize training provided on the job. *Hands-on* experience, alone or in combination with other methods, appears to be an essential component of these programs.

TRAINING METHODS FOR OPERATIVE EMPLOYEES

In firms utilizing self-directed work teams, operative employees make many decisions previously reserved for management. Their jobs still differ, however, in that their primary role does not involve achieving goals through the efforts of others. Basically, they are the *other people*. Their contributions are essentially direct and collectively vital to the production of goods and services. Organizations rely heavily on their senior clerks, systems analysts, and other operative employees. Every position in an organization is necessary or it would not (or should not) exist. Therefore, training and development for operative employees must also be given high priority.

In this section, we discuss HRD methods that apply to the training of operative employees. However, these are not the only available methods; they are just an overview of methods commonly utilized. Recall the methods listed in Table 8-4 that are applicable to both management and operative employees.

On-the-Job Training

On-the-job training (OJT) is an informal approach to training that permits an employee to learn job tasks by actually performing them. Although some may not consider OJT to be a bona fide training method, it is the most commonly used approach to HRD. With OJT, there is no problem in later transferring what has been learned to the task. Individuals may also be more highly motivated to learn because it is clear to them that they are acquiring the knowledge needed to perform their jobs. At times, however, the emphasis on production may tend to detract from the training process. The trainee may feel so much pressure to perform that learning is negatively affected.

HRM IN ACTION

—I'VE ALWAYS DONE IT THAT WAY!

Lon Williams, the training and development manager, was studying the weekly training schedule when he heard a tap at his door. "Got a minute, Lon?" asked Joe Diver, production manager.

"Sure, come on in," said Lon. "What've you got?"

"You may know that I recently hired John Bryan, a retired Marine officer who wanted to begin his second career with us. John's military record was excellent, and I was shocked when I heard through the grapevine about his high-handed methods. Apparently, he still thinks he's in the Marines the way he bosses people around. When I spoke to John, he said, 'I've been successful for twenty years managing people and using these exact methods.' Lon, something has to be done. Do you have any ideas?"

How would you respond?

Both the manager and the trainee must recognize that OJT is a joint effort. In addition, the manager must create a climate of trust and open communication to make OJT effective.

Apprenticeship Training

Another approach, **apprenticeship training**, combines classroom instruction with on-the-job training. Such training is traditionally used in craft jobs, such as those of plumber, barber, carpenter, machinist, and printer. While in training, the employee earns less than the master craftsperson who is the instructor. The training period varies according to the craft. For instance, the apprenticeship training period for barbers is two years; for machinists, four years; and for pattern makers, five years.

German-owned Siemens Stromberg-Carlson has a background in apprenticeship training that spans 100 years. The firm's program at its Lake Mary, Florida, plant involves both high school students and students from Seminole Community College. The high school students work at Siemens three hours a day, twice a week. Community college students complete a two-and-a-half-year curriculum while working 20 hours a week.[32] Employees recruited from the apprenticeship program are expected to *hit the ground running*. Siemens' experience had shown that this was not possible with other recruits.[33]

Simulators

Simulators are training devices of varying degrees of complexity that model the real world. They range from simple paper mock-ups of mechanical devices to computerized simulations of total environments. Human resource development specialists may use simulated sales counters, automobiles, and airplanes. Although simulator training may be less valuable than on-the-job training for some purposes, it has certain advantages. A prime example is the training of airline pilots: Simulated training crashes do not cost lives or deplete the firm's fleet of jets.

Vestibule Training

Vestibule training takes place away from the production area on equipment that closely resembles equipment actually used on the job. For example, a group of lathes may be located in a training center where the trainees will be instructed in their use. A primary advantage of vestibule training is that it removes the employee from the pressure of having to produce while learning. The emphasis is on learning the skills required by the job.

JOB TRAINING PARTNERSHIP ACT

The **Job Training Partnership Act (JTPA)** provides training through local-level partnerships between business and government. It results in the largest single training effort sponsored by the federal government.[34] The program provides several billion dollars in funds each year to the states, which, in turn, give grants to local governments and private entities. Job training and employment services are then provided for economically disadvantaged adults and youth, dislocated workers, and other persons who face exceptional employment hurdles. The act first became operational in 1983 with the goal of moving the unemployed into permanent, unsubsidized, self-sustaining jobs. Initially criticized for inadequate cost controls and failure to target the most disadvantaged individuals, the act was amended in 1992 to address these problems.

JTPA programs are overseen by the Private Industry Council (PIC). PIC members represent business, education, labor, rehabilitation and economic development agencies, community-based organizations, and public employment services. More than half of its members come from the business community. These business-led organizations assist in allocating funds to local training and employment services. On-the-job training programs are also offered. In OJT programs, the sponsoring business firms are reimbursed for a portion of their cost for training eligible new hires. OJT places participants in jobs that are determined by the PIC to be in high demand in their area. The purpose of all JTPA training is to provide better employment, higher earnings, increased skills, and decreased welfare dependency for participants. The ultimate goal is to improve the quality of the workforce and to enhance the nation's productivity.[35]

USES OF VARIOUS HUMAN RESOURCE DEVELOPMENT METHODS

A study of organizations with 100 or more employees revealed the percentage of firms using various training methods (see Figure 8-6). As may be seen, the top two methods are videotapes and lectures. Even though firms are slightly more likely to use videotapes than lectures, the figures do not imply that employees as a whole spend more time watching videos than listening to lectures. The question on the survey was "Do you use it?" not "How much do you use it?" Figure 8-6 also shows that other methods used by more than 50 percent of responding organizations include one-on-one instruction, slides, role plays, and audiotapes.[36]

FIGURE 8-6
Frequency of Use of Human Resource Development Methods

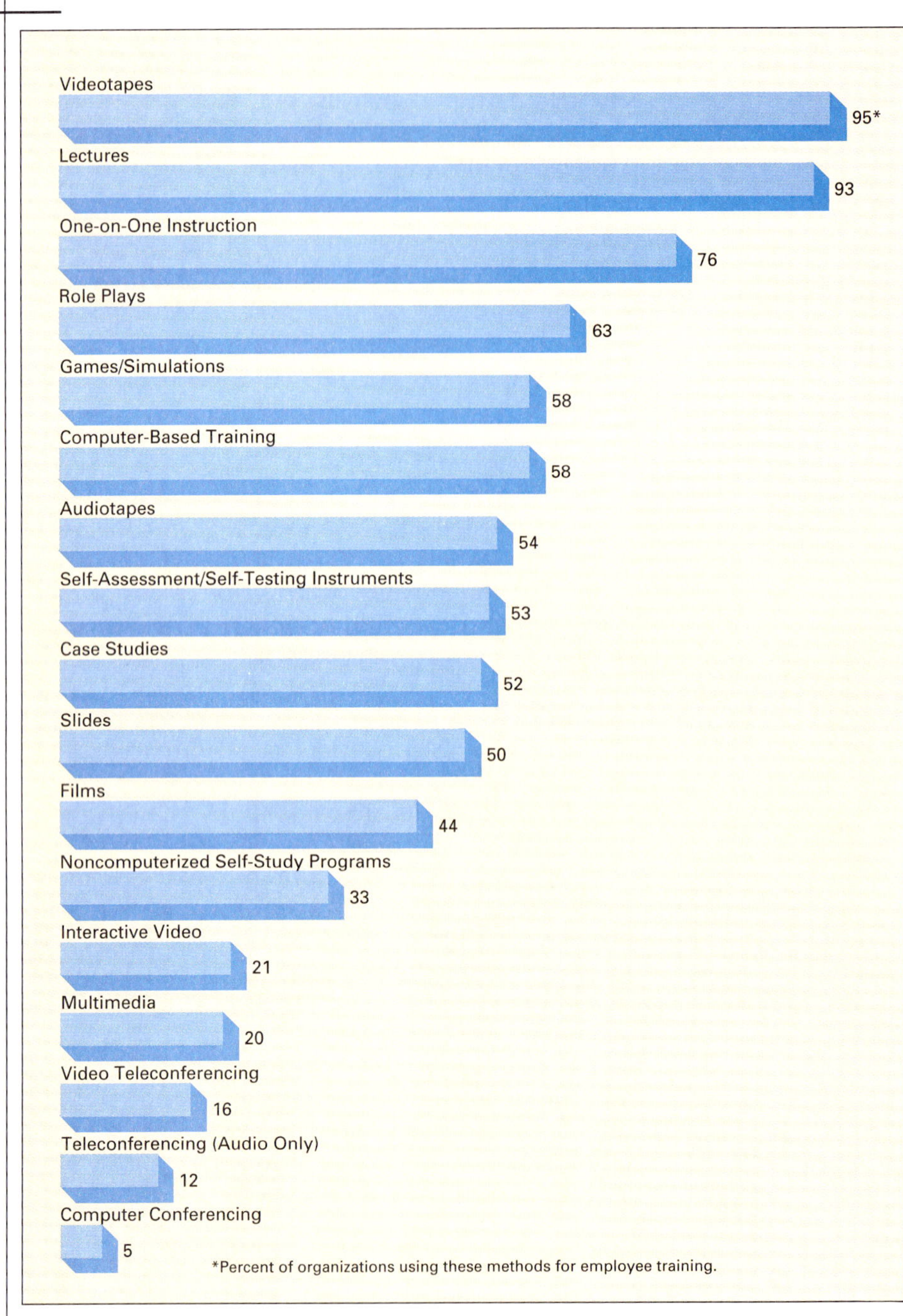

Source: Paul Froiland, "Who's Getting Trained?" *Training* (October 1993): 57.

HUMAN RESOURCE DEVELOPMENT MEDIA

Organizations utilize various media to enhance their training programs. In this context, **media** are special methods of communicating ideas and concepts in training and development. Multimedia presentations, using the computer in conjunction with video and/or other media, appear to offer tremendous potential as previously discussed. More conventional media include videotapes, films, closed-circuit television, slide projectors, overhead and opaque projectors, flip charts, and chalkboards.

Visual aids can greatly facilitate learning, and they play an important role in training and development. This function is emphasized when you consider that while 75 percent of what we learn is learned by sight, approximately 75 percent of what we hear is forgotten within two days.[37] One of the most commonly used HRD methods, the lecture, may be more effective when complemented with the use of overhead transparencies or a video. These media have the potential to gain and maintain trainee interest and attention.

IMPLEMENTING HUMAN RESOURCE DEVELOPMENT PROGRAMS

A perfectly conceived training program can fail if management cannot convince the participants of its merits. Participants must believe that the program has value and will help them achieve their personal and professional goals. The credibility of HRD specialists may depend on a series of successful programs.

Implementing HRD programs is often difficult. One of the reasons is that managers are typically action oriented and feel that they are too busy for HRD. According to one management development executive, "Most busy executives are too involved chopping down the proverbial tree to stop for the purpose of sharpening their axes. . . . " Another difficulty in program implementation is that qualified trainers must be available. In addition to possessing communication skills, the trainers must know the company's philosophy, its objectives, its formal and informal organization, and the training program's goals. Human resource development requires more creativity than perhaps any other human resource specialty.

A new program must be monitored carefully, especially during its initial phases. Training implies change, which employees may resist vigorously. Others may sit back waiting, perhaps even hoping, that the program will fail. Participant feedback is vital at this stage because there will be *bugs* in any new program. The sooner these problems are resolved, the better the chances for success.

The HRD manager often has unique problems in implementing training programs. For example, it may be difficult to schedule the training around present work requirements. Unless the employee is new to the firm, he or she undoubtedly has specific full-time duties to perform. Although it is the line manager's job to have positions covered while an employee is in training, the HRD manager must assist with this problem.

Another difficulty in implementing HRD programs is record keeping. Records should be maintained on all training the employee receives and how well he or she performs during training and on the job. This information is important in terms of measuring program effectiveness and charting the employee's progress in the company.

Training conducted outside the organization requires considerable coordination. Consider the coordination required to get managers from all parts of the country to participate in an HRD program in Storrs, Connecticut, for instance. The logistics and costs involved in this type of undertaking can be significant.

EVALUATING HUMAN RESOURCE DEVELOPMENT

Although corporate America spends billions of dollars a year on employee training, there is no clear consensus within the training community on how to determine its value. Obviously, the credibility of HRD can be greatly enhanced by showing that the organization benefits tangibly from such programs. Thus, the HRD department must document its efforts and clearly show that it provides a valuable service. The documentation should be in the form of memoranda to management, written reports of activities, and any other evidence that indicates a quality product.[38]

Organizations have taken several approaches to determining the worth of specific programs. These involve evaluations of (1) the participants' opinions of the program, (2) the extent to which participants have learned the material, (3) the participants' ability to apply the new knowledge, and (4) whether the stated training goals have been achieved.

Participants' Opinions

Evaluating an HRD program by asking the participants' opinions of it is an inexpensive approach that provides an immediate response and suggestions for improvements. The basic problem with this type of evaluation is that it is based on opinion rather than fact. In reality, the trainee may have learned nothing but perceives that a learning experience occurred. For example, Tom Dickson has just completed a three-day executive seminar in Honolulu. At the conclusion of the program, Tom was given a brief questionnaire that, in essence, asked him whether the seminar was beneficial. It is difficult to imagine Tom or any of his fellow participants downgrading this training program. Even if it had been conducted in a less exotic location, a brief break from the hectic part of an executive's job can be a welcome relief. Participants' perceptions of the value of such programs may prove useful, but they must be interpreted cautiously.

Extent of Learning

Some organizations administer tests to determine what the participants in an HRD program have learned. The pretest-posttest, control group design is one evaluation procedure that may be used. In this procedure, the same test is used before and after training. It also calls for both a control group (which does not receive the training) and an experimental group (which does). Trainees are randomly assigned to each group. Differences in pretest and posttest results between the groups are then attributed to the training provided.

Behavioral Change

Tests may indicate fairly accurately what has been learned, but they give little insight into desired behavioral changes. For example, it is one thing for a manager to learn about motivational techniques but quite another matter for this person to apply the new knowledge. Consider the situation involving Pat Sittel:

> Pat Sittel sat in the front row at the supervisory training seminar her company sponsored. The primary topic of the program was empowering employees. As the lecturer made each point, Pat would nod her head in

agreement. She thoroughly understood what was being said during the two-day period of the seminar. At the end of the program, Pat returned to her department and continued the management style she had followed for ten years; one that involved little empowerment of anyone except herself. Although she had understood the material presented in the seminar, Pat's failure to apply what she had learned didn't benefit the organization.

Accomplishment of HRD Objectives

Still another approach to evaluating HRD programs involves determining the extent to which stated objectives have been achieved. For instance, if the objective of an accident prevention program is to reduce the number and severity of accidents by 15 percent, comparing accident rates before and after training provides a useful measurement of success. The problem is that many programs dealing with broader topics are more difficult to evaluate. A group of executives may, for example, be sent to a state university for a one-week course in management and leadership development. *Before* and *after* performance appraisals of the participants may be available. Following the course, the managers may actually perform at a higher level, but other variables may distort the picture. For instance, a mild recession may force the layoff of several key employees; a competing firm may be successful in luring away one of the department's top engineers; or the company president could pressure the employment director to hire an incompetent relative. These and many other factors could cause the performance level of the group to decline, even though the managers had benefited from the HRD program.

In evaluating HRD programs, managers should strive for proof that the program is effective. While such proof may be difficult to establish, the effect on performance should at least be estimated to show whether the training achieved its desired purpose. In spite of problems associated with evaluation, the human resource manager must continue to strive for solid evidence of HRD's contributions in achieving organizational goals.

A GLOBAL PERSPECTIVE

Effective employee initiation is essential for employee success. Two vital components of employee initiation are orientation and training. Orientation is the guided adjustment of new employees to the company, the job, and the work group, and training is designed to permit learners to acquire knowledge and skills needed for their present jobs.

Orientation for new employees to the company, the job, and the work group varies in its degree of complexity, but global orientation will almost certainly be more complex than any domestic program. Because of the extreme cost of global staffing and the staggering cost of failed expatriate assignments, global orientation takes on increased importance.[39] Orientation for new global employees is critical. It must incorporate an introduction to the organizational (and perhaps national) cultures of all parties that the individual is likely to encounter. Such an introduction should also include an overview of the history, traditions, and corporate values of partners, if any. Then, it should include a description of the new venture, its organization, and its management structure, followed by an introduction of the employee to the manager, department, and coworkers.[40]

Orientation cannot be a sketchy overview of the basics. It should be an in-depth process that has been thoroughly planned in advance, taking a long-term approach that includes provisions for follow-up and evaluation. The benefits of such programs are just now beginning to become evident. Two years after developing such a system, Corning, Inc., showed a 69 percent reduction in voluntary turnover among new hires, an 8:1 benefit/cost ratio in the first year, and a 14:1 ratio annually thereafter.[41]

Training in the United States differs markedly from that provided in foreign countries. American employers tend to emphasize training for more highly educated employees. In contrast, German firms control training through financial support of technical schools, apprenticeship programs, and on-the-job training. Approximately 70 percent of German workers who do not attend college receive such training. Sweden and other industrial nations also supply more training than in the United States.[42] Japanese firms have historically not emphasized training as much as many countries in other industrialized nations. For decades, because of a strong sense of loyalty and respect for authority on the part of workers, the Japanese have needed only basic technical training. However, with new attitudes among younger workers, who are more inclined to job-hop for additional economic benefits, much more formal training is needed. Training expenditures reflect an awareness of this challenge. In 1980, the Japanese spent an average of only $200 per employee, but by 1990, this expenditure had doubled. In fact, some large firms spend as much as $1,200 per person. Survey results of Japanese firms with more than 500 employees reveal that Japanese firms now understand, and are starting to really emphasize training:[43] Specifically, more than 90 percent of new employees receive orientation training, 85 percent of the firms have employee-development plans, 80 percent supply follow-up training within one year, 80 percent of newly assigned managers receive primary management training, 80 percent of middle managers obtain management development training, 70 percent of firms offer new employee training within two to three weeks of employment, and 60 percent assign orientation homework after a person is hired but before he or she reports to work.

Both the General Motors-Toyota NUMMI joint venture and the Chrysler-Mitsubishi Diamond Star alliance made new employee orientation and training high priorities. Each joint venture spent millions of dollars on orientation and training long before it formally started its manufacturing operations in the United States. The success of these companies suggests that international alliances should expend as much effort preparing new employees to deal with the social context of their jobs (and to cope with the insecurities and frustrations of a new learning situation) as they do developing the technical skills that employees need to perform effectively.[44]

SUMMARY

Change involves moving from one condition to another, and it will affect individuals, groups, and entire organizations. Basically, the impetus for change comes from a belief that the organization and its human resources can be more productive and successful after change occurs. Reducing resistance to change is crucial to success. The change sequence does not end when a change is implemented. A new and flexible position capable of dealing with present requirements and adapting to further change must be developed. The final phase of the change sequence involves evaluating the effectiveness of the specific human resource development method chosen.

Human resource development (HRD) is planned, continuous effort by management to improve employee competency levels and organizational performance through training and development programs. Training is designed to permit learners to acquire knowledge and skills needed for their present jobs. Development involves learning that looks beyond today and today's job; it has a more long-term focus. The general human resource development process that helps facilitate change involves the following steps: determine HRD needs, establish specific objectives, select HRD methods, select HRD media, implement HRD programs, and evaluate HRD programs.

Orientation is the guided adjustment of new employees to the company, the job, and the work group. There are essentially three different stages in an effective orientation program. During the first stage, general information about the organization is provided. The employee's immediate supervisor usually is responsible for the second stage of orientation. The third stage involves evaluation and follow-up, which are conducted by the human resource department in conjunction with the immediate supervisor.

Management development consists of all learning experiences resulting in an upgrading of skills and knowledge required in current and future managerial positions. Coaching is an on-the-job approach to management development in which the manager is given an opportunity to teach on a one-to-one basis. Mentoring is an on-the-job approach to management development in which the trainee is given the opportunity to learn on a one-to-one basis from more experienced organizational members. Simulations that represent actual business situations are referred to as business games. The case study is a training method that utilizes simulated business problems for trainees to solve. The conference method, or discussion method, is a widely used instructional approach that brings together individuals with common interests to discuss and attempt to solve problems. Behavior modeling utilizes live demonstrations or videotapes to illustrate effective interpersonal skills and how managers function in various situations. In-basket training is a simulation in which the participant is given a number of business papers, such as memoranda, reports, and telephone messages, which would typically cross a manager's desk. An internship program is a recruitment method whereby university students divide their time between attending classes and working for an organization. In role playing, participants are required to respond to specific problems they may actually encounter in their jobs. Job rotation involves moving employees from one job to another to broaden their experience. A teaching method that provides instruction without the intervention of an instructor is called programmed instruction (PI). Computer-based training takes advantage of the speed, memory, and data manipulation capabilities of the computer for greater flexibility. Videoconferencing and satellite classrooms are also used for training. Although lacking the glitz of newer approaches, the classroom lecture continues to be effective for certain types of employee training.

In firms utilizing self-directed work teams, operative employees make many decisions previously reserved for management and need training. On-the-job training (OJT) is an informal approach to training that permits an employee to learn job tasks by actually performing them. Apprenticeship training combines classroom instruction with on-the-job training. Simulators are training devices of varying degrees of complexity that model the real world. Vestibule training takes place away from the production area on equipment that closely resembles equipment actually used on the job.

The Job Training Partnership Act (JTPA) provides training through local-level partnerships between business and government. It results in the largest single training effort sponsored by the federal government.

Organizations have taken several approaches to determining the worth of specific programs. These involve evaluations of (1) the participants' opinions of the program, (2) the extent to which participants have learned the material, (3) the participants' ability to apply the new knowledge, and (4) whether the stated training goals have been achieved.

QUESTIONS FOR REVIEW

1. What are the steps involved in the organization change sequence?
2. What can the manager do to reduce resistance to change?
3. Define and explain the scope of human resource development (HRD).
4. What are the general purposes of HRD?
5. Describe the HRD process.
6. Define *orientation* and explain the importance of employee orientation to a firm.
7. Define *management development*. Why is it important?
8. List and describe the primary methods used in management development.

9. What methods are used primarily to train operative employees?

10. What are some of the means of evaluating HRD programs? Discuss.

HRM SIMULATION

Training is another major element of the simulation. Training programs prepare an employee for new job responsibilities, provide general managerial and career development training, and update an employee's technical skills. Currently, your organization does not have any training programs. Failure to train a person who has been promoted will result in a higher than normal turnover rate in that level, reduced productivity, and decreased morale when the employee fails at his or her new job and must be placed back in his or her old position.

ABC VIDEO CASE

CULTURAL REVOLUTION TAPE 1, NUMBER 13

Many companies in the United States are not as prepared as they should be for competing in the global marketplace. Much of their workforce is not sufficiently well educated to meet the challenge from other nations. In the town of Orville, Ohio, on the edge of Amish country, there is a one-hundred year old machine parts factory that was on the edge of ruin until all 290 employees started studying together. All Will-Burt Company employees are required to take a year of classes held on company premises and on company time. The school concept was the invention of Harry Featherstone, Will-Burt chairman. The idea was that if everyone would get into the same classroom, then everyone would learn that everyone is equal and everybody has the same problems. By learning math, they would be able to communicate better with one another about the machine specs that allowed Will-Burt to make its defects almost disappear. A two-year business management course was added, resulting in an overlapping of knowledge that led to greater precision and quality in their product.

HRM INCIDENT 1

—WHAT TO DO?

"I'm a little discouraged," said Susan Matthews to the training officer, George Duncan. "I keep making mistakes running the new printing press. It's a lot more complicated than the one I operated before, and I just can't seem to get the hang of it." "Well, Susan," responded George, "maybe you're just not cut out for the job. You know that we sent you to the two-week refresher course in Atlanta to get you more familiar with the new equipment."

"Yes," said Susan, "they had modern equipment at the school, but it wasn't anything like this machine." "What about the factory rep?" asked George. "Didn't he spend some time with you?" "No, I was on vacation at that time," said Susan.

George responded, "Have you asked your boss to get him back for a day or two?" "I asked him," said Susan, "but he said training was your responsibility. That's why I'm here." After she was gone, George began writing a letter to the printing press manufacturer.

Questions

1. What steps in the HRD process has the company neglected?
2. Is George taking the proper action? What would you do?

HRM INCIDENT 2

—MANAGEMENT SUPPORT OF HRD?

As the initial training session began, John Robertson, the hospital administrator, spoke of the tremendous benefits he expected from the management development program the hospital was starting. He also complimented Brenda Short, the human resource director, for her efforts in arranging the program. As he finished his five-minute talk, he said, "I'm not sure what Brenda has in store for you, but I know that management development is important, and I'll expect each of you to put forth your best efforts to make it work." Mr. Robertson then excused himself from the meeting and turned the program over to Brenda.

For several years Brenda had been trying to convince Mr. Robertson that the supervisors could benefit from a management development program. She believed that many problems within the hospital were management related. Reluctantly, Mr. Robertson had agreed to authorize funds to employ a consultant. Through employee interviews and self-administered questionnaires completed by the supervisors, the consultant attempted to identify development needs. The consultant recommended twelve four-hour sessions emphasizing communication, leadership, and motivation. Each session was to be repeated once so that supervisors who missed it the first time could attend the second offering.

Mr. Robertson had signed the memo that Brenda had prepared, directing all supervisors to support the management development program. There was considerable grumbling, but all the supervisors agreed to attend. As Brenda replaced Mr. Robertson at the podium, she could sense the lack of interest in the room.

Questions

1. Have any serious errors been made so far in the management development program? What would you have done differently?
2. What advice do you have for Brenda at this point to help make the program effective?

DEVELOPING HRM SKILLS

AN EXPERIENTIAL EXERCISE

Human resource development (HRD) is very important to any organization as it faces change and deals with the continual development of its employees. Training, an integral part of the HRD process, can often be used to improve employee productivity. However, effective training cannot occur in a vacuum; therefore, training requires the support and understanding of the entire organization.

This day will be a training day, with the training specialist from the main office attempting to train an unwilling supervisor. The training specialist has almost completed this very difficult task and is looking forward to the last training session. All of the supervisors in this training session have risen through the ranks and have a definite dislike of college graduates. In addition, they all believe that they are experts on training in their areas. The training specialist just wants to get through this last briefing. As with the other supervisors, he'll show this supervisor the basics and then go back to the main office where people are more receptive. As with the others, if no in-depth questions are asked, he'll provide no additional details. He really doubts if the main office really expects improvement anyway. This operation seems to be going OK as it is.

The supervisor involved in this training session is really opposed to the training specialist trying to tell the supervisors how to train. It really grinds on this individual's nerves that since the company was bought out, the supervisors must do things their way. This person is scheduled to meet with the training specialist to learn how to train. The rumor mill has it that the training specialist is some twenty-one-year-old college grad. According to this supervisor, "I was training my people before this person was born. All of a sudden, we can't do anything right. I look forward to my private session with that individual. I'm going to reeducate the college grad on training."

Two individuals will play roles in this exercise: one to serve as the training specialist and the other to play the supervisor. Each participant should carefully follow his or her role. All students not playing roles should carefully observe the behavior of both participants. Your instructor will provide the participants with additional information necessary to complete the exercise.

NOTES

1. Owen Linstein and James Mauro, "Tom Peters . . . and the Healthy Corporation," *Psychology Today* 26 (March/April 1993): 57.

2. Leonard Ackerman, "Whose Ox Is Being Gored?" *HRMagazine* 36 (February 1991): 96.

3. William Fitzgerald, "Training Versus Development," *Training and Development* 46 (May 1992): 81.

4. Ibid.

5. Paul Froiland, "Who's Getting Trained?" *Training* (October 1993): 53.

6. Bob Filipczak, "Training Budgets Boom," *Training* (October 1993): 37–38.

7. "Industry Report," *Training* (October 1993): 29–30.

8. Ronald Henkoff, "Companies that Train Best," *Fortune* 127 (March 22, 1993): 62–63.

9. Stephenie Overman, "Ethan Allen's Secret Weapon," *HRMagazine* 39 (May 1994): 61.

10. "Skills for Success," *The Olsten Forum™ on Human Resource Issues and Trends*, The Olsten Corporation, Fall 1994, 7.

11. Kenneth N. Wexley and Gary P. Latham, *Developing and Training Human Resources in Organizations*, 2nd edition (New York: Harper-Collins Publishers, Inc., 1991): 36.

12. Kenneth M. Nowack, "A True Training Needs Analysis," *Training and Development Journal* 45 (April 1991): 69.

13. Ibid.

14. Samuel Greengard, "How Technology Is Advancing HR," *Personnel Journal* 72 (September 1993): 85.

15. Ron Zemke, "Employee Orientation: A Process, Not a Program," *Training* 26 (August 1989): 34–35.

16. Leslie Brokaw, "The Enlightened Employee Handbook," *Inc* 13 (October 1991): 49.

17. Karen Bridges, Gail Hawkins, and Keli Elledge, "From New Recruit to Team Member," *Training and Development* 47 (August 1993): 55–57.

18. Ron Zemke, "Employee Orientation: A Process, Not a Program," 34.

19. Diana Reed-Mendenhall and C. W. Millard, "Orientation: A Training and Development Tool," *Personnel Administrator* 25 (August 1980): 42–44.

20. Paul G. Wilhelm, "Employment at Will Harms Productivity," *HRMagazine* 35 (September 1990): 88.

21. William K. Fitzgerald and Scott Allen, "Personal Empowerment Key to Manager's Development," *HRMagazine* 38 (November 1993): 84–85.

22. Philip J. Harkins and David Giber, "Linking Business and Education Through Training," *Training and Development Journal* 43 (October 1989): 69.

23. Paul Froiland, "Who's Getting Trained?" 60.

24. Don Barnes, "What Is This Thing Called Mentoring?" *National Underwriter* 94 (May 28, 1990): 9.

25. William M. Fox, "Getting the Most from Behavior Modeling Training," *National Productivity Review* 7 (Summer 1988): 238.

26. Samuel Greengard, "How Technology is Advancing HR," 81.

27. "Computers in Training," *Training* 28 (October 1991): 51.

28. La Tresa Pearson, "Is CD-ROM About to Bloom?" *Training* 30 (November 1993): 5–7.

29. Samuel Greengard, "How Technology is Advancing HR," 84.

30. "Interactive Satellite Learning Improves Training Programs," *Personnel Journal* 72 (September 1993): 86.

31. Michael Emery and Margaret Schubert, "A Trainer's Guide to Videoconferencing," *Training* 30 (June 1993): 59–61.

32. After eleven months' training in Siemens' Florida program, American apprentices scored higher on their intermediary tests than their German counterparts. This finding suggests that American youths may be more talented than they are often given credit for.

33. Beth Rogers, "The Making of a Highly Skilled Worker," *HRMagazine* 39 (July 1994): 62–63.

34. Stephenie Overman, "Government Helps Retrain Displaced Workers," *HRMagazine* 38 (October 1993): 42.

35. Kathleen Barnes, "Government Program Supports On-the-Job Training," *HR Focus* 71 (June 1994): 12.

36. Jack Gordon, "Where the Training Goes," *Training* 27 (October 1990): 54–55.

37. Martin M. Broadwell, *The Supervisor as an Instructor*, 3rd edition (Reading, Mass.: Addison-Wesley, 1978): 85.

38. Jack Asgar, "Give Me Relevance or Give Me Nothing," *Training* 27 (July 1990): 49.

39. Mike Fergus, "Employees on the Move," *HRMagazine* 36 (May 1990): 45.

40. Wayne F. Cascio and Manuel G. Serapio, Jr., "Human Resources Systems in an International Alliance: The Undoing of a Done Deal?" *Organizational Dynamics* 19 (Winter 1991): 68.

41. Ibid.

42. Bernard W. Anderson, "Training to Succeed," *Black Enterprise* 21 (April 1991): 40.

43. Miyo Umeshima and Ron Dalesio, "More Like US," *Training and Development* 17 (March 1993): 28–29.

44. Wayne F. Cascio and Manuel G. Serapio, Jr., "Human Resources Systems in an International Alliance: The Undoing of a Done Deal?" 69.

CHAPTER 9

Corporate Culture and Organization Development

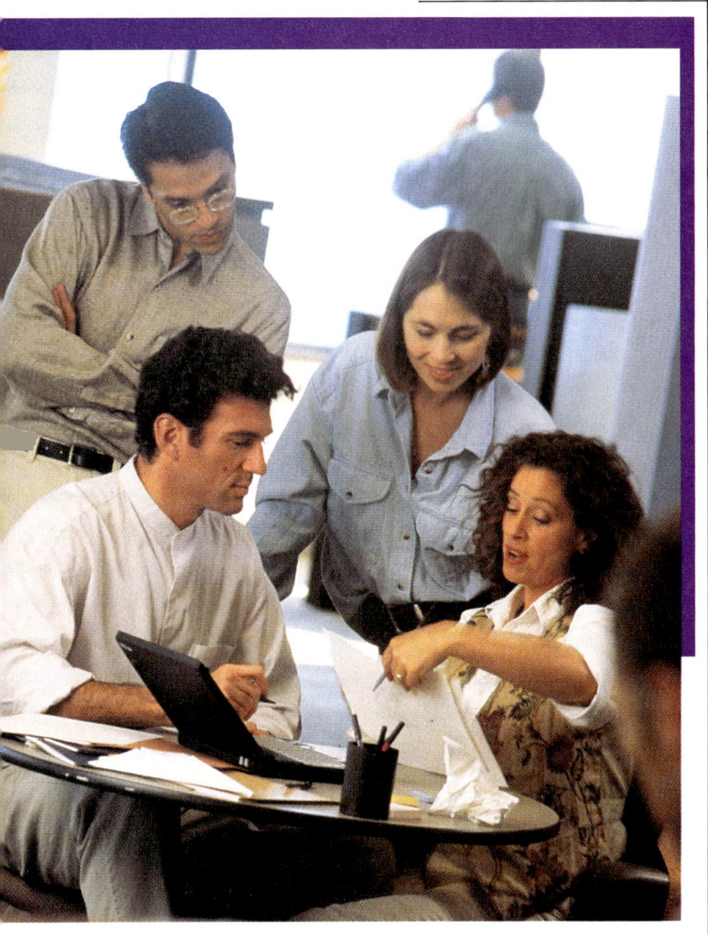

KEY TERMS

Corporate culture 270
Organization development (OD) 277
Survey feedback 278
Quality circles 280
Management by objectives (MBO) 280
Transactional analysis (TA) 282
Quality of work life (QWL) 283
Sensitivity training 284
Total quality management (TQM) 285
Team building 289

CHAPTER OBJECTIVES

1. Define corporate culture and describe the factors that interact to affect corporate culture.
2. Explain the various types of cultures, describe the participative culture, and state the importance of changing the corporate culture.
3. Define organization development (OD) and explain the traditional organization development methods.
4. Describe the organization development methods of total quality management and team building.
5. Explain the use of consultants in organization development and state the ways that managers can evaluate OD programs.

During the past four years, the profits of International Motor Corporation have declined sharply. Teddy McCoy, International's CEO, is especially concerned about the results of an attitude survey, which revealed that 60 percent of International's employees were dissatisfied with their jobs. Teddy felt certain this condition was directly related to an excessive number of product recalls and employee turnover. In a recent board meeting, he asserted, "With competition from both domestic and foreign corporations increasing, broad changes are needed throughout the firm if International is to survive and prosper. If we maintain the status quo, we may go under."

In all likelihood, International Motor Corporation requires an organization-wide human resource development program. In this chapter, we first define *corporate culture* and then present factors that determine corporate culture. Next, we describe types of cultures and the participative culture. Then, we discuss organization development methods, including total quality management and team building. Finally, we cover the use of consultants and organization development evaluation.

CORPORATE CULTURE DEFINED

When beginning a new job, an employee may soon hear, "This is the way to do things around here." This bit of informal communication refers to something more formally known as corporate culture.[1] **Corporate culture** is the system of shared values, beliefs, and habits within an organization that interacts with the formal structure to produce behavioral norms. It is the pattern of basic assumptions, values, norms, and artifacts shared by organizational members.[2] Corporate culture embodies the values and standards that guide people's behavior. It determines the organization's overall direction. Corporate culture governs what the company stands for, how it allocates resources, its organizational structure, the systems it uses, the people it hires, the fit between jobs and people, the results it recognizes and rewards, and what it defines as problems and opportunities and how it deals with them.[3]

Corporate culture is similar in concept to meteorological climate. Weather is described by such variables as temperature, humidity, and precipitation; similarly, corporate culture reflects such characteristics as friendliness, supportiveness, and risk taking. Each individual forms perceptions of the job and organization over a period of time as he or she works under the general guidance of a superior and a set of organizational policies. A firm's culture has an impact on employee job satisfaction, as well as on the level and quality of employee performance. However, each employee may assess the nature of an organization's culture differently. One person may perceive the culture negatively, and another may view it positively. Employees who are quite dissatisfied may even leave an organization in the hope of finding a more compatible culture.

According to Anthony Jay, an eminent researcher in the field of corporate culture, "It has been known for some time that corporations are social institutions with customs and taboos, status groups, and pecking orders. But they are also political institutions, autocratic and democratic, peaceful and warlike, liberal and paternalistic."[4] What Jay was writing about, although the term had not then achieved broad usage, was *corporate culture*. Businesses are being forced to make many changes to stay competitive. They must find ways to improve quality, increase speed of operations, and adopt a customer orientation. These changes are so fundamental that they must take root in a company's very essence, which means in its culture.[5] Corporate culture is an integral part of accomplishing an organization's mission and objectives; therefore, the factors that determine corporate culture are also crucial to success.

FACTORS THAT INFLUENCE CORPORATE CULTURE

The culture of a corporation evolves from the examples set by top management. It stems largely from what these executives do, not what they say. In addition, other factors can interact to shape the culture of a firm. Among those factors are work groups, managers' and supervisors' leadership styles, organizational characteristics, and administrative processes (see Figure 9-1). As in most management situations, the external environment also influences corporate culture.

One of the external environmental factors that greatly impacts a firm is competing in a global business environment. The corporate culture of Citicorp had always "overprized vision and undervalued hands-on, day-to-day management" until global pressures started to mount. Citicorp discovered that profits, more than any one single factor, are essential for global success. Combining an effective corporate culture, which keys on effectively coping with the global environment and at the same time being profitable, is what all global companies must strive for.[6]

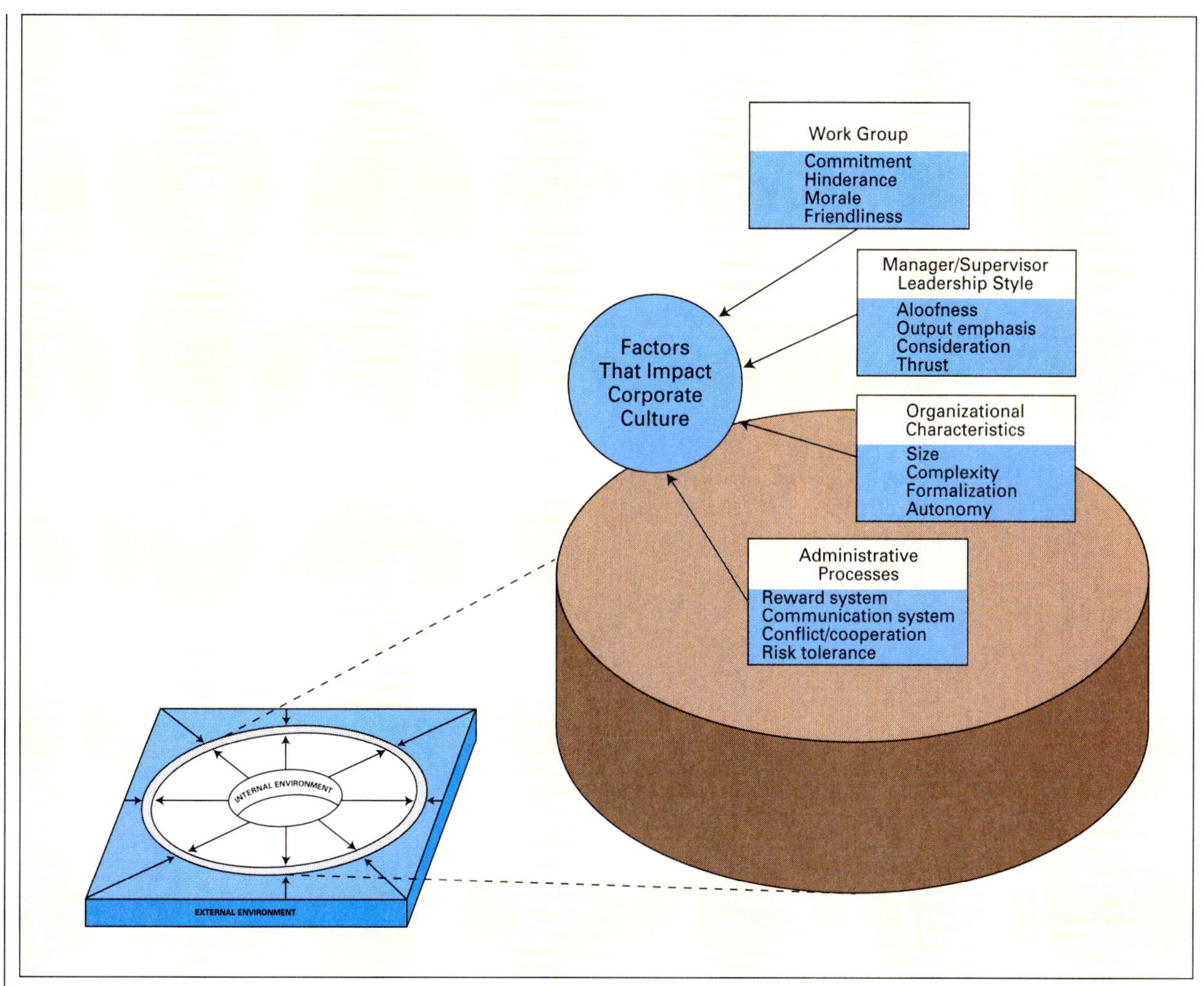

FIGURE 9-1 Factors That Influence Corporate Culture

Work Group

The character of the immediate work group will affect one's perception of the nature of corporate culture. For example, commitment to the mission of the work group directly influences cultural perceptions. Commitment refers to whether or not the group is really working. If people in the work group are just going through the motions of work, it is difficult for an individual member to obtain high levels of output and satisfaction. Hindrance may also occur when individuals work together as a group. Hindrance is concerned with the degree of busywork (work of doubtful value) given to the group. Morale and friendliness within the group also affect the environment of the work group and the perceived nature of the corporate culture.

Manager/Supervisor Leadership Style

The leadership style of the immediate supervisor will have a considerable effect on the culture of the group, and vice versa. If the manager is aloof and distant in dealing with subordinates, this attitude could have a negative influence on the organization. If the supervisor is always pushing for output, this too alters the environment. Consideration is a desirable leadership characteristic that can positively influence group effectiveness. Thrust—managerial behavior characterized by hard work and example setting—is also a positive influence on the group.

Organizational Characteristics

The type of culture that develops can also be affected by organizational characteristics. For example, organizations vary on such attributes as size and complexity. Large organizations tend toward higher degrees of specialization and impersonalization. Labor unions often find that large firms are easier to organize than smaller ones because smaller firms tend to be closer and have more informal relationships among employees and management. Complex organizations tend to employ a greater number of professionals and specialists, which alters the general approach to solving problems. Organizations also vary in the degree to which they write things down and attempt to program behavior through rules, procedures, and regulations. They can be distinguished, too, on the basis of the degree of decentralization of decision-making authority, which affects the degree of autonomy and employee freedom.

Administrative Processes

Corporate culture may be affected by administrative processes. Firms that can develop direct links between performance and rewards tend to create cultures conducive to achievement. Communication systems that are open and free flowing tend to promote participation and creative atmospheres. The general attitudes that exist toward the tolerance of conflict and the handling of risk have considerable influence on teamwork. They also affect the amount of innovation and creativity.

From these and other factors, organization members develop a subjective impression of what kind of place the organization is to work in. This im-

HRM IN ACTION

—BREAKING UP THE TEAM

Wayne, Don, and Robert were supervisors with a small chain of fifteen convenience stores in north Dallas. Each had responsibility for five stores and reported directly to the company president. But actually they all just worked as a team. Wayne coordinated the scheduling of clerks at all fifteen stores, Don took care of inventory control and purchasing, and Robert took responsibility for recruiting and hiring. Otherwise, they each just did whatever needed to be done.

Things changed markedly within just a year. The president, wishing to relieve himself of daily details, promoted Robert to vice president. Another supervisor, Phillip, was hired to manage Robert's five stores. At first, everything went well. But soon Robert, who was much more involved in store management than the president had been, told the three supervisors he wanted each of them to take care of his own five stores.

Wayne, Don, and Phillip initially resisted Robert's frequent orders and demands. After a few *chewing outs*, though, the men decided to do as Robert wanted. They rarely saw one another, and each took care of all aspects of store operations, as well as filling in for clerks who were late or sick. There were frequent problems, however. Robert accused the three supervisors of working against him and threatened them with dismissal if operations did not get better. Wayne, Don, and Phillip saved him the trouble; they quit within days of one another. The president fired Robert a few days later.

Explain the corporate culture that existed before and after Robert's promotion to vice president.

pression will affect performance, satisfaction, creativity, and commitment to the organization.

TYPES OF CULTURES

At times, an organization must alter its culture in order to succeed or influence events just to survive. This was necessary at IBM when the computer industry changed so drastically in the 1980s and early 1990s. However, alterations made to the corporate culture should always improve the current situation.

Management must be aware of the types of corporate culture that a firm may wish to emulate—and why one particular culture may prove superior to another. Most behavioralists advocate an open and participative culture. Some go so far as to contend that such a culture is best for all situations. This type of culture is characterized by the following characteristics:

- trust in subordinates
- open communication
- considerate and supportive leadership
- team problem solving
- worker autonomy
- information sharing
- high output goals

Many U.S. businesses are culturally permissive and, therefore, embrace behavioralist principles. They have been guided by the philosophy that organization members who are free to choose among alternatives make the soundest decisions. When employees are asked to give up some of their individuality for the common good, the end result is often reinforcement of the status quo.

The opposite of the open and participative culture is a closed and autocratic one. It, too, may be characterized by high output goals. But such goals are more likely to be declared and imposed on the organization by autocratic and threatening leaders. The greater rigidity in this culture results from strict adherence to a formal chain of command, narrower spans of management, and stricter individual accountability. The emphasis is on the individual rather than on teamwork. Employees often simply go through the motions and do as they are told.

A GLOBAL PERSPECTIVE

Often when a U.S. corporation goes global, it forms an alliance with a company in the host country. Once an alliance is formed, it is essential that the corporate cultures and management styles of the partners blend together as quickly as possible.[7] Corporate culture is the system of shared values, beliefs, and habits within an organization that interacts with the formal structure to produce behavioral norms. Corporate culture embodies the values and standards that guide people's behavior and determines the organization's overall direction. Long-term success means having a corporate culture that supports the goals of the organization and effectively deals with the business environment. As a firm becomes more and more global in nature, it becomes more difficult to have a supportive corporate culture. Alliances are useful for all partners because collaboration makes it possible to share the costs and risks of doing business, and it enables companies to share financial resources, technology, production facilities, marketing expertise, and, of course, human resources.

The AT&T alliance with Olivetti was plagued with difficulties because of a failure to blend the partners' divergent corporate cultures and management styles. Robert Kavner, an AT&T senior executive, blames the problems on differences in these areas. Kavner has said, "I don't think we or Olivetti spent enough time understanding the behavior of the other partner. We knew that our cultures were different but we never really penetrated. We would get angry and they would get upset."[8] Problems may occur in international alliances when people from different organizations and national cultures work together.[9]

As was previously mentioned, the corporate culture of Citicorp has always "overprized vision and undervalued hands-on, day-to-day management, which to many Citibankers has looked an awful lot like work." Citicorp's corporate culture did not focus on making a profit, but rather it has been run for growth and revenue generation. Citicorp's corporate culture has changed, and now the focus is on profits; no longer can Citicorp survive with the cultural attitude that it "could buy everything, fix anything, and do it all at once." Globally no corporation has that much money, including Citicorp. The company discovered what other successful global companies are aware of, that profits are essential for global success. Combining an effective corporate culture that keys on effectively coping with the global environment, and at the same time being profitable, is what all global companies must strive for.[10]

THE PARTICIPATIVE CULTURE

The prevailing managerial approach in many organizations is highly structured. Consequently, most attempts to alter organizational culture have been directed toward opening it up and making it more participative.

Values of Participation

The value of involving more people in the decision-making process relates primarily to productivity and morale. Increased productivity can result from the stimulation of ideas and encouragement of a greater cooperative effort. Psychologically involved employees will often respond to shared problems with innovative suggestions and unusually productive effort.

Open and participative cultures are often used to improve employee morale and satisfaction. Specific benefits to be derived include the following:

- increased acceptability of management's ideas
- increased cooperation between management and staff
- reduced turnover
- reduced absenteeism
- reduced complaints and grievances
- greater acceptance of changes
- improved attitudes toward the job and the organization

In general, greater employee participation seems to have a direct and immediate effect on employee morale. Employees take more interest in the job and the organization. They tend to accept—and sometimes initiate—change not only because they understand the necessity for it, but also because they are more secure as a result of knowing more about the change. Most experience and research indicates a positive relationship between employee participation and measures of morale, turnover, and absenteeism. However, little evidence has been presented that suggests a positive relationship between job satisfaction and productivity. Therefore, if productivity is not adversely affected by participation, the supplementary benefits alone may make participation

Open and participative cultures are often used to improve employee morale and satisfaction.

worthwhile. However, if productivity actually fell, management would have to carefully scrutinize its organizational and managerial approach.

Limitations of Participation

Despite its benefits, the participative approach to decision making has certain prerequisites and limitations. The requirements for greater participation in decision making are (1) sufficient time, (2) adequate ability and interest on the part of the participants, and (3) adherence to restrictions generated by the present structure and system.

If immediate decisions are required, time may not be available for group participation. The manager may be forced to decide what to do and issue directives accordingly. Participation calls for some measure of self discipline instead of leaning on others. In addition, participation requires that the subordinate learn to handle freedom and the supervisor learn to trust the subordinate.

Whether greater involvement in decision making can be developed depends largely on the abilities and interests of the participants, both subordinates and managers. Obviously, if the subordinate knows or cares nothing about a subject, there is little reason to consult that person. As organizations and technology become increasingly complex, and as management becomes more professional, employee participation will likely involve more cooperation seeking or information sharing. However, not all employees want to participate in decisions about their work. Managers must face the fact that some workers do not seek and will not accept more job responsibility and involvement.

CHANGING THE CORPORATE CULTURE

Environmental factors, such as governmental action, workforce diversity, and global competition, often require a firm to change its culture and even make a clean break with the past. For example, the culture of AT&T is distinctly different from that of just a few years ago when it virtually monopolized its industry. After being dismantled by the government, the firm has had to deal with aggressive competitors and in doing so develop a new modus operandi.

A diverse American workforce reflects the increasing diversity of its population. In order to maximize the advantages of diversity—particularly the talents of women and minorities—efforts are being made to create a culture in which each employee has the opportunity to contribute and to advance in the organization based on excellent performance. HR professionals know that critical factors, such as retention, motivation, and advancement, are highly dependent upon how employees react to their firm's culture.

A recent survey of a group of managers with high representations of women and minority employees identified several problem areas inherent in counterproductive cultures.[11]

- *Fighting stereotypes.* The number one problem faced by women and minority managers related to frustrations in coping with gender and race stereotypes.
- *Discrimination and harassment.* Whether experiencing discrimination personally or witnessing it, managers reported that such incidents caused them to question whether they fit in with the firm.
- *Exclusion and isolation.* Women and minority managers are often excluded from social activities and left out of informal communication networks.
- *Work-family balance.* Women managers expressed the view that playing the game often requires compromising personal values and conforming to the expectations of others.
- *Career development.* A mere look around the organization to witness the few women and minority managers results in concerns about opportunities for career progression.

The above problem areas illustrate legitimate concerns that organizations must consider in revamping their corporate cultures. Taken together, women and minorities represent a majority of employees entering the workforce. If the talents of these key groups are to be utilized to the fullest, corporate cultures of the future must reflect their needs.

Global competition is another key factor impacting corporate cultures. Few firms have escaped the competitive pressure from foreign firms. This pressure has greatly increased the need for improved quality, competitive pricing, and better customer service. Since these critical factors are so dependent upon a firm's culture, the culture itself must be changed if the firm is to survive, much less prosper.

In changing a firm's culture, as much of the organization should be involved as possible. The chief executive officer should be proactively involved. The necessity of the change, along with the goals sought, should be clearly communicated to all organizational members. They, too, should be involved either directly or indirectly. Change of this magnitude is often called organization development. This topic is discussed in the next section.

ORGANIZATION DEVELOPMENT

We have examined various factors that affect employees' behavior on the job. To bring about desired changes in these factors and behavior, organizations must be transformed into market-driven, innovative, and adaptive systems if they are to survive and prosper in the highly competitive global environment of the next decade. Many firms are beginning to face this urgent need by practicing organization development, an HRD approach that involves the entire system. **Organization development (OD)** is an organization-wide application of behavioral science knowledge to the planned development and reinforcement of a firm's strategies, structures, and processes for improving its effectiveness.[12]

Organization development applies to an entire system, such as a company or a plant. Early applications of the approach focused on employee satisfaction. It appears that employee and organizational performance are now being emphasized as well. Although OD does not produce a blueprint for how things should be done, it does provide an adaptive strategy for planning and implementing change. In addition, OD ensures a long-term reinforcement of change. Organization development may involve changes in the firm's strategy, structure, and processes. A firm's strategy entails how it relates to its wider environment and how to improve those relationships. In dealing with structure, the focus is on how people are grouped in the organization. The firm's processes include methods of communication and solving problems.[13]

Several OD methods are discussed in the following sections. Traditional ones will be discussed first. Then, the approaches getting the most attention today—total quality management and team building—will be presented.

TRADITIONAL ORGANIZATION DEVELOPMENT METHODS

Traditional organization development intervention methods include survey feedback, team building, quality circles, management by objectives, job enrichment, transactional analysis, quality of work life, and sensitivity training. These techniques may be combined to provide a strategic approach to organization development.

Survey Feedback

Survey feedback is a process of collecting data from an organizational unit through the use of a questionnaire or survey. A developing trend has been to combine survey feedback, a powerful intervention in its own right, with other OD interventions.[14]

Survey feedback generally involves the following steps:

- Members of the organization, including top management, are involved in planning the survey.
- The survey instrument is administered to all members of the organizational unit.
- The OD consultant analyzes the data, tabulates results, suggests approaches to diagnosis, and trains participants in the feedback process.
- Data feedback begins at the top level of the organization and flows downward to groups reporting at successively lower levels.
- Feedback meetings provide an opportunity to discuss and interpret data, diagnose problem areas, and develop action plans.[15]

An example of a management survey feedback instrument is provided in Figure 9-2. This instrument is used to analyze management performance in leadership, motivation, communication, decision making, goals, control, and other critical areas. Employees are asked to check—along a continuum—the point that best describes their organization. They are also asked to indicate their views of a desired state. Averaging the responses and charting them gives an organizational profile. Referring again to Figure 9-2, note that the present state of leadership is perceived as being quite negative. The employees surveyed apparently felt that their company's leadership was *condescending*. The consensus was that the leader should show *substantial* confidence in subordinates (the desired state).

		Present State		Desired State	
LEADERSHIP	How much confidence is shown in subordinates?	None	Condescending	Substantial	Complete
	How free do they feel to talk to superiors about your job?	Not at All	Not Very	Rather	Fully
	Are subordinates' ideas sought and used, if worthy?	Seldom	Sometimes	Usually	Always
MOTIVATION	Is predominant use made of (1) fear, (2) threats, (3) punishment, (4) rewards, (5) involvement?	1, 2, 3 Occasionally 4	4, Some 3	4, Some 3 and 5	5, 4, based on group-set goals
	Where is responsibility felt for achieving organization's goals?	Mostly at Top	Top and Middle	Fairly General	All Levels
COMMUNICATION	How much communication is aimed at achieving organization's objectives?	Very Little	Little	Quite a Bit	A Great Deal
	What is the direction of information flow?	Downward	Mostly Downward	Down and Up	Down, Up and Sideways
	How is downward communication accepted?	With Suspicion	Possibly with Suspicion	With Caution	With an Open Mind
	How accurate is upward communication?	Often Wrong	Censored for the Boss	Limited Accuracy	Accurate
	How well do superiors know problems faced by subordinates?	Know Little	Some Knowledge	Quite Well	Very Well
DECISIONS	At what level are decisions formally made?	Mostly at Top	Policy at Top, Some Delegation	Broad Policy at Top, More Delegation	Throughout but Well Integrated
	What is the origin of technical and professional knowledge used in decision making?	Top Management	Upper and Middle	To a Certain Extent Throughout	To a Great Extent Throughout
	Are subordinates involved in decisions related to their work?	Not at all	Occasionally Consulted	Generally Consulted	Fully Involved
	What does the decision making process contribute to motivation?	Nothing, Often Weakens It	Relatively Little	Some Contribution	Substantial Contribution
GOALS	How are organizational goals established?	Orders Issued	Orders, Some Comment Invited	After Discussion, by Orders	By Group Action (Except in Crisis)
	How much covert resistance to goals is present?	Strong Resistance	Moderate Resistance	Some Resistance at Times	Little or None
CONTROL	How concentrated are review and control functions?	Highly at Top	Relatively Highly at Top	Moderate Delegation to Lower Levels	Quite Widely Shared
	Is there an informal organization resisting the formal one?	Yes	Usually	Sometimes	No—Same Goals as Formal
	What are cost, productivity and other control data used for?	Policing, Punishment	Reward and Punishment	Reward, Some Self-Guidance	Self-Guidance Problem Solving

FIGURE 9-2 An Example of a Survey Feedback Questionnaire

Source: Adapted by permission of the publisher, from *Organizational Development for Operating Managers* by Michael E. McGill, 232. Copyright 1977, by AMACOM, a division of American Management Association, New York. All rights reserved.

Quality Circles

Another OD approach is the use of quality circles. **Quality circles** are groups of employees who voluntarily meet regularly with their supervisors to identify production problems and recommend solutions. These recommendations are then presented to higher level management for review, and the approved actions are implemented with employee participation.

In Japan, millions of workers participate in quality circles, which results in billions of dollars saved annually. Even though the corporate culture in the United States is different, an increasing number of firms are adapting the quality circle concept to their operations. In fact, larger firms may have several hundred quality circles.

In spite of numerous successful applications, the quality circle concept has not worked well for some organizations. In order to implement a successful quality circle program, the firm must set clear goals for the program, gain top management's support, and create a climate conducive to participative management. In addition, a qualified manager must be selected for the program, and the program's goals must be communicated to all concerned. Individuals participating in the program must receive quality circle training.

Management by Objectives

Management by objectives (MBO) is a philosophy of management that emphasizes the setting of agreed-on objectives by superior and subordinate managers and using these objectives as the primary basis for motivation, evaluation, and self control. As a management approach that encourages managers to anticipate and plan for the future, MBO directs efforts toward attainable goals. It deemphasizes guessing or making decisions based on hunches.

Since MBO emphasizes participative management approaches, it has been called a philosophy of management. Within this broader context, MBO becomes an important method of organization development. It focuses on the achievement of individual and organizational goals. The participation of individuals in setting goals and the emphasis on self-control promote not only personal development but also organizational development.

Management by objectives is a dynamic process that must be continuously reviewed, modified, and updated. Top management must both initiate the MBO process by establishing long-range goals (see Figure 9-3) and support the process. For example, the president and vice president of human resources (superior and subordinate) may jointly establish the firm's HRM long-range goals and intermediate and short-range objectives. At this point, the president and vice president mutually agree on the subordinate's performance objectives and action plans, which outline how the objectives will be achieved. The subordinate proceeds to work toward his or her goals. At the end of the appraisal period, both parties review the subordinate's performance and determine what can be done to overcome any problems encountered. Goals are then established for the next period and the process is repeated.

From an organization development standpoint, MBO offers numerous potential benefits. It does the following:

- provides an opportunity for development of managers and employees
- increases the firm's ability to change
- provides a more objective and tangible basis for performance appraisal and salary decisions
- results in better overall management and higher performance levels
- provides an effective overall planning system

FIGURE 9-3
The MBO Process

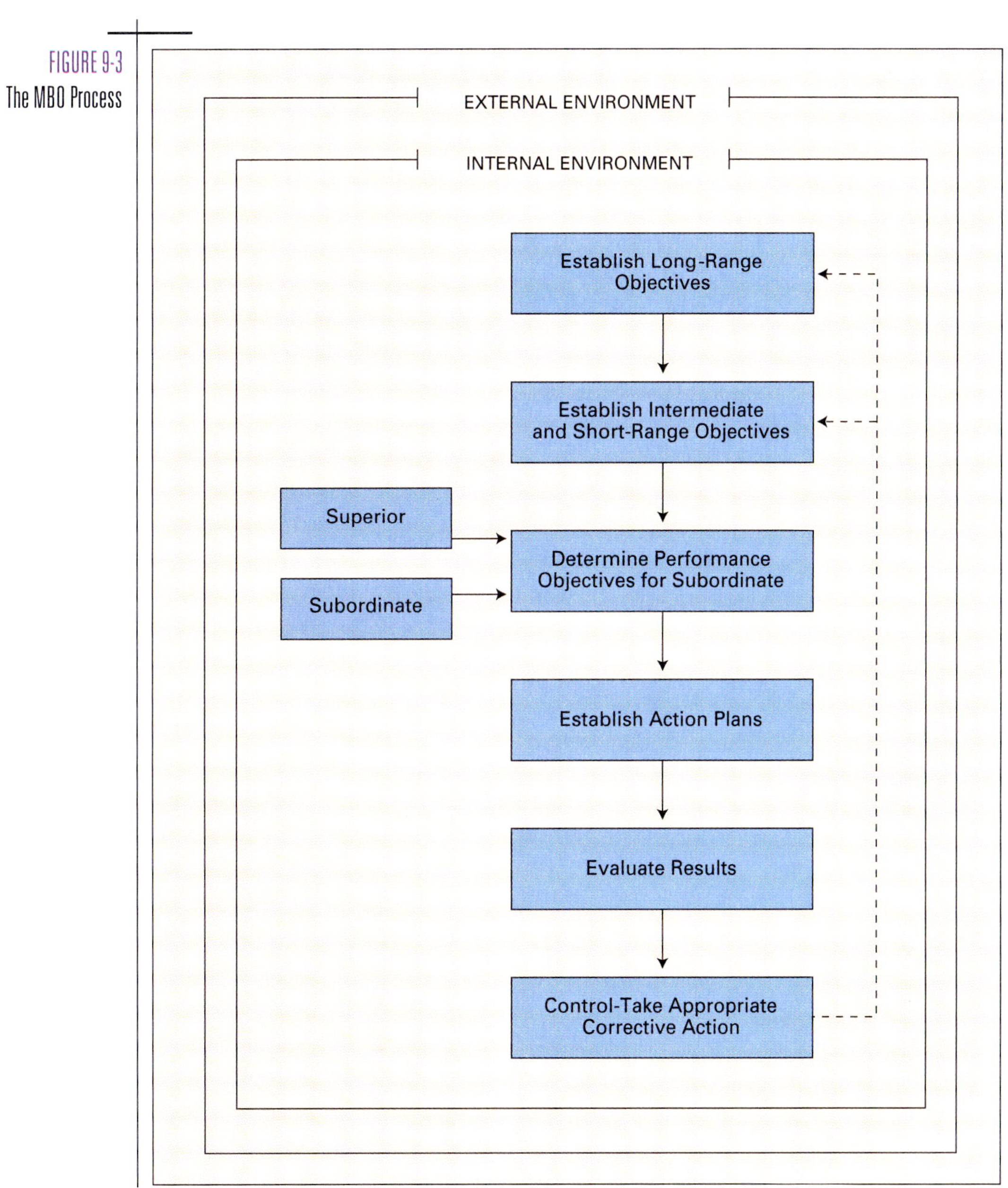

- forces managers to establish priorities and measurable targets or standards of performance
- clarifies the specific roles, responsibilities, and authority of employees
- encourages the joint participation of employees and managers in establishing objectives
- promotes accountability
- lets individuals know clearly what is expected of them
- improves communication within the organization
- helps identify promotable managers and employees
- increases employee motivation and commitment

While there are potential benefits to be realized, certain problems are associated with MBO. Without the full support of top management, for example, it is bound to fail. This commitment may be difficult to obtain because implementing such a system often takes from three to five years. In addition, goals may be difficult to establish. Another potential weakness is a tendency to concentrate on short-term plans. For example, short-term objectives may be achieved at the expense of long-term goals. The system also has the potential to create a seemingly insurmountable paper mill if it is not closely monitored. Finally, some managers believe that MBO is excessively time consuming. The process forces people to think ahead and be capable of seeing how their goals and actions fit into the overall picture. This is not an easy task for some managers, but it is one that can prove quite beneficial.

Job Enrichment

As defined in Chapter 4, job enrichment is the deliberate restructuring of a job to make it more challenging, meaningful, and interesting. It emphasizes accomplishing significant tasks so that the employee can feel a sense of achievement. Job enrichment takes an optimistic view of employee capabilities. Its use presumes that individuals have the ability to perform more difficult and responsible tasks than they are currently performing. Furthermore, it assumes that most people will respond favorably if given the opportunity to accomplish challenging tasks and will also be motivated to be more productive. When job enrichment is applied on a broad scale, it becomes an important OD method.

When jobs are restructured to increase responsibility and challenge, employees continually develop while performing them. The nature of these jobs actually requires that employees keep their skills up-to-date.

Transactional Analysis[16]

Although it is not currently a popular OD intervention, transactional analysis was used for a number of years as a technique for teaching behavioral principles. **Transactional analysis (TA)** is a method that considers each individual's three ego states—the Parent, the Adult, and the Child—in helping people understand interpersonal relations. It provides a system for forming a mental image of the emotions and thought processes used by people interacting in either a social or business setting. It can be most useful in permitting an employee to understand where a customer or fellow employee *is coming from* and to respond appropriately.[17]

The interaction of ego states can have a significant impact on behavior in organizations. If organizational members are able to recognize the ego state affecting a given communication, they may be able to respond appropriately. In light of today's increased need for training employees in customer service, this approach to OD may have renewed relevance.

Quality of Work Life

A concept that has many implications for employee anticipation is called **quality of work life (QWL)**. QWL is the degree to which members of a work organization are able to satisfy their most important personal needs through organizational experiences. QWL programs encompass many strategies, including job redesign, autonomous work groups, and worker participation in decision making. A basic assumption is that such programs will increase job satisfaction and worker motivation, which in turn will lead to increased productivity.[18]

Any firm that wants to develop a QWL program must first determine the goals it wants to achieve with the program. Therefore, citing a list of appropriate activities (as is done with MBO programs) is difficult. The goals and actions undertaken are the joint responsibility of management, the union, and other members of the organization.

However, certain guidelines may be helpful in initiating QWL efforts. Generally, QWL improvement efforts call for the following:

- An understanding that they are not short-term, quick fix programs that should be undertaken lightly.
- Organizations to forge new definitions of "how we work in this organization" when initiating QWL efforts.
- The willing participation of people at all levels of the organization.
- A commitment from the organization's leaders that goes beyond the rhetoric of endorsement and support and that must be demonstrated daily.
- Organizations to communicate and integrate their strategic goals into the day-to-day business operations.
- Management and labor leaders to work with their constituencies to examine and resolve internal issues before moving on to cooperative problem solving in joint committees. (Management's demonstrated commitment in addressing its own issues and barriers can contribute substantially to supportive and responsible behaviors and actions on the part of others within the organization.)
- New approaches and processes in most organizations. (These processes are never static and require constant attentiveness and responsiveness to developments as they occur.)[19]

The results of research conducted on QWL programs have provided mixed results. Although many successes have been reported, it is often difficult to determine the variable responsible for production increases. HR managers need to recognize that a QWL program is an experiment and that there is no conclusive evidence to ensure that it will be successful.[20]

Sensitivity Training

An OD technique designed to make us more aware of ourselves and our impact on others is referred to as **sensitivity training**. It is quite different from traditional forms of training, which stress the learning of a predetermined set of concepts.[21]

Sensitivity training features a group—often called a training group or T-group—in which there is no preestablished agenda or focus. The trainer's purpose is merely to serve as a facilitator in this unstructured environment. Participants are encouraged to learn about themselves and others in the group. Some objectives of sensitivity training are to increase the following:

1. Self-awareness and insight into the participant's behavior and its meaning in a social context.
2. Sensitivity to the behavior of others.
3. Awareness and understanding of the types of processes that facilitate or inhibit group functioning and the interactions between different groups.
4. Diagnostic skills in social, interpersonal, and intergroup situations.
5. The participant's ability to intervene successfully in intergroup or intragroup situations so as to increase member satisfaction, effectiveness, and output.
6. The participant's ability to analyze continually his or her own interpersonal behavior in order to achieve more effective and satisfying interpersonal relationships.[22]

When sensitivity training begins, there is no agenda—and no leaders, no authority, and no power positions. Essentially, a vacuum exists until participants begin to talk. Through dialogue people begin to learn about themselves and others. Participants are encouraged to look at themselves as others see them. Then, if they want to change, they can attempt to do so.

Although the purpose of sensitivity training (to assist individuals to learn more about how they relate to other people) cannot be questioned, the technique has been roundly criticized. It is clear that sensitivity training often involves anxiety-provoking situations as stimulants for learning. In addition, some critics believe that it is one matter for participants to express true feelings in the psychological safety of the laboratory but quite another to face their coworkers back on the job.[23] Information learned in a sensitivity group may prove to be irrelevant or even damaging unless the participant returns to an organizational environment that supports the use of that knowledge. Individuals may be encouraged to be more open and supportive in the T-group, but when they return to their jobs, they often have not really changed. In addition, participants often undergo severe emotional stress during training. Sensitivity training flourished in the 1970s. Use of poorly trained, uncertified trainers may be the primary reason for the decline in popularity of this method.

TOTAL QUALITY MANAGEMENT

Total Quality Management (TQM) is a commitment to excellence by everyone in an organization that emphasizes excellence achieved by teamwork and a process of continuous improvement.

Today most companies have "total quality" programs that integrate every department from manufacturing to marketing and research in the effort to improve. Implied in the concept is a commitment to be the best and provide the highest quality products and services that meet or exceed the hopes of the customer. Businesses are making many changes to stay competitive. They are constantly seeking ways to improve quality, increase speed of operations, and adopt a customer orientation. These changes are so fundamental that they must take root in a company's very essence, which means in its *culture*.

TQM often involves major cultural changes. It requires a new way of thinking and strong leadership at all levels. Individuals throughout the organization must be inspired to do things differently. They must understand what needs to be done and why, and this takes strong leadership.

The Objectives of TQM

As world market share shifted away from U.S. producers, forward thinking American managers recognized the necessity for change. Since 1960, more than half of the world market share had been lost to other international producers in a number of product lines. These lines included athletic equipment, automobiles, cameras, computer chips, industrial robots, medical equipment, optical equipment, radial tires, stereos, and television sets. Something had to be done, so TQM was employed.

The ultimate goal of TQM is to alter the process by improving customer satisfaction. Instead of being content with the status quo, employees at all levels continually seek alternative methods or technologies that will improve existing processes. TQM provides a strategy for reducing the causes of poor quality and thereby increasing productivity.

TQM is a process of continuously improving quality over the long run. In the short run, once each of the linked processes within a firm is operating at or above a desired level of quality, reliance on costly inspection practices can be reduced or eliminated altogether. Attention can then be turned to monitoring the overall process to determine the sources of variation still present. If these sources are also eliminated, then the process can be more precise and fewer defects or errors produced. In the customer's view, quality will have exceeded the expected level. The customer, more than satisfied, will probably remain a customer. The increased employee participation required by TQM creates a new role for all organizational members. Top management, middle managers, first-level supervisors, and all workers must embrace the philosophy and work to ensure its acceptance throughout the organization. Operative employees are consulted for assistance in determining and analyzing sources of process variation, and they are relied on to develop proposals for reducing or eliminating them.

Cultural change must precede or accompany the introduction of total quality management. And the organizational culture required to support the concepts of TQM is not likely to be changed quickly. Five to ten years is generally needed for such changes in the top management value system to permeate the organization. TQM is not a body of regulations and cannot be forced on employees. Since a company's culture is largely a product of positively reinforced behavior, the route to change is almost always through education and training.[24] In addition to training and development activities, employee selection practices will be a central component in implementing the TQM philosophy. As Robert Costello, former undersecretary of defense for acquisition, stated, "The ultimate goal is to ingrain basic cultural change to a depth where the slogan TQM will fade and, in its wake, the principles and practices of TQM will remain as a permanent, normal way of conducting business in the United States."[25]

Quality and TQM

The concept of quality in a TQM environment is based on the customer being served to the maximum degree possible. Quality means the product meets all requirements. Adherence to the concepts of TQM means that before any product is produced, the producer must first know precisely the requirements the product must meet. Only those products that meet all of the conditions are produced and delivered to the customer. A product that meets ninety-nine out of one hundred requirements is defective and should not be shipped to the customer.

The concept of quality differs with the type of company involved. For example, the definition of quality would be different at McDonald's than it would be at the Ritz in Paris. The seller must understand the customer. Even a perfect product cannot do more than it was designed to do. A Chevy should not outperform a Rolls even if both are perfect. However, the customer should be able to get what he or she is willing to pay for, and maybe a little more.

With TQM, how a process is implemented is as important as what the process includes. Many organizations still work under a departmentalized approach in which some employees plan improvements, others carry out the work, and still others inspect to see if procedures and results are correct. With TQM, all employees are committed to improving the quality of their product or service so that customers' needs are not only met but exceeded.

Until recently, many efforts to improve and gain a competitive advantage were delayed by the mistaken belief that better quality costs more.[26] The historical approach was to add more inspection steps. In an inspection-oriented plant, more than half of all workers are somehow involved in finding and reworking rejects.[27] A company using TQM should inspect a product in the design phase. The product is engineered in the manufacturing process to be stable and reliable. As Genichi Taguchi said, "To improve quality, you need to look upstream in the design stage. At the customer level, it's too late."[28]

TQM accomplishes just what Taguchi suggested. Under a system of TQM, managers are looking upstream to improve quality by focusing on the design stage, before the product reaches the customer level. When TQM is used, firms design quality into the product. Less emphasis is given to inspection and more emphasis is given to *front-end* planning and design. Certainly TQM does not advocate elimination of all inspection. Eliminating the cause of a defect is more important than continuing to reject defective parts. Josh Hammond, president of the American Quality Foundation, has pointed to a study in which more than half the U.S. companies reported that executive pay will soon be pegged in part to quality.[29]

Managerial Mistakes in Implementing TQM

In a recent survey of 500 manufacturing and service companies that use TQM, only 36 percent believed that TQM was significantly improving their competitiveness.[30] Many practitioners admit that the image of TQM is tarnished and is not the quick fix that U.S. management often seeks.[31] As with many management innovations, the concept is not the cause of the failure. Rather, it is how the concept is implemented.

A major mistake that is often made in implementing TQM results from a lack of top management support. A TQM program needs to be pushed from the top down and constantly tested from the bottom up. Lack of management support assumes various forms. For example, it is management's responsibility to maintain a constancy of purpose; problem solving is impossible when management's priorities are constantly changing.

A lack of patience or need for instant gratification will also doom a TQM program. Sometimes, management does not fully understand how to implement a necessary objective, relying on tentative objectives while searching for a case study to follow for firm objectives. No case study will be an exact fit for a particular company's needs. Each situation requires its own set of objectives. In some cases, management tries to legislate TQM. Such attempts to force improvement on the system will not work—in large part because they encourage the perception that TQM is yet another soon-to-be discredited *magic solution*. Management must change its style before the rest of the organization can be expected to respond.

There will always be bias when management evaluates its own corporate culture, usually resulting in an overly optimistic view of the quality of the environment. Failure to address this actively at all levels will shut off the flow of ideas and the problem-solving activities. In the chain of command, it only takes one individual or one level to ruin the system. Most often, this occurs at the supervisor level. Bias can be even more dangerous, however, if it occurs at higher levels in the organization.

There is also the tendency by management to take shortcuts, especially with employee training. Workers typically can be taught how to fill in control charts in less than four hours. It takes far longer to ground workers in the overall philosophy and to provide them with the statistical knowledge they need to understand and interpret the charts. Since computers can be used to complete the control charts, managers often use automation as the excuse for failing to train workers properly. Another common shortcut is dispensing with problem-solving teams. Many managers view them as unproductive and a waste of time—especially when it is already the responsibility of individuals who are already in place to solve problems. Bypassing problem-solving teams results in many barriers to TQM remaining.[32]

TEAM BUILDING AND SELF-DIRECTED TEAMS

At Volvo's two radically innovative factories, a fixed rather than moving assembly line is the norm. Gone are the days of the moving assembly line introduced by Henry Ford three-quarters of a century ago. In Sweden, the close supervision and machine pacing of work on the assembly lines were major sore points with employees. At Volvo's newer plants, "work teams build cars much like doctors operate on a patient. Each car frame sits on its individual rotating holder while the assembly crew attach the pieces. Instead of foreman and engineers, ordinary workers manage the shop floor." This radical change was brought about because Sweden's highly educated and well-trained labor force does not like to work in conventional factories.

This factory environment is conducive to so-called self-management. Volvo gives workers sixteen weeks' training before they are allowed to get close to a car, and sixteen months more of on-the-job orientation. In Sweden, at two Volvo plants, functional work teams assemble entire cars and assist in certain management activities. The work teams at these two innovative Volvo automobile plants assemble large units of a car without much supervision from managers. At the Kalmar plant, fifteen or twenty people are grouped into teams that build cars without a moving assembly line. Each team builds a large section of a car, with a work cycle of thirty minutes. According to Volvo management, productivity is higher at Kalmar than at the large, conventional assembly plant at Gothenburg. Uddevalla goes much further with functional work teams. The Uddevalla facility is divided into six assembly plants, each of which has eight teams. Teams basically manage themselves, handling scheduling, quality control, hiring, and other duties normally performed by supervisors. There are no first-line supervisors and only two tiers of management. Each team has a spokesperson who reports to one of the six plant managers. These six individuals report directly to the company president.

In Sweden, as in many countries, the move toward utilization of functional work teams is increasing. Basically, in Sweden the *old way* of running automakers and other large industrial companies is outmoded. However, this approach to automobile manufacturing is not perfect. Problems have occurred with some assembly teams. Workers have reported *friction* and disagreements among team members that have created a certain degree of conflict. Still, few wish to go back to the old way with supervisors making all the decisions. In Sweden, as in all countries, the environment surrounding the workforce is extremely important and must be designed to encourage employees to put forth effort in the pursuit of organizational goals. The combination of motivated work teams and aggressive marketing has allowed Volvo to be more profitable globally, as well as in the United States.[33]

Individualism has deep roots in American culture. This trait has been a virtue and will continue to be an asset in our society. Now, however, there are work situations that make it imperative to subordinate individual autonomy in favor of cooperation with a group. While lives in an industrial setting are not normally in jeopardy, jobs certainly are. Performance by teams has been shown to be clearly superior in performing many of the tasks required by organizations. The building of effective teams, therefore, has become a business necessity.

Much training effort must be expended prior to efficient and effective functioning of work teams. Fortunately, most managers know this. A conscious effort to develop effective work groups throughout the organization is referred to as **team building**. Team building utilizes self-directed teams, each composed of a small group of employees responsible for an entire work process or segment. Team members work together to improve their operation or product, to plan and control their work, and to handle day-to-day problems. They may even become involved in broader, company-wide issues, such as vendor quality, safety, and business planning.[34] Team building is one of the more popular approaches to OD. For instance, Team Saturn, the revolutionary approach to car manufacturing that has resulted in the Saturn automobile being named by J.D. Powers & Associates as the best built car in the United States, is based upon the concept of teamwork. Unlike other General Motors plants, Saturn is really built upon a team effort, not just an exercise in lip service. Line worker Deborah Wikaryasz could not believe the difference between teamwork at Saturn and at the Cadillac plant where she worked previously. Wikaryasz is very impressed with the environment at Saturn, stating, "We don't have the backstabbing and the yelling." Her team not only assembles fixtures on the left side of each Saturn, but they also hire workers, approve parts from suppliers, and handle administrative matters such as its budget. Wikaryasz is proud that her team, "keeps down costs and passes the savings along to customers." This plant was started from scratch with a team approach calling for all team members to be selected from the best General Motors had to offer. At Saturn, teams were kept small and were composed of people with complementary skills, who were committed to the common purpose of not compromising quality.[35]

A recent survey conducted by a human resources consulting firm found that 27 percent of the respondents currently use self-directed teams. Half of the respondents predicted that the majority of their workforce will be organized in teams within the next five years. The reason? Teams produce extra performance results![36]

Advocating the use of teams years before they became commonplace, Douglas McGregor identified characteristics of effective management teams (see Table 9-1). His version of an effective team emphasizes an informal organizational culture that is relatively free from tension. The team's decision-making process involves much discussion and broad participation. Communications are open, with an emphasis placed on listening to the views of others. Members feel free to disagree but do so in an atmosphere of acceptance. The team pursues goals that its members understand and accept.

Effective work teams focus on solving actual problems while building efficient management teams. The team building process begins when the team leader defines a problem that requires organizational change (see Figure 9-4). The team diagnoses the problem to determine the underlying causes. These causes may be related to breakdowns in communication, inappropriate leadership styles, deficiencies in the organizational structure, or other

TABLE 9-1
Characteristics of Effective Teams

1. The atmosphere, which can be sensed in a few minutes of observation, tends to be informal, comfortable, and relaxed. There are no obvious tensions.
2. There is a lot of discussion in which virtually everyone participates, but it remains pertinent to the task of the group.
3. The task or the objective of the group is well understood and accepted by the members.
4. The members listen to each other! The discussion does not have the quality of jumping from one idea to another unrelated one. Every idea is given a hearing. People are not afraid of seeming foolish by expressing a creative thought even if it seems fairly extreme.
5. There is disagreement. The group is comfortable with this and shows no signs of having to avoid conflict or to keep everything light and on a plane of sweetness. Disagreements are not suppressed or overridden by premature group action. Individuals who disagree do not appear to be trying to dominate the group or to express hostility. Their disagreement is an expression of a genuine difference of opinion, and they expect a hearing in order to find a solution.
6. Most decisions are reached by a kind of consensus in which it is clear that everybody is in general agreement and willing to go along.
7. Criticism is frequent, frank, and relatively comfortable. There is little evidence of personal attack, either open or hidden. The criticism has a constructive flavor in that it is oriented toward removing an obstacle that prevents the group from getting the job done.
8. People freely express their feelings as well as their ideas on both the problem and the group's operation. There is little pussyfooting; there are few hidden agendas. Everybody appears to know quite well how everybody else feels about any matter under discussion.
9. When action is taken, clear assignments are made and accepted.
10. The chairperson of the group does not dominate it, nor to the contrary, does the group defer unduly to him or her. In fact, the leadership shifts from time to time, depending on the circumstances. At various times, different members, because of their knowledge or experience, are in a position to act as "resources" for the group. The members utilize them in this fashion and they occupy leadership roles while they are thus being used. There is little evidence of a struggle for power as the group operates. The issue is not who controls but how to get the job done.
11. The group is conscious of its own operations. Frequently, it will stop to examine how well it is doing or what may be interfering with its operation. The problem may be a matter of procedure, or it may be that an individual's behavior is interfering with the accomplishment of the group's objectives. Whatever the problem, it is openly discussed until a solution is found.

Source: Adapted from Douglas McGregor, *The Human Side of Management* (New York: McGraw-Hill, 1960), 232–235. Reprinted by permission of the McGraw-Hill Book Company.

factors. The team then considers alternative solutions and selects the most appropriate one. The result of open and frank discussions is likely to be commitment to the proposed course of action. The interpersonal relations developed by team members improve the chances for implementing the change. Team building is a process in which participants and facilitators experience increasing levels of trust, openness, and willingness to explore core issues that affect excellent team functioning.[37]

The American Society for Training and Development (ASTD) conducted a survey that asked for the areas most improved through the use of trained self-directed teams. The factors that had noticeably or significantly

FIGURE 9-4
The Team Building Process

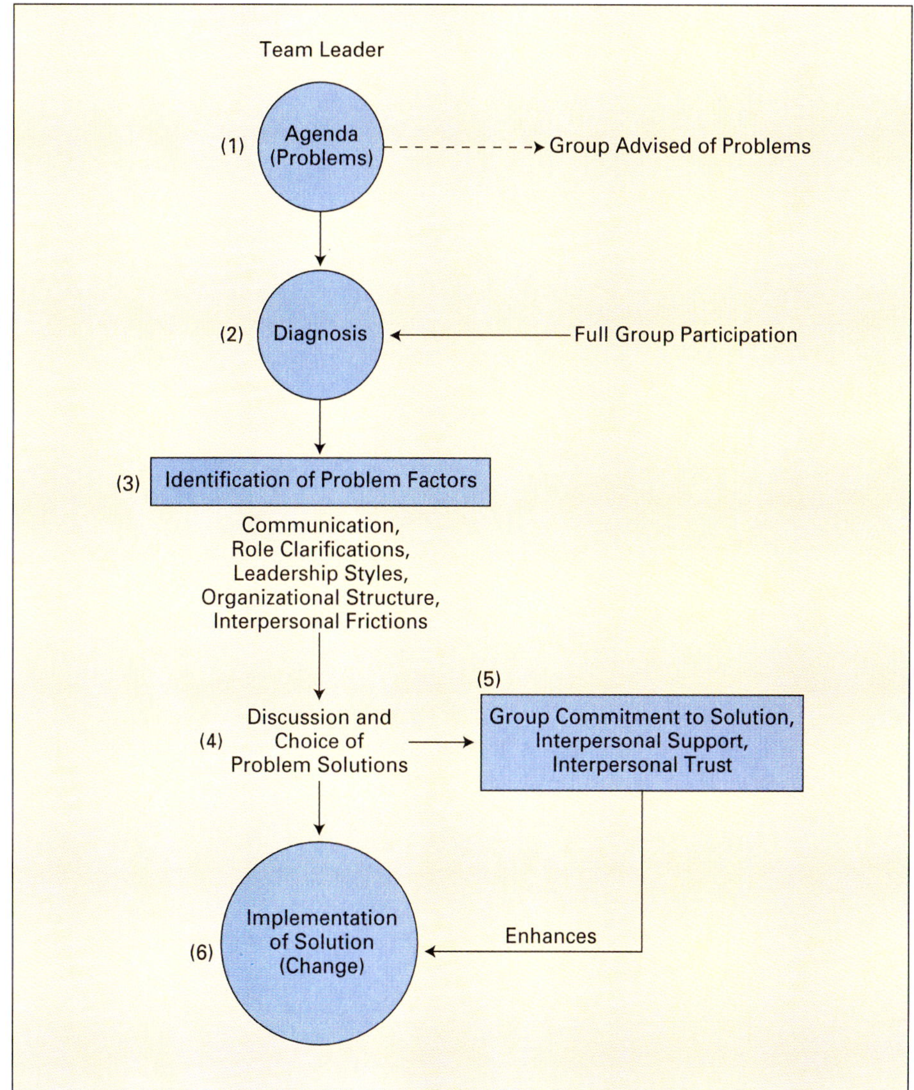

Source: Reproduced by permission from Michael A. Hitt, R. Dennis Middlemist, and Robert L. Mathis, *Management: Concepts and Effective Practice*, 3rd ed. (St. Paul, Minn.: West, 1989), 453.

improved are in the following list. The figure in parentheses indicates the percentage of respondents who felt the factor had improved.[38]

- productivity (77%)
- quality (72%)
- job satisfaction (65%)
- customer service (57%)
- waste reduction (55%)

USE OF CONSULTANTS

Organization development efforts rely heavily on the use of qualified consultants who work with teams from the firm's management and work teams. The consultant—a facilitator—assists both types of groups in identifying goals and solving problems that interfere with goal achievement. The consultant is also responsible for helping guide implementation of planned change.

A consultant may come from within the organization or from the outside. The role of the consultant is to utilize his or her specialized knowledge in making proposals for intervention in the organization's activities. Consultants assist managers in bringing about change in areas such as communication, leadership styles, and motivational techniques.

Management frequently believes that an outside expert brings objectivity to a situation and obtains acceptance and trust from organizational members more easily. However, another approach is to utilize internal consultants (employees of the firm) as effective change agents. Proponents of this tactic believe that the internal consultant, who knows both the formal and informal nature of the organization, can often produce desired results at a lower cost.

ORGANIZATION DEVELOPMENT PROGRAM EVALUATION

When an OD effort has been implemented, the following question must be asked: "Did anything happen as a result of this experience?" All too often the answer is: "We don't know." Evaluation of an OD effort is more difficult than determining whether an employee has learned to operate a particular piece of equipment. Nevertheless, management should evaluate the effort. The company has probably invested a considerable amount of time and money in the program and deserves to know whether it has produced tangible benefits.

One means of measuring program effectiveness is to assess changes in meeting performance criteria. Some of the factors to be measured might include (1) productivity, (2) absenteeism rate, (3) turnover rate, (4) accident rate, (5) costs, and (6) scrap. An improvement in these and other areas may mean that the OD yielded desired results. For instance, a lower turnover rate might mean that workers are more satisfied with their work and have chosen to remain with the firm. Lower costs per unit produced suggests that workers may be paying more attention to their work. Although such evaluative data are useful, they probably will not provide the entire answer.

Effectiveness should not be measured only when the program has been completed. Rather, questionnaires should be administered periodically over an extended period of time. Evaluation is a continuous process in which performance criteria are considered in order to measure the effect of the change effort. As early as the 1950s, OD was identified as a promising and effective approach to organizational change. This appraisal has been proven accurate by the successful utilization of OD by many organizations.

SUMMARY

Corporate culture is the system of shared values, beliefs, and habits within an organization that interacts with the formal structure to produce behavioral norms. The organization's reward system identifies the types of behavior and attitudes that are important for success.

Corporate culture evolves from the examples of top management, stemming largely from what they do, not what they say. Other factors also interact to shape the culture of a firm. Organizational characteristics, administrative processes, organizational structure, and management style help shape corporate culture.

Most behavioralists advocate an open and participative culture. Some contend that such a culture is best for all situations. The opposite of the open and participative culture is a closed and autocratic one. This culture's greater rigidity results from strict adherence to a formal chain of command, a narrower span of control, and stricter individual accountability.

The prevailing managerial approach in many organizations is highly structured. Consequently, most attempts to alter organizational culture have been directed at creating a culture that is more open and participative. Open and participative cultures often improve employee morale and satisfaction.

Despite the benefits of a participative approach, greater employee participation in decision making involves certain prerequisites and limitations. The requirements for greater participation in decision making are (1) sufficient time, (2) adequate ability and interest on the part of the participants, and (3) adherence to restrictions generated by the present structure and system.

Organization development (OD) applies behavioral science knowledge to an organization-wide effort to improve effectiveness. Some traditional OD techniques include survey feedback, quality circles, management by objectives, job enrichment, transactional analysis, quality of work life, and sensitivity training. Newer OD techniques include total quality management and team building. Some of these techniques may be combined to provide a strategic approach to organization development.

Organization development efforts rely heavily on the use of qualified consultants who work with groups of managers and workers from throughout the organization. The consultant is a facilitator who helps the groups identify goals and solve problems that interfere with goal achievement. The consultant may also be responsible for helping guide implementation of planned change.

One method of measuring program effectiveness is to assess changes in meeting performance criteria. Some of the factors measured might include (1) productivity, (2) absenteeism rate, (3) turnover rate, (4) accident rate, (5) costs, and (6) scrap. An improvement in these and other areas may mean that the OD effort has led to improvements.

QUESTIONS FOR REVIEW

1. Define *corporate culture*. What factors determine corporate culture?
2. Does a participative culture improve productivity? Defend your answer.
3. What are the values of an open and participative culture?
4. What are the limitations of participation?
5. Define each of the following terms:
   a. *Organization development*
   b. *Survey feedback*
   c. *Quality circles*
   d. *Job enrichment*
   e. *Quality of work life*
   f. *Transactional analysis*
   g. *Sensitivity training*
   h. *Total quality management*
   i. *Team building*
6. How can organization development programs be evaluated?
7. Explain the use of consultants in organization development.

HRM SIMULATION

In Incident H in the *Simulation Players Manual*, the CEO has asked your team to make a recommendation concerning the use of self-managed work teams in his organization. Your team has a wide variety of choices, so study them carefully and make your recommendation to the CEO.

ABC VIDEO CASE

SELF-DIRECTED WORK TEAMS TAPE 1, NUMBER 4

When the HELLFIRE missle plant outside Atlanta, Georgia, was losing money in the late 1980s, the company took action. Paul Smith, the general manager of the Tactical Systems Division, was sent on a week-long seminar based on the teachings of Edward Deming and the Japanese style of management he inspired. Smith came back a convert: "They were talking just to the kind of problems that we were having and that was improving our quality and getting our costs down." So Smith made the plant more like a commercial business. He also made it more self-managing. Instead of supervisors calling all the shots on the shop floor, the workforce was divided into two self-managing teams composed of ten to fifteen workers.

Says Jim Lake, Director of Operation HELLFIRE, "The bottom-line now is that this group decides what is acceptable quality within the group." For example, management had blamed workers for too many circuit board defects—the workers' team blamed it on the assembly machines. New machines were brought in and now the number of defect free circuit boards is almost 100 percent. The most radical example of the workers' new self-management was a decision made in one of the secret assembly rooms. The workers decided that there was not enough of a backlog of orders for the optical guidance components to allow both of the rooms to run economically, so they voted to close one for two weeks. Smith says, "Some of them took voluntary vacation, some went out without pay, but that team made the decision to take two weeks off. And we were amazed." One reason for such initiative is the Gain-Share Program. A percentage of any cost savings is passed back to the employees as a bonus.

HRM INCIDENT 1

—IMPLEMENTING TEAM BUILDING

When Bruce McDaniel retired because of ill health in 1991, he appointed his twenty-six year old son, Jim, president of the family firm. The company, McDaniel Corporation of Marietta, Georgia, marketed a line of hospital beds. The company manufactured the metal frames for the beds and purchased hydraulic items, springs, and certain other parts. The company also sold hospital furniture items and maintained a crew to repair the McDaniel beds. Employment at the firm totaled about 500.

With an MBA degree from Georgia State University and two years' experience with the company, Jim was eager to take over. He believed that his college training and work experience had prepared him well. One of the first things Jim wanted to do was to give decision-making authority to the managers. He remarked, "I felt this would let me pay attention to the big picture while the day-to-day problems were solved lower in the organization." He felt that one effective tool for helping him shift more authority downward in the organization would be the use of work teams.

Bruce McDaniel had been president and owner of McDaniel Corporation for thirty years. During that time, the firm had grown from a small hospital supply company with three employees to its present size. Bruce had been a hard worker, often putting in fifteen hours a day. Jim said that his dad was a "pleasant autocrat" because the elder McDaniel insisted on making every important decision, but Bruce had such an affable personality that no one objected.

For a while, Jim tried to behave pretty much as his father had, giving managers firm decisions on matters they brought to him. But about a month after his father's retirement, Jim called a meeting to tell the managers that the firm was going to introduce work teams throughout the organization. He made a brief presentation to them about how the teams would be set up. He especially emphasized that they would have to give more responsibility to the work teams and that he expected all supervisors to assist in team building.

Questions

1. Does the proper environment presently exist for developing work teams? Explain.
2. Discuss any likely pitfalls to the development of work teams.

HRM INCIDENT 2

CLOSE TO THE VEST

For the past few years, sales at Glenco Manufacturing had been falling, reflecting an industry-wide decline. During this time, Glenco had actually been able to increase its share of the market slightly. Although forecasts indicated that demand for its products would improve in the future, Joe Goddard, the company president, believed that something needed to be done immediately to help the firm survive this temporary slump. As a first step, he employed a consulting firm to determine whether reorganization might be helpful.

A team of five consultants arrived at the firm. They told Mr. Goddard that they first had to gain a thorough understanding of the current situation before they could make any recommendations. Mr. Goddard assured them that the company was open to them. They could ask any questions that they thought were necessary.

The grapevine was full of rumors virtually from the day the consulting group arrived. One employee was heard to say, "If they shut down the company, I don't know if I could take care of my family." Another worker said, "If they move me away from my friends, I'm going to quit."

When workers questioned their supervisors, they received no explanations. No one had told the supervisors what was going on. The climate began to change to one of fear. Rather than being concerned about their daily work, employees worried about what was going to happen to the company and their jobs. As a result, productivity dropped drastically.

A month after the consultants departed, an informational memorandum was circulated throughout the company. It stated that the consultants had recommended a slight modification in the top levels of the organization to achieve greater efficiency. No one would be terminated. Any reductions would be the result of normal attrition. By this time, however, some of the best workers had already found other jobs, and company operations were severely disrupted for several months.

Questions

1. Why did the employees tend to assume the worst about what was happening?
2. How could this difficulty have been avoided?

DEVELOPING HRM SKILLS

AN EXPERIENTIAL EXERCISE

In every organization, human resource professionals work with many individuals and groups. Cooperation is a must if the tasks involved in human resource management are to be accomplished effectively. The Blue-Green exercise provides students with the opportunity to experience some of the interrelationships that occur in a structured setting, such as an organization or work group.

The Blue-Green exercise is one of the best to use when working with a relatively large group. In fact, it is not recommended for groups of fewer than twelve persons. It has been successfully used with groups as large as forty persons. This exercise works equally well with groups of people who have been working together for some time and with heterogeneous groups whose members barely know one another. Its impact, however, is probably greater when dealing with people who are supposed to work together. The language used by the person in charge of conducting the exercise is extremely important, so participants should listen carefully to the rules.

Those who participate in this exercise usually find it quite enlightening; it has been repeated many times over the years. The total group will be divided into four subgroups of as nearly equal size as possible. These subgroups will be called *teams* and be designated as Team A-1, Team A-2, Team B-1, and Team B-2. Your instructor will provide the participants with additional information necessary to participate. Enjoy the classic Blue-Green exercise.

OTES

1. Arthur Sharplin, *Strategic Management* (New York: McGraw-Hill, 1985): 102.

2. Thomas G. Cummings and Christopher G. Worley, *Organization Development and Change,* 5th edition (Minneapolis/St. Paul: West Publishing Company, 1993): 526.

3. Frank Petrock, "Corporate Culture Enhances Profits," *HRMagazine* 35 (November 1990): 64–66.

4. Anthony Jay, *Management and Machiavelli* (New York: Holt, Rinehart and Winston, 1967): 231.

5. Brian Dumaine, "Creating a New Company Culture," *Fortune* 121 (January 15, 1990): 127.

6. Carol J. Loomis, "The Reed That Citicorp Leans On," *Fortune* 128 (July 12, 1993): 90–93.

7. Wayne F. Cascio and Manuel G. Serapio, Jr., "Human Resources Systems in an International Alliance: The Undoing of a Done Deal?" *Organizational Dynamics* 19 (Winter 1991): 65.

8. Ibid., 67–68.

9. Ibid., 68.

10. Carol J. Loomis, "The Reed That Citicorp Leans On," ibid.

11. Benson Rosen and Kay Lovelace, "Fitting Square Pegs into Round Holes," *HRMagazine* 39 (January 1994): 86–93.

12. Thomas G. Cummings and Christopher G. Worley, *Organization Development and Change*, 2.

13. Ibid.

14. Ibid., 136–137.

15. Ibid., 137.

16. The material on transactional analysis is abridged and adapted from Thomas A. Harris, M.D., *I'm O.K.—You're O.K.* Copyright 1967, 1968, and 1969 by Thomas A. Harris, M.D. Reprinted by permission of Harper & Row Publishers, Inc.

17. David J. Lill and John T. Rose, "Transactional Analysis and Personal Selling: A Primer for Banks," *Journal of Commercial Bank Lending* 70 (February 1988): 57.

18. Barbara Mandell, "Does a Better Worklife Boost Productivity?" *Personnel* 66 (October 1989): 49.

19. Ibid., 27.

20. Ibid., 49.

21. James L. Gibson and John M. Ivancevich, *Organizations: Behavior, Structure, Processes*, 4th edition (Plano, Texas: Business Publications, 1982): 580–581.

22. John P. Campbell and Marvin D. Dunnette, "Effectiveness of T-Group Experiences in Managerial Training and Development," *Psychological Bulletin* 70 (August 1968): 23–104.

23. Irwin L. Goldstein, *Training in Organizations: Needs Assessment, Development, and Evaluation*, 2nd edition (Monterey, Calif.: Brooks/Cole Publishing Company, 1986): 243.

24. Ellis Pines, "TQM Training: A New Culture Sparks Change at Every Level," *Aviation Week and Space Technology* 132 (May 21, 1990): S38.

25. Ellis Pines, "From Top Secret to Top Priority: The Story of TQM," *Aviation Week and Space Technology* 132 (May 21, 1990): S24.

26. Otis Port and John Carey, "Questing for the Best," *Business Week Bonus Issue, The Quality Imperative* (October 11, 1991): 10.

27. Ibid.

28. Karen Lowry Miller and David Woodruff, "A Design Master's End Run around Trial and Error," *Business Week Bonus Issue, The Quality Imperative* (October 25, 1991): 24.

29. Otis Port and John Carey, "Questing for the Best," 14.

30. Otis Port, John Carey, Kevin Kelly, and Stephanie Anderson Forest, "Quality," *Business Week* (November 30, 1992): 68.

31. . . . "TQM Worth It," *HRMagazine* 38 (August 1993): 30.

32. Adapted from Howard J. Weiss and Mark E. Gershon, *Production and Operations Management*, 2nd edition (Needham Heights, Mass.: Allyn and Bacon, 1993): 783–4.

33. This case is a composite of a number of accounts, among them: Jonathan Kapstein and John Hoerr, "Volvo's Radical New Plant: 'The Death of the Assembly Line?'" *Business Week* (August 28, 1989): 92–93; David Bartal, "Volvo's Back-to-the-Future Factory," *U.S. News & World Report* 107 (August 21, 1989): 42; Leigh Bruce and Jack Burton, "Strained Alliances," *International Management* 45 (May 1990): 29; and Patricia Sellers, "The Best Way to Reach Your Buyers," *Fortune* 128 (Autumn/Winter 1993): 14–17.

34. Richard Wellins and Jill George, "The Key to Self-Directed Teams," *Training and Development Journal* 45 (April 1991): 27.

35. David Woodruff, James B. Treece, Sunita Wadekar Bhargava, and Karen Lowry Miller, "Saturn," *Business Week* (August 17, 1992): 88.

36. Shari Caudron, "Are Self-Directed Teams Right for Your Company?" *Personnel Journal* 72 (December 1993): 78.

37. Donna Robbins, "The Dark Side of Team Building," *Training and Development* 47 (December 1993): 17.

38. Richard Wellins and Jill George, "The Key to Self-Directed Teams," ibid.

CHAPTER 10

Career Planning and Development

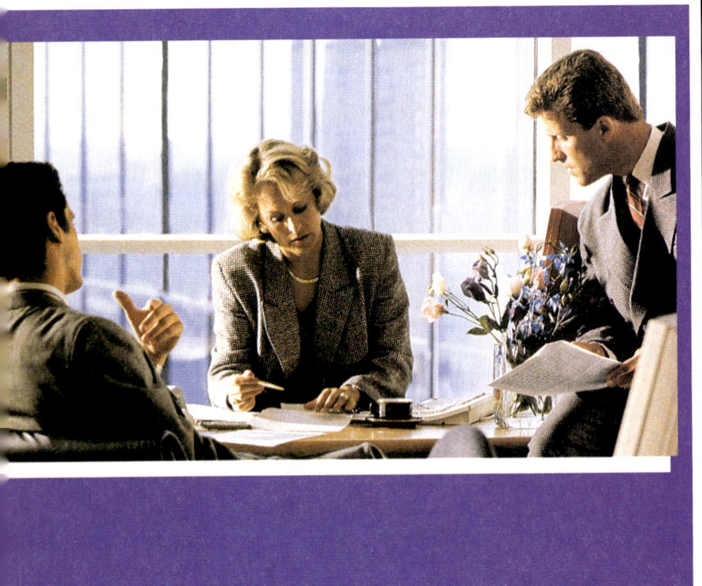

KEY TERMS

Career 300
Career planning 300
Career path 300
Career development 300
Career anchors 302
Self-assessment 305
Strength/weakness balance sheet 305
Likes and dislikes survey 305
Organizational career planning 307
Traditional career path 308
Network career path 310
Dual career path 310
Plateauing 313

CHAPTER OBJECTIVES

1. Define career planning and career development and describe factors affecting career planning.
2. Explain the importance of individual career planning and how a thorough self-assessment is crucial to career planning.
3. Explain the nature of career planning, discuss career paths, and describe plateauing.
4. Describe career development and describe the avenues available for beginning a career in human resources.

Bob Allen and Thelma Gowen, both supervisors at American Bank of New York, were having a cup of coffee and discussing a point of mutual concern in the employee lounge. Bob said, "I'm beginning to get frustrated. When I joined American four years ago, I really felt that I could make a career here. Now I'm not so sure. I spoke with the boss last week about where I might be in the next few years, and all she kept saying was, 'There are all kinds of possibilities.' I need more than that. I'd like to know what specific opportunities might be available if I continue to do a good job. I'm not sure if I want to spend my career in this job. I know we have cut out several management levels in the last couple of years, but there may be better chances for advancing my knowledge in other areas. This is a big company."

Thelma replied, "I'm having the same trouble. She told me, 'You are doing a great job, and we want you to stay at American.' I'd also like to know what other jobs are available if I get the proper training."

Obviously, American Bank has no career planning and development program. Bob is frustrated, and Thelma wants to know what career avenues are available to her. Lacking this knowledge, they may decide not to remain with the bank. Career planning and development are also important to a company because they ensure that people with the necessary skills and experience will be available when needed.

In this chapter, we first discuss the concept of career planning and development. Next, we identify several factors that affect career planning and discuss the nature of career planning. Then, we address individual career planning, career paths, and plateauing. Following this, we describe career development and the methods used in career planning and development. We devote the last part of the chapter to how a person might begin a career in human resources.

CAREER PLANNING AND DEVELOPMENT DEFINED

A **career** is a general course that a person chooses to pursue throughout his or her working life. **Career planning** is an ongoing process whereby an individual sets career goals and identifies the means to achieve them. The major focus of career planning should be on matching personal goals and opportunities that are realistically available. Career planning should not concentrate only on advancement opportunities since the present work environment has reduced many of these opportunities. Also, from a practical standpoint, there never were enough high-level positions to make upward mobility a reality for everyone. At some point, career planning needs to focus on achieving psychological successes that do not necessarily entail promotions.

Individual and organizational careers are not separate and distinct. A person whose individual career plan cannot be followed within the organization will probably leave the firm sooner or later. Or, if opportunities are not available elsewhere, a person may *leave* the firm by permitting productivity to decline. Thus, organizations should assist employees in career planning so that both can satisfy their needs. A **career path** is a flexible line of movement through which an employee may move during employment with a company. Following an established career path, the employee can undertake career development with the firm's assistance. **Career development** is a formal approach taken by the organization to ensure people with the proper qualifications and experience are available when needed. Career planning and development benefit both the individual and the organization.

FACTORS AFFECTING CAREER PLANNING

Several factors affect a person's view of a career. The individual should recognize and consider the most important factors when planning a career. In this section we describe three such factors: life stages, career anchors, and the environment.

Life Stages

People change constantly and, thus, view their careers differently at various stages of their lives. Some of these changes result from the aging process and others from opportunities for growth and status. The basic life stages are shown in Figure 10-1.

The first stage is that of establishing identity. A person typically reaches this stage between the ages of ten and twenty. The individual explores career alternatives and begins to move into the adult world. Stage two involves growing and getting established in a career. This stage usually lasts from ages twenty to forty. During this stage, a person chooses an occupation and establishes a career path. The third stage, self-maintenance and self-adjustment, generally lasts to age fifty and beyond. At this point, a person either accepts life as it is or makes adjustments. Career change and divorce occur during this phase because people seriously question the quality of their lives. The final stage is that of decline. Diminishing physical and mental capabilities may accelerate this stage. A person may have lower aspirations and less motivation during the decline stage, resulting in additional career adjustments.

Even though most individuals have career development needs throughout their working lives, the majority of developmental activities are directed at new, younger workers. Since the last amendment to the Age Discrimination in Employment Act, there has been no mandatory retirement age, and, therefore, the self-maintenance and self-adjustment stage is likely to be extended. Consequently, future employees will probably need career develop-

FIGURE 10-1
Life Stages

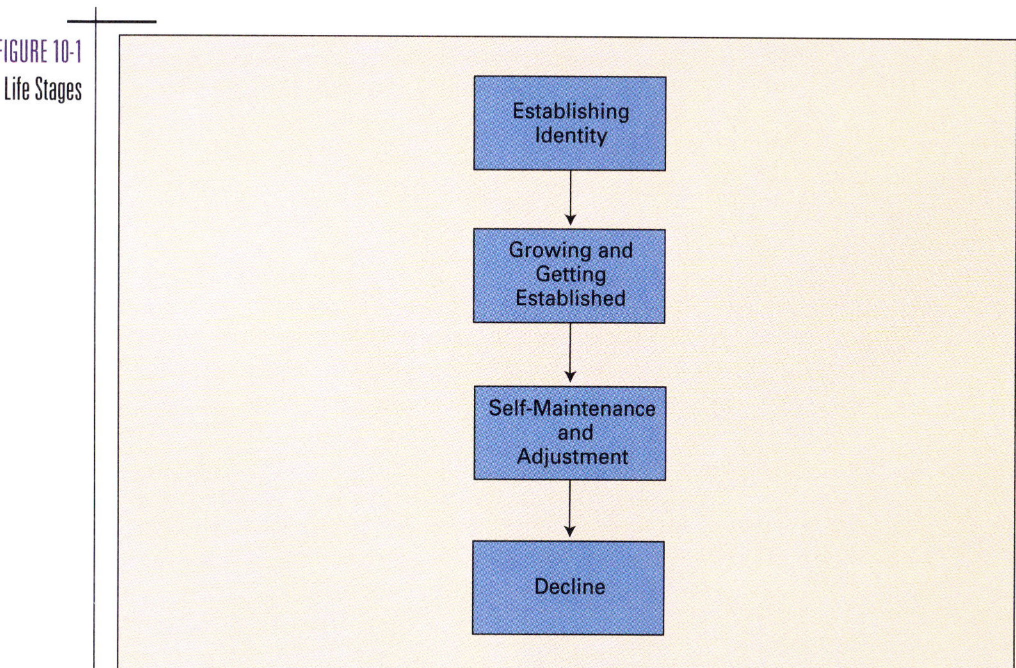

Source: Adapted from James W. Walker, *Human Resource Planning* (New York: McGraw-Hill Book Company, 1980). Used with permission of the McGraw-Hill Book Company.

ment as much in later years as they do in the initial years of their working lives. Also, as a result of downsizing and the elimination of layers of management in organizations, development has become much more important as workers are expected to accomplish a wider variety of tasks.

Career Anchors

All of us have different aspirations, backgrounds, and experiences. Our personalities are molded, to a certain extent, by the results of our interactions with our environments. Edgar Schein's research identified five different motives that account for the way people select and prepare for a career. He called them **career anchors.**[1]

1. *Managerial Competence.* The career goal of managers is to develop qualities of interpersonal, analytical, and emotional competence. People using this anchor want to manage people.
2. *Technical/Functional Competence.* The anchor for technicians is the continuous development of technical talent. These individuals do not seek managerial positions.
3. *Security.* The anchor for security-conscious individuals is to stabilize their career situations. They often see themselves tied to a particular organization or geographical location.
4. *Creativity.* Creative individuals are somewhat entrepreneurial in their attitude. They want to create or build something that is entirely their own.
5. *Autonomy and Independence.* The career anchor for independent people is a desire to be free from organizational constraints. They value autonomy and want to be their own boss and work at their own pace.

One of the implications of these career anchors is that companies must be flexible enough to provide alternative paths to satisfy people's varying needs.

The Environment

The work environment in which career planning takes place has changed rapidly in recent years. Across the country, and around the world, downsizing has occurred. Workers and managers alike are being displaced in massive numbers. Therefore, a very important factor affecting career planning is the work environment individuals confront. As Charles W. Sweet, president of A.T. Kearney's executive recruiting firm in Chicago, Illinois, said, "The way people approached their careers in the past is history. It will never, never, never return."[2] For many workers, career planning involves planning ways to retain their present job in this drastically changing work environment. Such a change in environment was dramatically emphasized by William Bridges, author of *JobShift*, when he stated, "We used to read predictions that by 2000 everyone would work 30-hour weeks, and the rest would be leisure. But as we approach 2000 it seems more likely that half of us will be working 60-hour weeks and the rest of us will be unemployed."[3]

CAREER PLANNING

The process by which individuals plan their life's work is referred to as career planning. Through career planning, a person evaluates his or her own abilities and interests, considers alternative career opportunities, establishes career goals, and plans practical development activities.

In addition to a self-assessment, an individual would be wise to follow the guidelines presented in Table 10-1 to prepare for a new career path. Career planning should begin with a person's placement in an entry-level job and initial orientation. Management will observe the employee's job performance and compare it with job standards. At this stage, strengths and weaknesses will be noted, enabling management to assist the employee in making a tentative career decision. Naturally, this decision can be altered later as the process continues. This tentative career decision is based on a number of factors, including personal needs, abilities and aspirations, and the organization's needs. Management can then schedule human resource development programs that relate to the employee's specific needs. For instance, a person who wants a career in human resources may require some legal training.

TABLE 10-1
Fourteen Steps on a New Career Path

1. **Accept the new values of the workplace by showing how you can help a company meet its bottom-line needs**: increasing profits, cutting costs, increasing productivity and efficiency, improving public relations, even getting new clients. . . .

2. **Continually look for newer and better ways to be of more value to your employer**. Too many who did a good job fifteen or twenty years ago are today doing the same thing and thinking that they are still doing a good job. Your company has changed; you need to change with it.

3. **Don't keep yourself stuck in an 'information vacuum.'** Today you can no longer afford to be unaware of what is happening to your company, industry, your community, your country, or, for that matter, the world. . . .

4. **Don't be reactive**. Those who are successful today are those who prepare ahead of time, anticipate problems and opportunities, and get ready.

5. **Continually seek out a new education**. Expanded knowledge, increased information, and new skills are appearing at record pace. Those who are successful are those who find out what new skills and knowledge they need and who are taking the extra time and trouble to learn them. The others simply will not be competitive.

6. **Develop significant career and financial goals and detailed plans to reach them**. Otherwise, you are vulnerable.

7. **Avoid a state of denial**. When a person is in denial, he or she will ignore signs that something is wrong. Denial is one of the major reasons why people become immobilized and are not prepared for a problem or a change in the company.

8. **Prepare for survival in your present career and for taking the next job or career step**. Have you explored alternatives? Are your job search skills those of today, or are you using antiquated job search methods?

Source: Sander I. Marcus and Jotham G. Friedland, "Fourteen Steps on a New Career Path," *HRMagazine* 38 (March 1993): 55–56.

TABLE 10-1 (continued)
Fourteen Steps on a New Career Path

9. Become motivated by your goals, not by anger, fear, or hopelessness. In difficult and uncertain career situations, it is human nature to have strong feelings. The problem is that too many of us let those feelings guide our actions and our words.

10. Market yourself aggressively. Whether you have a job or are looking for a job, today's world demands that in order to survive and be successful, you must learn to market yourself: network with others, let others know the good work that you do, and don't burn your bridges by making unnecessary enemies. In particular, learn to market yourself within your present company.

11. Improve your motivation and commitment. Employers are no longer looking for those who are good enough, they are looking for those who are the most highly motivated. Demand and get the best out of yourself. Go to seminars and get counseling if there is a motivational block. Rejuvenate your enthusiasm and demonstrate it at work.

12. Place your weaknesses and inadequacies in perspective; do not allow them to loom so large in your mind that all you can see when you look in the mirror is failure. Remember that no one is without weaknesses, inadequacies, and mistakes.

13. Realize that to survive and prosper in today's world, your primary job is to change yourself. You are the one who has to keep up with your training and education. You are the one who has to learn new skills in networking. You are the one who has to develop a different perspective on your career and your employment.

14. There's no reason HR professionals can't take advantage of the same professional counseling and guidance available to others. Give yourself the edge and you can confidently move forward to define the career path you want.

Remember that career planning is an ongoing process. It takes into consideration the changes that occur in people, in organizations, and in the environment. This type of flexibility is absolutely necessary in today's dynamic organizational environment. Not only do the firm's requirements change, but individuals may choose to revise their career expectations. Some prefer the old-fashioned way—up. But in today's less vertical corporate world, workers may have to consider other directions that may eventually lead to a higher plane. For example, they can move sideways, with no change in salary or title, to a more dynamic department; leave the company perhaps for a more rewarding career elsewhere; remain in the same position and try to enhance their skills and explore new horizons; or move down to a job that may carry less weight but promises more growth.[4]

Individual Career Planning

Career planning begins with self-understanding. Then, the person is in a position to establish realistic goals and determine what to do to achieve these goals. This action also lets the person know whether his or her goals are realistic.

Learning about oneself is referred to as **self-assessment**. Anything that could affect one's performance in a future job should be considered. Realistic self-assessment may help a person avoid mistakes that could affect his or her entire career progression. Often an individual accepts a job without considering whether it matches his or her interests and abilities. This approach often results in failure. A thorough self-assessment will go a long way toward helping match an individual's specific qualities and goals with the right job or profession.

Some useful tools include a strength/weakness balance sheet and a likes and dislikes survey. However, any reasonable approach that assists self-understanding is helpful.

Strength/Weakness Balance Sheet. A self-evaluation procedure, developed originally by Benjamin Franklin, that assists people in becoming aware of their strengths and weaknesses is called a **strength/weakness balance sheet**. Employees who understand their strengths can use them to maximum advantage. By recognizing their weaknesses, individuals avoid having to utilize those qualities or skills. Furthermore, by recognizing weaknesses, individuals are in a better position to overcome them. This attitude is summed up by the statement, "If you have a weakness, understand it and make it work for you as a strength; if you have a strength, do not abuse it to the point where it becomes a weakness."

To use a strength/weakness balance sheet, the individual lists strengths and weaknesses as he or she perceives them. This is quite important because believing, for example, that a weakness exists can equate to a real weakness. Thus, a person who believes that he or she will make a poor first impression when meeting someone will probably make a poor impression. The perception of a weakness often becomes a self-fulfilling prophesy.

The mechanics for preparing the balance sheet are quite simple. To begin, draw a line down the middle of a sheet of paper. Label the left side *strengths* and the right side *weaknesses*. Record all perceived strengths and weaknesses. You may find it difficult to write about yourself. Remember, however, that no one else need see the results. The primary consideration is complete honesty.

Figure 10-2 shows an example of a strength/weakness balance sheet. Obviously, Wayne (the person who wrote the sheet) did a lot of soul-searching in making these evaluations. Typically, a person's weaknesses will outnumber strengths in the first few iterations. However, as the individual repeats the process, some items that first appeared to be weaknesses may eventually be recognized as strengths and should then be moved from one column to the other. A person should devote sufficient time to the project to obtain a fairly clear understanding of his or her strengths and weaknesses. Typically, the process should take a minimum of one week. The balance sheet will not provide all the answers regarding a person's strengths and weaknesses, but many people have gained a better understanding of themselves by completing it.

Likes and Dislikes Survey. An individual should also consider likes and dislikes as part of a self-assessment. A **likes and dislikes survey** assists individuals in recognizing restrictions they place on themselves. For instance,

FIGURE 10-2
Strength/Weakness Balance Sheet

Strengths	Weaknesses
Work well with people.	Get very close to few people.
Like to be given a task and get it done in my own way.	Do not like constant supervision.
Good manager of people.	Don't make friends very easily with individuals classified as my superiors.
Hard worker.	Am extremely high-strung.
Lead by example.	Often say things without realizing consequences.
People respect me as being fair and impartial.	Cannot stand to look busy when there is no work to be done.
Tremendous amount of energy.	Cannot stand to be inactive. Must be on the go constantly.
Function well in an active environment.	Cannot stand to sit at a desk all the time.
Relatively open-minded.	Basically a rebel at heart but have portrayed myself as just the opposite. My conservatism has gotten me jobs that I emotionally do not want.
Feel comfortable in dealing with high-level businesspersons.	Am sometimes nervous in an unfamiliar environment.
Like to play politics. (This may be a weakness.)	Make very few true friends.
Get the job done when it is defined.	Not a conformist but appear to be.
Excellent at organizing other people's time. Can get the most out of people who are working for me.	Interest level hits peaks and valleys.
Have an outgoing personality—not shy.	Many people look on me as being unstable. Perhaps I am. Believe not.
Take care of those who take care of me. (This could be a weakness.)	Divorced.
Have a great amount of empathy.	Not a tremendous planner for short range. Long-range planning is better.
Work extremely well through other people.	Impatient—want to have things happen fast.
	Do not like details.
	Do not work well in an environment where I am the only party involved.

Source: Wayne Sanders.

some people are not willing to live in certain parts of the country, and such feelings should be noted as a constraint. Some positions require a person to spend a considerable amount of time traveling. Thus, an estimate of the amount of time a person is willing to travel would also be helpful. Recognition of such self-imposed restrictions may reduce future career problems. Another limitation is the type of firm an individual will consider working for. The size of the firm might also be important. Some people like a major organization whose products are well-known; others prefer a smaller organization, believing that the opportunities for advancement may be greater or that the environment is better suited to their tastes. All factors that could affect an individual's work performance should be listed in the likes and dislikes survey. An example of this type of survey is shown in Figure 10-3.

A self-assessment, such as this one, helps a person understand his or her basic motives, setting the stage for pursuing a management career or seeking

FIGURE 10-3
Likes and Dislikes Survey

Likes	Dislikes
Like to travel.	Do not want to work for a large firm.
Would like to live in the East.	Will not work in a large city.
Enjoy being my own boss.	Do not like to work behind a desk all day.
Would like to live in a medium-size city.	Do not like to wear suits all the time.
Enjoy watching football and baseball.	
Enjoy playing racquetball.	

Source: Wayne Sanders.

further technical competence. A person with little desire for management responsibilities should probably not accept a promotion to supervisor or enter management training. People who know themselves can more easily make the decisions necessary for successful career planning. Many people get sidetracked because they choose careers based on haphazard plans or the wishes of others rather than on what they believe to be best for themselves.

Getting to know oneself is not a singular event. As individuals progress through life, priorities change. Individuals may think they know themselves quite well at one stage of life and later begin to see themselves quite differently. Therefore, self-assessment should be viewed as a continuous process. Career-minded individuals must heed the Red Queen's admonition to Alice: "It takes all the running you can do, to keep in the same place."[5] This admonition is so very true in today's work environment.

Organizational Career Planning

The primary responsibility for career planning rests with the individual.[6] However, organizations should actively assist in the process. From the organization's viewpoint, career planning involves a conscious attempt to maximize a person's potential contributions. Firms that promote career planning programs for their employees reap many benefits.

The process of establishing career paths within a firm is referred to as **organizational career planning**. Firms should undertake organizational career planning programs only when the programs contribute to achieving basic organizational goals. Therefore, the rationale and approach to career planning programs varies among firms. This is more important in today's environment in which traditional vertical mobility has been stifled in many organizations. In most organizations, career planning programs are expected to achieve one or more of the following objectives:

- More effective development of available talent. Individuals are more likely to be committed to development that is part of a specific career plan. This way they can better understand the purpose of development.
- Self-appraisal opportunities for employees considering new or nontraditional career paths. Some excellent workers do not view the traditional upward mobility as a career option since firms today have fewer and fewer promotion options available. Other workers see themselves in

dead-end jobs and seek relief. Rather than lose these workers, a firm can offer career planning to help them identify new and different career paths.

- More efficient development of human resources within and among divisions and/or geographic locations. Career paths should be developed that cut across divisions and geographic locations.
- A demonstration of a tangible commitment to EEO and affirmative action. Adverse impact can occur at virtually any level in an organization. Firms that are totally committed to reducing adverse impact often cannot find qualified women and minorities to fill vacant positions. One means of overcoming this problem is an effective career planning and development program. Frequently, affirmative action programs require companies to set up career development programs for women and minorities.
- Satisfaction of employees' personal development needs. Individuals who see their personal development needs being met tend to be more satisfied with their jobs and the organization.
- Improvement of performance through on-the-job training experiences provided by horizontal and vertical career moves. The job itself is the most important influence on career development. Each job can provide different challenges and experiences.
- Increased employee loyalty and motivation, leading to decreased turnover. Individuals who believe that the firm is interested in their career planning will be more likely to remain with the organization.
- A method of determining training and development needs. If a person desires a certain career path and does not presently have the proper qualifications, this identifies a training and development need.[7]

All these objectives may be desirable. But successful career planning depends on a firm's ability to satisfy those that it considers most crucial to employee development and the achievement of organizational goals.

CAREER PATHS

Recall that a career path is a flexible line of progression through which an employee typically moves during employment with a company. Career paths have historically focused on upward mobility within a particular occupation. One of four types of career paths may be used: traditional, network, lateral skill, and dual.

Traditional Career Path

The **traditional career path** is one in which an employee progresses vertically upward in the organization from one specific job to the next. The assumption is that each preceding job is essential preparation for the next higher level job. Therefore, an employee must move, step-by-step, from one job to the next to gain needed experience and preparation.

One of the biggest advantages of the traditional career path is that it is straightforward. The path is clearly laid out, and the employee knows the specific sequence of jobs through which he or she must progress.

HRM IN ACTION

—A LEGITIMATE COMPLAINT?

Five years ago when Bobby Bret joined Crystal Productions as a junior accountant, he felt that he was on his way up. He had just graduated with a B+ average from college, where he was well liked by his peers and the faculty. As an officer in several student organizations, Bobby had shown a natural ability to get along with people as well as to get things done. He remembered what Roger Friedman, the controller at Crystal, had told him when he was hired, "I think you will do well here, Bobby. You've come highly recommended. You are the kind of guy who can expect to move right up the ladder."

Bobby felt that he had done a good job at Crystal, and everybody seemed to like him. In addition, his performance appraisals had been excellent. However, after five years he was still a junior accountant. He had applied for two senior accountant positions that had come open, but they were both filled by people hired from outside the firm. When the accounting supervisor's job came open two years ago, Bobby had not applied. He was surprised when his new boss turned out to be a hotshot graduate of State University whose only experience was three years with a Big Six accounting firm. Bobby had hoped that Ron Green, a senior accountant he particularly respected, would get the job.

On the fifth anniversary of his employment at Crystal, Bobby decided it was time to do something. He made an appointment with Mr. Friedman. At that meeting Bobby explained he had worked hard to obtain a promotion and shared his frustration about having been in the same job for so long. "Well," said Mr. Friedman, "you don't think that you were all that much better qualified than the people we have hired, do you?" "No," said Bobby, "but, I think I could have handled the senior accountant job. Of course, the people you have hired are doing a great job too." The controller responded, "We just look at the qualifications of all the applicants for each job and, considering everything, try to make a reasonable decision."

Do you believe that Bobby has a legitimate complaint? Explain.

Today, however, the traditional approach has become flawed because of business trends and changes in the workforce. Some of these factors include the following:

- a massive reduction in management ranks due to mergers, downsizing, stagnation, growth cycles, and reengineering
- extinction of paternalism and job security
- erosion of employee loyalty
- a work environment where new skills must constantly be learned

The certainties of yesterday's business methods and growth have vanished in many industries, and neither organizations nor individuals can be assured of ever regaining them.

Network Career Path

The **network career path** contains both a vertical sequence of jobs and a series of horizontal opportunities. The network career path recognizes the interchangeability of experience at certain levels and the need to broaden experience at one level before promotion to a higher level. This approach more realistically represents opportunities for employee development in an organization than does the traditional career path. The vertical and horizontal options lessen the probability of blockage. One disadvantage of this type of career path is that it is more difficult to explain to employees the specific route their careers may take for a given line of work.

Lateral Skill Path

Traditionally, a career path was viewed as moving upward to higher levels of management in the organization. The previous two career path methods focused on such an approach. The availability of these two options has diminished considerably in recent years. But, this does not mean that an individual has to remain in the same job for life. There are often lateral moves within the firm that can be taken to allow an employee to become revitalized and find new challenges. No pay or promotion is involved, but employees can increase their value to the organization and also revitalize themselves.

Dual Career Path

The dual career path was originally developed to deal with the problem of technically trained employees who had no desire to move into management through the normal procedure for upward mobility in an organization. The **dual career path** recognizes that technical specialists can—and should be allowed to—contribute their expertise to a company without having to become managers. In organizations, such as National Semiconductor, a high-tech worldwide firm headquartered in Santa Clara, California, a dual career approach was set up to encourage and motivate individual contributors in engineering, sales, marketing, finance, human resources, and other areas.[8] Individuals in these fields can increase their specialized knowledge, make contributions to their firms, and be rewarded without entering management. Whether on the management or technical side of the path, compensation would be comparable at each level.

The dual career path is becoming increasingly popular. In our high-tech world, specialized knowledge is often as important as managerial skill.

Rather than creating poor managers out of competent technical specialists, the dual career path permits an organization to retain both highly skilled managers and highly skilled technical people.[9]

Dow Corning has created what they describe as multiple ladders. As may be seen in Figure 10-4, individuals can progress upward in research, technical service and development, and process engineering without being forced into management roles.

Adding Value to Retain Present Job

Adding value to retain a person's present job may seem to be a strange topic to include under the heading of career planning. But, today's workers need to develop a plan whereby they are viewed as continually *adding value* to the organization. William J. Morin, chairman of the outplacement firm Drake Beam Morin, said, "Employees will have to anticipate where they can add value to their companies and take charge of their own destiny."[10] If they cannot add value, the company does not need them. Workers must anticipate what tools will be needed for success in the future and obtain these skills. These workers must look across company lines to other organizations to determine what skills are transferable, and then go and get them. Essentially, today's workers must manage their own careers as never before. According to Pat Milligan, a partner at Towers Perrin, a human resources consulting firm, the new attitude among companies is: "There will never be job security. You will be employed by us as long as you add value to the organization, and you are continuously responsible for finding ways to add value. In return, you have the right to de-

Level	Managerial	Research	Technical Service and Development	Process Engineering
	Vice President, R&D			
	Director			
VIII	Manager	Senior Research Scientist	Senior Development Scientist	Senior Process Engineering Scientist
VII	Manager	Research Scientist	Development Scientist	Process Engineering Scientist
VI	Section Manager	Associate Research Scientist	Associate Development Scientist	Associate Process Engineering Scientist
V	Group Leader	Senior Research Specialist	Senior TS&D Specialist	Senior Engineering Specialist
IV		Research Specialist	TS&D Specialist	Senior Project Engineer
III		Project Chemist	TS&D Representative	Project Engineer
II		Associate Project Chemist	TS&D Engineer	Development Engineer
I		Chemist	Engineer	Engineer

FIGURE 10-4 Multiple Ladders at Dow Corning

Source: Charles W. Lentz, "Dual Ladders Become Multiple Ladders at Dow Corning," *Research Technology Management* 33 (May-June 1990): 28.

mand interesting and important work, the freedom and resources to perform it well, pay that reflects your contribution, and the experience and training needed to be employable here or elsewhere."[11]

As a worker increases his or her value to an organization, the value in the overall job market also increases. In today's work environment, the definition of *job security* is being able to go out and find another job. It might be called enlightened self-interest. A person must discover what companies need and then develop the necessary skills to meet these needs. As one Avon executive stated, "Always be doing something that contributes significant, positive change to the organization. That's the ultimate job security."[12] For many workers, the only tie that binds a worker to the company is a common commitment to success and growth.

Job Revitalization and Career Enhancement

Many organizations are not able to reward workers with raises and promotions and remain competitive in the new global workplace. This climate has often caused productivity to suffer and absenteeism to soar. Says Chevron's head of personnel development, Sarah Clemens, "We're working to help people revitalize their jobs in a way that will benefit them and the company."[13] Companies need to reinvigorate diminished and demoralized ranks. They are trying to spur productivity by offering employees a host of ways to spice up their jobs with additional training, lateral moves, short sabbaticals, and compensation based on a person's contribution, not title.[14]

Compensation is another way flattened organizations are spurring enthusiasm. *Broad banding*, as the concept is called, rewards people with raises unaccompanied by promotions. The more skills you acquire and use, the more you can earn—even if you do not jump to the next rung on the corporate ladder.[15]

As companies reduce the levels of management, lower the number of workers employed, and increase the pressure on those who remain, lateral moves have become the commonest way to reenergize the troops. Chevron, which has slimmed down by 6,500 employees in the past two years, has redeployed more than 1,000 people to different areas of the company. As CEO Kenneth Derr puts it, "That's not as easy as it sounds. Relocation and retraining expenses can run around $75,000 a person." General Motors, which by 1995 had cut its vast white-collar workforce nearly in half to about 70,000, is paying some $10 million a year for 6,100 employees to be retrained and to enhance their skills in everything from carpentry to the nuts and bolts of automotive design.[16]

Career Path Information

Information regarding career options and opportunities must be available before individuals can begin to set realistic career objectives. One way to provide this information is to develop career path data for each job. This information can be developed from job descriptions, based on historical trends within the organization, or based on similarities to other jobs in the same job family. Career path information is particularly useful because it does the following:

1. Shows each employee how his or her job relates to other jobs.
2. Presents career alternatives.

3. Describes educational and experience requirements for a career change.
4. Points out the orientations of other jobs.[17]

PLATEAUING

A problem for many individuals who aspire to move upward in an organization is plateauing. **Plateauing** occurs when an employee's job functions and work content remain the same because of a lack of promotional opportunities with the firm. It has been estimated that 99 percent of the workforce has experienced plateauing at least once in their career.[18] Plateauing has become more common recently because many organizations are downsizing, hierarchies are flattening, and the baby boom generation is just reaching its prime. In addition, women and minorities are now competing for positions that once were not available to them.

Between 1950 and 1976, many companies offered extraordinary opportunities for advancement. However, the picture today is quite different, as a large number of people with similar educational backgrounds compete for fewer promotions. In our society, promotion has always been an important measure of success. Thus, plateauing will present new challenges for those involved with career planning and development.

Several approaches may be used to deal with this problem. As previously mentioned, one possibility is to move individuals laterally within the organization. Although status or pay may remain unchanged, the employee is given the opportunity to develop new skills. Firms that want to encourage lateral movement may choose to utilize a skill-based pay system that rewards individuals for the type and number of skills they possess. Another approach, which we have already discussed, is job enrichment. This approach rewards (without promoting) an employee by increasing the challenge of the job, giving the job more meaning and giving the employee a greater sense of accomplishment. Today roughly one in ten midsized to large companies offers such enrichment opportunities.

Exploratory career development is yet another way of dealing with plateauing. It gives an employee the opportunity to test ideas in another field without committing to an actual move. Demotions have long been associated with failure, but limited promotional opportunities in the future may make them more legitimate career options. If the stigma of demotion can be removed, more employees—especially older workers—might choose to make such a move. In certain instances, this approach might open up a clogged promotional path and, at the same time, permit a senior employee to escape unwanted stress without being thought a failure.

CAREER DEVELOPMENT

As previously mentioned, a career path is a flexible line of movement through which an employee may move during employment with a company. Career development is a formal approach taken by the organization to ensure that people with the proper qualifications and experience are available when needed. Thus, career development includes any and all activities that prepare a person for satisfying the needs of the firm both now and in the future. Today's workers realize that if they do not continuously add value to the organization, their future with the firm is greatly diminished. Essentially everyone in the company could be involved.[19] Career development usually involves both formal and informal means. Career devel-

Workers of today realize that if they do not continuously add value to the organization, their future with the firm is greatly diminished.

opment programs may be conducted in-house or by outside sources, such as professional organizations or colleges and universities.

In-house programs are usually planned and implemented by a training and development unit within the firm's human resource department. Line managers are also frequently utilized to conduct program segments. Outside the company, such organizations as the Society for Human Resource Management and the American Management Association are active in conducting conferences, seminars, and other types of career development programs.

Certain principles should be observed with regard to career development. First, the job itself has the greatest influence on career development. When each day presents a different challenge, what is learned on the job may be far more important than formally planned development activities. Second, the type of developmental skills that will be needed is determined by specific job demands. The skills needed to become a first-line supervisor will likely differ from those needed to become a middle manager. Third, development will occur only when a person has not yet obtained the skills demanded by a particular job. If the purpose of a transfer is to develop an employee further—and the individual already possesses the necessary skills for the new job—little or no learning will take place. Finally, the time required to develop the necessary skills can be reduced by identifying a rational sequence of job assignments for a person.

Responsibility for Career Development

Many key individuals must work together if an organization is to have an effective career development program. Management must first make a commitment to support the program by making policy decisions and allocating resources to the program. Human resource professionals are then responsible for implementing the career development program by providing the necessary information, tools, guidance, and program liaison with top management.

The worker's immediate supervisor is responsible for providing support, advice, and feedback. Through the supervisor, a worker can find out how supportive of career development the organization actually is. Finally, individual employees are ultimately responsible for developing their own careers.[20] "You can lead a horse to water but you can't make it drink" is an appropriate analogy for career development.

METHODS OF ORGANIZATION CAREER PLANNING AND DEVELOPMENT

Organizations can assist individuals in career planning and development in numerous ways. Some currently utilized methods, most of which are used in various combinations, are listed here:

- *Superior/Subordinate Discussions.* The superior and subordinate jointly agree on career planning and development activities. The resources made available to achieve these objectives may well include development programs. Human resource professionals are often called on for assistance, as are psychologists and guidance counselors. Colleges and universities often provide such services.

- *Company Material.* Some firms provide material specifically developed to assist their workers in career planning and development. Such material is tailored to the firm's special needs.
- *Performance Appraisal System.* The firm's performance appraisal system can also be a valuable tool in career planning. Noting and discussing an employee's weaknesses can uncover development needs. If overcoming a particular weakness seems difficult or even impossible, an alternate career path may be the solution.
- *Workshops.* Some organizations conduct workshops lasting two or three days for the purpose of helping workers develop careers within the company. Employees define and match their specific career objectives with the needs of the company.

A GLOBAL PERSPECTIVE

According to a survey of U.S. expatriate executives conducted by Richard A. Guzzo of the University of Maryland/College Park, an estimated 20 percent of the personnel sent abroad return prematurely; many others endure global assignments but are ineffective in their jobs and social lives, and often must endure broken marriages. The study advises companies to hire a professional relocation service to help ease moves for managers abroad.[21] The main reason for these problems is culture shock, resulting in anxieties regarding customs and security that appear when an individual deals with a foreign culture. Culture shock is frequently accompanied by medical and personal problems, which often continue after the employee returns home. According to the Guzzo study, nonfinancial support is more important to expatriates than money. More than 80 percent of respondents said they were satisfied with their financial perks. However, many respondents faulted their companies for not doing more to prepare them for the shock of living in another culture, to help a spouse find a job, or to plan how the overseas assignment would fit into their career path.[22]

Returning employees nearly always experience less decision-making ability, reduced autonomy, lower pay, and fewer perks. It is also estimated that about one-quarter of all American expatriates do not ever regain a position in the firm upon returning from foreign assignments. Others leave the company immediately, take demotions, or relocate.[23] Many of these consequences result because of the failure of the organization to prepare the person properly with appropriate cross-cultural adaptation skills. Research indicates that success in overseas work assignments depends on the possession of personal skills, people skills, and perceptual skills. Personal skills are those techniques and attributes that facilitate the expatriate's mental and emotional well-being. They include means of finding solitude, such as meditation, prayer, and physical exercise routines, which tend to decrease the employee's stress level. An ability to manage time, to delegate, and to manage responsibilities are also essential personal skills.[24]

BEGINNING A CAREER IN HUMAN RESOURCES

Individuals desiring a career in human resources may enter the field in one of two basic ways: They may go to work in another field and later transfer to human resources; or they may obtain an entry-level position in human resources. In order to assist in solving this dilemma, we asked human resource practitioners in various firms the following questions:

1. Which entry-level position in your firm would be most helpful if a person desires to progress into human resources?
2. What types of education or experience are most desirable for these entry-level positions?
3. Which human resource entry-level position would best assist a person's career progression in your firm?

As you can see in Table 10-2, the responses to these questions were not consistent. Some firms clearly stress work in other functional areas before an employee moves into human resources, whereas others believe in direct entry into the human resource area.

Entry-Level Positions in Other Fields

Executives in numerous firms believe that an employee should gain experience in another field before moving into human resources. They believe that potential human resource professionals need varied exposure in the company to be effective in human resource positions; that is, they feel that such exposure can increase the person's credibility in dealing with other managers. Trans World Airlines, for one, selects human resource specialists from among their experienced reservation salespeople.

Entry-Level Positions in Human Resources

Not all firms require broad-based experience for those entering human resources. In fact, the number of individuals entering the human resource field directly appears to be increasing. This trend may be the result, in part, of specialized knowledge currently expected of human resource professionals. Firms that need people who can be productive very quickly in human resources do not feel that basic training time is available.

Several firms believe that the compensation specialty provides excellent entry-level positions. For example, the Grumman Corporation identifies salary administration as the best entry-level position "because it affects almost every aspect of human resource work and company operations." Management of Teledyne, Inc. believes that "starting in wage and salary provides an individual with exposure to relationships of job classifications throughout the company," and that this background is helpful to the human resource practitioner.

The nature of the firm's business may also affect the best human resource entry-level position. Labor-intensive organizations—those that have high labor costs relative to total operating costs—appear to emphasize staffing and recruitment positions in which interviewing skills are important. For instance, Denny's Inc. lists the *interviewer* as being the best human resource entry-level position. Walt Disney Productions also identifies the *human resource interviewer* position as one of the best.

Entry-Level Positions: An Overview

Practitioners do not agree as to the most appropriate entry-level position for individuals aspiring to a job in human resources. A position considered best by

TABLE 10-2 Careers in Human Resource Management

COMPANY	ENTRY-LEVEL POSITION	EDUCATION/EXPERIENCE
A. B. Dick Company	*Assistant Hourly Employment Manager	Bachelor's degree for all positions
	Shop Foreman	
	Assistant Salary Administrator	
Bristol-Myers Products	Human Resource Assistant	Bachelor's degree with two or three years' experience in general human resource work
Conoco, Inc.	*Human Resource Trainee	Bachelor's or master's degree in human resource administration, industrial relations, organizational development, business, or engineering
	Any position with Conoco	
Denny's, Inc.	*Interviewer	Bachelor's degree in business or two years in human resource interviewing
	Wage and Salary Analyst	Bachelor's degree and one year of experience in human resources, preferably with compensation experience
	Human Resource Administrator	Bachelor's degree and/or two years' experience in human resources
GAF Corporation	*Production Supervisor	B.S.I.E., B.S.M.E., B.B.A.
	Industrial Engineer	B.A. with relevant coursework
	Wage and Salary Analyst	B.S. with relevant coursework
	Safety Specialist	
General Cable Technologies	Assistant Plant Industrial Relations Manager	B.S. in industrial relations
	Compensation Analyst	B.S. in industrial relations
Gerber Products Company	*Supervisor Trainee	Four years of college
	*Administrative Trainee	Four years of college
Grumman Corporation	*Salary Analyst	Bachelor's degree in any of a variety of concentrations including psychology, business, and data processing
	Employment Interviewer	
	Career Development Analyst	
Hartmarx	Human Resource Assistant	Bachelor's or master's degree in business, human resources, or employee relations
	Compensation Assistant	
	Employee Relations Assistant	
	Human Resource Director (small plant or store)	

*Indicates best entry-level position.

TABLE 10-2 (continued) Careers in Human Resource Management

COMPANY	ENTRY-LEVEL POSITION	EDUCATION/EXPERIENCE
International Paper Company	*Supervisor—Employee Relations	B.S. or B.A. in human resource or industrial management
	Administrator—Industrial Relations	B.S. or B.A. in industrial labor relations, or B.S. in industrial management
	Entry-level specialist assigned to the Corporate Human Resources Department	
Manville Corporation	*Employee Relations Supervisor	Bachelor's degree and some plant experience desirable
	*Plant Supervisor	
	*Benefits Clerk	
Motorola, Inc.	*Employment Interviewer	B.S. or B.A.; no experience
Nabisco Brands, Inc.	*Human Resource Assistant (Field)	Bachelor's degree in such fields as business or psychology
Rockwell International Corporation	Supervisory Trainee (Field)	M.B.A. in human resources or industrial relations
	Industrial Relations Trainee	
Shell Oil Company	Employee Relations Analyst	Bachelor's or master's degree in human resources or industrial relations preferred
Squibb Corporation	Human Resource Assistant (nonexempt recruiting)	Two or three years' experience in human resource related activities preferred
Stokely-Van Camp, Inc.	Employee Relations—Management Trainee	Master's degree (preferably in human resources)
Teledyne, Inc.	*Wage and Salary Representative	B.A. or human resource or financial administrative experience
	Labor Relations Representative	B.A. or general plant or human resource administrative experience
Trans World Airlines	Reservation Sales Agent	High school diploma, customer contact, and sales experience
USX	Labor Relations Trainee	Law degree
	Employee Relations Trainee	Master's degree, certification, experience
	Line Operations Management Trainee	Technical degree plus leadership
Walt Disney Productions	Human Resource Interviewer	People skills; B.A. and/or equivalent
	Human Resource Assistant	Salaried experience and statistical orientation
	Wage and Salary Analyst	

*Indicates best entry-level position.

one firm may not be viewed the same way by another. The nature of the firm's business or of top management's human resource philosophy may account for these differences. Some firms stress the need for operating experience before entering human resources. Others believe that direct entry into human resources provides a more suitable beginning. People with ability who truly desire a position in human resources will likely be given the opportunity. It is no longer sufficient or desirable for organizations to employ human resource people who desire a career in human resources simply because they "like people" and "enjoy helping others." In fact, people who see this as their primary role are usually unsuccessful as professional human resource managers.

SUMMARY

A career is a general course a person chooses to pursue throughout his or her working life. Career planning is an ongoing process whereby the individual sets career objectives and identifies the means to achieve them. Career paths are flexible lines of movement through which an employee may move during employment with a company. Career development is an organization's formal approach to ensuring that people with the proper qualifications and experience are available when needed.

Several factors, including life stages, career anchors, and the environment, affect a person's view of a career. People change constantly and, thus, view their careers differently at various stages of their lives. Edgar Schein's research identified five different motives that account for the way people select and prepare for a career, which he called career anchors: managerial competence, technical/functional competence, security, creativity, and autonomy and independence. The work environment in which career planning takes place has changed rapidly in recent years. Across the country, and around the world, downsizing has occurred. Workers and managers alike are being displaced in massive numbers.

Learning about oneself is referred to as self-assessment. Two useful tools in this endeavor include a strength/weakness balance sheet and a likes and dislikes survey.

The process of establishing career paths within a firm is referred to as organizational career planning. Firms should undertake organizational career planning programs only when the programs contribute to achieving basic organizational goals. Depending on the organization and the nature of the jobs involved, one of three types of career paths may be used—traditional, network, and dual.

Plateauing is a career condition that occurs when job functions and work content remain the same because of a lack of promotional opportunities within the firm. Plateauing has become more common recently because many organizations are downsizing, hierarchies are flattening, and the baby boom generation is just reaching its prime.

Organizations can assist individuals in numerous ways with their career planning and development. Some currently used methods, most of which are used in various combinations, are superior/subordinate discussion, company materials, performance appraisal systems, and workshops.

For individuals desiring a career in human resources, there are two basic ways of entering the field: from another field or directly into an entry-level position in human resources. Practitioners do not agree as to the best way to obtain an entry-level human resource position. However, people with ability who truly desire to obtain a position in human resources will likely be given the opportunity.

QUESTIONS FOR REVIEW

1. Define the following terms:
   a. *Career*
   b. *Career planning*
   c. *Career path*
   d. *Career development*
2. Identify and discuss the basic life stages that people pass through.
3. List and briefly define the five types of career anchors.
4. How should a strength/weakness balance sheet and a likes and dislikes survey be prepared?
5. What kind of questions should a person involved in career planning attempt to answer?
6. What objectives are career planning programs expected to achieve?
7. What are the types of career paths? Briefly describe each.

8. Define *plateauing*. How does plateauing affect human resource management?
9. Identify and describe some of the methods of organizational career planning and development.
10. What are the two basic means for entering the field of human resources? Why might a firm favor one means over the other?

HRM SIMULATION

Incident F in the *Simulation Players Manual* involves training and development. Your team has several requests for training and/or management development on its desk. Your team must make a decision concerning which, if any, it will fund.

ABC VIDEO CASE

CINCINNATI RETRAINING PROGRAM TAPE 1, NUMBER 11

Workers are facing being laid-off on a daily basis across the nation. At General Electric's aircraft engine plant, outside Cincinnati, Ohio, 2,500 people have just received the news. These newly unemployed workers, however, feel better about their chances for financial survival due to what some believe is the best job retraining program in the country. Members of the "Cooperative Partners" program range from the city's biggest employer to a small software firm. All are partners at the Cincinnati Technical College, where cooperative education links paid, real-life work experience with classroom instruction. The success rate of 98 percent proves that the program helps cooperative students find skilled jobs.

HRM INCIDENT 1

IN THE DARK

"Could you come to my office for a minute, Bob?" asked Terry Geech, the plant manager. "Sure, be right there," said Bob Glemson. Bob was the plant's quality control director. He had been with the company for four years. After completing his degree in mechanical engineering, he worked as a production supervisor and then as a maintenance supervisor, prior to moving to his present job. Bob thought he knew what the call was about.

"Your letter of resignation catches me by surprise," began Terry. "I know that Wilson Products will be getting a good person, but we sure need you here, too." "I thought about it a lot," said Bob, "but there just doesn't seem to be a future for me here." "Why do you say that?" asked Terry. "Well," replied Bob, "the next position above mine is yours. Since you're only 39, I don't think it's likely that you'll be leaving soon." "The fact is that I *am* leaving soon," said Terry. "That's why it's even more of a shock to learn that you're resigning. I think I'll be moving to the corporate office in June of next year. Besides, the company has several plants that are larger than this one, and we need good people in those plants from time to time, both in quality control and in general management." "Well, I heard about an opening in the Cincinnati plant last year," said Bob, "but by the time I checked, the job had already been filled. We never know about opportunities in the other plants until we read about the incumbent in the company paper."

"All this is beside the point now. What would it take to get you to change your mind?" asked Terry. "I don't think I will change my mind now," replied Bob, "because I've given Wilson Products my word that I'm going to join them."

Questions

1. Evaluate the career planning and development program at this company.
2. What actions might have prevented Bob's resignation?

HRM INCIDENT 2

DECISIONS, DECISIONS

A nervous Jerry Fox was ushered into the Levitt Corporation president's office by the secretary. In the office he encountered Allen Anderson, the human resource manager, and Mr. Gorman, the vice president. Jerry was flattered when Mr. Gorman stood to shake his hand.

"I'll make this short and sweet," Mr. Gorman said. "You probably have heard that Allen plans to retire at the end of next year. In preparing for the staff changes, we would like to move you in as his assistant to get some cross-training experience." Jerry responded, "Why me, Mr. Gorman? I'm a purchasing coordinator; I've never even worked in the human resource area."

"Well," replied Mr. Gorman, "we've been watching you carefully. I have personally reviewed your qualifications. From the company's standpoint, we know you can do the job. We need people who have been out in the company and can bring fresh perspectives to the human resource area." Mr. Gorman instructed Jerry to discuss the idea with Allen. Then he said he had to leave for another meeting. As he shook Jerry's hand, he said, "We would like to coordinate your transition from the purchasing department to make it as smooth as possible for everyone, and I know you're involved in some priority projects over there. Allen will get back with me on a time frame after you and he talk."

Jerry was thirty-two and he had been with Levitt for seven years. His business administration degree, from Arizona State, had included a heavy concentration in behavioral science courses, which he thought probably was a factor in his selection. But he had worked only in purchasing. After three successful years as a buyer, he had been promoted to purchasing coordinator with responsibility for supervising eight buyers and a small clerical staff.

Jerry knew he was respected throughout the company. This was especially true in the production department, which had a great deal of interaction with purchasing. The production manager made no secret of his high regard for Jerry. Jerry also had taken time to get to know members of the finance and research department. His purpose in pursuing all of these relationships, though, was to help him do his purchasing job better. He had no idea at all that he would be considered for a job in the human resource department.

Questions

1. How should Jerry respond to the new assignment? Discuss.
2. What are the main qualifications for a senior human resource manager? Discuss Jerry's apparent qualifications for such a job.

DEVELOPING HRM SKILLS

AN EXPERIENTIAL EXERCISE

Career planning and development is extremely important to many individuals. Workers want to know how they fit into the future of the organization. Employees who believe that they have a future with the company are often more productive than those who do not. This exercise is designed to assist in understanding what it takes for a certain human resource professional to climb the organizational ladder. This climb is partially dependent on the individual's self-perceptions and perceptions of past experiences with the company. This exercise provides one method of individual career planning for the human resource manager described in the scenario below.

The individual being evaluated is thirty-five years old and is at a career crossroads. Upon self-reflection and appraisal at a birthday party, the person realizes that while only moderate success in ten years with the organization has been achieved, few others in the organization of comparable age and experience have any more *book or common sense intelligence*. In fact, the company is inundated with middle and upper level managers who are much older and often less intelligent, and who seem to spend an inordinate amount of time at the country club.

Assume that you are this person and have set your sights on an important human resource middle management position in the next five to seven years, and a top management position with your organization in the next ten to fifteen years. You have figured out there are twenty factors that determine upward movement in your organization. You are now trying to decide which are the most important for survival and success and which are the least important. This decision will determine whether you take the career crossroad to organizational survival and success or the crossroad to career failure and stagnation.

Each student will be given a list of twenty factors. You will rank the importance of each factor for your survival and success in the organization. Write the number *1* beside the *most important factor,* the number *2,* beside the *second most important factor*, and so on through the number *20*, the *least important factor.*

Everyone in the class can participate in this exercise. Each student will complete Exhibit 1, *Business Survival and Success Factors*, as he or she believes the individual described in the scenario would. Your instructor will provide the participants with additional information necessary to complete the exercise.

NOTES

1. Edgar Schein, "How 'Career Anchors' Hold Exectives to Their Career Paths," *Personnel* 52 (May-June 1975): 11–24.
2. Louis S. Richman, "How to Get Ahead in America," *Fortune* 129 (May 14, 1994): 46.
3. William Bridges, "The End of the JOB," *Fortune* 130 (September 19, 1994): 62.
4. Jaclyn Fierman, "Beating the Midlife Career Crisis," *Fortune* 128 (September 6, 1993): 54.

5. Lewis Carroll, *Through the Looking Glass* (New York: Norton, 1971): 127.

6. Lewis Newman, "Career Management Starts with Goals," *Personnel Journal,* 68 (April 1989): 91.

7. Milan Moravec, "A Cost-Effective Career Planning Program Requires a Strategy," *Personnel Administrator* 27 (January 1982): 29.

8. Milan Moravec and Beverly McKee, "Designing Dual Career Paths and Compensation," *Personnel* 67 (August 1990): 5.

9. Donald L. Caruth, Robert M. Noe III, and R. Wayne Mondy, *Staffing the Contemporary Organization* (New York: Praeger Publishers, 1990): 253–254.

10. Louis S. Richman, "How to Get Ahead in America," 47.

11. Brian O'Reilly, "The New Deal: What Companies and Employees Owe One Another," *Fortune* 129 (June 13, 1994): 44.

12. Louis S. Richman, "How to Get Ahead in America, 49.

13. Jaclyn Fierman, "Beating the Midlife Career Crisis," ibid.

14. Ibid., 53–54.

15. Ibid.

16. Ibid., 58.

17. Donald L. Caruth, Robert M. Noe III, and R. Wayne Mondy, *Staffing the Contemporary Organization,* 42.

18. Susan Sonnesyn Brooks, "Moving Up Is Not the Only Option," *HRMagazine* 39 (March 1994): 79.

19. Zandby B. Leibowitz and Sherry H. Mosley, "Career Development Works Overtime at Corning, Inc.," *Personnel* 67 (April 1990): 38.

20. Loretta D. Foxman and Walter L. Polsky, "Aid in Employee Career Development," *Personnel Journal* 69 (January 1990): 22.

21. Daniel B. Moskowitz, "How to Cut It Overseas," *International Business* (October 1992): 76, 78.

22. Ibid.

23. Mark E. Mendenhall and Gary Oddon, "The Overseas Assignment: A Practical Look" *Business Horizons* 31 (September/October 1988): 78–79.

24. Ibid.

CHAPTER 11

Performance Appraisal

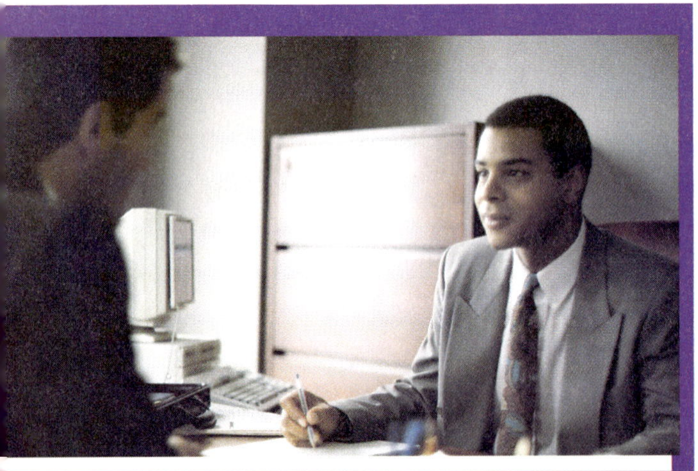

KEY TERMS

CHAPTER OBJECTIVES

1. Define performance appraisal, identify its uses, and describe the performance appraisal process.
2. Identify who is usually responsible for performance appraisal, typical appraisal periods, and various methods used.
3. List the problems that have been associated with performance appraisal and the characteristics of an effective appraisal system.
4. Describe the legal implications of performance appraisal and explain the appraisal interview.
5. Describe how assessment centers are used to assess an employee's management potential.

"Doug, we simply must increase our productivity," exclaimed Marco Ghignoni, vice president of production for Block and Becker. "If we don't, the foreign competition is 'going to eat our lunch.' Worker productivity hasn't declined much, but our people seem to have little incentive to work together to improve it."

"I agree with you Marco," said Doug Overbeck, vice president for human resources. "We really don't have a good system for evaluating team results while at the same time recognizing differences in individual performance. I'm convinced that our team approach in manufacturing is sound. But, it does bring us new problems with performance appraisal and our reward system. We need to take some action in these areas—and fast!"

Marco and Doug had begun to realize a need for identifying both team and individual performance. When a performance appraisal system is geared totally toward individual results, it is not surprising that employees show little interest in working in teams.[1] On the other hand, individual contributions must also be taken into account.

We begin this chapter by defining *performance appraisal* and describing its uses. We then explain the performance appraisal process and the responsibility for appraisal. We follow this with a discussion of the performance appraisal period, methods, and problems. Next, we describe the characteristics of an effective appraisal system, the legal implications, the appraisal interview, and assessment centers. The overall purpose of this chapter is to emphasize the importance of performance appraisal as it relates to organizational effectiveness and its special implications for developing the firm's human resources.

PERFORMANCE APPRAISAL DEFINED

Nothing is more discouraging for a top producer in a work group than to receive the same pay increase as a marginal employee. A major incentive to do superior work is destroyed. At the same time, if work is organized around groups, and team effort is vital, the performance of the team must also be considered. It is vital for managers to realize that performance evaluation must be comprehensive and that it is a continuous process rather than an event that happens once a year.[2] **Performance appraisal (PA)** is a formal system of periodic review and evaluation of an individual's or team's job performance.[3]

Conducting performance appraisals is probably the most frustrating task in the field of human resource management. When HR professionals are asked about their appraisal system, a frequent response is "We are working on a new one" or "We are thinking about working on a new one." A study involving ninety-two Ohio firms with a performance appraisal system in place revealed that approximately 65 percent were in some way dissatisfied with their system.[4] Another source suggested that more than 80 percent of firms were dissatisfied with their appraisal systems.[5] General disenchantment with appraisal systems was expressed by one human resource executive who described the process as a "search for the Holy Grail!" An even more negative view was presented by a prominent management guru who called the performance appraisal process one of management's seven deadly diseases.[6]

Since PA is so often perceived as a negative, frustrating activity—and one which seemingly eludes mastery—why don't organizations just throw in the towel? Actually, some might just do this if managers did not have to make decisions about developmental needs, promotions, pay raises, terminations, transfers, admission to training programs, and areas with legal ramifications. If managers could be guaranteed that they would never be required to defend themselves in court against wrongful termination suits or charges of discrimination, perhaps PA would not be such a critical management task.

However, considering the multiple needs for PA data, most organizations are led to one conclusion: Although it is a difficult process to devise and administer, there is a genuine organizational and employee need to conduct performance appraisals.

For the reasons mentioned, developing an effective performance appraisal system has been, and will continue to be, a high priority of human resource management. In this effort, it must be remembered that performance appraisal is not an end in itself but rather the means to achieve a higher performance level. At the same time, evaluators must take into account system factors that are outside the control of employees but may affect their performance.

Performance appraisal is one of many human resource activities that must be essentially owned by line managers. Human resource professionals obviously play a critical role in developing and coordinating PA systems. However, for the process to be successful, line personnel must be key players in the system. Approached in this manner, PA has the best chance for successful implementation.

USES OF PERFORMANCE APPRAISAL

For many organizations, the primary goal of an appraisal system is to improve performance. However, other goals may be sought as well. A potential problem, and possibly a primary cause of much dissatisfaction with PA, may result from expecting too much from one appraisal plan. In developing a new appraisal system to fit a changed corporate culture, Eastman Chemical Company found that it needed three separate assessments: one to address development and coaching, another specifically for compensation, and a third for selection.[7]

A system that is properly designed and communicated can help achieve organizational objectives and enhance employee performance.[8] In fact, PA data are potentially valuable for use in numerous human resource functional areas.

Human Resource Planning

In assessing a firm's human resources, data must be available that describe the promotability and potential of all employees, especially key executives. Management succession planning is a key concern for all firms. A well-designed appraisal system provides a profile of the organization's human resource strengths and weaknesses to support this effort.

Recruitment and Selection

Performance evaluation ratings may be helpful in predicting the performance of job applicants. For example, it may be determined that successful managers in a firm (identified through PA) exhibit certain behaviors when performing key tasks. These data may then provide benchmarks for evaluating applicant responses obtained through behavior description interviews (discussed in Chapter 7). Also, in validating selection tests, employee ratings may be used as the variable against which test scores are compared. In this instance, correct determination of the selection test's validity would depend on the accuracy of appraisal results.

Human Resource Development

A performance appraisal should point out an employee's specific needs for training and development. For instance, if Mary Jones' job requires skill in technical writing, and she receives a marginal evaluation on this factor, additional training in written communication may be indicated. If the human resource manager finds that a number of first-line supervisors are having difficulty in administering discipline, training sessions addressing this problem may be suggested. By identifying deficiencies that adversely affect performance, human resource and line managers are able to develop HRD programs that permit individuals to build on their strengths and minimize their deficiencies. An appraisal system does not guarantee that employees will be properly trained and developed. However, the task of determining training and development needs is assisted when appraisal data are available.

Career Planning and Development

Career planning and development may be viewed from either an individual or organizational viewpoint. In either case, PA data are essential in assessing an employee's strengths and weaknesses and in determining potential. Managers may use such information to counsel subordinates and assist them in developing and implementing their career plans.

Compensation Programs

Performance appraisal results provide a basis for rational decisions regarding pay increases. Most managers believe that outstanding job performance should be rewarded tangibly with raises. They believe that "what you reward is what you get." To encourage good performance, a firm should design and implement a fair performance appraisal system and then reward the most productive workers and teams accordingly.

Internal Employee Relations

Performance appraisal data are also frequently used for decisions in several areas of internal employee relations, including motivation, promotion, demotion, termination, layoff, and transfer. For example, self-esteem is essential for motivation. Therefore, appraisal systems must be designed and implemented in a way to maintain employees' self-esteem. PA systems that result in brutally frank descriptions of performance result in demotivating people.[9]

An employee's performance in one job may be useful in determining his or her ability to perform another job on the same level, as is required in the consideration of transfers. Or, when the performance level is unacceptable, demotion or even termination may be appropriate. When employees working under a labor agreement are involved, employee layoff is typically based on seniority. However, when management has more flexibility, an employee's performance record may be a more significant criterion.

Assessment of Employee Potential

Some organizations attempt to assess employee potential as they appraise job performance. It has been said that the best predictors of future behavior are past behaviors. However, an employee's past performance in a job may not accurately indicate future performance in a higher level or different position. The best salesperson in the company may not have what it takes to become a successful district sales manager. The best computer programmer may, if promoted, be a disaster as a data processing manager. Over-emphasizing technical skills and ignoring other equally important skills is a common error in promoting employees into management jobs. Recognition of this problem has led some firms to separate the appraisal of performance, which focuses on past behavior, from the assessment of potential, which is future oriented. These firms have established *assessment centers*, which will be discussed in a later section.

THE PERFORMANCE APPRAISAL PROCESS

Many of the external and internal environmental factors discussed in Chapter 2 can influence the appraisal process. Legislation, for example, requires that appraisal systems be nondiscriminatory. In the 1977 case of *Mistretta v Sandia Corporation* (a subsidiary of Western Electric Company, Inc.), a federal district court judge ruled against the company, stating, "There is sufficient circumstantial evidence to indicate that age bias and age based policies appear throughout the performance rating process to the detriment of the protected age group." The *Albermarle Paper v Moody* case supported validation requirements for performance appraisals, as well as for selection tests. Organizations should avoid using any appraisal method that results in a disproportionately negative impact on a protected class.[10]

The labor union is another external factor that might affect a firm's appraisal process. Unions have traditionally stressed seniority as the basis for promotions and pay increases. They may vigorously oppose the use of a management designed performance appraisal system that would be used for these purposes.

Management should select those specific performance appraisal goals that it believes to be most important and can be realistically achieved.

Factors within the internal environment can also affect the performance appraisal process. For instance, the type of corporate culture can serve to assist or hinder the process. In today's dynamic organizations, which increasingly utilize teams to perform jobs, overall team results, as well as individual contributions, must be recognized. A closed, nontrusting culture does not provide the environment required for either individual or team effort. In such an environment, performance will suffer even though individual workers may try to do a good job. Recognizing the true contributions in such an environment may be quite difficult.

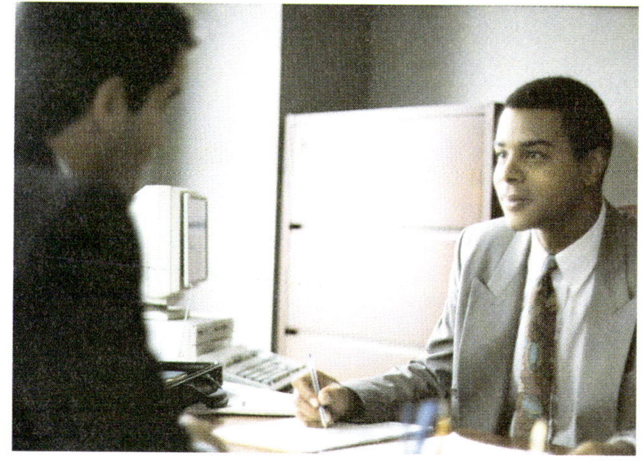

Identification of specific goals is the starting point for the PA process (see Figure 11-1). An appraisal system will not likely be able to serve every purpose desired effectively. Therefore, management should select those specific PA goals it believes to be most important and can be realistically achieved. For example, some firms may want to stress employee development, whereas other organizations may want to focus on admin-

FIGURE 11-1
The Performance Appraisal Process

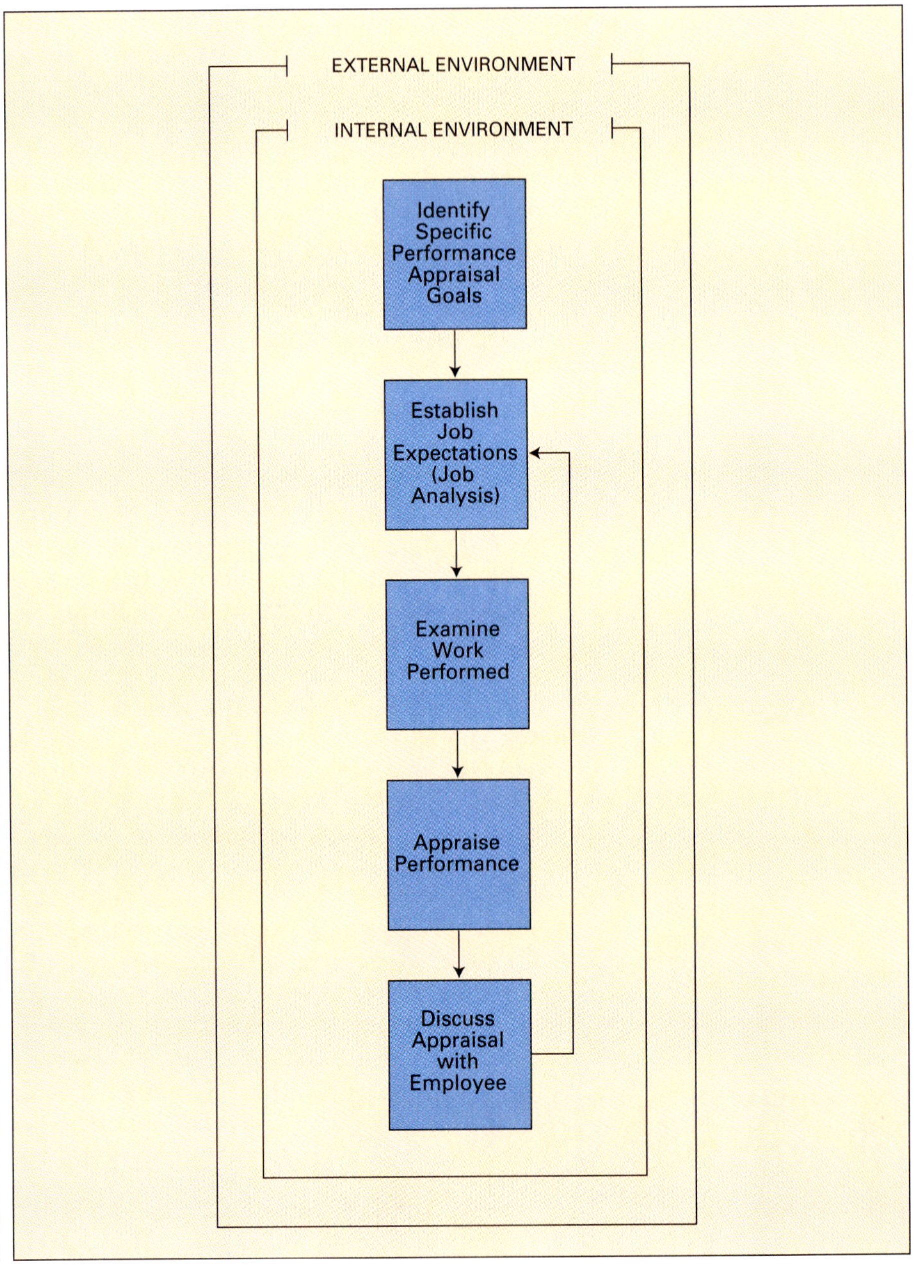

istrative decisions, such as pay adjustments. Too many performance appraisal systems fail because management does not determine specifically what it wants the system to accomplish. Management often expects too much from one method.

After specific appraisal goals have been established, workers and teams must understand what is expected from them in their tasks. Informing employees what is expected of them is a most important employee relations task.

At the end of the appraisal period, the appraiser observes work performance and evaluates it against established performance standards. The evaluation results are then communicated to the workers. The performance evaluation discussion with the supervisor serves to reestablish job requirements.

RESPONSIBILITY FOR APPRAISAL

In most organizations, the human resource department is responsible for coordinating the design and implementation of performance appraisal programs. However, it is essential that line managers play a key role from beginning to end. These individuals will likely have responsibility for actually conducting the appraisals, and they must directly participate in the program if it is to succeed. Several possibilities exist as to who will actually rate the employee, some of which are presented next.

Immediate Supervisor

An employee's immediate supervisor has traditionally been the most common choice for evaluating performance. This continues to be the case, and there are several valid reasons for such an approach. In the first place, the supervisor is usually in the best position to observe the employee's job performance. Another reason is that the supervisor has the responsibility for managing a particular unit. When the task of evaluating subordinates is given to someone else, the supervisor's authority may be undermined. Finally, subordinate training and development is an important element in every manager's job and—as previously mentioned—appraisal programs and employee development are often closely related.

On the negative side, the immediate supervisor may emphasize certain aspects of employee performance and neglect others. Also, managers have been known to manipulate evaluations to justify their pay increases and promotion decisions. Also, in project or matrix organizations, the functional supervisor may not have the opportunity to observe performance sufficiently to evaluate it. However, in most instances, the immediate supervisor will probably continue to be involved in evaluating performance. Organizations will seek alternatives, however, because of the organizational innovations that have occurred and a desire to broaden the appraisal's perspective.

Subordinates

Some managers have concluded that evaluation of managers by subordinates is feasible. They reason that subordinates are in an excellent position to view their superior's managerial effectiveness. Advocates of this approach believe that supervisors will become especially conscious of the work group's needs and will do a better job of managing. Critics are concerned that the manager will be caught up in a popularity contest or that employees will be fearful of reprisal. If this approach has a chance for success, one thing is clear: Anonymity of the evaluators must be guaranteed. This might be particularly difficult in a small department if any demographic data are included in the evaluation that could easily identify raters.

Peers

Peer appraisal has long had proponents who believed that such an approach is reliable if the work group is stable over a reasonably long period of time and performs tasks that require considerable interaction. Organizations, encouraged by TQM concepts, are increasingly using teams, including those that are self-directed. Therefore, it is likely that peer rating within such groups will also grow in popularity. The advantages of evaluations conducted by team members include[11]:

- Team members know each other's performance better than anyone and can, therefore, evaluate more accurately.
- Peer pressure is a powerful motivator for team members.
- Members who recognize that peers within the team will be evaluating their work show increased commitment and productivity.
- Peer review involves numerous opinions and is not dependent upon one individual.

Problems with peer evaluations include the time required for conducting them and the difficulty that may be experienced in distinguishing between individual and team contributions. In addition, some team members may feel uncomfortable appraising their coworkers. PA training would also be needed for team members as it is for anyone evaluating performance.

Peer evaluation works best in a participative culture. However, the approach is not always satisfactory even in this type of environment. Quaker Oats had such a plan in one of its plants for ten years before it crashed. An explanation for the plan's demise was, "There was no incentive for people to be strict about it." One of the success stories comes from W.L. Gore, of Newark, Delaware. Gore's associates (not called employees) are organized in work teams that handle performance problems. They also perform other traditional human resource functions, such as hiring and firing. With the rapid growth in using self-directed work teams, peer appraisal is expected to grow in popularity.[12]

Group Appraisal

Group appraisal involves the use of two or more managers who are familiar with the employee's performance to evaluate it as a team. For instance, if a person regularly works with the data processing manager and the financial manager, these two individuals might jointly make the evaluation. An advantage of this approach is that it injects a degree of objectivity by utilizing *outside parties*. A disadvantage is that it diminishes the role of the immediate supervisor. Also, it may be difficult to get managers together for a group appraisal because of other demands on their time.

Self-Appraisal

At one small firm, 300 wage earners evaluate themselves using a rating scale with seventeen specific factors. Each employee's tutor also evaluates the employee, and the two are then required to reconcile significant differences.[13] If employees understand the objectives they are expected to achieve and the standards by which they are to be evaluated, they are—to a great extent—in the best position to appraise their own performance. Many people know what they do well on the job and what they need to improve. If they are given the opportunity, they will objectively criticize their own performance and take action needed to improve it.[14] Also, because employee development is self-development, employees who appraise their own performance may become more highly motivated. Self-appraisal has great appeal to managers who are primarily concerned with employee participation and development.

Combinations

The approaches just described are not mutually exclusive. In fact, organizations are beginning to involve multiple sources including both external and internal customers. Using these sources is known as *360-degree feedback*. One firm, Milwaukee Mutual Insurance Company, uses a combination of supervisor, self- and peer assessment. The firm has found that this approach, which it calls *consensus review process*, produces more meaningful appraisals.[15]

An appraisal system involving multiple evaluators will naturally take more time and, therefore, be more costly. A high degree of trust among participants and training in the appraisal system are needed regardless of how it is conducted. These factors may take on increased importance when a combination of raters are involved. Nevertheless, the way firms are being organized may require innovative alternatives to traditional top-down appraisals.

THE APPRAISAL PERIOD

Performance evaluations are usually prepared at specific intervals. While there is nothing magic about the interval, in most organizations these evaluations are made either annually or semiannually. Individuals are often evaluated just before the end of the probationary period. Evaluating new employees several times during their first year of employment is also a common practice. The following are the evaluation periods for three companies:

- The New York Times Company evaluates all its guild and nonunion employees annually. Craft unions are not included in this process.
- Cessna Aircraft Company appraises all monthly salaried employees and all weekly salaried supervisors approximately once a year.
- General Mills, Inc., evaluates all employees annually, except for operative, nonexempt employees, who are evaluated each six months.

The appraisal period may begin with each employee's date of hire, or all employees may be evaluated at the same time. Although both practices have advantages, staggered appraisals may have greater merit if an organizational unit has many members. There may not be sufficient time to evaluate each employee adequately if all appraisals are conducted at the same time.

PERFORMANCE APPRAISAL METHODS

Managers may choose from among several appraisal methods. The type of performance appraisal system utilized depends on its purpose. If the major emphasis is on selecting people for promotion, training, and merit pay increases, a traditional method, such as rating scales, may be appropriate. Collaborative methods, such as MBO, are designed to assist employees in developing skills and becoming more effective.[16]

Rating Scales

A widely used appraisal method, which rates employees according to defined factors, is called the **rating scales method**. Using this approach, judgments about performance are recorded on a scale. The scale is divided into categories—normally 5-7 in number—which are often defined by adjectives, such as *outstanding*, *average*, or *unsatisfactory*. While an overall rating may be provided, this method generally allows for the use of more than one performance criterion. One reason for the popularity of the rating scales method is its simplicity, which permits many employees to be evaluated quickly.

The factors chosen for evaluation are typically of two types: job-related and personal characteristics. Note that in Figure 11-2 job-related factors include quantity and quality of work, whereas personal factors include such attributes as dependability, initiative, adaptability, and cooperation.[17] The rater (evaluator) completes the form by indicating the degree of each factor that is most descriptive of the employee and his or her performance.

Some firms provide space for the rater to comment on the evaluation given for each factor. This practice may be especially encouraged, or even required, when the rater gives either the highest or lowest rating. For instance, if an employee is rated *unsatisfactory* on initiative, the rater provides written justification for this low evaluation. The purpose of this type of requirement is to avoid arbitrary and hastily made judgments.

As you can see in Figure 11-2, each factor and each degree have been defined. In order to receive an *exceptional* rating for the factor *quality of work*, a person must consistently exceed the prescribed work requirements. The more precisely the various factors and degrees are defined, the better the rater can evaluate worker performance. Evaluation agreement throughout the organization is achieved when each rater interprets the factors and degrees in the same way.

Many rating scale performance appraisal forms also provide for an assessment of the employee's growth potential. The form shown in Figure 11-2 contains four categories relating to a person's potential for future growth and development. They range from *now at or near maximum performance in present job* to *no apparent limitations*. Although there are drawbacks in attempting to evaluate both past performance and future potential at the same time, this practice is often followed.

Critical Incidents

The **critical incident method** requires that written records be kept of highly favorable and highly unfavorable work actions. When such an action affects the department's effectiveness significantly, either positively or negatively, the manager writes it down. It is called a critical incident. At the end of the appraisal period, the rater uses these records, along with other data, to evaluate employee performance. With this method, the appraisal is more likely to cover the entire evaluation period and not, for example, focus on the last few weeks or months. However, if a supervisor has many employees to rate, the time required for recording behaviors may become excessive.

FIGURE 11-2
Rating Scales Method of Performance Appraisal

Employee's Name ______________________

Job Title ______________________

Department ______________________

Supervisor ______________________

Evaluation Period:
From __________ to __________

Instructions for Evaluation:
1. Consider only one factor at a time. Do not permit rating given for one factor to affect decision for others.
2. Consider performance for entire evaluation period. Avoid concentration on recent events or isolated incidents.
3. Remember that the average employee performs duties in a satisfactory manner. An above average or exceptional rating indicates that the employee has clearly distinguished himself or herself from the average employee.

EVALUATION FACTORS	Unsatisfactory. Does not meet requirements.	Below average. Needs improvement. Requirements occasionally not met.	Average. Consistently meets requirements.	Good. Frequently exceeds requirements	Exceptional. Consistently exceeds requirements.
QUANTITY OF WORK: Consider the volume of work achieved. Is productivity at an acceptable level?					
QUALITY OF WORK: Consider accuracy, precision, neatness, and completeness in handling assigned duties.					
DEPENDABILITY: Consider degree to which employee can be relied on to meet work commitments.					
INITIATIVE: Consider self-reliance, resourcefulness, and willingness to accept responsibility.					
ADAPTABILITY: Consider ability to respond to changing requirements and conditions.					
COOPERATION: Consider ability to work for, and with, others. Are assignments, including overtime, willingly accepted?					

POTENTIAL FOR FUTURE GROWTH AND DEVELOPMENT:
- ☐ Now at or near maximum performance in present job.
- ☐ Now at or near maximum performance in this job, but has potential for improvement in another job, such as: ______________________
- ☐ Capable of progressing after further training and experience.
- ☐ No apparent limitations.

EMPLOYEE STATEMENT: I agree ☐ disagree ☐ with this evaluation
Comments:

____

____

Employee ______________________ Date ______________________

Supervisor ______________________ Date ______________________

Reviewing Manager ______________________ Date ______________________

Essay

In the **essay method**, the rater simply writes a brief narrative describing the employee's performance. This method tends to focus on extreme behavior in the employee's work rather than routine day-to-day performance. Ratings of this type depend heavily on the evaluator's writing ability. Some supervisors, because of their excellent writing skills, can make even a marginal worker sound like a top performer. Comparing essay evaluations might be difficult because no common criteria exist. However, some managers believe that the essay method is not only the simplest but also the best approach to employee evaluation.

Work Standards

The **work standards method** compares each employee's performance to a predetermined standard or expected level of output. Standards reflect the normal output of an average worker operating at a normal pace. Work standards may be applied to virtually all types of jobs, but they are most frequently used for production jobs. Several methods may be utilized in determining work standards, including time study and work sampling.

An obvious advantage of using standards as appraisal criteria is objectivity. However, in order for employees to perceive that the standards are objective, they should understand clearly how the standards were set. It follows that the rationale for any changes to the standards must also be carefully explained.

Ranking

In using the **ranking method**, the rater simply places all employees from a group in rank order of overall performance. For example, the best employee in the department is ranked highest, and the poorest is ranked lowest. A major difficulty occurs when individuals have performed at comparable levels.

Paired comparison is a variation of the ranking method in which the performance of each employee is compared with every other employee in the group. The comparison is often based on a single criterion, such as overall performance. The employee who receives the greatest number of favorable comparisons is ranked highest.

Some professionals in the field argue for use of a comparative approach, such as ranking, whenever human resource decisions are made. For example, these professionals feel that employees are not promoted because they achieve their objectives but rather because they achieve them better than others in their work group. Such decisions go beyond a single individual's performance and, therefore, should be considered on a broader basis.

Forced Distribution

In the **forced distribution method**, the rater is required to assign individuals in the work group to a limited number of categories similar to a normal frequency distribution. As an example, employees in the top 10 percent are placed in the highest group, the next 20 percent in the following group, the next 40 percent in the middle group, the next 20 percent in the second to lowest group, and the remaining 10 percent in the lowest category. This approach is based on the rather questionable assumption that all groups of employees will have the same distribution of excellent, average, and poor performers. If one department has all outstanding workers, the supervisor would likely be hard pressed to decide who should be placed in the lower categories.

Forced-Choice and Weighted Checklist Performance Reports

The **forced-choice performance report** requires that the appraiser choose from a series of statements about an individual those that are most or least descriptive of the employee. One difficulty with this method is that the descriptive statements may be virtually identical.

Using the **weighted checklist performance report**, the rater completes a form similar to the forced-choice performance report, but the various responses have been assigned different weights. The form includes questions related to the employee's behavior, and the evaluator answers each question either positively or negatively. The evaluator is not aware of each question's weight, however.

As with forced-choice performance reports, the weighted checklist is expensive to design. Both methods strive for objectivity, but the evaluator does not know which items contribute most to successful performance. Employee development, therefore, cannot result from this approach.

Behaviorally Anchored Rating Scales

The **behaviorally anchored rating scale (BARS) method** combines elements of the traditional rating scales and critical incidents methods. Using BARS, job behaviors derived from critical incidents—effective and ineffective behavior—are described more objectively. Individuals familiar with a particular job identify its major components. They then rank and validate specific behaviors for each of the components. Because BARS typically requires considerable employee participation, it may be accepted more readily by both supervisors and subordinates.

In BARS, various performance levels are shown along a scale and described in terms of an employee's specific job behavior. For example, suppose the factor chosen for evaluation is "Ability to Absorb and Interpret Policies." On the *very positive* end of this factor might be "This interviewer could be expected to serve as an information source concerning new and changed policies for others in the organization." On the *very negative* end of this factor might be "Even after repeated explanations, this interviewer could be expected to be unable to learn new procedures." There might be several levels in between the very negative and very positive levels. Instead of using adjectives at each scale point, BARS uses behavioral anchors related to the criterion being measured. This modification clarifies the meaning of each point on the scale. Instead of providing a box to be checked for a category such as *very positive* performance, the BARS method provides examples of such behavior. This approach facilitates discussion of the rating because specific behaviors can be addressed.[18] This method was developed to overcome weaknesses in other evaluation methods. Reports on the effectiveness of BARS are mixed, and it does not seem to be superior to other methods in overcoming rater errors or in achieving psychometric soundness.[19] A specific deficiency is that the behaviors used are activity oriented rather than results oriented. This poses a potential problem for supervisors because they must rate employees who are performing the activity but not necessarily accomplishing the desired goals.

Management by Objectives

As previously discussed, the MBO concept values and utilizes employee contributions. It is also a potentially effective method of evaluating an employee's performance. In traditional approaches to performance appraisal, personal traits of employees are often used as criteria for evaluating performance. In addition, the role of the evaluating supervisor is similar to that of a judge. With MBO, the focus of the appraisal process shifts from the worker's personal attributes to job performance. The supervisor's role changes from that of an umpire to that of a counselor and facilitator. Also, the employee's function changes from that of passive bystander to that of active participant.

Individuals jointly establish objectives with their superiors, who then give them latitude in how to achieve the objectives. Jointly established goals make the employee an involved part of the process. This ownership of objectives increases the likelihood that they will be met.[20] At the end of the appraisal period, the employee and supervisor meet for an appraisal interview. They first review the extent to which the objectives have been achieved and then review the actions needed to solve remaining problems. Under MBO, the supervisor keeps communication channels open throughout the appraisal period. The problem-solving discussion during the appraisal interview is merely another conversation designed to assist the worker in progressing according to plan. At this time, objectives are established for the next evaluation period, and the process is repeated.

PROBLEMS IN PERFORMANCE APPRAISAL

Many performance appraisal methods have been severely criticized. The rating scales method seems to have received the greatest attention. In all fairness, many of the problems commonly mentioned are not inherent in the method but, rather, reflect improper usage. For example, raters may be inadequately trained, or the appraisal device actually used may not be job related.

Lack of Objectivity

A potential weakness of traditional performance appraisal methods is that they lack objectivity. In the rating scales method, for example, commonly used factors, such as attitude, loyalty, and personality, are difficult to measure. In addition, these factors may have little to do with an employee's job performance.

Some subjectivity will always exist in appraisal methods. However, the use of job-related factors does increase objectivity. Employee appraisal based primarily on personal characteristics may place the evaluator—and the company—in untenable positions with the employee and EEO guidelines. The firm would be hard pressed to show that these factors are job related.

Halo Error

Halo error occurs when the evaluator perceives one factor as having paramount importance and gives a good or bad overall rating to an employee based on this one factor. For example, David Edwards, accounting supervisor, placed a high value on *neatness*, which was a factor used in the company's performance appraisal system. As David was evaluating the performance of his senior accounting clerk, Carl Curtis, he noted that Carl was not a very neat individual and gave him a low ranking on this factor. David also permitted, consciously or unconsciously, the low ranking on neatness to carry over to other factors, giving Carl undeserved low ratings on all factors. Of course, if Carl was very neat, the opposite could have occurred. Either way, the halo error does a disservice to the employee involved and the organization.

Leniency/Strictness

Giving undeserved high ratings is referred to as **leniency**. This behavior is often motivated by a desire to avoid controversy over the appraisal. It is most prevalent when highly subjective (and difficult to defend) performance criteria are used, and the rater is required to discuss evaluation results with employees. Leniency may result in several organizational problems. When deficiencies are not discussed with employees, they may not understand the need to improve their performance and the status quo will continue. Other employees, especially those who are doing a good job, may resent lenient evaluations, especially if promotions and pay increases are involved. Finally, an organization will find it difficult to terminate a poor performing employee if he or she has a record of satisfactory evaluations.[21]

Being unduly critical of an employee's work performance is referred to as **strictness**. Although leniency is usually more prevalent than strictness, some managers apply an evaluation more rigorously than the company standard. This behavior may be due to a lack of understanding of various evaluation factors. When one manager is overly strict on an entire unit, workers in that unit suffer with regard to pay raises and promotion. Strictness applied to a particular individual has the potential for charges of discrimination.

One study revealed that more than 70 percent of responding managers believe that inflated and lowered ratings are intentionally given to subordinates. Table 11-1 shows these managers' explanations for their rationale. The results suggest that the validity of many performance appraisal systems is flawed. Evaluator training should be provided to emphasize the negative consequences of rater errors.

Central Tendency

Central tendency is a common error that occurs when employees are incorrectly rated near the average or middle of the scale. Some rating scale systems require the evaluator to justify in writing extremely high or extremely low ratings. In these instances, the rater may avoid possible controversy or criticism by giving only average ratings.

TABLE 11-1
Reasons for Intentionally Inflating or Lowering Ratings

Inflated Ratings

- The belief that accurate ratings would have a damaging effect on the subordinate's motivation and performance
- The desire to improve an employee's eligibility for merit raises
- The desire to avoid airing the department's dirty laundry
- The wish to avoid creating a negative permanent record of poor performance that might hound the employee in the future
- The need to protect good performers whose performance was suffering because of personal problems
- The wish to reward employees displaying great effort even when results are relatively low
- The need to avoid confrontation with certain hard-to-manage employees
- The desire to promote a poor or disliked employee up and out of the department

Lowered Ratings

- To scare better performance out of an employee
- To punish a difficult or rebellious employee
- To encourage a problem employee to quit
- To create a strong record to justify a planned firing
- To minimize the amount of the merit increase a subordinate receives
- To comply with an organization edict that discourages managers from giving high ratings

Source: Clinton Longenecker and Dean Ludwig, "Ethical Dilemmas in Performance Appraisal Revisited," *Journal of Business Ethics* 9 (December 1990): 963. Reprinted by permission of Kluwer Academic Publishers.

Recent Behavior Bias

Virtually every employee knows precisely when he or she is scheduled for a performance review. Although his or her actions may not be conscious, an employee's behavior often improves and productivity tends to rise several days or weeks before the scheduled evaluation. It is only natural for a rater to remember recent behavior more clearly than actions from the more distant past. However, performance appraisals generally cover a specified period of time, and an individual's performance should be considered for the entire period.

Personal Bias

Supervisors doing performance appraisals may have biases related to their employees' personal characteristics, such as race, religion, gender, disability, or age. While federal legislation protects such employees, discrimination continues to be an appraisal problem.

Discrimination in appraisal can be based on many factors in addition to those mentioned. For example, mild-mannered people may be appraised more harshly simply because they do not raise serious objections to the results. This type of behavior is in sharp contrast to the *hell raisers* who often confirm the adage, "the squeaking wheel gets the grease."

Judgmental Role of Evaluator

Supervisors conducting performance evaluations are at times accused of "playing God" with their employees. In some instances, supervisors control virtually every aspect of the process. Manipulation of evaluations by managers to justify their pay increase and promotion decisions is one example of how supervisors may abuse the system. They make decisions about the ratings and often try to sell their version to the employees. The highly judgmental role of some evaluators often places employees on the defensive. Such relationships are hardly conducive to employee development, morale, and productivity.

HRM IN ACTION

—THE PRESSURE IS THERE

"Bill, you're the human resource manager, and I have a human resource problem that I need your advice on," said Marvin Alexander, production supervisor for Service International. "Tom has worked for me for four years. He is likable and never misses a day of work. However, he is strictly mediocre at his job, despite numerous retraining attempts, conferences, and even incentives. I hear that the company is preparing for a reduction in force. As I was working on Tom's appraisal this morning, he stuck his head in the door, handed me three cigars, and said that his wife had just had triplets. That sure puts pressure on me."

If you were Bill, how would you respond?

Validation studies of an appraisal system may be the most direct and certain approach for determining whether the system is satisfactory. However, such studies can be costly and time consuming. Also, many smaller firms will simply not have a sufficient number of positions to meet technical validation requirements.

CHARACTERISTICS OF AN EFFECTIVE APPRAISAL SYSTEM[22]

It is unlikely that any appraisal system will be totally immune to legal challenge. However, systems that possess certain characteristics may be more legally defensible. But being *legal* is not enough in performance appraisal. The purpose is not only to abide by the law but to have a system that is ethical. An honest assessment of performance should be sought that permits the mutual development of a plan to improve individual and group performance. The system must honestly inform people how they stand with the organization.[23] The following factors assist in accomplishing this purpose.

Job-Related Criteria

The criteria used for appraising employee performance must be job related. The *Uniform Guidelines* and court decisions are quite clear on this point. More specifically, job information should be determined through job analysis. Subjective factors, such as initiative, enthusiasm, loyalty, and cooperation, are obviously important. However, they virtually defy definition and measurement. Unless such factors as these can be clearly shown to be job related, they should not be used in formal evaluations.

Performance Expectations

Managers must clearly explain performance expectations to their subordinates in advance of the appraisal period. Otherwise, it is not reasonable to evaluate employees using criteria that they know nothing about.

The establishment of highly objective work standards is relatively simple in many areas, such as manufacturing, assembly, and sales. However, for many other types of jobs, this task is more difficult. Still, evaluation must take place, and performance expectations, however elusive, should be defined in understandable terms.

Standardization

Employees in the same job category under the same supervisor should be appraised using the same evaluation instrument. It is also important that appraisals be conducted regularly for all employees. In addition, the appraisals should cover similar periods of time. Although annual evaluations are most common, they are conducted more frequently by many forward-thinking firms. Feedback sessions and appraisal interviews should be regularly scheduled for all employees.

Another aspect of standardization is formal documentation. Employees should sign their evaluations. If the employee refuses to sign, the manager should document this behavior. Records should also include a description of employee responsibilities, expected performance results, and the way these data will be viewed in making appraisal decisions. However, smaller firms are not expected to maintain performance appraisal systems that are as formal as those used by large organizations. The courts reason that objective criteria are not as important in firms with fewer than thirty employees because a smaller firm's top managers are more familiar with their employees' work.[24]

Qualified Appraisers

Responsibility for evaluating employee performance should be assigned to the individual, or individuals, who directly observe at least a representative sample of job performance. Usually, this person is the employee's immediate supervisor. However, as previously discussed, other approaches are gaining in popularity.

Situations that lessen the immediate supervisor's ability to appraise performance objectively include those found in matrix organizations. In these firms, certain employees may be formally assigned to a supervisor but actually work under various project managers. Also, a supervisor who is in a new position may have insufficient knowledge of employee performance initially. In such instances, multiple raters may be used.

In order to ensure consistency, appraisers must be well trained. Training should emphasize that performance appraisal is a significant component of every manager's job. Training should also stress that a primary task of the supervisor is to ensure that subordinates understand what is expected of them. In addition, training itself is an ongoing process. It responds to changes in the appraisal system and to the fact that supervisors, for various reasons, may deviate from established procedures. Training should cover how to rate employees and conduct appraisal interviews and should include written instructions. These instructions should be rather detailed and stress the importance of making objective and unbiased ratings.

Open Communication

Most employees have a strong need to know how well they are performing. A good appraisal system provides highly desired feedback on a continuing basis. A worthwhile goal is to avoid surprises during the appraisal interview. Even though the interview presents an excellent opportunity for both parties to exchange ideas, it should not serve as a substitute for day-to-day communication. On the other hand, a performance appraisal system should allow immediate access to information on key employees. The PA also alerts managers to individuals who may be risking termination if they do not improve their performance. The system permits HR professionals to take proactive measures, such as providing training or transfers, to salvage those who are not performing satisfactorily.

Employee Access to Results

For the many appraisal systems that are designed to improve performance, withholding appraisal results would be unthinkable. Employees simply could not perform better without having access to this information. Also, permitting employees to review appraisal results allows them to detect any errors that may have been made. Or the employee may simply disagree with the evaluation and may want to challenge it formally. Employees who receive a substandard appraisal should be offered the necessary training and guidance. Supervisors must make an effort to salvage marginal employees. Employees in this category should, however, be told specifically what will happen if their performance does not improved.

As a result of the Federal Privacy Act of 1974, employees of the federal government and federal contractors must be given access to their employment files, which may include performance appraisal data. While this requirement does not currently apply to all employees in the private sector, there are good reasons—aside from the threat of broader legislation coverage—for allowing such access. Most importantly, employees will not trust a system they do not understand. Secrecy will invariably breed suspicion and, thereby, thwart efforts to obtain employee participation.

Due Process

In connection with a formal challenge, ensuring due process is vital. A formal procedure should be developed—if one does not exist—to permit employees to appeal appraisal results that they consider inaccurate or unfair. They must have a procedure for pursuing their grievances and having them addressed objectively.

LEGAL IMPLICATIONS

Wrongful termination suits increased more than a hundredfold during the past decade. Employees won 64 percent of those cases brought to jury trial. The average award in these cases was $733,000, but awards in the millions of dollars were not uncommon. With the enactment of the Americans with Disabilities Act and the new civil rights legislation, employers must prepare for more discrimination lawsuits and jury trials. This preparation must include a legally defensible performance appraisal system.[25]

A review of court cases makes it clear that perfect appraisals are not expected from employers. It is also not anticipated that supervisory discretion should be removed from the process. However, the courts normally require the following four conditions to exist:

1. *Either the absence of adverse impact on members of certain groups or validation of the process.* As with the selection process, an invalid performance appraisal system has the potential to have a negative impact on members of certain groups.
2. *A review process that prevents one manager from directing or controlling a subordinate's career.* The performance appraisal should be reviewed and approved by someone or some group higher in the organization.
3. *The rater must have personal knowledge and contact with the employee's job performance.* This requirement may appear to be too obvious, but there are instances in which the rater does not have an adequate opportunity to observe employee performance. When this type of situation exists, the chances of a valid appraisal are virtually nonexistent.
4. *The use of formal appraisal criteria that limit the manager's discretion.* A system is needed that forces managers to base evaluations on certain predetermined criteria.

Mistakes in appraising performance and decisions based on appraisal results can have serious repercussions. For example, an employer may be vulnerable to a negligent retention claim if an employee who gets an unsatisfactory evaluation is kept on the payroll, and he or she causes injury to a third party. In this instance, the firm's liability might be reduced if the substandard performer had received training designed to overcome the deficiencies.[26] In addition, discriminatory allocation of money for merit pay increases can result in costly legal action brought against a firm. In settling cases, courts have held employers liable for back pay, court costs, and other costs related to training and promoting certain employees in protected classes.

While it is unlikely that any appraisal system will be totally immune to legal challenge, systems that possess the characteristics previously discussed are apparently more legally defensible. At the same time, these items can provide a more effective means for achieving performance appraisal goals.

THE APPRAISAL INTERVIEW

The Achilles' heel of the entire evaluation process is the appraisal interview itself.[27] In spite of the problems involved, supervisors usually conduct a formal appraisal interview at the end of an employee's appraisal period. This interview is essential for employee development. However, effective performance appraisal systems require more than this single interview. Instead, supervisors should maintain a continuous dialogue with employees emphasizing their own responsibility for development and management's supportive role.

A successful appraisal interview should be structured in a way that allows both the supervisor and the subordinate to view it as a problem-solving rather than a fault-finding session. The supervisor should consider three basic purposes when planning an appraisal interview: discussing the employee's performance, assisting the employee in setting objectives, and suggesting means for achieving these objectives. For instance, a worker may be rated as average on the factor *quality of production*. In the interview, both parties should agree as to the specific improvement needed during the next appraisal period. In suggesting ways to achieve a higher level objective, the supervisor might recommend specific actions.

The interview should be scheduled soon after the end of the appraisal period. Employees usually know when their interview should take place, and their anxiety tends to increase when it is delayed. Interviews with top performers are often pleasant experiences for all concerned. However, supervisors may be reluctant to meet face-to-face with poor performers. They tend to postpone these anxiety-provoking interviews.

The amount of time devoted to an appraisal interview varies considerably with company policy and the position of the evaluated employee. Although costs must be considered, there is merit in conducting separate interviews for discussing (1) employee performance and development, and (2) pay increases. Many managers have learned that as soon as pay is mentioned in an interview it tends to dominate the conversation. For this reason, a rather common practice is to defer pay discussions for one to several weeks after the appraisal interview. At American Express's IDS Financial Services unit in Minneapolis, most employees receive formal evaluations at the end of each year. The salary review is conducted one day to three weeks later. Avon Products and Harley-Davidson have also separated their performance and salary evaluations at some locations.[28]

Conducting an appraisal interview is often one of management's more difficult tasks. It requires tact and patience on the part of the supervisor. Praise should be provided when warranted, but it can have only limited value if not clearly deserved. Criticism is especially difficult to give. So-called constructive criticism is often not perceived that way by the employee. Yet it is difficult for a manager at any level to avoid criticism when conducting appraisal interviews. The supervisor should realize that all individuals have some deficiencies that may not be changed easily, if at all. Continued criticism may lead to frustration and have a damaging effect on employee development. Again, this possibility should not allow undesirable employee behavior to go unnoticed. However, discussions of sensitive issues should focus on the deficiency, not the person. Threats to the employee's self-esteem should be minimized whenever possible.

A serious error that a supervisor sometimes makes is to surprise the subordinate by bringing up some past mistake or problem. For example, if an incident had not been previously discussed, it would be most inappropriate for the supervisor to state, "Two months ago, you failed to coordinate your plans properly for implementing the new automated resume review procedure." Good management practice and common sense dictate that such situations be dealt with when they occur and not be saved for the appraisal interview.

The entire performance appraisal process should be a positive experience for the employee. In practice, however, it often is not. Negative feelings can often be traced to the appraisal interview and the manner in which it was conducted by the supervisor. Ideally, employees will leave the interview with positive feelings about the supervisor, the company, the job, and themselves. The prospects for improved performance will be bleak if the employee's ego is deflated. Past behavior cannot be changed, but future performance can. Specific plans for the employee's development should be clearly outlined and mutually agreed on. Cessna Aircraft Company has developed several hints for supervisors that have been helpful in conducting appraisal interviews (see Figure 11-3).

A GLOBAL PERSPECTIVE

A performance appraisal system mandates a formal periodic review and evaluation of an employee's job performance. A general management survey on perceptions of national management style was given to 707 managers representing diverse industries from the United States, Indonesia, Malaysia, and Thailand. Results on survey items relating to the design of performance appraisal systems revealed significant differences in the management styles of these countries. Such differences may translate into distinct differences in the optimal management of performance appraisal, thus suggesting important reservations about the transferability of traditional performance appraisal principles across cultural boundaries. The appropriate performance appraisal system design needs of Pacific Rim managers may not be satisfied by traditional Western guiding principles. Possible cultural forces within each of the Pacific Rim countries are examined in order to gain an understanding of the significant differences. For example, the rating of Thai managers closest to the traditional position on several

FIGURE 11-3
Suggestions for Conducting Appraisal Interviews

1. Give the employee a few days' notice of the discussion and its purpose. Encourage the employee to give some preparatory thought to his or her job performance and development plans. In some cases, have employees read their written performance evaluation prior to the meeting.
2. Prepare notes and use the completed performance appraisal form as a discussion guide so that each important topic will be covered. Be ready to answer questions employees may ask about why you appraised them as you did. Encourage your employees to ask questions.
3. Be ready to suggest specific developmental activities suitable to each employee's needs. When there are specific performance problems, remember to "attack the problem, not the person."
4. Establish a friendly, helpful, and purposeful tone at the outset of the discussion. Recognize that it is not unusual for you and your employee to be nervous about the discussion, and use suitable techniques to put you both more at ease.
5. Assure your employee that everyone on Cessna's management team is being evaluated so that opportunities for improvement and development will not be overlooked and each person's performance will be fully recognized.
6. Make sure that the session is truly a discussion. Encourage employees to talk about how they feel they are doing on the job, how they might improve, and what developmental activities they might undertake. Often an employee's viewpoints on these matters will be quite close to your own.
7. When your appraisal differs from the employee's, discuss these differences. Sometimes employees have hidden reasons for performing in a certain manner or using certain methods. This is an opportunity to find out if such reasons exist.
8. These discussions should contain both constructive compliments and constructive criticism. Be sure to discuss the employee's strengths as well as weaknesses. Your employees should have clear pictures of how you view their performance when the discussions are concluded.
9. Occasionally the appraisal interview will uncover strong emotions. This is one of the values of regular appraisals; since they can bring out bothersome feelings, they can be dealt with honestly. The emotional dimension of managing is very important. Ignoring it can lead to poor performance. Deal with emotional issues when they arise because they block a person's ability to concentrate on other issues. Consult Personnel for help when especially strong emotions are uncovered.
10. Make certain that your employees fully understand your appraisal of their performance. Sometimes it helps to have an employee orally summarize the appraisal as he or she understands it. If there are any misunderstandings, they can be cleared up on the spot. Ask questions to make sure you have been fully understood.
11. Discuss the future as well as the past. Plan with the employee specific changes in performance or specific developmental activities that will allow fuller use of potential. Ask what you can do to help.
12. End the discussion on a positive, future-improvement-oriented note. You and your employee are a team, working toward the development of everyone involved.

Source: Used with the permission of Cessna Aircraft Company.

questions may be attributed to the fact that only 47 percent of the respondents were educated in Thailand.[29]

The development of an appropriate global performance appraisal system will undoubtedly be a complex process, but an effective global system is essential for credible employee evaluations.[30] Valid performance appraisal is difficult enough to achieve in the United States; evaluating overseas employees makes a normally complex problem nearly impossible. What usually works in one culture might not work in another.[31] What is a strength in one culture might be considered a weakness in another. When performance appraisals are done overseas, the issue of what performance standards to use comes into question. Differences in performance appraisal practices are almost always necessary. An improper performance appraisal system can create a great deal of misunderstanding and personal offense.[32]

Such problems can be partially avoided if human resource management professionals take the following actions. First, managers should determine the purpose of the appraisal—whether it is to enhance administrative decision making or to enhance the personal development of the employee. Second, whenever possible, performance objectives for job assignments or tasks should be developed. Third, managers must allow more time to achieve results in an overseas assignment. Finally, the objectives of the appraisal system should be flexible and responsive to potential markets and environmental contingencies. As with a domestic performance appraisal system, a global one should result in a realistic review and evaluation of the employee's job performance.[33]

ASSESSMENT CENTERS

Many employee performance appraisal systems evaluate an individual's past performance and at the same time attempt to assess his or her potential for advancement. Other organizations have developed a separate approach for assessing potential. This process often takes place in what is appropriately referred to as an assessment center.

An **assessment center** requires employees to perform activities similar to those they might encounter in an actual job. These simulated exercises are based on a thorough job analysis. The assessors usually observe the employees somewhere other than their normal workplace over a certain period of time. The assessors selected are typically experienced managers who both participate in the exercises and evaluate performance. Assessment centers are used increasingly to (1) identify employees who have higher level management potential, (2) select first-line supervisors, and (3) determine employee developmental needs. Assessment centers are used by more than 1,000 organizations,[34] including small firms and large corporations, such as General Electric Company, J. C. Penney Company, Ford Motor Company, and AT&T. An advantage of the assessment center approach is the increased reliability and validity of the information provided. Assessment centers have been shown to be more successful than aptitude tests in predicting performance.[35]

A typical schedule for General Electric's Supervisory Assessment Center (SAC) is shown in Table 11-2. The SAC program is used for selecting new employees and assessing the management potential of current employees.

TABLE 11-2
Typical Schedule for General Electric Company's Supervisory Assessment Center

Day 1

Approximately four hours per candidate are required for the background interview and an in-basket exercise. The interview covers such traditional areas as work experience, educational background, and leadership experience. The in-basket exercise provides an opportunity for the individual to demonstrate how he or she would handle administrative problems including day-to-day "fire-fighting." All Day 1 activities are scheduled on an individual basis and are typically administered by persons in Employee Relations.

Day 2

An additional four hours are devoted to group and individual exercises. Group exercises related to reallocation of resources allow an individual's performance to be observed as the candidate solves problems in peer group situations. In the individual exercises each candidate assumes the role of a supervisor to handle four typical work-related problems. Six operating managers serve as the SAC staff for Day 2 activities. They observe and evaluate the performance of six candidates. The staff completes structured rating forms on each candidate's performance immediately following each exercise. After all exercises have been completed and the candidates dismissed, the staff conducts an overall evaluation of each individual's potential for a supervisory position. Over fifty pieces of data from each candidate's performance are reviewed along with information obtained from the interview. The staff then arrives at a consensus decision and a recommended course of action for each candidate.

Source: Used with permission of the General Electric Company.

Note the number of exercises that are utilized in evaluating a participant's behavior.

An evaluation of the General Electric SAC process revealed the following:

> The SAC was based on a job analysis of a supervisor's job and is considered to have content validity.[36] The SAC provides all candidates an equal opportunity to demonstrate their skills and does not discriminate against any employee group. For example, a study of more than 1,000 candidates from fourteen company locations showed that the success ratios were acceptable for caucasians, minorities, and women. Those individuals who scored highest in the SAC are the same individuals who have subsequently received the greatest number of job promotions. Thus, one area of predictive validity of the SAC was demonstrated.

As many as half a dozen assessors may evaluate each participant, as at General Electric. The participant's position in the organization often determines the amount of time spent in the center. First-line supervisory candidates may only spend a day or two, whereas more time may be needed for those being considered for middle management and executive jobs. After the session is over, the participants return to their jobs, and the assessors prepare their evaluations. Interestingly, because the assessors are often not full-time members of the human resource development staff, they frequently gain further insight into how managers in their organization should function. And even though a primary purpose of assessment centers is to identify management potential, the J. C. Penney experience indicates that the "participants gain valuable insights into their own strengths, weaknesses, and interests." These insights permit management and the individual to make plans for the employee's development.

Accurately assessing potential and evaluating performance are critical to productivity. Yet systems poorly conceived or improperly implemented can actually impair employee performance. PA definitely presents management with a double-edged sword. However, as long as productivity must be improved and decisions made in such areas as pay increases, promotions, and transfers, organizations must strive for the best system possible.[37]

SUMMARY

Performance appraisal is a system that provides a periodic review and evaluation of an individual's or group's job performance. The overriding purpose of performance appraisal is to improve the organization's effectiveness. Identification of specific objectives provides the starting point for the performance appraisal process. Because an appraisal system cannot serve all purposes, a firm should select those specific objectives it desires to achieve. Next, workers must understand what is expected of them on the job. Supervisors normally discuss with employees the major duties contained in their job descriptions.

Work performance is observed and periodically evaluated against previously established job performance standards. The results of the evaluation are then discussed with the workers. The performance evaluation interview serves to reestablish job requirements in the employee's mind. The process is dynamic and ongoing. The human resource department is responsible for designing and coordinating the performance appraisal process. However, line managers must play a central role in the process for it to be successful. The person (or persons) who actually conduct performance appraisals varies from company to company. The rating of the employee may be done by the immediate supervisor (most commonly), subordinates, peers, a group, the employee (as self-appraisal), or a combination of these people.

Performance appraisal methods include (1) rating scales, (2) critical incidents, (3) essay, (4) work standards, (5) ranking, (6) forced distribution, (7) forced-choice and weighted checklist performance reports, (8) behaviorally anchored rating scales, and (9) management by objectives. Problems associated with these performance appraisal methods include lack of objectivity, halo error, leniency, strictness, central tendency, recent behavior bias, personal bias, and the judgmental role of the evaluator "playing God."

At the end of the appraisal period, the evaluator usually conducts a formal appraisal interview with the employee. The key to a successful interview is to structure it so that both the manager and the subordinate will approach it as a problem-solving, rather than a fault-finding, session. This interview is essential for achieving employee development but does not replace the need for a continuous dialogue between employee and management.

Certain appraisal system practices have successfully withstood legal challenges. Because improperly constituted systems can result in costly legal action against a firm, appraisal systems must be based on job content.

An assessment center requires employees to perform activities similar to those that they might confront in an actual job. Assessment centers are being used increasingly for (1) identifying employees who have higher level management potential, (2) selecting first-line supervisors, and (3) determining employees' developmental needs.

QUESTIONS FOR REVIEW

1. Define *performance appraisal* and briefly discuss the basic purposes of performance appraisal.
2. What are the basic steps in the performance appraisal process?
3. Many different people can conduct performance appraisals. Briefly describe the various alternatives.
4. Briefly describe each of the following methods of performance appraisal:
   a. Rating scales
   b. Critical incidents
   c. Essay
   d. Work standards
   e. Ranking
   f. Forced distribution
   g. Forced-choice and weighted checklist performance reports
   h. Behaviorally anchored rating scales
   i. Management by objectives
5. What are the various problems associated with performance appraisal? Briefly describe each.
6. Why should employee performance and development be discussed separately from pay increases?
7. What are the characteristics of an effective appraisal system?
8. What are the legal implications of performance appraisal?
9. Why is the following statement often said: "The Achilles' heel of the entire evaluation process is the appraisal interview itself."
10. Describe how an assessment center could be used as a means of performance appraisal.

HRM SIMULATION

Your firm does not currently have a formal performance appraisal system. Some employees complain that the supervisors and managers give raises and perks to those they like and not necessarily to those who are most productive. A formal system could be established and maintained, but it costs money. However, decreased turnover, increased morale, and higher productivity might result.

In addition, in Incident E in the *Simulation Players Manual*, the CEO has instructed your team to recommend a system of performance appraisal for supervisors and managers. Choosing an appraisal system is not difficult but explaining your rationale may be more demanding.

ABC VIDEO CASE

PAYING FOR PERFORMANCE TAPE 2, NUMBER 1

The public feels betrayed by members of Congress who made $125,000 but who overdrew their accounts at the House bank in spite of subsidized barbershops, pharmacies, and reserved parking at the airport. The public felt betrayed by the administration, when the vice president flew a government jet to a golf game. And the public also felt betrayed by the group with the largest paychecks in America—corporate CEOs.

Big pay, golden parachutes, and ballooning bonuses make many people angry. Stockholders are increasingly upset with CEOs who get salary increases without having them linked to performance. Citizens are calling for responsibility in spending, and Congress, in the hot seat, is calling for accountability on declining stock value. When Westinghouse lost money, its CEO got a raise—increasing his earnings to more than $5 million. Even though some corporate boards are listening and cutting the CEO's pay, Congress has bills in the Senate to give shareholders a direct say, which will allow stockholders to know exactly how much they are paying their CEOs. There is a new standard emerging for corporate accountability.

HRM INCIDENT 1

—LET'S GET IT OVER WITH

"There, at last it's finished," thought Tom Baker, as he laid aside the last of twelve performance appraisal forms. It had been a busy week for Tom, who supervises a road maintenance crew for the Georgia Department of Highways.

The governor, in passing through Tom's district a few days earlier, had complained to the area superintendent that repairs were needed on several of the highways. Because of this, the superintendent assigned Tom's crew an unusually heavy workload. In addition, Tom received a call from the personnel office that week telling him that the performance appraisals were late. Tom explained his predicament, but the personnel specialist insisted that the forms be completed right away.

Looking over the appraisals again, Tom thought about several of the workers. The performance appraisal form had places for marking *quantity of work*, *quality of work*, and *cooperativeness*. For each characteristic, the worker could be graded *outstanding, good, average, below average,* or *unsatisfactory*. Since Tom's crew had completed all of the extra work assigned for that week, he marked every worker *outstanding* in *quantity of work*. He marked Joe Blum *average* in *cooperativeness* because Joe had questioned one of his decisions that week. Tom had decided to patch a pothole in one of the roads, and Joe thought the small section of road surface ought to be broken out and replaced. Tom did not include this in the remarks section of the form, though. As a matter of fact, he wrote no remarks on any of the forms.

Tom felt a twinge of guilt as he thought about Roger Short. He knew that Roger had been sloughing off, and the other workers had been carrying him for quite some time. He also knew that Roger would be upset if he found that he had been marked lower than the other workers. Consequently, he marked Roger the same to avoid a confrontation. "Anyway," Tom thought, "these things are a pain in the neck, and I really shouldn't have to bother with them."

As Tom folded up the performance appraisals and put them in the envelope for mailing, he smiled. He was glad he would not have to think about performance appraisals for another six months.

Question

1. What weaknesses do you see in Tom's performance appraisals?

HRM INCIDENT 2

—PERFORMANCE APPRAISAL?

As the production supervisor for Sweeny Electronics, Mike Mahoney was generally well regarded by most of his subordinates. Mike was an easygoing individual who tried to help his employees any way he could. If a worker needed a small loan until payday, he would dig into his pocket with no questions asked. Should an employee need some time off to attend to a personal problem, Mike would not dock the individual's pay; rather, he would take up the slack himself until the worker returned.

Everything had been going smoothly, at least until the last performance appraisal period. One of Mike's workers, Bill Overstreet, had been experiencing a large number of personal problems for the past year. Bill's wife had been sick much of the time and her medical expenses were high. Bill's son had a speech impediment and the doctors had recommended a special clinic. Bill, who had already borrowed the limit the bank would loan, had become upset and despondent over his general circumstances.

When it was time for Bill's annual performance appraisal, Mike decided he was going to do as much as possible to help him. Although Bill could not be considered anything more than an average worker, Mike rated him outstanding in virtually every category. Because the firm's compensation system was tied heavily to the performance appraisal, Bill would be eligible for a merit increase of 10 percent in addition to a regular cost of living raise.

Mike explained to Bill why he was giving him such high ratings, and Bill acknowledged that his performance had really been no better than average. Bill was very grateful and expressed this to Mike. As Bill left the office, he was excitedly looking forward to telling his friends about what a wonderful boss he had. Seeing Bill smile as he left gave Mike a warm feeling.

Questions

1. From Sweeny Electronics' standpoint, what difficulties might Mike Mahoney's performance appraisal practices create?
2. What can Mike do now to diminish the negative impact of his evaluation of Bill?

DEVELOPING HRM SKILLS

AN EXPERIENTIAL EXERCISE

Performance appraisal is an essential aspect of human resource management. It is a formal system that provides a periodic review and evaluation of an individual's or team's job performance. Developing an effective performance appraisal system is difficult. However, some managers do not take PA as seriously as they should. Such attitudes are counterproductive, and they frequently lower individual and group productivity.

Larry Beavers, supervisor of an electrical department, has a busy day scheduled, but he needs to squeeze in the last of his performance appraisals. They are due today, and he only needs to get one more signature. Upon arriving for work he thinks, "I hate doing performance appraisals. It is the worst part of a supervisor's job. But it does allow me to point out deficiencies that the workers must be aware of if they are to improve their performance. The guy I'm appraising today has always exceeded his quotas, he is very helpful to the workers he likes, and he is excellent on the new computerized production setup; but if he wants to advance, he will need to change his behavior. He seems to have problems working with the females on the line, and he doesn't seem to be very open-minded. Also, on September 23, he failed to secure his work area. This guy really has problems. Maybe our talk will do some good; either way I need to get this done. On the positive side, this is the last performance appraisal until next year."

Today Alex Martin gets his performance appraisal, and he is excited about it. Before the meeting with Larry, his supervisor, he thinks, "I've been very good on the new computerized setup, and very helpful to my friends on the line, and this will help me get my promotion. I expect that the boss saved my performance appraisal for last to praise my performance and to recommend me for that promotion I've been deserving for some time. I've been passed over for promotion for too long, this has been a great year for me, and this will cap off a year of excellent performance."

When these two get together, it will be a meeting of two quite different minds, and in all likelihood, the meeting will be filled with disagreement, dissatisfaction, and maybe even hard feelings. This exercise will require active participation from two of you. One person will play the supervisor conducting the performance appraisal, and the other will be the evaluated employee. Only two can play; the rest of you should observe carefully. Your instructor will provide the participants with additional information necessary to complete the exercise.

NOTES

1. "The Team Building Tool Kit," *Compensation and Benefits Review* 26 (March/April 1994): 67.
2. Peter M. Tafti, "Face to Face," *Training and Development Journal* 44 (November 1990): 68.
3. R. Wayne Mondy, Robert M. Noe III, and Robert E. Edwards, "What the Staffing Function Entails," *Personnel* 63 (April 1986): 55.
4. Charles Lee, "Smoothing Out Appraisal Systems," *HRMagazine* 35 (March 1990): 72, 76.
5. Clive Fletcher, "Appraisal: An Idea Whose Time Has Gone?" *Personnel Management* 25 (September 1993): 34.
6. Kenneth P. Carson, Robert L. Cardy, and Gregory H. Dobbins, "Upgrade the Employee Evaluation Process," *HRMagazine* 37 (November 1992): 88.
7. Robert C. Joines, Steve Quisenberry, and Gary W. Sawyer, "Business Strategy Drives Three-Pronged Assessment System," *HRMagazine* 38 (December 1993): 68–70.
8. Robert J. Sahl, "Design Effective Performance Appraisals," *Personnel Journal* 69 (October 1990): 60.
9. Robert C. Joines, Steve Quisenberry, and Gary W. Sawyer, "Business Strategy Drives Three-Pronged Assessment System," 70.
10. Robert V. Romberg, "Performance Appraisal, 1: Risks and Rewards," *Personnel* 63 (August 1986): 20.
11. "The Team Building Tool Kit," 68.
12. Mathew Budman and Berkeley Rice, "The Rating Game," *Across the Board* 31 (February 1994): 34–38.
13. "How Johnsonville Shares Profits on the Basis of Performance," *Harvard Business Review* 68 (November-December 1990): 74.
14. James G. Goodale, "Seven Ways to Improve Performance Appraisals," *HRMagazine* 38 (May 1993): 80.
15. Mathew Budman and Berkeley Rice, "The Rating Game," 35.
16. Robert L. Taylor and Robert A. Zawaki, "Trends in Performance Appraisal: Guidelines for Managers," *Personnel Administrator* 29 (March 1984): 71.
17. Because the system depicted makes liberal use of personal factors that may not be job related, it has been described by one reviewer as "a good example of a poor method."
18. J. Peter Graves, "Let's Put Appraisal Back in Performance Appraisal, Part I," *Personnel Journal* 61 (November 1982): 848–849.
19. Stephen J. Carroll and Craig E. Schneier, *Performance Appraisal and Review Systems: The Identification, Measurement, and Development of Performance in Organizations* (Glenview, Ill.: Scott, Foresman, 1982): 117.
20. Jay T. Knippen, "Boost Performance Through Appraisals," *Business Credit* 92 (November-December 1990): 27.
21. Barbara H. Holmes, "The Lenient Evaluator Is Hurting Your Organization," *HRMagazine* 38 (June 1993): 75–76.
22. Portions of this section were adapted from Ronald G. Wells, "Guidelines for Effective and Defensive Performance Appraisal Systems," *Personnel Journal* 61 (October 1982): 776–782.
23. Larry L. Axline, "Ethical Considerations of Performance Appraisals," *Management Review* 83 (March 1994): 62.
24. Barry J. Baroni, "The Legal Ramifications of Appraisal Systems," *Supervisory Management* 27 (January 1982): 41–42.
25. Karen Matthes, "Will Your Performance Appraisal System Stand Up in Court?" *HR Focus* 69 (August 1992): 5.
26. David I. Rosen, "Appraisals Can Make—or Break—Your Court Case," *Personnal Journal* 71 (November 1992): 115.

27. C. O. Colvin, "Everything You Always Wanted to Know about Appraisal Discrimination," *Personnel Journal* 60 (October 1981): 758–759.

28. Julie Amparano Lopez, "Companies Split Reviews on Performance and Pay," *Wall Street Journal* (May 10, 1993): B1.

29. Charles M. Vance, Shirley R. McClaine, David M. Boje, and H. Daniel Stage, "An Examination of the Transferability of Traditional Performance Appraisal Principals Across Cultural Boundaries," *Management International Review* (Fourth Quarter, 1992): 313–326.

30. Wayne F. Cascio and Manuel G. Serapio, Jr., "Human Resources Systems in an International Alliance: The Undoing of a Done Deal?" *Organizational Dynamics* 19 (Winter 1991): 70.

31. Mark E. Mendenhall and Gary Oddon, "The Overseas Assignment: A Practical Look," *Business Horizons* 31 (September/October, 1988): 81.

32. Ibid., 70.

33. Ibid.

34. *General Electric Assessment Center Manual*, General Electric Company.

35. Peter Rea, Julie Rea, and Charles Moomaw, "Use Assessment Centers in Skill Development," *Personnel Journal* 69 (April 1990): 126.

36. Content validity is inherent in the assessment center process when the exercises developed are based on job analysis. This type of validity is acceptable according to the *Uniform Guidelines*.

37. Gary English, "Tuning Up for Performance Management," *Training and Development Journal* 45 (April 1991): 56.

CHAPTER 12 Financial Compensation

KEY TERMS

Compensation 358
Direct financial compensation 358
Indirect financial compensation 358
Nonfinancial compensation 358
Equity 359
External equity 360
Internal equity 360
Employee equity 360
Team equity 360
Pay leaders 361
Going rate 361
Pay followers 362
Labor market 362
Benchmark job 363
Cost-of-living allowance (COLA) 364
Exempt employees 366
Job evaluation 368
Ranking method 369
Classification method 369
Factor comparison method 370
Point method 371
Hay guide chart-profile method 374
Job pricing 381
Pay grade 381
Wage curve 382
Pay range 383
Comparable worth 386
Pay compression 388

CHAPTER OBJECTIVES

1. Define compensation and explain the concept of compensation equity.
2. Describe the organization and the labor market as determinants of financial compensation.
3. Define job evaluation and describe the basic job evaluation methods.
4. Describe the employee as a determinant of financial compensation and explain the factors associated with job pricing.
5. Describe the compensation issues of comparable worth, pay secrecy, and pay compression.

Earl Lewis and his wife are full of excitement and anticipation as they leave their home for a shopping trip. Earl had just learned his firm was implementing a new variable pay system, and his long record of high performance would finally pay off. He looked forward to the opportunity to increase his income so that he could purchase some needed items for a new home.

Inez Scoggin's anxiety over scheduled minor surgery was somewhat relieved. Her supervisor has assured her that a major portion of her medical and hospitalization costs will be covered by the firm's health insurance plan.

Trig Ekeland, executive director of the local YMCA, returns home dead tired from his job each evening no earlier than six o'clock. His salary is small compared to the salaries of many other local managers who have similar responsibilities. Yet Trig is an exceptionally happy person who believes that his work with youth, civic leaders, and other members of the community is extremely important and worthwhile.

Joanne Abrahamson has been employed by a large manufacturing firm for eight years. Although her pay is not what she would like it to be, her job in the accounts payable department enables her to have contact with some of her best friends. She likes her supervisor and considers the overall working environment to be great. Joanne would not trade jobs with anyone she knows.

Compensation and benefits are obviously important to Earl Lewis and Inez Scoggin, as they are to most employees. However, for Trig and Joanne, other factors in a total compensation package also assume great importance. These components include a pleasant work environment and job satisfaction. Because it has many elements, compensation administration is one of management's most difficult and challenging human resource areas.

We begin this chapter with an overview of compensation and an explanation of compensation equity. Next, we discuss determinants of individual financial compensation, including the influence of the organization and the labor market. This is followed by a discussion of the job and the role of job evaluation. The impact of a final determinant, the employee, is presented next. We devote the final portion of the chapter to job pricing and other compensation issues.

COMPENSATION: AN OVERVIEW

Compensation refers to every type of reward that individuals receive in return for their labor. The components of a total compensation program are shown in Figure 12-1. **Direct financial compensation** consists of the pay that a person receives in the form of wages, salaries, bonuses, and commissions. Earl Lewis just received word that by continuing his high level of performance he may now increase the size of his paycheck. **Indirect financial compensation** (benefits) includes all financial rewards that are not included in direct compensation. Inez Scoggin will receive indirect financial compensation because her company provides for a major portion of her medical and hospital costs. As you can see in Figure 12-1, this form of compensation includes a wide variety of rewards that are normally received indirectly by the employee.

Nonfinancial compensation consists of the satisfaction that a person receives from the job itself or from the psychological and/or physical environment in which the person works. Trig Ekeland and Joanne Abrahamson are receiving important forms of nonfinancial compensation. Trig is extremely satisfied with the job he performs. This type of nonfinancial compensation consists of the satisfaction received from performing meaningful job-related tasks. Joanne's job permits her to have contact with close friends. This form of nonfinancial compensation involves the psychological and/or physical environment in which the person works.

All such rewards comprise a total compensation program. In order to remain competitive, organizations must reward performance outcomes that are required to achieve its key goals.[1] In determining effective rewards, the uniqueness of employees must be considered. People have different reasons for working, and the most appropriate compensation package depends on those reasons. When individuals are being stretched to provide food, shelter, and clothing for their families, money may well be the most important reward. However, some people work many hours each day, receive little pay,

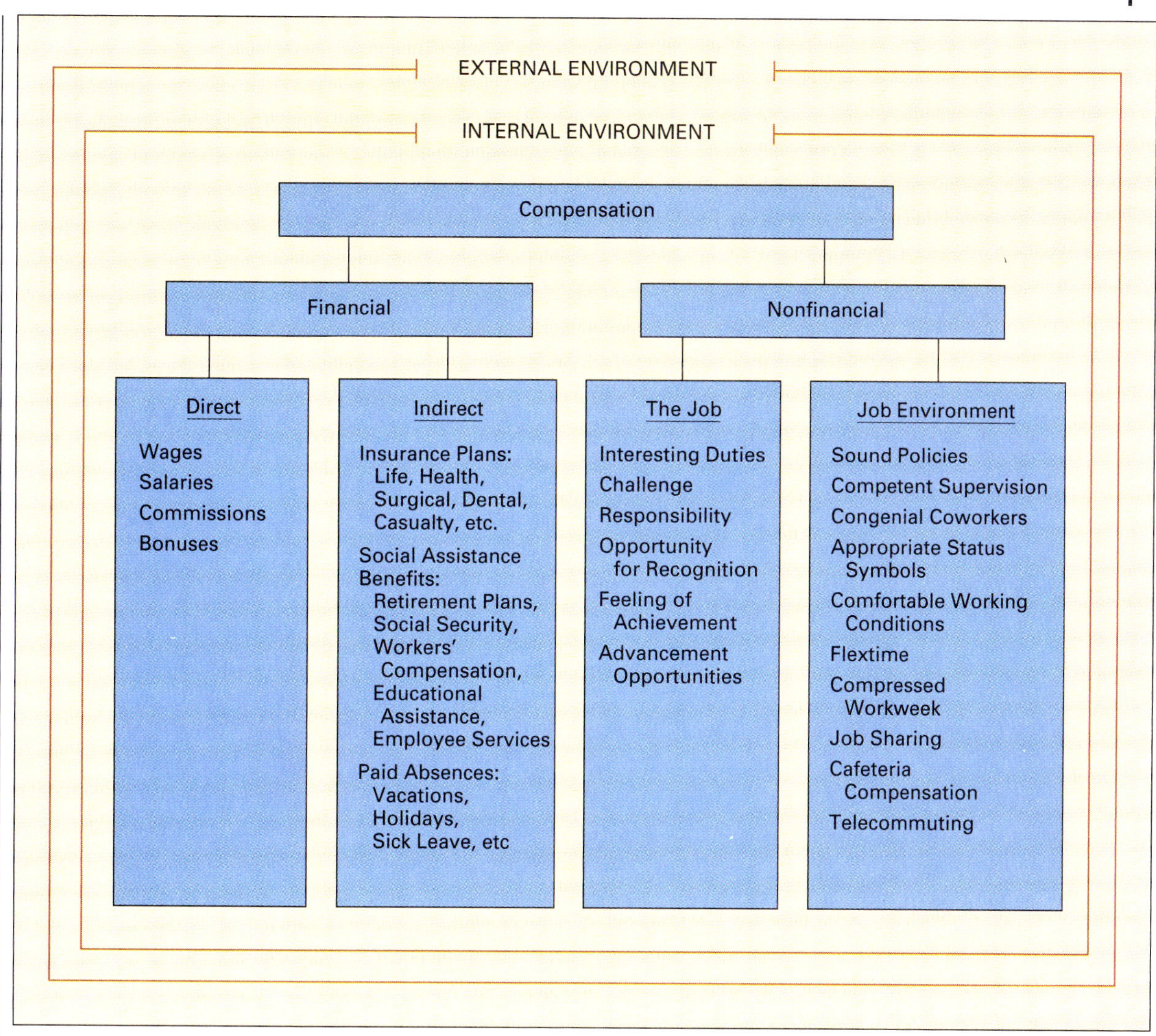

FIGURE 12-1 Components of a Total Compensation Program

and love their work. To a large degree, adequate compensation is in the mind of the receiver. It is often more than the financial compensation received in the form of a paycheck.

COMPENSATION EQUITY

Organizations must attract, motivate, and retain competent employees. Since achievement of these goals is largely accomplished through a firm's compensation system, organizations must strive for compensation equity. **Equity** is workers' perceptions that they are being treated fairly. Compensation must be fair to all parties concerned and be perceived as fair. When chief executives are paid millions of dollars in one year and receive huge bonuses along with *golden parachutes*, serious questions arise as to what constitutes fairness within an organization.

External equity exists when a firm's employees are paid comparably to workers who perform similar jobs in other firms. Compensation surveys enable organizations to determine the extent to which external equity is present. **Internal equity** exists when employees are paid according to the relative value of their jobs within an organization. Job evaluation is a primary means for determining internal equity. **Employee equity** exists when individuals performing similar jobs for the same firm are paid according to factors unique to the employee, such as performance level or seniority. **Team equity** is achieved when more productive teams are rewarded greater than less productive groups. Performance levels may be determined through appraisal systems, which were discussed in the previous chapter.

Inequity in any category can result in severe morale problems. If employees feel they are being compensated unfairly, they may restrict their efforts or even leave the firm. In either event, the organization's overall performance is damaged. Regarding employee equity, for example, suppose that two accountants in the same firm are performing similar jobs, and one is acknowledged to be far superior to the other in performance. If both workers receive equal pay increases, employee equity does not exist and the more productive employee is likely to be unhappy. Most workers are concerned with pay equity, both internal and external. From an employee relations perspective, internal pay equity is probably more important. Employees simply have more information about pay matters within their own organization, and these data are used to form perceptions of equity.[2] On the other hand, an organization must be competitive in the labor market to remain viable. External equity, therefore, must always be a prominent consideration. The difficulty in maintaining equity on all fronts has long been an organizational dilemma.

DETERMINANTS OF INDIVIDUAL FINANCIAL COMPENSATION

Compensation theory has never been able to provide a completely satisfactory answer to what an individual is worth for performing jobs. While no scientific approach is available, a number of relevant factors are typically used to determine individual pay. These determinants are shown in Figure 12-2. The organization, the labor market, the job, and the employee all have an impact on job pricing and the ultimate determination of an individual's financial compensation.[3]

THE ORGANIZATION AS A DETERMINANT OF FINANCIAL COMPENSATION

Managers tend to view financial compensation as both an expense and an asset. It is an expense in the sense that it reflects the cost of labor. In service industries, for example, labor costs account for more than 50 percent of all expenses. However, financial compensation is an asset when it induces employees to put forth their best efforts and to remain in their jobs. Compensation programs have the potential to influence employee work attitudes and behavior, encouraging workers to be more productive.[4] Improved performance, increased productivity, and lower turnover are sought by all managers, which accounts for the serious attention compensation receives from top management.

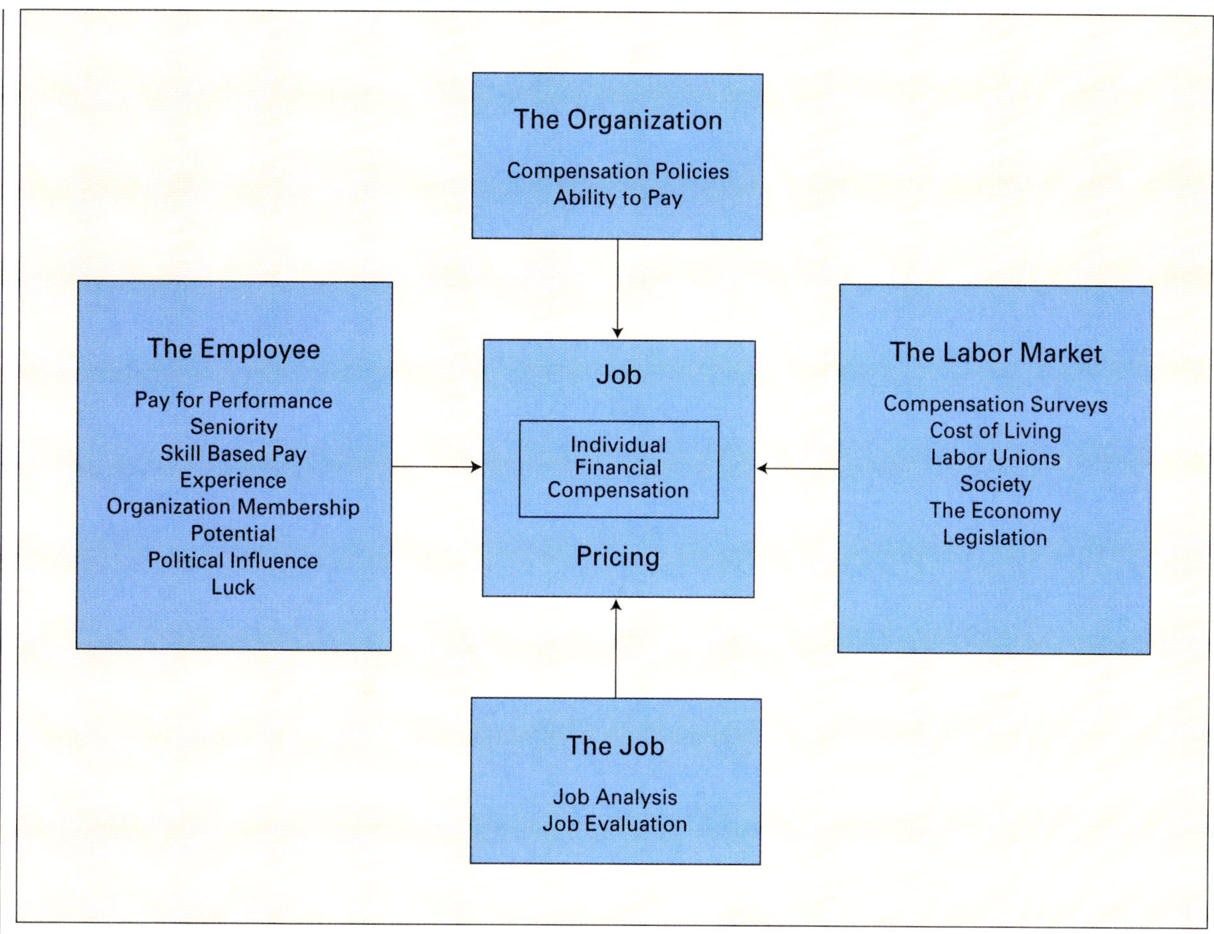

FIGURE 12-2 Primary Determinants of Individual Financial Compensation

Corporate culture has a major influence on an individual's financial compensation. An organization often establishes—formally or informally—compensation policies that determine whether it will be a pay leader or a pay follower, or it strives for an average position in the labor market. **Pay leaders** are those organizations that pay higher wages and salaries than competing firms. Such organizations expect to have lower per unit labor costs. They feel that they will be able to attract high-quality, productive employees. Higher paying firms usually attract more and better qualified applicants than do lower paying companies in the same industry.

The **going rate** is the average pay that most employers provide for the same job in a particular area or industry. Many organizations have a policy that calls for paying the going rate. In such firms, management believes it can employ qualified people and still remain competitive by not having to raise the price of goods or services. Employers with this policy may be overlooking the possibility of hiring more proficient workers. Yet, many firms have jobs that require only average employee qualifications. An assembly line worker who tightens four bolts every minute and a half is an example. In this situation, an excellent employee may not be any more productive than one with only average ability. Thus, a person's productive potential may be limited by the nature of the work assigned.

Companies that choose to pay below the going rate because of poor financial condition or a belief that they simply do not require highly capable employees are **pay followers**. Difficulties often occur when this policy is followed. Consider the case of Melvin Denney:

> Melvin Denney managed a large, but financially strapped farming operation in the Southwest. Although no formal policies had been established, Melvin had a practice of paying the lowest wage possible. For example, one of his farmhands, George McMillan, was paid minimum wage. During a period of three weeks, George wrecked a tractor, severely damaged a combine, and stripped the gears in a new pickup truck. George's actions prompted Melvin to remark, "George is the most expensive darned employee I've ever had."

As Melvin discovered, paying the lowest wage possible did not save money—actually, it was quite expensive. In addition to hiring unproductive workers, organizations that are pay followers may have a high turnover rate as their most qualified employees leave to join organizations that pay more. Equally important, in situations where incompetent or disgruntled employees come in contact with customers, they may not provide the kind of customer service management desires. If management does not treat its employees well, their customers may also suffer, and this spells disaster for any firm in today's competitive global environment.

The organizational level in which compensation decisions are made can also have an impact on pay. These decisions are often made at a high management level to ensure consistency. However, there are advantages to making pay decisions at lower levels where better information may exist regarding employee performance. Top level executives err when they make decisions in isolation from lower level managers.

An organization's assessment of its ability to pay is also an important factor in determining pay levels. Financially successful firms tend to provide higher than average compensation.[5] However, an organization's financial strength establishes only the upper limit of what it will pay. To arrive at a specific pay level, management must consider other factors.

THE LABOR MARKET AS A DETERMINANT OF FINANCIAL COMPENSATION

Potential employees located within the geographical area from which employees are recruited comprise the **labor market**. Labor markets for some jobs extend far beyond the locality of a firm's operations. An aerospace firm in Seattle, Washington, for example, may be concerned about the labor market for engineers in Wichita, Kansas, or Orlando, Florida. Managerial and professional employees are often recruited from a wide geographical area. In fact, nationwide recruitment is not unusual for certain skills. As mentioned in Chapter 6, some firms engage in global recruitment for top executives.

Moreover, pay for jobs within various markets may vary considerably. Secretarial jobs, for example, may carry an average salary of $29,000 per year in a large, urban community but only $18,000 or less in a small, rural town. Compensation managers must be aware of these differences in order to compete successfully for employees. The going wage, or prevailing rate, is an important guide in determining pay. Many employees view it as the standard for judging the fairness of their firm's compensation practices.

Compensation Surveys

Large organizations routinely conduct compensation surveys to determine prevailing pay rates within labor markets. These surveys provide the low, high, and average salaries for a given position. They give a good sense of what other companies are paying employees in various jobs. A Bureau of National Affairs study found that 93 percent of employers used salary surveys to determine pay levels; 55 percent of the respondents believed them to be essential or absolutely necessary.[6]

Compensation surveys provide information for establishing both direct and indirect compensation. The decisions that must be made prior to conducting a compensation survey include determining (1) the geographic area of the survey, (2) the specific firms to contact, and (3) the jobs to include. The geographic area to be included in the survey is often determined from employment records. Data from this source may indicate maximum distance or time that employees are willing to travel to work. Also, the firms to be contacted in the survey are often from the same industry but may also include others—regardless of industry—that compete for the same skills. Because obtaining data on all jobs in the organization may not be feasible, the human resource department often surveys only benchmark jobs. A **benchmark job** is one that is well known in the company and industry, one that represents the entire job structure, and one in which a large percentage of the workforce is employed.

A primary difficulty in conducting a compensation survey involves determining comparable jobs. Recall that organizing work and designing jobs can be done in many different ways. A job in one company may only roughly resemble a job with a similar title in another. For this reason, job titles have little value in compensation surveys. Instead, the analyst must use well-written job descriptions when requesting compensation data.

There are other ways to obtain compensation data in a given labor market. Some professional organizations periodically conduct surveys. The U.S. Bureau of Labor Statistics also makes yearly surveys and provides data by area, industry, and job type. In addition, a number of journals, such as *Compensation and Benefits Review* and *Hospital Administration*, report compensation information periodically. Some organizations choose to use other sources, even though they are large enough to afford surveys. Several life insurance companies, for example, use compensation data provided by the Life Office Management Association. These companies may supplement these data with survey information supplied by other organizations, such as Hay, Mercer Meidinger Hansen, the Society for Human Resource Management, and the American Management Association.

Cost of Living

The logic for using cost of living as a pay determinant is simple: When prices rise over a period of time and pay does not, *real pay* is actually lowered. A pay increase must be roughly equivalent to the increased cost of living if a person is to maintain a previous level of real wages. For instance, if someone earns $24,000 during a year in which the average rate of inflation is 5 percent, a $100 per month pay increase will be necessary merely to maintain that person's standard of living.

People living on fixed incomes (primarily the elderly and the poor) are especially hard hit by inflation, but they are not alone; most employees also suffer financially. Recognizing this problem, some firms index pay increases to the inflation rate. Some firms will sacrifice *merit money* to provide across-the-board increases designed to offset the results of inflation.

Labor Unions

An excerpt from the Wagner Act, which is discussed in Chapter 15, prescribes the areas of mandatory collective bargaining between management and unions as "wages, hours, and other terms and conditions of employment." These broad bargaining areas obviously have great potential impact on compensation decisions. The union affects company compensation policies in three important areas: (1) the standards used in making compensation decisions, (2) wage differentials, and (3) payment methods.[7]

When a union uses comparable pay as a standard in making compensation demands, the employer must obtain accurate labor market data. When a union emphasizes cost of living, management may be pressured to include a **cost-of-living allowance (COLA)**. This is an escalator clause in the labor agreement that automatically increases wages as the U.S. Bureau of Labor Statistics cost-of-living index rises.

Unions may also attempt to create, preserve, or even destroy pay differentials between wages for craft workers and unskilled workers. The politics of a given situation will determine the direction taken. For instance, if the unskilled workers have the largest union membership, an attempt may be made to eliminate pay differentials.

Management may want to use incentive plans to encourage greater productivity. However, decisions to implement such plans may be scrapped if the union strongly opposes this approach. Employee acceptance of such a plan is essential for successful implementation, and union opposition may make it unworkable.

Society

Compensation paid to employees often affects a firm's pricing of its goods or services. For this reason, consumers may also be interested in compensation decisions. At times in the past, the government has responded to public opinion and stepped in to encourage businesses to hold down wages and prices. The process of *jawboning,* initiated by President John F. Kennedy in the early 1960s, involved using the prestige of the presidency to informally pressure large companies and unions to "hold the line."

Businesses in a given labor market are also concerned with the pay practices of new firms locating in their area. For instance, when the management of a large electronics firm announced plans to locate a branch plant in a relatively small community, it was confronted by local civic leaders. Their questions largely concerned the wage and salary rates that would be paid. Subtle pressure was applied to keep the company's wages in line with other wages in the community. The electronics firm agreed to begin operations with initial compensation at a lower level than it usually paid, but the firm's management made it clear that a series of pay increases would be given over a period of two years to maintain its own *pay leader* policy.

The Economy

The economy definitely affects financial compensation decisions. For example, a depressed economy generally increases the labor supply. This, in turn, serves to lower the going wage rate. In most cases, the cost of living will rise in an expanding economy. Because the cost of living is commonly used as a pay standard, the economy's health exerts a major impact on pay decisions. Labor unions, government, and society are all less likely to press for pay increases in a depressed economy, but attitudes change as conditions improve.

Legislation

Federal and state laws can also affect the amount of compensation a person receives. Next, we describe some of the more significant pieces of federal legislation in this area.

Davis-Bacon Act of 1931. The Davis-Bacon Act of 1931 was the first national law to deal with minimum wages. The act requires federal construction contractors with projects valued in excess of $2,000 to pay at least the prevailing wages in the area. The Secretary of Labor has the authority to make this determination, and the prevailing wage is often the average local union rate. Davis-Bacon has come under fire, with critics claiming that it has resulted in excessive construction cost overruns. Critics have also charged that the act is inflationary and obstructs minority hiring because of its limitation of one apprentice for every three full-time journeymen on a job.

Social Security Act of 1935, as Amended. The Social Security Act established a federal payroll tax to fund unemployment and retirement benefits. The act also set up the Social Security Administration. Employers were required to share equally with employees the cost of old age, survivors, and disability insurance. Employers were required to pay the full cost of unemployment insurance. Unemployment benefits are paid through agencies in each of the fifty states for a minimum period of twenty-six weeks.

Walsh-Healy Act of 1936. The Walsh-Healy Act of 1936 requires companies with federal supply contracts exceeding $10,000 to pay prevailing wages. The act also requires one and a half times the regular pay rate for hours over eight per day or forty per week.

Fair Labor Standards Act of 1938, as Amended. The most significant law affecting compensation is the Fair Labor Standards Act of 1938 (FLSA). The act establishes a minimum wage, requires overtime pay and record keeping, and provides standards for child labor. This act is administered by the Wage and Hour Division of the U.S. Department of Labor (DOL). The basic requirements of the act apply to more than 73 million full-time and part-time workers in the private and public sectors.[8]

The act provided for a minimum wage of not less than $4.25 an hour. It also required overtime payment at the rate of one and one-half times the employee's regular rate after forty hours of work in a 168-hour period. Although most organizations and employees are covered by the act, certain classes of employees are specifically exempt from overtime provisions. However, nonexempt employees, many of whom are paid salaries, must receive overtime pay.

Exempt employees are categorized as executive, administrative, and professional employees and outside salespersons. An executive employee is essentially a manager (such as a production manager) with broad authority over subordinates. An administrative employee, while not a manager, occupies an important staff position in an organization and might have a title such as systems analyst or assistant to the president. A professional employee performs work requiring advanced knowledge in a field of learning, normally acquired through a prolonged course of specialized instruction. This type of employee might have a title such as company physician, legal counsel, or senior statistician. Outside salespeople sell tangible or intangible items away from the employer's place of business. Employees in jobs not conforming to these definitions are considered nonexempt.

Failure to comply with provisions of the FLSA can become very expensive. For example, failure to classify jobs properly as *exempt* or *nonexempt* may result in substantial fines. Not long ago, the Department of Labor and a New Jersey dairy and convenience chain entered a consent decree that required the firm to pay $4.4 million in back wages to 20,000 present and former employees. The firm was charged with violations of overtime and minimum wage provisions. This case emphasizes the critical importance of conducting job analysis and writing accurate job descriptions. In another suit, Burger King was charged with repeated violations of the child labor provisions. The firm was allegedly permitting minors to work more hours than allowed under the FLSA, to work hours restricted under the law, and to work at jobs considered hazardous. These revelations resulted from a DOL crackdown called "Operation Child Watch." During this program, 3,400 investigations were conducted, and approximately 1,400 businesses were found to be in violation of the FLSA.[9]

Equal Pay Act of 1963. The Equal Pay Act of 1963 (an amendment to the FLSA) has also influenced the field of compensation. In 1972, amendments expanded the act to cover employees in executive, administrative, professional, and outside sales force categories, as well as employees in most state and local governments, hospitals, and schools. The purpose of this legislation is to prohibit discrimination in pay on the basis of gender. The act has teeth, as evidenced by the millions of dollars paid to women employees to compensate them for past discriminatory pay policies.

The act applies to all organizations and employees covered by the FLSA, including the exempt categories. The act requires equal pay for equal work for both men and women. *Equal work* is defined as work requiring equal skill, effort, and responsibility that is performed under the same or similar working conditions. The act does not prohibit the establishment of different wage rates based on seniority or a merit system. Also permitted are pay systems based on the quantity or quality of production and differentials based on any factor other than gender. The act's effect has become less significant because a violation of the Equal Pay Act may also be a violation of Title VII of the Civil Rights Act.

Employee Retirement Income Security Act of 1974. Passed in 1974, the Employee Retirement Income Security Act (ERISA) is one of the most complex pieces of federal compensation legislation ever to be passed. The purpose of the act is described as follows:

> It is hereby declared to be the policy of this act to protect . . . the interests of participants in employee benefit plans and their beneficiaries . . . by establishing standards of conduct, responsibility and obligations for fiduciaries of employee benefit plans, and by providing for appropriate remedies, sanctions, and ready access to the federal courts.[10]

Note that the word *protect* is used here because the act does not force employers to create employee benefit plans. It does set standards in the areas of participation, vesting of benefits, and funding for existing and new plans. Numerous existing retirement plans have been altered in order to conform to this legislation.

Consolidated Omnibus Budget Reconciliation Act of 1985 (COBRA). COBRA requires employers to continue specified health insurance coverage at group rates for certain employees and their families following termination of employment. Traditionally, employers receive a tax deduction for expenses paid or incurred for any group health plan. The act does not allow such deductions unless each *qualified beneficiary* under the group health plan who would lose coverage as a result of a *qualifying event* is entitled to elect continuation coverage under the plan within the election period. A qualifying event is (1) termination of the covered employee (except in cases of gross misconduct), (2) a reduction in hours of the covered employee, (3) the death of the covered employee, (4) the divorce or legal separation of the covered employee from his or her spouse, (5) eligibility of the covered employee for Medicare benefits, and (6) a child ceasing to be a dependent. The requirements of COBRA do not apply to a group health plan for any calendar year in which employers employed fewer than 20 employees on a typical business day.

THE JOB AS A DETERMINANT OF FINANCIAL COMPENSATION

The jobs people are given to do are a major determinant of the amount of financial compensation they will receive. Organizations pay for the value they attach to certain duties, responsibilities, and other job-related factors (such as working conditions). Management techniques utilized for determining a job's relative worth include job analysis, job descriptions, and job evaluation.

Job Analysis and Job Descriptions

Before an organization can determine the relative difficulty or value of its jobs, it must first define their content, which it normally does by analyzing jobs. Recall from Chapter 4 that job analysis is the systematic process of determining the skills and knowledge required for performing jobs. Recall, also, that the job description is the primary by-product of job analysis, consisting of a written document that describes job duties and responsibilities. Job descriptions are used for many different purposes, including job evaluation. Job descriptions are essential to all job evaluation methods, and their success depends largely on their accuracy and clarity.

Job Evaluation

Job evaluation is that part of a compensation system in which a firm determines the relative value of one job in relation to another. The basic purpose of job evaluation is to eliminate internal pay inequities that exist because of illogical pay structures. For example, a pay inequity exists if the mailroom supervisor earns more money than the accounting supervisor. More specifically, job evaluation has the potential to do the following:

- Identify the organization's job structure.
- Bring equity and order to the relationships among jobs.
- Develop a hierarchy of job value that can be used to create a pay structure.
- Achieve a consensus among managers and employees regarding jobs and pay within the firm.[11]

The concept of internal pay equity previously discussed is closely related to the purposes of job evaluation. Although individuals may be concerned with external equity, they basically believe that their pay should be commensurate to their contributions relative to the pay and contributions of fellow employees performing comparable work. They quickly become unhappy when they perceive that someone in the organization receives more pay for performing the same or lower level work.

The human resource department is usually responsible for administering job evaluation programs. However, actual job evaluation is typically done by committee. The committee often consists of managers from different functional areas. A typical committee might include the human resource director as chairperson and the vice presidents for finance, production, and marketing. However, the composition of the committee usually depends on the type and level of the jobs that are being evaluated. In all instances, it is important for the committee to keep personalities out of the evaluation process and to remember it is the job that should be evaluated, not the person(s) performing the job.

Small- and medium-sized organizations often lack job evaluation expertise and may elect to use an outside consultant. When employing a qualified consultant, management should require that the consultant develop an internal job evaluation program and train company employees to administer it properly.

Organizations use four basic job evaluation methods: ranking, classification, factor comparison, and point. There are innumerable variations of these methods.[12] A firm often chooses one method and modifies it to fit its particular needs. The ranking and classification methods are nonquantitative, whereas the factor comparison and point methods are quantitative approaches.

Ranking Method. The simplest of the four job evaluation methods is the ranking method. In the **ranking method**, the raters examine the description of each job being evaluated and arrange the jobs in order according to their value to the company. The procedure is essentially the same as that discussed in Chapter 11 regarding the ranking method for performance appraisal. The only difference is that jobs, not people, are being evaluated. The first step in this method—as with all the methods—is conducting job analysis and writing job descriptions.

Classification Method. The **classification method** involves defining a number of classes or grades to describe a group of jobs. In evaluating jobs by this method, the raters compare the job description with the class description. The class description that most closely agrees with the job description determines the classification for that job. For example, in evaluating the job of word processing clerk, the description might include these duties:

1. Data enter letters from prepared drafts.
2. Address envelopes.
3. Deliver completed correspondence to unit supervisor.

Assuming that the remainder of the job description includes similar routine work, this job would most likely be placed in the lowest job class.

The best-known example of the classification method is the federal government's civil service system. This system originally had eighteen grades

(GS-1 to GS-18). At the bottom of the scale (GS-1), the nature and typical duties of the job are very simple and routine. Jobs become progressively more difficult through GS-18, which involves high level executive tasks. The federal government now has a single gradeless structure called the Senior Executive Service (SES), which has replaced the super grades GS-16 to GS-18.[13]

Clearly defining grade descriptions for many diverse jobs is difficult. For this reason, the federal government has implemented a Factor Evaluation System (FES). This system combines three methods of job evaluation: ranking, factor comparison, and point. However, the FES is not the only job evaluation plan used within the federal government. As with private industry, the government's approach is to select and adapt systems according to specific needs.[14]

Factor Comparison Method. The factor comparison method is somewhat more complex than the two previously discussed qualitative methods. In the **factor comparison method**, raters need not keep the entire job in mind as they evaluate; instead, they make decisions on separate aspects, or factors, of the job. A basic underlying assumption is that there are five universal job factors:

- Mental requirements, which reflect mental traits, such as intelligence, reasoning, and imagination.
- Skills, which pertain to facility in muscular coordination and training in the interpretation of sensory impressions.
- Physical requirements, which involve sitting, standing, walking, lifting, and so on.
- Responsibilities, which cover such areas as raw materials, money, records, and supervision.
- Working conditions, which reflect the environmental influences of noise, illumination, ventilation, hazards, and hours.[15]

The committee first ranks each of the selected benchmark jobs on the relative degree of difficulty for each of the five factors. The committee then allocates the total pay rates for each job to each factor based on the importance of the respective factor to the job. This step is probably the most difficult to explain satisfactorily to employees because the decision is highly subjective.

A job comparison scale, reflecting rankings and money allocations, is developed next (see Figure 12-3). All jobs shown, except for programmer analyst, are original benchmark jobs. The scale is then used to rate other jobs in the group being evaluated. The raters compare each job, factor by factor, with those appearing on the job comparison scale. Then, they place the jobs on the chart in an appropriate position. For example, assume that the committee is evaluating the job of programmer analyst. The committee determines that this job has fewer mental requirements than that of systems analyst but more than those of programmer. The job would then be placed on the chart between these two jobs at a point agreed on by the committee. In this example, the committee evaluated the mental requirements factor at

	Mental	Skill	Physical	Responsibility	Working Conditions
$4.00	Systems Analyst			Systems Analyst	
3.80	(Programmer Analyst)				
3.50	Programmer				
3.00				Programmer	
2.50	Console Operator	Data Entry Clerk Console Operator Programmer			
2.00		Systems Analyst		Console Operator	
1.50	Data Entry Clerk			Data Entry Clerk	Data Entry Clerk Console Operator Systems Analyst Programmer
1.00			Data Entry Clerk Systems Analyst Programmer Console Operator		
.50					
.00					

FIGURE 12-3 Job Comparison Scale

$3.80 (a point between the $4.00 and $3.40 values that had been allocated to the benchmark jobs of systems analyst and programmer, respectively). The committee repeats this procedure for the remaining four factors and then for all jobs to be evaluated. Adding the values of the five factors for each job yields the total value for the job.

The factor comparison method provides a systematic approach to job evaluation. However, at least two problems with it should be noted. The assumption that the five factors are universal has been questioned because certain factors may be more appropriate to some job groups than others. Also, while the steps are not overly complicated, they are somewhat detailed and may be difficult to explain.

Point Method. In the **point method**, raters assign numerical values to specific job components, and the sum of these values provides a quantitative

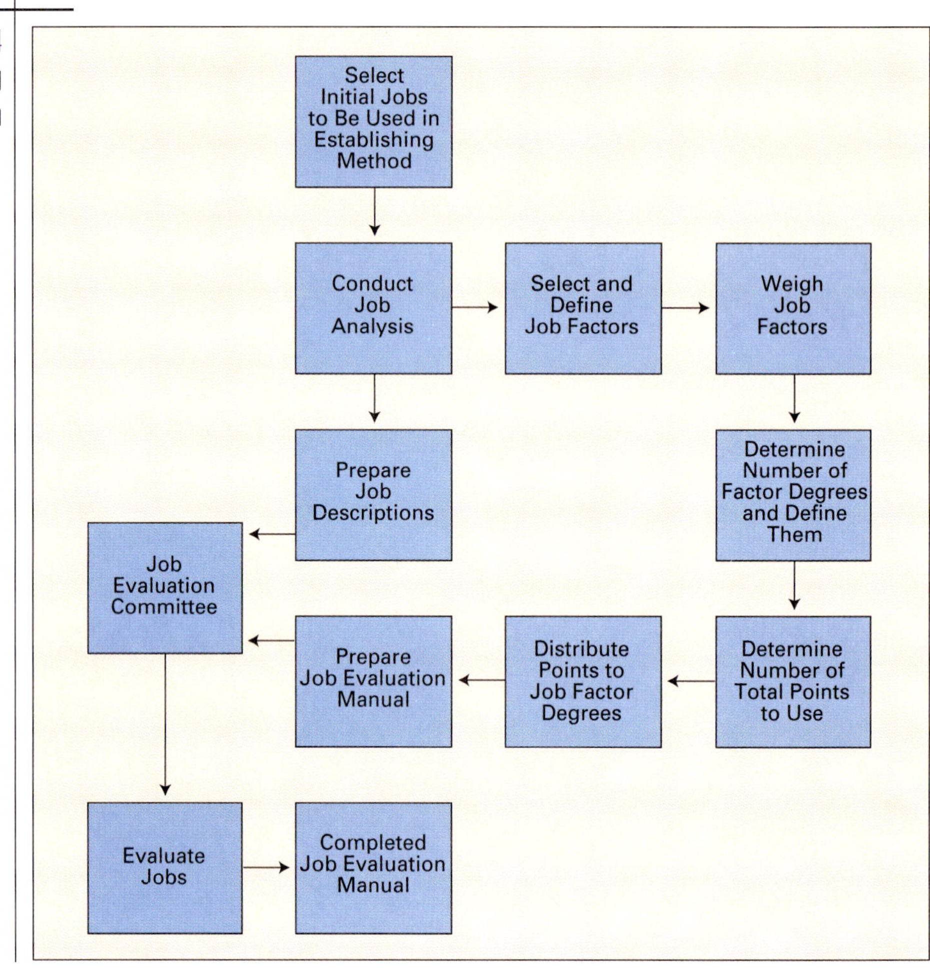

FIGURE 12-4
Procedure for Establishing the Point Method of Job Evaluation

assessment of a job's relative worth.[16] Many job evaluation plans in use today by large and small firms are some variation of the point method.

The point method requires selection of job factors according to the nature of the specific group of jobs being evaluated. Normally, organizations develop a separate plan for each group of similar jobs (job clusters) in the company. Production jobs, clerical jobs, and sales jobs are examples of job clusters. The procedure for establishing a point method is illustrated in Figure 12-4. After determining the group of jobs to be studied, analysts conduct job analysis and write job descriptions. The job evaluation committee will later use these descriptions as the basis for making evaluation decisions.

Next, the analysts select and define the factors to be used in measuring job value. These factors become the standards used for the evaluation of jobs. They can best be identified by individuals who are thoroughly familiar with the content of the jobs under consideration. Education, experience, job knowledge, mental effort, physical effort, responsibility, and working conditions are examples of factors typically used. Each factor should be significant in helping to differentiate jobs. Factors that exist in equal amounts in all jobs obviously would not serve this purpose. As an example, in evaluating a company's clerical jobs, the working conditions factor would be of little value in differentiating jobs if all jobs in the cluster had approximately the same working conditions. The number of factors used varies with the job cluster under consideration. It is strictly a subjective judgment made by the committee.

The committee must establish factor weights according to their relative importance in the jobs to be evaluated. For example, if experience is considered quite important for a particular job cluster, this factor might be weighted as much as 35 percent. Physical effort (if used at all as a factor in an office cluster) would likely be low—perhaps less than 10 percent.

The next consideration is to determine the number of degrees for each job factor and define each degree. Degrees represent the number of distinct levels associated with a particular factor. The number of degrees needed for each factor depends on job requirements. If a particular cluster required virtually the same level of formal education (a high school diploma, for example)—a smaller number of degrees would be appropriate compared to some jobs in the cluster that required advanced degrees.

The committee then determines the total number of points to be used in the plan. The number may vary, but 500 or 1,000 points may work well. The use of a smaller number of points (for example, 50) would not likely provide the proper distinctions among jobs, whereas a larger number (such as 50,000) would be unnecessarily cumbersome. The total number of points in a plan indicates the maximum points that any job could receive.

The next step is to distribute point values to job factor degrees (see Table 12-1). As you can see, factor 1 (education) has five degrees, factor 2 (responsibility) has four, factor 3 (physical effort) has five, and factor 4 (working conditions) has three. Maximum points for each factor are easily calculated by multiplying the total points in the system by the assigned weights. For example, the maximum points any job could receive for education would be 250 (50 percent weight multiplied by 500 points). If the interval between factors is to be a constant number, points for the minimum degree may take the value of the percentage weight assigned to the factor.

TABLE 12-1
Overview of the Point System (500-Point System)

		DEGREE OF FACTOR				
JOB FACTOR	WEIGHT	1	2	3	4	5
1. Education	50%	50	100	150	200	250
2. Responsibility	30%	30	70	110	150	
3. Physical effort	12%	12	24	36	48	60
4. Working conditions	8%	8	24	40		

For instance, the percentage weight for education is 50 percent, so the minimum number of points would also be fifty. The degree interval may be calculated by subtracting the minimum number of points from the maximum number, and dividing by the number of degrees used minus 1. For example, the interval for factor 1 (education) is:

$$\text{Interval} = \frac{250 - 50}{5 - 1} = 50$$

As you can see in Table 12-1, the interval between each degree for education is 50.

This approach to determining the number of points for each degree is referred to as *arithmetic progression*. An arithmetic progression is simple to understand and explain to employees. In the example, it is assumed that the factors have been defined so that the intervals between the degrees are equal. However, if this is not the case, another method, such as a geometric progression, may be more appropriate.

The next step involves preparing a job evaluation manual. Although there is no standard format, the manual often contains an introductory section, factor and degree definitions, and job descriptions. As a final step, the job evaluation committee then evaluates jobs in each cluster by comparing each job description with the factors in the job evaluation manual. Point plans have been criticized for the amount of time and effort required to design them and for supporting traditional bureaucratic management.[17] However, a redeeming feature of the method is that, once developed, the plan may be used over a long period of time. The procedure for using an established point method is presented in Figure 12-5. As new jobs are created and the contents of old jobs substantially changed, job analysis must be conducted, and job descriptions rewritten. The job evaluation committee evaluates the jobs and updates the manual. Only when job factors change, or for some reason the weights assigned become inappropriate, does the plan become obsolete.

The Hay Guide Chart-Profile Method (Hay Plan).[18] A highly refined version of the point method is the **Hay guide chart-profile method**. The Hay Plan uses the factors of know-how, problem solving, accountability, and, where appropriate, working conditions. Point values are assigned to these factors to determine the final point profile for any job.

Know-how is the total of all knowledge and skills needed for satisfactory job performance. It has three dimensions: the amount of practical, specialized, or scientific knowledge required; the ability to coordinate many functions; and the ability to deal with and motivate people effectively.

Problem solving is the degree of original thinking required by the job for analyzing, evaluating, creating, reasoning, and making conclusions. Problem solving has two dimensions: the thinking environment in which problems are solved (from strict routine to abstractly defined), and the thinking challenge presented by the problems (from repetitive to uncharted). Problem solving is expressed as a percentage of know-how, since people use what they know to think and make decisions.

Accountability is the responsibility for action and accompanying consequences. Accountability has three dimensions: the degree of freedom the job incumbent has to act, the job impact on end results, and the extent of the monetary impact of the job.

The Hay Plan is an extremely popular approach to determining compensation. It is used by some 5,000 employers worldwide, including 130 of the 500 largest U.S. corporations.[19] The popularity of the Hay Plan gives it an important advantage: It facilitates job comparison between firms. Thus, the method serves to determine both internal and external equity.

THE EMPLOYEE AS A DETERMINANT OF FINANCIAL COMPENSATION

In addition to the organization, the labor market, and the job, factors related to the employee are also essential in determining pay equity. We discuss each of these factors in this section.

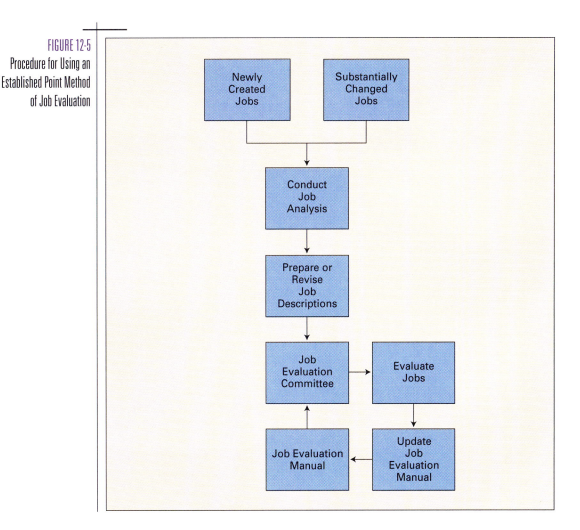

FIGURE 12-5
Procedure for Using an Established Point Method of Job Evaluation

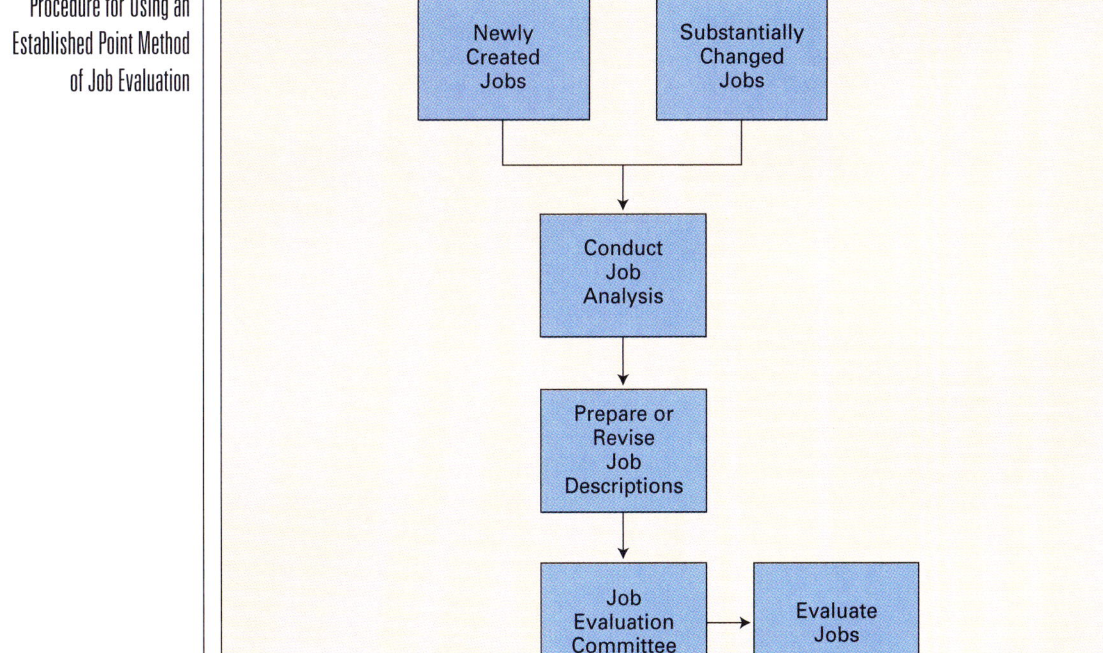

There are many factors related to the employee that have a major impact in determining financial compensation.

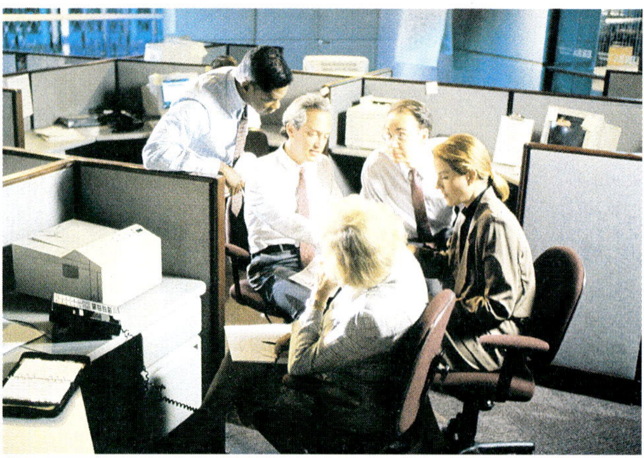

Pay for Performance

Rewarded behavior tends to be repeated. What you reward is generally what you get. It has been stated that the greatest obstacle to the success of today's organizations is that firms are not rewarding the behavior they need.[20] With increasing domestic and international competition, a high level of performance from each employee is essential. For this reason, pay for performance is spreading fast, especially for middle managers. Such plans are now used for some employees at seven out of ten large U.S. firms.[21] While senior executives have their compensation tied to overall corporate results and factory workers often participate in gain-sharing bonuses, middle managers and other workers between the executive suite and the factory floor are often not provided with similar incentives. Now, such companies as AT&T and General Mills are using pay for performance to get impressive results from these employees.

Competitive pressures are bringing about changes even in Japan, where historically people work as a group and the achievers often carry the laggards. A survey of 500 companies found that 14.6 percent had merit pay systems in 1992, up from 10.4 percent a year earlier. Some Japanese companies are departing from seniority-based pay systems and introducing merit pay, in which those who perform better are paid more. Currently, most of these firms are limiting the system to managers. The rationale for this change is to save on labor costs and to promote individual accountability. Managers in such firms as Honda, Fujitsu, and Fujisawa Pharmaceutical are writing specific goals and holding employees accountable for meeting them.[22]

The most common type of pay for performance is the annual bonus, which may be tied to the firm's overall performance, the results of a business unit, the manager's individual performance, or a combination of all three. Since 1988, the number of domestic firms offering variable pay to all salaried employees rose from 47 percent to 68 percent. These firms also provide more in incentive compensation than in salary increases. Use of bonuses, in addition to eliciting better performance, also provides an advantage to the employer in that these amounts are not added to base pay; they must be earned each year. This permits a firm to restrict fixed costs while providing an incentive for improved performance.[23] Merit pay increases based on a previous employment period but added perpetually to base pay are difficult to justify. One executive proposed that merit pay should consist of an increased amount of salary in exchange for an employee promise to perform satisfactory future work of a specified and mutually agreed upon complexity.[24] The apparent point is that past performance cannot be motivated.

Some of the advantages that have been cited for using performance-based pay include the following[25]:

- Increases job satisfaction.
- Increases productivity.
- Reduces avoidable absenteeism.
- Decreases voluntary turnover.
- Improves the quality of the employee mix.

Top performers are attracted to firms that base pay on performance. At Continental Bank of Chicago—in an uncommon practice for the financial services industry—commercial bankers are paid bonuses based on performance. Their HR head claims, "We're attracting far more entrepreneurial people."[26]

A downside to the use of bonuses based on organizational performance occurs when overall business performance turns sour. Such a plan was abandoned at a division of DuPont several years ago. When profits declined and paychecks shrunk, the firm was pressured by employees to revert to its previous system. Another problem encountered with pay for performance involves the amount of money firms use. When, for example, mediocre performance is rewarded with a 3 percent increase and superior performance receives 5 percent, there is no real incentive to be *superior.* The failure to differentiate adequately among performance levels may explain why some organizations are unhappy with the results of their pay for performance plans.

A prerequisite for any pay system tied to performance is a sound performance appraisal program. In such cases, an organization must have a valid means of determining varying performance levels. Difficulties associated with this requirement may also explain problems some firms have with pay for performance programs.

While across-the-board dollar or percentage pay increases are still common, this approach is slowly losing ground. Compensation increases are to a greater extent now being based on other factors, such as achievement of performance goals.

Seniority

The length of time an employee has been associated with the company, division, department, or job is referred to as *seniority*. While management generally prefers performance as the primary basis for compensation changes, labor unions tend to favor seniority. They believe the use of seniority provides an objective and fair basis for pay increases. Many union leaders believe performance evaluation systems are too subjective and permit management to reward favorite employees arbitrarily.

An acceptable performance-seniority compromise might be to permit employees to receive pay increases to the midpoints of their pay grades on the basis of seniority. The rationale is that workers performing at an acceptable level should eventually receive the average wage or salary of their pay grades. However, progression beyond the midpoint should be based on performance. This practice would permit only the outstanding performers to reach the maximum rate for the grade, and it reflects the initial rationale for rate ranges.

Skill-Based Pay

Most compensation systems focus on the value of jobs that have been evaluated to determine their relative worth to the organization, so that they can be priced accordingly. *Skill-based pay*, or pay for knowledge, is a system that compensates employees on the basis of job-related skills and knowledge they possess, not for their job titles. It is one of the fastest growing innovations in the United States; in fact, it is estimated that more than 50 percent of all Fortune 500 companies use skill-based pay with at least some employees.[27] The purpose of this approach is to encourage employees to gain additional skills that will increase their value to the organization and improve its competitive position. Today's downsizing and elimination of many middle management jobs have left fewer promotional opportunities. Room for growth needs to be possible within jobs, and employees should be motivated by factors other than promotions and titles.

McDonnell Douglas Helicopter Company, in Mesa, Arizona, determined that their automatic wage progression system was not working well. In developing an alternative—a pay for skills program—they found that the program should be done by teams rather than individuals. The Implementation Team was multidisciplinary and included a compensation specialist, an organizational development expert, a trainer, a systems analyst and an employee relations professional. The purpose of this team was to provide leadership, create guidelines, facilitate the development process, and coordinate plan approvals. Its first task was to establish the structure for the Development Teams, which were formed for each job family and involved both hourly employees and managers. The purpose of these teams included identifying relevant skills, determining how these skills would be verified, and deciding the type of training required. A majority of employees and managers at McDonnell Douglas have positive feelings about the new program, which has resulted in productivity improvements greater than anticipated.[28]

When employees obtain additional job relevant skills, both individuals and the departments they serve may benefit. Employees may receive both tangible and intangible rewards: pay increases, job security, greater mobility, and the satisfaction of being more valuable. Acquiring additional skills also allows employees the opportunity to increase their earnings without the necessity of being moved permanently to a higher level job. This factor gains additional importance in a highly competitive environment in which promotional opportunities are more limited than in the past. Organizational units are provided with a greater degree of versatility in dealing with absenteeism and turnover.

Skill-based pay is often used with autonomous work groups or other job enrichment programs. A high commitment to human resource development is necessary to implement such a program successfully. In addition, employees involved in skill-based pay programs must have the desire to grow and increase their knowledge and skills.

While skill-based pay appears to have advantages for both employer and employee, there are some challenges for management. Adequate training opportunities must be provided or else the system can become a demotivator. Since research has revealed that it takes an average of only three years for a worker to reach a maximum level in a skill-based pay system, what will keep employees motivated? One answer has been coupling the plan with a pay for performance system. An additional challenge associated with skill-based pay is that payroll costs will escalate. It is conceivable that a firm could have, in addition to high training and development costs, a very expensive workforce possessing an excess of skills.[29] However, a survey conducted by Towers Perrin indicated that more than 70 percent of the employers surveyed reported lower operating costs and other significant benefits were achieved from their pay for skills programs.[30]

Experience

Regardless of the nature of the task, experience has great potential for enhancing a person's ability to perform. This potential can be realized if the experience acquired is positive. Knowledge of the basics is usually a prerequisite for enabling experience to be effective. This is true for a person starting to play golf, learn a foreign language, or manage people in organizations. People who express pride in their long tenure as managers may be justified in their sentiments but only if their experience has been positive. Those who have been bull-of-the-woods autocrats for a dozen years or so would likely not find their experience highly valued by a Malcolm Baldrige Award winning firm. Nevertheless, experience is often indispensable for gaining the insights necessary for performing many tasks.

Employees are often compensated on the basis of their experience. This practice is justified if the experience has been positive and is relevant to the job to be performed.

Membership in the Organization

Some components of individual financial compensation are given to employees without regard to the particular job they perform or their level of productivity. These rewards are provided to all employees simply because they are members of the organization. For example, an average performer occupying a job in pay grade 1 may receive the same number of vacation days, the same amount of group life insurance, and the same reimbursement for educational expenses as a superior employee working in a job classified in pay grade 10. In fact, the worker in pay grade 1 may get more vacation time if he or she has been with the firm longer. Rewards based on organizational membership are intended to maintain a high degree of stability in the workforce and to recognize loyalty.

Potential

Potential is useless if it is never realized. However, organizations do pay some individuals based on their potential. In order to attract talented young people to the firm, the overall compensation program must appeal to those with no experience or any immediate ability to perform difficult tasks. Many young employees are paid well because they have the potential to become a first-line supervisor, manager of compensation, vice president of marketing, or possibly even CEO.

College graduates typically do not have significant business experience for employment managers to examine. Lacking such a record, organizations turn elsewhere for factors to predict the success of the graduate. Grades in college may be considered if they can be shown to be job relevant. Of course, other factors might also indicate potential. Student employment of virtually any type is considered positive by many employers because of the opportunity it provides for displaying important job relevant behaviors. Information may also be sought about leadership performance in student professional or social organizations.

Political Influence

Political influence is a factor that obviously should not be used to determine financial compensation. However, to deny that it exists would be unrealistic. It is disheartening to hear someone say, "It's not what you know, it's who you know." Yet there is an unfortunate element of truth in that statement. To varying degrees in business, government, and not-for-profit organizations, a person's *pull* or political influence may sway pay and promotion decisions. It may be natural for a manager to favor a friend or relative in granting a pay increase or promotion. Whether it is natural or not, if the person receiving the reward is not truly deserving, this fact will soon become known throughout the work group. This practice can have a devastating impact on employee morale. Employees want—and are demanding—equitable treatment. However, there is nothing equitable about a person receiving a promotion and/or pay increase based strictly on politics. The practice should be strictly avoided.

Luck

You have undoubtedly heard the expression, "It certainly helps to be in the right place at the right time." There is more than a little truth in this statement as it relates to a person's compensation. Positions are continually coming open in firms. Realistically, there is no way for managers to foresee many of the changes that occur. For instance, who could have known that the purchasing agent, Joe Flynch, an apparently healthy middle-aged man, would suddenly die of a heart attack? Although the company may have been grooming several managers for Joe's position, none may be capable of immediately assuming the increased responsibility. The most experienced person, Tommy Loy, has been with the company only six months. Tommy had been an assistant buyer for a competitor for four years. Because of his experience, Tommy receives the promotion and the increased financial compensation. Tommy Loy was lucky; he was in the right place at the right time.

When asked to explain their most important reasons for success and effectiveness as managers, two chief executives responded candidly. One said, "Success is being at the right place at the right time and being recognized as having the ability to make timely decisions. It also depends on having good rapport with people, a good operating background, and the knowledge of how to develop people." The other replied, "My present position was attained by being in the right place at the right time with a history of getting the job done." Both executives recognize the significance of luck combined with the ability to perform. Their experiences lend support to the idea that luck works primarily for the efficient employee.

JOB PRICING

The primary considerations in pricing jobs are the organization's policies, the labor market, and the job itself. If allowances are to be made for individual factors, they too must be considered. Recall that the process of job evaluation results in a job hierarchy. It might reveal, for example, that the job of senior accountant is more valuable than the job of computer operator, which, in turn, is more valuable than the job of senior invoice clerk. At this point, the relative value of these jobs to the company is known, but their absolute value is not. Placing a dollar value on the worth of a job is called **job pricing**. It takes place after the job has been evaluated, and the relative value of each job in the organization has been determined. However, as shown in Figure 12-2, additional factors should be considered in determining the job's absolute value. Firms often use pay grades and pay ranges in the job pricing process.

Pay Grades

A **pay grade** is the grouping of similar jobs to simplify the job pricing process. It is much more convenient for organizations to price fifteen pay grades rather than 200 separate jobs. The simplicity of this approach is similar to a college or university's practice of grouping grades of 90 to 100 into an *A* category, grades of 80 to 89 into a *B*, and so on. A false implication of preciseness is also avoided. While job evaluation plans may be systematic, none is scientific.

Plotting jobs on a scatter diagram is often useful in determining the appropriate number of pay grades. In Figure 12-6, each dot on the scatter diagram represents one job as it relates to pay and evaluated points, which reflect its worth. By following this procedure, it is likely that a certain point

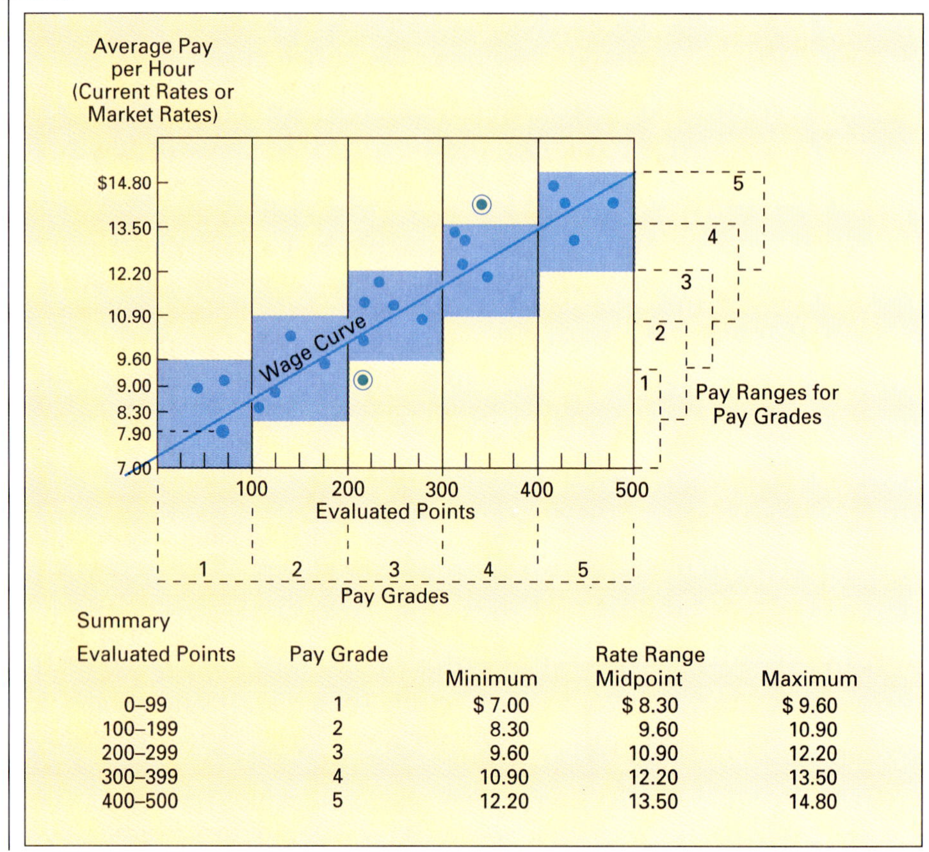

Summary

Evaluated Points	Pay Grade	Minimum	Rate Range Midpoint	Maximum
0–99	1	$ 7.00	$ 8.30	$ 9.60
100–199	2	8.30	9.60	10.90
200–299	3	9.60	10.90	12.20
300–399	4	10.90	12.20	13.50
400–500	5	12.20	13.50	14.80

FIGURE 12-6
Scatter Diagram of Evaluated Jobs Illustrating the Wage Curve, Pay Grades, and Rating Ranges

spread will work satisfactorily (100 points used in this illustration). Each dot represents one job but may involve dozens of individuals who fill that one job. The large dot at the lower left represents the job of data entry clerk, which was evaluated at 75 points. The data entry clerk's hourly rate of $7.90 represents either the average wage currently being paid for the job or its market rate. This decision depends on how management wants to price its jobs.

A **wage curve** (or pay curve) is the fitting of plotted points in order to create a smooth progression between pay grades. The line that is drawn to minimize the distance between all dots and the line—a line of best fit—may be straight or curved. However, when the point system is used (normally considering only one job cluster), a straight line is the usual result, as in Figure 12-6. This wage line can be drawn either freehand or by using a statistical method. Some compensation specialists use the former because it is simpler.

Pay Ranges

After pay grades have been determined, the next decision is whether all individuals performing the same job will receive equal pay or whether pay ranges will be used. A **pay range** includes a minimum and maximum pay rate with enough variance between the two to allow for significant pay difference. Pay ranges are generally preferred over equal pay because they allow employees to be paid according to length of service and performance. Pay then serves as a positive incentive. When pay ranges are used, a method must be developed to advance individuals through the range. Although many organizations grant pay increases based on seniority, others hold the view that only outstanding performers should be allowed to advance to the top of their pay ranges.

Referring again to Figure 12-6, note that anyone can readily determine the minimum, midpoint, and maximum pay rates per hour for each of the five pay grades. For example, for pay grade 5, the minimum rate is $12.20, the midpoint is $13.50, and the maximum is $14.80. The minimum rate is normally the *hiring in* rate that a person receives when joining the firm. The maximum pay rate represents the maximum that an employee can receive for that job, regardless of how well the job is performed. A person at the top of a pay grade will have to be promoted to a job in a higher pay grade in order to receive a pay increase unless (1) an across-the-board adjustment is made, or (2) the job is reevaluated and placed in a higher pay grade. This situation has caused numerous managers some anguish as they attempt to explain the pay system to an employee who is doing a tremendous job but is at the top of a pay grade. Consider this situation:

> Everyone in the department realized that Martha Wilson was the best secretary in the company. At times, she appeared to do the job of three secretaries. Bill Merideth, Martha's supervisor, was especially impressed. Recently, he had a discussion with the human resource manager to see what could be done to get a raise for Martha. After Bill described the situation, the human resource manager's only reply was, "Sorry, Bill. Martha is already at the top of her pay grade. There is nothing you can do except have her job upgraded or promote her to another position."

Situations such as Martha's present managers with a perplexing problem. Many would be inclined to make an exception to the system and give Martha a salary increase. However, this action would violate a basic principle, which holds that every job in the organization has a maximum value, regardless of how well it is performed. In addition, making exceptions to the compensation plan could soon result in widespread pay inequities.

The rate ranges established should be large enough to provide an incentive to do a better job. At times, pay differentials may need to be greater to be meaningful, especially at higher levels. There may be logic in having the rate range become increasingly wide at each consecutive level (see Figure 12-7). Consider, for example, what a $100 per month salary increase would mean to a file clerk earning $1,200 per month (an 8.3 percent increase) and to a senior cost accountant earning $3,000 per month (a 3.3 percent increase). Assuming an inflation rate of 5 percent, the file clerk's real pay would increase somewhat while the cost accountant would obviously fall behind.

FIGURE 12-7
Rate Ranges on Percentage Spreads

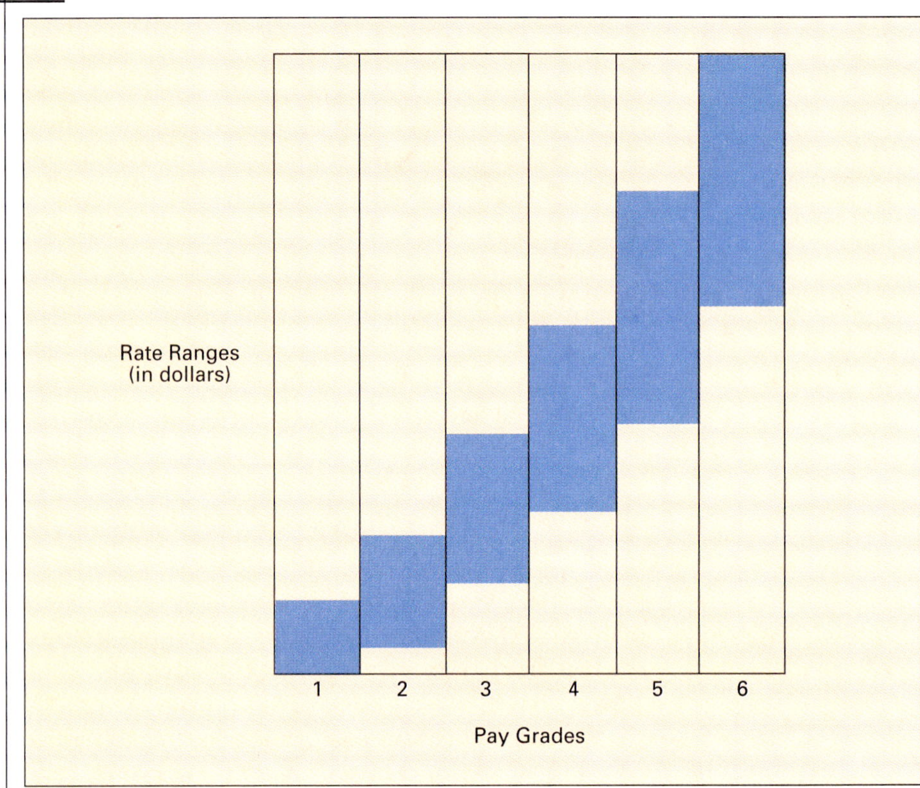

Some workplace conditions do not favor pay ranges. For instance, in a situation in which all or most jobs are routine, with little opportunity for employees to vary their productivity, a single, or fixed, rate system may be more appropriate. When single rates are used, everyone working the same job receives the same pay, regardless of seniority or productivity.

Adjusting Pay Rates

When pay ranges have been determined and jobs assigned to pay grades, it may become obvious that some jobs are overpaid and others underpaid. Underpaid jobs are normally brought to the minimum of the pay range as soon as possible. Referring again to Figure 12-6, you can see that a job evaluated at about 225 points and having a rate of $9.00 per hour is represented by a circled dot immediately below pay grade 3. The job was determined to be difficult enough to fall in pay grade 3 (200-299 points). However, employees working in the job are being paid 60 cents per hour less than the minimum for the pay grade ($9.60 per hour). Two jobs in pay grade 2 are paid more than $9.00. Good management practice would be to correct this inequity as rapidly as possible by placing the job in the proper pay grade and increasing the pay of those who work that job.

Overpaid jobs present more of a problem. An overpaid job for pay grade 4 is illustrated in Figure 12-6 (note the circled dot above pay grade 4). Employees in this job earn $14.00 per hour, or 50 cents more than the maximum for the pay grade. This type of overpayment, as well as the kind of underpayment discussed above is referred to as a *red circle rate*.

An ideal solution to the problem of an overpaid job is to promote the employee. This might be a reasonable approach if the employee is qualified for a higher rated job and a job opening is available. Another possibility would be to bring the job rate and employee pay into line through a pay cut. This type of action may appear logical, but it is not consistent with good management practice. This action would punish employees for a situation they did not create. Somewhere in between these two possible solutions is a third: To freeze the rate until across-the-board pay increases bring the job into line. If the past few decades are an indication of the future, rising pay levels will eventually solve this problem.

A GLOBAL PERSPECTIVE

Designing total compensation programs for expatriates and local nationals is especially ticklish. In the United States, many firms have a single policy that covers all employees. However, firms overseas may have numerous standards depending on the employee's situation. For example, allowances may be given for the number of children in a household, or an allowance may be provided for transportation if the employee lives a certain distance from the workplace but not if they live close by. Base pay may appear to be low at first glance, but the benefits package is often much better when allowances for social conditions are considered.[31]

HRM IN ACTION

—A COMPENSATION PROBLEM?

Lynn Marlow, the data processing manager for National Insurance Company, was perplexed as she spoke to Graham Johnston, the human resource manager. Lynn said, "I have trouble recruiting programmers and systems analysts. The data processing center employs a total of forty-five people, including ten programmers and four systems analysts. During the past six months, seven programmers and three systems analysts have quit. The people who left were experienced and competent. Their major reasons for leaving the company were better salaries and greater advancement opportunities elsewhere. Because of the shortage of experienced programmers and analysts, the replacements hired by the company possess little prior experience. This situation has caused the data processing center to run continuously behind schedule."

How should Graham respond?

Several questions arise when considering compensation levels for global employees. In the case of alliances, should the compensation system of the partners be linked, or will they be synthesized into a common system? Will compensation rates be adjusted for local markets or tied to similar jobs in the partner's home country? Often each partner in a venture has an established pay policy, and those policies differ. At the very least, partners in such ventures should reach an agreement on the broad objectives of a compensation program for employees.[32]

Global compensation programs should be designed to establish and maintain a consistent relationship between the compensation of employees in all international alliances. The programs should also maintain compensation levels that are reasonable in relation to the practices of leading competitors. Failure to establish a uniform compensation policy can result in predictably adverse results, especially for employees doing the same jobs. Such compensation systems will inevitably lead to low morale, motivational problems, and less productive employees.[33] Apparently the financial compensation provided to most expatriate managers is satisfactory. According to a survey by Richard A. Guzzo, 80 percent of the respondents were satisfied with their financial perks. The same respondents, however, were not pleased with their *nonfinancial* support, such as properly preparing them for overseas assignments and developing an appropriate career path.[34]

OTHER COMPENSATION ISSUES

Several issues that affect compensation deserve special mention. These issues include comparable worth, pay secrecy, and pay compression. We will examine these issues next.

Comparable Worth

The comparable worth, or pay equity, theory extends the concept of the Equal Pay Act. While the act requires equal pay for equal work, comparable worth advocates prefer a broader interpretation: requiring equal pay for comparable worth even if market rates and job duties differ. **Comparable worth** requires the value for dissimilar jobs, such as company nurse and welder, to be compared under some form of job evaluation, and pay rates for both jobs to be assigned according to their evaluated worth. Although the Supreme Court has ruled that comparable worth is not required by law, the 1992 Democratic platform endorsed the concept.[35] In addition, a number of state and local governments have passed legislation that mandates pay equity.

The basic premise of comparable worth is that jobs traditionally held by women are paid less than those traditionally held by men, even though both types of jobs may make equal contributions to the organization's goals. Specifically, as of 1992, women working full time earned 75 percent of men's earnings.[36] Jobs that have historically been filled by women pay less, and when employers use market data for establishing pay rates, the pay differentials are perpetuated.

Opponents of comparable worth contend that the earnings gap reflects an overall statistic and does not compare the earnings of two people performing the same job. They state that the gender difference is explainable by such variables as education, job experience, and women's tendency to rank pay as less important than flexible scheduling and good working conditions.[37]

Comparable worth detractors note that existing law prohibits employers from paying a woman at a lower rate than a man for doing the same work. A more effective solution, they suggest, would be vigorous enforcement of equal opportunity and equal pay laws. In addition, women should be encouraged to enter nontraditional occupations and be provided with equal access to education, training programs, and employment. Also, efforts should be continued to promote a nondiscriminatory socialization process for children. This view holds that these alternatives, rather than artificially raising the price of labor for special groups, will address the problem of gender discrimination.[38]

Perhaps the greatest fear of implementing comparable worth standards is the cost of replacing market forces of supply and demand with a government-imposed system of job evaluation. Estimates of costs vary, but they range into the billions of dollars per year. Proponents of comparable worth reject market pricing of jobs because they believe that markets reflect bias against occupations traditionally held by women.

The goal of nondiscriminatory pay practices is one that every organization should seek to achieve for ethical and legal reasons. Whether comparable worth is an appropriate solution remains to be seen.

Pay Secrecy

Organizations tend to keep their pay rates secret for various reasons. If a firm's compensation plan is illogical, secrecy may indeed be appropriate because only a well-designed system can stand careful scrutiny. An open system would almost certainly require managers to explain the rationale for pay decisions to subordinates.

Secrecy can have negative results, however. If compensation data are not freely communicated to employees, the grapevine will likely do the job. While the grapevine is fast, it sometimes lacks accuracy and can become the source of misinformation and misunderstanding.[39] In addition, managers who are unaware of pay rates in their firm tend to overestimate the pay of managers around them and to underestimate what higher level managers make. Such perceptions destroy much of the motivation intended in a differential pay system and indirectly contribute to turnover.[40]

Ideally, a firm will strive to develop a logical pay system, which reflects both internal and external equity. Employees in the process should participate to the greatest extent feasible. Compensation managers should take the lead in ensuring that employees understand the bases for their pay. Obviously, management cannot make all employees happy. The dissatisfaction and costs associated with a secret pay system, however, seem to make it a highly questionable practice.

Pay Compression

Organizations normally strive for both internal and external pay equity. In practice, however, this is often difficult or even impossible to accomplish.

For example, in order to attract an engineer to a firm, an unusually high salary may have to be paid. Individuals possessing the skills needed to perform this job are in short supply relative to the demand for their services. Therefore these workers, and others in similar situations, are able to command higher salaries.

But how does the hiring of this type of employee affect internal equity? Other jobs within the firm may have greater value to the firm—as determined by job evaluation—but are now paid less than some engineers. In this instance, the firm sacrificed internal equity because it had little choice in the matter, assuming that it had to fill the engineer's job.

Situations of this type may also result in a troublesome problem called pay compression. **Pay compression** occurs when workers perceive that the pay differential between their pay and that of employees in jobs above or below them is too small. It can be created in several ways, including the hiring of new employees at pay rates comparable to, or higher than, those of current employees who have been with the firm for several years. Making pay adjustments at the lower end of the job hierarchy without commensurate adjustments at the top is also a common cause of pay compression.

Pay compression may also result from granting pay increases on a flat cents-per-hour basis over a long period of time. Percentage increases, on the other hand, maintain relative differences in pay rates. The result of compression is usually dissatisfaction on the part of employees in higher level jobs. With a flattened pay curve, there is less financial incentive for employees to strive for promotion.

SUMMARY

Compensation refers to the rewards that individuals receive in return for their labor. Direct financial compensation consists of the pay a person receives in the form of wages, salary, bonuses, and commissions. Indirect financial compensation (benefits) includes all financial rewards that are not included in direct compensation. Nonfinancial compensation is the satisfaction a person receives directly from the job or from the psychological and/or physical job environment. All these types of compensation comprise a total compensation program.

Equity refers to the perception by workers that they are being treated fairly. External equity exists when employees performing jobs within a firm are paid at levels comparable to those paid for similar jobs in other firms. Internal equity exists when employees are paid according to the relative value of their jobs within the organization. Job evaluation is a primary means for determining internal equity. Employee equity exists when individuals performing similar jobs in the same firm are paid according to factors unique to the employee, such as productivity.

Many factors interact with and affect compensation. The organization, the labor market, the job, and the employee all have an impact on determining the individual's financial compensation.

Job evaluation is that part of a compensation system which a firm uses to determine the relative value of its jobs. The basic purpose of job evaluation is to eliminate internal pay inequities that exist because of illogical pay structures. Organizations use four basic job evaluation methods: ranking, classification, factor comparison, and point. The ranking and classification methods are qualitative, whereas the factor comparison and point methods are quantitative approaches.

Placing a dollar value on the worth of a job is called job pricing. Jobs are priced after they have been evaluated and the relative value of each job in the organization has been determined. A pay grade is the grouping of similar jobs to simplify the job pricing process. A pay range includes a minimum and maximum pay rate, with enough variance between the two to allow for significant pay difference. Pay ranges allow employees to be paid according to length of service and performance levels. When pay ranges are used, a method must be developed to advance individuals through the range. Global compensation issues include—in the case of alliances—how the pay systems of partners are to be related. In these situations, an agreement should be reached concerning the broad objectives of the compensation system.

Several issues that affect compensation deserve special mention, including comparable worth, pay secrecy, and pay compression. Comparable worth requires the value for dissimilar jobs to be compared under some form of job evaluation and pay rates to be assigned according to their evaluated worth. Organizations tend to keep their pay rates secret for various reasons. Pay compression occurs when workers perceive that the differential between their pay and that of employees in jobs above or below them is too small.

QUESTIONS FOR REVIEW

1. Define each of the following terms:
   a. *Compensation*
   b. *Direct financial compensation*
   c. *Indirect financial compensation*
   d. *Nonfinancial compensation*
2. Distinguish among external equity, internal equity, employee equity, and team equity.
3. What are the primary determinants of financial compensation? Briefly describe each.
4. Distinguish among a pay follower, a pay leader, and a going-rate organization.
5. How has government legislation affected compensation?
6. Give the primary purpose of job evaluation.
7. Distinguish among the four basic methods of job evaluation: ranking, classification, factor comparison, and point.
8. What is the purpose of job pricing? Discuss this briefly.
9. State the basic procedure for determining pay grades.
10. What is the purpose of establishing pay ranges?
11. Describe the various factors relating to the employee in determining pay and benefits.
12. Describe each of the following concepts:
    a. Comparable worth
    b. Pay secrecy
    c. Pay compression

HRM SIMULATION

The wage rates for your organization are somewhat below the average for the local community. In this simulation, you will be making decisions for five levels of employees. Although decisions concerning the level of wages and benefits are not traditionally the sole responsibility of the human resource manager, the CEO has given your team the responsibility of making compensation decisions, within certain constraints.

Incident G in the *Simulation Players Manual* involves Compensation Plans. Your team has been concerned for quite some time about the turnover rate in your organization. While the rate has improved somewhat, your team believes the cost of turnover is too high, especially for experienced employees. What type of compensation plan will your team recommend?

ABC VIDEO CASE

BALANCING WORK AND FAMILY TAPE 1, NUMBER 2

Now that the baby boom is over, and skilled workers are in such demand, women are entering the workforce in record numbers. A quiet, but dramatic, revolution is occurring in the redefinition of work. Traditional career paths are being replaced, and company benefits are being restructured. Every survey shows that child care is the number one problem for employees. Four thousand employers now offer some form of child care assistance. In one example, five New York based companies pay for a trained worker to go to an employee's home when a child is sick or the normal care arrangements break down. According to Arnold Hiatt of Stride Rite, "Offering child care is not diluting our earnings; in fact, it's improving our earnings." For two decades, Stride Rite's on-site day care has helped the shoe manufacturer attract better employees, reduce turnover, and improve productivity. Stride Rite is now opening a second day care center for those workers who care for elderly relatives. This is the latest company benefit. With the population aging, an increasing number of workers are being faced with the responsibility of caring for aged family members.

The most progressive companies are offering their workers flexibility through work hours, leave, and part-time work. Addressing these issues is necessitated by changing demographics in the labor market. The number of family friendly companies is growing, but most employees do not enjoy any of these benefits. Some companies state that providing these kinds of benefits is too expensive and not equitable, and that business should not be involved in family matters. But, increasingly, these views are considered short sighted. The new demographics are a reality. Companies that do not help employees balance work and family will simply lose out against those companies that do.

HRM INCIDENT 1

—IT'S JUST NOT FAIR!

During a Saturday afternoon golf game with his friend Randy Dean, Harry Neil discovered that his department had hired a recent university grad as a systems analyst—at a starting salary almost as high as Harry's. Although Harry was good natured, he was bewildered and upset. It had taken him five years to become a senior systems analyst and to attain his current salary level at Trimark Data Systems. He had been generally pleased with the company and thoroughly enjoyed his job.

The following Monday morning Harry confronted Dave Edwards, the human resource director, and asked if what he had heard was true. Dave apologetically admitted that it was and attempted to explain the company's situation: "Harry, the market for systems analysts is very tight, and in order for the company to attract qualified prospects, we have to offer a premium starting salary. We desperately needed another analyst, and this was the only way we could get one."

Harry asked Dave if his salary would be adjusted accordingly. Dave answered, "Your salary will be reevaluated at the regular time. You're doing a great job, though, and I'm sure the boss will recommend a raise." Harry thanked Dave for his time but left the office shaking his head and wondering about his future.

Questions

1. Do you think Dave's explanation was satisfactory? Discuss.
2. What action do you believe the company should have taken with regard to Harry?

HRM INCIDENT 2

—JOB EVALUATION: WHO OR WHAT?

David Rhine, compensation manager for Farrington Lingerie Company, was generally relaxed and good natured. Although he was a no-nonsense, competent executive, David was one of the most popular managers in the company. This Friday morning, however, David was not his usual self. As chairperson of the company's job evaluation committee, he had called a late morning meeting at which several jobs were to be considered for reevaluation. The jobs had already been rated and assigned to pay grade 3. But the office manager, Ben Butler, was upset that one of the jobs was not rated higher. To press the issue, Ben had taken his case to two executives who were also members of the job evaluation committee. The two executives (production manager Bill Nelson and general marketing manager Betty Anderson) then requested that the job ratings be reviewed. Bill and Betty supported Ben's side of the dispute, and David was not looking forward to the confrontation that was almost certain to occur.

The controversial job was that of receptionist. Only one receptionist position existed in the company, and it was held by Beth Smithers. Beth had been with the firm twelve years—longer than any of the committee members. She was extremely efficient, and virtually all the executives in the company, including the president, had noticed and commented on her outstanding work. Bill Nelson and Betty Anderson were particularly pleased with Beth because of the cordial manner in which she greeted and accommodated Farrington's customers and vendors, who frequently visited the plant. They felt that Beth projected a positive image of the company.

When the meeting began, Dave said, "Good morning. I know that you're busy, so let's get the show on the road. We have several jobs to evaluate this morning, and I suggest we begin . . . " Before he could finish his sentence, Bill interrupted, "I suggest we start with Beth." Betty nodded in agreement. When David regained his composure, he quietly but firmly asserted, "Bill, we are not here today to evaluate Beth. Her supervisor does that at performance appraisal time. We're meeting to evaluate jobs based on job content. In order to do this fairly, with regard to other jobs in the company, we must leave personalities out of our evaluation." David then proceeded to distribute copies of the receptionist job description to Bill and Betty, who were obviously very irritated.

Questions

1. Do you feel that David was justified in insisting that the job, not the person, be evaluated? Discuss.
2. Do you believe that there is a maximum rate of pay for every job in an organization, regardless of how well the job is being performed? Justify your position.
3. Assuming that Beth is earning the maximum of the range for her pay grade, in what ways can she obtain a salary increase?

DEVELOPING HRM SKILLS

AN EXPERIENTIAL EXERCISE

In the future, one of the key issues concerning pay may be comparable worth. If comparable worth should become federal law, organizations will have to base salaries and wages on job evaluation scores. Salaries and wages will be determined by the requirements of the job itself—skills required, knowledge required, effort required, working conditions, and responsibilities—rather than the workings of the labor market. Then, equal pay for different jobs of the same value will have to be determined not by looking at the *going rate* in the marketplace, but rather at the job's difficulty, importance, and the training required to properly perform it. This exercise has been developed to impart an understanding and appreciation of the concept of comparable worth.

The concept of comparable worth is based on three premises:

1. That it is possible to compare different jobs and establish a *correct pay* relationship for them.
2. That the pay established by the supply and demand of the job market is often inequitable and discriminatory, especially with regard to pay for women.
3. That the government and the courts must intervene to ensure that pay relationships are corrected and made equitable.

Based on Exhibit 1 (which you will be given a copy of) and these three premises, determine the following:

1. Which of the following jobs would you consider *comparable*? (Select a job from the second list, and write it beside the job on the first list to which you feel it *compares*.)
2. What average monthly salary would you assign to each position?

After ten minutes everyone will sign their exhibits and turn them in. Then, three participants with dissimilar comparisons will list their comparisons and salaries on the chalkboard, and the debriefing process will begin.

NOTES

1. Vicki Fuehrer, "Total Reward Strategy: A Prescription for Organizational Survival," *Compensation and Benefits Review* 26 (January-February 1994): 45.

2. George J. Meng, "Link Pay to Job Evaluation," *Personnel Journal* 69 (March 1990): 104.

3. Edward J. Giblin, Geoffrey A. Wiegman, and Frank Sanfilippo, "Bringing Pay Up to Date," *Personnel* 67 (November 1990): 17.

4. George T. Milkovich and Jerry M. Newman, *Compensation*, 4th edition (Homewood, Ill.: Richard D. Irwin, 1993): 3.

5. David W. Belcher and Thomas J. Atchison, *Compensation Administration*, 2nd edition (Englewood Cliffs, N.J.: Prentice Hall, 1987): 127.

6. Joseph E. McKendrick, Jr., "Salary Surveys: Roadmaps for the Volatile Employment Scene of the 1990s," *Management World* 19 (March-April 1990): 18–20.

7. Cyril C. Ling, *The Management of Personnel Relations* (Homewood, Ill.: Richard D. Irwin, 1965): 146–151.

8. Bruce R. Belrose, "Defining Fair Compensation," *Association Management* 42 (October 1990): 64.

9. Jill Kanin-Lovers, "Revisiting the Fair Labor Standards Act," *Journal of Compensation and Benefits* 6 (November-December 1990): 48.

10. *U.S. Statutes at Large* 88, Part I, 93rd Congress, 2nd Session, 1974: 833.

11. Roger J. Plachy, "The Case for Effective Point-Factor Job Evaluation, Viewpoint I," *Personnel* 64 (April 1987): 31.

12. George T. Milkovich and Jerry M. Newman, *Compensation*, 119.

13. Richard I. Henderson, *Compensation Management: Rewarding Performance*, 6th edition (Englewood Cliffs, N.J.: Prentice Hall, 1994): 216.

14. George T. Milkovich and Jerry M. Newman, *Compensation*, 124.

15. John A. Patton, C. L. Littlefield, and Stanley A. Self, *Job Evaluation: Text and Cases*, 3rd edition (Homewood, Ill.: Richard D. Irwin, 1964): 115.

16. Donald L. Caruth, *Compensation Management for Banks* (Boston: Bankers Publishing Company, 1986): 65.

17. Edward E. Lawler III, "What's Wrong with Point-Factor Job Evaluation," *Personnel* 64 (January 1987): 39–40.

18. George T. Milkovich and Jerry M. Newman, *Compensation*, 152–155.

19. Ibid., 135.

20. Tom Brown, "Does Compensation Add Up?" *Industry Week* 239 (August 20, 1990): 13.

21. Denise M. Topolnicki, "To Earn More in 1994, You'll Need to Perform for Your Pay," *Money* 23 (January 1994): 16.

22. Andrew Pollack, "Japanese Starting to Link Pay to Performance, Not Tenure," *New York Times* (October 2, 1993): 1.

23. Shawn Tully, "Your Paycheck Gets Exciting," *Fortune* 126 (November 1, 1993): 83–84.

24. Donald Brookes, "Merit Pay, The Hoax," *HRMagazine* 38 (February 1993): 117.

25. John A. Parnell, "Five Reasons Why Pay Must Be Based on Performance," *Supervision* 52 (February 1991): 7.

26. Shawn Tully, "Your Paycheck Gets Exciting," 96.

27. Shari Caudron, "Master the Compensation Maze," *Personnel Journal* 72 (June 1993): 64F.

28. Bradford A. Johnson and Harry H. Ray, "Employee-Developed Pay System Increases Productivity," *Personnel Journal* 72 (November 1993): 112–118.

29. Shari Caudron, "Master the Compensation Maze," 64G–64I.

30. Survey Report: Skill-Based Pay Can Pay Off," *HR Focus* 69 (October 1991): 6.

31. Stephenie Overman, "Going Global," *HRMagazine* 38 (September 1993): 49.

32. Wayne F. Cascio and Manuel G. Serapio, Jr., "Human Resources Systems in an International Alliance: The Undoing of a Done Deal?" *Organizational Dynamics* 19 (Winter 1991): 70.

33. Ibid., 71.

34. Daniel B. Moskowitz, "How to Cut It Overseas," *International Business* (October 1992): 76, 78.

35. Steven E. Rhoads, "Pay Equity Won't Go Away," *Across the Board* 30 (July-August 1993): 38.

36. Ibid.

37. Ibid.

38. Julie M. Buchanan, "Comparable Worth: Where Is It Headed?" *Human Resources: Journal of the International Association for Personnel Women* 2 (Summer 1985): 12.

39. Dallas Brozik, "The Importance of Money and the Reporting of Salaries," *Journal of Compensation and Benefits* 9 (January/February 1994): 52–63.

40. Edward E. Lawler III, *Pay and Organizational Effectiveness: A Psychological View* (New York: McGraw-Hill, 1971): 174–175, 196–197.

CHAPTER 13

Benefits and Other Compensation Issues

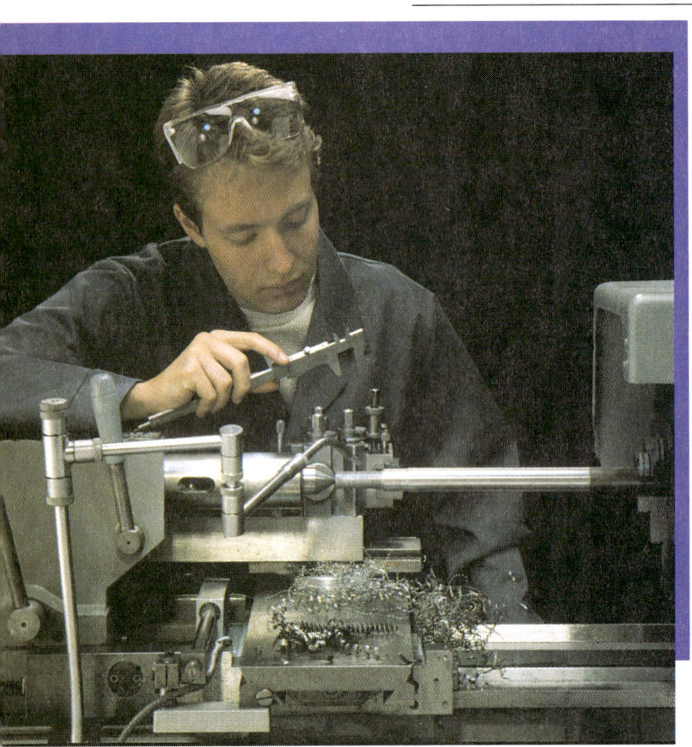

KEY TERMS

Benefits 396
Health Maintenance Organizations (HMOs) 401
Preferred Provider Organizations (PPOs) 401
Capitation 401
Utilization review 402
Defined benefit plan 402
Defined contribution plan 403
401(k) plan 403
Employee stock ownership plan (ESOP) 403
Premium pay 404
Hazard pay 404
Shift differential 404
Incentive compensation 406
Straight piecework plan 407
Standard hour plan 407
Profit sharing 408
Scanlon Plan 410
Stock option plan 412
Perquisites (perks) 412
"Golden parachute" contract 412
Workplace flexibility 418
Flextime 418
Compressed workweek 419
Job sharing 419
Flexible compensation plans 419
Telecommuting 422
Modified retirement 423

CHAPTER OBJECTIVES

1. Define benefits and describe their importance to the total compensation program.
2. Describe legally required and voluntary benefits.
3. Explain the various incentive compensation programs that are available.
4. Describe how compensation for executives, professionals, and sales representatives is determined.
5. Describe compensation in growth companies and explain the many forms of nonfinancial compensation that employees are beginning to expect.
6. Explain what is meant by the term nonfinancial compensation and describe what companies are doing to improve workplace flexibility.

John Hicks, a college dropout, is a senior credit clerk at Ajax Manufacturing Company. A bright young man, John has been with Ajax for four years. He has received excellent performance ratings in each of the several positions he has held with the firm. However, during his last appraisal interview, John's supervisor implied that promotion to a higher level job would require additional formal education. Because John appeared to be receptive to the idea, his supervisor suggested that he check with human resources to learn the details of Ajax's educational assistance policy.

Arnold Anderson, Bob Minnis, and Mason Kearby are all employed as shipping clerks for Mainstreet Furniture Company. Arnold and Bob are energetic young people who consistently work hard each day. Both earn about $8.50 per hour. Mason is a "good ole boy" who spends most of his time flipping quarters with dock workers and talking with anyone who will listen. Yesterday, work was piling up in the department, and Arnold and Bob were working furiously to keep up. Mason was nowhere to be found. "Arnold," Bob said disgustedly, "the pay here just isn't fair. We do twice as much work as Mason, yet he makes as much as we do." "I know," Arnold acknowledged, "but we all punch in and out at the same time."

Liz Anne Miller is a divorcee and the mother of three elementary school children. She works as an illustrator for Busiform Company to support her family. Her normal working hours are from 8:00 a.m. to 5:00 p.m., Monday through Friday. The children's school begins each weekday morning at 9:00 a.m.

and ends at 3:30 p.m. Satisfactory arrangements had been made for the children after school. However, Liz faced an almost impossible task of transporting them to school in the morning and arriving at her job on time. The school's principal permitted the children to enter the building at 7:45 each morning to wait until classes began, but Liz was afraid that she couldn't count on this practice to continue indefinitely. When Busiform management announced implementation of a new system of flexible working hours, Liz was delighted.

Although these anecdotes may seem to have little in common, each relates to the broad area of compensation. John is investigating the possibility of continuing his education through his company's educational assistance program. Arnold and Bob are angry because a less productive worker makes as much money as they do. Liz believes that the new flexible working hours will solve a difficult problem in caring for her children.

We begin the chapter with a discussion of benefits, both mandated and voluntary. Next, we present various types of incentive compensation systems, followed by a discussion of special pay considerations that are provided to executives, professionals, and sales representatives. Then, we describe compensation in growth companies, nonfinancial compensation that stems from the job itself, and workplace flexibility. The overall purpose of this chapter is to emphasize the significance of benefits in a total compensation system and to provide an overview of other important issues associated with compensation programs.

BENEFITS (INDIRECT FINANCIAL COMPENSATION)

Most organizations recognize that they have a responsibility to provide their employees with insurance and other programs for their health, safety, security, and general welfare (see Figure 13-1). These programs are called **benefits** and include all financial rewards that generally are not paid directly to the employee. Benefits cost the firm money, but employees usually receive them indirectly. For example, an organization may spend $3,200 a year as a contribution to the health insurance premiums for each nonexempt employee. The employee does not receive money but does obtain the benefit of health insurance coverage. This type of compensation has two distinct advantages: (1) it is generally nontaxable to the employee, and (2) in the case of insurance, the premium rates are much less for large groups of employees than for individual policies.

Generally speaking, benefits are provided to employees because of their membership in the organization. Benefits are typically not related to employee productivity and, therefore, do not serve as motivation for improved performance. However, an attractive benefit package can assist in the recruitment and retention of a qualified workforce.

The cost of benefits is high and is growing rapidly, costing employers more than $1,000 billion in 1990. A typical worker who earns $30,000 per year will receive approximately $11,700 (39 percent) indirectly in the form

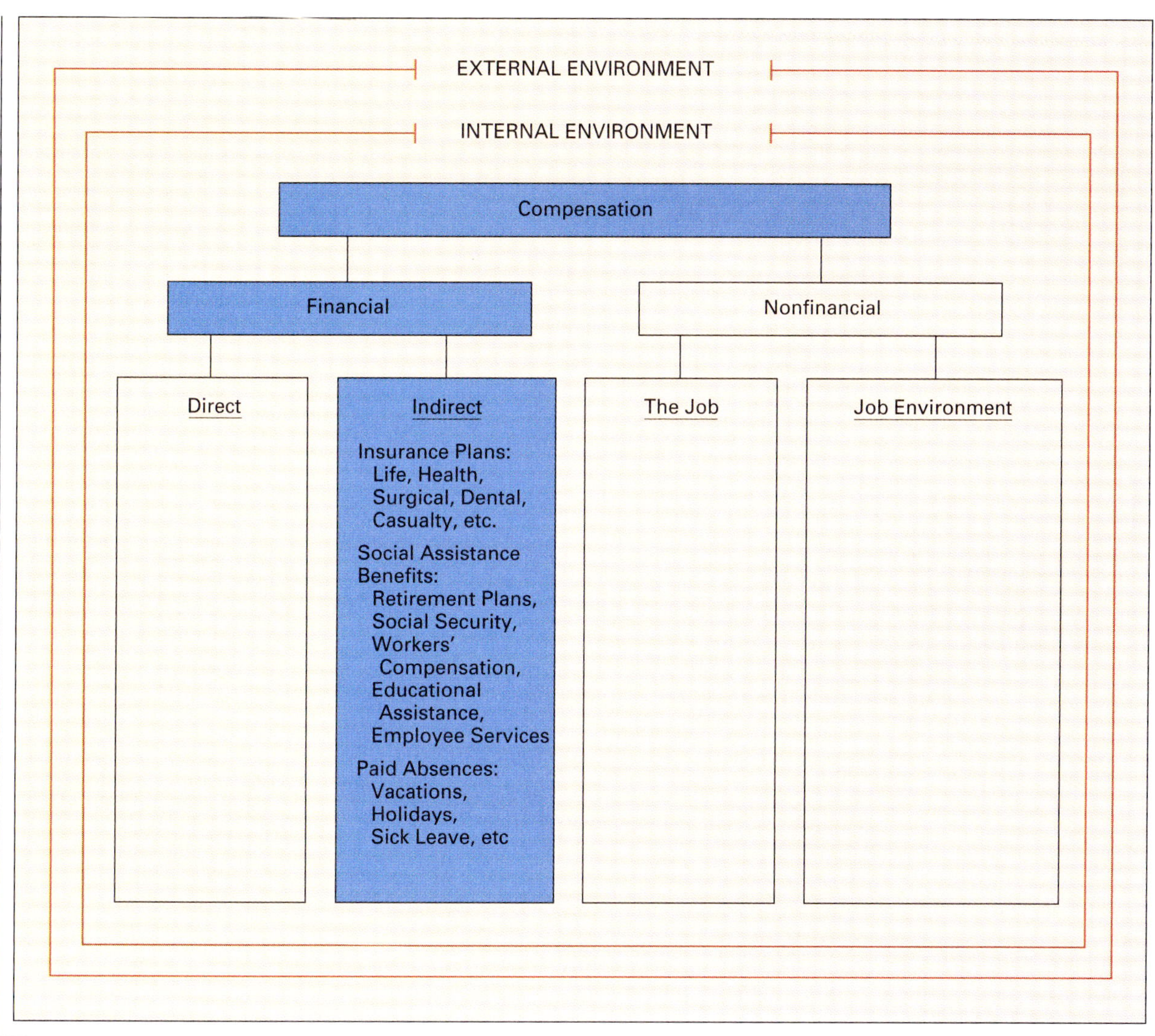

FIGURE 13-1 Typical Benefits in a Total Compensation Program

of benefits. Within the next decade, the percentage of benefits to wages and salaries may reach 50 percent.[1] This proportion no doubt accounts for the much less frequent use of the term *fringe benefits*. In fact, the benefits that employees receive today are significantly different from those of just ten years ago.

LEGALLY REQUIRED BENEFITS

While most employee benefits are provided at the employer's discretion, others are required by law. These benefits currently account for about 9 percent of total compensation costs. They are, in order of relative costs: Social Security, workers' compensation, and unemployment insurance. The future comparative importance of these benefits will depend on how the United States deals with rising health care costs and with long-term custodial care for elderly citizens.[2]

Social Security

The Social Security Act of 1935 created a system of retirement benefits. Subsequent amendments to the act added other forms of protection, such as disability insurance, survivors benefits, and, most recently, Medicare. Disability insurance protects employees against loss of earnings resulting from total disability. Survivors benefits are provided to certain members of an employee's family when he or she dies. These benefits are paid to the widow or widower and the unmarried children of the deceased employee. Unmarried children may be eligible for survivors benefits until they are eighteen years old. In some cases, students retain eligibility until they are nineteen. Medicare provides hospital and medical insurance protection for individuals sixty-five years of age and older and for those who have become disabled.

While employees must pay a portion of the cost, the employer makes an equal contribution for Social Security coverage. It is the employer's part that is considered a benefit. In 1937, workers paid 1 percent of the first $3,000 they earned—a maximum of $30. At that time, only 40 percent of American workers were covered. During the first forty years of Social Security's existence, the maximum tax increased to $965.25. From 1977 to 1987, the maximum tax almost tripled, and projections indicate steady increases in the future. In 1991, a dual tax rate was imposed for the first time: 6.2 percent for cash benefits and 1.45 percent for Medicare. The total tax rate of 7.65 percent applied to a maximum taxable wage of $53,400. The rate for Medicare, 1.45 percent, applied to earnings exceeding $53,400, up to a maximum of $125,000, making the maximum tax $5,123.30. While the tax rates have remained constant, the taxable wage for cash benefits has increased each year up to $60,600 in 1994, and the lid was removed for the Medicare portion. The 1.45 percent tax will now apply to all earnings without a maximum limit. Today, approximately 95 percent of the workers in this country pay into and may draw Social Security benefits.

The normal retirement age under social security will be increased after the turn of the century. Beginning with employees who reach age sixty-two in the year 2000, the retirement age will be increased gradually until 2009, when it reaches age sixty-six. After stabilizing at this age for a period of time, it will again increase in 2027 when it reaches age sixty-seven. These changes will not affect Medicare, with full eligibility under this program holding at age sixty-five.

Unemployment Compensation

An individual laid off by an organization covered by the Social Security Act may receive unemployment compensation for up to twenty-six weeks. While the federal government provides certain guidelines, unemployment compensation programs are administered by the states, and the benefits vary state by state. A payroll tax paid by employers funds the unemployment compensation program.

Workers' Compensation

Workers' compensation benefits provide a degree of financial protection for employees who incur expenses resulting from job-related accidents or illnesses. As with unemployment compensation, the various states administer individual programs, which are subject to federal regulations. Employers pay the entire cost of workers' compensation insurance; their premium expense is directly tied to their past experience with job-related accidents and illnesses. This situation should encourage employers actively to pursue health and safety programs, which are topics discussed in Chapter 14.

Consolidated Omnibus Budget Reconciliation Act (COBRA)

The Consolidated Omnibus Budget Reconciliation Act became law in 1986. This act requires, among other things, that most employers in the private sector make available to terminated or retired employees and their families continued health benefits for a period of time, usually eighteen months. The cost of these benefits, however, must be borne by the former employee. In many instances, employees will utilize coverage from their next employer or their spouse's employer. In either case, the cost will almost always be less.

Family and Medical Leave Act of 1993 (FMLA)

The Family and Medical Leave Act requires employers to provide eligible employees with a total of twelve weeks' leave during any twelve-month period for several family and medical situations. These conditions include:

- birth, adoption, or foster care of a child
- caring for a spouse, child, or parent with a serious health condition
- serious health condition of the employee

All federal, state, and private employers with fifty or more employees within seventy-five miles of a workplace are covered by the act. Employees must have worked at least twelve months or 1,250 hours in the previous year to be eligible.

While the act has obvious benefits for employees, some negative aspects have been noted. A survey of HR professionals revealed general dissatisfaction with portions of the act. For example, 42 percent of those surveyed said they would like to eliminate leave benefits for intermittent leave and reduced work schedules. The act is also complex, requiring many firms to seek outside expertise to assist in complying with the law.[3]

VOLUNTARY BENEFITS

Organizations voluntarily provide numerous benefits. These benefits may be classified as (1) payment for time not worked, (2) health and security benefits, (3) employee services, and (4) premium pay. Generally speaking, such benefits are not legally required. They may result from unilateral management decisions in some firms and from union-management negotiations in others.

Payment for Time Not Worked

In providing payment for time not worked, employers recognize that employees need time away from the job for many purposes. Included in this category are paid vacations, payment for holidays not worked, paid sick leave, jury duty, national guard or other military reserve duty, voting time, and bereavement time. It is also common for organizations to provide payments to assist employees in performing civic duties.

Some payments for time not worked are provided for time off taken during work hours. Common benefits in this area include rest periods, coffee breaks, lunch periods, cleanup time, and travel time.

Paid Vacations. Payment for time not worked serves important compensation goals. For instance, paid vacations provide workers with an opportunity to rest, become rejuvenated, and, hopefully, become more productive. They may also encourage employees to remain with the firm. Paid vacation time typically increases with seniority. For example, employees with six months' service might receive one week of vacation; employees with one year of service, two weeks; ten years' service, three weeks; and fifteen years' service, four weeks.

Vacation time may also vary with organizational rank. For instance, a senior level executive, regardless of time with the firm, may be given a month of vacation. With an annual salary of $120,000, this manager would receive a benefit of approximately $10,000 each year while not working. A junior accountant earning $36,000 a year might receive two weeks of vacation time worth about $1,500.

Sick Leave. Each year many firms allocate, to each employee, a certain number of days of sick leave, which they can use when ill. Employees who are too sick to report to work continue to receive their pay up to the maximum number of days accumulated. As with vacation pay, the number of sick leave days often depends on seniority.

Some sick leave programs have been severely criticized. At times, these programs have been abused by individuals calling in sick when all they really wanted was additional paid vacation. In order to counter this situation, some firms require a doctor's statement after a certain number of sick leave days have been taken.

Health and Security Benefits

Health and security benefits are often included as part of an employee's indirect financial compensation. Specific areas include health care, disability protection, dental and vision care, retirement benefits, supplemental unemployment benefits, and life insurance.

Health Care. Benefits for health care represent the most expensive and fastest growing cost in the area of indirect financial compensation. Health care costs in the United States were estimated to be almost $1 trillion in 1994.[4] A number of factors have combined to create this situation: an aging population, a growing demand for medical care, increasingly expensive medical technology, a lack of price controls, and inefficient administrative processes. While the federal government struggles to reform the health care system, consumers have moved the industry toward affordable options. Employers and health care institutions have taken steps to control costs. For example, after health care costs had soared well above inflation rates for two decades, employers' health care costs—on the average—fell 1.1 percent in 1994. Although smaller businesses had an average increase of 6.5 percent, large employers with more than 500 workers experienced decreases averaging 1.9 percent. Reversal of this costly trend has been attributed to a surge in the use of managed care systems.[5] These networks are comprised of doctors and hospitals who agree to accept negotiated prices. Employees are given financial incentives to use the facilities within the network. Today, more than half of all insured employees in the United States participate in some kind of managed care plan, and the trend continues.[6]

In addition to self-insurance and traditional commercial insurers, which supply indemnity insurance covering bills from any provider, employers may utilize one of several options. **Health Maintenance Organizations (HMOs)** cover all services for a fixed fee. However, control is exercised over which doctors and health facilities may be used. *Managed Indemnity* is a health care plan that provides coverage from any provider. Some restrictions are placed on patients, however. For example, patients may be required to obtain clearance prior to surgery. *Point-of-Service* permits a member to select a provider within the network, or, for a lower level of benefits, go outside the network. **Preferred Provider Organizations (PPOs)** are a more flexible managed care system. While incentives are provided to members to use services within such a system, out-of-network providers may be utilized at greater cost. Currently, PPOs are used to cover more individuals than other plans—more than one-third of all persons in 1992. PPOs are also gaining in popularity faster than other health care plans.[7]

Capitation is an approach to health care where providers negotiate a rate for health care for a covered life over a period of time. It presumes that doctors have an incentive to keep patients healthy and avoid costly procedures when they are paid per patient rather than per service. This approach, long the domain of HMOs, is moving into other managed care systems. Capitation appears to control costs, reduce paperwork, and require providers to work within a budget. It also shifts some of the financial risk to the doctors. If providers' costs exceed the cost of providing care, doctors suffer a loss. This systems shifts the incentive for physicians away from providing care toward limiting care. This change has prompted critics to fear that such plans compromise quality. In spite of this concern, some experts believe that market pressure is making capitation inevitable.[8]

In addition to doctor office visits, health insurance typically includes hospital room and board costs, service charges, and surgical fees. Coverage for these benefits may be paid in part, or totally, by the employer.

Many plans provide for major medical benefits to cover extraordinary expenses that result from long-term or serious health problems. The use of *deductibles* is a common feature of medical benefits. For example, the employee may have to pay the first $200 of medical bills before the insurance takes over payment. In order to control health care costs, a number of firms have increased the amount of deductibles and/or reduced the scope of insurance coverage.

Health insurance premiums alone amount to a sizeable portion of the total payroll. In a further attempt to curb medical costs, many firms use some type of utilization review service. **Utilization review** is a process that scrutinizes medical diagnoses, hospitalization, surgery, and other medical treatment and care prescribed by doctors. The reviewer, often a registered nurse, explores alternatives to the treatment provided, such as outpatient treatment or admission on the day of surgery. The objective of this process is, of course, to hold down costs.

Disability Protection. Workers' compensation protects employees from job related accidents and illnesses. Some firms, however, provide additional protection that is more comprehensive. As previously discussed, a firm's sick leave policy may provide full salary for short-term health problems. When these benefits expire, a short-term disability plan may become operative and provide pay equivalent to 50 to 70 percent of regular pay. Short-term disability plans may cover periods for up to six months.

When the short-term plan runs out, a firm's long-term plan may become active; such a plan may provide 50 to 66 percent of an employee's wages. Although only about one-third of American businesses provide this type of insurance, the plans that do exist pay for periods from two years to the life of the employee.[9]

Dental and Vision Care. Dental and vision care are relative newcomers to the list of potential health benefits. However, a majority of large U.S. employers now provide dental insurance, and an increasing number of firms have vision care as part of a benefits program. Both type of plans are typically paid for entirely by the employer except for a deductible, which may amount to $25 to $50 per year.

Dental plans may cover, for example, 70 to 100 percent of the cost of preventive procedures (including semi-annual examinations) and 50 to 80 percent of restorative procedures (including crowns, bridgework, etc.). Some plans also include orthodontic care. Vision care plans may cover all or part of the cost of eye examinations and glasses.

Retirement Plans. Private retirement plans provide income for employees who retire after reaching a certain age or having served the firm for a specific period of time.[10] Pension plans are vitally important to employees because Social Security was not designed to provide complete retirement income. Over the next thirty years, the U.S. population will be dominated by older people who are either retired or approaching retirement. Therefore, retirement financing will become a primary issue for individuals, employers, and governments.[11]

Retirement plans are generally either defined benefit plans or defined contributory plans.[12] In a **defined benefit plan**, the employer agrees to provide a specific level of retirement income that is either a fixed dollar amount or a percentage of earnings. An employee's seniority in the firm may determine the specific figure. Plans that are considered generous typically provide pensions equivalent to 50 to 80 percent of an employee's final earnings. Use of this type of retirement plan has declined rapidly in the recent past as companies strive to cut costs.

A **defined contribution plan** is a retirement plan that requires specific contributions by an employer. The final benefit, however, depends upon the investment success of the pension fund. A **401(k) plan** is a defined contribution plan in which employees may defer income up to a maximum amount allowed. The maximum amount permitted is tied to the consumer price index. Employers typically match employee contributions 50 cents for each dollar deferred. As 401(k) plans become the primary form of retirement income plan, sponsoring firms are making them more flexible by permitting more frequent transfers between investment accounts. Companies are also helping employees make more informed investment choices and at the same time encouraging them to invest less conservatively.[13]

An **employee stock ownership plan (ESOP)** is a defined contribution plan in which a firm makes a tax deductible contribution of stock shares or cash to a trust. The trust then allocates the stock to participating employee accounts on the basis of employee earnings. When used as a retirement plan, employees receive income at retirement based on the value of the stock at that time. If the firm's stock performance has fared well, this type of defined contribution plan will be satisfactory. However, since stock value may decline in value as well, the results may be disastrous. An expanded discussion of ESOPs is provided later in this chapter.

Profit sharing, if the distribution of funds is deferred until retirement, is another form of defined contribution plan. It will also be discussed later in this chapter.

The Employee Retirement Income Security Act of 1974 (ERISA), discussed in the previous chapter, was passed to strengthen existing and future retirement programs. Mismanagement of retirement funds was the primary factor in the need for this legislation. Many employees were entering retirement only to find that retirement income they anticipated was not available. The act's basic intent was to ensure that retired employees receive deserved pensions.

Supplemental Unemployment Benefits (SUB). Supplemental unemployment benefits first appeared in auto industry labor agreements in 1955. They are designed to provide additional income for employees receiving unemployment insurance benefits. These plans have spread to many other industries and are usually financed by the company. They tend to benefit newer employees since layoffs are normally determined by seniority. For this reason, employees with considerable seniority are often not enthusiastic about SUB.

Life Insurance. Group life insurance is a benefit commonly provided to protect the employee's family in the event of his or her death. Although the cost of group life insurance is relatively low, some plans call for the employee to pay part of the premium. Coverage may be a flat amount (for instance, $20,000) or based on the employee's annual earnings. For example, a worker earning $30,000 per year may have $60,000 worth of group life coverage. Typically, members of group plans do not have to show evidence of insurability. This provision is especially important to older employees and those with physical problems. Many of these employees may find the cost of individual insurance to be prohibitive.

Employee Services

Organizations offer a variety of benefits that can be termed *employee services*. These benefits include company-subsidized food services, financial assistance for employee-operated credit unions, legal and income tax aid, club memberships, athletic and recreational programs, discounts on company products, moving expenses, parking spaces, and tuition rebates on educational expenses. Employee assistance programs (EAPs), wellness programs, and physical fitness programs, all of which are discussed in Chapter 14, also represent important benefits in this category. Such benefits can greatly enhance the employment relationship.

Premium Pay

Premium pay is compensation paid to employees for working long periods of time or working under dangerous or undesirable conditions. As we mentioned in Chapter 12, payment for overtime is required for nonexempt employees who work beyond forty hours in a given week. However, some firms pay overtime for hours worked beyond eight in a given day and pay double time—or even more—for work on Sundays and holidays.

Hazard Pay.

Additional pay provided to employees who work under extremely dangerous conditions is called **hazard pay**. A window washer for skyscrapers in New York City might well be given extra compensation because of dangerous working conditions. Military pilots receive extra money in the form of flight pay because of the hazards involved.

Shift Differentials.

A **shift differential** is paid to employees for the inconvenience of working undesirable hours. This type of pay may be provided on the basis of additional cents per hour. For example, employees who work the second shift (*swing shift*), from 4:00 p.m. until midnight, might receive $0.50 per hour above the base rate for that job. The third shift (*graveyard shift*) often warrants an even greater differential; for example, an extra $0.70 per hour may be paid for the same job. Shift differentials are sometimes based on a percentage of the employee's base rate.

Other Benefits

Several other benefits have become popular as part of benefit packages. One example is subsidized day care centers. Here, the firm provides facilities for young children of employees either at no cost or for a modest fee. Parents typically transport the children to and from the center. While there, the children engage in supervised play and receive meals. This benefit is an effective recruitment aid and helps to reduce absenteeism. The need for such programs is emphasized by the fact that in 1950 only 12 percent of women with children under age 6 were in the labor force. That figure has now risen to almost 60 percent.[14] The number of firms providing child care assistance is growing rapidly.

In a novel version of day care, Stride Rite, the footwear retailer, established the first on-site day care center open both to children and to elderly dependents of employees. Lancaster Laboratories, a scientific research firm, opened a center not only to elderly dependents but also to disabled dependents of all ages.[15]

To ensure that all of its employees can afford to send their children to college, RJR Nabisco has a benefit program that provides tuition loan guarantees and company-matched savings. More than half a dozen firms, including Kodak and Merck, offer job counseling and referrals to spouses of relocated employees.[16]

In an attempt to conserve energy and relieve traffic congestion, some firms transport workers to and from work. Participating employees pay a portion of the cost and ride in company vans or buses. Employees often find this service a very convenient, attractive alternative to driving in heavy traffic.

There is generally no such thing as a free lunch. However, the exception to this rule is provided by a few firms that provide company-paid cafeterias. What they hope to gain in return is increased productivity, less wasted time, increased employee morale, and, in some instances, a healthier workforce. Most firms that offer free or subsidized lunches feel that they get a high payback in terms of employee relations. Hewitt Associates, Northwestern Mutual Life, and Alliance Capital Management Corporation are among the firms that provide this benefit. Keeping the lunch hour to a minimum is an obvious advantage, but employees also appreciate the opportunity to meet and mix with people they work with. Making one entree a "heart healthy" choice and listing the calories, fat, cholesterol, and sodium content in food is also appealing to a large number of employees. Healthy meals may result in a payoff, too. At Alliance, for example, lunch costs $5 to $6 per employee per day. However, the firm has seen about a 20 percent reduction in medical claims, and its insurance premiums have not increased even though the average rise has been about 15 percent in their area of operations.[17]

Communicating Information About the Benefits Package

Employee benefits can help a firm recruit and retain a quality workforce. Management depends on an upward flow of information from employees in order to know when benefit changes are needed. In addition, because employee awareness of benefits is often severely limited, the program information must be communicated downward. Regardless of the technical soundness of a benefits program, a firm simply cannot get its money's worth if its employees do not know what they are receiving. Workers may even become resentful if they are not frequently reminded of the value of the company's benefits. Employees may resent having to pay a portion of some benefits and overlook the larger picture of what they receive and the substantially greater costs borne by their employer.

The Employee Retirement Income Security Act provides still another reason for communicating information about a firm's benefits program. This act requires organizations with a pension or profit-sharing plan to provide employees with specific data at specified times. The act further mandates that the information be presented in an understandable manner and include the following details:

- the kind of plan
- eligibility requirements
- amount of benefits due at specific times and payment options
- surviving dependents' benefits
- how the pension trust is invested
- who is responsible for managing the plan[18]

Naturally, organizations can go beyond what is legally required. Many firms, such as the Southland Corporation, did so even before ERISA's enactment. Southland's report provides each employee with a compensation and benefits profile.

INCENTIVE COMPENSATION

A significant U.S. economic dilemma in recent years has been its productivity growth rate relative to other nations. This problem has given even greater importance to human resource management. Productivity growth stems not only from capital assets but also from the proper utilization of human resources. Pay for performance is one of the best means for motivating people and encouraging increased productivity.[19] While compensation is most often determined by how much time an employee spends at work, compensation programs that relate pay to productivity are referred to as **incentive compensation**. The basic purpose of all incentive plans is to improve employee productivity in order to gain a competitive advantage. To do this, the firm must utilize various rewards and focus on the needs of employees as well as the firm's business goals.[20] Productive workers, such as Arnold Anderson and Bob Minnis (mentioned at the beginning of the chapter), probably would prefer to be paid on the basis of their output. In fact, they may not maintain their high performance level for long if they are not paid in this way. Money can serve as an important motivator for those who value it—and many individuals do. However, a clear relationship must exist between performance and pay if money is to serve as an effective motivator.

Pay for performance is one of the best means for motivating people and encouraging increased productivity.

Output standards must be established before any type of incentive system can be introduced. These standards are a measure of work that an average, well-trained employee, working at a normal pace, should be able to accomplish in a given period of time. For example, a firm may determine that employees in a particular department should be able to produce five finished parts per hour. The standard then becomes five. Time study specialists in industrial engineering or methods departments have historically been responsible for establishing work standards. Increasingly, teams comprised of individuals who *own* various processes are playing a major role in this area. Regardless of how standards are determined, incentive compensation offers a more direct approach to balancing pay and performance. This type of compensation can be offered on an individual, group, or companywide basis.

Individual Incentive Plans

Many individual incentive plans have been used in an attempt to improve worker productivity and a firm's profitability. Under an incentive plan, if Arnold Anderson produces more than Mason Kearby (another employee performing the same job), Arnold would be paid more for producing more.

A predetermined amount of money is paid for each unit produced under a **straight piecework plan**. The piece rate is calculated by dividing the standard hourly output into the job's pay rate. For example, if the standard output is 0.04 hour per unit, or 25 units per hour, and the job's pay rate is $5 per hour, the piece rate would be $0.20. Thus, an employee who produced at the rate of 280 units per day would earn $56 in an eight-hour day. Most incentive plans in use today have a guaranteed base. In this example, it would be the $5 per hour rate.

The straight piecework plan is the most commonly used incentive system.[21] It is simple, and employees can easily understand it. One possible weakness (which is minimized by the use of computers) is that any change in the overall pay scale necessitates computing new piece rates for every job. The standard hour plan was devised to overcome this problem.

The **standard hour plan** is an individual incentive plan under which time allowances are calculated for each unit of output. Again, assuming that 25 units per hour, or 0.04 hour per unit, is the standard output, $5 the hourly job rate, and eight hours the time worked per day, an employee would have an allowance of 0.04 hour per unit of output (instead of a piece rate of $0.20 per unit). An employee producing at the rate of 280 units per day would receive an allowance of 0.04 hour per unit for all units produced in a day. Therefore, in an eight-hour day, this employee would earn 11.2 standard hours (280 units x 0.04 hour per unit). The pay for the day would be 11.2 standard hours x $5 per hour, or $56. The standard hour plan has the characteristics of the straight piecework plan; however, its advantage is that piece rates need not be recalculated for every pay rate change.

One potential problem with both the straight piecework plan and the standard hour plan is related to the output standard. Often, industrial engineers establish the standard, which the workers may distrust. Employees may also view with considerable skepticism any change in the standard, although it may be justified in the eyes of management. Moreover, when individual output cannot be easily distinguished, group and companywide plans offer alternatives to individual incentive plans.

Group (or Team) Incentive Plans

As we suggested earlier, paying individual incentives is not always feasible. Work is often organized in such a manner that productivity results from team effort. It is then difficult, if not impossible, to determine each individual's contribution. In this event, if incentives are used, they must be provided to the team. For example, if the team produced 100 units over standard, each member would receive incentive compensation on a pro rata basis.

Team incentives have both advantages and disadvantages. For instance, in the assembly of electrical transformers, ten employees may be working on one phase of the operation. They must work together to accomplish the overall task successfully. If nine employees perform their tasks but one does not, the productivity of the entire group may suffer. However, the peer pressure exerted in such a situation can be so great that the affected individual will either conform to the group's standards or leave the group. Group incentive plans tend to foster teamwork and often encourage peers to serve as counselors and coaches for new members. Team members tend to lend a helping hand when it is needed.

Companywide Plans

In baseball, an outstanding pitcher or a great outfield is not the standard by which a team is judged. The standard is the team's overall win-loss record. The criterion for success focuses on the team's performance, not the achievements of individuals. In business, companywide plans offer a feasible alternative to the incentive plans previously discussed. Companywide plans may be based on the organization's productivity, cost savings, or profitability. To illustrate the concept of companywide plans, we will discuss profit sharing, employee stock ownership plans, and the Scanlon Plan.

Profit Sharing.

Profit sharing is a compensation plan that results in the distribution of a predetermined percentage of the firm's profits to employees. Many firms use this type of plan to integrate the employee's interests with those of the company. Profit sharing plans can aid in recruiting, motivating, and retaining employees, which usually enhances productivity.

There are several variations of profit sharing plans, but the three basic forms are current, deferred, and combination.[22]

- *Current plans* provide payment to employees in cash or stock as soon as profits have been determined.
- *Deferred plans* involve placing company contributions in an irrevocable trust to be credited to the account of individual employees. The funds are normally invested in securities and become available to the employee (or his or her survivors) at retirement, termination, or death.
- *Combination plans* permit employees to receive payment of part of their share of profits on a current basis, while payment of part of their share is deferred.

Normally, most full-time employees are included in a company's profit-sharing plan after a specified waiting period. Vesting determines the amount of *profit* an employee actually owns in his or her account and is often established on a graduated basis. For example, an employee may become 25 percent vested after being in the plan for two years; 50 percent vested after three years; 75 percent vested after four years; and 100 percent vested after five years. This approach to vesting may tend to reduce turnover by encouraging employees to remain with the company.

Profit sharing tends to tie employees to the economic success of the firm. Reported results include increased efficiency and lower costs. However, in recent years the Employee Retirement Income Security Act and the introduction of employee thrift plans have slowed the growth of profit sharing plans. Also, variations in profits have had an impact. For example, if the company does not make sufficient profits for several years, employees may not benefit from the plan. This may be a special problem when employees have become accustomed to receiving added compensation from profit sharing or when the plan itself represents a major part of the firm's benefits program.

Employee Stock Ownership Plan (ESOP). A companywide incentive plan whereby the company provides its employees with common stock is called an employee stock ownership plan (ESOP). While nearly 43 percent of firms responding to a recent survey stated that their companies have an ESOP, only 1 percent of these were formed within the previous year. In fact, 23 percent of the responding firms that did not have an ESOP indicated that they had eliminated their plan within the past five years. Only 4 percent of the firms without an ESOP are considering introducing one. The reason for this cooling interest at many firms is that they already provide stock to employees through other benefit programs. Interestingly, virtually all firms with ESOPs (96 percent) state that their employees like the plan, and 75 percent reported that since establishing ESOPs, their companies' stock value has risen.[23]

Many of the benefits of profit sharing plans have also been cited for ESOPs. Specifically, ESOP advocates have suggested that employees obtain a stake in the business and become more closely identified with the firm—a relationship that theoretically increases motivation.

Although the potential advantages of ESOPs are impressive, critics point out the dangers of employees having "all their eggs in one basket." Employees would be in a vulnerable position should their company fail.

HRM IN ACTION

—UPPING THE STANDARDS?

"Did you realize that we spent more than $70,000 on our incentive program last year?" asked Pat Shelton, production manager. She was talking to the human resource manager, Jerry Kemp. Pat continued, "For a company our size, we sure spend a lot of money for what we get. Frankly, I think the employees are paid too much. What do you think about upping the standards a bit for receiving incentive pay? It could save the company a lot of money."

If you were Jerry, how would you respond?

Scanlon Plan. The **Scanlon Plan** is a gain-sharing plan designed to bind employees to the firm's performance. Gain-sharing plans (also known as productivity incentives, team incentives, and performance sharing incentives) generally refer to incentive plans that involve many or all employees in a common effort to achieve a firm's productivity objectives.

The Scanlon Plan was developed by Joseph Scanlon in 1937, and it continues to be a successful approach to group incentive, especially in smaller firms. Employees are financially rewarded for savings in labor costs that result from their suggestions. These suggestions are evaluated by employee-management committees. Savings are calculated as a ratio of payroll costs to the sales value of what that payroll produces. If the company is able to reduce payroll costs through increased operating efficiency, it shares the savings with its employees.

The Scanlon Plan differs from other gain-sharing programs by emphasizing the empowerment of employees. Adoption of the plan necessitates a commitment to a particular value system and management philosophy. There are four basic Scanlon Plan principles:[24]

1. *Identity.* To focus on employee involvement, the firm's mission or purpose must be clearly articulated.
2. *Competence.* The plan requires the highest standards of work behavior and a continual commitment to excellence.
3. *Participation.* The plan provides a mechanism for using the ideas of knowledgeable employees and translating these into productivity improvements.
4. *Equity.* Equity is achieved when three primary stakeholders—employees, customers, and investors—share financially in the productivity increases resulting from the program.

Such firms as Herman Miller, Ameritech, Martin Marietta, Donnelly Mirrors, Motorola, and Boston's Beth Israel Hospital are realizing benefits from the Scanlon Plan. They have created formal participative means for soliciting suggestions and are sharing the revenue resulting from increases in productivity. According to the Scanlon Plan Association, plans resulted in an average gain of $1,914 per employee in 1992 for its members and cost only $135 per employee to administer.[25]

EXECUTIVE COMPENSATION

Executive skill largely determines whether a firm will prosper, survive, or fail. Therefore, providing adequate compensation for these managers is vital. A critical factor in attracting and retaining the best managers is a company's program for compensating executives.[26]

Determining Executive Compensation

In determining executive compensation, firms typically prefer to relate salary growth for the highest level managers to overall corporate performance. For the next management tier, firms tend to integrate overall corporate performance with market rates and internal considerations to come up with compensation factors. For lower level managers, salaries are often determined on the basis of market rates, internal pay relationships, and individual performance.

In general, the higher the managerial position, the greater the flexibility managers have in designing their jobs. Management jobs are often difficult to define because of their diversity. And when they are defined, they are often described in terms of anticipated results rather than tasks or how the work is accomplished. Thus, market pricing may be the best approach to use in determining executive pay for several reasons. For one thing, such jobs are critically important to the organization, and the people involved are highly skilled and difficult to replace. In addition, the firm often has a considerable investment in developing managers. Even though the market may support a high wage decision, managers comprise a relatively small percentage of the total workforce, and the overall impact on total labor costs will be small. Finally, because of their numerous outside contacts, managers are likely to know the going market rates.

In using market pricing, organizations utilize compensation survey data to determine pay levels for a representative group of jobs. These data may be obtained from such sources as William M. Mercer, the American Management Association, and Sibson & Company, Inc. Some organizations also adapt point and factor comparison methods of job evaluation to determine the relative value of management jobs.

Types of Executive Compensation

Executive compensation often has five basic elements: (1) base salary, (2) short-term incentives or bonuses, (3) long-term incentives and capital appreciation plans, (4) executive benefits, and (5) perquisites.[27] The way an executive compensation package is designed is partially dependent on the ever changing tax legislation.

Base Salary. Although it may not represent the largest portion of the executive's compensation package, salary is obviously important. It is a factor in determining the executive's standard of living. Salary also provides the basis for other forms of compensation. For example, the amount of bonuses and certain benefits may be based on annual salary.

Short-Term Incentives or Bonuses. Payment of bonuses reflects a managerial belief in their incentive value. Today, virtually all top executives receive bonuses tied to base salary. The popularity of this compensation component has risen rapidly in recent years.

Long-Term Incentives. The stock option is a long-term incentive designed to integrate further the interests of management with those of the organization. The sentiments of some boards of directors may be revealed in results from a recent survey of large industrial and service corporations. One firm in six, of the firms surveyed, require top executives to hold some of the company's stock. Most commonly, CEOs are required to hold shares worth four to five times their base salary. One firm, J. C. Penney, has a stricter requirement. Its CEO must hold seven times his or her annual salary. Certain other J. C. Penney managers are required to hold stock worth one-half their salary by 1998.[28] While the motivational value of stock ownership seems logical, research on the subject has not been conclusive.

Although various types of plans exist, the typical **stock option plan** gives the manager the option to buy a specified amount of stock in the future at or below the current market price. This form of compensation is advantageous when stock prices are rising. However, there are potential disadvantages to stock option plans. A manager may feel uncomfortable investing money in the same organization in which he or she is building a career. As with profit sharing, this method of compensation is popular when a firm is successful. But during periods of decline when stock prices fall, the participants may become disenchanted.

Executive Benefits. Executive benefits are generally more generous than those received by other employees because the benefits are tied to managers' higher salaries. However, current legislation (ERISA) does restrict the value of executive benefits to a certain level above those of other workers.

Perquisites. **Perquisites (perks)** are any special benefits provided by a firm to a small group of key executives and designed to give the executives something extra. In addition to status, these rewards either are not considered as earned income or are taxed at a lower level than ordinary income.[29] Some of the more common perks include the following:

- a company-provided car
- accessible, no cost parking
- limousine service—the chauffeur may also serve as a bodyguard
- kidnap and ransom protection
- counseling assistance—including financial and legal services
- professional meetings and conferences
- spouse travel
- use of company plane and yacht
- home entertainment allowance
- special living accommodations away from home
- club memberships
- special dining privileges
- season tickets to entertainment events
- special relocation allowances
- use of company credit cards
- medical expense reimbursement—coverage for all medical costs
- reimbursement for children's college expenses
- no- and low-interest loans[30]

A **"golden parachute" contract** is a perquisite that protects executives in the event their firm is acquired by another firm. Such executives, if negatively affected, may receive maximum agreed-to payouts under both short- and long-term incentive plans. Perquisites extend a firm's benefit program on an individual basis.

The high level of compensation for top executives has received increased attention in recent years. For example, Charles Locke, CEO for Morton International, received almost $26 million in total compensation in 1994. The second highest paid CEO that year was James L. Donald, of DSC Communications, who received almost $24 million. Although a record number of executives—537 of 742—earned more than $1 million, the top pay was just a fraction of that earned in 1993 by Michael Eisner, Walt Disney's CEO. Mr. Eisner's total compensation that year was an astounding $203 million, an amount almost equal to the GNP of Grenada. While 1994 saw a dramatic decrease in the compensation of the highest paid CEOs, signs do not point to a trend in this direction. On the contrary, the latest pay contracts involving generous stock options suggest "you ain't seen nothing yet."[31]

Many people, including lower level employees, view compensation packages such as these as unjustified or downright obscene. However, the answer to the question, "Are executives overpaid?" is difficult if not impossible to determine. Consider the case of Mr. Donald. When he joined DSC in 1981, the firm had only five employees, no commercial products, and a market value of under $10 million. DSC now employs more than 5,410 employees and has a market worth of $3.5 billion.[32] Perhaps this level of performance explains the lack of employee or shareholder revolt in successful companies.

COMPENSATION FOR PROFESSIONALS[33]

Professionals are initially paid for the knowledge they bring to the organization. Therefore, compensation programs for professionals are administered somewhat differently from those for managers.

Many professional employees eventually become managers. However, for those who do not aspire to a management career, some organizations have created a dual compensation track. This approach provides a separate pay structure for professionals, which overlaps the managerial pay structure. With this system, high performing professionals are not required to enter management to obtain greater pay. Some firms face serious organizational problems when a highly competent and effective professional feels compelled to become a manager for more pay and is unable to perform well in this capacity.

Professional career curves, shown in Figure 13-2, have been developed for determining compensation for professional jobs. These curves are based on the assumption that the more experience an individual has, the higher his or her earnings should be. However, as the figure shows, varying performance levels are also considered. For example, an individual with eight years' experience (see the boxed area) may earn from less than $3,300 per month to more than $5,925 depending on his or her performance appraisal rating (employee rating *E* being the highest and rating *A* the lowest). Career curves are similar to pay grades, which we discussed in Chapter 12.

SALES COMPENSATION

Because designing compensation programs for sales employees involves unique considerations, some executives assign this task to the sales staff rather than to human resources. However, many gen-

FIGURE 13-2
Professional Career Curves

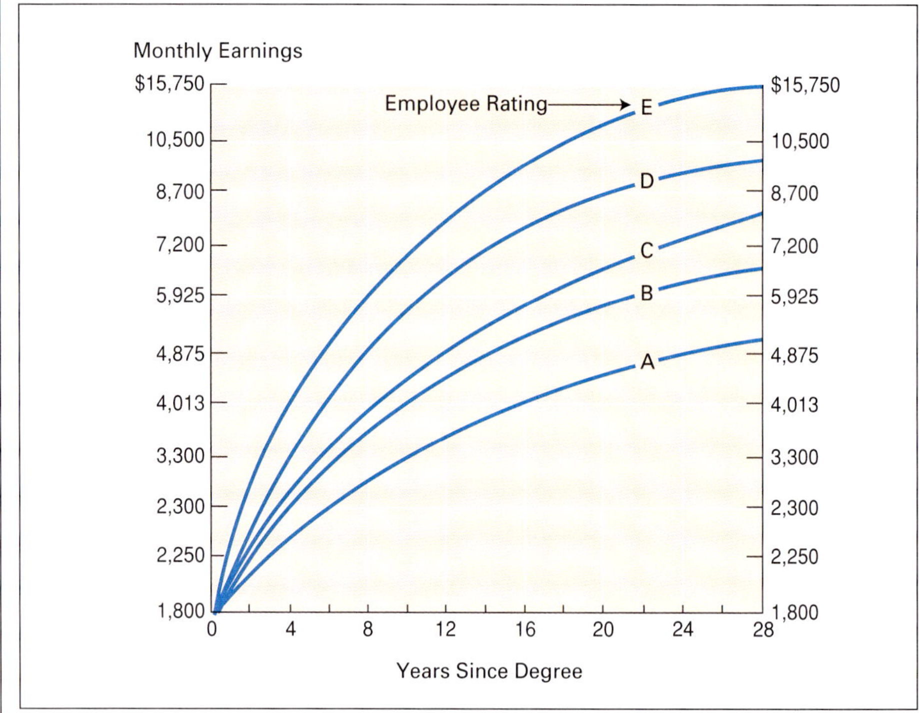

Source: Robert E. Sibson, *Compensation,* 5th edition (New York: American Management Association, 1990): 279. Reprinted by permission of the publisher from *Compensation* by Robert E. Sibson, ©1990 AMACOM, a division of American Management Association, NY. All rights reserved.

eral compensation practices apply to sales jobs. For example, job content, relative job worth, and job market value should be determined.

The straight salary approach is at one extreme in sales compensation. In this method, salespersons receive a fixed salary regardless of their sales levels. Organizations use straight salary primarily when they stress continued product service after the sale. For instance, many sales representatives who deal largely with the federal government are compensated in this manner.

At the other extreme, the person whose pay is totally determined as a percentage of sales is on straight commission. If no sales are made, the person working on straight commission receives no pay. On the other hand, the highly productive salesperson can earn a great deal of money.

Between these extremes is the endless variety of part-salary, part-commission combinations. The possibilities increase when various types of bonuses are added to the basic compensation package. The emphasis given to either commission or salary depends on several factors, including the organization's philosophy toward service, the nature of the product, and the amount of time required to close a sale.

In addition to salary, commissions, and bonuses, salespersons often receive other forms of compensation that are intended to serve as added incentives. Sales contests that offer television sets, refrigerators, or expense-paid vacations to exotic locations are common.

If any one feature sets sales compensation apart from other programs, it is the emphasis on incentives. The nature of sales work often simplifies the problem of determining individual output. Sales volume can usually be related to specific individuals, a situation that encourages payment of incentive compensation. Also, experience in sales compensation practices over the years has supported the concept of directly relating rewards to performance.

COMPENSATION IN GROWTH COMPANIES

The compensation approach for both executives and other employees in growth companies is basically different from average companies. Annual cash incentives are used but not as the primary inducement. The typical bonus for CEOs in growth companies, as a percent of salary, is roughly the same as the traditional 40 to 50 percent. In growth companies, the primary incentive is through stock options. On the average, growth companies provide two to three times as many shares for their executive stock programs as nongrowth companies. In addition, growth companies share stock with essentially all employees, not just executives.[34]

The focus of growth companies' compensation packages is clearly on providing equity. They apparently want everyone in the organization to focus on building the company's financial strength and to share in the company's success. While causality between employee equity and growth has not been established, many entrepreneurial managers view it as an important factor in their firm's success.

NONFINANCIAL COMPENSATION

In recent years, many American workers have essentially been able to satisfy their basic physiological and safety needs. Therefore, their interests have tended to include factors in addition to money as compensation. As employees receive sufficient cash to provide for basic necessities (and then stereos, color TVs, VCRs, PCs, and so on), they are inclined to desire rewards that will satisfy higher order needs. Specifically, social, ego, and self-actualization needs are becoming more important. These needs may be satisfied through the job itself and/or the job environment. Figure 13-3 shows the basic nonfinancial elements of the total compensation package.

The Job

As previously described, a job consists of a group of tasks that must be performed for an organization to achieve its goals. The demise of the job as a way of organizing work has been predicted in some quarters because of rapidly changing duties in a dynamic environment.[35] However, it seems that as long as tasks must be completed by humans, a job—by whatever name—will be necessary whether performed by employees, temps, part-timers, consultants, or contract workers. As long as employees are required by organizations, a major human resource management objective will be to match job requirements satisfactorily with employee abilities and aspirations. There is no question that as many jobs become increasingly complex, this challenge will also increase in difficulty.

Although the task of job design is typically performed by other organizational units, human resource management has a distinct responsibility for recruiting, selecting, and placing individuals in those jobs. Also, a good case could be made for directly involving human resources professionals in the task of job design. Offering the employee a "good" job can be an important part of nonfinancial compensation. Because of this, a number of organizations have become actively engaged in job enrichment, which we discussed in Chapters 4 and 9.

The job is a central issue in many theories of motivation, and it is also a vital component of a total compensation program. Employees may receive important rewards by performing meaningful jobs. This type of reward is intrinsic in nature, but management arranges required tasks into job content; therefore, the job's compensation possibilities are largely controlled by the organization. The selection and placement processes are extremely impor-

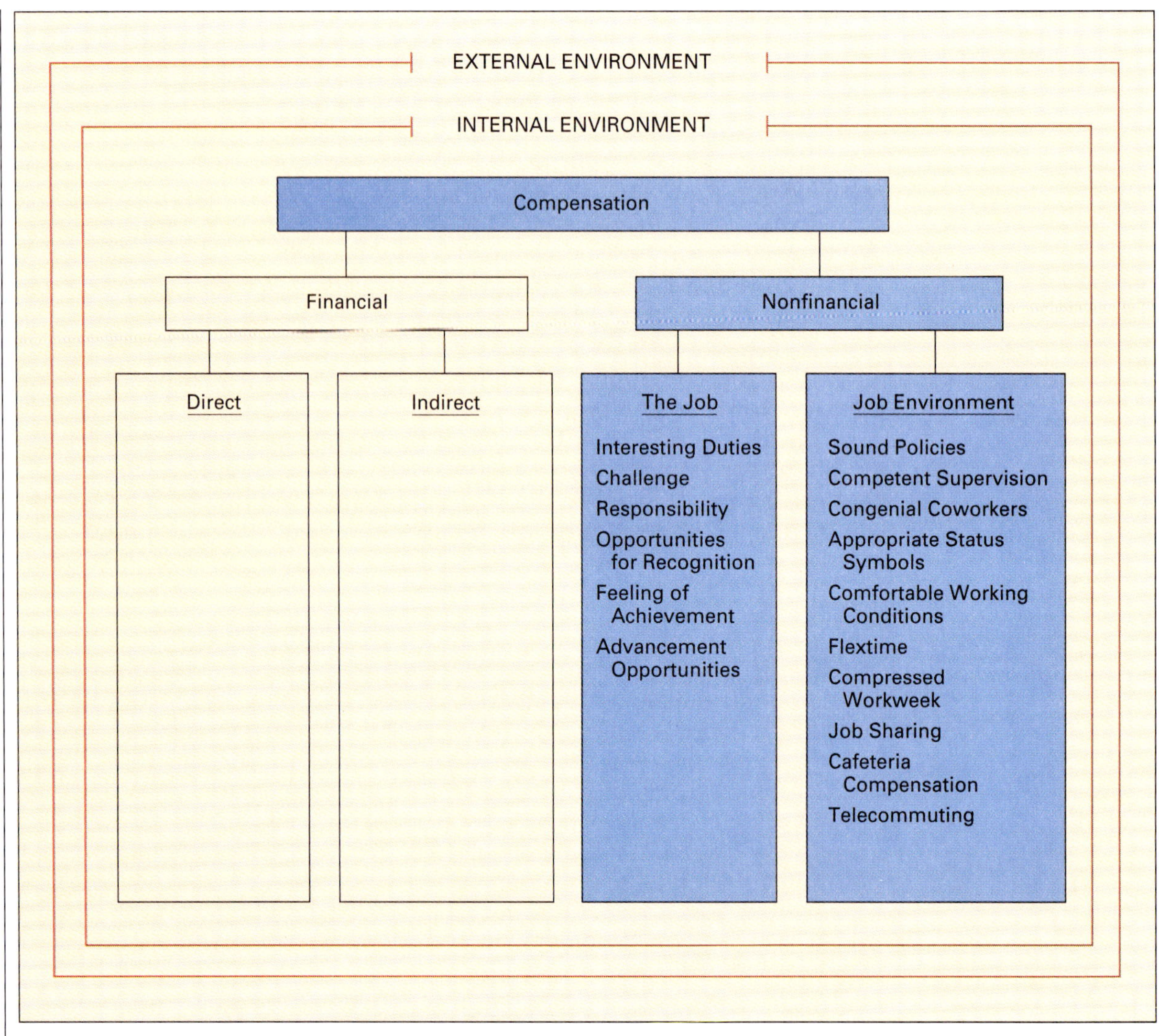

FIGURE 13-3 Nonfinancial Elements of a Total Compensation Program

tant in this context. The collection of tasks comprising a job that is challenging to one person may be quite boring to another, and failure to recognize this fact often leads to major problems.

The Job Environment

The job environment is also an important aspect of nonfinancial compensation. We discussed the significance of a warm, supportive corporate culture in Chapter 9. Many organizations have only "paid lip service" to making jobs more rewarding. However, other companies have made concerted efforts to improve many of the factors that surround the job. These factors are discussed next.

Sound Policies. Human resource policies and practices expressing management's sincerity in its employee relationships can serve as positive rewards. For example, fostering stable employment reflects a company's respect for its employees. If a firm's policies show consideration—rather than disrespect, fear, doubt, or lack of confidence—the result can be rewarding to both the employees and the organization.

Competent Supervision. Nothing in the job environment can be so demoralizing to employees as an incompetent supervisor. Successful organizations offer continuing programs that emphasize supervisory and executive development. These programs ensure, insofar as possible, the continuity of sound leadership and management.

Congenial Coworkers. Although a few individuals in this world may be quite self-sufficient and prefer to be left alone, such an attitude is not prevalent. Most people possess, in varying degrees, a desire to be accepted by their work group. This acceptance helps them satisfy basic social needs. It is very important that management, in its staffing efforts, be concerned with developing compatible work groups.

Appropriate Status Symbols. At times, employees compare the size of their offices with those of their peers or they measure the distance from their offices to the CEO's office. When such extreme behavior occurs, it is time to examine the firm's policy regarding status symbols. While these symbols may be appropriate in achieving certain purposes—such as providing incentives for employees to progress in the firm—management must take care not to overemphasize them. However, status symbols (such as office size, desk size and quality, other office furnishings, floor covering, office location, title, parking space, or make of company car) can serve as compensation because they often appeal to employees' ego needs. Some organizations tend to minimize the use of status symbols, but other firms use them liberally. A crucial point to remember in providing such rewards is to furnish them equitably.

Comfortable Working Conditions. Good working conditions are taken for granted in many organizations today. However, a brief return to non-air-conditioned offices would quickly remind us of their importance. The view that working conditions can be a form of compensation is reinforced by pay plans that increase the financial reward for jobs that entail relatively poor working conditions.

WORKPLACE FLEXIBILITY

A relatively new, but highly significant aspect of nonfinancial compensation relates to creating flexibility in the workplace to meet the needs of an increasingly diverse workforce. **Workplace flexibility** entails a number of options given to employees that are designed to provide them with greater control over their jobs and job environments. Included in this category are flextime, the compressed workweek, job sharing, flexible compensation, telecommuting (or flexplace), regular part-time work, and modified retirement.

Flextime

The practice of permitting employees to choose, with certain limitations, their own working hours is referred to as **flextime**. It was introduced in Germany in the late 1960s and has since spread throughout Europe and the United States. In a survey involving companies of all sizes, from all industries, and from every region of the United States and Canada, flextime was reported being used by 30 percent of the responding firms. This was double the number reporting use of the system in 1977.[36]

In a flextime system, employees work the same number of hours per day as they would on a standard schedule. However, they are permitted to work these hours within what is called a *band width*, which is the maximum length of the workday (see Figure 13-4). *Core time* is that part of the day when all employees must be present. *Flexible time* is the time period within which employees may vary their schedules. A typical schedule permits employees to begin work between 6:00 a.m. and 9:00 a.m. and to complete their workday between 3:00 p.m. and 6:00 p.m.

Perhaps flextime's most important feature is that it allows employees to schedule their time to minimize conflicts between personal needs and job requirements. Remember the incident described at the beginning of the chapter involving Liz Miller, who had scheduling problems. Flextime allows Liz to arrive at work later, after taking her children to school.

With flextime, personal needs can be accommodated without employees being tempted to use sick leave illegitimately. Flextime also permits employees to work at hours when they feel they can function best. It caters to those who are early risers or to those who prefer to work later in the day. The

FIGURE 13-4
Illustration of Flextime

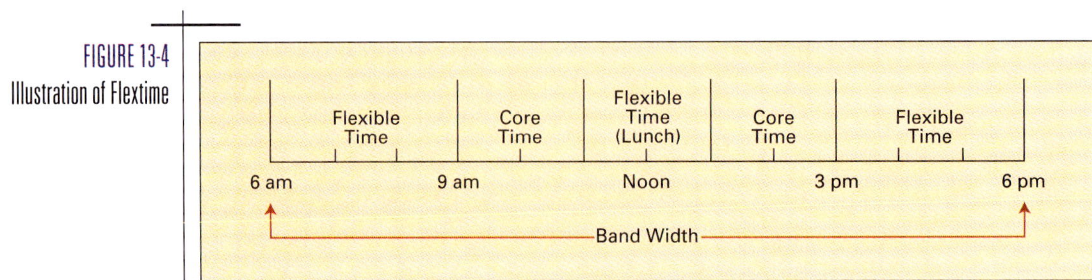

public also seems to reap benefits from flextime. Transportation services, recreational facilities, medical clinics, and other services can be better utilized as a result of reduced competition for service at conventional peak times. Benefits accruing to organizations are also impressive. Studies at such firms as Johnson and Johnson and AT&T indicate that assisting employees resolve work and family conflicts not only boosts morale, but also increases productivity. Johnson and Johnson found that absenteeism among employees who used flextime and family leave policies was on average only half that for the workforce as a whole.[37]

Flextime is not suitable for all types of organizations. For example, its use may be severely limited in assembly line operations and companies utilizing multiple shifts. However, flextime is feasible in many situations, benefitting both the employee and the employer. Clearly, the use of such plans as flextime are compatible with the desire of employees (especially younger ones) to have greater control over their work situations.

The Compressed Workweek

Any arrangement of work hours that permits employees to fulfill their work obligation in fewer days than the typical five-day workweek is referred to as the **compressed workweek**. A common compressed workweek is four ten-hour days. Working under this arrangement, employees have reported greater job satisfaction. In addition, the compressed workweek offers the potential for better use of leisure time for family life, personal business, and recreation. Employers in some instances have cited such advantages as increased productivity and reduced turnover and absenteeism. In other firms, however, work scheduling and employee fatigue problems have been encountered. In some cases, these problems have resulted in lower product quality and reduced customer service. Some organizations have even reverted back to the conventional five-day week after experiencing problems with the compressed workweek. Apparently, overall acceptance of the compressed workweek is not as clear-cut as with flextime.

Job Sharing

Job sharing is an approach to work that is attractive to people who want to work fewer than forty hours per week. In job sharing, two part-time people split the duties of one job in some agreed-on manner and are paid according to their contributions. From the employer's viewpoint, compensation is paid for only one job, but creativity is obtained from two employees. The total financial compensation cost may be greater because of the additional benefits provided; however, this expense may be offset by increased productivity. Job sharing may be especially attractive to individuals who have substantial family responsibilities and to older workers who wish to move gradually into retirement.

Flexible Compensation (Cafeteria Compensation)

Flexible compensation plans permit employees to choose from among many alternatives in deciding how their financial compensation will be allocated. Employees are given considerable latitude in determining, for example, how much they will take in the form of salary, life insurance, pension contributions, and other benefits. Cafeteria plans permit flexibility in allowing each employee to determine the compensation package that best satisfies his or her particular needs.

Twenty years ago or so firms offered a uniform package that generally reflected a "typical" employee. The common prototype was a married male, forty years old, with a nonworking wife, two dependent children, and a heavily mortgaged home. Today, the workforce has become considerably more heterogeneous, and this prototype is no longer typical.[38] To accommodate such diversity, flexible compensation plans appear to provide a satisfactory solution. A recent study shows that flexible compensation programs are becoming increasingly popular among employers. It is estimated that approximately 1,500 medium-to-large firms have such programs in place in the United States.[39]

The rationale behind cafeteria plans is that employees have individual needs and preferences. A sixty-year-old man would probably not desire maternity benefits in an insurance plan. At the same time, a twenty-five-year-old woman who regularly jogs three miles each day might not place a high value on a parking space near the firm's entrance. Some of the possible compensation vehicles utilized in a cafeteria approach are shown in Table 13-1.

Obviously, organizations cannot permit employees to select all their financial compensation vehicles. For one thing, benefits required by law must be provided. In addition, it is probably wise to require that each employee have core benefits, especially in areas such as retirement and medical insurance. Some guidelines would likely be helpful for most employees in the long run. However, the freedom to select highly desired benefits would seem to maximize the value of an individual's compensation. Involvement in the determination of tailored compensation plans should also effectively communicate the cost of benefits to employees.

TRW has had a flexible compensation program since 1974. The program was inspired by a general belief that employees should have more flexibility and self-determination in shaping their compensation packages. The plan developed at TRW is based on the following principles:

- The core plan will be available to each employee at the company's expense.
- Plans that are better, but more costly than the current plan, will be developed and made available at the employee's expense.
- Plans that provide less coverage, and that are less costly than the current plan, will be developed and an employee given credit toward other benefits or given the difference in cash.
- The core plan will be reviewed annually and will be maintained at a competitive level.
- Additional choices will be added as experience is gained and as new elements of the total compensation package can be defined on a choice basis.

TABLE 13-1 Compensation Vehicles Utilized in a Cafeteria Compensation Approach

Accidental death, dismemberment insurance	Health maintenance organization fees
Birthdays (vacation)	Home health care
Bonus eligibility	Hospital-surgical-medical insurance
Business and professional membership	Incentive growth fund
Cash profit sharing	Interest-free loans
Club memberships	Long-term disability benefit
Commissions	Matching educational donations
Company medical assistance	Nurseries
Company provided automobile	Nursing home care
Company provided housing	Outside medical services
Company provided or subsidized travel	Personal accident insurance
Day care centers	Price discount plan
Deferred bonus	Recreation facilities
Deferred compensation plan	Resort facilities
Dental and eye care insurance	Sabbatical leaves
Discount on company products	Salary continuation
Education costs	Savings plan
Educational activities (time off)	Scholarships for dependents
Free checking account	Severance pay
Free or subsidized lunches	Sickness and accident insurance
Group automobile insurance	Stock appreciation rights
Group homeowners' insurance	Stock bonus plan
Group life insurance	Stock purchase plan

Choices in the current plan include health care, hospital, surgical, maternity, supplemental accident, and major medical benefits. Future possibilities for expanded areas of choice are retirement supplement, group auto and homeowners' insurance, and long-term disability compensation.

In spite of new legislative restrictions, the number of flexible compensation programs is increasing, primarily because such plans provide substantial advantages for both employer and employee. For example, United Hospitals, a health care system in the Philadelphia area, implemented a program to control the escalation of health care costs. During the first three years of the plan, the firm avoided increases in health care costs of almost $8 million. The system also proved to be valuable in recruiting and retaining professional employees. In addition, the flexible program was acknowledged as a major factor in defeating a unionization attempt.[40]

While flexible compensation programs add to the organization's administrative burden, advantages seem to outweigh shortcomings. Therefore, systems of this type will likely become more common in the future.

Telecommuting

Telecommuting allows employees (teleworkers) to work at home or at least in a location away from the office. In fact, modern communications and data processing technologies permit people to work just about anywhere they want. Such workers perform their tasks over data lines tied to a computer as if they were at the office. Telecommuters generally are information workers. They accomplish jobs that require, for example, analysis, research, writing, budgeting, data entry, or computer programming.[41]

Using a personal computer located in the employee's home and connected by telephone to a computer network, both training and job duties are carried out without loss of efficiency and quality. An example of a telecommuting job is that of business application programmer. The following advantages have been cited for both employee and employer:

- Permits effective use of human resources.
- Eliminates the need for office space.
- Provides flexible working hours.
- Eliminates costs associated with travel to and from work.
- Enhances intellectual functioning.
- Permits a higher level of self-care for severely disabled employees.
- Reduces costs of health care.
- Increases employees' self-concept and confidence levels.
- Provides a means for reentering a traditional work environment.

Commuting distances are not a factor for teleworkers. Therefore, firms may hire the best employees available anywhere in the country. The size of the U.S. workforce should also increase with the ability of telecommuting to expand the utilization of disabled workers and workers with small children. In 1993, an estimated 7.6 million people were working at home during normal business hours and approximately $4.7 billion was expended for telecommuter technology.[42] This represents a substantial increase of the 4.4 million people telecommuting in 1991.

In addition to corporate employees, free-lance consultants are setting up shop in resorts and backwoods communities such as Telluride, Steamboat Springs and Durango, Colorado, and Buffalo, Wyoming. Such communities welcome these highly educated teleworkers with open arms as they represent a significant economic boost. As the Information Superhighway is ushered in over the next decade, the numbers of these professionals could increase substantially.[43]

While telecommuting has many advantages, it also has some potential pitfalls. For example, ties between employees and their firms may be weakened, and successful programs will require a higher degree of trust between employees and their supervisors. One manager noted that maintaining discipline among the teleworkers was the biggest management challenge since some employees may be inclined to stall in completing projects. This potential problem may be dealt with by imposing many intermediate deadlines until the project is completed.[44]

In addition to the way people are supervised, firms considering telecommuting will need to think about changes in other policy areas as well. Questions such as the following will need to be addressed:

- Will compensation and benefits be affected? If so, how?
- Who will be responsible for workers injured at home?
- What about responsibility for purchasing and providing insurance coverage for equipment?
- How will taxes be affected by telecommuting?
- Will overtime be allowed?
- Will security be provided for the telecommuter's work? How?
- Will the firm have safety requirements for the home?

These kinds of questions seem to suggest that telecommuting poses insurmountable problems. However, there are not many examples of unsuccessful telecommuting. Experience has provided two caveats, however. Telecommuting should not be used as a means to reduce other standard benefits provided to employees. Also, telecommuting should not be implemented in areas where the supervisor is opposed to the concept.[45]

Regular Part-Time Work

Use of part-time workers on a regular basis has begun to gain momentum in the United States. This approach adds many highly qualified individuals to the labor market by permitting both employment and family needs to be addressed. Part-time employees have historically been regarded as second class workers. This perception must be changed if a part-time program is to be successful.

Modified Retirement

Modified retirement is an option that permits older employees to work fewer than regular hours for a certain period of time preceding retirement. This option allows an employee to avoid an abrupt change in lifestyle and more gracefully move into retirement.

In order to prosper with a diverse workforce, organizations will need to develop workplace flexibility. This shift is apparently being resisted in some firms. For example, in some organizations, people who take flexible schedules are viewed as committing career suicide. The long held view that "presence equals productivity" remains part of many corporate cultures.[46] Flexible options seem to work best in TQM environments, which are characterized by freedom, trust, responsibility, and respect.[47] It is encouraging that some organizations are altering traditional approaches to jobs and work not only to cut costs, but also to ease conflicts between work and family responsibilities and to attract and retain qualified people.[48] If these goals are achieved, it seems reasonable that organizations will become more productive.

A GLOBAL PERSPECTIVE

As executive talent is transferred across national borders, a host of human resource issues must be addressed and resolved. A major challenge facing human resources in international transfers is designing a benefits package that will assure the U.S. expatriate that his or her benefits will be equal or fair in relation to what they would have been in the United States. The human resource professional will have to ascertain whether the executive can be maintained under the current group health programs while on assignment in the foreign country. Perhaps the greatest challenge involves unraveling the complexities of the expatriate's Social Security benefits and retirement plans.[49]

Typically, employees from the parent country receive a salary, an overseas premium of up to 50 percent, relocation allowances, and living expense allowances. Normally, individuals from the parent country receive higher pay than workers from the host country. These differentials tend to create resentment and reduce cooperation. Many Americans have found their standard of living and social class is considerably better in foreign countries than it had been at home. The drop in living standards when they return may create some difficulties. An important incentive for U.S. citizens to accept assignments in foreign countries is the opportunity to exclude a portion of their income earned in the foreign country from U.S. income taxes. Internal Revenue Service (IRS) regulations allow a U.S. citizen to exclude certain income earned while working in a foreign country, provided the individual resides in the foreign country twelve months or longer. The IRS issued a decision in 1985 on the taxation of U.S. citizens working abroad. In 1988, the exclusion was $85,000, and it reached a peak of $95,000 in 1990. To qualify for this exclusion, a taxpayer must have a tax home in a foreign country for 330 days of foreign presence.[50]

Employee benefits often vary drastically from country to country or from industry to industry. In Europe, for instance, it is common for employees to receive added compensation in proportion to the number of their family members or the degree of their unpleasant working conditions. In Japan, a supervisor whose weekly salary is only $500 may also receive benefits that include family income allowances, housing or housing loans, subsidized vacations, year-end bonuses that can equal three months' pay, and profit sharing.[51] Japanese CEOs averaged $872,646 in compensation in 1991, just about one-fourth of the pay of U.S. CEOs. In Japan, the CEO makes about 32 times the pay of the average factory worker. In the United States, that gap is much wider, roughly 157 times. As to what accounts for the Japanese restraint, one American executive feels it is largely a function of Japan's group style of management. He cites instances where Japanese executives of Western firms have declined individual bonuses on the grounds that business results are a joint effort and rewards should be shared.[52]

Successful management of employee benefits in a multinational corporation depends on various factors. Perhaps the most important factor is a corporate policy statement that outlines specific instructions for the development, approval, and administration of all benefits plans. This policy statement should clearly establish that no benefits plan is to be implemented or changed by a foreign subsidiary without prior approval of the corporate benefits department. Employee benefits covered by the policy statement should include any payment of company funds to employees other than base salary, such as pensions, medical and life insurance, vacations, and severance pay.[53]

In drafting the policy statement, two general objectives must be kept in mind. First, the organization's overall welfare must be given primary consideration. Second, employee benefits must be competitive on the international level if a multinational corporation is to attract and retain the dynamic, aggressive kind of leadership that is required to be successful.[54]

SUMMARY

Most organizations recognize a responsibility to their employees by providing programs covering their health, safety, security, and general welfare. These programs are called benefits and include all financial rewards that generally are not paid directly to the employee. Legally required benefits include Social Security, unemployment compensation, and workers' compensation.

A seemingly endless number of benefits are provided voluntarily by organizations. These benefits may be classified as (1) payment for time not worked, (2) employee health and security benefits, (3) employee services, and (4) premium pay.

Compensation is most often determined by how much time an employee spends at work. Compensation programs that relate pay to productivity provide an incentive for greater individual and work group productivity.

Companywide incentive plans include profit sharing, employee stock ownership plan (ESOP), and the Scanlon Plan. The latter is the most popular plan of its type.

Executive compensation often has five basic elements: (1) base salary, (2) short-term incentives or bonuses, (3) long-term incentives and capital appreciation plans, (4) executive benefits, and (5) perquisites.

Professionals are initially compensated primarily for the knowledge they bring to the organization. Many professional employees eventually become managers. For those who do not want to move into management, some organizations have created a dual compensation track.

Compensation programs for sales employees involve unique considerations, but general compensation practices, such as job content, relative job worth, and job market value, still apply to sales jobs.

Compensation in growth companies is different from that of average firms. Growth companies use stock options as the primary incentive. In addition, the stock is shared with all employees, not just executives.

As employees receive sufficient cash to provide for basic necessities, they tend to want rewards that will satisfy higher order needs. Specifically, social, ego, and self-actualization needs become more important. These needs may be satisfied by the job itself and/or the job environment.

Permitting employees to choose, within certain limits, their own working hours is known as flextime. Any arrangement that permits employees to work full time but for fewer days than the typical five-day workweek is called a compressed workweek. In job sharing, two part-time people split the duties of one job in some agreed-on manner and are paid according to their contributions. Flexible compensation plans permit employees to choose from among many alternatives in allocating their financial compensation. Telecommuting permits employees to work at home and communicate via computer and telephone.

QUESTIONS FOR REVIEW

1. Define *benefits*. What are the general purposes of benefits?
2. Which benefits are required by law?
3. What are the basic categories of voluntary benefits? Give an example of each type.
4. Distinguish among premium pay, hazard pay, and shift differential pay.
5. What is meant by the term *incentive compensation*? When would an individual incentive plan, as opposed to a group incentive plan, be used?
6. Define the following terms:
   a. *Straight piecework plan*
   b. *Standard hour plan*
   c. *Profit sharing*
   d. *Employee stock ownership plan (ESOP)*
   e. *Scanlon Plan*
7. What are major determinants of compensation for executives? List and define the primary types of executive compensation.
8. Why are nonfinancial compensation considerations becoming so important?
9. Distinguish between flextime and the compressed workweek.

HRM SIMULATION

Your organization offers very meager benefits to its employees. These benefits are currently 11 percent of wages and include Social Security tax (FICA), unemployment insurance, a low-benefit, high-deductible health care plan, and workers' compensation insurance. Some possible new benefits include life insurance, dental care, pension plans, cafeteria plans, and sick leave. Your team will need to analyze your firm's benefits and decide what, if any, new benefits are needed.

ABC VIDEO CASE

CHANGING BENEFITS TAPE 2, NUMBER 3

Employers are moving away from paternalizing their employees with the traditional pension plan. They are switching from government insured defined pension plans, with employees knowing how much they will be getting at retirement, to defined contribution plans, with pensions dependent upon how well particular investments do.

Higher paid employees found that they would get a better return with a 401(k) plan. As a result, some employees are getting lump sum settlements instead of the monthly check. Investment counselors are worried that with poor money management, these employees will get into financial trouble in their retirement years.

HRM INCIDENT 1

A DOUBLE-EDGED SWORD

The decline in oil prices during the mid-1980s adversely affected many industries. Profits were down for all major oil companies and many of their suppliers. Few new orders were received by the producers of drilling fluids, for example, and many existing orders were canceled or scaled back. As a supplier of drilling fluids, Beta Chemical Company's sales plummeted. Beta, located in Lafayette, Louisiana, supplies such companies as Texaco, Shell, and Pennzoil, as well as independent oil drillers, often called *wildcatters*.

Beta had implemented a comprehensive profit-sharing plan in the 1970s, after several years of rapidly increasing sales and profits. The decision was based largely on an attitude survey of the employees at Beta, which showed that they strongly preferred profit sharing over other benefits.

In the early 1990s, the compensation plan at Beta provided for base wages about 20 percent below wage levels for similar jobs in Lafayette. But half of the company profits were paid out each quarter as a fixed percentage of employee wages. Distributed profits averaged more than 50 percent of base wages. This caused average total compensation at Beta to be 20 percent above that of the area. Because of the high pay, Beta remained a popular employer, able to take its pick from a long waiting list of applicants.

Benefits were kept to a minimum at Beta. There was no retirement plan and a very limited medical plan designed to cover catastrophic illnesses only. Employees considered this a good bargain, though, in light of the above average compensation.

Profits at Beta were down markedly in 1992, and the profit-sharing bonus was less than half the historical average. Earnings declined further for the first two quarters of 1994. By midyear, it was clear the company would be in the red for the entire second half. A board meeting was called in late August to discuss the profit sharing program. One director made it known that he felt the company should drop profit sharing. The human resource director, Vince Harwood, was asked to sit in at the board meeting and to make a presentation suggesting what the company should do about compensation.

Questions

1. Evaluate the compensation plan at Beta.
2. If you were Mr. Harwood, what would you recommend for the short-term? For the long-term?

HRM INCIDENT 2

—A BENEFITS PACKAGE DESIGNED FOR WHOM?

Wayne McGraw greeted Robert Peters, his next interviewee, warmly. Robert had an excellent academic record and appeared to be just the kind of person Wayne's company, Beco Electric, was seeking. Wayne is the university recruiter for Beco and had already interviewed six graduating seniors at Centenary College.

Based on the application form, Robert appeared to be the most promising candidate to be interviewed that day. He was twenty-two years old and had a 3.6 grade point average with a 4.0 in his major field, industrial management. Not only was Robert the vice president of the Student Government Association, but he was also activities chairman for Kappa Alpha Psi, a social fraternity. The reference letters in Robert's file revealed that he was both very active socially and a rather intense and serious student. One of the letters, from Robert's employer the previous summer, expressed satisfaction with Robert's work habits.

Wayne knew that discussion of pay could be an important part of the recruiting interview. But he did not know which aspects of Beco's compensation and benefits program would appeal most to Robert. The company has an excellent profit sharing plan, although 80 percent of profit distributions are deferred and included in each employee's retirement account. Health benefits are also good. The company's medical and dental plan pays almost 100 percent of costs. A company lunchroom provides meals at about 70 percent of outside prices, although few managers take advantage of this. Employees get one week of paid vacation after the first year and two weeks after two years with the company. In addition, there are twelve paid holidays each year. Finally, the company encourages advanced education, paying for tuition and books in full and often allowing time off to attend classes during the day.

Questions

1. What aspects of Beco's compensation and benefits program are likely to appeal to Robert? Explain.
2. Is the total compensation package likely to be attractive to Robert? Explain.

DEVELOPING HRM SKILLS

AN EXPERIENTIAL EXERCISE

Due to a downward trend in business and resulting financial constraints over the last two years, Straight Manufacturing Company has been able to grant only cost-of-living increases to its employees. However, the firm has just signed a lucrative three-year contract with a major defense contractor. As a result, management has formed a salary review committee to award merit increases to deserving employees. Since members of the salary review committee have only $13,500 of merit money, deciding who will receive merit increases will be difficult. Louis Convoy, Sharon Kubiak, J. Ward Archer, Ed Wilson, C.J. Sass, and John Passante have been recommended for raises.

Louis Convoy, financial analyst, has an undergraduate business degree and is currently working on an MBA. His previous work experience has allowed him to develop several outstanding financial contacts.

Sharon Kubiak, HRM administrative assistant, began as a secretary and after three years with the organization was promoted to her present position. Because her first position was that of secretary, her current salary is not at the range commensurate with her new position and responsibilities.

J. Ward Archer, assistant plant manager, worked three years as a production supervisor after obtaining his undergraduate degree in business. He then received an MBA degree from Harvard two years ago. He is viewed by many as a "successful fast tracker."

Ed Wilson, production supervisor, has been with the organization for nine years, the last two of which he has been a production supervisor. Last year he virtually single-handedly prevented a wildcat strike. To become a member of management as a production supervisor, Ed took a pay cut in comparison to his union wages.

C.J. Sass, director of computer services, has a doctoral degree in computer science and was hired away from a business college at a leading eastern university three years ago. Two and a half years ago he introduced a corporatewide Human Resource Information System that has refined the internal recruiting and promotion policies of the organization.

John Passante, district sales manager, has been with the organization for twelve and a half years. In his tenth year with the organization, John was promoted to his current position, and he has done a fine job.

Six students will serve on the salary review committee. While the committee would like to award significant merit increases to all those who have been recommended, there are limited funds available for raises. The committee must make a decision as to how the merit funds will be distributed. Your instructor will provide the participants with additional information necessary to complete the exercise.

NOTES

1. Richard I. Henderson, *Compensation Management: Rewarding Performance,* 6th edition (Englewood Cliffs, N.J.: Prentice Hall, 1994): 525.
2. George L. Stelluto and Deborah P. Klein, "Compensation Trends into the 21st Century," *Monthly Labor Review* 113 (February 1990): 44.
3. Stephenie Overman, "HR Complains of Family-Leave Headaches," *HRNews* 13 (September 1994): 5, 10.
4. Carol J. Loomis, "The Real Action in Health Care," *Fortune* 130 (July 11, 1994): 149.
5. Ron Winslow, "Employers' Costs Slip as Workers Shift to HMOs," *The Wall Street Journal* (February 14, 1995): A3, A5.
6. Carol J. Loomis, "The Real Action in Health Care," ibid.
7. Ibid., 150–151.
8. Suzanne Woolley, Michele Galen, Ann T. Palmer, "Physician, Restrain Thyself," *Business Week* (September 13, 1993): 32.
9. George T. Milkovich and Jerry M. Newman, *Compensation,* 4th edition (Homewood, Ill.: Richard D. Irwin, Inc., 1993): 446–447.
10. Except for certain exempt executives, the ADEA prohibits mandatory retirement at any specific age.
11. "Visions: Funding Retiree Benefits," *HRMagazine* 36 (February 1991): 87.
12. George T. Milkovich and Jerry M. Newman, *Compensation*: 438–439.
13. "Trends in Compensation," *HRMagazine* 38 (April 1993): 31.
14. Dan Cordtz, "Hire Me, Hire My Family," *Finance World* 159 (September 18, 1990): 77.

15. Lani Luciano, "The Good News About Employee Benefits," *Money* 21 (June 1992): 94.

16. Ibid., 94.

17. Julie Cohen Mason, "Whoever Said There Was No Such Thing as a Free Lunch?" *Management Review* 83 (April 1994): 60–62.

18. Robert Krogman, "Is Your Company Getting the Most Out of Its Benefit Program?" *Personnel Administrator* 25 (May 1980): 45–46.

19. *Pay for Performance* (Chicago: Commerce Clearing House, Inc., 1990): 7.

20. Michael Leibman and Harold P. Weinstein, "Money Isn't Everything," *HRMagazine* 35 (November 1990): 48–51.

21. George T. Milkovich and Jerry M. Newman, *Compensation*: 359.

22. J. D. Dunn and Frank M. Rachel, *Salary Administration: Total Compensation Systems* (New York: McGraw-Hill, 1971): 261–262.

23. "ESOP's Ebbing Momentum, *Institutional Investor* 27 (June 1993): 211.

24. Steven E. Markham, K. Dow Scott, and Walter G. Cox, Jr., "The Evolutionary Development of a Scanlon Plan," *Compensation and Benefits Review* 24 (March/April 1992): 50–51.

25. Glenn Rifkin, "Gainsharing Programs," *Harvard Business Review* 72 (May/June 1994): 10.

26. *Executive Compensation* (Chicago: Commerce Clearing House, Inc., 1990): 5.

27. George T. Milkovich and Jerry M. Newman, *Compensation*: 552.

28. Jennifer Files, "More Firms Require Execs to Own Stock," *The Dallas Morning News* (June 24, 1994): 1D–13D.

29. Since the late 1970s, the IRS has required firms to place a value on more perks and has recognized them as imputed income.

30. Richard I. Henderson, *Compensation Management: Rewarding Performance*: 505–506.

31. "CEO Pay: Ready for Takeoff," *Business Week* (April 24, 1995): 88–90.

32. Ibid., 90.

33. Adapted by permission of the publisher from *Compensation* by Robert E. Sibson, © 1990 AMACOM, a division of American Management Association, NY. All rights reserved.

34. John D. McMillan and Chris Young, "Sweetening the Compensation Package," *HRMagazine* 35 (October 1990): 36–39.

35. William Bridges, "The End of the Job," *Fortune* (September 19, 1994): 62–74.

36. Joseph E. McKendrick, Jr., "Stretching Time in '89," *Management World* 18 (July-August 1989): 10.

37. Michele Galen, Ann Therese Palmer, and Alice Cuneo, "Work and Family," *Business Week* (June 28, 1993): 82.

38. Robert M. McCaffery, "Organizational Performance and the Strategic Allocation of Indirect Compensation," *Human Resource Planning* 12, no. 3 (1989): 230.

39. Jennifer J. Laabs, "Flex Programs Meet Company and Employee Needs," *Personnel Journal* 72 (July 1993): 16.

40. M. Michael Markowich, "Flex Still Works," *Personnel Journal* 69 (December 1990): 62.

41. Michael Alexander, "Travel-Free Commuting," *Nation's Business* 78 (December 1990): 33.

42. Mitch Betts, "Telecommuter Quandry: Who Buys the PC?" *Computerworld* 27 (November 8, 1993): 41.

43. Sandra D. Atchison, "The Care and Feeding of 'Lone Eagles'," *Business Week* (November 15, 1993): 58.

44. Sharon Nelton, "A Flexible Style of Management," *Nation's Business* 81 (December 1993): 29.

45. Ibid., 70–71.

46. Arlene Johnson, "Fear of Flexing," *Across the Board* 29 (May 1992): 55.

47. Linda Thornburg, "Change Comes Slowly," *HRMagazine* 39 (February 1994): 49.

48. Michael A. Verespej, "The Anytime, Anyplace Workplace," *Industry Week* 243 (July 4, 1994): 37–38.

49. Gary E. Jenkins, "Beyond the Borders: The Human Resource Professional in a Global Economy," *Employment Benefit Plan Review* (May 1993): 43–44.

50. Marion Gajek and Monica M. Sabo, "The Bottom Line: What HR Managers Need to Know about the New Expatriate Regulations," *Personnel Administrator* 31 (February 1986): 87.

51. Wayne F. Cascio and Manuel G. Serapio, Jr., "Human Resources Systems in an International Alliance: The Undoing of a Done Deal?" *Organizational Dynamics* 19 (Winter 1991): 71.

52. Robert Neff, "What Do Japanese CEOs Really Make," *Business Week* (April 26, 1993): 60–61.

53. Neil B. Krupp, "Managing Benefits in Multinational Organizations," *Personnel* 63 (September 1986): 76.

54. Ibid.

A Safe and Healthy Work Environment

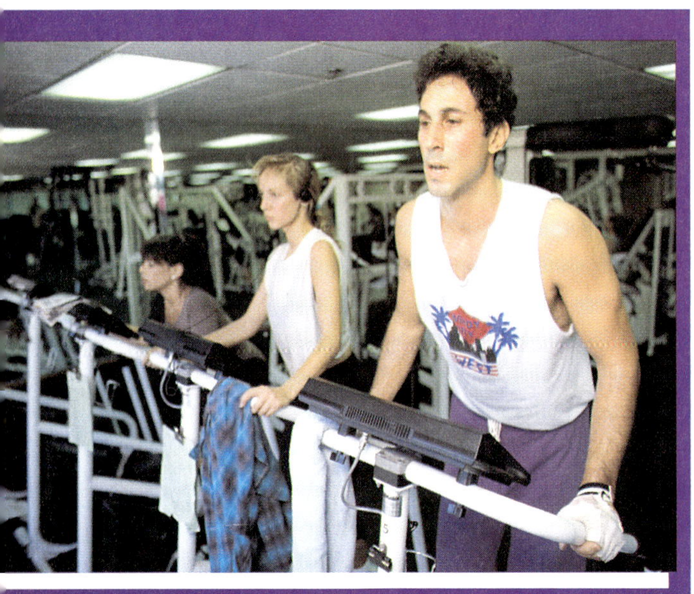

KEY TERMS

Safety 432
Health 432
Frequency rate 440
Severity rate 441
Ergonomics 441
Cumulative trauma disorders 442
Carpal tunnel syndrome 442
Stress 444
Burnout 446
Role ambiguity 447
Role conflict 447
Job overload 447
Hypnosis 449
Biofeedback 449
Transcendental meditation (TM) 449
Alcoholism 453
Employee assistance program (EAP) 455
AIDS (acquired immune deficiency syndrome) 456

CHAPTER OBJECTIVES

1. Describe the nature and role of safety and health and explain the Occupational Safety and Health Act.
2. Explain the importance of safety programs in business operations, describe cumulative trauma disorders and workplace violence, and explain health and wellness programs.
3. State the nature of stress and the importance of stress management in business today and describe why burnout is of major concern to management.
4. Describe physical fitness programs, alcohol abuse programs, drug abuse programs, and employee assistance programs.
5. Describe the possible impact of smoking and AIDS in the workplace.

Dionne Moore, safety engineer for Sather Manufacturing, was walking through the plant when she spotted a situation that immediately caught her attention. Several employees had backed out of a room where several chemicals were used in a critical manufacturing process. Dionne inspected the room but couldn't determine that anything was wrong or even different from any other day. She was puzzled as to why the workers were reluctant to resume their tasks. As it turned out, the employees were not only hesitant to return to work, but also they were adamant in maintaining that conditions in the room were unhealthy. Dionne and the group's supervisor discussed the situation and wondered whether they should order the people to resume work since the department was already behind schedule.

Bob Byrom, CEO for Aztec Enterprises, is concerned about his vice president for marketing, thirty-eight-year-old Cecil Weeks. The two had just returned from a short walk to the corporate attorney's office to discuss plans for an overseas joint venture. As they returned to Bob's office, Cecil's face was flushed, he was breathing hard, and he had to take a chair to rest. This really alarmed Bob because he didn't think that such a brief bit of exercise should tire anyone, especially someone as apparently healthy as Cecil. Bob knew that the firm couldn't afford to do without Cecil's expertise even for a short time during its expansion plans.

Dionne and Bob are each involved with but a few of the many critical areas related to employee safety and health. Dionne realizes safety is a major concern in her organization and that she must constantly strive to maintain a safe and healthy work environment. Bob's experience has caused him to realize the serious ramifications of losing a key executive due to an illness or even death.

We begin this chapter with definitions of *safety* and *health* and an overview of the Occupational Safety and Health Act. Then, we discuss the following issues: safety programs, cumulative trauma disorders, workplace violence, health and wellness programs, stress management, burnout, and programs for physical fitness, alcohol abuse, and drug abuse. Employee assistance programs are presented next, and the chapter ends with discussions of smoking in the workplace and AIDS.

THE NATURE AND ROLE OF SAFETY AND HEALTH

In our discussion, **safety** involves protecting employees from injuries caused by work-related accidents. **Health** refers to employees' freedom from physical or emotional illness. The human resource professional is vitally concerned with these aspects of employment. Safety and health problems seriously affect both the productivity and quality of work life. Employee accidents and illnesses can dramatically lower a firm's effectiveness and employee morale. Although line managers are primarily responsible for maintaining a safe and healthy work environment, human resource professionals provide staff expertise to help them deal with these issues. In addition, the human resource manager is frequently responsible for coordinating and monitoring specific safety and health programs.

THE OCCUPATIONAL SAFETY AND HEALTH ACT

For years, industrial safety has been a major problem that seemingly resists solution. Prior to 1971, it was regulated primarily by workers' compensation laws of the various states. When Congress passed the Occupational Safety and Health Act of 1970, it quickly become one of the most controversial laws affecting human resource management. There is little doubt that the act's intent is justified. For example, who could argue with the act's goal: "To assure, so far as possible, every working man and woman in the nation safe and healthful working conditions and to preserve our human resources"? Individual organizations must attain this goal if they are to reach their full productive potential. The act's basic requirements designed to achieve this goal are summarized in Table 14-1.

The act's enforcement by the Occupational Safety and Health Administration (OSHA) dramatically altered management's role in the area of safety and health. Total penalties assessed in a recent fiscal year exceeded $89 million, up 30 percent from the previous year.[1] Financial penalties such as these serve as pointed reminders to industry of the benefits of maintaining safe and healthy working conditions. Skyrocketing costs for workers' compensa-

TABLE 14-1 Job Safety and Health Protection

The Occupational Safety and Health Act of 1970 provides job safety and health protection for workers through the promotion of safe and healthful working conditions throughout the nation. Requirements of the act include the following:

Employers

Each employer must furnish to each of his or her employees a place of employment free from recognized hazards that are causing or are likely to cause death or serious harm to employees; and shall comply with occupational safety and health standards issued under the act.

Employees

Each employee shall comply with all occupational safety and health standards, rules, regulations, and orders issued under the act that apply to his or her own actions and conduct on the job. The Occupational Safety and Health Administration (OSHA) of the Department of Labor has the primary responsibility for administering the act. OSHA issues occupational safety and health standards, and its Compliance Safety and Health Officers conduct job site inspection to ensure compliance with the act.

Inspection

The act requires that a representative of the employer and a representative authorized by the employees be given an opportunity to accompany the OSHA inspector for the purpose of aiding the inspection. Where there is no authorized employee representative, the OSHA Compliance Officer must consult with a reasonable number of employees concerning safety and health conditions in the workplace.

Complaint

Employees or their representatives have the right to file a complaint with the nearest OSHA office requesting an inspection if they believe unsafe or unhealthful conditions exist in their workplace. OSHA will withhold, on request, names of employees complaining. The act provides that employees may not be discharged or discriminated against in any way for filing safety and health complaints or otherwise exercising their rights under the act. An employee who believes he or she has been discriminated against may file a complaint with the nearest OSHA office within thirty days of the alleged discrimination.

Citation

If upon inspection OSHA believes an employer has violated the act, a citation alleging such violations will be issued to the employer. Each citation will specify a time period within which the alleged violation must be corrected. The OSHA citation must be prominently displayed at or near the place of alleged violation for three days, or until it is corrected, whichever is later, to warn employees of dangers that may exist there.

Proposed Penalty

The act provides for mandatory penalties against employers of up to $7,000 for each serious violation and for optional penalties of up to $1,000 for each nonserious violation. Penalties of up to $7,000 per day may be proposed for failure to correct violations within the proposed time period. Also, any employer who willfully or repeatedly violates the act may be assessed penalties of up to $70,000 for each such violation. Criminal penalties are also provided for in the act. Any willful violation resulting in the death of an employee, upon conviction, is punishable by a fine of not more than $70,000 or by imprisonment for not more than six months, or by both. Conviction of an employer after a first conviction doubles these maximum penalties.

Voluntary Activity

While providing penalties for violations, the act also encourages efforts by labor and management, before an OSHA inspection, to reduce injuries and illnesses arising out of employment. The Department of Labor encourages employers and employees to reduce workplace hazards voluntarily and to develop and improve safety and health programs in all workplaces and industries. Such cooperative action would initially focus on the identification and elimination of hazards that could cause death, injury, or illness to employees and supervisors. There are many public and private organizations that can provide information and assistance in this effort, if requested.

Source: OSHA Bulletin (poster) (Washington, D.C.: U.S. Department of Labor).

tion insurance, the expense of training new workers, and the fact that risky jobs command higher pay also keep safety and health issues on management's mind.[2]

TABLE 14-2 Industries with the Highest Injury and Illness Incidence Rates in 1990 and 1991

Industry	1990 Rank	1990 Incidence Rate*	1991 Rank	1991 Incidence Rate*
Meat packing plants	2	42.4	1	45.5
Shipbuilding and repairing	1	46.2	2	44.1
Metal sanitary ware	3	31.5	3	42.0
Gray and ductile iron foundries	4	30.5	4	31.3
Household appliances, n.e.c.	14	24.2	5	30.7
Motor vehicles and car bodies	7	26.8	6	28.3
Automotive stampings	5	29.3	7	27.5
Truck trailers	16	24.0	8	25.5
Special product sawmills, n.e.c.	12	25.2	9	25.1
Steel foundries, n.e.c.	19	23.5	10	24.1
Primary aluminum	8	26.4	11	23.5
Prefabricated wood buildings	9	25.8	11	23.5
Truck and bus bodies	24	22.1	13	23.4
Poultry slaughtering and processing	6	26.9	14	23.1
Structural wood members, n.e.c.	13	24.5	15	22.9
Mobile homes	10	25.4	15	22.9
Metal barrels, drums, and pails	10	25.4	17	22.1
Motorcycles, bicycles, and parts	31	18.0	18	22.0
Malt	27	21.1	19	21.7
Flat glass	16	24.0	19	21.7
Secondary nonferrous metals	15	24.1	21	21.6
Aluminum foundries	23	22.2	22	21.3
Railroad equipment	25	21.8	23	21.1
Mattresses and bedsprings	30	18.8	24	21.0
Fresh or frozen prepared fish	21	22.5	24	21.0
Fabricated structural metal	18	23.6	26	20.9
Aluminum die-castings	26	21.4	26	20.9
Sausages and other prepared meats	20	22.7	28	20.8
Iron and steel forgings	22	22.4	29	20.7
Travel trailers and campers	28	20.3	29	20.7
Leather tanning and finishing	29	19.2	31	20.4
Private sector, total		**8.8**		**8.4**

*The incidence rate represents the number of injuries and illnesses per 100 full-time workers. The abbreviation n.e.c. stands for *not elsewhere classified.*

Source: U.S. Bureau of Labor Statistics, *Occupational Injuries and Illnesses in the United States by Industry*, annual.

While attempting to tighten its procedures, OSHA is also emphasizing the preventive effect of its inspections. For example, all companies employing more than ten workers are now required to maintain data regarding hazardous substances in the workplace. In addition, these companies must display warning labels when applicable.

The agency has historically concentrated on high risk industries, such as meat packing and shipbuilding, in which there is greater potential for reducing injuries and illnesses (see Table 14-2) than other industries. OSHA's inspections were made primarily in response to complaints. Under a new policy, it will focus on work sites that are most exposed to three risks: problems with confined space, construction materials containing lead, and tuberculosis. The organizations primarily affected will include health care facilities, nursing homes, construction companies, and manufacturers whose products or processes contain dangerous chemicals. While many of the firms in these categories are small businesses, OSHA's director has emphasized that these firms will not be punished for violations if they seek OSHA's assistance in correcting any problems.[3]

Since its inception, OSHA has simplified many of its rules. For instance, instead of requiring that a fire extinguisher be a certain number of inches above the floor, the rule now states only that it has to be readily accessible. In addition, numerous inappropriate rules have been eliminated.

Although positive steps have been taken in the area of safety, a controversial safety and health reform bill has been proposed. This legislation, if enacted, would be the first amendment to OSHA. It would mandate safety and health committees in all companies with eleven or more employees and felony penalties for serious violations of the act. Since the business community is apparently unified in its opposition to the act, this attempt to reform OSHA may not take place.[4]

SAFETY

The National Safety Council estimates that 8,500 workers were killed on the job in 1992.[5] The cost of job-related accidents is substantial—almost $116 billion that year alone (see Table 14-3). It may surprise some managers to discover that motor vehicle accidents are the number one cause of death on the job. A Bureau of Labor Statistics study found that of the deaths from workplace injuries in 1992, one-third occurred as the result of either automobile accidents or homicide.[6]

Job-related deaths and injuries of all types extract a high toll in terms of human misery. The significant financial costs are often passed along to the consumer in the form of higher prices. Thus, everyone is affected (directly or indirectly) by job-related deaths and injuries. Although many businesses had elaborate safety programs years before the Occupational Safety and Health Act was passed, a large number of firms did not establish formal safety programs until it was enacted.

The Focus of Safety Programs

Safety programs may be designed to accomplish their purposes in two primary ways. The first approach is to create a psychological environment and attitudes that promote safety. Accidents can be reduced when workers consciously or subconsciously think about safety. This attitude must permeate

TABLE 14-3
Job-Related Accident Costs

Work Accident Costs

The true cost to the nation, to employers, and to individuals of work-related deaths and injuries is much greater than the cost of workers' compensation insurance alone. The figures presented below show the National Safety Council's estimates of the total costs of occupational deaths and injuries. Cost estimating procedures were revised for the 1993 edition of *Accident Facts*. In general, cost estimates are not comparable from year to year. As additional or more precise data become available, they are used from that year forward. Previously estimated figures are not revised.

Total cost in 1992 .... $115.9 billion

Includes wage and productivity losses of $62.5 billion, medical costs of $22.0 billion, and administrative expenses of $14.5 billion. Includes employer costs of $10.2 billion, such as the money value of time lost by workers other than those with disabling injuries, who are directly or indirectly involved in accidents, and the cost of time required to investigate accidents, write up accident reports, etc. Also includes damage to motor vehicles in work accidents of $3.4 billion and fire losses of $3.3 billion.

Cost per worker $990

This figure indicates the value of goods or services each worker must produce to offset the cost of work injuries. It is *not* the average cost of a work injury.

Cost per death $780,000

Cost per disabling injury $27,000

These figures include estimates of wage losses, medical expenses, administrative expenses, and employer costs, and exclude property damage costs except to motor vehicles.

Source: Accident Facts (Chicago, Ill.: National Safety Council, 1993): 35.

the firm's operations, and a strong company policy emphasizing safety and health is crucial. For example, a major chemical firm's policy states: "It is the policy of the company that every employee be assigned to a safe and healthful place to work. We strongly desire accident prevention in all phases of our operations. Toward this end, the full cooperation of all employees will be required." As the policy infers, no one person is assigned the task of making the workplace safe. It is everyone's job, from top management to the lowest level employee, and everyone should be encouraged to come up with solutions to safety problems. Accident prevention requires a sustained effort by everyone, but unfortunately, the following adage often applies: "Everyone's responsibility becomes no one's responsibility." Therefore, the firm's managers, who can authorize the safety effort be carried out, must take the lead. The unique role of management is made clear by the fact that OSHA places the responsibility for employee safety primarily on the employer.

The second approach to safety program design is to develop and maintain a safe physical working environment. Here, the environment is altered to prevent accidents. Even if Joe, a machine operator, has danced the night away and can barely keep his eyes open, the safety devices on his machine will help protect him. It is in this area that OSHA has had its greatest influence. For instance, the agency's guidelines for power transmission apparatus are shown in Table 14-4. Through procedures such as these, and those developed by individual organizations, an attempt is made to create a physical environment in which accidents cannot occur.

Developing Safety Programs

Organizational safety programs require planning for prevention of workplace accidents. Plans may be relatively simple, as for a small retail store, or more complex and highly sophisticated, as for a large automobile assembly plant. Regardless of the organization's size, top management's support is essential if safety programs are to be effective. The top executives in a firm should be aware of the tremendous economic losses that can result from accidents.

Some of the reasons for top management's support of a safety program are listed in Table 14-5. As you can see, the lost productivity of a single injured worker is not the only factor to consider. Every phase of human resource management is involved. For instance, the firm may have difficulty in recruitment if it gains a reputation for having hazardous working conditions. Employee relations may be seriously eroded if workers believe that management does not care enough about them to make their workplace safe. Compensation may also be affected if the firm must pay a premium to attract qualified applicants and retain valued employees. Maintaining a stable workforce may become very difficult if the workplace is perceived as hazardous.

TABLE 14-4

Office of Safety and Health Administration Guidelines for Power Transmission Apparatus

Power Transmission Apparatus
All belts, pulleys, shafts, flywheels, couplings, and other moving power transmission parts must be securely guarded.
A flywheel located so that any part is seven feet or less above a floor or platform must be guarded with an enclosure of sheet, perforated, or expanded metal, or woven wire. It must also be fenced in with guard rails.
All exposed parts of horizontal shafting must be enclosed in a metal or wire cage on a frame of angle iron or iron pipe securely fastened to the floor or frame of the machine. If wire mesh forms the enclosure, it should be the type in which the wires are strongly fastened at every cross point, either by welding, soldering, or galvanizing.
Projecting shaft ends must be guarded by nonrotating caps or safety sleeves.
Pulleys or sheaves seven feet or less from the floor must be guarded with metal or wire mesh enclosures.
Horizontal, vertical, and inclined belt, rope, and chain drives must be enclosed in metal or wire mesh cages. The same applies to chains, sprockets, couplings, and gears.
Guards for horizontal overhead belts must run the entire length of the belt and follow the line of the pulley to the ceiling. This also applies to overhead rope and chain drives.

Source: Essentials of Machine Guarding (Washington, D.C.: U.S. Department of Labor, Office of Safety and Health Administration, July 1975), OSHA no. 2227: 10, 12.

The Superfund Amendments Reauthorization Act, Title III (SARA—the hazard communication standard), requires businesses to communicate more openly about the hazards associated with the materials they use and produce and the wastes they generate. SARA has been around for several years. However, it appears that many firms do not have a satisfactory program in place. Each year for the past five years, this standard leads the list of OSHA violations. During the past federal fiscal year, almost 30,000 citations were issued for basic violations, such as lack of a written hazard communication program, lack of appropriate employee training, and unavailability of data sheets to alert users of dangers associated with hazardous materials. Dealing with this standard appears to be relatively simple and inexpensive except when its provisions are ignored.[7]

Managers in unionized firms should recognize that a collective bargaining agreement—even if it contains both no-strike and grievance arbitration clauses—does not prohibit an employee walkout if objective evidence of abnormally dangerous working conditions exists. Managers in union-free firms should be aware that their employees' right to walk out when hazardous working conditions exist is also protected by the Labor Management Relations Act. Whether the firm is unionized or union-free, it is an unfair labor practice to interfere with workers' rights in regard to safe working conditions.

One way to strengthen a safety program is to include employee input, which provides workers with a sense of accomplishment. To prevent accidents, each worker must make a personal commitment to safe work prac-

TABLE 14-5
Reasons for Management's Support of a Safety Program

- *Personal loss.* Most individuals strongly prefer not to be injured. The physical pain and mental anguish associated with injuries is always unpleasant and may even be traumatic. Of much greater concern is the possibility of permanent disablement or even death.
- *Financial loss to injured employees.* Most employees are covered by company insurance plans or personal accident insurance. However, an injury may result in financial losses not covered by the insurance.
- *Lost productivity.* When an employee is injured, there will be a loss of productivity to the firm. In addition to obvious losses, there are often hidden costs. For example, a replacement may need additional training to replace the injured employee. Even when a person can be moved into the injured employee's position, efficiency may suffer.
- *Higher insurance premiums.* Workers' compensation insurance premiums are based on the employer's history of insurance claims. The potential for savings related to employee safety provides a degree of incentive to establish formal programs.
- *Possibility of fines and imprisonment.* Since the enactment of the Occupational Safety and Health Act, a willful and repeated violation of its provisions may result in serious penalties.
- *Social responsibility.* Many executives feel responsible for the safety and health of their employees. A number of firms had excellent safety programs years before OSHA existed. They understand that safety is in the best interest of the firm.

tices. A team concept, wherein employees watch out for each other as a moral obligation, is a worthy goal. One way to develop this is to form safety teams consistent with TQM initiatives. Participation in such teams helps form positive attitudes, and employees develop a sense of ownership of the program. The committee may become involved not only with safety issues but also with ways to improve productivity. Employee feedback is essential, and good safety performance must be rewarded.

Companies with effective safety programs strive to involve virtually everyone in the firm. Line managers are normally responsible for controlling conditions that cause accidents. As part of this responsibility, they must set the proper safety example for other employees. If a supervisor fails to use safety devices when demonstrating use of equipment, subordinates may feel that the devices are not really necessary. The line manager's attitude can also affect a worker's attitude toward safety training. Comments such as "O.K., we may as well go to that boring safety meeting," are not likely to elicit enthusiastic support from subordinates. Supervisors can show support for the safety program by conscientiously enforcing safety rules and by closely conforming to the rules themselves.

In many companies, one staff member coordinates the overall safety program. Some major corporations have risk management departments that anticipate losses associated with safety factors and prepare legal defenses in the event of lawsuits. Such titles as safety director and safety engineer are common. One of the safety director's primary tasks is to provide safety training for company employees. This involves educating line managers about the merits of safety and recognizing and eliminating unsafe situations. Although the safety director operates essentially in an advisory capacity, a well-informed and assertive director may have considerable power in the organization.

While internally conducted safety audits of a firm's practices may seem sensible, a recent ruling by a federal judge in Alabama may give managers second thoughts. The ruling stated that the secretary of labor had the authority to subpoena records of such company conducted audits. These audits may reveal many areas requiring expensive improvements. It has been suggested that management should not initiate a self-audit program unless it is prepared to provide the resources necessary to fix any detected problems.[8]

Accident Investigation

Accidents can happen even in the most safety conscious firms. Each accident, whether or not it results in an injury, should be carefully evaluated to determine its cause and to ensure that it does not recur. The safety engineer and the line manager jointly investigate accidents. One of the responsibilities of any supervisor is to prevent accidents. To do so, the supervisor must learn—through active participation in the safety program—why accidents occur, how they occur, where they occur, and who is involved. Supervisors gain a great deal of knowledge about accident prevention by helping prepare accident reports.

Safety should also be emphasized during the training and orientation of new employees. The early months of employment are often critical because, as Table 14-6 shows, work injuries decrease substantially with length

TABLE 14-6
Accident Rates by Length of Service

LENGTH OF SERVICE	MEN*	WOMEN*
1 month	10.64	8.78
2–3 months	5.90	5.47
4–6 months	3.41	3.31
7–12 months	1.72	1.84
2–3 years	0.84	0.95
4–5 years	0.43	0.46
6–10 years	0.21	0.23
11–25 years	0.06	0.05
26–35 years	0.02	0.01

*Rates are expressed as the average percentage per month of work injuries, by length of service, for 218,446 men and 52,136 women in ten states, 1976–1977.

Source: Norman Root and Michael Hoefer, "The First Work-Injury Data Available from New BLS Study," *Monthly Labor Review* 102 (January 1979): 77. Reprinted by permission.

of service. Note that the pattern is consistent for both men and women. This knowledge should lead supervisors to stress safety as they train new employees.

Evaluation of Safety Programs

Perhaps the best indicator that a safety program is succeeding is a reduction in the number and severity of accidents. Thus, program evaluation involves more than counting the number of accidents; it must also consider their severity. Such statistics as frequency and severity rates are often used in program evaluation. The **frequency rate** is expressed by the following formula, which yields the number of lost-time accidents per million person-hours worked:

$$\text{Frequency} = \frac{\text{Number of lost-time accidents}}{\text{Number of person-hours worked during the period}} \times 1{,}000{,}000$$

Although this formula is often used, OSHA has developed one that is conceptually different:

$$\text{Incident rate} = \frac{\text{Number of injuries and/or illnesses}}{\text{Total hours worked by all employees during reference year}} \times 200{,}000$$

In this formula, the constant (200,000) represents the base for 100 full-time equivalent workers at 40 hours per week, 50 weeks per year. The major differences between this formula and the first one are that OSHA considers both injuries and illnesses and uses a base for reporting injury frequency rates of 100 full-time employees (as opposed to 1 million person-hours).

The **severity rate** indicates the number of days lost because of accidents per million person-hours worked. It is expressed by the following formula:

$$\text{Severity rate} = \frac{\text{Number of person-days lost}}{\text{Number of person-hours worked during the period}} \times 1{,}000{,}000$$

In addition to program evaluation criteria, an effective reporting system is needed to ensure that accidents are recorded. When a new safety program is initiated, the number of accidents may decline significantly. However, some supervisors may be failing to report certain accidents to make the statistics for their units look better. Proper evaluation of a safety program depends on the accurate reporting and recording of data.

To be of value, the conclusions derived from an evaluation must be used to improve the safety program. Gathering data and permitting this information to collect dust on the safety director's desk will not solve problems or prevent accidents. The results of the evaluation must be transmitted upward to top management and downward to line managers in order to generate improvements.

Safety and Health Trends

According to recent reports, organizations are spending an increasing amount of money on safety. There are a number of reasons for this trend:[9]

- *Profitability.* Employees can only produce while they are on the job. In addition to reducing payouts related to rising medical costs, other factors, such as lost production, recruiting, and training, add to a firm's expenses.
- *Employee Relations.* Firms with good safety records have an effective vehicle for attracting and retaining good employees.
- *Reduced Liability.* An effective safety program can reduce corporate and executive liability for charges when employees are injured.
- *Marketing.* A good safety record may well provide companies with a competitive edge. Recruiting of employees may be facilitated, and the winning of contracts may also be aided.
- *Productivity.* An effective safety program may boost morale and productivity while simultaneously reducing rising costs.

There is a payoff for sound safety and health programs. Work sites with excellent safety and health programs can expect lost workday rates to run between 20 and 40 percent of the industry average.[10]

One specific safety and health approach that seems destined to become more common is the increased use of ergonomics. **Ergonomics** is the study of human interaction with tasks, equipment, tools and the physical environment. Through ergonomics, an attempt is made to fit the machine to the person, rather than require the person to adjust to the machine. The desired result is to reduce operator fatigue and discomfort. The Bureau of Labor Statistics reports that more than 50 percent of all occupational illnesses reported in 1990 were related to repetitive trauma, which may result in cumulative trauma disorders. In dealing with this problem, OSHA has increased its budget and staff to concentrate on ergonomics issues. Ergonomic standards are being established for all industries.[11]

CUMULATIVE TRAUMA DISORDERS

Cumulative trauma disorders include injuries to the back and upper extremities. As such, they are a primary target of ergonomics. **Carpal tunnel syndrome** is a specific problem caused by repetitive flexing and extension of the wrist. A nerve in the wrist may be pinched, resulting in the inability to differentiate hot and cold by touch and loss of strength in the fingers.

Many cumulative trauma disorders result from using computers. It has been estimated that by the year 2000, 75 percent of all jobs will involve the use of computers. Another factor that may contribute to the increase of repetitive trauma relates to aging of the workforce. By the year 2050, at least one-third of the U.S. population will be fifty-five years old or older. Since older workers have decreased muscle performance, flexibility, and joint mobility, cumulative trauma disorders could reasonably be expected to increase.

Companies with employees who suffer from cumulative trauma disorders stemming from their jobs may experience considerable costs. In fact, employers are currently paying as much as $20 billion a year in workers' compensation claims, lost productivity, and other expenses related to cumulative trauma disorders. In addition, employees may also have a disability claim under the Americans with Disabilities Act if one or more "major life activities" are substantially limited. There are compelling reasons for employers to develop a comprehensive preventive program designed to avoid cumulative trauma disorders.[12]

WORKPLACE VIOLENCE

Homicides, according to the National Institute for Occupational Safety and Health (NIOSH), account for at least 750 deaths each year. Sales workers experience the most job-related homicides, followed by service workers and then executives, administrators, and managers. Forty percent of occupational deaths for women are homicides. This high percentage reflects the fact that women normally are not employed in high risk occupations but do work in retail, where the homicide rate is high due to easy access by strangers.[13] Although automobile accidents and homicides may occur during working hours and are, therefore, job related, they do not necessarily reflect a dangerous workplace that is easily controlled by management. Nevertheless, workplace violence of all types, including beatings, serious injury, rape, and harassment, cost employers and others $4.2 billion in 1992. Violence results in lost business, lost productivity from injured workers, and increases in lawsuits stemming from negligent security claims. Workers' compensation insurance premiums are also typically increased in companies that have experienced violence.[14]

Few firms, even today, are adequately prepared to deal with the threat of workplace violence. However, courts have ruled that employers owe a duty of care for their employees, customers, and business associates and to take reasonable steps to prevent violence on their premises.[15]

HEALTH AND WELLNESS PROGRAMS

The reason for a firm to be concerned about its employees' health becomes obvious when employee worth is calculated. For instance, how valuable is Cecil Weeks, the vice president mentioned at the beginning of the chapter? If he becomes ill and cannot participate in his firm's strategic planning, his company will be seriously disadvantaged. Health problems not only affect individuals but also an organization's profitability.

In addition to management and government initiatives, union support has also hastened the establishment of more effective health programs. Unions are placing industrial health issues high on their list of demands in collective bargaining. Rather than concentrating on security and pay, unions now also seek gains in such areas as health care and recreational facilities.

Environmental factors play a major role in the development of physical and mental disorders. The traditional view that health is dependent on medical care and is simply the absence of disease is changing. Today, many individuals perceive that optimal health can be achieved through environmental safety, organizational changes, and different lifestyles. Infectious diseases, over which the individual has little control, are not the problem they once were. For example, from 1900 to 1970, the death rate from major infectious diseases dropped dramatically. However, the death rate from major chronic diseases, such as heart disease, cancer, and stroke, increased by more than 250 percent.[16] Although chronic lifestyle diseases are much more prevalent today, people have a great deal of control over many of them. These are the health problems related to smoking, excessive stress, lack of exercise, obesity, and alcohol and drug abuse.

A formal company wellness program involves more than merely dispensing aspirin and bandages. As with a safety program, it should reflect a company philosophy that emphasizes the value of its human assets. Many of the procedures used in establishing an effective safety program are also applicable to a company wellness program. A firm with the reputation of having a healthy work environment is in a stronger position to achieve many other human resource objectives. For instance, recruitment may be easier because more people want to work for the company. Employee and management relations may also improve when workers believe that the company is genuinely concerned about them.

Back and neck injuries, sprains, and strains are among the most common and costly problems in industry. For this reason, many wellness programs began with a focus on physical fitness or were actually developed out of a company-sponsored physical fitness program. While physical fitness continues to be an important component of most major wellness programs, the movement is now toward a more holistic approach to improving health. Another important element in wellness programs is stress management.

STRESS MANAGEMENT

A notable trend within U.S. industry is an increasing concern for employees' emotional well-being. Managers are becoming more aware that long-term productivity depends largely on the dedication and commitment of the company's employees. Another reason is that employees increasingly hold their employers liable for emotional problems they claim are work related. In fact, during the past few years, stress-related mental disorders have become the fastest growing occupational disease. A recent Gallup survey found that each year 25 percent of a company's workforce suffers from anxiety disorders or a stress-related illness.[17] For various reasons, programs dealing with stress and its related problems are becoming increasingly popular.

Stress is the body's nonspecific reaction to any demand made on it. It affects people in different ways and is, therefore, a highly individual condition. Certain events may be quite stressful to one person but not to another. Moreover, the effect of stress is not always negative. For example, mild stress actually improves productivity, and it can be helpful in developing creative ideas. Although everyone lives under a certain amount of stress, if it is severe enough and persists long enough, it can be harmful. In fact, stress can be as disruptive to an individual as any accident. It can result in poor attendance, excessive use of alcohol or other drugs, poor job performance, or even overall poor health. There is increasing evidence indicating that severe, prolonged stress is related to the diseases that are leading causes of death—coronary heart disease, stroke, hypertension, cancer, emphysema, diabetes, and cirrhosis; stress may even lead to suicide. Stress costs U.S. industry billions of dollars each year in lost wages and treatment of related disorders.

Aside from humanitarian reasons, the economic factor is sufficient to gain management's interest in helping employees manage stress. A legal factor may provide still another reason. One manager filed suit against his company, charging that his physical ailments (including a heart attack) were caused by the pressure of his job. The man won his case, and the company was ordered to make a cash settlement.

The National Institute for Occupational Safety and Health has studied stress as it relates to work. The organization's research indicates that some jobs are generally perceived as being more stressful than others. The twelve most stressful jobs are listed in Table 14-7. The common factor among these jobs is lack of employee control over work. Workers in such jobs may feel trapped and that they are treated more like machines than people. Some of the less stressful jobs are held by workers who have more control over their jobs, such as college professors and master craftspersons.

The fact that certain jobs are being identified as more stressful than others has important managerial implications. Managers are responsible for recognizing significantly deviant behavior and referring employees to health professionals for diagnosis and treatment. Some signs that may indicate problems include impaired judgment and effectiveness, rigid behavior, medical problems, increased irritability, excessive absences, emerging addictive behaviors, lowered self-esteem, and apathetic behavior. In addition, managers should monitor their employees' progress and provide them with the incentive to succeed. They should inform employees that there are rewards for lifestyle changes and that the advantages of such changes are greater

TABLE 14-7
Stressful Jobs

The Twelve Jobs with the Most Stress	
1. Laborer	7. Manager/administrator
2. Secretary	8. Waitress/waiter
3. Inspector	9. Machine operator
4. Clinical lab technician	10. Farm owner
5. Office manager	11. Miner
6. Supervisor	12. Painter
Other High-Stress Jobs (in Alphabetical Order)	
Bank teller	Nurse's aide
Clergy member	Plumber
Computer programmer	Policeperson
Dental assistant	Practical nurse
Electrician	Public relations worker
Fire fighter	Railroad switchperson
Guard	Registered nurse
Hairdresser	Sales manager
Health aide	Sales representative
Health technician	Social worker
Machinist	Structural-metal worker
Meatcutter	Teacher's aide
Mechanic	Telephone operator
Musician	Warehouse worker

Source: From a ranking of 130 occupations by the federal government's National Institute for Occupational Safety and Health.

than the costs involved. Stress may result in many complex problems, but it can generally be handled successfully. In the following section, we describe burnout, a condition that often results from organizational and individual failure to deal with stress effectively.

Burnout

Consider this scenario:

> Cheryl Weaver supervises fifty people in the administrative department of a large bank. She is normally a competent and conscientious manager with a reputation for doing things right and on time. Until recently, Cheryl had been strongly considered as a candidate for the position of vice president of administration. However, things have changed. Cheryl behaves differently. She can't seem to concentrate on her work and appears to be a victim of "battle fatigue." "Oh, Cheryl," a coworker advised, "you'll make it. You've always been so strong." But Cheryl shocked her associate when she responded, "I don't want to be told I'll make it on my own. I already know I can't."

Cheryl does not know exactly what has caused her run-down condition. She feels that she is at her wit's end and desperately needs assistance. Cheryl apparently is the victim of a stress-related phenomenon known as burnout. **Burnout** is a state of fatigue or frustration, which stems from devotion to a cause, way of life, or relationship that did not provide the expected reward. In essence, burnout is the perception that an individual is giving more than he or she is receiving—whether it is money, satisfaction, or praise.

Burnout is often associated with a midlife or mid-career crisis, but it can happen at different times to different people. A key factor in burnout is unrealistic expectations. When people strive excessively to achieve unattainable goals, they may experience a feeling of helplessness—that no matter what they do they will not succeed. When this occurs, they may lose their motivation to perform. Although some employees try to hide their problems, there are some shifts in behavior that indicate dissatisfaction. They may start procrastinating or go to the opposite extreme of taking on too many assignments. They may lose things and become increasingly scatterbrained. Individuals who are normally amiable may turn irritable. They may become cynical, disagreeable, or even pompous, or develop paranoia.[18]

Individuals in the helping professions, such as teachers and counselors, seem to be susceptible to burnout because of their jobs, whereas others may be vulnerable because of their upbringing, expectations, or personalities. Burnout is frequently associated with people whose jobs require working closely with others under stressful and tension-filled conditions. A study by Northwestern National Life Insurance Company found that burnout occurs at higher levels in firms which had substantially cut employee benefits, changed ownership, required overtime, or reduced the workforce.[19]

Any employee may experience burnout, and no one is exempt. The dangerous part of burnout is that it is contagious. A highly cynical and pessimistic burnout victim can quickly transform an entire group. Therefore, it is important that the problem be dealt with quickly. Once it has begun, it is difficult to stop.

Warning signals of burnout are (1) irritability, (2) forgetfulness, (3) frustration, (4) fatigue, (5) procrastination, (6) tension, or (7) increased alcohol or drug use.[20] Other symptoms might include recurring health problems, such as ulcers, back pain, or frequent headaches. The burnout victim is often unable to maintain an even balance of emotions; unwarranted hostility may occur in totally inappropriate situations.

Burnout is a problem that should be dealt with before it occurs. In order to do so, managers must be aware of potential sources of stress. These sources exist both within and outside the organization.

Sources of Stress

Regardless of its origin, stress possesses devastating potential. While some factors are controllable to varying degrees, others are not. In the following section, we discuss some of the primary sources of stress.

The Family. Although a frequent source of happiness and security, the family can also be a significant stressor. As a result, nearly one-half of all marriages end in divorce, which is often quite stressful. When divorce leads to single parenthood, the difficulties may be compounded.

Children are one of life's great sources of happiness. Yet, consider the effect of an infant awakening parents in the middle of the night with a severe asthma attack! This type of incident would certainly cause anxiety levels to rise significantly. Academic or extreme social adjustment problems for a teenager can also create much anguish for the entire family.

A relatively recent phenomenon is the dual career family. When both husband and wife have job and family responsibilities, traditional roles are altered. What happens when one partner is completely content with a job and the other is offered a desired promotion requiring transfer to a distant city? At best, these circumstances are beset with difficulties.

Financial Problems. Problems with finances may place an unbearable strain on the employee. For some, these problems are persistent and never quite resolved. Unpaid bills and bill collectors can create great tension and play a role in divorce or poor work performance.

Living Conditions. Stress levels may be higher for people who live in densely populated areas. These people face longer lines, endure more hectic traffic jams, and contend with higher levels of air and noise pollution. Urban life has many advantages, but the benefits are not without costs—often in the form of stress.

Corporate Culture. Generally speaking, corporate culture has a lot to do with stress. The CEO's leadership style often sets the tone. An autocratic CEO who permits little input from subordinates may create a stressful environment. Or a weak CEO may encourage subordinates to compete for power, resulting in internal conflicts. Certain firms have even been considered stressful because the CEO insists on superior performance.

Even in the healthiest corporate culture, stressful relationships among employees can occur. Employee personality types vary and, combined with differing values and belief systems, this may so impair communication that stress is inevitable. Also, competition encouraged by the organization's reward system for promotion, pay increases, and status may add to the problem.

Role Ambiguity. **Role ambiguity** exists when an employee does not understand the content of the job. The employee may feel stress when he or she does not perform certain duties expected by the supervisor, or when he or she attempts to perform tasks that are a part of someone else's job. These situations often result from role ambiguity, a condition that can be quite threatening to an employee and produce feelings of insecurity.

Role Conflict. **Role conflict** occurs when an individual is placed in the position of having to pursue opposing goals. For example, a manager may be expected to increase production while having to decrease the size of the workforce. Attaining both goals may be impossible, and stress is likely to result.

Job Overload. When employees are given more work than they can reasonably handle, they become victims of **job overload**. A critical aspect of this problem is that the best performers in the firm are often the ones most affected. These individuals have proven that they can perform more, so they are given more to do. At its extreme, work overload results in burnout.

Working Conditions. The physical characteristics of the workplace, including the machines and tools used, can create stress. Overcrowding, excessive noise, poor lighting, and poorly maintained work stations and equipment can all adversely affect employee morale and increase stress. Something as apparently benign as an antiquated photocopier that does not always work properly can create great stress when an important report must be assembled and sent to the CEO first thing in the morning.

Managerial Work. The nature of managerial work may itself be a source of stress. According to one management consultant, as many as half of today's business managers may suffer undue stress on the job.[21] Responsibility for people, conducting performance appraisals, coordinating and communicating layoffs, and conducting outplacement counseling can create a great deal of stress for some people. Consider human resource managers (or business school deans) who feel they must change their driving patterns, arrival times and even automobiles when they fear for their safety because of layoffs at their organizations.[22]

A study of human resource executives in the Southwest determined that female HR professionals felt considerably more stress as a result of organizational politics. This was the only significant difference found in sources of stress for men and women. The reason for this phenomenon could relate to the exclusion of many women from political networks.[23]

It is important for managers to be aware of sources of stress. It is equally important that they implement programs to deal with stress effectively.

Coping with Stress

A number of programs and techniques may effectively prevent or relieve excessive stress. General organizational programs, while not specifically designed to cope with stress, may, nevertheless, play a major role. The programs and techniques listed in Table 14-8 are discussed in the chapters of this text as indicated. Their effective implementation will achieve these results:

- A corporate culture that holds anxiety and tension to an acceptable level is created. Employee inputs are sought and valued, employees are given greater control over their work, and communication is emphasized.
- Each person's role is defined, yet care is taken not to discourage risk takers and those who want to assume greater responsibility.
- Individuals are given the training and development they need to successfully perform current and future jobs. Equal consideration is given to achieving personal and organizational goals. Individuals are trained to work as effective team members and to develop an awareness of how they and their work relate to others.
- Employees are assisted in planning for career progression.

- Employees participate in making decisions that affect them. They know what is going on in the firm, what their particular roles are, and how well they are performing their jobs.
- Employee needs, financial and nonfinancial, are met through an equitable reward system.

Table 14-8 also identifies several specific techniques that individuals can utilize to deal with stress. These methods include hypnosis, biofeedback, and transcendental meditation.

Hypnosis is an altered state of consciousness that is artificially induced and characterized by increased receptiveness to suggestions. A person in a hypnotic state may, therefore, respond to the hypnotist's suggestion to relax. Hypnosis can help many people cope with stress. The serenity achieved through dissipation of anxieties and fears can restore an individual's confidence. A principal benefit of hypnotherapy is that peace of mind continues after the person awakens from a hypnotic state. This tranquility continues to grow, especially when the person has been trained in self-hypnosis.

Biofeedback is a method that can be used to control involuntary bodily processes, such as blood pressure or heart rate. For example, using equipment to provide a visual display of blood pressure, individuals may learn to lower their systolic blood pressure levels.

Transcendental meditation (TM) is a stress-reduction technique whereby a secret word or phrase (mantra) provided by a trained instructor is mentally repeated while an individual is comfortably seated. Repeating the mantra over and over helps prevent distracting thoughts. It has successfully produced the following physiologic changes: decreased oxygen consumption, decreased car-

TABLE 14-8
Organizational Programs and Techniques That Can Be Effective in Coping with Stress

	CHAPTER
General Organizational Programs	
Job analysis	4
Human resource development	8
Effective communication, motivation, and leadership styles (corporate culture)	9
Organization development	9
Career planning and development	10
Performance appraisal	11
Compensation	12, 13
Specific Techniques	
Hypnosis, transcendental meditation, and biofeedback	14
Specific Organizational Programs	
Physical fitness, alcohol and drug abuse, and employee assistance programs	14

bon dioxide elimination, and decreased breathing rate. Transcendental meditation results in a decreased metabolic rate and a restful state.

Stress Abatement Through Ergonomics

Ergonomics, the science of how people interact with their work environment, is now more than a simple buzzword. Managers are beginning to realize that tailoring the office to the human physiology can enhance productivity and help avoid health problems and some types of work-related stress. What should managers do to assure an ergonomically sound workplace that will help enhance productivity? Experts believe that the place to start is with chairs. A good ergonomic chair lets you sit with your thighs parallel to the floor and your feet flat on the floor. Computers are the alleged cause of numerous repetitive stress injuries; their positioning and accessibility are critical. The top of the monitor should be at, or slightly below, eye level so that employees are not continually tilting their heads to read the top of the screen. The keyboard should ideally be at elbow level. Light is the final major factor in the world of office ergonomics. The ideal lighting arrangement is a combination of soft indirect overhead light that does not cause glare and task lights that provide strong direct light for immediate work. The most common lighting problem is that the office is too bright. Also, position each computer screen so that no light falls directly on the screen. Basically, to maximize productivity and limit stress, an ergonomic office must be designed and employees must be given frequent breaks.[24]

Table 14-8 also lists organizational programs designed specifically to deal with stress and related problems. These include physical fitness, alcohol and drug abuse, and employee assistance programs, which will be discussed later in the chapter.

A GLOBAL PERSPECTIVE

The international movement of employees can be a major stressor for expatriates. It is vitally important that human resource professionals properly prepare employees to cope with the stress they will encounter because of global assignments. Expatriates often experience stress from the moment they learn of global assignments until well after returning home.

Stress is evident in almost any work environment, but it is usually quite high in the global arena. Inappropriately addressing global stressors can result in failure and a disinterested employee. Culture shock is the main stressor, resulting in such maladies as poor job performance, unhappy social lives, broken marriages, change in sex drives, eating binges, bouts with depression, nervousness, anger and aggression, substance abuse, homesickness, impatience with family members, and insomnia. Stress arising from differences in business practices, standards, values, and norms guiding behavior is inherent in international business. These differences are evident when comparing business activities in developed countries to those in developing countries and when examining issues of worker health, safety, and environmental issues. Human resource management practices must prepare expatriates to deal with the norms, values, goals, and objectives of the host country.[25]

Human resource professionals should work to limit the impact of relocation stress by properly preparing individuals for overseas assignments.

Global assignments for unprepared employees are costly to the individual involved and quite costly to the organization.

PHYSICAL FITNESS PROGRAMS

Although few organizations have fully staffed facilities, thousands of U.S. business firms have exercise programs designed to help keep their workers physically fit. From management's viewpoint, this effort makes a lot of sense. Loss of productivity resulting from coronary heart disease costs U.S. businesses billions of dollars annually. The total cost to society is even higher because of lost tax revenue, health care costs, and the expense involved in finding and training replacements. Company-sponsored fitness programs often reduce absenteeism, accidents, and sick pay. There is increasing evidence that if employees stick to company fitness programs, they will experience better health, and the firm will have lower costs. Table 14-9 lists some positive effects that result from physical fitness and wellness programs.

TABLE 14-9
Examples of Benefits of Physical Fitness and Wellness Programs

- At DuPont, heart attacks dropped from 6.47 per 1,000 persons in 1957 to 2.83 in 1983.
- In San Diego, the health care expenses for school employees and fire fighters average $548 less for fitness program participants.
- The fitness program at SpeedCall Corporation resulted in a 65 percent decline in smoking and a 50 percent drop in the number of insurance claims filed by those who quit smoking.
- Weyerhaeuser Company claimed savings of about $8 million in two years through a program designed to enhance employee health.
- At Control Data Corporation, nonexercisers cost the company an additional $115 per year each in health care costs.
- Dallas school teachers involved in a fitness program took an average of three fewer sick days per year. This saved almost $500,000 a year in substitute teacher pay alone.
- At Tenneco, the average insurance claim for exercising women was less than half that for nonexercising women ($639.07 vs. $1,535.83). Similar statistics exist for men.
- At Tenneco, a high percentage of excellent performers are also exercisers; a large number of low performers are nonexercisers.
- Lockheed Missiles and Space Company estimates that it saved $1 million in life insurance costs over a five-year period through its wellness programs.
- Absenteeism at Lockheed was 60 percent lower for exercisers than for nonexercisers.
- The turnover rate at Lockheed is 13 percent lower among regular exercisers.

Source: Otto H. Chang and Cynthia Boyle, "Fitness Programs: Hefty Expense or Wise Investment?" *Management Accounting* 20 (January 1989): 47. Reprinted by permission. Published by Institute of Management Accountants (formerly National Association of Accountants), 10 Paragon Drive, Montvale, N.J. 07645.

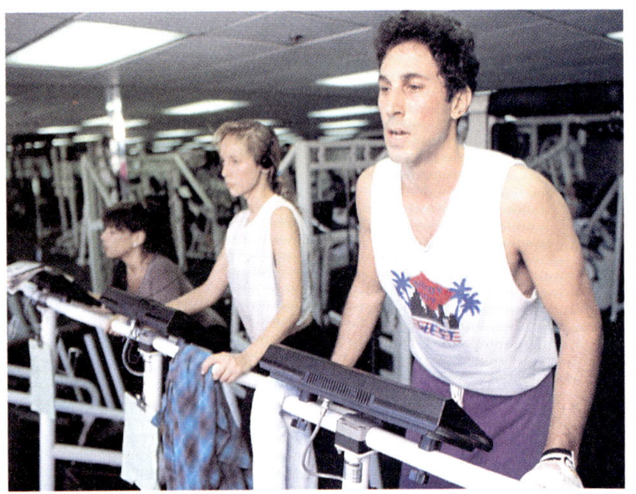

Company-sponsored fitness programs often reduce absenteeism, accidents, and sick pay.

The Xerox Program

Xerox Corporation currently has in-house physical fitness centers at locations throughout the United States. The Xerox programs are designed to help employees avoid coronary heart disease and other degenerative disorders. A fitness program, carefully designed for each individual, helps people feel and look better. As an added benefit, it also enhances their self-concept. A program manager of executive fitness at Xerox has stated, "We are concerned about the ever increasing costs of medical and insurance premiums, but beyond that, we have an obligation to our people as people."

A specific Xerox executive fitness program emphasizes four areas: (1) cardiovascular fitness, (2) flexibility, (3) relaxation by means of biofeedback, and (4) weight conditioning. In the cardiovascular training program, the motorized treadmill is the primary tool. The bicycle ergometer is also used, along with biofeedback training. Biofeedback, which was mentioned earlier, is a process whereby an individual monitors his or her own physiological states (such as pulse rate, skin temperature, blood pressure, muscular tension, and brain waves) through the use of bioinstruments. Electrodes placed over selected muscles during exercise indicate the level of muscular tension. By listening to an audio tone, individuals can actually measure and then relax the tension existing in a specific muscle.

Flexibility (the range of movement in a joint or joints) is achieved by using static methods. Static stretching holds muscles and connective tissues at their greatest length, thereby helping to relax them. Joint flexibility helps prevent the aches and pains that are common with aging.

Relaxation by means of biofeedback is also an important aspect of the exercise program. Appropriate exercise has been shown to have a greater effect on relaxation than the use of tranquilizers.

Xerox's weight conditioning program is used to strengthen major muscle groups and joints. The lifting of heavy weights, especially for middle-aged individuals, is carefully avoided; relatively light weights and frequent repetition are emphasized instead.

Programs at Kimberly-Clark and Tenneco

At Kimberly-Clark Corporation, approximately 1,200 employees participate in a health management program. A staff of twenty-three full-time health care professionals administers this program, utilizing a $2.5 million facility. Prior to admission, employees undergo a physical and medical history exam. Each employee then receives an individualized health prescription. The program at Kimberly-Clark began after its top management made a commitment to reduce health care costs.

Tenneco's 100,000 square-foot facility in Houston, Texas, cost $11 million. The facility includes racquetball courts, dressing rooms, exercise equipment, a sauna, and a whirlpool bath. It also features indoor gardens, employee dining rooms, and a conference and training center for 264 people.[26] Tenneco's emphasis on physical fitness can be attributed to a former CEO who underwent double bypass heart surgery over a decade ago. He suffered from severe angina due to a high cholesterol, high fat diet. After surgery, the CEO completely changed his diet and started running three miles a day.[27]

Physical fitness programs are also feasible for smaller companies. For example, such companies can often avoid large construction costs by converting unused rooms into aerobic centers. The price of a well-rounded facility of this type ranges from about $3,500 to $10,000. Other firms choose to join a commercial fitness center, which may charge, for example, an initial fee of $4,000 and annual dues of $1,000.[28]

ALCOHOL ABUSE PROGRAMS

Alcoholism is a disease characterized by uncontrolled and compulsive drinking that interferes with normal living patterns. It is a significant problem and can both result from and cause excessive stress. Although our society attaches a stigma to the disease of alcoholism, in 1956 the American Medical Association described it as treatable.

An individual may feel that drinking improves his or her ability to cope. However, alcohol rarely improves performance; to the contrary, it almost always impairs performance. As a person starts to drink excessively, the drinking itself results in greater stress. This increased stress is dealt with by more drinking, creating a vicious cycle. Alcohol abuse affects people at every level of society, from top-level managers to vagrants. It is also one of the most difficult conditions to detect. Sometimes a person progresses to advanced stages of alcohol abuse before perceiving that he or she may actually be an alcoholic. By then, the person's career may be on the verge of destruction. Early signs of alcohol abuse are especially difficult to identify. Often the symptoms are nothing more than an increasing number of absences from work. Over a period of time, productivity may begin to decline, or accidents may occur more frequently. A normally pleasant person can become highly disagreeable. Although alcohol abuse poses many problems for all concerned, no longer does it result in automatic termination. In fact, an increasing number of firms are establishing alcohol abuse programs, and supervisors are now being trained to cope with this health problem. In many instances, alcohol abuse programs are combined with more comprehensive wellness programs.

DRUG ABUSE PROGRAMS

As with alcohol, cocaine and other mind-altering drugs have impacted the workplace. According to the National Institute on Drug Abuse, almost 70 percent of the nation's illicit drug users are employed. In some instances, problems associated with drug abusers may consume as much as 35 percent of a firm's profits.[29] Chemically dependent employees exhibit behaviors that distinguish them from drug-free workers; some of these include being late to work three times more often, asking for time off at least twice as often, absent two and a half times as often, using three times the average amount of health care benefits, filing five times as many workers' compensation claims, and having accidents more than three and a half times as often.[30] Any one of these behaviors taken individually does not necessarily suggest that an individual is on drugs. It is when these behaviors are observed as a pattern that drug abuse may exist.

Numerous firms have recognized that drug problems pervade our society and have taken positive action to deal with them. A major goal of many firms is to ensure that drug abusers are not hired. However, if a person becomes an abuser after employment, a supervisor may be forced to resort to discipline for work-related irregularities, such as absenteeism and low productivity. All supervisors should be trained to look for signs of drug abuse. And if there is evidence that the problem does exist, the employee should be required to report to the medical department, where a bona fide attempt will be made to salvage the person. However, failure to comply with the supervisor's direction should reasonably result in discharge.

The medical department works with employees or refers them to appropriate agencies for treatment. If an employee assistance program exists, it may be able to deal with the problem. In any event, there should be an ongoing educational program that constantly reminds employees of the dangers of drug abuse.

Texas Instruments has recently implemented a comprehensive drug-free policy. The policy is simple: "There will be no use of any illegal drug. There will be no illicit use of a legal drug." The difficult part is not formulating the policy but rather implementing it. This aspect has four standards:

- Implementation of the policy must be unbiased. All employees will be treated the same way.
- Policy implementation must assure accuracy. It must contain a system of checks and balances that prevents or detects errors.
- Employees must understand the policy. They must realize the rationale behind the policy.
- Employees must be able to explain the policy. This assures not only understanding of the policy but also elicits their support of it.[31]

The Alcohol, Drug Abuse, and Mental Health Administration (ADAMHA) estimated that annual productivity losses from drug and alcohol abuse cost

HRM IN ACTION

—A COMPENSATION DILEMMA

"I just don't know what to do about Robert Lewis," said Marty Fagetti, the production supervisor, to Eli Richard, the human resource manager. "Lately I've noticed that Robert has missed work frequently. Even when he shows up, he is usually late. His eyes are always bloodshot, and he seems to move in slow motion. He also doesn't hang around with the old gang anymore. Again, today, he didn't show up for work. I just received a call from the police saying he was in the detoxification center and wanted us to be called."

If you were Eli, what action would you suggest?

employers almost $100 billion in 1986. This is an increase from $60 billion in 1983 and $46 billion in 1979. In the 1990s, the annual cost could reach $200 billion.[32]

The alternative to having a preemployment drug testing program is to hire other companies' rejects. According to an American Management Association (AMA) survey, the percentage of firms that test for drugs was almost 85 percent in 1993. Since the AMA began its annual survey in 1987, there has been a 300 percent increase in drug testing. Testing for cause—where there is reasonable suspicion of drug abuse and after employees have been involved in accidents—increased more than 400 percent. Random drug testing increased by 1,200 percent.

Drug programs are apparently more effective when drug testing is combined with other programs. For example, employee communication efforts and supervisory training can improve the chances for success. Family outreach efforts have also been shown to reduce the *test positive rate*.[33]

EMPLOYEE ASSISTANCE PROGRAMS

An **employee assistance program (EAP)** is a comprehensive approach that many organizations have taken to deal with numerous problem areas, including marital or family difficulties, job performance problems, stress, emotional or mental health issues, financial troubles, alcohol and drug abuse, and grief and loss. More recently, some EAPs have also become concerned with HIV and AIDS, eldercare, workplace violence, and natural disasters, such as earthquakes, floods, and tornadoes.[34] In an EAP, a firm either provides in-house professional counselors or refers employees to an appropriate community social service agency. Typically, most or all of the costs—up to a predetermined amount—are borne by the employer. The EAP concept includes a response to personal psychological problems that interfere with both an employee's well-being and overall productivity. The purpose of EAPs is to provide emotionally troubled employees with the same consideration and assistance given employees having physical illnesses.

In 1958, employee assistance counseling was offered by fewer than fifty American firms. Now, one-third of all U.S. firms provide access to an EAP counselor. Among Fortune 500 companies, 70 percent furnish such a service. Overall, 17,000 organizations sponsor EAPs.[35] These programs are being set up primarily to increase worker productivity and reduce costs. For example, one chief operating officer stated that a well-run EAP will return a minimum of three dollars for every dollar spent on the program. He hastens to add, however, that it cannot happen unless the employer is committed to promoting the program, educating employees and managers, and eliminating the stigma of the program from the environment.[36] Advantages claimed for EAPs include lower absenteeism, decreases in workers' compensation claims, and fewer accidents.

To get more mileage from an EAP, supervisors must receive training designed to provide specialized interpersonal skills for recognizing troubled employees and referring them to the firm's EAP. Addicted employees are often experts at denial and deception, and they can fool even experienced counselors. The problem of making EAP referrals is further compounded because supervisors often identify more with their workers than with management and do not want their employees to think they are on a witch-hunt. One study found that typical supervisors in public and private sector organizations covered up for troubled employees for a period of from eight to twelve years.[37]

SMOKING IN THE WORKPLACE[38]

One of the most controversial health issues facing employers today is environmental tobacco smoke (ETS). While many smokers remain adamant that smoking is not harmful, the Environmental Protection Agency has recently determined that ETS is a class A carcinogen, which puts it in the same cancer causing category as asbestos and benzene. The American Heart Association estimates that secondhand, or passive, smoke kills 53,000 nonsmokers each year by causing cancer, heart disease, and other smoke-related illnesses. In fact, smoking is the leading cause of preventable death, resulting in more deaths than the combined toll from AIDS, cocaine, heroin, alcohol, fire, automobile accidents, homicide, and suicide.

Numerous studies have concluded that workplace smoking not only is hazardous to employees' health, but also is detrimental to the firm's financial health. Increased costs of insurance premiums, higher absenteeism, and lost productivity cost the U.S. economy $65 billion a year. These factors, along with rising opposition from nonsmokers and widespread local and state laws, have spurred many firms into action, and the trend continues. For example, one recent survey indicated that in 1991, 32 percent of all companies banned smoking at work. By 1993, 56 percent had eliminated workplace smoking. A separate study indicated that by the year 2002, no less than 96 percent of the companies surveyed had a goal to be smoke-free.[39]

The development of no-smoking policies should take place over time, giving employees time to adjust. As a first step, firms should consider establishing employee teams consisting of both smokers and nonsmokers. Distinct smoking areas should be designated. Because of the high cost of installing ventilation systems, permitting smoking outdoors only may be the most feasible choice. Smoking-cessation classes should be offered to smokers along with reimbursement for those who actually stop smoking as a result. The final step would be implementing a totally smoke-free environment.

AIDS IN THE WORKPLACE

AIDS (acquired immune deficiency syndrome) is a disease that undermines the body's immune system, leaving the person susceptible to a wide range of fatal diseases. AIDS has become a worldwide epidemic with the potential to kill more people than the Black Plague did during the Middle Ages.[40] Since the first AIDS case was reported in the United States, the disease has claimed more than 78,000 lives. The number is expected to grow since AIDS affects every population regardless of race, gender, age, or sexual orientation. A direct effect on business is that it drains the pool of healthy adults of working age. An overwhelming majority of AIDS victims are between the ages of twenty and forty-nine.[41]

Although AIDS has become more feared than cancer, a relatively small percentage of firms have established formal policies to deal with it. In a study of AIDS practices and policies, 82 percent of the respondents expressed a need to engage in some education effort for their employees. However, only 28 percent have actually informed workers about AIDS.[42] For humanitarian and legal reasons, business practices will undoubtedly change.

It is apparent that some firms historically did not want to treat AIDS differently from other major illnesses. In one important respect, however, AIDS does differ significantly from all other diseases: It is always fatal. This fact no doubt accounts for both rational and irrational fears. Employees often hesitate to work with someone they believe has the disease, in spite of the law and despite assurance from medical experts that the disease cannot be transmitted through casual contact. At this time, it seems that the most aggressive action being taken by businesses regarding AIDS is in developing information programs that emphasize how to avoid contracting the disease.

There are only two ways that an individual can contract AIDS. The first is through the exchange of body fluids during sexual activity. The second is through exposure to contaminated blood in a manner that permits it to enter one's bloodstream. Outside of health care, workplace exposure to blood is rare. Therefore, there is no rational reason for employees to fear working with someone who has AIDS or who has been exposed to the virus.

The problem is that workers are not always rational. Their fear of the disease can result in the employer facing business interruption (if employees refuse to work with an AIDS victim) or unlawful discrimination under the Americans with Disabilities Act (if the employer discharges the ill person).

The need for educating employees is obvious. They must understand how the AIDS virus is transmitted and that it is not transmitted through casual contact. Only then can employees be assured that they are protected from this awful disease.

Firms that do provide AIDS training sessions for their employees often use more than one technique. Among the methods used are seminars, workshops, discussion groups, articles in employee publications, videotapes, literature in the company library, and health fairs. Providing training sessions is a commendable first step. However, it is quite clear that business organizations, in concert with the federal government, must soon deal more directly with this deadly disease. If human resources is truly the heart of the organization, as one HR executive has suggested, the chief human resource officer will be the catalyst in this effort.

SUMMARY

Safety involves protecting employees from injuries caused by work-related accidents. Health refers to the employees' freedom from physical or emotional illness. Prior to 1971, safety was regulated primarily by the workers' compensation laws of the various states. When Congress passed the Occupational Safety and Health Act, it quickly became one of the most controversial laws affecting human resource management.

One approach to safety programs is to create a psychology of promoting safety. Another approach is to develop and maintain a safe working environment. Evaluation of safety programs involves measuring both the frequency and severity of accidents. Promoting employee health has led many firms to develop wellness programs, which start with initial applicant screening and continue throughout workers' employment.

Cumulative trauma disorders include injuries to the back and upper extremities. Carpel tunnel syndrome is a specific problem caused by repetitive flexing and extension of the wrist. Many cumulative trauma disorders result from using computers. Workplace violence of all types includes beatings, serious injury, rape, and harassment.

Stress is the body's nonspecific reaction to any demand made on it. Everyone lives under some stress, which can be positive if not excessive but can be damaging when it is excessive. Burnout is a state of fatigue or frustration, which stems from devotion to a cause, way of life, or relationship that did not provide the expected reward. Stress can be managed, and many firms are helping employees deal with it in various ways.

Company-sponsored fitness programs often reduce absenteeism, accidents, and sick pay. Employees who are physically fit are more alert and productive, and their morale is higher.

Alcoholism is a disease characterized by uncontrolled and compulsive drinking that interferes with normal living patterns. It is a significant problem and can both result from and cause excessive stress. Numerous firms have recognized that drug problems exist and have taken positive action to deal with them. An employee assistance program (EAP) is a comprehensive approach that many organizations have taken to deal with burnout, alcohol and drug abuse, and other emotional disturbances. One of the most controversial health issues facing employers today is environmental tobacco smoke (ETS). AIDS (acquired immune deficiency syndrome) is a disease that destroys the body's immune system, leaving the person susceptible to a wide range of fatal diseases.

QUESTIONS FOR REVIEW

1. Define *safety* and *health*.
2. Describe the purpose of the Occupational Safety and Health Act.
3. What effect does workplace violence have on an organization?
4. What are the primary ways in which safety programs are designed? Discuss.
5. What are some measurements that would suggest the success of a firm's safety program?
6. What are the purposes of health and wellness programs?
7. Why should a firm attempt to identify stressful jobs? What could an organization do to reduce the stress associated with a job?
8. Why should a firm be concerned with employee burnout?
9. What are some signs that a supervisor might look for in identifying alcohol abuse?
10. Explain why employee assistance programs are being established.
11. What concerns should a manager have regarding smoking and AIDS in the workplace?

HRM SIMULATION

One of the problems facing the human resources director of your firm is an accident rate higher than it should be. Some of the causes of this are a higher-than-average turnover rate, a less-than-satisfactory morale level, and a lack of any type of accident prevention or safety program. The accident rate for the organization (as measured by employee-days lost per 1 million employee-hours) is 494. The industry average accident rate is also 494. However, both of these rates are above local accident rates and those of many other industries. Your team has the option of implementing a program and budget to deal with this problem. As always, there is a cost associated.

In Incident I, several proposals have been submitted concerning health, assistance, and wellness issues. Your team will have the task of studying these proposals and making a recommendation.

ABC VIDEO CASE

A SAFE AND HEALTHY WORKPLACE? TAPE 2, NUMBER 7

In an era when it is easier to get a gun than a job, some fired employees are reaching for a gun in an effort to cope. The typical employee with violence potential is male, white, middle-aged, and lives alone. Workplace murder is now one of the fastest growing kinds of murder in this country. In fact, the incidence of workplace murder has doubled. More and more people are angry and bitter. Facing job loss, they want revenge. Because of the difficulties of identifying which employee might retaliate with violence, and the economic pressures for more layoffs, it is more important than ever that companies pay as much attention to firing employees as they do hiring them.

HRM INCIDENT 1

TO TEST OR NOT TO TEST

John Hicks, human resource manager of Miller Chemical Company, had just read a report of a case filed in district court against a large neighboring company. One of that company's truck drivers had been involved in an accident in which two people were killed. The driver was tested by the police, and evidence of cocaine use was found.

John discussed the matter with the company president, Patsy Swain, who was familiar with the case. "Ms. Swain," he said, "I think we should adopt a policy of drug screening as part of all preemployment physicals." She replied, "I'm not sure that the testing requirement could be defended if we ever had a serious legal complaint. But the company could be in trouble if employee drug use led to negligence in some of these plant jobs." John asked, "What about the testing program for current employees? Should it be made a part of the annual physicals? Annual physicals are not really mandatory now, but we can make them so."

Questions

1. What is the primary purpose of a testing program such as the one John wants to establish?
2. What would Miller Chemical do if an employee became a drug abuser after employment?

HRM INCIDENT 2

A STAR IS FALLING

"Just leave me alone and let me do my job," said Manuel Gomez. Dumbfounded, Bill Brown, Manuel's supervisor, decided to count to ten and not respond to Manuel's comment. As he walked back to his office, Bill thought about how Manuel had changed over the past few months. He had been a hard worker and extremely cooperative when he came to work for Bill two years earlier. The company had sent Manuel to two training schools and had received glowing reports about his performance in each of them.

Until about a year ago, Manuel had a perfect attendance record and was an ideal employee. At about that time, however, he began to have personal problems, which resulted in a divorce six months later. Manuel had requested a day off several times to take care of personal business. Bill had attempted to help in every way he could without getting directly involved in Manuel's personal affairs. But Bill was aware of the strain Manuel must have experienced as his marriage broke up and he and his wife engaged in the inevitable disputes over child custody, alimony payments, and property.

During the same time period, top management initiated a push for improving productivity. Bill found it necessary to put additional pressure on all his workers, including Manuel. He tried to be considerate, but he had to become much more performance-oriented, insisting on increased output from every worker. As time went on, Manuel began to show up late for work and actually missed two days without calling Bill in advance. Bill attributed Manuel's behavior to extreme stress. Because Manuel had been such a good worker for so long, Bill excused the tardiness and absences, only gently suggesting that Manuel should try to do better.

Sitting at his desk, Bill thought about what might have caused Manuel's outburst a few minutes earlier. Bill had simply suggested to Manuel that he shut down the machine he was operating and clean up the surrounding area. This was a normal part of Manuel's job and something he had been careful to do in the past. Bill felt the disorder around Manuel's machine might account for the increasing number of defects in the parts he was making. "This is a tough one. I think I'll talk to the boss about it," thought Bill.

Questions

1. What do you think is likely to be Manuel's problem? Discuss.
2. If you were Bill's boss, what would you recommend that he do?

DEVELOPING HRM SKILLS

AN EXPERIENTIAL EXERCISE

At times, workers have personal problems that negatively influence their work and that may make the workplace unsafe. When this occurs, both managers and human resource professionals may be required to become involved to maintain a safe and healthy work environment. Dealing with one's own personal problems is often difficult, and assisting employees in dealing with their personal problems can be even more taxing on managers. However, since a problem employee can have a negative effect on workforce productivity, such a situation must be addressed by individuals involved in human resource management. This exercise should provide a better understanding of how to handle a most difficult issue—that of resolving employee problems.

"I'm going to do it, and I'm going to do it today. This has gone on long enough!" thought Annette Dommert, the data processing manager. "I can't put it off any longer. I realize that Walter has been with the company for fourteen years, and with this department for eleven of those years, but this drinking thing is out of hand. Lately, the problem is affecting other members of the work group. His friends are covering up pretty well for him, but that is causing their productivity to go down. Evidently Walter is not going to be able to work things out, and the situation will only get worse. We are going to meet today and resolve this matter one way or the other; he's dry or he's out! I am not a villain, and I really want him to work things out, but this is causing the department problems."

Walter Hollingsworth, a programmer in the data processing department, was concerned. He thought, "I heard from a friend in the boss's office that I am going to get chewed out about my drinking. I have always gotten my work done, but I guess I've let things slip lately. I know I can lick this problem. I'm going to straighten myself out, and when I meet with the boss I'll admit that I drink too much sometimes; everybody does. Drinking has only recently affected my work. I'll do better in the future. I've been with the company for fourteen years, and with this division for eleven of those years. Only one problem in all those years makes me a good risk. I can do it, and I deserve a chance. The boss should be compassionate."

If you are a sensitive person, you may want to play a role in this exercise. Two students will actively participate. One will play Annette and one will play Walter. The rest of you should observe carefully. Your instructor will provide any additional information necessary to participate.

NOTES

1. Brad Lee Thompson, "OSHA Bounces Back," *Training* 28 (January 1991): 46.

2. "No Accident," *The Wall Street Journal* (November 3, 1993): A22.

3. "OSHA to Mix a Little Mercy with Latest Crackdown," *The Wall Street Journal* (February 1, 1994): B2.

4. Michael A. Verespej, "Will Reich's Support Bring OSHA Reform?" *Industry Week* 243 (January 3, 1994): 66.

5. National Safety Council, Itasca, IL, *Accident Facts* annual (1993 edition): 34.

6. Stephenie Overman, "Driving the Safety Message Home," *HRMagazine* 39 (March 1994): 58.

7. Neville C. Tompkins, "At the Top of OSHA's Hit List," *HRMagazine* 38 (July 1993): 54.

8. Neville C. Tompkins, "Conduct Constructive Safety Audits," *HRMagazine* 38 (July 1993): 55–56.

9. Robert Pater, "Safety Leadership Cuts Costs," *HRMagazine* 35 (November 1990): 46.

10. "To OSHA, 'Workplace Safety Is Good Business,'" *Risk Management* 36 (October 1989): 172.

11. Marilyn Joyce, "Ergonomics Will Take Center Stage During '90s and into New Century," *Occupational Health and Safety* 60 (January 1991): 31–32.

12. Michael J. Lotito and Francis P. Alvarez, "Integrate Claims Management with ADA Compliance Strategy," *HRMagazine* 38 (August 1993): 86–92.

13. Linda Thornburg, "When Violence Hits Business," *HRMagazine* 38 (July 1993): 45.

14. Helen Frank Bensimon, "Violence in the Workplace," *Training and Development Journal* 48 (January 1994): 27–31.

15. Daniel Weisburg, "Preparing for the Unthinkable," *Management Review* 83 (March 1994): 58.

16. Cathy J. Brumback, "EAPs—Bringing Health and Productivity to the Workplace," *Business* 37 (April-June 1987): 42.

17. David S. Allen, "Less Stress, Less Litigation," *Personnel* 67 (January 1990): 32.

18. Patti Watts, "Are Your Employees Burnout-Proof?" *Personnel* 67 (September 1990): 12–13, 20.

19. Ron Zemke, "Workplace Stress Revisited," *Training* 28 (November 1991): 35–39.

20. "How to Avoid Burnout," *Training* 30 (February 1993): 16.

21. "Half of Managers Suffer Work Stress," *Supervision* 51 (July 1990): 10.

22. Jennifer Laabs, "Surviving HR Burnout," *Personnel Journal* 71 (April 1992): 85.

23. Debra L. Nelson, James C. Quick, and Michael A. Hitt, "What Stresses HR Professionals?" *Personnel* 67 (August 1990): 36–39.

24. Pam Black, "A Home Office That's Easier on the Eyes—and the Back," *Business Week* (August 17, 1992): 112–113.

25. Mark C. Butler and Mary B. Teagarden, "Strategic Management of Worker Health, Safety, and Environmental Issues in Mexico's Maquiladora Industry," *Human Resource Management* (Winter 1993): 479–503.

26. Otto H. Chang and Cynthia Boyle, "Fitness Programs: Hefty Expense or Wise Investment?" *Management Accounting* 20 (January 1989): 46.

27. Faye Rice, "How Execs Get Fit," *Fortune* 122 (October 22, 1990): 147.

28. Ibid.

29. Bill Oliver, "How to Prevent Drug Abuse in Your Workplace," *HRMagazine* 38 (December 1993): 79–80.

30. Ibid., 79.

31. Bill Oliver, "Do You Drug Test Your Employees?" *HRMagazine* 35 (October 1990): 57.

32. Cheryl Thieme, "Better-Bilt Builds a Substance Abuse Program That Works," *Personnel Journal* 69 (August 1990): 52.

33. Bill Oliver, "How to Prevent Drug Abuse in Your Workplace": 81–82.

34. Sharon A. Haskins and Brian H. Kleiner, "Employee Assistance Programs Take New Directions," *HR Focus* 71 (January 1994): 16.

35. William R. Tracey, editor, *Human Resource Management and Development Handbook,* 2nd edition (New York: AMACOM, a Division of American Management Association, 1994): 696.

36. Peggy Stuart, "Investments in EAPs Pay Off," *Personnel Journal* (February 1993): 54.

37. Mark Ralfs and John M. Morley, "Turning Employee Problems into Triumphs," *Training and Development Journal* 44 (November 1990): 73.

38. Jennifer Laabs, "Companies Kick the Smoking Habit," *Personnel Journal* 73 (January 1994): 38–43.

39. Ibid., 38.

40. Throughout history there have been several major epidemics of bubonic plague. In the 1300s, the infamous Black Plague destroyed one-fourth of Europe's population.

41. Laura B. Pincus and Shefali M. Trivedi, "A Time for Action: Responding to AIDS," *Training and Development* 48 (January 1994): 46.

42. Ibid., 47.

CHAPTER 15 The Labor Union

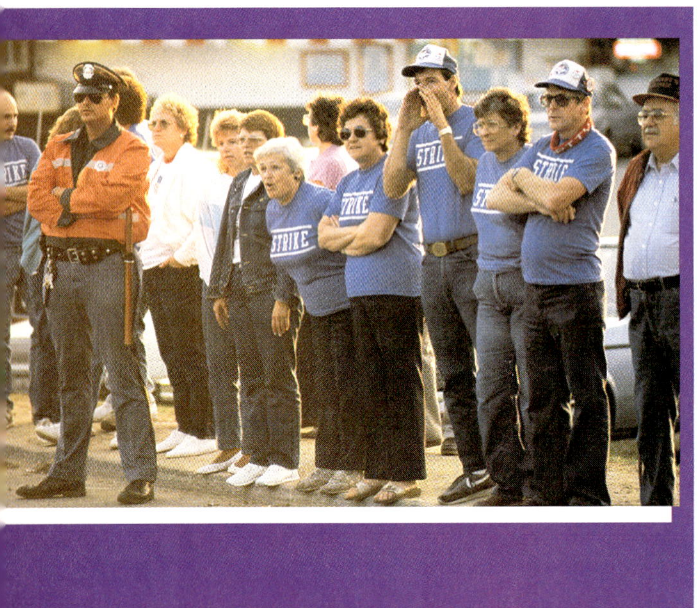

KEY TERMS

Conspiracy 464	Local union 480
Injunction 465	Craft union 480
Yellow-dog contract 465	Industrial union 480
Right-to-work laws 469	National union 481
New collar workers 475	Collective bargaining 483
Committee on Political Education (COPE) 476	Bargaining unit 483
Two-tier wage system 477	Authorization card 484

CHAPTER OBJECTIVES

1. Describe the history of the labor movement.
2. Explain the most significant union objectives, identify the reasons why employees join unions, and describe the basic structure of the union.
3. Explain what is involved in establishing the collective bargaining relationship.
4. Describe signs of a troubled labor movement and discuss why there is a growing legalistic approach to collective bargaining.
5. Describe the future of unionism and collective bargaining in a global economy.

Robert Sweeney, president of United Technologies, was disturbed and disappointed. He had just been informed by the National Labor Relations Board that a majority of his employees had voted to have the union represent them. The past months had been difficult ones, with charges and counter charges being made by both management and labor. The vote had been close, with only a few votes tipping the scales in favor of labor.

He looked at the human resource manager, Marthanne Bello, and said, "I don't know what to do. The union will demand so much that we can't possibly be competitive."

Marthanne replied, "Just because the union has won the right to be represented doesn't mean that we have to accept all their terms. I believe that a reasonable contract can be negotiated. I know many of those guys, and I am sure that we can work out a contract that will be fair to both sides."

Robert Sweeney is not only troubled, but he is also misinformed about the necessary impact of collective bargaining. Employees have decided to unionize, but this in no way mandates management acceptance of contractual terms that would adversely impact the health and profitability of the company.

We begin this chapter with a history of the labor movement in the United States and the legislation relating to it. Next, we discuss the objectives of unions, the reasons why employees join unions, and the multilevel organizational structure of unions. Then, we address the steps used to establish a collective bargaining relationship. Finally, we review the signs of a troubled labor movement, the growing legalistic approach to collective bargaining, and the future of unionism and collective bargaining in a global economy.

THE LABOR MOVEMENT BEFORE 1930

Unions are not a recent development in American history. The earliest unions originated toward the end of the eighteenth century, about the time of the American Revolution. Although these early associations had few characteristics of present day labor unions, they did bring workers in craft or guild-related occupations together to consider problems of mutual concern. These early unions were local in nature and usually existed for only a short time.[1]

Development of the labor movement has been neither simple nor straightforward. Instead, unionism has experienced as much failure as success. Employer opposition, the impact of the business cycle, the growth of American industry, court rulings, and legislation have exerted their influence in varying degrees at different times. As a result, the history of the labor movement has somewhat resembled the swinging of a pendulum. At times, the pendulum has moved in favor of labor and, at other times, it has swung toward the advantage of management. In most segments of the economy, management has the power to exert its will upon labor, but only a few smart managers have exercised control and even tried to work with labor for mutual gain.[2] Such trade agreements as NAFTA and GATT may have very adverse effects on unions if certain expert predictions are accurate.

Prior to the 1930s, the trend definitely favored management. The courts strongly supported employers in their attempts to thwart the organized labor movement. This was first evidenced by the use of criminal and civil conspiracy doctrines derived from English common law. A **conspiracy**, generally defined, is the combination of two or more persons who band together to prejudice the rights of others or of society (e.g., by refusing to work or demanding higher wages). An important feature of the conspiracy doctrine is that an action by one person, though legal, may become illegal when carried out by a group.[3] In 1806, the year in which the conspiracy doctrine was first applied to labor unions, the courts began to influence the field of labor relations.[4] From 1806 to 1842, seventeen cases went to trial charging labor unions with conspiracies. These cases resulted in the demise of several unions and certainly discouraged other union activities. The conspiracy doctrine was softened considerably by the decision in the landmark case *Commonwealth v Hunt* in 1842. In that case, Chief Justice Shaw of the Supreme Judicial Court of Massachusetts contended that labor organizations were legal. Thus, in order for a union to be convicted under the conspiracy doctrine, it had to be shown that the union's objectives were unlawful or that the means employed to gain a legal end were unlawful. To this day, the courts continue to exert a profound influence on both the direction and character of labor relations.

Other tactics used by employers to stifle union growth were injunctions and yellow-dog contracts. An **injunction** is a prohibiting legal procedure used by employers to prevent certain union activities, such as strikes and unionization attempts. A **yellow-dog contract** was a written agreement between the employee and the company made at the time of employment, prohibiting a worker from joining a union or engaging in union activities. Each of these defensive tactics, used by management and supported by the courts, severely limited union growth.

In the latter half of the nineteenth century, the American industrial system started to grow and prosper. Factory production began to displace handicraft forms of manufacturing. The Civil War gave the factory system a great boost. Goods were demanded in quantities that only mass production methods could supply. The railroads developed new networks of routes spanning the continent and knitting the country into an economic whole. Employment was high, and unions sought to organize workers in both new and expanding enterprises. Most unions during this time were small and rather weak, and many did not survive the economic recession of the 1870s. Union membership rose to 300,000 by 1872 and then dropped to 50,000 by 1878.[5] This period also marked the rise of radical labor activity and increased industrial strife as unions struggled for recognition and survival.[6]

Out of the turbulence of the 1870s emerged the most substantial labor organization that had yet appeared in the United States. The Noble Order of the Knights of Labor was founded in 1869 as a secret society of the Philadelphia garment workers. After its secrecy was abandoned and workers in other areas were invited to join, it grew rapidly, reaching a membership of more than 700,000 by the mid-1880s. Internal conflict among the Knights' leadership in 1881 gave rise to the nucleus of a new organization that would soon replace it on the labor scene.[7] That organization was the American Federation of Labor (AFL).

Devoted to what is referred to as either "pure and simple unionism," or "business unionism," Samuel Gompers of the Cigarmakers Union led some twenty-five labor groups representing skilled trades to found the AFL in 1886. Gompers was elected the first president of the AFL, a position he held until his death in 1924 (except for one year, 1894-95, when he adamantly opposed tangible support for the strikers of the Pullman group). He is probably the single most important individual in American trade union history. The AFL began with a membership of some 138,000 and doubled that number during the next twelve years.[8]

In 1890, Congress passed the Sherman Anti-Trust Act, which marked the entrance of the federal government into the statutory regulation of labor organizations. Although the primary stimulus for this act came from public concern over business's monopoly power, court interpretations soon applied its provisions to organized labor. Later, in 1914, Congress passed the Clayton Act (an amendment to the Sherman Act), which, according to Samuel Gompers, was the Magna Carta of Labor. The intent of this act was to remove labor from the purview of the Sherman Act. Again, judicial interpretation nullified that intent and left labor even more exposed to lawsuits.[9] Nonetheless, as a result of industrial activity related to World War I, the AFL grew to almost 5 million members by 1920.[10]

During the 1920s, labor faced legal restrictions on union activity and unfavorable court decisions. The one exception to such repressive policies was the passage and approval of the Railway Labor Act of 1926. This was the first time that the government declared without qualification the right of private employees to join unions and bargain collectively through representatives of their own choosing without interference from their employers. The act also set up special machinery for the settlement of labor disputes. Although the act covered only employees in the railroad industry (a later amendment extended coverage to the airline industry), it foreshadowed the extension of similar rights to other classes of employees in the 1930s.

THE LABOR MOVEMENT AFTER 1930

The 1930s found the United States in the midst of the worst depression in its history. The unemployment rate rose as high as 25 percent.[11] The sentiment of the country began to favor organized labor as many people blamed business for the agony that accompanied the Great Depression. The pendulum began to swing away from management and toward labor. This swing was manifested by several acts and actions that supported the cause of unionism.

Anti-Injunction Act (Norris-LaGuardia Act)—1932

The Great Depression caused a substantial change in the public's thinking about the role of unions in society. Congress reflected this thinking in 1932 with the passage of the Norris-LaGuardia Act. It affirms that U.S. public policy sanctions collective bargaining and approves the formation and effective operation of labor unions.[12] While this act did not outlaw the use of injunctions, it severely restricted the federal courts' authority to issue them in labor disputes. It also made yellow-dog contracts unenforceable in the federal courts.[13]

National Labor Relations Act (Wagner Act)—1935

In 1933, Congress made an abortive attempt to stimulate economic recovery by passing the National Industry Recovery Act (NIRA). Declared unconstitutional by the U.S. Supreme Court in 1935, the NIRA did provide the nucleus for legislation that followed it. Section 7a of the NIRA proclaimed the right of workers to organize and bargain collectively. Congress did not, however, provide procedures to enforce these rights.[14]

Undeterred by the Supreme Court decision and strongly supported by organized labor, Congress speedily enacted a comprehensive labor law, the National Labor Relations Act (Wagner Act). This act, approved by President Roosevelt on July 5, 1935, is one of the most significant labor-management relations statutes ever enacted. Drawing heavily on the experience of the Railway Labor Act of 1926 and Section 7a of the NIRA, the act declared legislative support, on a broad scale, for the right of employees to organize and engage in collective bargaining. The spirit of the Wagner Act is stated in Section 7, which defines the substantive rights of employees:

> Employees shall have the right to self-organization, to form, join, or assist labor organizations, to bargain collectively through representatives of their own choosing, and to engage in other concerted activities, for the purpose of collective bargaining or other mutual aid or protection.

The rights defined in Section 7 were protected against employer interference by Section 8, which detailed and prohibited five management practices deemed to be unfair to labor:

1. Interfering with or restraining or coercing employees in the exercise of their right to self-organization.
2. Dominating or interfering in the affairs of a union.
3. Discriminating in regard to hire or tenure or any condition of employment for the purpose of encouraging or discouraging union membership.
4. Discriminating against or discharging an employee who has filed charges or given testimony under the act.
5. Refusing to bargain with chosen representatives of employees.

The National Labor Relations Board (NLRB) was created by the National Labor Relations Act to administer and enforce the provisions of the act. The NLRB was given two principal functions: (1) to establish procedures for holding bargaining-unit elections and to monitor the election procedures, and (2) to investigate complaints and prevent unlawful acts involving unfair labor practices. However, current NLRB election procedures are often cumbersome because of technicalities employers can use to delay elections for years.[15] Much of the NLRB's work is delegated to thirty-three regional offices throughout the country.

In recent years, many labor leaders have expressed their dismay with the composition of the NLRB. Some feel that past Republican administrations made it easier for employers to beat unions by changing the way labor law is interpreted and enforced.

Following passage of the Wagner Act, union membership increased from approximately 3 million to 15 million between 1935 and 1947.[16] The increase was most conspicuous in industries utilizing mass production methods. New unions in these industries were organized on an industrial basis rather than a craft basis, and members were primarily unskilled or semiskilled workers. An internal struggle developed within the AFL over the question of whether unions should be organized to include all workers in an industry or strictly on a craft or occupational basis. In 1935, ten AFL-affiliated unions and the officers of two other AFL unions formed the Committee for Industrial Organization to promote the organization of workers in mass production and unorganized industries. The controversy grew to the point that in 1938 the AFL expelled all but one of the Committee for Industrial Organization unions. In November of 1938, the expelled unions held their first convention in Pittsburgh, Pennsylvania, and reorganized as a federation of unions under the name of Congress of Industrial Organizations (CIO). The new federation included the nine unions expelled from the AFL and thirty-two other groups established to recruit workers in various industries. John L. Lewis, president of the United Mine Workers, was elected the first president of the CIO.[17]

The rivalry generated by the two large federations stimulated union organizing efforts in both groups. With the ensuing growth, the labor movement gained considerable influence in the United States. However, many individuals and groups began to feel that the Wagner Act favored labor too much. This shift in public sentiment was in part related to a rash of costly strikes following World War II. Whether justified or not, much of the blame for these disruptions fell on the unions. It is interesting to note that even now few American managers have accepted the right of unions to exist, even though that is guaranteed by the 1935 Wagner Act. In fact, in the past twelve years, U.S. industry has conducted one of the most successful antiunion wars ever.[18]

Labor Management Relations Act (Taft-Hartley Act)—1947

In 1947, with public pressure mounting, Congress overrode President Truman's veto and passed the Labor Management Relations Act (Taft-Hartley Act). The Taft-Hartley Act extensively revised the National Labor Relations Act and became Title I of that law. A new period in the evolution of public policy regarding labor began. The pendulum had begun to swing toward a more balanced position between labor and management.

Some of the important changes introduced by the Taft-Hartley Act included the following:

1. Modifying Section 7 to include the right of employees to refrain from union activity as well as engage in it.
2. Prohibiting the closed shop (the arrangement requiring that all workers be union members at the time they are hired) and narrowing the freedom of the parties to authorize the union shop (the situation in which the employer may hire anyone he or she chooses, but all new workers must join the union after a stipulated period of time).
3. Broadening the employer's right of free speech.
4. Providing that employers need not recognize or bargain with unions formed by supervisory employees.
5. Giving employees the right to initiate decertification petitions.
6. Providing for government intervention in "national emergency strikes."

Another significant change extended the concept of unfair labor practices to unions. Labor organizations were to refrain from the following:

1. Restraining or coercing employees in the exercise of their guaranteed collective bargaining rights.
2. Causing an employer to discriminate in any way against an employee in order to encourage or discourage union membership.
3. Refusing to bargain in good faith with an employer regarding wages, hours, and other terms and conditions of employment.
4. Engaging in certain types of strikes and boycotts.
5. Requiring employees covered by union-shop contracts to pay initiation fees or dues "in an amount which the Board finds excessive or discriminatory under all circumstances."
6. "Featherbedding," or requiring that an employer pay for services not performed.

One of the most controversial elements of the Taft-Hartley Act is its Section 14b, which permits states to enact right-to-work legislation. **Right-to-work laws** are laws that prohibit management and unions from entering into agreements requiring union membership as a condition of employment. Twenty-one states, located primarily in the South and West, have adopted such laws, which are a continuing source of irritation between labor and management.[19] Much of the impetus behind the right-to-work movement is provided by the National Right to Work Committee, based in Springfield, Virginia.

For about ten years after the passage of the Taft-Hartley Act, union membership expanded at about the same rate as nonagricultural employment. But all was not well within the organized labor movement. Since the creation of the CIO, the two federations had engaged in a bitter and costly rivalry. Both the CIO and the AFL recognized the increasing need for cooperation and reunification. In 1955, following two years of intensive negotiations between the two organizations, a merger agreement was ratified, the AFL-CIO became a reality, and George Meany was elected president. In the years following the merger, the labor movement faced some of its greatest challenges.

Labor-Management Reporting and Disclosure Act (Landrum-Griffin Act)—1959

Corruption had plagued organized labor since the early 1900s. Periodic revelations of graft, violence, extortion, racketeering, and other improper activities aroused public indignation and invited governmental investigation. Even though the number of unions involved was small, every disclosure undermined the public image of organized labor as a whole.[20] Corruption had been noted in the construction trades and Laborers, Hotel and Restaurant, Carpenters, Painters, East Coast Longshoremen, and Boilermakers unions. The inability of the labor movement to deal with massive corruption and racketeering may be evidence of deep-seated union problems.[21] For example, the International Brotherhood of Teamsters faced a change of leadership in the late 1980s because of its alleged ties to organized crime.[22]

Scrutiny of union activities is a focal point in today's labor environment, but it began to intensify immediately after World War II. Ultimately, inappropriate union activities led to the creation in 1957 of the Senate Select Committee on Improper Activities in the Labor or Management Field, headed by Senator McClellan of Arkansas. Between 1957 and 1959, the McClellan Committee held a series of nationally televised public hearings that shocked and alarmed the entire country. As evidence of improper activities mounted—primarily against the Teamsters and Longshoremen/Maritime unions—the AFL-CIO took action.

In 1957, the AFL-CIO expelled three unions (representing approximately 1.6 million members) for their practices. One of them, the Teamsters, was the largest union in the country.

In 1959, largely as a result of the recommendations of the McClellan Committee, Congress enacted the Labor-Management Reporting and Disclosure Act (Landrum-Griffin Act). This act marked a significant turning point in the involvement of the federal government in internal union affairs. The Landrum-Griffin Act spelled out a "Bill of Rights of Members of Labor Organizations" designed to protect certain rights of individuals in their relationships with unions. The act requires extensive reporting on numerous internal union activities and contains severe penalties for violations. Employers are also required to file reports when they engage in activities or make expenditures that might undermine the collective bargaining process or interfere with protected employee rights. In addition, the act amended the Taft-Hartley Act by adding additional restrictions on picketing and secondary boycotts.[23]

In 1974, Congress extended coverage of the Taft-Hartley Act to private, not-for-profit hospitals. This amendment brought within the jurisdiction of the National Labor Relations Board some two million employees. Proprietary (profit-making) health care organizations were already under NLRB jurisdiction. The amendment does not cover government-operated hospitals; it applies only to the private sector.

Even though the AFL-CIO merger was completed in 1955, internal conflict remained. The Teamsters expulsion was followed in 1968 by the disaffiliation of the second largest union in the country, the United Automobile Workers (UAW). This split was caused primarily by personality and philosophical clashes between Walter Reuther, president of the UAW, and Meany. Shortly thereafter the UAW and the Teamsters formed the Alliance of Labor Action (ALA) with the possible aim of developing a rival federation.[24] The ALA lasted only until the untimely death of Walter Reuther in a plane crash in 1970. The UAW reaffiliated with the AFL-CIO in July 1981. The Teamsters Union was allowed to reaffiliate in October 1987, when it brought its 1.6 million members back into the AFL-CIO.[25]

Overall, the fall of "Big Labor" has been dramatic since the 1970s.[26] Despite the reaffiliation of the Teamsters with the AFL-CIO, union membership dropped from about one-third of the nonfarm workforce in 1950 to 15.8 percent in 1994.[27] As shown in Figure 15-1, the unionized share of the private workforce had shrunk to about 11 percent by 1994.[28] Unions have also won

FIGURE 15-1
Percentage of the Private Workforce That is Unionized

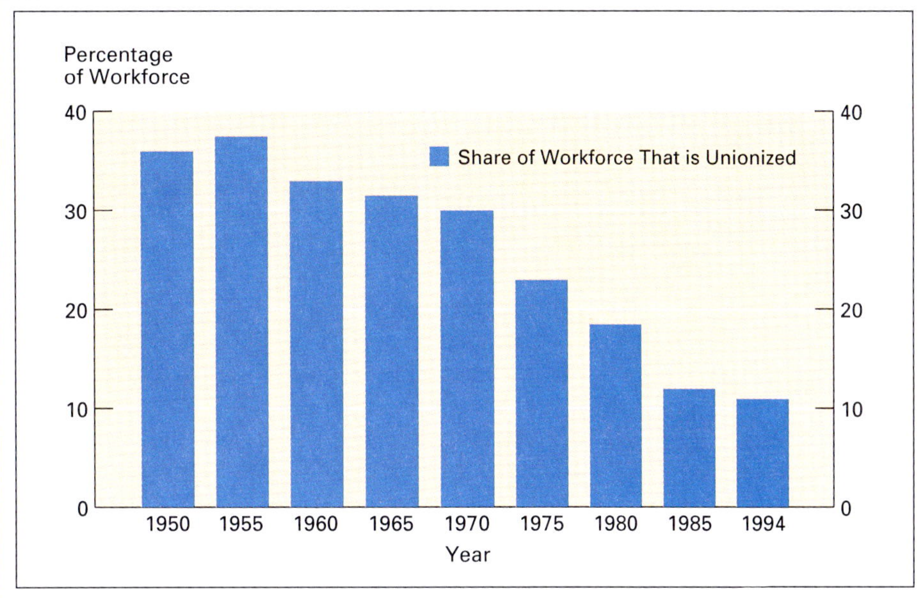

Source: Labor Department.

fewer and fewer representation elections as collective bargaining agents in recent years.[29]

THE PUBLIC SECTOR

Government (public sector) employees are generally considered a class apart from private-sector workers. This is reflected in their exclusion from coverage of general labor legislation.[30] However, like their counterparts in private industry, government employees have demonstrated a persistence in organizing in order to gain an effective voice in the terms and conditions of their employment. The unionized share of government workers is now approximately 37 percent, more than double that of the private sector.[31] Employee involvement and participation in decision making is much more accepted in the public sector than in the private sector. Quality management programs are on the rise in the public sector because a true union/management partnership is much closer to being a reality than it is in the private sector. In the public sector, employee involvement and participation are accepted as critical factors in achieving quality improvements and enhancing organizational effectiveness. The U.S. Department of Labor's "Employee-Involvement/Quality Improvement" is a quality improvement program that is actually working. This program, which is a true partnership between management and labor, has improved the productivity of the departments involved and the working lives of participating employees. In the program, employees and managers work in teams, and together make recommendations and decisions to benefit everyone concerned.[32]

For many years the federal government had no well-defined policy on labor-management relations regarding its own employees. In order to address this situation, President Kennedy issued Executive Order 10988 in 1962. Section 1(a) of the order stated:

> Employees of the federal government shall have, and shall be protected in the exercise of, the right, freely and without fear of penalty or reprisal, to form, join and assist any employee organization or to refrain from any such activity.

For the first time in the history of the federal civil service, a uniform, comprehensive policy of cooperation between employee organizations and management in the executive branch of government was established. Employees were permitted to organize and negotiate human resource policies and practices and matters affecting working conditions that were within the administrative discretion of the agency officials concerned. However, Public Law 84-330, passed in 1955, made it a felony to strike against the U.S. government.[33]

Executive Order 10988 established the basic framework for collective bargaining in federal government agencies. Subsequent EOs revised and improved this framework and brought about a new era of labor relations in the public sector.[34] In fact, the federal government codified the provisions of those EOs and transferred them to Title VII of the Civil Service Reform Act of 1978. This act regulates most of the labor-management relations in the federal service. It establishes the Federal Labor Relations Authority (FLRA), which is modeled on the National Labor Relations Board. The intent of the FLRA is to bring the public sector model in line with that of the private sector. Requirements and mechanisms for recognition and elections, dealing with impasses, and handling grievances are covered in the act.

The U.S. Postal Service is not subject to Title VII of the Civil Service Reform Act of 1978. It was given independent government agency status by the Postal Reorganization Act of 1970. Postal employees were given collective bargaining rights comparable to those governing private industry. National Labor Relations Board rules and regulations controlling representation issues and elections are applicable to the postal service. Unfair labor practice provisions are also enforced by the NLRB. However, the right to strike is prohibited, and union-shop arrangements are not permitted.

Labor Relations and Bargaining Patterns

There is no uniform pattern to state and local labor relations and bargaining rights. Some states have no policy at all, whereas a haphazard mixture of statutes, resolutions, ordinances, and civil service procedures exists in others. However, public-employer legislation passed by state and local government accelerated noticeably after the issuance of EO 10988 in 1962.[35] By 1984, forty-one states and the District of Columbia had collective bargaining statutes covering all or some categories of public employees. By 1980, thirty-eight states had passed some form of legislation that obligates state agencies and local governments to permit their public employees to join unions and to recognize bona fide labor organizations. Prior to 1960, just a handful of states had such legislation. The diversity of state labor laws makes it difficult to generalize about the legal aspects of collective bargaining at the state and local levels.

Unilateral determination of the conditions of employment by public employers is increasingly being questioned. These decisions—made without worker input—are being questioned not only by government workers, but also by the unions and associations that represent them. Placed in the middle between their employees and the general public, state and local governments are being forced to specify in clearer terms the collective bargaining rights of workers.[36]

Employee Associations

Membership in public-sector professional and state employee associations greatly exceeds private-sector unionization.[37] The largest of the employee associations, the National Education Association (NEA), has become the largest and most powerful "union" in the United States.[38]

In the past, employee associations were concerned primarily with the professional aspects of employment and avoided any semblance of unionism. In recent years, this approach has changed as public- and private-sector unions have actively organized both professional and government employees. Many employee associations now enthusiastically pursue collective bargaining relationships.

The greater public-sector penetration of unions in recent years indicates that the process of unionization in the public sector differs from that in the private labor market. One factor that accounts for membership gains is clearly the role played by government employee associations, particularly at the state and local level. Challenged by established unions, the associations either merged with unions or transformed themselves into collective bargaining organizations. Many are becoming de facto unions, as with the NEA. Another reason that membership gains were made so quickly was the encouragement union organizations received from public-sector management.[39] Next, we discuss the global sector.

A GLOBAL PERSPECTIVE

Although the future of unionism abroad seems much brighter than domestic unionism, the future is not as bright as it was even in the early 1990s. According to economist Richard Freeman, unionism fell in some countries in the 1980s, but no country had the same consistent abrupt drop experienced by U.S. unions. While unionism has waned in the United States, it has maintained much of its strength abroad. Even though unions in all countries have been under increasing pressure in recent decades because of slowing productivity, lower economic growth, rapid technological changes, and a shift toward a free market system, unionism in the United States has suffered the most.[40]

In the United States, the rate of unionism has fallen to 15.8 percent, in Sweden the rate is 96 percent, 51 percent in the United Kingdom, 45 percent in Italy, 43 percent in Germany, 36 percent in Canada, and 28 percent in Japan.[41] Although the overseas rates appear impressive, as free market systems spread throughout the world, the strength of unions overseas will continue to decline. Problems between labor and management are beginning to intensify, resulting in labor-management strife similar to the U.S. labor-management relationship in the '80s and '90s. In France, the government and Air France strikers experienced major conflict when the government announced plans to layoff 4,000 workers. In Germany, IG Metall's 3.3 million members vowed to fight cancellation of the national labor contract, and workers protested Deutsche Aerospace's plans to close six plants and lay off 26,000 workers. In Italy, strikes erupt daily and seem bound to worsen.[42]

In the past, the critical difference between U.S. unions and their overseas counterparts was that U.S. unions managed to win much higher wages than those received by nonunion workers. That gap was 20 to 25 percent in the United States compared with 10 percent or less abroad. This pronounced gap gave U.S. employers a major incentive to oppose unions and establish nonunion operations. In addition, foreign unions were generally less adversarial with management and less focused on wage gains. Instead, they concentrated on worker councils and participative decision making. However, because of recent developments, such as the Economic Communities' economic union, increasing global competition, and souring global unemployment, management and union cooperation (which has been commonplace overseas) is beginning to change to an adversarial relationship similar to that in the United States. The tide of union membership overseas may well be on a downturn.[43]

UNION OBJECTIVES

As previously indicated, the labor movement has a long history in the United States. Although each union is a unique organization seeking its own objectives, several broad objectives characterize the labor movement as a whole:

1. To secure and, if possible, improve the living standards and economic status of its members.
2. To enhance and, if possible, guarantee individual security against threats and contingencies that might result from market fluctuations, technological change, or management decisions.
3. To influence power relations in the social system in ways that favor and do not threaten union gains and goals.
4. To advance the welfare of all who work for a living, whether union members or not.[44]
5. To create mechanisms to guard against the use of arbitrary and capricious policies and practices in the workplace.

The underlying philosophy of the labor movement is that of organizational democracy and an atmosphere of social dignity for working men and women. In order to accomplish these objectives, most unions recognize that they must strive for continued growth and power. Although growth and power are related, we will discuss them separately to identify the impact of both factors on unionization.

Growth

To maximize its effectiveness, a union must strive for continual growth. Members pay dues, which are vital to promoting and achieving union objectives. Obviously, the more members the union enlists, the more dues they pay to support the union and the labor movement. Thus, an overall goal of most unions is continued growth. But, as we previously mentioned, the percentage of union members in the workforce is declining. Most union leaders are concerned about this trend. Much of a union's ability to accomplish its objectives is derived from strength in numbers. For this reason, unions must continue to explore new sources of potential members. Unions are now directing much of their attention to organizing the service industries, professional employees, and government employees.

Even with these efforts, union membership is expected to decline in the future, accompanied by a continual decline in labor's political and bargaining strength.[45] While there is a glimmer of hope for unions, the "mild" resurgence of unionism, predicted in the late 1980s, has failed to materialize, possibly partially because of the new collar worker class. **New collar workers** are younger, better educated, and more independent, and appear to be particularly susceptible to issues related to job security. In order to grow appreciably in the private sector, union acceptance by this new worker segment is necessary. However, these workers are well under fifty years of age, while the average union member is well over fifty. In addition, these new collar workers believe that seniority rules protect older workers at their expense.[46] While new collar workers are concerned with job security issues, many in this group believe such security can only be provided by cooperative employers.[47]

Power

Every indication is that management continues to improve its power base in relation to organized labor.[48] Most observers agree that the power base of organized labor will continue to erode. We define *power* here as the amount of external control that an organization is able to exert. As we mentioned previously, a union's power is influenced to a large extent by the size of its membership and the possibility of future growth. However, we also have to consider other factors when assessing the future power base of unions.

The importance of the jobs held by union members significantly affects union power. For instance, an entire plant may have to be shut down if unionized machinists performing critical jobs decide to strike. Thus, a few strategically located union members may exert a disproportionate amount of power. A union's power can also be determined by the type of firm that is unionized. Unionization of truckers, steel workers, or farm workers can affect the entire country and, subsequently, enhance the union's power base. Through control of key industries, a union's power may extend to firms that are not unionized. For instance, in some areas of the country, the power of trucking unions extends well beyond firms that the truckers serve. Firms that depend on deliveries by the trucking industry may yield to union pressures in order to continue receiving services. Recently, however, even such traditionally powerful unions as the Teamsters have relinquished power. The Teamsters have been much more amenable, agreeing to contracts that provide for less wage and benefit gains.[49] In addition, only eight of the top fifty unionized carriers that dominated the less-than-truckload carriage business in the 1980s are left. Additionally, according to Gary Yablon, a financial analyst with Wertheim Schroeder, "We are facing the demise of the unionized segment of the industry." More and more traditional strongholds of union dominance are wavering badly.[50] Another problem that must be overcome in traditional unionized firms is the low level of union membership among female workers, which has consistently been much lower than male workers.[51]

By achieving power, a union is capable of exerting its force in the political arena. The political arm of the AFL-CIO is the **Committee on Political Education (COPE)**. Founded in 1955, COPE's purpose is to support politicians friendly to the cause of organized labor. The union recommends and assists candidates who will best serve its interests. Union members also encourage their friends to support those candidates. The larger the voting membership, the greater a union's influence with politicians. With "friends" in government, the union is in a stronger position to maneuver against management.

As reduced union strength contributes to weaker unions at the bargaining table, labor leaders will strive to increase their political clout. This slowdown in union gains, coupled with declining union membership and organizing activities, caused unions to compensate by attempting to increase their political activity.[52]

Even though unions have taken their political knocks over the past decade, they remain a fairly potent political force. The AFL-CIO and five of its largest affiliates spent more than $16.5 million through political action committees in previous national elections. Unions can provide many members to staff phone banks and organize campaigns. The unions' long association with such narrow issues as picketing rules and organizing regulations have given way to more popular campaigns for plant-closing legislation, child care, and family leave.[53] Unions' political activity will continue to parallel their changing philosophy toward a desire for "more government intervention" in the U.S. economy and society.[54]

As unions become more political, an internally explosive situation could be brewing, because the overall goals of public and private sector unions are different. Over the long term, these goals may conflict. According to an AFL-CIO committee: "This is because private-sector unions, with the help of government intervention, want to raise members' income. To the extent they are successful, their members become subject to higher taxes, which their fellow public-sector unions will want to push even higher."[55] Regardless of the internal impact of an increased emphasis on political activities, the inevitability of union political involvement is a reality.

WHY EMPLOYEES JOIN UNIONS

Individuals join unions for many different reasons, which tend to change over time. They may involve job, personal, social, or political considerations. It would be impossible to discuss them all, but the following are some of the major reasons: dissatisfaction with management, need for a social outlet, opportunity for leadership, forced unionization, and peer pressure.

Dissatisfaction with Management

Every job holds the potential for real dissatisfactions. Each individual has a boiling point that can trigger him or her to consider a union as a solution to real or perceived problems. Unions look for problems in organizations and then emphasize the advantages of union membership as a means of solving them. In fact, management now has immense power, because "kicking tail and taking names is a lot easier when jobs are at a premium," as they now are. As one industrial relations manager puts it, "It is tempting for some of our managers to say, 'It's our turn; we've got the club.'" Basically, many experts believe that when this attitude prevails, "Management organizes unions." Management must exercise restraint and use its power to foster management and labor cooperation for the benefit of all concerned.[56] Some of the more common reasons for employee dissatisfaction are described in the following paragraphs.

Compensation. Employees want their compensation to be fair and equitable. Wages are important to them because they provide both the necessities and pleasures of life. If employees are dissatisfied with their wages, they may look to a union for assistance in improving their standard of living. However, the ability of unions to make satisfactory gains in income has been severely hampered in the past few years. Of the contracts settled in 1993, it was quite interesting to note that agreements resulted in wage gains, that were, on average, smaller than those specified in the contracts they replaced. Even more disturbing to unions officials is that this is the second consecutive year of wage and benefits declines, and that the 1993 increase represented the smallest gain since 1987.[57]

An important psychological aspect of compensation involves the amount of pay an individual receives in relation to that of other workers performing similar work. If an employee perceives that management has shown favoritism by paying someone else more to perform the same or a lower level job, the employee will likely become dissatisfied. Union members know precisely the basis of their pay and how it compares with others. In the past, pay inequities, with seniority as the accepted criterion for fairness, were generally accepted by union members, but with the growth of the new collar worker class, this may well be perceived as grossly unfair, further decreasing union membership.[58]

Two-Tier Wage System. The **two-tier wage system** is a wage structure that reflects lower pay rates for newly hired employees compared to those received by established employees performing similar jobs. This system is one of the most controversial developments in collective bargaining and is currently being used by fewer and fewer companies. In many cases, the system has caused high turnover and worker morale problems, and is, therefore, often counterproductive. However, some companies are still using the two-tier system basically to survive. Employees hired by United Airlines after January 1, 1994, received lower salaries and far fewer benefits. According to Sandra O'Neal, 10 to 20 percent of companies nationwide use some type of two-tier compensation package. However, Ms. O'Neal agrees that two-tier compensation arrangements are "never sought after unless there's a real issue of survival involved."[59] Some companies, such as Ford, do not use a two-tier system per se, but do pay new hires less than current employees; however, they make up the difference normally within three years, resulting in a two-tier system of sorts.[60]

Job Security. Historically, young employees have been less concerned with job security than older workers. The young employee seemed to think, "If I lose this job, I can always get another." But as young employees have witnessed management consistently terminating older workers to make room for younger, more aggressive employees, the latter have begun to think about job security. If the firm does not provide its employees with a sense of job security, workers may turn to a union. Generally speaking, employees are more concerned than ever before about job security due largely to a decline in employment in such key industries as automobiles, rubber, and steel. Unfortunately for union organizing attempts, while new collar workers appear to be particularly susceptible to job security issues, many in this group believe security can only be provided by cooperative employers, and not by unions.[61]

In recent years, the United Automobile Workers (UAW) union has had one of the strongest systems of job security in industrial America. Job guarantees at the "Big Three" automakers protect workers with at least one year's seniority from everything but sales decline.[62] In 1993, this guarantee was continued at the expense of lower COLAs and cutbacks in, or elimination of, profit sharing and bonus benefits.[63] The concern over job security was translated into legislation in 1988, with the enactment by Congress of a plant closing bill that requires employers to give advance notification prior to plant closings. Even with this legislation, plant closings have taken place and manufacturing facilities have continued to move outside the continental United States.

Management's Attitude. People like to feel they are important. They do not like to be considered a commodity that can be bought and sold. Thus employees do not like to be subjected to arbitrary and capricious actions by management. In some firms, management is insensitive to the needs of its employees. When this situation occurs, employees may perceive they have little or no influence in job-related matters. Workers who feel they are not really part of an organization are prime targets for unionization.

Management's attitude may be reflected in such small actions as how bulletin board notices are written. Memos addressed "To All Employees" instead of "To Our Employees" may indicate managers that are indifferent to employee needs. Such attitudes likely stem from top management, but they are noticed initially by employees in the actions of first-line supervisors. Workers may notice that supervisors are judging people entirely on what they can do, how much they can do, and when they can do it. Employees may begin to feel they are being treated more as machines than people. Supervisors may fail to give reasons for unusual assignments and may expect employees to dedicate their lives to the firm without providing adequate rewards. The prevailing philosophy may be: "If you don't like it here, leave." A management philosophy such as this, which does not consider the needs of employees as individuals, makes the firm ripe for unionization.

The Xerox Corporation appears to realize the importance of considering the needs of employees. Ron Blackwell of the ATCWU (which represents Xerox employees) commends the company's philosophy of cooperation by commenting: "Many companies talk about cooperation, but few are willing to take the steps to make it work. Xerox is a farsighted company in terms of the effective relationship unions and management can have when they cooperate." He says the firm realizes that in order to have employee cooperation, management has to give workers recognition as human beings.[64] Management must keep in mind that unions would never have gained a foothold if management had not abused its power.[65] Once again it is worth restating that many experts believe that "management organizes unions."

A Social Outlet

By nature, many people have strong social needs. They generally enjoy being around others who have similar interests and desires. Some employees join a union for no other reason than to take advantage of union-sponsored recreational and social activities that members and their families find fulfilling. Some unions now offer day care centers and other services that appeal to working men and women and increase their sense of solidarity with other union members. People who develop close personal relationships, in either a unionized or union-free organization, will likely stand together in difficult times. However, since the new collar worker core is dissatisfied with the concept of seniority, this basic tenet of unionism may well discourage younger workers from seeking affiliation with unions.[66]

Providing Opportunity for Leadership

Some individuals aspire to leadership roles, but it is not always easy for an operative employee to progress into management. However, employees with leadership aspirations can often satisfy them through union membership. As with the firm, the union also has a hierarchy of leadership, and individual members have the opportunity to work their way up through its various levels. Employers often notice employees who are leaders in the union, and it is not uncommon for them to promote such employees into managerial ranks as supervisors.

Forced Unionization

It is generally illegal to require that an individual join a union prior to employment. However, in the twenty-nine states without right-to-work laws, it is legal for an employer to agree with the union that a new employee must join the union after a certain period of time (generally thirty days) or be terminated. This is referred to as a *union-shop agreement.* However, data are not available to indicate the number of employees who become union members because of these compulsory agreements.

Peer Pressure

Many individuals will join a union simply because they are urged to do so by other members of the work group. Friends and associates may constantly remind an employee that he or she is not a member of the union. In the past, this social pressure from peers was difficult to resist, but as the age gap between workers increases and the educational gap broadens, peer pressure becomes less and less of an issue. Quite possibly, rejection of these employees by current union members is much less of a sanction than in the past. In extreme cases, union members threaten nonmembers with physical violence and sometimes carry out these threats.

UNION STRUCTURE

The labor movement has developed a multilevel organizational structure over time. This complex of organizations ranges from local unions to the principal federation, the AFL-CIO. Each level has its own officers and ways of managing its affairs. Many national unions have intermediate levels between the national and the local levels. In this section, however, we describe only the three basic elements of union organization: (1) the local union, (2) the national union, and (3) the federation, or AFL-CIO.

The Local Union

The basic element in the structure of the American labor movement is the **local union** (or simply, the local). To the individual union member, it is the most important level in the structure of organized labor. Through the local, the individual deals with the employer on a day-to-day basis. There are approximately 65,000 locals in the United States, most of which are affiliated with one of the 170 or so national or international unions. The latter are generally organized along industry or craft lines,[67] and ninety-four are affiliated with the AFL-CIO.

There are two basic kinds of local unions: craft and industrial. A **craft union**, such as the Carpenters and Joiners union, is typically composed of members of a particular trade or skill in a specific locality. Members usually acquire their job skills through an apprenticeship training program. An **industrial union** generally consists of all the workers in a particular plant or group of plants. The type of work they do and the level of skill they possess are not a condition for membership in the union. An example of an industrial union is the United Auto Workers.

The local union's functions are many and varied. Administering the collective bargaining agreement and representing workers in handling grievances are two quite important activities. Other functions include keeping the membership informed about labor issues, promoting increased membership, maintaining effective contact with the national union, and, when appropriate, negotiating with management at the local level.

The National (or International) Union

The most powerful level in the union structure is the national union. As we stated previously, most locals are affiliated with national unions. Some national unions are called *international unions* because they have affiliated locals in Canada.

A **national union** is composed of local unions, which it charters. As such, it is the parent organization to local unions. The local union—not the individual worker—holds membership in the national union. The national union is supported financially by each local union, whose contribution is based on its membership size.

The national union is governed by a national constitution and a national convention of local unions, which usually meets every two to five years. The day-to-day operation of the national union is conducted by elected officers, aided by an administrative staff. The national union is active in organizing workers within its jurisdiction, engaging in collective bargaining at the national level, and assisting its locals in their negotiations. In addition, the national union may provide numerous educational and research services for its locals, dispense strike funds, publish the union newspaper, provide legal counsel, and actively lobby at national and state levels.

Mega Union Merger

On July 27, 1995, the United Auto Workers (UAW), the United Steelworkers of America, and the International Association of Machinists promised to merge within the next five years, creating the largest union in the United States. Merger advocates contend that the consolidation will bring together the kind of technical resources, innovation, and efficient operations that will create the "new, high-performance union" members desire. In addition, with more than 2 million members, ranging from aerospace workers to cannery employees, the proposed union would have considerably more political and economic clout than any of the three unions have now. Although the merger still requires rank-and-file approval, it has been approved by each union's board. Some analysts doubt the merger will go through, but even the possibility of such a mega merger is major union news.

AFL-CIO

The American Federation of Labor and Congress of Industrial Organizations (AFL-CIO) is the central trade union federation in the United States. It represents the interests of labor and its member national unions at the highest level. The federation does not engage in collective bargaining; however, it provides the means by which member unions can cooperate to pursue common objectives and attempt to resolve internal problems faced by organized labor. The federation is financed by its member national unions and is governed by a national convention, which meets every two years.

As shown in Figure 15-2, the structure of the AFL-CIO is complex. The federation has state bodies in all fifty states and Puerto Rico. In addition, national unions can affiliate with one or more of the trade and industrial de-

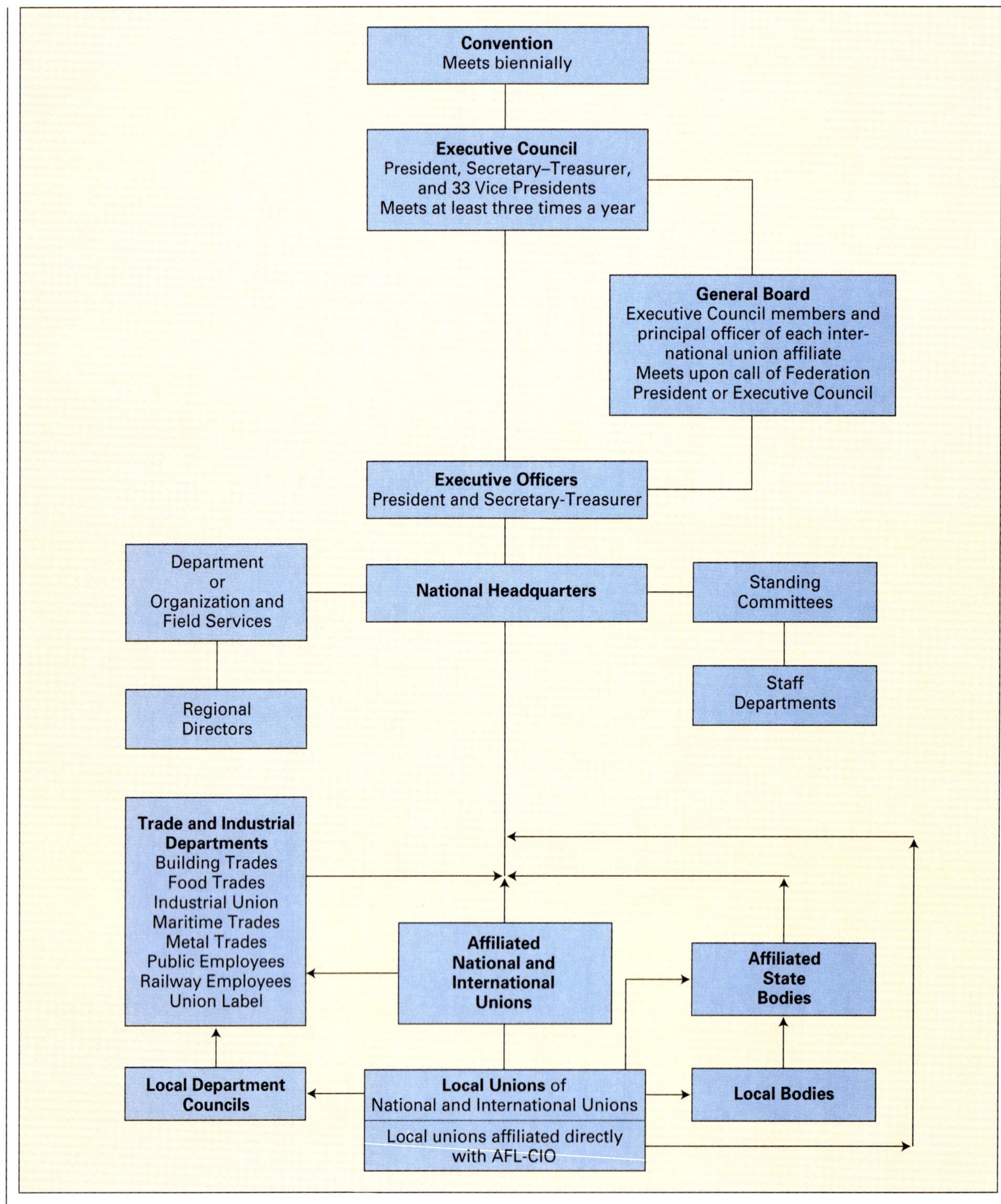

FIGURE 15-2 The Structure of the AFL-CIO

Source: Bureau of Labor Statistics, *Directory of National Unions and Employee Associations,* 1980.

partments. These departments seek to promote the interests of specific groups of workers who are in different unions but who have common interests. The federation's major activities include the following:

1. Improving the image of organized labor.
2. Extensive lobbying on behalf of labor interests.
3. Politically educating constituencies and others through COPE.
4. Resolving disputes between national unions.
5. Policing internal affairs of member unions.

The AFL-CIO is a loosely knit organization of more than ninety national unions. It has little formal power or control. The member national unions remain completely autonomous and decide their own policies and programs. Not all national unions are members of the federation. In fact, one of the largest unions, the Teamsters, was expelled in 1957 and did not rejoin the AFL-CIO until October 1987. In the late 1970s, affiliated unions represented approximately 17 million members, or about 78 percent of all union members in the United States.[68] Currently, the AFL-CIO represents approximately 14 million members.[69]

ESTABLISHING THE COLLECTIVE BARGAINING RELATIONSHIP

The primary law governing the relationship of companies and unions is the National Labor Relations Act, as amended.[70] Collective bargaining is one of the key parts of the act. Section 8(d) of the act defines **collective bargaining** as:

> The performance of the mutual obligation of the employer and the representative of the employees to meet at reasonable times and confer in good faith with respect to wages, hours, and other terms and conditions of employment, or the negotiation of an agreement, or any question arising thereunder, and the execution of a written contract incorporating any agreement reached if requested by either party, but such obligation does not compel either party to agree to a proposal or require the making of a concession.

The act further provides that the designated representative of the employees shall be the exclusive representative for all the employees in the unit for purposes of collective bargaining. A **bargaining unit** consists of a group of employees, not necessarily union members, recognized by an employer or certified by an administrative agency as appropriate for representation by a labor organization for purposes of collective bargaining. A unit may cover the employees in one plant of an employer, or it may cover employees in two or more plants of the same employer. Although the act requires the representative to be selected by the employees, it does not require any particular procedure to be used so long as the choice clearly reflects the desire of the majority of the employees in the bargaining unit. The employee representative is normally chosen in a secret ballot election conducted by the NLRB. When a union desires to become the bargaining

FIGURE 15-3
The Steps That Lead to Forming a Bargaining Unit

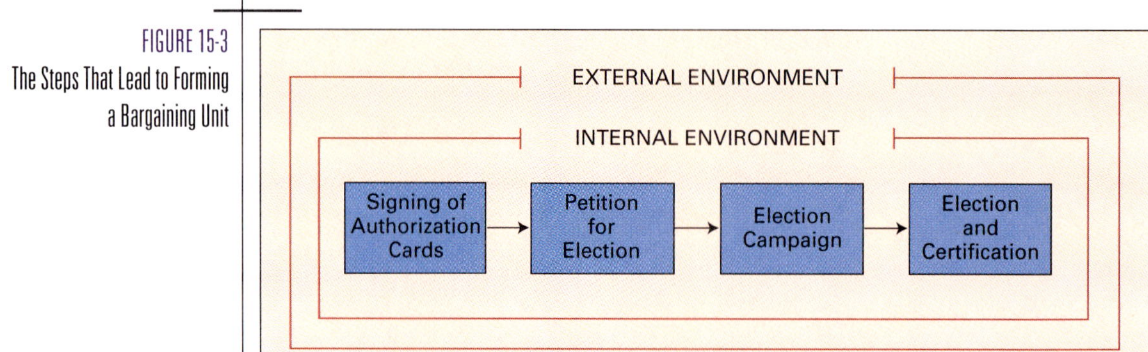

representative for a group of employees, several steps leading to certification have to be taken (see Figure 15-3). External and internal factors can affect the process. The primary external factors are legislation (most recently NAFTA and GATT) and the union, and the prevailing corporate culture can affect the internal environment. According to Geoff Armstrong, Director General of IPM, a major British firm, the collective bargaining process should be conducted with an appreciation that "flexibility and change are essential to organizational success and survival."[71]

Signing of Authorization Cards

A prerequisite to forming a recognized bargaining unit is to determine whether there is sufficient interest on the part of employees. Evidence of this interest is expressed when at least 30 percent of the employees in a work group sign an authorization card. The **authorization card** is a document indicating that an employee wants to be represented by a labor organization in collective bargaining. Most union organizers will not proceed unless at least 50 percent of the workers in the group sign cards. An authorization card used by the International Association of Machinists and Aerospace Workers is shown in Figure 15-4.

Petition for Election

After the authorization cards have been signed, a petition for an election may be made to the appropriate regional office of the NLRB. When the petition is filed, the NLRB will conduct an investigation. The purpose of the investigation is to determine, among other things, the following:

1. Whether the Board has jurisdiction to conduct an election.
2. Whether there is a sufficient showing of employee interest to justify an election.
3. Whether a question of representation exists (for example, the employee representative has demanded recognition, which has been denied by the employer).

4. Whether the election will include appropriate employees in the bargaining unit (for instance, the Board is prohibited from including plant guards in the same unit with the other employees).
5. Whether the representative named in the petition is qualified (for example, a supervisor or any other management representative may not be an employee representative).
6. Whether there are any barriers to an election in the form of existing contracts or prior elections held within the past twelve months.[72]

If these conditions have been met, the NLRB will ordinarily direct that an election be held within thirty days. Election details are left largely to the agency's regional director. Management is prohibited from making unusual concessions or promises that would encourage workers to vote against union recognition.

Election Campaign

When an election has been ordered, both union and management usually promote their causes actively. Unions will continue to encourage workers to join the union, and management may begin a campaign to tell workers the benefits of remaining union-free. The supervisor's role during the campaign is crucial. Supervisors need to conduct themselves in a manner that avoids violating the law and committing unfair labor practices. Specifically, they

FIGURE 15-4
An Authorization Card

YES, I WANT THE IAM

I, the undersigned, an employee of

(Company) ______________________

hereby authorize the International Association of Machinists and Aerospace Workers (IAM) to act as my collective bargaining agent with the company for wages, hours, and working conditions.

NAME (print)______________________ DATE ____________

ADDRESS (print)______________________

CITY____________ STATE__________ ZIP____________

DEPT.____________ SHIFT__________ PHONE__________

Classification ______________________

SIGN HERE ✗______________________

NOTE: THIS AUTHORIZATION IS TO BE SIGNED AND DATED IN EMPLOYEE'S OWN HANDWRITING. YOUR RIGHT TO SIGN THIS CARD IS PROTECTED BY FEDERAL LAW.

Source: The International Association of Machinists and Aerospace Workers.

should be aware of what can, and cannot, be done in the pre-election campaign period. In many cases, it is not so much what is said by the supervisor as how it is said.[73] Human resource professionals can give supervisors a lot of help in these matters. Throughout the campaign, supervisors should keep upper management informed about employee attitudes.

Theoretically, both union and management are permitted to tell their stories without interference from the other side. At times, the campaign becomes quite intense. Election results will be declared invalid if the campaign was marked by conduct that the NLRB considers to have interfered with the employee's freedom of choice. Examples of such conduct are:

- An employer or a union threatening loss of jobs or benefits to influence employees' votes or union activities.
- An employer or a union misstating important facts in the election campaign when the other party does not have a chance to reply.
- Either an employer or a union inciting racial or religious prejudice by inflammatory campaign appeals.
- An employer firing employees to discourage or encourage their union activities or a union causing an employer to take such an action.
- An employer or a union making campaign speeches to assembled groups of employees on company time within twenty-four hours of an election.

Election and Certification

The NLRB monitors the secret-ballot election on the date set. Its representatives are responsible for making sure that only eligible employees vote and for counting the votes. Following a valid election, the Board will issue a certi-

HRM IN ACTION

—USING HER INFLUENCE?

Sandy Marshall, one of the workers in the plant, has just come to see the human resource manager, Lonnie Miller, for advice. Apparently, a union organizer approached her yesterday and asked her to help with the union organizing effort. Lonnie knows that lately there have been growing tensions and a lot of talk about unions. He has even seen what appear to be authorization cards being passed about. Lonnie knows that if Sandy starts working for the union, she will have a lot of influence. She seems to be a natural leader, and Lonnie thinks she is supervisory material.

What advice should Lonnie give Sandy?

fication of the results to the participants. If a union has been chosen by a majority of the employees voting in the bargaining unit, it will receive a certificate showing that it is now the official bargaining representative of the employees in the unit. However, the right to represent employees does not mean, as was assumed by Robert Sweeney in the scenario at the beginning of this chapter, the right to dictate terms to management that would adversely affect the organization. The bargaining process does not require either party to make concessions; it only compels them to bargain in good faith.

Union Strategies in Obtaining Bargaining Unit Recognition

Unions may use various strategies to obtain recognition by management. Unions generally try to make the first move because this places management in the position of having to react to union maneuvers. The search for groups of employees to organize involves a continuous effort by union leaders. To begin a drive, unions often look for disaffection. Union organizers recognize that if employees generally have an overall positive attitude toward management, organizing employees will be extremely difficult.

Some situations indicate that employees are ripe for organizing:

- a history of unjustified and arbitrary treatment of employees
- compensation below the industry average
- lack of concern for employee welfare

A union does not normally look at isolated conditions of employee unrest. Rather, it attempts to locate general patterns of employee dissatisfaction. Whatever the case, the union will probably not make a major attempt at organizing unless it believes that it has a good chance of success.

The union may take numerous approaches in getting authorization cards signed. One effective technique is first to identify workers who are not only dissatisfied but also influential in the firm's informal organization. These individuals can assist in developing an effective organizing campaign. Information is obtained through the grapevine regarding who was hired, who was fired, and management mistakes in general. Such information is beneficial to union organizers as they approach company employees. Statements such as these are common: "I hear Bill Adams was fired today. I also understand that he is well liked. No way that would have happened if you had a union."

Ultimately, the union must abandon its secret activities. Sooner or later management will discover the organizing attempt. At this point, union organizers may station themselves and other supporters at company entrances and pass out *throwsheets* or campaign literature proclaiming the benefits of joining the union and emphasizing management weaknesses. They will talk to anyone who will listen in their attempt to identify union sympathizers. Employees who sign authorization cards are then encouraged to convince their friends to sign also. The effort often mushrooms, yielding a sufficient number of signed authorization cards before management has time to react.

Union efforts continue even after the election petition has been approved by the NLRB. Every attempt is made by the organizers to involve as many workers from the firm as possible. The outside organizers would prefer to take a back seat and let company employees convince their peers to join the union. Peer pressure typically has a much greater effect on convincing a person to join a union than outside influence does. Whenever possible, unions utilize peer pressure to encourage and expand unionization.

SIGNS OF A TROUBLED LABOR MOVEMENT

The declines that began in the early 1980s are continuing into the mid-1990s and may continue well into the year 2000. Overall union membership by occupation and by industry continues to decline, but at a slower rate.[74] As we have mentioned earlier in this chapter, the percentage of unionized workers in the private sector was a mere 11 percent in 1994, and union membership was down to 15.8 percent of the overall nonfarm workforce.[75]

In the 1970s, elections to form unions were running at the rate of 7,000 a year, but now are less than half that rate.[76] The legacy of the Reagan administration, which created the perception that unions were weak and encouraged the anti-labor environment of the 1980s, apparently continues to linger.[77]

These are not encouraging signs for those who support unionism, but in 1989 there were some significant events which indicated that the tide might be turning. However, by 1994, the tide had not yet turned, and, in fact, appeared to have worsened somewhat. Also, with the passage of NAFTA, there appears to be a major threat to American unionism just across the border. Unions are bracing to absorb the shock that will result from the movement of major full-fledged manufacturing from the United States to Mexico. Many companies with unionized employees are carefully studying the feasibility of moving their manufacturing operations across the border. The Thompson Consumer Electronics firm already employs some 5,500 Mexican workers, and that was prior to the passage of NAFTA. The projected cost to

Fading union strength will not enable management to deal with workers in a free and unrestricted manner.

organized labor of NAFTA and GATT could be the loss of thousands of union jobs. Continued downward pressure on wages and additional losses in union membership are expected in the U.S. manufacturing sector because of the passage of NAFTA and GATT.

North American Free Trade Agreement (NAFTA)

NAFTA creates a free trade zone encompassing Canada, the United States, and Mexico. All five ex-presidents were in favor of NAFTA, as was the sitting president. Multimedia star Rush Limbaugh was also for NAFTA. Former President George Bush negotiated the agreement, President Clinton supported it, and the Republicans pushed it through Congress. According to supporters, this agreement will open new markets and expand the growth of U.S. exports. The effect on Canada is expected to be minimal, but commerce between the United States and Mexico could expand dramatically. Labor opposed NAFTA because it believed that the loss of jobs to the low wage Mexican labor pool was inevitable. On the other hand, the loss to the United States in terms of jobs could be offset by higher exports to Mexico. The bottom line is that labor opposed NAFTA, and labor lost.[78]

General Agreement on Tariffs and Trade (GATT)

GATT is a 124-nation trade agreement that cuts tariffs by an average of 38 percent worldwide and creates a powerful World Trade Organization to moderate trade practices and disputes. Labor opposed GATT because it predicted additional job losses, but President Clinton supported GATT because he believed it will create new jobs and result in an annual increase of $150 million in U.S. economic growth a decade from now, when the agreement is fully implemented. So will GATT mean new job creation and significant economic growth or will it lead to massive manufacturing job losses, as predicted by the unions? The answer is as yet unknown, but the reality of labor suffering another major defeat on the heels of its NAFTA defeat is a stark reality.[79]

Since the mid-1980s, employers have had the upper hand when dealing with unions, but fading union strength will not enable management to deal with workers in a free and unrestricted manner. Some business leaders believe they will get a union-free environment, but they may well inherit a legalistic system instead. Unionism seems to be declining, but legalized worker protection is a growing trend.

THE GROWING LEGALISTIC APPROACH

The specter of increasing government regulation has reappeared since the closing days of the Reagan administration. With the passage of recent legislation, such as the Worker Adjustment and Retraining Notification Act (WARN), the Employee Polygraph Protection Act of 1988, the Clean Air Act of 1991, and the Americans With Disabilities Act and the Civil Rights Act of 1991, it has become clear that Congress and the White House are willing to place more legal restrictions on business. Unions have been strong proponents of such legislation, but in some ways the mere existence of such laws limits what unions can provide to potential members.[80] Recent emergence of an employee rights movement has the potential to shape revolutionary changes in the workplace and the way companies manage people. As nonunion sentiment intensifies, the courts and state legislatures are becoming the most effective champions of employee rights. As union membership declines, so does union political and legal clout. However, according to Harvard labor law specialist Paul C. Weiler, employee rights will be protected by a legalistic system.[81] A web of legislation is growing at the national, state, and local levels and in all aspects of the work environment. Legislation has been developed with regard to the following: right-to-know laws; whistle-blower protection; prohibition against a mandatory retirement age; notice requirements of plant shutdowns; severance for workers affected by plant shutdowns; employee privacy protection; enhanced standards for a safe and healthful workplace; protection against discrimination in hiring, promotion, and discharge; prohibitions against sex discrimination in pay; retirement security protection; national minimum wage; and limitations on company ability to discharge and discipline employees for union activity.

Not only has this web of legal protection weakened the need for union protection, this growing network of legal protection could eventually replace collective bargaining in many industries. However, top AFL-CIO officials refuse to accept legislation as an acceptable substitute for bargaining or the suggestion that unions are in permanent decline. Regardless of the state of unionism, the employee rights movement will continue to expand, providing employees with more influence in their work.[82] Companies and unions that fail to recognize this latest movement are ignoring what appears to be an inevitable part of future work environments.

THE FUTURE OF UNIONISM AND COLLECTIVE BARGAINING IN A GLOBAL ECONOMY

The future of unionism is changing, sometimes quite rapidly. In fact, unionism and collective bargaining in the United States have changed even since 1990. Global competition no longer allows highly structured bargaining that links wages and benefits to macroeconomic factors, rather than to company-specific performance.[83] In the early days of the growth of the U.S. economy, the railroads developed new networks for routes spanning the continent and knitted the country into an economic whole. Similarly, the trading ties with other countries have united the world into an economic whole. No longer can the processes of collective bargaining and unionism be considered domestic issues; they must be considered in the global spectrum. Even foreign countries are experiencing downward shifts in union membership percentages. Even though union membership rates are still high in many Western European countries, indications are that union membership rates will continue to decline. Specifically, annual declines of between 5 and 7 percent are becoming fairly common. Younger members are placing a higher priority on advancement and job security issues and a lower priority on the importance of being affiliated with unions. "The solidarity between the employees across the firm's borders has been replaced by a loyalty between the employer and parts of the employees," says one expert. Currently, in many foreign countries the "labor market is extremely divided," which may signal a shift toward declining union power and influence overseas.[84]

Recent developments, such as the two-tier wage system, increased management flexibility, gain-sharing, and employee identification with productivity, are necessary to compete effectively in a global environment. These factors must, therefore, be considered in many collective bargaining situations and will affect the future of unionism in the United States. The President's Commission on Industrial Competitiveness summarized changes needed to compete in the global economy. Adherence to the following changes would foster a new era of management-labor cooperation, and may help unions survive into the year 2000:

- Labor-management cooperation is essential. The new cooperative relationships will maximize productivity by involving employees and their elected representatives in the decision-making process.
- Employee incentives must be strengthened to reward the efforts of individual employees and to emphasize the linkage between compensation and performance.
- Displaced workers must be handled in a more resourceful manner. Employers must be encouraged to strengthen their commitment to employee security and will be required to provide early notification of plant closings. All parties should work toward the goal of reemployment.
- Improved work skills must be developed by training employees to compete effectively in the job market. Specifically, employers should be encouraged to take a more systematic approach in their training activities.[85]

Obviously, times have changed and will continue to change, and labor and management must evolve to compete in the global economy. Neither labor nor management should attempt to hold on to the practices of the past because today's global economy will not tolerate such entrenched behavior. Once again, it is interesting to note that changes in the labor climate are even occurring overseas, where unions have traditionally been quite strong. Recession is impacting global economies, and with automation of computer operations, downsizing, and outsourcing, more and more nontechnical jobs are being threatened both in the United States and abroad.

SUMMARY

The labor movement has not enjoyed simple and straightforward progress. Prior to the 1930s, attitudes definitely favored management. This was first evidenced by the use of criminal and civil conspiracy doctrines derived from English common law. Other tactics used by employers to stifle union growth were injunctions and yellow-dog contracts. In 1890, Congress passed the Sherman Anti-Trust Act. This marked the entrance of the federal government into the statutory regulation of labor organizations. Later, in 1914, Congress passed the Clayton Act (an amendment to the Sherman Act), the intent of which was to remove labor from the purview of the Sherman Act. During the 1920s, labor faced legal restrictions on union activity and unfavorable court decisions. The one exception to such repressive policies was enactment of the Railway Labor Act of 1926.

The pendulum began to swing away from management and toward labor after 1930. Congress passed the Norris-LaGuardia Act in 1932, affirming the use of collective bargaining and approving the formation of labor unions. In 1933, Congress made an abortive attempt to stimulate economic recovery by passing the National Industry Recovery Act (NIRA). Undeterred by a Supreme Court decision and strongly supported by organized labor, Congress speedily enacted a comprehensive labor law, the National Labor Relations Act (Wagner Act) in 1935. Drawing heavily on the experience of the Railway Labor Act of 1926 and Section 7a of the NIRA, the act declared legislative support, on a broad scale, of the right of workers to organize and engage in collective bargaining. However, recently employers have violated the Wagner Act and illegally fired union employees with impunity. In 1947, with public pressure mounting, Congress overrode President Truman's veto and passed the Labor Management Relations Act (Taft-Hartley Act), which extensively revised the National Labor Relations Act. One of the most controversial elements of the Taft-Hartley Act permits states to enact right-to-work legislation. Right-to-work laws are laws that prohibit management and unions from agreements requiring union membership as a condition of employment. In 1959, Congress enacted the Labor-Management Reporting and Disclosure Act (Landrum-Griffin Act), which spelled out a "Bill of Rights of Members of Labor Organizations" designed to protect certain rights of individuals in their relationships with unions.

Government employees are generally considered a class apart from private-sector workers. This is reflected in their exclusion from the coverage of general labor legislation. Membership in public-sector professional and state employee associations greatly exceeds private-sector unionization.

Most unions recognize that they must strive for continued growth and power. A union's power is influenced to a large extent by the size of its membership and the possibility of future growth. However, union growth and power continue to decline.

Individuals join unions for many different reasons, which tend to change over time. Some of the major reasons are dissatisfaction with management, need for a social outlet, opportunity for leadership, forced unionization, and peer pressure.

The labor movement has developed a multilevel organizational structure that includes (1) the local union, (2) the national union, and (3) the federation, or AFL-CIO. The basic element in the structure of the American labor movement is the local union, of which there are two basic kinds: craft and industrial. A national union is composed of local unions, which it charters. The American Federation of Labor and Congress of Industrial Organizations (AFL-CIO) is the main trade union federation in the United States.

A bargaining unit consists of a group of employees recognized by an employer as appropriate for representation by a labor organization for purposes of collective bargaining. A prerequisite to forming a recognized bargaining unit is to determine whether there is sufficient interest on the part of employees. After authorization cards have been signed, a petition for an election may be made to the appropriate regional office of the National Labor Relations Board (NLRB). The NLRB monitors a secret ballot election.

Unionism and collective bargaining will change in the future as labor-management cooperation becomes more the norm than the exception. Global competition will no longer allow highly structured bargaining that links wages and benefits to macroeconomic factors, rather than to company-specific performance.

Many signs point to serious trouble in the labor movement, including the two recently passed so-called anti-union agreements, NAFTA and GATT. Fundamental indicators of union growth and survival are declining. As antiunion sentiment grows, however, a legalistic approach to employee protection appears to be replacing collective bargaining.

QUESTIONS FOR REVIEW

1. Describe the development of the labor movement in the United States.
2. List the unfair labor practices by management that were prohibited by the Wagner Act.
3. What union actions were prohibited by the Taft-Hartley Act?
4. In what way does unionization of the public sector differ from unionization of the private sector?
5. Why would unions strive for continued growth and power? Discuss.
6. What are the primary reasons for employees joining labor unions?
7. What steps must a union take in attempting to form a bargaining unit? Briefly describe each step.
8. Describe the ways unions might go about gaining bargaining unit recognition.
9. Discuss the signs of a troubled labor movement.
10. Describe the process of collective bargaining and unionism in a global economy.

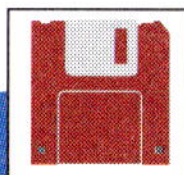

HRM SIMULATION

Incident L in the *Human Resources Management Simulation Players Manual* deals with unionization. Three weeks ago the Amalgamated Workers Union began organizing efforts with the workers in your organization. The CEO has given your team the responsibility of combatting this perceived threat. Numerous options are available, so your team needs to study them carefully and make its recommendation.

ABC VIDEO CASE

GM: TROUBLE AT THE WORLD'S LARGEST CAR MAKER TAPE 1, NUMBER 9

After losing 4.5 billion dollars in 1991, General Motors was forced to close twenty-one plants and lay off 74,000 workers. One issue was the choice of closing either the Willow-Run plant in Ypsilanti, Michigan, or the Arlington, Texas, plant. Willow-Run employees were confident that their plant would remain open due to their high productivity and quality. An Arlington union/management proposal created the attitude that management and workers were a team, working together to make cars. Flexibility in cutting costs and quality improvement were stated as key points in choosing Arlington over Willow-Run. Some auto analysts said that the local union did not offer enough to keep the Willow-Run plant open.

HRM INCIDENT 1

WORK RULES

Jerry Sharplin eagerly drove his new company pickup onto the construction site. He had just been assigned by his employer, Lurgi-Knost Construction Company, to supervise a crew of sixteen equipment operators, oilers, and mechanics. This was the first unionized crew Jerry had supervised, and he was unaware of the labor agreement in effect that carefully defined and limited the role of supervisors. As he approached his work area, he noticed one of the cherry pickers (a type of mobile crane with an extendable boom) standing idle with the operator beside it. Jerry pulled up beside the operator and asked, "What's going on here?"

"Out of gas," the operator said.

"Well, go and get some," Jerry said.

The operator reached to get his thermos jug out of the toolbox on the side of the crane and said, "The oiler's on break right now. He'll be back in a few minutes."

Jerry remembered that he had a five-gallon can of gasoline in the back of his pickup. So he quickly got the gasoline, climbed on the cherry picker, and started to pour it into the gas tank. As he did so, he heard the other machines shutting down in unison. He looked around and saw all the other operators climbing down from their equipment and standing to watch him pour the gasoline. A moment later he saw the union steward approaching.

Questions

1. Why did all the operators shut down their machines?
2. If you were Jerry, what would you do now? Explain.

HRM INCIDENT 2

—UNION APPEAL

In late 1994, a vigorous union-organizing campaign was under way at Dodge Tube Company in Rochester, North Carolina. The management at Dodge was strongly antiunion and made no bones about it. Roger Verdon was a general supervisor at Dodge, with the responsibility for four supervisors and about eighty machine operators and helpers. Roger had become increasingly incensed as the union's organizing attempts became more apparent.

At first, fliers and other promotional literature had been handed out at the plant gates. There had been an increasing number of complaints, many of which Roger felt were caused by the union-organizing activity. The workers in general had become more belligerent, Roger thought, and he saw indications of more and more secret communication. Workers who had previously been his friends seemed to have pulled away. While they were not unfriendly, they typically limited their conversation with him to office matters.

Roger felt that Dodge was a good employer and treated its people fairly. Discipline was administered by supervisors on the spot. Helpers were paid minimum wage, but few stayed in that position very long. Most helpers were either fired or promoted to machine operator within about six months. The machine operators were placed in pay grades 1, 2, or 3 at the discretion of the supervisor. Supervisors were encouraged to base pay grade assignments only on job proficiency. Most of the supervisors were required to participate in the company's management training program. Those who were not college graduates were required to complete a correspondence course in management from the University of Maryland during their first six months as supervisors.

The company had an aggressive health and safety program. Workers in noisy areas were required to wear earplugs, and a worker who failed to do so was immediately fired. The same was true of safety glasses in areas involving grinding, drilling, or chipping. The workers in and around the tube-cleaning area were required to wear respirators because an OSHA inspector had cited the company for the amount of particulate matter in the air.

One day in early December, Roger observed what he considered to be the "last straw." He saw a worker from another part of the plant walking through his area handing out cards to the workers. Bob asked to see one of the cards and realized that it was a union authorization card. He decided to have a meeting with his supervisors.

Questions

1. What factors could have produced union-organizing activity?
2. What can Roger do about it?

DEVELOPING HRM SKILLS

AN EXPERIENTIAL EXERCISE

Unionization is often met with mixed feelings by all concerned. Management is usually opposed to such efforts. Beth Morrison, the production manager of the heavy motors division of MNP Corporation, knows that upper management does not care much for unions. Senior officials believe this unionizing effort is not good for anybody involved with the company and that the union wants to turn the employees against them. Upper management also feels that a union will destroy the company's competitive edge—something that has happened to many other firms. The firm must do everything possible to circumvent this union-organizing effort, but it must do so in line with NLRB guidelines.

Beth thought, "I've got to meet with Ray Miller, the supervisor over in section 4 today. He is a little too eager about stopping the union. We don't want this union, but we also don't want the NLRB breathing down our necks. Indirect threats are okay, but direct threats can get us in trouble. Ray must understand the ground rules and apply those rules to stop this union. Obviously, we don't want the union, but no supervisor can threaten loss of jobs or benefits or fire anybody, at least until after the election. I'm going to tell Ray that if his employees ask his opinion, he should definitely discourage workers from unionizing."

If you are either in favor of or opposed to unions, there is a role for you here. One of you will play the production manager, and another will play the supervisor. The rest of you should observe carefully. Your instructor will provide the participants with additional information

NOTES

1. *Brief History of the American Labor Movement* (Washington, D.C.: U.S. Department of Labor Statistics, Bulletin 1000, 1970): 1.

2. Sam F. Parigi, Frank J. Cavaliere, and Joel L. Allen, "Improving Labor Relations in an Era of Declining Union Power," *Review of Business* 14 (Winter 1992): 31–35.

3. Benjamin J. Taylor and Fred Witney, *Labor Relations Law,* 5th edition (Englewood Cliffs, N.J.: Prentice Hall, 1987): 12–13.

4. Ibid., 14–18.

5. *Brief History of the American Labor Movement,* 9.

6. Foster Rhea Dulles, *Labor in America,* 3rd edition (New York: Crowell, 1966): 114–125.

7. Ibid., 126–149.

8. *Brief History of the American Labor Movement,* 15–16.

9. E. Edward Herman, Alfred Kuhn, and Ronald L. Seeber, *Collective Bargaining and Labor Relations* (Englewood Cliffs, N.J.: Prentice Hall, 1987): 32–34.

10. *Brief History of the American Labor Movement,* 27.

11. *Historical Statistics of the United States, Colonial Times to 1970,* Bicentennial Edition, Part I (Washington, D.C.: U.S. Bureau of the Census, 1975): 126.

12. Benjamin J. Taylor and Fred Witney, *Labor Relations Law,* 78–81.

13. Ibid., 81–85.

14. Ibid., 150–151.

15. Sandra Atchison and Aaron Bernstein, "A Silver Bullet for the Union Drive at Coors?" *Business Week* (July 11, 1988): 61–62.

16. *Brief History of the American Labor Movement,* 65.

17. Ibid., 29–33.

18. Aaron Bernstein, "Why America Needs Unions But Not the Kind It Has Now," *Business Week* (May 23, 1994): 70–82.

19. Right-to-work states include Alabama, Arizona, Arkansas, Florida, Georgia, Idaho, Iowa, Kansas, Louisiana, Mississippi, Nebraska, Nevada, North Carolina, North Dakota, South Carolina, South Dakota, Tennessee, Texas, Utah, Virginia, and Wyoming.

20. Foster Rhea Dulles, *Labor in America,* 382–383.

21. Herman Benson, "Union Democracy," in *Unions in Transition* (San Francisco: ICS Press, 1988): 343.

22. Harris Cooingwood, "The Teamsters' Vacuum at the Top," *Business Week* (July 25, 1988): 41.

23. *Brief History of the American Labor Movement,* 58–61.

24. Ibid., 139.

25. "The AFL-CIO: A Tougher Team with the Teamsters," *Business Week* (November 9, 1987): 110.

26. Gene Koretz, "Why Unions Thrive Abroad—But Wither in the U.S." *Business Week* (September 10, 1990): 26.

27. Aaron Bernstein, "Why America Needs Unions But Not the Kind It Has Now," ibid.

28. Ibid.

29. Ibid.

30. Examples include the Social Security Act, the Fair Labor Standards Act, and the National Labor Relations Act, as amended.

31. Gene Koretz, "Why Unions Thrive Abroad—But Wither in the U.S.," ibid.

32. Jim Armshaw, David Carnevale, and Bruce Waltuck, "Union-Management Partnership in the U.S. Department of Labor," *Review of Public Personnel Administration* 13 (Summer 1993): 94–101.

33. Section 305 of the Labor Management Relations Act of 1947 also makes it unlawful for government employees to participate in any strike.

34. They are Executive Order 11491 (effective January 1, 1970); EO 11616 (effective November 1971); EO 11636 (effective December 1971); and EO 11828 (effective May 1975).

35. E. Edward Herman, Alfred Kuhn, and Ronald L. Seeber, *Collective Bargaining and Labor Relations,* 407.

36. Benjamin J. Taylor and Fred Witney, *Labor Relations Law,* 649.

37. Leo Troy, "The Rise and Fall of American Trade Unions: The Labor Movement from FDR to RR" in *Unions in Transition* (San Francisco: ICS Press, 1988): 85.

38. Walter Galenson, "The Historical Role of American Trade Unionism" in *Unions in Transition* (San Francisco: ICS Press, 1988): 88.

39. Leo Troy, "The Rise and Fall of American Trade Unions," 85.

40. Gene Koretz, "Why Unions Thrive Abroad—But Wither in the U.S.," 26.

41. David A. Dilts, "The Future of Labor Arbitrators," *Arbitration Journal* 48 (June 1993): 24–31.

42. Stewart Toy, John Rossant, and Patrick B. Oster, "Strike Fever Hits Europe," *Business Week* (November 8, 1993): 50–51.

43. Ibid.

44. Edwin F. Beal and James P. Begin, *The Practice of Collective Bargaining,* 5th edition (Homewood, Ill.: Richard D. Irwin, 1982): 91.

45. Ibid., 20–22.

46. Sam F. Parigi, Frank J. Cavaliere, and Joel L. Allen, "Improving Labor Relations in an Era of Declining Union Power," ibid.

47. Ibid.

48. R. Wayne Mondy and Shane R. Premeaux, "The Labor/Management Power Relationship Revisited," *Personnel Administrator* 30 (May 1985): 52.

49. Edward J. Wasilewski, "Compensation Gains Moderated in 1993 Private Industry Settlements," *Monthly Labor Review* 177 (May 1994): 46–56.

50. Kurt C. Hoffman, "Death Knell Sounds for Union LTL's," *Distribution* (March 1994): 64.

51. Flora Carapellucci, "Realizing Women's Potential," *Work & People* (June 1992): 25–28.

52. Leo Troy, "The Rise and Fall of American Trade Unions," 104.

53. Susan B. Garland, "Why Democrats Still Want to Wear the Union Label," *Business Week* (March 5, 1990): 37.

54. Stan Crock, "The Duke Is Still Playing Hard-to-Get with Labor," *Business Week* (August 29, 1988): 39.

55. "The Changing Situation of Workers and Their Unions," A Report by the AFL-CIO Committee on the Evolution of Work (Washington, D.C.: AFL-CIO, February 1985).

56. Scott Seegert and Brian H. Kleiner, "The Future of Labor-Management Relations," *Industrial Management* 35 (March/April 1993): 15–16.

57. Edward J. Wasilewski, "Compensation Gains Moderated in 1993 Private Industry Settlements," ibid.

58. Sam F. Parigi, Frank J. Cavaliere, and Joel L. Allen, "Improving Labor Relations in an Era of Declining Union Power," ibid.

59. Deborah Shalowitz Cowans, "Two-Tier Compensation," *Business Insurance* 28 (March 14, 1994): 3, 20.

60. "Contracts Describe Benefit Plans in Automobile, Steel Industries," *Employee Benefits Plan Review* 48 (January 1994): 48–49.

61. Sam F. Parigi, Frank J. Cavaliere, and Joel L. Allen, "Improving Labor Relations in an Era of Declining Union Power," ibid.

62. Wendy Zellner, "All the Ingredients for Disaster Are There," *Business Week* (April 16, 1990): 28.

63. Edward J. Wasilewski, "Compensation Gains Moderated in 1993 Private Industry Settlements," ibid.

64. Ibid.

65. Ibid., 14.

66. Sam F. Parigi, Frank J. Cavaliere, and Joel L. Allen, "Improving Labor Relations in an Era of Declining Union Power," ibid.

67. Daniel K. Benjamin, "Combination of Workmen: Trade Unions in the American Economy" in *Unions in Transition* (San Francisco: ICS Press, 1988): 104.

68. *Directory of National Unions and Employee Associations* (Washington, D.C.: U.S. Department of Labor, Bureau of Labor Statistics, Bulletin 2079, September 1980): 73.

69. *The Wall Street Journal* 89 (April 14, 1992): 1.

70. Other names for this act are the Labor Management Relations Act of 1947 and the Taft-Hartley Act.

71. Sid Kessler, "Is There Still a Future for Unions?" *Personnel Management* 25 (July 1993): 24–30.

72. *A Guide to Basic Law and Procedures under the National Labor Relations Act* (Washington, D.C.: U.S. Government Printing Office, October 1978): 11–13.

73. Art Bethke, R. Wayne Mondy, and Shane R. Premeaux, "Decertification: The Role of the First-Line Supervisor," *Supervisory Management* 31 (February 1986): 21–23.

74. Sam F. Parigi, Frank J. Cavaliere, and Joel L. Allen, "Improving Labor Relations in an Era of Declining Union Power," ibid.

75. Ibid.

76. Aaron Bernstein, "Why America Needs Unions But Not the Kind It Has Now," 70–82.

77. Anne Ritter, "Are Unions Worth the Bargain?" *Personnel* 67 (February 1990): 12.

78. Laurence I. Barrett, Michael Duffy, Laura Lopez, and Joseph R. Szczesny, Time Daily News Summary-America Online, *Time, Inc.* (November 11, 1993): 2–5.

79. Ibid., 1.

80. Sam F. Parigi, Frank J. Cavaliere, and Joel L. Allen, "Improving Labor Relations in an Era of Declining Union Power," ibid.

81. Ibid., 74.

82. Ibid., 77.

83. Alexander B. Trowbridge, "A Management Look at Labor Relations" in *Unions in Transition* (San Francisco: ICS Press, 1988): 417.

84. Bengt Abrahamsson, "Union Structural Changes," *Economic and Industrial Democracy* 14 (August 1993): 399–421.

85. "Global Competition: The New Reality," vol. 2, *Report of the President's Commission on Industrial Competitiveness* (Washington, D.C.: U.S. Government Printing Office, 1985): 137–160.

CHAPTER

16 Collective Bargaining

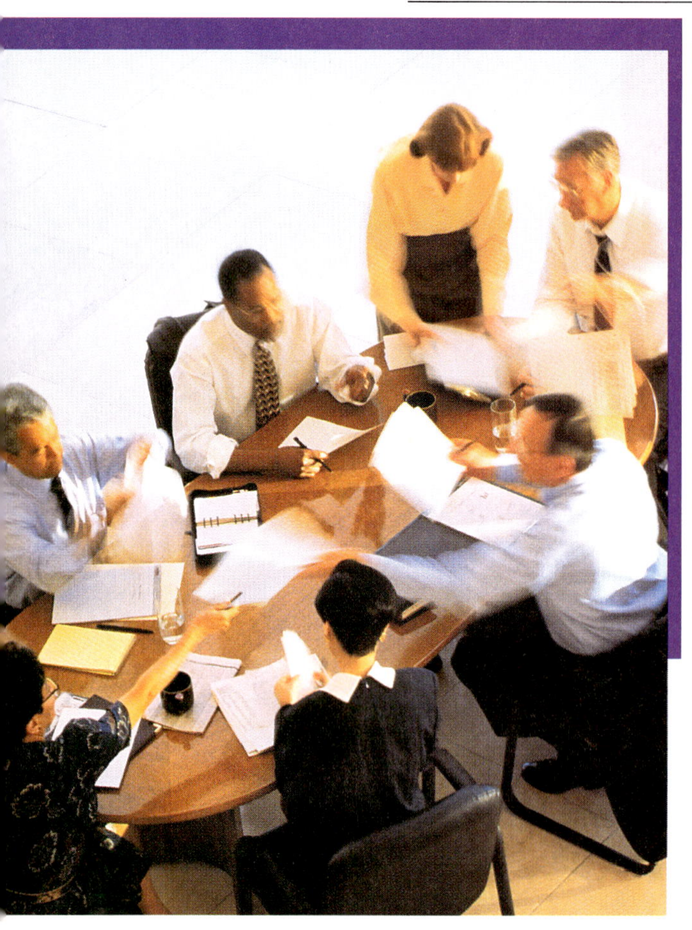

KEY TERMS

Mandatory bargaining issues 508
Permissive bargaining issues 508
Prohibited bargaining issues 508
Closed shop 513
Union shop 513
Agency shop 514
Open shop 514
Checkoff of dues 514
Beachhead demands 518
Mediation 519
Arbitration 519
Strike 520
Boycott 521
Secondary boycott 521
Lockout 521

CHAPTER OBJECTIVES

1. Discuss the collective bargaining process, describe the role of the human resource manager in it, and explain the psychological aspects of collective bargaining.
2. Describe what both labor and management do as they prepare for negotiations.
3. Explain typical bargaining issues and the process of negotiating.
4. Identify and describe ways to overcome breakdowns in negotiations and describe what is involved in ratifying and administering the agreement.
5. Discuss the future of collective bargaining.

Barbara Washington, the chief union negotiator, was meeting with company representatives on a new contract. Both the union team and management had been preparing for this encounter for a long time. Barbara's deep concern was whether union members would support a strike vote if one were called. Sales for the industry were generally down because of imports. In fact, there had even been some layoffs at competing firms. The union members' attitude could be described as "Get what you can for us, but don't rock the boat." She hoped, however, that skillful negotiating could win concessions from management.

In the first session, Barbara's team presented its demands to management. The team had determined that pay was the main issue, and a 20 percent increase spread over three years was demanded. Management countered by saying that since sales were down it could not afford to provide any pay raises. After much heated discussion, both sides agreed to reevaluate their positions and to meet again in two days. Barbara met with her negotiating team in private, and it decided to decrease the salary demand slightly. The team felt that the least they could accept was a 15 percent raise.

At the next meeting, Barbara presented the revised demands to management. They were not well received. Bill Thompson, the director of industrial relations, began by saying, "We cannot afford a pay increase in this contract, but we will make every attempt to ensure that no layoffs occur. Increasing wages at this time will virtually guarantee a reduction in the workforce."

Barbara's confidence collapsed. She knew that there was no way that the general membership was willing to accept layoffs and that a strike vote would be virtually impossible to obtain. She asked for a recess to review the new proposal.

Barbara is experiencing the negotiating crunch that has existed for several years in the United States. The power pendulum has swung in favor of management, making it very difficult for union negotiators to bargain effectively with management on certain issues, including pay increases.

We devote the first portion of this chapter to the collective bargaining process and the human resource manager's role in it. Then, we describe the psychological aspects of collective bargaining and preparing for negotiations. Next, we address bargaining issues, negotiating the agreement, and overcoming breakdowns in negotiations, before discussing the ratification and administration of the agreement. We conclude the chapter with a section on the future of collective bargaining.

THE COLLECTIVE BARGAINING PROCESS

The collective bargaining process is fundamental to management-labor relations in the United States. According to Nobel laureate Gary S. Becker, a conservative economist at the University of Chicago, "Some kind of union behavior is bad, but unions that help workers bargain collectively instead of individually perform a legitimate role that's not counter to social efficiency."[1] Extensive collective bargaining activity occurs each year, but the outcomes of collective bargaining have been disappointing to unions in recent years. In 1994, major collective bargaining agreements for about 2.1 million workers under 395 major collective bargaining agreements were negotiated, which accounts for 38 percent of the 5.5 million workers under all major contracts in private industry. Such agreements covering 1,000 or more workers provided wage gains that were smaller than the contracts they replaced.[2]

Throughout the 1980s and into the mid-1990s, management had the power advantage in collective bargaining, a situation that is not expected to change in the foreseeable future. From the early 1980s until the mid-1990s, management has achieved their collective bargaining goals. Among the unusual features of collective bargaining settlements in the 1990s, which indicate increased management clout, were the large proportion of workers receiving very slight wage increases, the increasing number of performance-based contracts negotiated, the increasing importance of lump sum payments, and the large proportion of workers who were not covered by cost-of-living adjustments.[3] The number of strikes has also sharply declined, with major strikes involving 1,000 or more employees falling from an all-time high of a little more than 200 a year to only thirty-five last year.[4] Some workers, particularly younger, better educated workers, believe that if harm is done to the employer, their job opportunities will be reduced. Other employees are avoiding strikes because they do not want to lose wages. Some workers fear that management will replace them with nonstriking employees.[5]

Even though collective bargaining is widely practiced, there is no precise format of what to do or how to do it. In fact, diversity is probably the most prominent characteristic of collective bargaining in the United States. The collective bargaining process, in general, is shown in Figure 16-1. As you can see, both external and internal environmental factors can influence the process. For instance, the form of the bargaining structure can affect the conduct of collective bargaining. The four major types of structure are (1) one company dealing with a single union, (2) several companies dealing with a single union, (3) several unions dealing with a single company, and (4) sev-

FIGURE 16-1
The Collective Bargaining Process

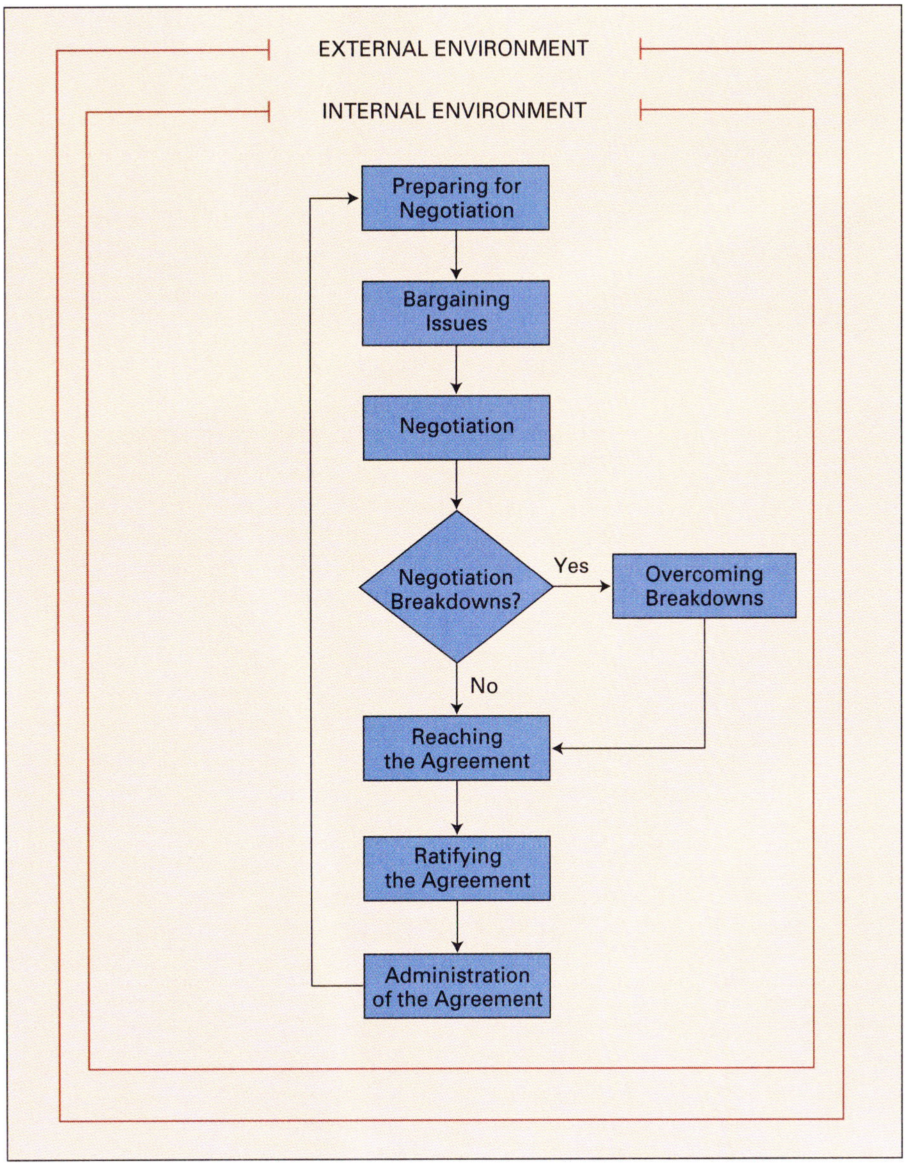

eral companies dealing with several unions. Most contract bargaining is carried out under the first type of structure.

The process can become quite complicated when several companies and unions are involved in the same negotiations. However, even when there is only one industry involved and one group of workers with similar skills, collective bargaining can be quite problematic. Major League Baseball is a perfect example of collective bargaining gone haywire. In 1994, players' salaries ($1.2 million annual average) soared to 58 percent of revenues from 43 percent in 1990. Meanwhile, the league's national TV revenue skidded from $365 million a year to perhaps $165 million annually. Despite these revenue slides and a projected $150 million loss in 1993, the players struck, rather than accept a salary cap proposed by the owners. In response to these circumstances, Donald M. Fehr, chief negotiator for the Major League Players Union, stated, "Once they (management) force us (players) out, it will probably be a long time before we're back." The result of this attitude was no baseball until just before the opening of the 1995 season. However, management did not give in, and neither did the players. Finally, acting under court orders, the owners let the players play baseball under the terms of the existing contract, and the players returned. After the aborted 1994 season, no World Series, and great hostility among the parties involved, no real progress has been made to resolve the labor issues faced by Major League Baseball. Both groups are resolute in their positions, but the collective bargaining process is thus far unsuccessful.[6]

Another environmental factor influencing collective bargaining is the type of union-management relationship that exists. In the case of Major League Baseball, the union-management relationship is obviously quite adversarial. When a group of workers decide they want union representation, changes occur in the organization. In the absence of a union, management exercises virtually unlimited authority, except for the limitations imposed by the growing web of employee legal rights protection. As noted in Chapter 15, these legal protections may well replace collective bargaining in the future. However, for the present, when a union becomes the bargaining representative, management must change its style of decision making to include union bargaining agents. When employees take collective action, such as slow downs and strikes, an adversarial relationship can be created, with varying degrees of conflict. Sloane and Witney list six types of union-management relations that may exist in an organization:

1. *Conflict.* Each challenges the other's actions and motivation; cooperation is nonexistent, and uncompromising attitudes and union militancy are present. For example, AK Steel's "Smiling Barracuda," President Tom Graham, is dead set against unions, and the union is determined to unionize his company as they have the rest of the industry. Open hostility and an old-style battle is the nature of the management-labor bargaining environment.[7]
2. *Armed truce.* Each views the other as antagonistic but tries to avoid head-on conflict; bargaining obligations and contract provisions are strictly interpreted.

3. *Power bargaining.* Management accepts the union; each side tries to gain an advantage from the other.
4. *Accommodation.* Each tolerates the other in a "live and let live" atmosphere and attempts to reduce conflict without eliminating it. Accommodation was the first step in the bargaining process that Xerox Corporation and its union embarked upon in 1982, but because of mutual cooperation, this process soon became one of *real* labor-management cooperation.[8]
5. *Cooperation.* Each side accepts the other, and both work together to resolve human resource and production problems as they occur. Cooperation was the next step in the bargaining process that eventually brought Xerox Corporation and its union into a new era of cooperation. The relationship between Xerox and the Amalgamated Clothing & Textile Workers Union (ACTWU) has resulted in Xerox bringing back 300 jobs from abroad to a new plant in Utica, New York, where Xerox expects higher quality and a savings of $2 million a year. Management cooperation goes to the point of providing internal financial statements to union officials and training them alongside management personnel.[9]
6. *Collusion.* Both "cooperate" to the point of adversely affecting the legitimate interests of employees, other businesses in the industry, and the consuming public; this involves conniving to control markets, supplies, and prices illegally and/or unethically.[10]

The nature and quality of union-management relations vary over time. The first three types of relationships mentioned are generally unsatisfactory; collusion is unacceptable, and cooperation has been rare in the past. Typically, U.S. union-management relations appear to be some form of accommodation. Indications are that cooperation will be the best approach to union-management bargaining in the 1990s and well into the future. According to Xerox CEO Paul A. Allaire, "If we have a cooperative model, the union movement will be sustained and the industries it's in will be more competitive." The bottom line in effective bargaining arrangements is the overwhelming issue of joint economic survival. Furthermore, the lessening of adversarial relationships and the increased cooperation in areas never possible in the past offer real future prospects for both management and labor.[11]

The relationship between some companies and unions (such as AK Steel and the United Steel Workers) is still quite adversarial, but more and more companies are forging cooperative relationships with their unions. As was previously mentioned, just such a cooperative relationship exists between Xerox and the ACTWU. Basically, "Xerox has a partnership with its unions." Xerox's union is "indivisible; they are not a separate part of the company." In this environment, the size of the union increased from approximately 3,000 manufacturing employees in 1990 to 6,200 by mid-1994. Ron Blackwell, the union representative for Xerox employees, commends the company's philosophy of cooperation. According to Blackwell, Xerox makes cooperation work. Management and employees at Xerox are bound together by a commitment to quality production, at lower costs. Xerox encourages employee participation in many ways, such as soliciting employee suggestions to uncover and solve problems and to design assembly lines so that individual employees can stop production without approval from a supervisor should difficulties be spotted.[12]

The acceptance of cooperative relationships between management and labor is spreading among the few dozen major companies that are developing real partnerships with labor. According to David H. Hoag, CEO of LTV Corporation, the union agreed to team methods and other efficiency measures for a union nominee on the board. Ford's head of cooperative labor programs goes beyond this sentiment and declares, "If unions were to disappear, the country would be in serious trouble." On the other hand, most employers could not agree less; they have never accepted unions, and they appear unwilling to accept them at this time. Basically, during the past twelve years, U.S. industry has conducted one of its most successful antiunion wars ever, and many managers appear eager to continue their assault on labor.[13]

These cooperative practices empower employees, foster pride in them, and help assure joint economic survival. Since both groups agree, now more than ever, that joint economic survival is most important, it is quite possible that past adversarial relationships will be replaced with cooperation. When both groups cooperate, everyone involved benefits, particularly unions. This could explain why unions are embracing cooperation with unprecedented enthusiasm. Unions are currently accepting the notion that they must reinvent themselves to embrace cooperation and balance better wages with efforts to help employers win competitive battles. This attitude will, no doubt, be an integral part of collective bargaining in the future.[14]

Depending on the type of relationship encountered, the collective bargaining process may be relatively simple, or it may be a long, tense struggle for both parties, as was the case with Major League Baseball. Veteran labor negotiator Robert J. Harding, a consulting firm executive, offers the following seven tips for successful collective bargaining:

1. Don't underestimate the importance of the first preparatory, nonadversarial meeting between labor and management representatives; use this opportunity to set the ground rules for future sessions.
2. Carefully document each meeting because accurate, well-organized notes can be quite useful in initial, and subsequent, contract negotiations.
3. If the CEO is well regarded by employees, consider including him or her in the sessions.
4. Within the bounds of law and propriety, develop a personal profile of each member of the committee who will take part in the collective bargaining process.
5. Accept negotiators as peers; never underestimate them.
6. Maintain strong communications with those individuals who best know the people most affected by the contract and the issues being discussed.
7. If negotiations break down, consider federal mediation.[15]

Regardless of the complexity of the bargaining issues, the ability to reach agreement is the key to any successful negotiation. Success requires good communication skills and an understanding of these seven negotiation tips.

As stated previously, the first step in the collective bargaining process is preparing for negotiations. This step is often extensive and ongoing for both union and management. After the issues to be negotiated have been determined, the two sides confer to reach a mutually acceptable contract. Although breakdowns in negotiations can occur, both labor and management have at their disposal tools and arguments that can be used to convince the other side to accept their views. It is interesting to note that successful unions—those that are growing—are unions that embrace cooperation and are more likely to avoid bargaining breakdowns. Basically, unions are giving up more ground than ever before in collective bargaining agreements, because many union officials have accepted the notion that increased wages and benefits result from cooperative work efforts, team management, and overall productivity gains. Wage increases are at their lowest levels in years, having fallen in 1992 and 1993. In addition, benefits are dropping, as are other costly rewards such as pension plan contributions.[16] Eventually, however, management and the union will reach an agreement that defines the rules of the game for the duration of the contract. The next step is for the union membership to ratify the agreement.

Note the feedback loop from "Administration of the Agreement" to "Preparing for Negotiation" in Figure 16-1. Collective bargaining is a continuous and dynamic process, and preparing for the next round of negotiations often begins the moment a contract is ratified.

THE HUMAN RESOURCE MANAGER'S ROLE

When a firm becomes unionized, the human resource manager's role tends to change rather significantly. In a unionized environment, the human resource manager must deal primarily with a union's organizational structure, consisting of union stewards and business agents, rather than with individual workers. The human resource manager is among those persons who must live with the consequences of the contract, and, therefore, he or she should be an integral part of the ultimate resolution of contractual issues. According to veteran negotiator Fritz Ihrig, if the human resource manager is a strong and capable individual, that person should actually negotiate the contract.[17] Successful negotiators must have a thorough understanding of what is going on and an appreciation of the human element of the collective bargaining process. It is also vitally important that the human resource manager remain involved in the human resource system to ensure effective implementation of the human resource strategy after collective bargaining is complete. The human resource manager must continually revise the strategy based upon problems and opportunities that occur in human resource strategy implementation to ensure success and properly prepare for the next round of collective bargaining negotiations.

Start-up plants offer a unique opportunity for human resource managers to be involved from the beginning to help ensure effective implementation of a human resource strategy. At the Saturn plant in Spring Hill, Tennessee, an integrated and active human resource strategy was vital for the car company's success. This strategy, which recognized that a "people oriented process" is essential for success, developed in part through the collective bargaining process and formed a proactive partnership with its peer departments and the United Automobile Workers (UAW).[18] However, by 1993, 29 percent of the 5,000 union workers voted to shift toward a traditional arm's-length adversarial relationship. Fueling this shift toward a more traditional labor-management relationship were such factors as recent hires being less committed to employee-participation ideals, employee burnout from fifty-hour weeks, growing ties between union and management officials, and scaling back on the training of new workers.[19] Obviously, as the focus moved away from the human resource component to the manufacturing component, union-management cooperation suffered.

Because the role of first-line supervisors is crucial, the human resource manager must maintain close contact with them before, during, and after collective bargaining. First-line supervisors administer the contract and know whether it is working well or if there are problems. Through an active and involved role, the human resource manager can limit problems such as animosity, fighting, games, role-playing, and a "stick it to them" mentality. Human resource managers who assume their proper roles in the collective bargaining process, including implementation, can make that process more beneficial to all concerned.

GLOBAL LABOR-MANAGEMENT RELATIONS

Before doing business in another country or entering into an international alliance, it is important to understand the characteristics of the industrial relations system in that country. For example, contrast the following two situations: In the first, a firm in Germany (where roughly 40 percent of the workforce is represented by unions domestically) forms an alliance with a firm in Sweden (where roughly 93 percent of the workforce is represented by a union domestically). Both partners are quite sympathetic to the workers' desires to be represented collectively; each firm accepts the idea that the workers want to be associated with national or international unions. In the second situation, a Japanese firm, whose U.S. plant is nonunionized, forms an alliance with a U.S. company, whose workers are members of a union. When asked for their most important concern about the partnership, the plant managers cited the fact that their alliance called for two companies with different industrial relations systems to work together.

Obviously, the industrial relations issues that human resources professionals must address in these two situations are quite different. It is critically important to understand the implications of (and agree to abide by) a particular type of industrial relations system before consummating an international alliance. Regardless of the union or nonunion status of the workers involved, it is imperative that the industrial relations issues that could decrease the productivity of the workforce be addressed prior to entering a country or forming an international alliance.[20]

It is much more common to encounter true cooperation between labor and management overseas than in the United States. In fact, according to John Hougham, chairman of Acas, a British company, "Trade union officials . . . are willing to join with management representatives in seeking to resolve problems, improve organizational effectiveness, and facilitate change through cooperation rather than conflict." In certain situations this level of cooperation will make the global human resource manager's job easier, allowing him or her to focus on other issues.[21]

PSYCHOLOGICAL ASPECTS OF COLLECTIVE BARGAINING

Prior to collective bargaining, both the management team and the union team have to prepare positions and accomplish certain tasks. Vitally important for those involved are the psychological aspects of collective bargaining. Psychologically, the collective bargaining process is often difficult because it is an adversarial situation and must be approached as such. It is "a situation that is fundamental to law, politics, business, and government, because out of the clash of ideas, points of view, and interests come agreement, consensus, and justice."[22]

In effect, those involved in the collective bargaining process will be matching wits with the competition, will experience victory as well as defeat, and will ultimately resolve problems, resulting in a contract. The role of those who meet at the bargaining table essentially involves the "mobilization and management of aggression" in a manner that allows them to hammer out a collective bargaining agreement.[23] Because those involved must "mobilize and manage aggression," their personalities have a major impact on the negotiation process. The attitudes of those who will be negotiating have a direct effect on what can be accomplished and how quickly a mutually agreed-on contract can be finalized. Problems are compounded by differences in the experience and educational backgrounds of those involved in the negotiation process. Finally, the longer, more involved, and intense the bargaining sessions are, the greater the psychological strain on all concerned will be.

Recent "scare tactics" have intensified the psychological pressures of collective bargaining. In order to break unions in the 1980s, management permanently replaced striking workers, a trend that continues in the 1990s. In the past couple of years, certain companies have placed advertisements and even hired permanent replacements during contract talks. This dramatically upped the ante since employees knew that a decision to strike could cost them their jobs. However, a recent NLRB ruling could limit the use of this tactic. In the past, employers replaced striking workers without taking a vote because the assumption was made that newly hired workers opposed the union. The NLRB ruled that replacement workers should be presumed to support the union.[24] If employers use a permanent replacement threat and this does not work, it may become even harder for management to ease the tensions between labor and management.[25] Some unions, such as the UAW, are reaching the bargaining table in a combative mood, all but stating that union members are quite willing to strike. One UAW negotiator viewed this approach as bringing all of the ingredients for disaster together.[26] As psychological pressures intensify, the gap between labor and management can easily widen, further compounding the problems of achieving mutual accommodation. Even in Britain, where unions have flourished for decades, union-management adversity is increasing. According to Sir Pat Lowry, Britain's labor minister, the role of current unions is to step in when workers resent the employers' insistence on their absolute and unqualified right to manage in whatever way they see fit. Thus, these psychological pressures are intensifying even overseas.[27]

PREPARING FOR NEGOTIATIONS

Because of the complex issues facing labor and management today, the negotiating teams must carefully prepare for the bargaining sessions. Prior to meeting at the bargaining table, the negotiators should thoroughly know the culture, climate, history, present economic state, and wage and benefits structure of both the organization and similar organizations.[28] Because the length of a typical labor agreement is three years, negotiators should develop a contract that is successful both now and in the future. This consideration should prevail for both management and labor, although it rarely does. During the term of an agreement, the two sides usually discover contract provisions that need to be added, deleted, or modified. These items become proposals to be addressed in the next round of negotiations.

Bargaining issues can be divided into three categories: mandatory, permissive, and prohibited. **Mandatory bargaining issues** fall within the definition of wages, hours, and other terms and conditions of employment (see Table 16-1). These issues generally have an immediate and direct effect on workers' jobs. A refusal to bargain in these areas is grounds for an unfair labor practice charge. **Permissive bargaining issues** may be raised, but neither side may insist that they be bargained over. For example, the union may want to bargain over health benefits for retired workers or union participation in establishing company pricing policies, but management may choose not to bargain over either issue. **Prohibited bargaining issues**, such as the issue of the closed shop, are statutorily outlawed.

The union must continuously gather information regarding membership dissatisfaction. The union steward is normally in the best position to collect such data. Because stewards are usually elected by their peers, they should be well-informed regarding union members' attitudes. The union steward constantly funnels information up through the union's chain of command, where the data are compiled and analyzed. Union leadership attempts to uncover any areas of dissatisfaction because the general union membership must approve any agreement before it becomes final. It would be foolish for union leaders to demand management concessions and have the members reject their proposals. Because they must be elected, union leaders will lose their positions if the demands they make of management do not represent the desires of the general membership.

Management also spends long hours preparing for negotiations. The many interrelated tasks that management must accomplish are presented in Figure 16-2. In this example, the firm allows approximately six months to prepare for negotiations. All aspects of the current contracts are considered, including flaws that should be corrected. When preparing for negotiations, management should listen carefully to first-line supervisors. These individuals must administer the labor agreement on a day-to-day basis and must live with any error that management makes in negotiating the contract. An alert

TABLE 16-1 Mandatory Bargaining Issues

- Wages
- Hours
- Discharge
- Arbitration
- Paid holidays
- Paid vacations
- Duration of agreement
- Grievance procedure
- Layoff plan
- Reinstatement of economic strikers
- Change of payment from hourly base to salary base
- Union security and checkoff of dues
- Work rules
- Merit wage increase
- Work schedule
- Lunch periods
- Rest periods
- Pension plan
- Retirement age
- Bonus payments
- Cancellation of seniority upon relocation of plant
- Discounts on company products
- Shift differentials
- Contract clause providing for supervisors keeping seniority in unit
- Procedures for income tax withholding
- Severance pay
- Nondiscriminatory hiring hall
- Plant rules
- Safety
- Prohibition against supervisor doing unit work
- Superseniority for union stewards
- Partial plant closing
- Hunting on employer's forest reserve where previously granted
- Plant closedown and relocation
- Change in operations resulting in reclassifying workers from incentive to straight time, or a cut in the workforce, or installation of cost-saving machinery
- Price of meals provided by company
- Group insurance—health, accident, life
- Promotions
- Seniority
- Layoffs
- Transfers
- Work assignments and transfers
- No-strike clause
- Piece rates
- Stock purchase plan
- Workloads
- Change of employee status to independent contractors
- Motor carrier-union agreement providing that carriers use own equipment before leasing outside equipment
- Overtime pay
- Agency shop
- Sick leave
- Employer's insistence on clause giving arbitrator right to enforce award
- Management rights clause
- Plant closing
- Job posting procedures
- Plant reopening
- Employee physical examination
- Truck rentals—minimum rental to be paid by carriers to employee-owned vehicles
- Arrangement for negotiation
- Change in insurance carrier and benefits
- Profit-sharing plan
- Company houses
- Subcontracting
- Production ceiling imposed by union

Source: Reed Richardson, "Positive Collective Bargaining," Chapter 7.5 of ASPA *Handbook of Personnel and Industrial Relations*, 7–121. Copyright 1979 by The Bureau of National Affairs, Inc., Washington, D.C. Reprinted by permission.

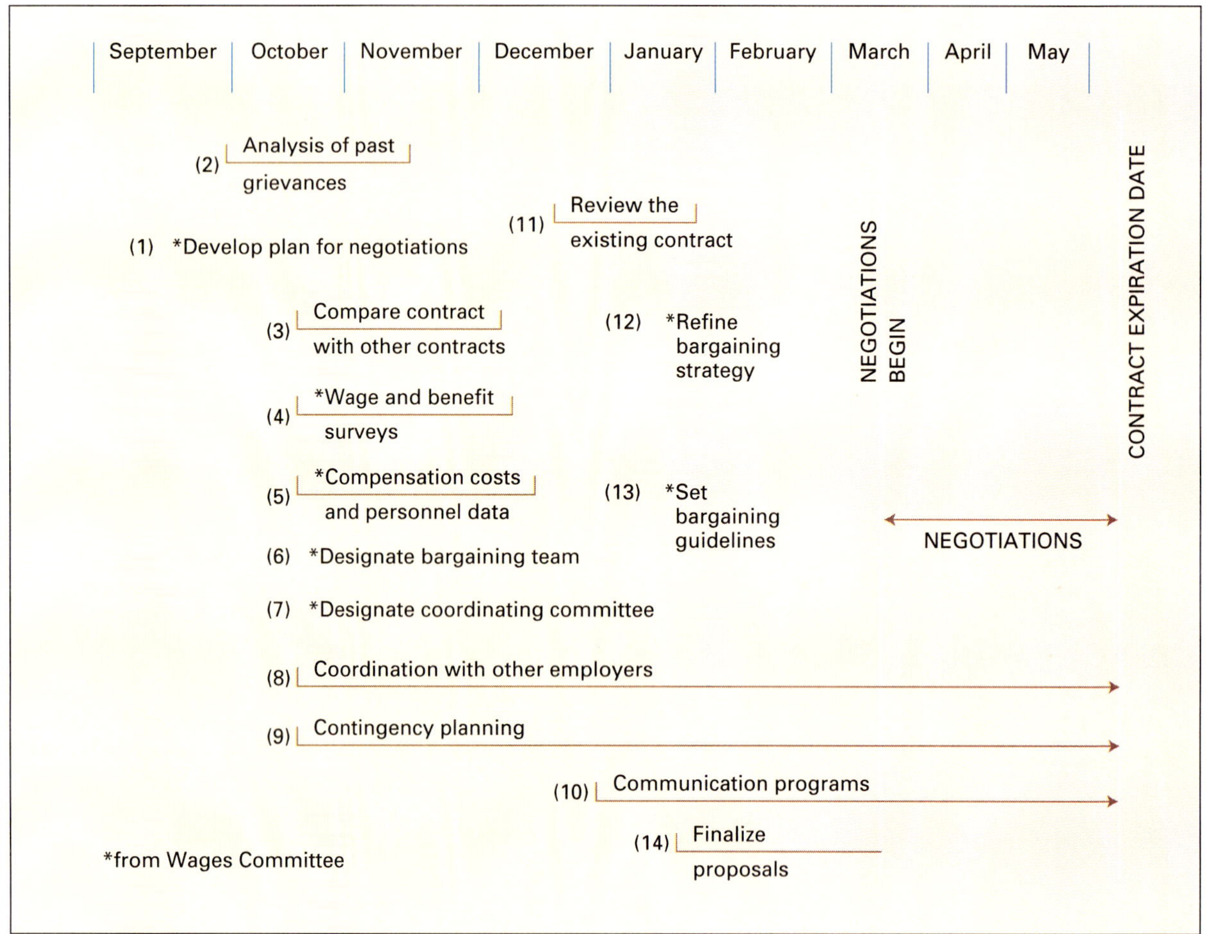

FIGURE 16-2 An Example of Company Preparations for Negotiations

Source: Adapted from Ronald L. Miller, "Preparations for Negotiations," *Personnel Journal,* Vol. 57, 38. Copyright January 1978. Reprinted with permission.

first-line supervisor is also able to inform upper management of the demands unions may plan to make during negotiations.

Management also attempts periodically to obtain information regarding employee attitudes. Surveys are often administered to workers to determine their feelings toward their jobs and job environment. When union and management representatives sit down at the bargaining table, both sides like to know as much as possible about employee attitudes.

Another part of preparation for negotiations involves identifying various positions that both union and management will take as the negotiations progress. Each side usually takes an initial extreme position, representing the conditions union or management would prefer. The two sides will likely determine absolute limits to their offers or demands before a breakdown in negotiations occurs. They also usually prepare fallback positions based on combinations of issues. Preparations should be detailed because clear minds often do not prevail during the heat of negotiations.

A major consideration in preparing for negotiations is selection of the bargaining teams. The makeup of the management team usually depends on the type of organization and its size. Normally, bargaining is conducted by labor relations specialists, with the advice and assistance of operating managers. Sometimes, top executives are directly involved, particularly in smaller firms. Larger companies utilize staff specialists (a human resource manager or industrial relations executive), managers of principal operating divisions, and in some cases, an outside consultant, such as a labor attorney. However, it is essential that the human resource manager become actively involved in the collective bargaining process whenever possible.

The responsibility for conducting negotiations for the union is usually entrusted to union officers. At the local level, the bargaining committee will normally be supplemented by rank-and-file members elected specifically for this purpose. In addition, the national union will often send a representative to act in an advisory capacity or even participate directly in the bargaining sessions. The real task of the union negotiating team is to develop and obtain solutions to the problems raised by the union's membership.

Traditional differences between management and union negotiating teams contribute additional friction to the collective bargaining process. Generally speaking, management negotiators are older and better educated than labor negotiators. From management's point of view, their people are more sophisticated and have a better understanding of the issues at hand than labor's team. The management negotiators are likely to be impatient with younger, not so well educated, and presumably less knowledgeable union representatives. On the other hand, labor representatives often perceive management as being less sensitive to the feelings of employees than to property rights and the realities of economic survival and future company growth.[29] As part of their preparation for collective bargaining, negotiators on both sides should fully appraise the makeup of the other team in terms of their strengths and weaknesses and bring this information to bear in the negotiations.

Finally, it is imperative that both groups appreciate the environment in which companies in the industry must operate. While there are environmental differences between industries, some basic similarities do exist. Rapid technological changes and ever increasing competitive global pressures are sweeping across western economies, making the partnership between labor and management more essential than ever. Labor must keep in mind that it is often at a bargaining disadvantage because of lower union membership rates, outmoded labor laws, and management inclination to transfer lower skilled/labor intensive jobs overseas. More and more the jobs remaining in the United States require specific skills, adaptability, and flexibility; traits that many traditional core union members historically lacked. Lastly, worker involvement is a reality and not an option for larger corporations. The *Journal of Commerce* noted that 80 percent of Fortune 500 companies, both union and nonunion, have established worker involvement programs, a necessity for the future of both global business and unions.[30]

BARGAINING ISSUES

The document that emerges from the collective bargaining process is known as a *labor agreement* or *contract.* It regulates the relationship between employer and employees for a specified period of time. Collective bargaining basically determines the relationship between labor and management. Even those who have been long-term foes of organized labor believe that the existence of organized labor and the collective bargaining process is essential. Senator Orrin G. Hatch (R-Utah), labor's archrival on Capital Hill for nearly two decades, believes that labor has value. Hatch still opposes organized labor, but according to him, "There are always going to be people who take advantage of workers. Unions even that out, to their credit. We need them to level the field between labor and management. If you didn't have unions, it would be very difficult for even enlightened employers not to take advantage of workers on wages and working conditions, because of (competition from) rivals."[31] Collective bargaining is an essential, but difficult task because each agreement is unique, and there is no standard or universal model. Despite many dissimilarities, certain topics are included in virtually all labor agreements. These topics include recognition, management rights, union security, compensation and benefits, grievance procedure, employee security, and job-related factors.

Recognition

This section usually appears at the beginning of the labor agreement. Its purpose is to identify the union that is recognized as the bargaining representative and to describe the bargaining unit—that is, the employees for whom the union speaks. A typical recognition section might read as follows:

> The XYZ Company recognizes the ABC Union as the sole and exclusive representative of the bargaining unit employees for the purpose of collective bargaining with regard to wages, hours, and other conditions of employment.

Management Rights

A section that is often, but not always, written into the labor agreement spells out the rights of management. If no such section is included, management may reason that it retains control of all topics not described as bargainable in the contract. The precise content of the management rights section will vary by industry, company, and union. When included, management rights generally involve three areas:

1. Freedom to select the business objectives of the company.
2. Freedom to determine the uses to which the material assets of the enterprise will be devoted.
3. Power to discipline for cause.[32]

In a brochure the company publishes for all of its first-line supervisors, AT&T describes management's rights when dealing with the union, including the following:

You should remember that management has all such rights except those restricted by law or by contract with the union. You either make these decisions or carry them out through contact with your people. Some examples of these decisions and actions are:

- To determine what work is to be done and where, when, and how it is to be done.
- To determine the number of employees who will do the work.
- To supervise and instruct employees in doing the work.
- To correct employees whose work performance or personal conduct fails to meet reasonable standards. This includes administering discipline.
- To recommend hiring, dismissing, upgrading, or downgrading of employees.
- To recommend employees for promotion to management.[33]

Management rights in collective bargaining could be somewhat restricted by a ruling by the NLRB stating that companies must bargain with workers prior to relocating their business operations. The new standard directs employers to bargain over proposed relocations unless they can prove (1) that labor costs were not a factor in the relocation decision or (2) that if labor costs were a consideration, other costs of staying were greater than any wage concessions the union could offer. If the union offered concessions that equaled the size of the financial gains of moving, employers have a bargaining obligation. However, if the relocation involves "a basic change in the nature of the employer's operation," employers do not have to bargain over relocation.[34]

Union Security

Union security is typically one of the first items negotiated in a collective bargaining agreement. The objective of union security provisions is to ensure that the union continues to exist and perform its functions. A strong union security provision makes it easier for the union to enroll and retain members. We describe some basic forms of union security clauses in the following paragraphs.

Closed Shop. A **closed shop** is an arrangement whereby union membership is a prerequisite to employment. Such provisions are generally illegal in the United States.

Union Shop. As we mentioned in Chapter 15, a **union shop** arrangement requires that all employees become members of the union after a specified period of employment (the legal minimum is thirty days) or after a union shop provision has been negotiated. Employees must remain members of the union as a condition of employment. The union shop is generally legal in the United States, except in states that have right-to-work laws.

Maintenance of Membership. Employees who are members of the union at the time the labor agreement is signed or who later voluntarily join must continue their memberships until the termination of the agreement, as a condition of employment. This form of recognition is also prohibited in most states that have right-to-work laws.

Agency Shop. An **agency shop** provision does not require employees to join the union; however, the labor agreement requires, as a condition of employment, that each nonunion member of the bargaining unit "pay the union the equivalent of membership dues as a kind of tax, or service charge, in return for the union acting as the bargaining agent.[35] The agency shop is outlawed in most states that have right-to-work laws.

Exclusive Bargaining Shop. Thirteen of the twenty-one states having right-to-work laws allow only exclusive bargaining shop provisions. Under this form of recognition, the company is legally bound to deal with the union that has achieved recognition, but employees are not obligated to join or maintain membership in the union or to contribute to it financially.

Open Shop. An open shop describes the absence of union security, rather than its presence. The **open shop**, strictly defined, is employment that has equal terms for union members and nonmembers alike. Under this arrangement, no employee is required to join or contribute to the union financially.

Dues Checkoff. Another type of security that unions attempt to achieve is the checkoff of dues. A checkoff agreement may be used in addition to any of the previously mentioned shop agreements. Under the **checkoff of dues** provision, the company agrees to withhold union dues from members' paychecks and to forward the money directly to the union. Because of provisions in the Taft-Hartley Act, each union member must voluntarily sign a statement authorizing this deduction. Dues checkoff is important to the union because it eliminates much of the expense, time, and hassle of collecting dues from each member every pay period or once a month.

Compensation and Benefits

This section typically constitutes a large portion of most labor agreements. The importance of compensation and benefits is illustrated in a survey of union members. Those surveyed ranked pay, pensions, and benefits as the second, third, and fifth most important compensation-related items.[36] Virtually any item that can affect compensation and benefits may be included in labor agreements. Some of the items frequently covered include the following:

- *Wage rate schedule.* The base rates to be paid each year of the contract for each job are included in this section. Figure 16-3 illustrates the average annual changes in wage rate adjustments for current and replaced contracts for private industry collective bargaining settlements covering 1,000 or more workers from 1983 to 1993.[37] At times, unions are able to obtain a cost-of-living allowance (COLA) or escalator clause in the contract in order to protect the purchasing power of employees' earnings. These clauses are generally related to the Consumer Price Index (CPI) prepared by the Bureau of Labor Statistics. However, the average COLA has increased at a smaller percentage in recent years.[38]

- *Overtime and premium pay.* Provisions covering hours of work, overtime pay, and premium pay, such as shift differentials, are included in this section.
- *Jury pay.* Some firms pay an employee's entire salary when he or she is serving jury duty. Others pay the difference between jury pay and the compensation that would have been earned. The procedure covering jury pay is typically stated in the contract.
- *Layoff or severance pay.* The amount that employees in various jobs and/or seniority levels will be paid if they are laid off or terminated is presented in this section.
- *Holidays.* The holidays to be recognized and the amount of pay that a worker will receive if he or she has to work on a holiday are specified.

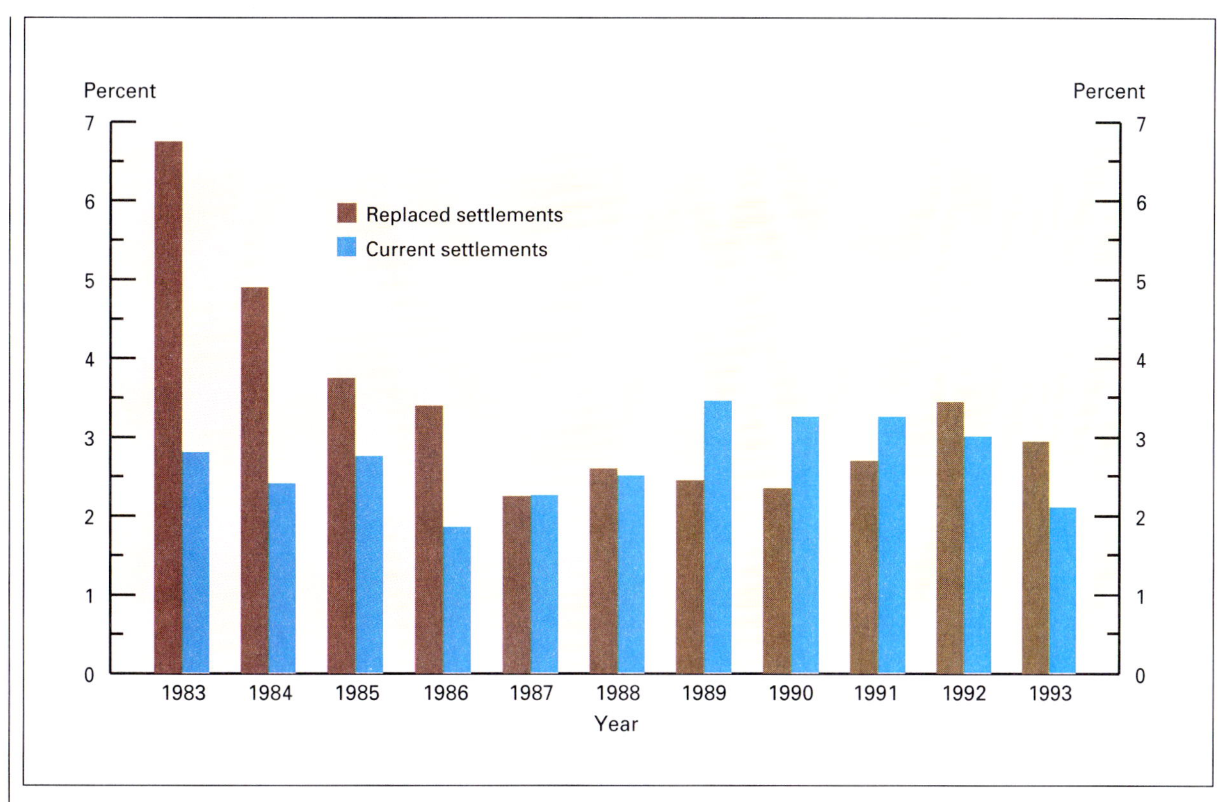

FIGURE 16-3 Average Annual Changes in Wage Rate Adjustments: Current vs Replaced Contracts

Source: Edward J. Wasilewski, "Compensation Gains Moderated in 1993 Private Industry Settlements," *Monthly Labor Review* (May 1994): 47.

In addition, the pay procedure for times when a holiday falls on a worker's nominal day off is provided.

- *Vacation.* This section spells out the amount of vacation that a person may take, based on seniority. Any restrictions as to when the vacation may be taken are also stated.
- *Family care.* This is a benefit that has been included in recent collective bargaining agreements. As previously discussed, AT&T and the Communications Workers of America (CWA) negotiated a contract that had landmark family-care provisions.

Grievance Procedure

A portion of most labor agreements is devoted to a grievance procedure. It contains the means whereby employees can voice dissatisfaction with and appeal specific management actions. Also included in this section are procedures for disciplinary action by management and the termination procedure that must be followed. We devote a portion of Chapter 18 to disciplinary action and the grievance process.

Employee Security

This section of the labor agreement establishes the procedures that cover job security for individual employees. According to a nationwide survey, employee security was the prime concern of union members.[39] Security continues to be a major concern for employees. Recent labor negotiations have dramatically focused on the security issue. As mentioned earlier, since 1990, labor agreements with the "Big Three" automakers included provisions to protect employee security. In 1993, settlements with the Big Three provided lower wage rate changes than those negotiated in the contracts they replaced, but the firms did fully restore funding for job security and supplemental unemployment benefits provided in 1990-1993 agreements.[40]

Seniority and grievance handling procedures are the key topics related to employee security. Seniority is determined by the amount of time that an employee has worked in various capacities with the firm. Seniority may be companywide, by division, by department, or by job. Agreement on seniority is important because the person with the most seniority, as defined in the labor agreement, is typically the last to be laid off and the first to be recalled. The seniority system also provides a basis for promotion decisions. When qualifications are met, employees with the greatest seniority will likely be considered first for promotion to higher level jobs. However, many new collar workers, who are younger and better educated, feel that seniority puts them at an unfair advantage, and they are, therefore, possibly less likely to join unions.

NEGOTIATING THE AGREEMENT

There is no way to ensure speedy and mutually acceptable results from negotiations. At best, the parties can attempt to create an atmosphere that will lend itself to steady progress and productive results. For example, the two negotiating teams usually meet at an agreed-on neutral site, such as a hotel. It is generally important that a favorable relationship be established early in order to avoid "eleventh hour" bar-

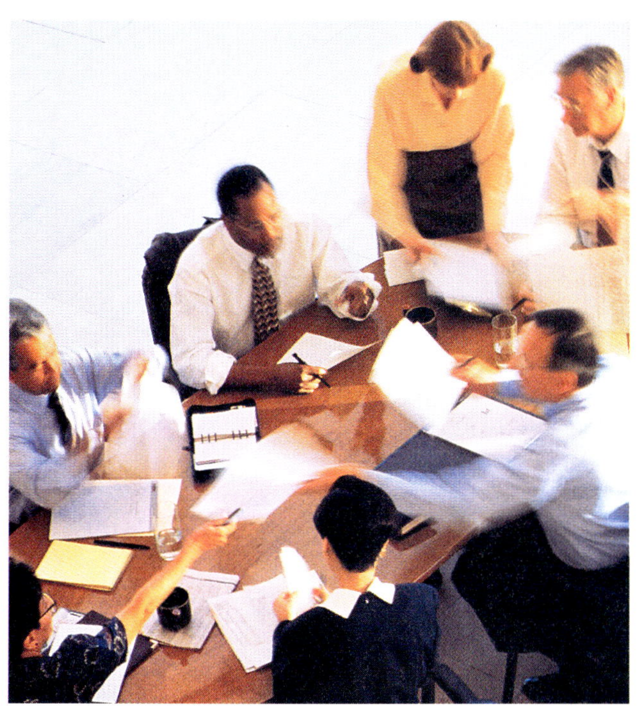

Negotiations should be conducted in the privacy of the conference room, not in the news media.

gaining.[41] It is equally important that union and management negotiators strive to develop and maintain clear and open lines of communication. Since collective bargaining is a problem-solving activity, good communication is essential to its success. Negotiations should be conducted in the privacy of the conference room, not in the news media. If the negotiators feel that publicity is necessary, joint releases to the media may avoid unnecessary conflict.

The negotiating phase of collective bargaining begins with each side presenting its initial demands. Because a collective bargaining settlement can be expensive for a firm, the cost of various proposals should be estimated as accurately as possible. Some changes can be quite expensive, and others cost little or nothing, but the cost of the various proposals being considered must always be carefully deliberated. The term *negotiating* suggests a certain amount of give-and-take, the purpose of which is to lower the other side's expectations. The union will bargain to upgrade its members' economic and working conditions. The company will negotiate to maintain or enhance profitability. One of the most costly components of any collective bargaining agreement is a wage increase provision. An example of the negotiation of a wage increase is shown in Figure 16-4.

In this example, labor initially demands a $0.40 per hour increase. Management counters with an offer of only $0.10 per hour. Both labor and management—as expected—reject each other's demand. Plan B calls for labor to lower its demand to a $0.30 per hour increase. Management counters with an offer of $0.20. The positions in Plan B are feasible to both sides, as both groups are in the bargaining zone. Wages within the bargaining zone are those that management and labor can both accept—in this case, an increase of between $0.20 and $0.30 per hour. The exact amount will be determined by the power of the bargaining unit and the skills of the negotiators.

The realities of negotiations are not for the weak of heart and at times are similar to a high-stakes poker game. A certain amount of bluffing and raising of the ante takes place in many negotiations. The ultimate bluff for the union would be when a negotiator says, "If our demands are not met, we are prepared to strike." Management's version of this bluff would be to threaten a lockout. We will discuss each of these tactics later; utilizing them is a form of power politics. The party with the greater leverage can expect to extract the most concessions. In recent years, management has gained negotiating power, with 84 percent of union members surveyed believing that management now has the upper hand in labor negotiations.[42]

Even though one party in the negotiating process may appear to possess the greater power, negotiators often take care to keep the other side from losing face. They recognize that the balance of power may switch rapidly. By

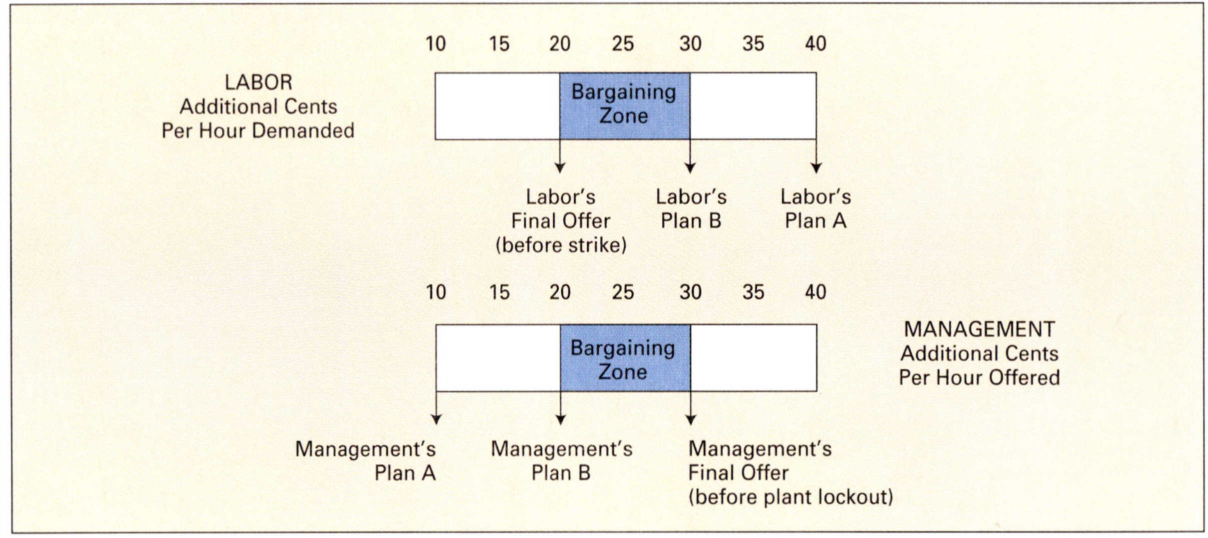

FIGURE 16-4 An Example of Negotiating a Wage Increase

the time the next round of negotiations occurs, the pendulum may be swinging back in favor of the other side. Even when management appears to have the upper hand, it may make minor concessions that will allow the labor leader to claim gains for the union. Management may demand that workers pay for grease rags that are lost (assuming that the loss of these rags has become excessive). In order to obtain labor's agreement to this demand, management may agree to provide new uniforms for the workers if the cost of these uniforms would be less than the cost of lost rags. Thus, labor leaders, although forced to concede to management's demand, could show the workers that they have obtained a concession from management.

As mentioned previously, each side usually does not expect to obtain all the demands presented in its first proposal. However, management must remember that a concession may be difficult to reverse in future negotiations. For instance, if management agreed to provide dental benefits, withdrawing these benefits in the next round of negotiations would be difficult. Labor, on the other hand, can lose a demand and continue to bring it up in the future. Demands that the union does not expect to receive when they are first made are known as **beachhead demands**.

BREAKDOWNS IN NEGOTIATIONS

At times negotiations break down, even though both labor and management may sincerely want to arrive at an equitable contract settlement. Several means of removing roadblocks may be used in order to get negotiations moving again. Breakdowns in negotiations can be overcome through third-party intervention, union strategies, and management strategies. Even with the lack of success of traditional collective bargaining, the caseload for third-party neutrals, such as arbitrators, has increased over the past four fiscal years. At this time, it appears there is no relationship between the number of collective bargaining agreements or the percentage of workers unionized and the number of cases submitted to third party neutrals.[43]

Third-Party Intervention

Often an outside person can intervene to provide assistance when an agreement cannot be reached and the two sides reach an impasse. The reasons behind each party's position may be quite rational. Or the breakdown may be related to emotional disputes that tend to become distorted during the heat of negotiations. Regardless of the cause, something must be done to continue the negotiations. The two basic types of third-party intervention are mediation and arbitration.

Mediation.

In **mediation**, a neutral third party enters a labor dispute when a bargaining impasse has occurred. The objective of mediation is to persuade the parties to resume negotiations and reach a settlement. A mediator has no power to force a settlement but can help in the search for solutions, make recommendations, and work to open blocked channels of communication. Successful mediation depends to a substantial degree on the tact, diplomacy, patience, and perseverance of the mediator. The mediator's fresh insights are used to get discussions going again.

Arbitration.

In **arbitration**, a dispute is submitted to an impartial third party for a binding decision. Arbitration is very much a part of many human resource managers' jobs. There are two principal types of union-management disputes: rights disputes and interests disputes. Those that involve disputes over the interpretation and application of the various provisions of an existing contract are referred to as *rights arbitration*. This type of arbitration is used in settling grievances. Grievance arbitration is common in the United States and is discussed in Chapter 18. The other type of arbitration, *interest arbitration*, involves disputes over the terms of proposed collective bargaining agreements. In the private sector, the use of interest arbitration as an alternative procedure for impasse resolution is not a common practice. Unions and employers rarely agree to submit the basic terms of a contract (such as wages, hours, and working conditions) to a neutral party for disposition. They prefer to rely on collective bargaining and the threat of economic pressure (such as strikes and lockouts) to decide these issues.

In the public sector, most governmental jurisdictions prohibit their employees from striking. As a result, interest arbitration is used to a greater extent in the public sector than in the private sector. Although there is no uniform application of this method, fourteen states have legislation permitting the use of interest arbitration to settle unresolved issues for public employees. In a number of states, compulsory arbitration of interest items is required at various jurisdictional levels.[44] A procedure used in the public sector is *final-offer arbitration*, which has two basic forms: package selection and issue-by-issue selection. In package selection, the arbitrator must select one party's entire offer on all issues in dispute. In issue-by-issue selection, the arbitrator examines each issue separately and chooses the final offer of one side or the other on each issue.[45]

Sources of Mediators and Arbitrators

The principal organization involved in mediation efforts, other than a state and local agency, is the Federal Mediation and Conciliation Service (FMCS). The FMCS was established as an independent agency by the Taft-Hartley Act in 1947. Either one or both parties involved in negotiations can seek the assistance of the FMCS, or the agency can offer its help if it feels that the situation warrants this. Federal law requires that the party wishing to change a contract must give notice of this intention to the other party sixty days prior to the expiration of a contract. If no agreement has been reached thirty days prior to the expiration date, the FMCS must be notified.

In arbitration, the disputants are free to select any person as their arbitrator so long as they agree on the selection. Most commonly, however, the two sides make a request for an arbitrator to either the American Arbitration Association (AAA) or the FMCS. The AAA is a nonprofit organization with offices in many cities. Both the AAA and the FMCS maintain lists of arbitrators. Only people who can show, through references, experience in labor-management relations and acceptance by both labor and management as neutrals are selected for inclusion on these lists.[46]

Union Strategies for Overcoming Negotiation Breakdowns

There are times when a union believes that it must exert extreme pressure to get management to agree to its bargaining demands. Strikes and boycotts are the primary means that the union may use to overcome breakdowns in negotiations.

Strikes. When union members refuse to work in order to exert pressure on management in negotiations, their action is referred to as a **strike**. A strike halts production, resulting in lost customers and revenue, which the union hopes will force management to submit to its terms.

The timing of a strike is important in determining its effectiveness. An excellent time is when business is thriving and the demand for the firm's goods or services is expanding. However, the union might be hard-pressed to obtain major concessions from a strike if the firm's sales are down and it has built up a large inventory. In this instance, the company would not be severely damaged.

Contrary to many opinions, unions prefer to use strikes only as a last resort. In recent years, many union members have been even more reluctant to strike because of the fear of being replaced. The Supreme Court ruled in 1989 that when a union goes on strike and the company hires replacements, the company does not have to lay off these individuals at the end of the strike. Even with the threat of replacement looming and union membership declining, organized labor was involved in fifty-one major strikes in 1989, up from a record low in 1988 of only forty strikes.[47] However, in 1993 the number of strikes was only 35, down from a little more than 200 a year in the 1970s.[48] Strikes are extremely expensive, not only for the employer, but also for the union and its members. In addition to fewer strikes, those that do occur are shorter in duration. For example, Local 2166 of the UAW and GM reached an agreement on a settlement for some 2,300 production and maintenance workers at a truck plant in Shreveport, Louisiana, after a very brief six-day strike. The basic issue was job security; however, the strike was not a firm threat but instead merely a "shot across the bows for the entire truck division."[49]

A union's treasury is often depleted by payment of strike benefits to its members. In addition, members suffer because they are not receiving their normal pay. Although strike benefits help, union members certainly cannot maintain a normal standard of living from these relatively minimal amounts. Sometimes during negotiations (especially at the beginning), the union may want to strengthen its negotiating position by taking a strike vote. Members often give overwhelming approval to a strike. This vote does not necessarily mean that there will be a strike, only that the union leaders now have the authority to call one if negotiations reach an impasse. A favorable strike vote can add a sense of urgency to efforts to reach an agreement.[50]

Successful passage of a strike vote has additional implications for union members. Virtually every national union's constitution contains a clause requiring the members to support and participate in a strike if one is called. If a union member fails to comply with this requirement, he or she can be fined. Therefore, union members place themselves in jeopardy if they cross a picket line without the consent of the union. Fines may be as high as 100 percent of wages for as long as union pickets remain outside the company. However, the Supreme Court has ruled that an employee on strike may resign from the union during a strike and avoid being punished by the union. More subtle measures, such as sickouts and work slowdowns, have been used successfully by union members in order to avoid the impact of a strike on the membership and still bring pressure on the company to meet union demands.

Boycotts. The boycott is another of labor's weapons to get management to agree to its demands. A **boycott** involves an agreement by union members to refuse to use or buy the firm's products. A boycott exerts economic pressure on management, and the effect often lasts much longer than that of a strike. Once shoppers change buying habits, their behavior will likely continue long after the boycott has ended. At times, significant pressures can be exerted on a business when union members, their families, and friends refuse to purchase the firm's products. This approach is especially effective when the products are sold at retail outlets and are easily identifiable by brand name. For instance, the decade-old boycott against Adolph Coors Company was effective because the product, beer, was directly associated with the company.[51] The practice of a union attempting to encourage third parties (such as suppliers and customers) to stop doing business with the company is known as a **secondary boycott**. This type of boycott was declared illegal by the Taft-Hartley Act.

Management's Strategies for Overcoming Negotiation Breakdowns

Management may also use various strategies to encourage unions to come back to the bargaining table. One form of action that is somewhat analogous to a strike is called a **lockout**. In a lockout, management keeps employees out of the workplace and may run the operation with management personnel and/or temporary replacements. Unable to work, the employees do not get paid. Although the lockout is used rather infrequently, the fear of a lockout may bring labor back to the bargaining table. A lockout is particularly effective when management is dealing with a weak union, when the union treasury is depleted, or when the business has excessive inventories.

Another course of action that a company can take if the union goes on strike is to operate the firm by placing management and nonunion workers in the striking workers' jobs. The type of industry involved has considerable effect on the impact of this maneuver. If the firm is not labor intensive and if maintenance demands are not high, such as at a petroleum refinery or a chemical plant, this practice may be quite effective. When it is utilized, management will likely attempt to show how production actually increases with the use of nonunion employees. For example, unionized employees at Southwestern Bell Telephone Company went on strike, and the company continued to provide virtually uninterrupted service to consumers. At times, management personnel will actually live in the plant and have food and other necessities delivered to them.

Another way management can continue operating a firm during a strike is to hire replacements for the strikers. Hiring replacements on either a temporary or a permanent basis is legal when the employees are engaged in an economic strike—that is, one that is a part of a collective bargaining dispute. However, a company that takes such a course of action risks inviting violence and creating bitterness among its employees, which may adversely affect the firm's performance long after the strike has ended.

RATIFYING THE AGREEMENT

Most collective bargaining leads to an agreement without a breakdown in negotiations or disruptive actions. Typically, agreement is reached before the current contract expires. After the negotiators have reached a tentative agreement on all contract terms, they prepare a written agreement covering those terms, complete with the effective and termination dates. The approval process for management is often easier than for labor. The president or CEO has usually been briefed regularly on the progress of negotiations. Any difficulty that might have stood in the way of obtaining approval has probably already been resolved with top management by the negotiators.

However, the approval process is more complex for the union. Until a majority of members voting in a ratification election approve it, the proposed agreement is not final. At times, union members reject the proposal, and a new round of negotiations must begin. In recent years, approximately 10 percent of all tentative agreements have been rejected when presented to the union membership. Many of these rejections might not have occurred if union negotiators had been better informed of the desires of the membership.

ADMINISTRATION OF THE AGREEMENT

Negotiating, as it relates to the total collective bargaining process, may be likened to the tip of an iceberg. It is the visible phase, the part that makes the news. The larger and perhaps more important part of collective bargaining is administration of the agreement, which the public seldom sees.[52] The agreement establishes the union-management relationship for the duration of the contract. Usually, neither party can change the contract's language until the expiration date, except by mutual consent. However, the main problem encountered in contract administration is uniform interpretation and application of the contract's terms. Administering the contract is a day-to-day activity. Ideally, the aim of both management and the union is to make the agreement work to the benefit of all concerned. Often this is not an easy task.

Management is primarily responsible for explaining and implementing the agreement. This process should begin with meetings or training sessions not only to point out significant features but also to provide a clause-by-clause analysis of the contract. First-line supervisors, in particular, need to know their responsibilities and what to do when disagreements arise.

Additionally, supervisors and middle managers should be encouraged to notify top management of any contract modifications or new provisions required for the next round of negotiations.

The human resource manager plays a key role in the day-to-day administration of the contract. He or she gives advice on matters of discipline, works to resolve grievances, and helps first-line supervisors establish good working relationships within the terms of the agreement. As mentioned previously, when a firm is unionized, the HRM function tends to change rather significantly and may even be divided into separate human resource and industrial relations departments. The Bendix Corporation provides an excellent example of this separation of activities. The company has both a vice president of human resources and a vice president of industrial relations (see Figures 16-5 and 16-6). In situations such as this, the vice president of human resources may perform all human resource management tasks with the exception of industrial relations. The vice president of industrial relations would likely deal

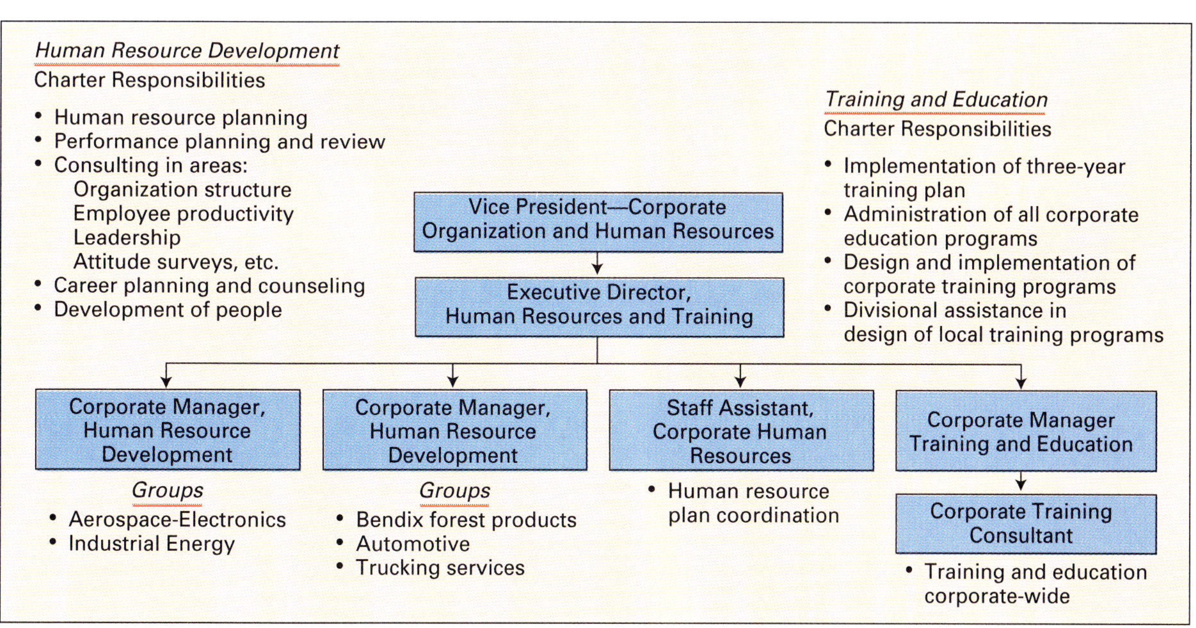

FIGURE 16-5 The Organization of the Human Resource Department at Bendix Corporation

Source: Bendix Corporation.

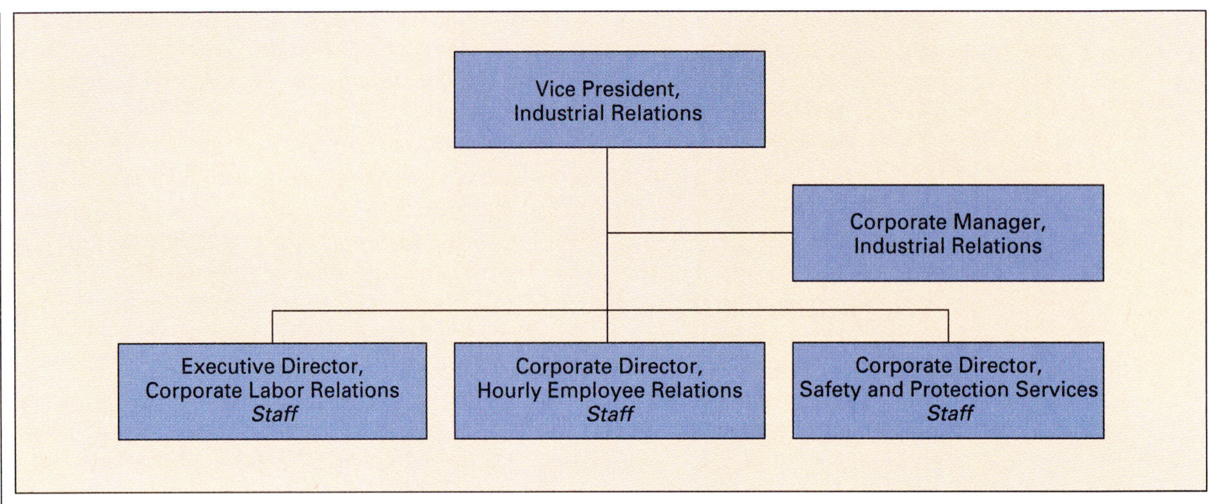

FIGURE 16-6 The Corporate Industrial Relations Department of Bendix Corporation by Functional Responsibility

Source: Bendix Corporation.

with all union-related matters. As one vice president of industrial relations stated:

> My first challenge is, wherever possible, to keep the company union-free and the control of its operations in the hands of corporate management at all levels. Where unions represent our employees, the problem becomes one of negotiating collective bargaining agreements that our company can live with, administering these labor agreements with the company's interests paramount (consistent with good employee relations), and trying to solve all grievances arising under the labor agreement short of their going to arbitration, without giving away the store.

THE FUTURE OF COLLECTIVE BARGAINING

The collective bargaining process and the labor movement have both changed in recent years. They no doubt will change further in the years ahead in response to forces of varying magnitude and conflicting perspectives.

Industrial and Occupational Change

Of the many environmental conditions that shape a firm's labor-management relations, none is more important than the market for the firm's goods or services and its own labor market.[53] In the early 1990s, the trend was toward increased competition within product markets. This trend has a strong international dimension, reflecting the growing interdependence of world markets, and will, in all likelihood, continue into the year 2000. Competition fosters innovation, opens up new market opportunities, and creates new jobs. Firms in mature markets, however, with fewer prospects for growth and expansion, cannot offer a wide variety of job opportunities. In such situations, employers and employees alike need to concern themselves with career transitions, job losses, and organizational restructuring. Historically, unions have had their greatest success in the manufacturing, mining, transportation, and construction industries. With the relative decline in importance of these industries and the relative growth in importance of service industries, union membership has decreased.

Major increases in employment have taken place in wholesale and retail trades; finance and insurance; general service industries; and federal, state, and local government. However, with the exception of government, these industries have had low union membership in the past.

The pattern of employment by occupation has also changed markedly over time. Major changes in white-collar occupations include increases in the number of professional and clerical employees. In blue-collar occupations, the proportion of operative employees increased through 1950; then a long-term decline occurred.[54]

It is also interesting to note that between 1955 and 1984 a larger proportion of industrial workers were assigned to nonproduction jobs, a trend that has continued into the 1990s.[55] The shift toward more professional, service, and white-collar occupations suggests that future employees may well have different expectations of their work. Not only may labor need to rethink its organizing strategy, but also management needs to sharpen its managerial skills in negotiating and team building.

In addition, as mentioned in Chapter 2, the composition of the labor force will change dramatically in the future. Union leadership will need to redefine organizing strategies to attract those who will account for future growth in the U.S. employment sector.

HRM IN ACTION

—IS IT COVERED IN THE CONTRACT?

"I think I might have messed up this morning," said the maintenance supervisor, Carlos Chaves, to Doug Williams, the industrial relations manager. "One of the workers in my section wasn't doing the job exactly according to specs, and I blew up and told him to hit the road. Five minutes later the union steward was in the office reading me the riot act. She said situations such as this are covered in our contract and that I was violating it. I had never spoken to the worker before about that particular offense, and the steward said the contract called for both oral and written warnings before terminations."

How would you respond?

A GLOBAL PERSPECTIVE

Unions often point to multinational corporations as an important cause of U.S. economic problems, especially unemployment. Obviously, both NAFTA and GATT will be singled out by unions as the main cause of the loss of additional manufacturing jobs. Many companies have located part or all of their operations outside the United States to take advantage of lower labor and material costs and favorable tax laws. Investment funds have been diverted to foreign operations, costing the U.S. economy jobs, but proponents of NAFTA and GATT believe that the increased exports that result from these agreements will increase the number of higher paying jobs in the United States.[56] Japanese and European firms have invested significantly in U.S. marketing and manufacturing, which has created new jobs here in the United States. As these firms hire American workers, some interesting collective bargaining situations are created. The key to global success, and the best way to deal with global competition, is through a real partnership between management and labor. Unions throughout the world must contribute with greater productivity and increased flexibility or their numbers will decline.[57]

Foreign competition has had major impacts on employment in several U.S. industries already. In the United States, the shoe, apparel, auto, steel, and rubber industries continue to lose jobs, and their remaining employees feel the effects at the bargaining table in terms of wage and work rule concessions.[58] Wage increases continue to increase at a smaller rate than before, and work rule concessions are basically accepted without much opposition.

If predictions are accurate, NAFTA will dramatically alter the nature of business in North America. Thousands of American producers, from small manufacturers to such global giants as the Eastman Kodak Company, are pouring into Mexico for low cost labor.[59] Partially because of NAFTA, Mexico may become the most popular location for U.S. manufacturers faced with global competition and pricing pressures.

NAFTA and cheap labor, combined with open markets and a government that seems capable of delivering both political and economic security, could mean that Mexico will be one of the world's best places to do business. According to Kodak President Donald F. Spielex, "By 2000, I see Mexico as being a Korea, but with an even wider industrial base."[60] NAFTA and these changes in Mexico may dramatically impact domestic unionism and permanently alter the nature of collective bargaining in the United States.

SUMMARY

Collective bargaining is fundamental to management-labor relations in the United States. Labor and management go through periods in which one has the power to dictate the majority of terms to the other party. In the foreseeable future, management is expected to maintain the power advantage in collective bargaining.

The structure of collective bargaining can affect how it is conducted. When a firm becomes unionized, the role of human resource management tends to change rather significantly. In major corporations in which the large majority of the operative employees belong to unions, the HRM function may even be divided into separate human resource and industrial relations departments.

There are three collective bargaining categories: mandatory, permissive, and prohibited. Mandatory bargaining issues fall within the definition of wages, hours, and other terms and conditions of employment. Permissive bargaining issues may be raised, but neither side may insist that they be bargained over. Prohibited bargaining issues are ones that are statutorily outlawed and, thus, illegal.

The document produced by the collective bargaining process is known as a labor agreement or contract. It regulates the relationship between the employer and the employees for a specified period of time. Certain topics are included in virtually all labor agreements: recognition, management rights, union security, compensation and benefits, grievance procedure, employee security, and job-related factors. Union security is typically one of the first items negotiated in a collective bargaining agreement.

At times negotiations break down, even though both labor and management may sincerely want to arrive at an equitable contract settlement. Several means of removing roadblocks may be used in order to get negotiations moving again, including third-party intervention, union strategies, and management strategies.

The two basic types of third-party intervention are mediation and arbitration. Strikes and boycotts are the primary means the union may use to overcome a breakdown in negotiations. Management may also use various strategies to encourage unions to resume negotiations. In a lockout, management keeps employees out of the workplace and may run the operation with management personnel and/or temporary replacements. Management can continue operations during a strike by utilizing management personnel and hiring nonunion replacements for the strikers.

QUESTIONS FOR REVIEW

1. Describe the basic steps involved in the collective bargaining process.
2. Distinguish among mandatory, permissive, and prohibited bargaining issues.
3. Why is it said that "at times negotiations are similar to a high-stakes poker game?"
4. Define each of the following:
   a. *Closed shop*
   b. *Union shop*
   c. *Agency shop*
   d. *Maintenance of membership*
   e. *Checkoff of dues*
5. What are the primary means by which breakdowns in negotiations may be overcome? Briefly describe each.
6. What is the human resource manager's role in the collective bargaining process?
7. What is involved in the administration of a labor agreement?
8. What appears to be the future of collective bargaining?

HRM SIMULATION

The grievance procedure is usually determined in collective bargaining. This simulation offers an option for your firm to establish a formal grievance program—something it currently does not have. The grievance panel consists of an even number of employees and supervisors. Such programs increase morale by helping employees feel they have a "court of last resort." As with any decision, costs are involved.

ABC VIDEO CASE

THE UNION'S DIFFICULT DECISION
TAPE 2, NUMBER 6

The negotiators for the United Auto Workers (UAW) and General Motors (GM) have made an agreement to end a walkout that has idled thousands of workers. The effects of a strike at the Lords Town plant spread to all of GM's operations to cause parts shortages and work stoppage actions. GM has gotten tough with its nonunion workers, forcing them to forego merit pay increases and bonuses in addition to kicking in for their health insurance. This has caused some to feel that GM is going to get even tougher with the UAW.

According to Douglas Frasier, a former UAW president, "Certainly when you have the law, as it is now stated, where on one hand you give the workers the right to strike. . . . and you take it away with another by saying that if you strike we're going to replace your job permanently. . . . it doesn't provide for a level playing field."

More corporations are turning away from using union workers in manufacturing. Some people think this is a signal of a decreasing standard of living for American manufacturing workers. One survey stated that Americans are losing purchasing power year after year.

HRM INCIDENT 1

—MAYBE I WILL, AND MAYBE I WON'T

Yesterday Bill Brown was offered a job as an operator trainee with GEM Manufacturing. He had recently graduated from Milford High School in a small town in the Midwest. Since Bill had no college aspirations, upon graduation he moved to Chicago to look for a job.

Bill's immediate supervisor spent only a short time with him before turning over Bill to Gaylord Rader, an experienced operator, for training. After they had talked for a short time, Gaylord asked, "Have you given any thought to joining our union? You'll like all of our members."

Bill had not considered this. Moreover, he had never associated with union members, and his parents had never been members either. At Milford High, his teachers had never really talked about unions. The fact that this union operated as an open shop meant nothing to him. Bill replied, "I don't know. Maybe. Maybe not."

The rest of the day progressed much the same way, with several people asking Bill the same question. They were all friendly, but there seemed to be a barrier that separated Bill from the other workers. One worker looked Bill right in the eyes and said, "You're going to join aren't you?" Bill still did not know, but he was beginning to lean in that direction.

After the buzzer rang to end the shift, Bill went to the washroom. Just as he entered, David Clements, the union steward, also walked in. After they exchanged greetings, David said, "I hear that you're not sure about wanting to join our union. You and everyone else reaps the benefits of the work we've done in the past. It doesn't seem fair for you to be rewarded for what others have done. Tell you what, why don't you join us down at the union hall tonight for our beer bust? We'll discuss it more then."

Bill nodded yes and finished cleaning up. "That might be fun," he thought.

Questions

1. Why does Bill have the option of joining or not joining the union?
2. How are the other workers likely to react toward Bill if he chooses not to join? Discuss.

HRM INCIDENT 2

—WHAT'S CAUSING THE TURNOVER?

Alonzo Alexander, human resource manager for Hyatt Manufacturing, had a problem he did not know how to handle. His firm was unionized, and the relationship between management and the union had generally been good. The firm also had a strong affirmative action program, which required Alonzo to recruit women for jobs that had traditionally been filled by men. Hyatt had made major strides in implementing this program throughout the firm, with the notable exception of the machine department. There were only two women among the thirty-three operators in that department, both of whom had been hired within the past two months.

Alonzo had continued to locate numerous women applicants for the machine operator jobs. Some had trained at the local trade school and were obviously well qualified. A reasonable percentage of women were hired, but they never stayed long. Reviewing records of exit interviews with women who had quit the machine department, Alonzo categorized the main reasons given for leaving as follows: to take a better job (10 responses); pay not high enough (5); personal and family obligations (3); personal relationships on the job (2); and supervision (2).

When Alonzo interviewed coworkers of women who had quit, he felt that he got little cooperation. Typical comments were "They just had their feelings hurt too easily," and "They were treated like any other worker; if they couldn't hack it maybe they didn't belong here." At one point, the union steward told Alonzo that the continued questioning of workers could be considered harassment.

Questions

1. What action would you suggest Alonzo take? Discuss.
2. How might the union be involved in helping Alonzo solve the problem?

DEVELOPING HRM SKILLS

AN EXPERIENTIAL EXERCISE

A major part of the human resource manager's job is to advise managers at all levels regarding HR matters. The human resource manager's knowledge and experience are often required in dealing with union matters, especially in handling situations that have an impact on future unionization. This exercise provides additional insight into the importance of properly handling employee problems in a unionized environment.

The human resource manager, Gregory Menchew, works very closely with all the managers and employees in an attempt to settle problems before they become critical. Today one of the union stewards, Eugene Wilson, has called for an appointment with Gregory to voice a complaint. The HR manager has agreed to talk to Eugene, but prior to the conversation he wants to talk to the supervisor, Larry Bradley. That way Gregory can get both sides of the story. Gregory really hopes this is not a major problem, since it appears that the company is moving toward union decertification, which may be derailed if difficulties arise now.

Larry Bradley has been with the company for twelve years, the last four as a supervisor. He is a very safety-conscious supervisor with a reputation for strictly enforcing the rules. In Larry's opinion, because of this safety-consciousness, there has not been a lost-time accident in the division since he became the supervisor. There is a rule in the plant, well known to everyone, that every intersection is a "four-way stop" for forklift trucks. According to the labor-management agreement, even minor safety violations justify a three-day suspension and a written warning. Larry saw a forklift truck, with Charlie Fox at the wheel, come around a corner at a high speed and not stop at an intersection. Virtually no one except Charlie Fox and Larry were at the plant, but Larry suspended Charlie for three days and placed a written warning in his personnel folder.

Eugene Wilson was elected union steward last year, since when there have been few grievances, leaving him little to do. A couple of workers have brought complaints, but management was correct in each case and workers were told so. Eugene likes being the union steward and believes it might be tough to be reelected unless he can make a "show." In Eugene's opinion, Charlie Fox was improperly suspended for three days. Eugene has found his reelection platform.

Three individuals will participate in this exercise: one to serve as the human resource manager, one to serve as the supervisor, and another to play the role of union steward. Your instructor will provide the participants with additional information necessary to complete the exercise.

NOTES

1. Aaron Bernstein, "Why America Needs Unions But Not the Kind It Has Now," *Business Week* (May 23, 1994): 70–82.

2. Edward J. Wasilewski, "Compensation Gains Moderated in 1993 Private Industry Settlements," *Monthly Labor Review* 117 (May 1994): 46–56.

3. Ibid.

4. Aaron Bernstein, "Why America Needs Unions But Not the Kind It Has Now," ibid.

5. Edward J. Wasilewski, Jr., "Collective Bargaining in 1992: Contract Talks and Other Activity," *Monthly Labor Review* 115 (January 1992): 5.

6. Aaron Bernstein and David Greising, "Baseball's Strike Talk Turns Serious," *Business Week* (June 27, 1994): 34.

7. Keith L. Alexander and Stephen Baker, "The Steelworkers Vs. The Smiling Barracuda," *Business Week* (May 23, 1994): 26.

8. Aaron Bernstein, "Why America Needs Unions But Not the Kind It Has Now," ibid.

9. Ibid.

10. Arthur A. Sloane and Fred Witney, *Labor Relations*, 4th edition (Englewood Cliffs, N.J.: Prentice Hall, 1981): 28–35.

11. Aaron Bernstein, "Why America Needs Unions But Not the Kind It Has Now," ibid.

12. Anne Ritter, "Are Unions Worth the Bargain?" *Personnel* 67 (February 1990): 14, and Aaron Bernstein, "Why America Needs Unions But Not the Kind It Has Now," ibid.

13. Aaron Bernstein, "Why America Needs Unions But Not the Kind It Has Now," ibid.

14. Ibid.

15. Abby Brown, "Labor Contract Negotiations: Behind the Scenes," *Labor Relations: Reports from the Firing Line* (Plano, TX: Business Publications, 1988): 305–308.

16. "Why Labor Keeps Losing?" *Fortune* (July 11, 1994): 54.

17. Abby Brown, "An Interview with Fritz Ihrig," *Personnel Administrator* 31 (April 1986): 60.

18. James L. Lewandowski and William P. MacKinnion, "What We Learned at Saturn," *Personnel Journal* 71 (December 1992): 30–31.

19. David Woodruff, "Saturn: Labor's Love Lost?" *Business Week* (February 8, 1993): 122–123.

20. Ibid., 73.

21. Sid Kessler, "Is There Still a Future for Unions?" *Personnel Management* 25 (July 1993): 24–30.

22. Harry Levinson, "Stress at the Bargaining Table," *Labor Relations: Reports from the Firing Line* (Plano, TX: Business Publications, 1988): 310.

23. Ibid.

24. "HR Focus: Labor Relations: Court Sides with Unions," *Personnel* 67 (June 1990): 6–7.

25. Aaron Bernstein and Jim Bartimo, "Wrong Time for Scare Tactics?" *Business Week* (April 16, 1990): 28.

26. Wendy Zellner, "All the Ingredients for Disaster Are There," *Business Week* (April 16, 1990): 28.

27. Sid Kessler, "Is There Still a Future for Unions?" ibid.

28. Abby Brown, "An Interview with Fritz Ihrig," 56.

29. Harry Levinson, "Stress at the Bargaining Table," 312.

30. Editorial, *Journal of Commerce* (March 26, 1993), and Henry P. Guzda, "Workplace Partnerships in the United States and Europe," *Monthly Labor Review* 117 (October 1993): 67–72.

31. Aaron Bernstein, "Why America Needs Unions But Not the Kind It Has Now," ibid.

32. Edwin F. Beal and James P. Begin, *The Practice of Collective Bargaining,* 6th edition (Homewood, Ill.: Richard D. Irwin, 1982): 295–298.

33. *Management/Employee/Union Relations* (Dallas, TX: Southwestern Bell Telephone Company, December 1971): 3.

34. "NLRB Requires Firms to Bargain Before Relocating," *The Wall Street Journal* (June 17, 1991): A12.

35. Edwin F. Beal and James P. Begin, *The Practice of Collective Bargaining,* 286.

36. Shane R. Premeaux, R. Wayne Mondy, and Art L. Bethke, "Decertification: Fulfilling Unions' Destiny?" *Personnel Journal* 32 (June 1987): 148.

37. Edward J. Wasilewski, "Compensation Gains Moderated in 1993 Private Industry Settlements," ibid.

38. Ibid.

39. Anne Ritter, "Are Unions Worth the Bargain?" ibid.

40. Edward J. Wasilewski, "Compensation Gains Moderated in 1993 Private Industry Settlements," ibid.

41. Eleventh hour bargaining refers to last minute settlement attempts just prior to the expiration date of an existing agreement. Failure to reach agreement in this manner frequently results in a strike.

42. R. Wayne Mondy and Shane R. Premeaux, "The Labor/Management Power Relationship Revisited," *Personnel Administrator* 30 (May 1985): 55.

43. David A. Dilts, "The Future of Labor Arbitrators," *Arbitration Journal* 48 (June 1993): 24–31.

44. Benjamin J. Taylor and Fred Witney, *Labor Relations Law,* 4th edition (Englewood Cliffs, N.J.: Prentice Hall, 1983): 652–653.

45. Robert E. Allen and Timothy J. Keaveny, *Contemporary Labor Relations* (Reading, Mass.: Addison-Wesley, 1983): 558–559.

46. Donald Austin Woolf, "Arbitration in One Easy Lesson: A Review of Criteria Used in Arbitration Awards," *Personnel* 55 (September-October 1978): 76.

47. Gene Koretz and Celeste Whittaker, "More Picket Lines, Fewer Rank-and-Filers," *Business Week* (May 7, 1990): 24.

48. Aaron Bernstein, "Why America Needs Unions But Not the Kind It Has Now," ibid.

49. Developments in Industrial Relations, "Strike Ends At GM Truck Plant," *Monthly Labor Review* 117 (April 1994): 46.

50. Edwin F. Beal and James P. Begin, *The Practice of Collective Bargaining,* 221–222.

51. Sandra Atchison and Aaron Bernstein, "A Silver Bullet for the Union Drive at Coors?" *Business Week* (July 11, 1988): 61.

52. Harold W. Davey, *Collective Bargaining,* 3rd edition (Englewood Cliffs, N.J.: Prentice Hall, 1972): 141.

53. Thomas A. Kochan and Thomas A. Barocci, *Human Resource Management and Labor Relations* (Boston: Little, Brown, 1985): 528–529.

54. John A. Fossum, *Labor Relations,* 3rd edition (Plano, TX: Business Publications, 1985): 472–473.

55. Ibid., 475–477.

56. Laurence I. Barrett, Michael Duffy, Laura Lopez, and Joseph R. Szczesny, Time Daily News Summary-America Online, *Time, Inc.* (November 11, 1993): 1–5.

57. Henry P. Guzda, "Workplace Partnerships in the United States and Europe," ibid.

58. Stephen Baker, Elizabeth Weener, and Amy Borrus, "Mexico: A New Economic Era," *Business Week* (November 12, 1990): 103.

59. Ibid.

60. Ibid., 104.

CHAPTER 17

Union-Free Organizations

KEY TERMS

Open door policy 544	Ombudsperson 547
Grievance procedure 547	Decertification 548

CHAPTER OBJECTIVES

1. Explain why employees choose not to join a union and describe both the costs and benefits of unionization.
2. List and describe the various strategies and tactics a firm might use to maintain its union-free status.
3. Explain union decertification.
4. Describe the role of the human resource manager in a union-free organization.

Wayne Roberts recently joined Royal Airlines as a reservation agent in Dallas. Prior to this job, he had been employed by Muse Airline of New York. When Muse went out of business recently, Wayne was offered a job with Royal. The pay wasn't as good, and he seemed to be working harder, but he needed the job.

During his first week on the job, Wayne was talking with several workers on his shift: "I don't see why we don't have a union here. Who's going to represent us when management puts the screws on?" Wayne's conversation was quickly cut off by one of the other workers, who replied, "We don't believe in unions at Royal. Management has done a good job. If you believe you need a union to represent you, maybe you don't need to work here." Wayne nodded his head to indicate his understanding and decided not to mention his feelings about wanting a union again.

In an unrelated incident, Brad Carpet, general manager for Royal, was visibly upset. He had just walked through the Royal terminal and accidentally heard one of the supervisors severely reprimanding an employee in front of coworkers. Brad called the supervisor aside and said, "We're a union-free organization and hope to remain that way. What you just did was one of the fastest ways to create a feeling among our employees that they need a union."

These incidents describe some employee and management attitudes in union-free firms. Wayne Roberts discovered that many of his fellow employees feel they do not need to be represented by a union. On the other hand, Brad Carpet is quite concerned that the actions of one of his supervisors may create an atmosphere in which employees believe they do need a union. Employees of union-free firms comprise a major part of the labor force in the United States. Remaining union-free is the obvious choice of management. However, continuation of a union-free environment can be threatened by many work-related factors of which management must be acutely aware.

We begin this chapter with a discussion of the reasons that employees avoid joining unions. We then present a cost/benefit analysis of unionization, followed by a discussion of the strategies and tactics for maintaining a union-free status. We devote the final portion of the chapter to union decertification and the role of the human resource manager in a union-free organization.

WHY EMPLOYEES AVOID JOINING UNIONS

According to the heads of the Council of Economic Advisers, workers are satisfied if certain rewards are provided for employee performance. These rewards include productivity bonuses, job security, steps to build group cohesiveness (such as limiting the pay differences between workers and management), and employee rights (such as protection from arbitrary firings).

According to the Council's cohead, David I. Levine, "A union is one way to do [all] that, although it's [not] the only way."[1] However, it is in the best interest of management and employees that these rewards are provided. Not only will such behavior forestall unionization, but it will also help to maximize employee performance. Most employees in the United States do not belong to unions; in fact, currently only 15.8 percent of the workforce is unionized. This is less than one-half of the percentage of those unionized in the mid 1950s. Furthermore, if government employees are subtracted, a mere 11 percent of private-industry workers are represented by unions, a figure that could plunge to 4 or 5 percent by the year 2000.[2] Basically, employees avoid unions when the human resource system deals directly and effectively with employees and their needs, a situation that is even more so today than at any time in the past 50 years.[3] For quite some time, management has had the upper hand because, as Rutgers University Professor Leo Troy puts it, "Capital can go anywhere, labor cannot. Labor has been outmaneuvered."[4] Even with this advantageous position, management must sustain an environment in which labor cannot successfully organize in order to remain union-free. The old saying that "management gets what it deserves" is never more true than when a union successfully organizes a group of employees.[5] After the union arrives and successfully organizes, management usually recognizes the avoidable mistakes that led to unionization. However, a well-conceived and implemented employee relations system could substantially reduce the likelihood of unionization.[6] Acceptance that "environmental changes will forever conspire against the survival and growth of unions" will eventually result in the survival of unions, most probably in firms that dismiss the concept of equity and employee involvement.[7]

Employees do not join unions for several reasons, some of which are shown in Figure 17-1. In the first place, it costs money to be a union member. Typically, there is an initiation fee followed by dues that must be paid regularly. From time to time, there may also be special assessments. Although dues typically do not amount to more than 2 percent of before-tax pay, many individuals would rather use this money in other ways. A worker who makes $24,000 annually would pay dues of approximately $40 per month, in addition to the initiation fee and any special assessments.

Also, most employees think that unions are unnecessary. They believe that they should not have to depend on a third party to help satisfy their job-related needs. These individuals feel that their value to the organization should be judged on an individual basis; if their performance is superior, the rewards should be appropriate and direct. The workforce of the future will be made up of different types of workers, many of whom will naturally dismiss the covenants of unionism. New collar workers, who are younger, better educated, and more independent, are one segment of the workforce that is particularly susceptible to issues related to job security, and they have a very negative view of seniority. Fortunately, rewarding superior performance goes hand-in-hand with corporate global competitiveness and survival, and this is one of the most effective methods of remaining union-free.[8] New collar workers believe that joining a union is an admission that others control their destiny, thereby limiting their opportunities to maximize rewards.

FIGURE 17-1
Why Employees Do Not Join Unions

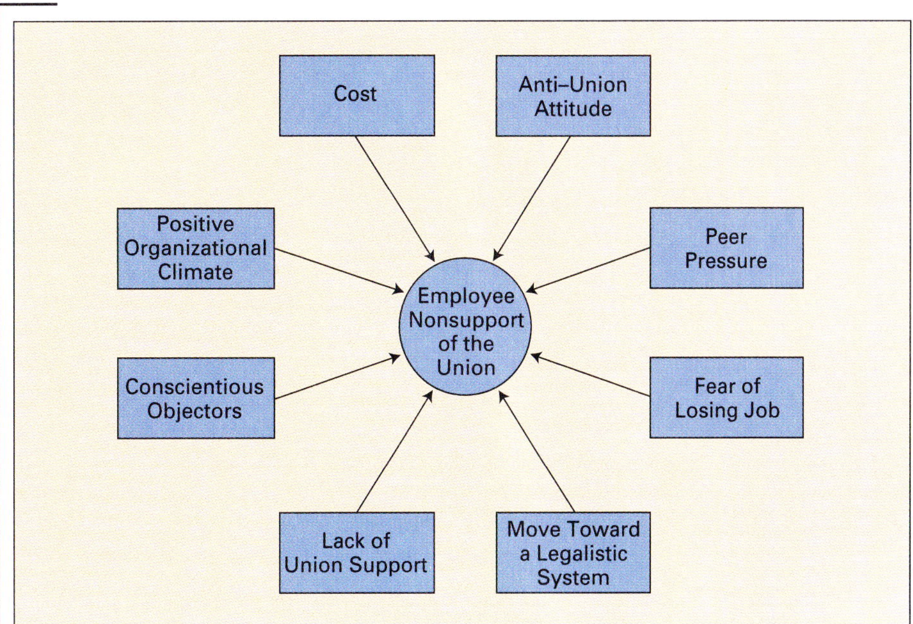

In addition, just as there may be peer pressure in some firms to encourage employees to join the union, in other instances there may be as much pressure against union affiliation. Even if an individual might desire to join a union, the informal work group may be powerful enough to stop the individual from joining. As Wayne Roberts discovered in the incident at the beginning of the chapter, the prevailing attitude of his coworkers to maintain a union-free status created extreme peer pressure on him to conform. Reprisals for union activities are illegal in the United States, but that has not stopped such activities. According to an analysis of the National Labor Relations Board figures, "unlawful firings occurred in one-third of all representation elections in the late 1980s, compared to 8 percent in the late 1960s."[9] Some employees would feel very insecure about their jobs if they engaged in union activities. Perhaps they have seen workers who supported a union receive what they perceive as unfair treatment from employers. A worker who can be easily replaced may decide not to take a chance on losing his or her job by supporting union activities. In fact, according to Harvard labor law specialist Paul C. Weiler, the real perception of risk by workers who think that "they'll be fired in an organizing campaign" is significant.[10]

Establishing a union is much like starting a business. The cost of starting and maintaining a union must be evaluated in relation to the revenue and other benefits to be gained. Under certain circumstances, a union may decide to expend little or no effort to create a new bargaining unit. For instance, a union would tend to favor organizing a unit of 500 skilled workers rather than a group of fifty semiskilled employees. Although the union might like to help the fifty employees, the cost of organizing and supporting their demands might be excessive.

Unions also recognize that there are certain industries, firms, and locations in the country with a tradition of resisting unions. For instance, in the Sunbelt states, unions commonly experience organizing difficulties. Additionally, unions believe that legislation such as NAFTA and GATT will continue to erode their traditional organizing base of manufacturing firms, leading to additional membership losses.[11] Also, a union may feel that additional attempts to unionize some organizations are a waste of money because previous efforts proved fruitless. Even with recent layoffs at IBM, for the first time in the company's history, attempts to organize at the computer giant and similar firms will probably prove fruitless.[12]

Some employees have religious or moral beliefs that preclude them from joining organizations. Because unions are organizations, such employees refuse to work for a firm where union membership is required.

As discussed in Chapter 15, the growing web of employee legal protection may well replace union representation in the future. In 1985, Harvard's Paul C. Weiler predicted that employee rights in the future will be protected by a legalistic rather than a collective bargaining system, and this prediction may well become a reality in the future.[13]

Finally, there may be factors within the company that keep employees from joining a union. The corporate culture (discussed in Chapter 9) may be one that encourages open communication and employee participation. Workers may have excellent relations with their supervisors. Trust may exist to the point that workers may feel that they do not need a third party to represent them in their dealings with management. When this attitude is prevalent, the employees identify strongly with the objectives of the company and are likely to resist organizing efforts.

COSTS AND BENEFITS OF UNIONIZATION

Valid reasons exist for management's acceptance or rejection of unionization, as shown in Figure 17-2. Now we will discuss the rationales for both philosophies.

Acceptance of Unionization Attempts

There may be times when resisting unionizing attempts is not advantageous. In such situations, management must set aside personal feelings and make decisions that are in the firm's best interest. For example, in certain areas of the United States, the maritime and construction unions often provide a ready source of labor from their hiring halls. A firm operating in one of these industries in an area that is strongly unionized may find it advantageous to accept unionization in order to obtain qualified workers.

In addition, there are situations in which union-management relationships are quite good and well established. In such instances, it may be prudent to keep a particular union. Otherwise, a more demanding union may take its place. Thus, management rationalizes that it can work within the present system, whereas the alternative, with a different union, may be uncertain. Unionized firms such as John Deere, AT&T, General Motors' Saturn Corporation, Scott Paper Company, and Xerox Corporation have prospered in recent years. For example, when faced with mounting competitive pressures and the need to dramatically cut costs, Scott Paper formed a committee of ten top officials from each side who "worked together to meet the needs of employees, customers, shareholders, the union, and the community." To accomplish its cost-cutting goal, Scott gave workers more decision-making power, and the union struck a true partnership with the company. This approach was so successful that other paper companies, such as Champion International Corporation, copied it. Cooperation between management and labor is a must if the labor force is to be trustful and receptive to manage-

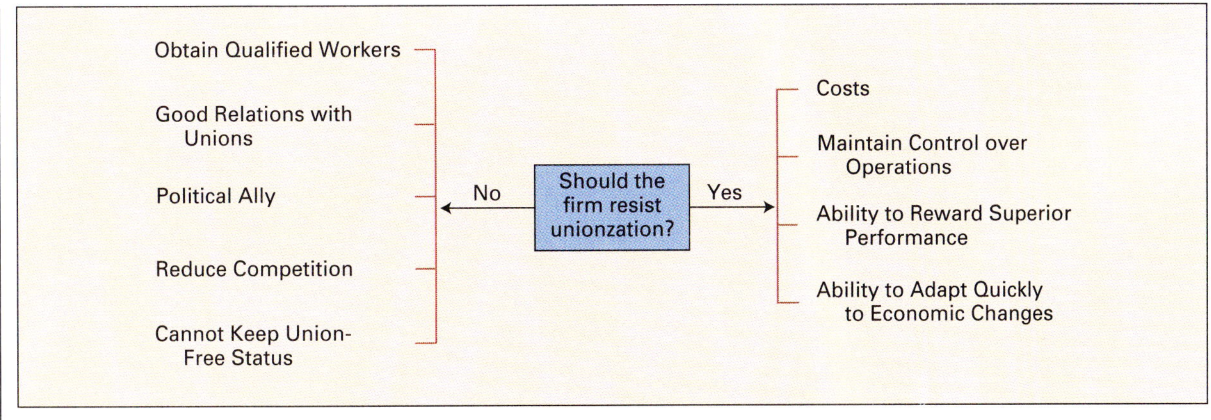

FIGURE 17-2 Should the Organization Resist Unionization?

ment's goals.[14] In addition, requirements of a new high performance workforce include employee trust and commitment, teamwork, and labor-management cooperation.

Management may also desire unionization of competing firms. If a competitor attempts to enter the industry by paying lower nonunion wages, the established firms will likely desire unionization of the new firm. Costs to firms producing similar products remain relatively constant when all are unionized. An additional factor determining whether a firm should resist unionization attempts involves a realistic appraisal of whether it can remain union-free. In some cases, the firm would have little hope of staying union-free. For example, a maritime company located in New York City would have little chance of remaining union-free. In such cases, it would probably be in the firm's best interest to begin developing a strategy for working with a union.

Resistance to Unionization Attempts

Although there may be valid reasons for a firm to accept unionization, a large majority of executives would prefer that their companies remain union-free. In fact, that is a major goal for many organizations. It is tempting for managers to say, "It's our turn; we've got the club." Basically, many experts believe that when this attitude prevails, "management organizes unions." But it remains true that the majority of managers prefer to operate without unions.[15] To remain union-free, management must exercise restraint and use its power to provide the performance-based rewards mentioned at the beginning of this chapter. Various reasons encourage management to remain union-free.

Costs. In the past, the compensation paid to union members was generally higher than that for nonunion workers, but this gap is narrowing, except for upper seniority union workers in long surviving firms. However, recent major collective bargaining agreements have resulted in lower wage rate increases than those negotiated in the contracts they replaced.[16] Both management and unions now realize that a cooperative effort and performance-based rewards are essential if firms are to remain competitive and survive.[17]

In general, unionization increases labor costs, but at an ever decreasing rate.[18] In the past, factors that contributed to such costs included: complex, payroll-padding work rules; work stoppages, strikes, and slowdowns; lengthy negotiations and the grind of arbitration cases; and layoff by seniority. However, the impact of these factors on costs is diminishing with every new collective bargaining agreement that is ratified. In addition, costs are being reduced because the working relationship between labor and management continues to be one of greater cooperation and mutual effort for mutual gain and survival.[19]

Maintaining Control over Operations. Management typically wants to operate without restrictive union work rules and other provisions that could reduce its authority. When a firm is unionized, management relinquishes some of its control. For example, with a union-free airline, a ticket agent may load baggage or fill in as a dispatcher or a scheduler during slow periods. This would not happen in a unionized firm, where job duties are often inflexible.

A union-free firm does not face costly strikes, which can be disastrous during critical periods. It avoids having its competitors step in and increase their market shares. The extended strikes of the past is one of the reasons the U.S. steel industry experienced such a decline in sales. Manufacturers, needing steel to produce their goods, tried Japanese and European steel and often continued to purchase from the foreign suppliers after the strikes were over. This scenario has been repeated many times in other industries.

Ability to Reward Superior Performance. Rewarding superior performance in a union-free organization is often much easier than in a unionized company. A study involving twenty-six nonunion firms revealed that company executives believe they achieve higher productivity than they would if they were organized.[20] In union-free organizations, promotions and salary increases may be based solely on performance instead of seniority. In a unionized organization, the compensation paid each worker is specified by the agreement, not based on performance.

Ability to Adapt Quickly. Most organizations experience fluctuations in demand for their products. Some firms undergo severe business downturns before the cycle reverses. Union-free firms are typically able to respond more easily to changing conditions. If wages must be reduced to remain competitive, the union-free firm can generally adjust them rapidly. The unionized firm is bound by the labor agreement and cannot lower wages unless the union agrees to a contract change. When the automobile industry was in severe difficulty because foreign products were less expensive and of better quality, management could not quickly lower wages to be competitive. Any wage concessions had to be negotiated. Often these negotiations were unsuccessful, partially resulting in the severe slump in the sale of U.S.-made automobiles throughout most of the 1980s.

When workers must be laid off as a result of declining demand, management in a union-free firm is able to lay off marginally productive employees. The seniority system determines who will be laid off in a unionized company, further diminishing management's ability to raise productivity. However, in the future a combination of declining union strength and competitive pressures will likely result in more flexible unions and less oppressive rules, such as the existence of seniority based reward systems.[21]

BUSTING UNIONS CAN NEGATIVELY IMPACT PROFITABILITY

A union-free organization is often viewed by management as the best environment in which to do business, but as unions become more cooperative, this could change in certain industries. However, should a company "bust" a union to become union-free? Is it better to break a union or to encourage cooperation between labor and management? Slight evidence is surfacing that supports the notion of remaining unionized but changing the organizational focus to one of labor-management cooperation. Firms such as Scott Paper and Xerox have already realized the benefits of mutual cooperation. Over the long haul, moderate behavior (by management when dealing with unions) is probably more efficient, particularly as union clout decreases.[22]

Industrial relations professor William N. Cooke surveyed fifty-six unionized manufacturers that either ousted unions or developed cooperative relations with them. After adjusting for such factors as changing market conditions, Cooke and a collaborator reached an unexpected conclusion. Employers that tried teamwork reported a 19 percent increase over the course of a decade in value added per employee, but combative employers experienced a 15 percent decline. Teamwork eventually brought Xerox Corporation and its union into a new era of cooperation. The relationship between Xerox and the Amalgamated Clothing & Textile Workers Union (ACTWU) has resulted in Xerox bringing back 300 jobs from abroad to a new plant in Utica, New York, where the company expects higher quality and a savings of $2 million a year.[23] *Value added* was defined as operating income plus inventory divided by the number of workers. Companies that experienced a decline eventually recovered from the decline, which was apparently caused by the huge cost of withstanding a union-busting strike. However, according to Cooke, "Our evidence suggests that cooperation seems to pay off the best, at least so far." It is unlikely that after many years of wielding significant power over unions that management will embrace unions and attempt to bring them into the fold (as the Japanese did at their Bridgestone tire plant in Warren County, Tennessee). However, some companies are embracing the concept of cooperative relationships between workers and managers, a strategy that has paid off at John Deere & Company.[24]

STRATEGIES AND TACTICS FOR REMAINING UNION-FREE

Some managers believe that the presence of a union is evidence of management's failure to treat employees fairly.[25] The factors that the AFL-CIO believes will significantly reduce chances of unionizing are listed in Table 17-1. According to a report published in *Unions in Transition,* certain similar characteristics help organizations remain union-free: competitive pay and strong benefits, a team environment, open communication, a pleasant work environment, and the avoidance of layoffs.[26] Currently, both organized labor and progressive management realize that these positive characteristics will be a part of future work environments regardless of the union status of a company.

If a firm's goal is to remain union-free, it must establish its strategy long before a union-organizing attempt begins. The development of long-term strategies and effective tactics for the purpose of remaining union-free is crucial because the employees' decision to consider forming a union is usually not made overnight. Negative attitudes regarding the company are typically formed over a period of time and well in advance of any attempt at unionization. A particular farm implement company is a perfect example of an organization that may be destined to have continual trouble with unions. Despite the fact that the firm's business is booming and their employees enjoy some of the most generous wage and benefit packages of any unionized firm, workers are unhappy. This company continues to harass workers by not allowing them to wear anti-upper management T-shirts and "Stop Scabs" buttons. Its management practices are so negative that the UAW is

TABLE 17-1
AFL-CIO: Factors That Reduce the Chances for Union Organizing

1. A conviction by employees that the boss is not taking advantage of them.
2. Employees who have pride in their work.
3. Good performance records kept by the company. Employees feel more secure on their jobs when they know their efforts are recognized and appreciated.
4. No claims of high-handed treatment. Employees respect firm but fair discipline.
5. No claim of favoritism that's not earned through work performance.
6. Supervisors who have good relationships with subordinates. The AFL-CIO maintains that this relationship of supervisors with people under them—above all—stifles organizing attempts.

Source: "What to Do When the Union Knocks," *Nation's Business* 54 (November 1966): 107. Copyright 1977 by Nation's Business. Reprinted by permission.

quickly winning back workers. It is unfortunate that petty actions by management, which had nothing to do with productivity gains, should create such problems and actually help unions organize.[27]

If a firm desires to remain union-free, it must borrow some of the union's philosophy. Basically, management must be able and willing to offer workers equal or better conditions than they could expect with a union, which is becoming easier and easier to do. Weakness in any critical area may be an open invitation to a union.[28] As shown in Figure 17-3, all aspects of an organization's operations are involved in maintaining its union-free status.

Effective First-Line Supervisors

Extremely important to an organization's ability to remain union-free is the overall effectiveness of its management, particularly its first-line supervisors. These supervisors represent the first line of defense against unionization. Their supervisory ability often determines whether unionization will be successful. The supervisor assigns work, evaluates each individual's performance, and provides praise and punishment. The manner in which he or she communicates with the employee in these and other matters can affect the individual's attitude toward the firm. Even though the first-line supervisor is the lowest level of management in the workplace, this person usually has more influence over employees than any other manager.

The supervisor also must communicate information about the firm to employees. Information regarding profits, sales, how the firm's products compare with those of competitors, and the like are important. The grapevine may reveal that sales are declining, which would likely disturb many workers. If the supervisor explains that sales are down across the industry but are expected to return to normal in the next quarter, employees might be less concerned.

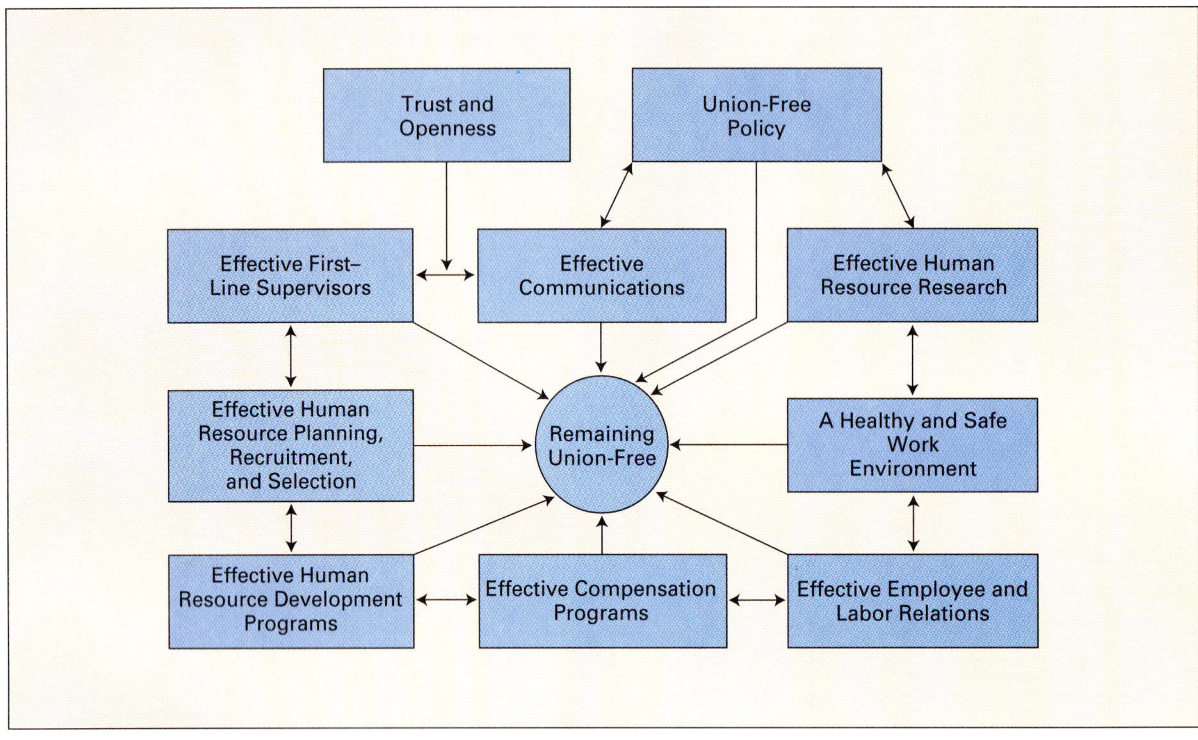

FIGURE 17-3 Factors Involved in Maintaining a Union-Free Status

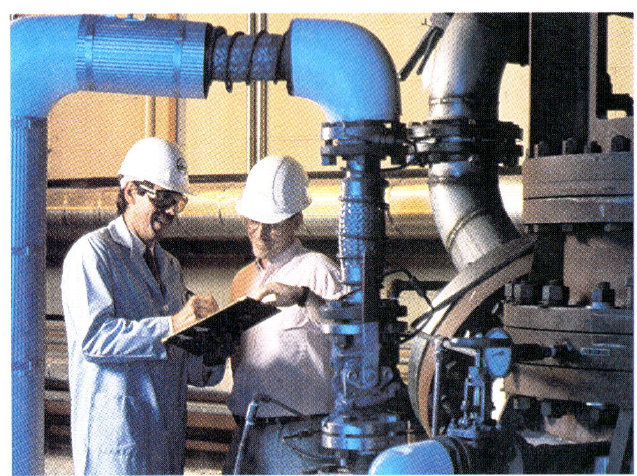

Extremely important to an organization's ability to remain union-free is the overall effectiveness of its management, particularly its first-line supervisors.

In order for a supervisor to communicate effectively with employees, he or she must possess timely and accurate information. If an employee is aware of company plans before the supervisor, the supervisor loses credibility. For instance, if top management changes a company policy regarding safety hats in a particular area and the supervisor is not told of the change, the supervisor might continue to tell employees to adhere to the old policy. Any disciplinary action resulting from such a situation would embarrass the supervisor.

The supervisor must also be adept at interpreting the signals of nonverbal communication. A well-trained supervisor can identify symptoms of unrest among employees. For instance, increasing signs of resentment, where there were none before, may indicate union activity. Emerging informal groups may also indicate unrest. The supervisor might notice that workers stop talking or change the subject when he or she approaches. A competent supervisor will notice these signs and report them immediately to upper-level management. There may be patterns of similar activities in other departments, suggesting an attempt at unionization. This knowledge can assist management in developing appropriate strategies and tactics.

One of the fastest ways to convert a nonunion person into a union advocate is to allow favoritism. To the worker, favoritism is equivalent to discrimination. The supervisor must establish an atmosphere in which the worker believes that he or she can receive fair treatment and equitable rewards.

Union-Free Policy

The fact that the organization's goal is to remain union-free should be clearly and forcefully communicated to all of its members. Such a policy statement might read as follows:

> Our success as a company is founded on the skill and efforts of our employees. Our policy is to deal with employees as effectively as possible, respecting and recognizing each of them as individuals.
>
> In our opinion, unionization would interfere with the individual treatment, respect, and recognition the company offers. Consequently, we believe a union-free environment is in the employees' best interest, the company's best interest, and the interest of the people served by the corporation.[29]

This type of policy evolves into a philosophy that affects everyone in the organization. All employees, from the lowest paid worker to top management, must understand it. No major human resource-related decision should be made without asking, "How will this affect our union-free status?" The union-free policy should be repeatedly communicated to every worker. Workers must be told why the company advocates the policy and how it affects them. This involves much more than sending a memo each year to all employees stating that the company's goal is to remain union free. Every means of effective communication may be needed to convince employees that the organization intends to remain union-free.

Effective Communication

One of the most important actions an organization that wants to remain union-free can take is to establish credible and effective communication. A very positive by-product of the movement toward participative management, cooperation, and teamwork is open and effective communication. Employees must be given the information they need to perform their jobs and then be provided feedback on their performance. Management should openly share information with workers concerning activities taking place within the organization.

In order to sustain employee cooperation in the pursuit of organizational goals and remain union-free, management must consider the needs of employees. Employees want and need to know the following:

- Their standing in relation to the formal authority structure.
- Their standing in relation to the informal organization with respect to individual status, power, acceptance, and so on.

HRM IN ACTION

PRESSING THE ISSUE

Allen Fender is human resource manager for ML Plastics, a small injection molding company near Wichita, Kansas. ML has been experiencing some worker unrest, and there have been hints of a unionizing attempt. As Allen rounded the corner in the mixing department one day, he heard Judy Morgan reprimanding one of her operators. Several other workers were watching the episode. Allen quickly figured out that the operator had spilled some oil near his machine and had failed to clean it up. The operator, obviously embarrassed, was trying to put oil absorbent on the spill. But Judy continued to press the issue. She said, "When you risk other people's safety around here, you are risking your job."

What should Allen do?

- Events that have a bearing on their own and the company's future economic security.
- Operational information that will enable them to develop pride in the job.

One approach taken to encourage open communication is the open-door policy. The **open-door policy** gives employees the right to take any grievance to the person next in the chain of command if the problem cannot be resolved by the immediate supervisor. Delta Air Lines is well known for its open-door policy, which enables employees to express their grievances. An effective open-door policy represents an attitude of openness and trust among people within the organization. It is counterproductive to state that an open-door policy exists and then punish an employee for bypassing his or her immediate supervisor. The employee must not fear that talking to the manager next in line will be detrimental to his or her career. Although it might seem that an open-door policy would result in wasted time for upper and middle managers, in most instances this has not proven to be the case. The mere knowledge that an employee can move up the chain of command with a complaint without fear of retribution often encourages the immediate supervisor and the employee to work out their differences.

Trust and Openness

Openness and trust on the part of managers and employees alike are important in order to remain union-free. The old expression "actions speak louder than words" is certainly valid for an organization that desires to remain union-free. Credibility, based on trust, must exist between labor and management, and this trust develops only over time. If employees perceive that the manager is being open and receptive to ideas, feedback is likely to be encouraged. Managers need this feedback to do their jobs effectively. However, if managers give the impression that their directives should never be questioned, communication will be stifled and credibility lost. Here again, the participative style that is becoming more pervasive will enhance trust, openness, and employee involvement, helping management to maintain a union-free organization.

One of the major factors in the success of Japanese businesses is said to be that managers trust not only their workers but also their peers and superiors. As a result, a simpler organizational structure than that generally used in the United States is possible. More levels of management result in higher overhead costs and more time-consuming decision making. Japanese firms assume that workers at all levels are competent and trustworthy. As a result, these firms do not have to employ highly paid executives to review the work of other highly paid executives.[30]

Effective Human Resource Planning, Recruitment, and Selection

A firm's ability to remain union-free relates closely to its human resource planning, recruitment, and selection practices. For instance, if a firm used only word-of-mouth from current employees as a recruiting source, a very homogeneous workforce of friends and relatives could develop. Such a workforce would likely have strong interpersonal relationships. However, should management take action against any worker, the work group might perceive this as an action against them all. For this reason, and others discussed in Chapter 6, the human resource manager recruits from a wide variety of sources.

The method of human resource planning used can have a major impact on the organization's susceptibility to unionization. If it is constantly hiring and terminating employees in reaction to fluctuating demand for its products, the firm may face unionization. However, a firm can often maintain stable employment with adequate planning.

Effective Human Resource Development Programs

Many employees want the opportunity to grow and advance within the organization. Employees can often attain these goals through training and development. At the Saturn plant in Spring Hill, Tennessee, an integrated and active human resource strategy that emphasized a "people-oriented process" was vital for Saturn's success. This strategy recognized the importance of training for all employees. However, when demand outpaced supply, new pressures were placed on the workforce, and training was scaled back. By 1993, these changes resulted in 29 percent of the 5,000 union workers voting to shift toward a traditional arm's-length adversarial relationship.[31] Obviously, as the focus moved away from the human resource component to the manufacturing component, problems surfaced.

A philosophy that is genuinely supportive of human resource development would extend from top management to the lowest-level employee. As we discussed in Chapter 8, the success of any companywide training and development program depends on the support and interest shown by top management. Management support is crucial because management attitudes will filter down and influence employees at other levels of the organization.

One important requirement of human resource development is that employees have a genuine desire for self-improvement. Some employees are content in their present positions, while others desire to develop their potential. New collar workers will probably thrive in a self-improvement oriented environment. These workers are younger and better educated and are highly motivated by job security. More employees will wish to improve their skills if they are able to see a relationship between increased training and higher pay and other rewards. An organization takes a giant step toward remaining union-free when it provides avenues for advancement in skill and status. The seniority system often denies union employees these opportunities.

Supervisors also need training to prepare them to deal with organizing attempts. If the union knows that supervisors have been thoroughly trained in the tactics of dealing with unionizing efforts, it may decide against organizing attempts. This type of training will also assist in preventing costly mistakes that could lead to charges of unfair labor practices during an organizing campaign. Training is necessary because the supervisor's actions can actually bind the employer. Ignorance on the part of the supervisor is no excuse for inappropriate behavior.

Effective Compensation Programs

The financial compensation that employees receive is the most tangible measure they have of their worth to the organization. If an individual's pay is substantially below that provided for similar work in the area, the employee will soon become dissatisfied. Compensation must remain relatively competitive if the organization expects to remain union-free.[32] This is becoming less of a problem now than in the past because of the slow rate of compensation growth for unionized employees, not only in salary but also in bonuses, COLAs, and contributions to pension plans.

The compensation program should be intelligently planned and communicated to all employees. They must understand what they are being compensated for and how the system works. If employees perceive the system as being unfair, they are ripe for unionizing activities. One of the primary covenants of unions is that seniority guides compensation and promotions, which is contrary to today's more competitive global business environment. In addition, many new workers may avoid unions simply to avoid such nonperformance-based reward systems. It appears that the goals of businesses and new workers in the 1990s are the same, which may result in mutual benefit for all concerned.

The same approach should be followed with regard to benefits. The organization need not have the best benefits in a geographic area or an industry to protect its union-free status. However, the benefits package must be competitive. Employees must know what benefits they are actually receiving. Too often management does not adequately inform employees about their benefits. When such a situation exists, the organization is wasting financial resources and jeopardizing its union-free status.

A Healthy and Safe Work Environment

An organization that gains a reputation for failing to maintain a safe and healthy work environment leaves itself wide open for unionization. For years, unions have campaigned successfully by convincing workers that the union will provide them with a safer work environment. In fact, labor organizations were leading advocates of the Occupational Safety and Health Act, and they continue to support this type of legislation.

Effective Employee and Labor Relations

No organization is free from employee disagreements and dissatisfaction. Therefore, a means of resolving employee complaints, whether actual or perceived, should be available. The **grievance procedure** is a formal process that permits employees to complain about matters affecting them. Most labor-management agreements contain formal grievance procedures, and union members regard handling grievances as one of the most important functions of a labor union. Until the early 1980s, grievance procedures were not as common in union-free organizations. However, since that time many nonunion firms have started grievance procedure programs. When employees do not have ways to voice their complaints and have them resolved, even small gripes may grow into major problems.

The grievance procedure is a way of keeping problems from becoming serious. Total commitment to such a policy needs to start with top management and be instilled in every manager. Supervisors should develop an attitude of wanting to resolve problems before they become formal complaints.[33] Employees who believe that management is concerned with resolving problems lack a major reason for needing a union.

A means of resolving grievances in union-free organizations is through the use of ombudspersons. This approach has been used for some time in Europe, and the practice is now becoming more popular in the United States. An **ombudsperson** is a complaint officer with access to top management, who hears employees' complaints, investigates them, and sometimes recommends appropriate action. Because of their access to top management, ombudspersons can often resolve problems swiftly. The Singer Company's ombudsperson system serves as an example. This program is described in Figure 17-4.

In recent years, the ombudsperson has assumed the additional duties of helping uncover scandals within organizations. Large defense contractors, such as McDonnell Douglas and General Electric, have used ombudspersons to respond to questions raised regarding product design safety or defense contract billings. Workers who believe that a problem exists can now bypass the supervisor and talk to the ombudsperson.[34]

Effective Human Resource Research

Human resource research can reveal changes in attitudes within the organization. One purpose of human resource research is the early identification of employee dissatisfaction. Corrective action should be taken before workers feel a need for a union to solve their problems. Ignored problems often encourage unionization.

Research may reveal symptoms of worker unrest. For instance, statistics that show an increase in the turnover rate may indicate growing employee dissatisfaction. Employee attitude surveys and exit interviews, as part of the research effort, can assist management in identifying the problems causing high turnover before they become critical.[35]

In A Less Than Perfect Universe . . .
See the Ombudsperson

An employee is fired for cause, disciplined, or perceives himself or herself a victim of discrimination. To reverse the decision or remedy the situation, the employee tries normal channels—but remains dissatisfied with the results.

In many organizations, the story would end here. At Singer, because of the Corporate Ombudsperson program started in 1976, the story can have another chapter or two. And, although the story may not necessarily have a happy ending, employees are guaranteed that they won't be subjected to harassment or retribution for contacting the Ombudsperson.

A concept borrowed from Scandinavia, the Ombudsperson function entails an impartial investigation of and assistance in equitably settling complaints. At Singer this corporatewide function is the responsibility of Harry P. Hancock, Jr., senior director, employee relations programs. "Because the program is informal rather than formal and the range of cases is varied," explains Mr. Hancock, "there is really no single modus operandi. I handle each case as it presents itself." The range of cases includes grievances about performance appraisals, involuntary discharge, sexual harassment, sexual discrimination, denial of promotion, formal reprimand, and conflict with or unfair treatment by a supervisor.

For the purpose of illustrating the thoroughness of the Ombudsperson proceedings, Mr. Hancock describes how he might deal with a discharge-for-cause case brought to his attention by an employee who had exhausted all normal channels and remained dissatisfied.

"In the investigation and evaluation," he explains, "we rely heavily on the division personnel staff. Our objective is to make sure that:

- The rule or policy allegedly broken by the employee has been published, posted, or otherwise made known to employees.
- The employee has been warned about any earlier infractions and given counseling.
- The employee has been given a reasonable length of time to improve performance.
- The proposed disciplinary action is appropriate to the infraction.
- Other employees charged with similar infractions have been treated in a similar manner."

If it is determined that the employee has been unfairly discharged, the case is discussed with the immediate supervisor who initiated the action. If the decision is not reversed or amended at this level—which it usually is—then the discussion is brought to successively higher levels. On the other hand, if it is judged that the decision was appropriate, the employee is so advised, and the case is closed.

Most problems are resolved, of course, through Singer's normal channels. Resolving a problem via normal channels includes an initial discussion with the immediate supervisor. If the issue is not settled at that level, then the matter is taken to higher levels, in the specific unit. Equal Opportunity coordinators, industrial relations personnel, and other employee relations specialists may become involved.

In cases of terminations of employees with more than ten years of continuous service, standard procedure requires that those terminations be approved by members of the Management Committee.

If employees, after having gone through normal channels, still believe that they have received unfair treatment, then they can bring the matter to the attention of the Ombudsperson.

FIGURE 17-4 Description of an Ombudsperson Program

Source: Used with Permission of the Singer Company.

Another indicator of employee dissatisfaction is the number of customer complaints received. For example, research that reveals increasing customer complaints because of lower quality might point to certain employees with problems that need resolving. Accident frequency, maintenance costs, and theft are other indicators of employee dissatisfaction.[36]

UNION DECERTIFICATION

Until 1947, once a union was certified, it was certified forever.[37] However, the Taft-Hartley Act made it possible for employees to decertify a union. This action results in a union losing its right to act as the exclusive bargaining representative of a group of employees. **Decertification** is essentially the reverse of the process that employees must follow to be recognized as an official bargaining unit. In recent years, many decertification elections have been held.

The 1980s and the mid-1990s were not good times for America's labor unions. Currently, organized labor's share of the workforce is only 15.8 percent. In addition, this decline occurred while the nation's workforce increased.

Union memberships are at the lowest levels in at least fifty years.[38] Also, a recent National Bureau of Economic Research report estimated that union membership in the private sector could drop below 5 percent by the year 2000 if present trends continue.[39] The two primary reasons for this decline are (1) decertification and (2) the U.S. economy's continuing shift to service industries. With the passage of NAFTA and GATT, the movement toward the service sector may well intensify, further diminishing union ranks.[40]

In light of this significant reduction in union ranks, the outcome of certification and decertification elections are of increasing concern to unions. Unions are winning fewer certification elections and are losing the majority of their decertification elections.[41] Some union leaders are concerned that the trend may even be spreading to larger firms. Should this occur, the foundation of the U.S. labor movement would be threatened even more. Not only would the total number of union members decline, but unions' hold on major domestic industries would be substantially reduced.[42] Decertification elections have been won in such well-known firms as Holiday Inn, Goodyear, Dow Chemical, Sears, American Airlines, and the Washington Post. However, smaller firms appear to be achieving the greatest won-lost decertification record. Perhaps this is because it is easier for management to reestablish trust with employees in smaller firms.

Decertification Procedure

The rules established by the NLRB spell out the conditions for filing a decertification petition. At least 30 percent of the bargaining unit members must petition for an election. As might be expected, this task by itself may be difficult because union supporters are likely to oppose the move strongly. Although the petitioners' names are supposed to remain confidential, many union members are fearful that their signatures on the petition will be discovered. Timing of the NLRB's receipt of the decertification petition is also critical. The petition must be submitted between sixty and ninety days prior to the expiration of the current contract. When all these conditions have been met, the NLRB regional director will schedule a decertification election by secret ballot.

The NLRB carefully monitors the events leading up to the election. Current employees must initiate the request for the election. If the NLRB determines that management initiated the action, it probably will not certify the election. After the petition has been accepted, however, management can support the decertification election attempt. If a majority of the votes cast are against the union, the employees will be free from the union. Strong union supporters are all likely to vote. Thus, if a substantial number of employees are indifferent to the union and choose not to vote, decertification may not occur.

Management and Decertification

When management senses employee discontent with the union, it often does not know how to react. Many times, management decides to do nothing, reasoning that it is best not to get involved or that it may even be illegal to do so. But if it does want to get involved, management can use a variety of legal tactics. If management really wants the union decertified, it must learn how to be active rather than passive.

Meetings with union members to discuss the benefits of becoming union-free have proven beneficial. In fact, such discussions are often cited as being the most effective campaign tactic. These meetings may be with individual employees, small groups, or even entire units. Management explains the benefits and answers employees' questions.

Management may also provide workers with legal assistance in preparing for decertification. Because the workers probably have never been through a decertification election, this type of assistance may prove invaluable. For example, the NLRB may not permit an election if the paperwork has not been properly completed. Management must always remember that it cannot initiate the decertification action; that is the workers' responsibility.

The most effective means of accomplishing decertification is to improve the corporate culture so that workers no longer feel the need to have a union. This cannot be done overnight, as mutual trust and confidence must be developed between workers and the employer.

If decertification is to succeed, management must eliminate the problems that initially led to unionization. Although many executives believe that pay and benefits are the primary reasons for union membership, these factors are probably not the real cause.[43] Failure to treat employees as individuals is often the primary reason for unionization. The real problems often stem from practices such as failing to listen to employees' opinions, dealing with workers unfairly and dishonestly, and treating employees as numbers and not as people. Many organizational attitudes and actions indicate to employees how the firm feels toward them, including the following:

- poor housekeeping
- poor supervision
- inadequate wage differentials among various skill levels
- inadequate preventive maintenance
- arbitrary company policies
- unfair promotional policies
- an ineffective complaint and discipline procedure[44]

Such problems may have initially led to unionization. Even if an organization desires to be union-free, it cannot become so immediately. Such unsatisfactory conditions must be eliminated, and this takes time. Now, and in the future, companies with these unsatisfactory conditions will not be able to compete in the global environment, and, therefore by default, such conditions will improve, as will labor-management relations.

THE ROLE OF THE HUMAN RESOURCE MANAGER

The human resource manager in a union-free firm has a somewhat different role than his or her counterpart in a unionized company. The tasks of the human resource manager in a unionized firm often revolve around contract negotiations and grievance handling. The human resource manager in a union-free firm must work toward creating an atmosphere in which workers do not feel the need for union representation. Human resource managers serve as the catalyst for developing and maintaining nonunion attitudes. In today's era of cooperation, teamwork, and the like, human resource managers become even more important players contributing to organizational success.

In the mid-1960s many senior labor relations professionals gave primary attention to stabilizing collective bargaining relationships. At that time, the most important force for change was the rise of laws and governmental regulations mandating nondiscrimination and affirmative action in employment. Affirmative action brought about rational human resource policies and practices, which resulted in management focusing on better employment relationships. The Conference Board survey on labor-management relations showed that preventing the spread of unionism and developing effective employee relations systems are more important to managers today than achieving sound collective bargaining results.[45] These changes in priority, along with the current emphasis on remaining or becoming union-free have increased HRM responsibilities, which, in turn, have given human resource managers greater corporate power and importance throughout the 1980s and 1990s.[46]

The desire for union-free operations and the greater emphasis on employee oriented policies have created a management perspective that emphasizes the individual employee over adversary labor relations. The union-free approach is basically a human resource system that bypasses the union and deals directly with the individual worker—and his or her needs. This human resource system matches compensation and benefits with worker performance, properly designs the organization and the workplace to enhance productivity and worker satisfaction, and involves employees in solving workplace problems and in making decisions.[47]

Remaining union-free requires a strong commitment by management at all levels, open communication, and trust. In many ways, the commitment necessary to maintain a union-free environment requires a much more demanding effort by the human resource professional. Some organizations may not maintain that commitment and, therefore, will become vulnerable to organizing efforts. The old maxim is still true: "Unions don't organize employees—managers do." They do this through mistakes, neglect, and (unfortunately) plain greed.[48] The human resource manager, therefore, must ensure that an employee relations system is created whereby employees are treated in a positive manner, allowing each individual to maintain his or her self-esteem and advance individually as the organization advances.

A GLOBAL PERSPECTIVE

Global human resource managers in union-free multinational organizations have much more difficult roles than their counterparts in union-free domestic companies. These individuals must work even harder to create an atmosphere in which workers will not feel the need for union representation. The 1980s were a difficult decade for many workers in this country, and these difficulties continue into the 1990s. Even unionized employees continue to receive much lower wage and benefit packages than they previously did, and givebacks are becoming fairly commonplace. Dislocations are no longer unusual. In fact, disgruntled employees filed a record number of wrongful discharge and job discrimination suits in the 1980s; unfair labor practice complaints also soared.[49] Even in such difficult times, U.S. workers did not turn to unions, and this trend may well continue throughout the 1990s. Employees apparently did not view union representation as a feasible solution to their problems. In such an environment, domestic human resource managers are under less pressure to create a human resource system that bypasses the union and deals directly with the needs of individual workers.[50]

This may very well be the time to develop a new worker-management relations approach that will involve a new "structure that furthers constant experimentation, development, and the flexibility to respond quickly to new ideas and needs providing incrementally better products." It is quite interesting to note that most workers desire "innovative forms of employee participation" to further mutual goals.[51] Now is the perfect time for global human resource managers to forward the goals of management since workers appear to embrace these ideals. In fact, sentiment regarding unions is clear, with two-thirds of the working population currently opposing unions.[52]

Until quite recently, the drastic decline in union membership in the United States appeared to be a uniquely American phenomenon. However, recently unions abroad have experienced problems, with some suffering annual membership losses of 5 to 7 percent. Even with these recent problems, global workers are much more likely to turn to unions when the union-free environment is not worker-oriented. In the past two decades, union membership in the United States has declined by approximately 50 percent; in the United Kingdom, the percentage fell to 51 percent; and in Japan it fell from 32 to 28 percent. Membership remained nearly the same in Germany, at 43 percent, and in Canada, at 36 percent.[53] Because of the relatively strong state of global unionization, a much more decisive effort by global human resource managers is needed to maintain a multinational's union-free status. Recent declines in union membership could afford human resource managers the opportunity to become union-free, assuming that management is willing to treat workers appropriately. Global organizations that do not maintain that commitment could become quite vulnerable to union-organizing efforts. Even more than their domestic counterparts, global human resource managers must ensure that effective employee relations systems are created whereby employees are treated in a positive manner.

SUMMARY

Most employees in the United States do not belong to unions. Their reasons for not joining are many and varied: it costs money to be a union member, many employees think that unions are unnecessary, and peer pressure against union affiliation may be exerted. Reprisals against employees for union activities are illegal in the United States.

Under certain circumstances a union may decide to expend little or no effort to establish a new bargaining unit. Unions also recognize that there are certain industries, firms, and locations in the country with an anti-union tradition. Moreover, the growing web of employee legal protection may take the place of union representation in the future.

Valid reasons exist for management's acceptance or rejection of a union. There may be times when resistance to organizing attempts is not advantageous. In addition, situations exist in which the relationship between management and the union is quite good and well established. Management may also desire unionization of competing organizations. Although there may be valid reasons for a firm to accept unionization, a large percentage of executives prefer that their companies remain union-free. To remain union-free, an organization must establish its strategy and tactics long before a union-organizing attempt begins.

Decertification means that a union has lost its right to act as the exclusive bargaining representative of a group of employees. The process is essentially the reverse of what a union must go through to be recognized as an official bargaining unit. Rules established by the National Labor Relations Board specify the procedures for filing a decertification petition and holding a decertification election. The human resource manager in a union-free firm has a somewhat different role from his or her counterpart in a unionized company. The tasks of the human resource manager in a unionized firm often revolve around contract negotiations and grievance handling. The human resource manager in a union-free firm must work toward creating an atmosphere in which workers do not feel the need for union representation. Human resource managers serve as the catalyst for developing and maintaining nonunion attitudes.

QUESTIONS FOR REVIEW

1. What are the most important reasons for employees not joining unions? Discuss each of them.
2. What are the reasons both for and against a firm resisting unionization attempts?
3. Briefly describe the factors involved in maintaining a union-free status.
4. What role does the first-line supervisor play in helping a firm remain union-free?
5. Describe the process of decertification.
6. How might the role of a human resource manager change if he or she moves from a unionized firm to a union-free firm? Discuss.

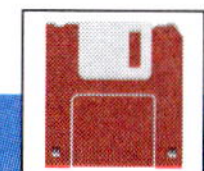

HRM SIMULATION

Providing fair treatment to all employees is one of the best ways of maintaining a union-free organization. Incident M in the *Simulation Players Manual* deals with a difficult situation involving employee discipline. Your team must study the options and make a difficult decision. Other employees will be watching your team to see if you are fair.

ABC VIDEO CASE

WORKER SURVIVAL TRAINING TAPE 1, NUMBER 8

Companies are sending their employees for survival training in an effort to help them learn how to conquer their fears. For about $250 each, employees are taught how to replace fear and uncertainty with confidence and self-esteem. Due to restructuring and downsizing, managers are being forced to work with teams of employees who have never worked together before. By sending the new team members on survival training programs, they can learn to communicate and work together in order to get the job done.

The Kodak Copier Western Division, hit by restructuring and lay-offs, sent its sales managers through this "tree training." The year the division took the course, it went from last in company sales to first.

HRM INCIDENT 1

—BEING FAIR

Ed Davis is a supervisor at the Paxma Manufacturing Company, a manufacturer of a special kind of filler material for packaging. Ed was transferred to his present job from another plant. He accepted the transfer because he felt it would provide a better opportunity for promotion. Ed's new section includes fifteen workers whose jobs are essentially identical. The workload of Paxma often fluctuates, requiring extensive use of overtime. This overtime is very popular among the workers, and Ed's predecessor had distributed it on a simple rotation basis.

When Ed took over, he felt that overtime should be a reward for excellent performance. He also felt that certain workers needed the overtime more than others. Ed did not discuss this with the workers but simply began to assign the overtime as he saw fit.

Everything seemed to be going well until the day Ed was called to the office of Mary Donnelly, the human resource manager. After a brief greeting, Mary said, "Ed, I hear through the grapevine that there's a good deal of dissension in your crew. Some of the workers feel they're not being given their fair share of overtime." Ed replied, "I assign everybody their share. It's just not always an equal share." "That may be true, Ed," said Mary, "but at least a couple of the workers believe that most of the overtime has been going to the three new people you've hired." "Who told you that?" asked Ed. "I don't think that is important," Mary answered, "but you need to think about whether there's any substance to the impression your workers have." "You may be right," said Ed. He admitted, "I suppose I could have unconsciously favored the people I personally selected."

Questions

1. Was it appropriate for the human resource manager to get involved in the line function of assigning overtime? Explain.
2. What would you do if you were Ed?

HRM INCIDENT 2

—OPEN THE DOOR!

Barney Cline, the new human resource manager for Ampex Utilities, was just getting settled in his new office. He had recently moved from another firm to take his new job. Barney had been selected over several in-house candidates and numerous other applicants because of his record of getting things done. He had a good reputation for working through people to get the job accomplished.

Barney's phone rang. The person on the other end of the line asked, "Mr. Cline, could I set up an appointment to talk with you?" "Certainly," Barney said, "when do you want to get together?" "How about after work? It might be bad if certain people saw me speaking to anyone in management," said the caller.

Barney was a bit puzzled, but he set up an appointment for 5:30 p.m., when nearly everyone would be gone. At the designated time, there was a knock on his door; it was Mark Johnson, a senior maintenance worker, who had been with the firm for more than ten years.

After the initial welcome, Mark began by saying, "Mr. Cline, several of the workers asked me to talk to you. Rumor has it that you're a fair person. The company says it has an open-door policy, but we're afraid to use it. Roy Edwards, one of the best maintenance workers in our section, tried it several months ago. They hassled him so much that he quit last week. We just don't know what to do to get any problems solved. There have been talks of organizing a union. We really don't want that, but something has to give."

Barney thanked Mark for his honesty and promised not to reveal the conversation. In the weeks following the conversation with Mark, Barney was able to verify that the situation existed just as Mark had described. There was considerable mistrust between managers and the operative employees.

Questions

1. What are the basic causes of the problems confronting Ampex Utilities?
2. How should Barney attempt to resolve this problem?

DEVELOPING HRM SKILLS

AN EXPERIENTIAL EXERCISE

Union-organizing attempts are a real challenge to human resource managers and first-line supervisors. During a recent conference on maintaining a union-free status, the point was stressed that supervisors are the key to preventing companies from being organized. Therefore, those in human resource management should maintain direct and continual contact with supervisors. This exercise is designed to give participants an opportunity to experience what goes on when a union is being considered.

Two committees, one employee group and one supervisor group, will discuss the prospects of unionization. Each committee must come up with a recommendation for or against unionization and state its reasons for the recommendation. The spokesperson for the employee group is Bob Jones, and the group members are Gerald Young, Julie Faire, and Tony Wells. Bob Jones is a very outspoken union advocate who has always believed this company should have a union. He believes wages are lower here than at unionized firms in the area, and he sees too much "brother-in-lawing" going on in the organization. He was also denied a raise recently, having been told that the boss just did not "feel" he deserved one.

This is Gerald Young's first job, but his father is the union steward of another company. Gerald's dad often says, "What you guys need over there is a good union." Last month when production standards were raised, Gerald's piece-rate bonus was wiped out. His dad says they do not pull such things in a unionized firm.

Julie Faire has been working here for several years, and the company has always been good to her. She had some family problems last year, and her boss let her off for several days. She wonders if a union could be better than her understanding boss.

Tony Wells is an old hand at the company, and he has seen lots of things come and go over the years. Tony's experience has been that if employees have enough guts to go to their supervisors directly they can usually get satisfaction. It seems to Tony that too many people today are looking for a "free lunch."

The spokesperson for the supervisor group, Charlie Neal, is very anti-union. Charlie is really fed up with all this union talk and believes that these people do not seem to know when they are well off. Charlie has been with the company for nearly twenty years and does not intend to put up with a union now. He believes the company should "get tough." Charlie has a pretty good idea of who is leading the union advocates. Charlie thinks that if the other supervisors will listen, it will be easy to find reasons to get rid of the troublemakers.

Beverly Woods has been a supervisor for only a few years, but previously she was a supervisor in a unionized company. Beverly has a healthy respect for unions and some feeling for how they get their power. Beverly feels that this is a great opportunity for the supervisors to get together with the employees and solve the employees' legitimate complaints. She believes this would be all it would take to convince employees that they do not need a union.

Depending on what is determined in the conference, there may be an agreement proposed that will prevent unionizing or that will create a delaying action such as a joint committee. There may be hard lines drawn leading to a showdown or even an immediate call for a union election. Once the groups have decided, the spokespersons will report their decisions. Your instructor will provide the participants with additional information necessary to complete the exercise.

NOTES

1. Aaron Bernstein, "Why America Needs Unions But Not the Kind It Has Now," *Business Week* (May 23, 1994): 70–82.
2. Ibid.
3. Alexander B. Trowbridge, "A Management Look at Labor Relations," in *Unions in Transition* (San Francisco: ICS Press, 1988): 415.
4. David Hage, "Unions Feel the Heat," *U.S. News* 116 (January 24, 1994): 57.
5. John P. Bucalo, Jr., "Successful Employee Relations," *Personnel Administrator* 31 (April 1986): 63.
6. Paul S. McDonough, "Maintaining a Union-Free Status," *Personnel Journal* 69 (April 1990): 108.
7. Dave Weil, *Turning the Tide: Strategic Planning for Labor Unions* (New York: Lexington Books, 1994): 255–256.
8. Sam F. Parigi, Frank J. Cavaliere, and Joel L. Allen, "Improving Labor Relations in an Era of Declining Union Power," *Review of Business* 14 (Winter 1992): 31–35.
9. Aaron Bernstein, "Why America Needs Unions But Not the Kind It Has Now," ibid.
10. Ibid.
11. Laurence I. Barrett, Michael Duffy, Laura Lopez, and Joseph R. Szczesny, Time Daily News Summary-America Online, *Time, Inc.* (November 11, 1993): 1–5.
12. "Unions Launch Campaign to Organize IBM: Task Likened to Putting 'Man on the Moon,'" *Daily Labor Record* (Washington, D.C.: The Bureau of National Affairs, January 22, 1987): A-1.
13. John Hoerr et al., "Beyond Unions," *Business Week* (July 8, 1985): 74.
14. Scott Seegert and Brian H. Kleiner, "The Future of Labor-Management Relations," *Industrial Management* 35 (March/April 1993): 15–16.
15. Ibid.
16. Edward J. Wasilewski, "Compensation Gains Moderated in 1993 Private Industry Settlements," *Monthly Labor Review* 117 (May 1994): 46–56.
17. David A. Dilts, "AFL-CIO: Unions Will Rise Again," *Arbitration Journal* 48 (June 1993): 27.
18. Edward J. Wasilewski, "Compensations Gains Moderated in 1993 Private Industry Settlements," ibid.
19. Scott Seegert and Brian H. Kleiner, "The Future of Labor-Management Relations," ibid.
20. Fred K. Foulkes, "How Top Nonunion Companies Manage Employees," *Harvard Business Review* 59 (September-October 1981): 90.
21. Richard Edwards, *Rights At Work: Employment Relations in the Post Union Era* (Washington, D.C.: The Brookings Institution, 1993): 132–146.
22. Aaron Bernstein, "Busting Unions Can Backfire on the Bottom Line," *Business Week* (March 18, 1991): 108.
23. Aaron Bernstein, "Why America Needs Unions But Not the Kind It Has Now," ibid.
24. Ibid.
25. Wiley I. Beavers, "Employee Relations Without a Union," in Dale Yoder and Herbert S. Heneman, Jr., eds., *ASPA Handbook of Personnel and Industrial Relations: Employee and Labor Relations,* vol. III (Washington, D.C.: The Bureau of National Affairs, 1976): 7–83.
26. Alexander B. Trowbridge, "A Management Look at Labor Relations," 415–416.
27. Kevin Kelly, "Cat Is Purring, But They're Hissing On The Floor," *Business Week* (May 16, 1994): 33.
28. Alexander B. Trowbridge, "A Management Look at Labor Relations," 417.
29. James F. Rand, "Preventive Maintenance Techniques for Staying Union-Free," *Personnel Journal* 59 (June 1980): 497.

30. "Trust: The New Ingredient of Management," *Business Week* (July 6, 1988): 104.

31. David Woodruff, "Saturn: Labor's Love Lost?" *Business Week* (February 8, 1993): 122–123.

32. James F. Rand, "Preventive-Maintenance Techniques for Staying Union-Free," 498.

33. George W. Bohlander and Harold C. White, "Building Bridges: Nonunion Employee Grievance Systems," *Personnel* 65 (July 1988): 62.

34. Michael Brody, "Listen to Your Whistleblower," *Fortune* 24 (November 1986): 77–78.

35. Wanda R. Embrey, R. Wayne Mondy, and Robert M. Noe, "Exit Interview: A Tool for Personnel Development," *Personnel Administrator* 24 (May 1979): 48.

36. Wiley I. Beavers, "Employee Relations Without a Union," 7-69–7-70.

37. 93 Daily Congressional Record 3954 (23 April 1947).

38. Gene Koretz, "Why Unions Thrive Abroad—But Wither in the U.S.," *Business Week* (May 7, 1990): 26.

39. Gene Koretz and Celeste Whittaker, "More Picket Lines, Fewer Rank-and-Filers," *Business Week* (May 7, 1990): 24.

40. Laurence I. Barrett, Michael Duffy, Laura Lopez, and Joseph R. Szczesny, Time Daily News Summary-America Online, ibid.

41. Woodruff Imberman, "How to Win a Decertification Election," *Management Review* 66 (September 1977): 38.

42. Ibid.

43. Ibid.

44. Ibid.

45. Alexander B. Trowbridge, "A Management Look at Labor Relations," 414.

46. Ibid.

47. David C. Metz, "12 Key Factors in Staying Union-Free—A Checklist for Employers," *CUE* 30 (Washington, D.C., 1989): 49–73.

48. Alexander B. Trowbridge, "A Management Look at Labor Relations," 417.

49. John Hoerr, "What Should Unions Do?" *Harvard Business Review* 69 (May-June 1991): 30–31.

50. David C. Metz, "12 Key Factors in Staying Union-Free," ibid.

51. Leo Troy, "Big Labor's Problems," *Business and Society Review* 24 (Fall 1993): 49–52.

52. "Why Labor Keeps Losing?" *Fortune* 130 (July 11, 1994): 54.

53. David A. Dilts, "The Future of Labor Arbitrators," *Arbitration Journal* 48 (June 1993): 24–31.

CHAPTER 18

Internal Employee Relations

KEY TERMS

Internal employee relations 560
Discipline 560
Disciplinary action 560
Progressive disciplinary action 564
Disciplinary action without punishment 565
Grievance 568
Employment at will 576
Demotion 577
Outplacement 579
Transfer 579
Promotion 580

CHAPTER OBJECTIVES

1. Define discipline and disciplinary action.
2. Identify and describe the steps involved in the disciplinary process, describe the approaches to discipline, and explain the administration of disciplinary action.
3. Explain how grievance handling is typically conducted under a collective bargaining agreement and in union-free firms.
4. State how termination conditions may differ when operative employees, executives, managers, or professionals are involved, and explain the concept of employment at will.
5. Explain demotion as an alternative to termination and describe the role of internal employee relations with regard to layoffs, transfers, promotions, resignations, and retirements.
6. Discuss the legal implications of internal employee relations and describe how multinational corporations cope with internal employee relations.

Bob Halmes, the production supervisor for American Manufacturing, was mad at the world when he arrived at work. Since the automobile mechanic had not repaired his car on time the day before, he had been forced to take a taxi to work this morning. Because no one was safe around Bob today, it was not the time for Phillip Martin, a member of Local 264, to report for work late. Without hesitation, Bob said, "You know our company can't tolerate this type of behavior. I don't want to see you around here anymore. You're fired." Just as quickly, Phillip replied, "You're way off base. Our contract calls for three warnings for tardiness. My steward will hear about this."

Bill Morton, a ten-year employee at Ketro Productions, arrived at the office of the human resource manager to turn in his letter of resignation. Bill was very upset with his supervisor. When the human resource manager, Robert Noll, asked what was wrong, Bill replied, "Yesterday, I made a mistake and set my machine up wrong. It was the first time in years that I'd done that. My boss chewed me out in front of my friends. I wouldn't take that from the president, much less a two-bit supervisor!"

These scenarios represent only two of the many situations that human resource managers confront when dealing with internal employee relations. Bob Halmes has just been reminded that his power to fire Phillip Martin has limits. The resignation of Bill Morton might have been avoided if his supervisor had not shown poor judgment and disciplined him in front of his friends.

In this chapter, we first define *internal employee relations*. Next, we discuss the reasons for disciplinary action, the disciplinary action process, approaches to disciplinary action, and the administration of disciplinary action. We then describe grievance handling under a collective bargaining agreement and for nonunion employees. This is followed by a review of termination, employment at will, demotion as an alternative to termination, layoffs, transfers, promotion, resignation, and retirement. Finally, the last portion of the chapter is devoted to legal implications of internal employee relations and internal employee relations in times of international crisis.

INTERNAL EMPLOYEE RELATIONS DEFINED

The status of most workers is not permanently fixed in an organization. Employees constantly move upward, laterally, downward, and out of the organization. In order to ensure that workers with the proper skills and experience are available at all levels, constant and concerted efforts are required to maintain good internal employee relations. A well-conceived and implemented employee relations program is very beneficial to both the organization and its employees. **Internal employee relations** comprises the human resource management activities associated with the movement of employees within the organization. These HRM activities include promotion, transfer, demotion, resignation, discharge, layoff, and retirement. Discipline and disciplinary action are also crucial aspects of internal employee relations.

DISCIPLINARY ACTION

Discipline is the state of employee self-control and orderly conduct and indicates the extent of genuine teamwork within an organization. **Disciplinary action** invokes a penalty against an employee who fails to meet established standards. Effective disciplinary action addresses the employee's wrongful behavior, not the employee as a person. Incorrectly administered disciplinary action is destructive to both the employee and the organization. Thus, disciplinary action should not be applied haphazardly.

A necessary but often trying aspect of internal employee relations is the application of disciplinary action. Disciplinary action is not usually management's initial response to a problem. Normally, there are more positive ways of convincing employees to adhere to company policies that are necessary to accomplish organizational goals. However, managers must administer disciplinary action when company rules are violated. Disciplinary policies afford the organization the greatest opportunity to accomplish organizational goals, thereby benefiting both employees and the corporation. Not only is there a need for such policies, but a process should also exist to assist employees in appealing disciplinary actions. Because disciplinary action involves interaction between human beings, the process is sometimes biased and emotional, and, therefore, such actions are not always justified. Unjustified action is unfair to the employee involved, is counterproductive, and has contributed to the loss of union-free status by some firms. It has also resulted in wildcat strikes, walkouts, and slow-downs in unionized firms. Even if employees do not react overtly to unjustified disciplinary actions, morale will likely decline, which can negatively affect the firm.

Despite management's desire to solve employee problems in a positive manner, at times this is not possible. A major purpose of disciplinary action is to ensure that employee behavior is consistent with the firm's rules. Rules are established to further the organization's objectives. When a rule is violated, the effectiveness of the organization is diminished to some degree, depending on the severity of the infraction. For instance, if a worker is late to work once, the effect on the firm may be minimal. Consistently being late is another matter because it negatively affects both the productivity of the worker and the morale of other employees. Supervisors must realize that disciplinary action can be a positive force for the company when it is applied responsibly and equitably. The firm benefits from developing and implementing effective disciplinary policies. Without a healthy state of discipline, or the threat of disciplinary action, the firm's effectiveness may be severely limited.

Disciplinary action can also help the employee become more productive, thereby benefiting him or her in the long-run. For example, if a worker is disciplined because of failure to monitor the quality of his or her output, and quality improves after the disciplinary action, it has been useful in the worker's development. Because of improved performance, the individual may receive a promotion or pay increase. The employee is reminded of what is expected and fulfills these requirements better. Effective disciplinary action can, therefore, encourage the individual to improve his or her performance, ultimately resulting in gain for that individual.

THE DISCIPLINARY ACTION PROCESS

The disciplinary action process is dynamic and ongoing. Because one person's actions can affect others in a work group, the proper application of disciplinary action fosters acceptable behavior by other group members. Conversely, unjustified or improperly administered disciplinary action can have a detrimental effect on other group members.

The disciplinary action process is shown in Figure 18-1. The external environment affects every area of human resource management, including disciplinary policies and actions. Changes in the external environment, such as technological innovations, may render a rule inappropriate and may even necessitate new rules. Laws and government regulations that affect company policies and rules are also constantly changing. For instance, the Occupational Safety and Health Act has caused many firms to establish safety rules.

Unions are another external factor. Specific punishment for rule violations is subject to negotiation and inclusion in the collective bargaining agreement. For example, the union may negotiate for three written warnings

FIGURE 18-1
The Disciplinary Action Process

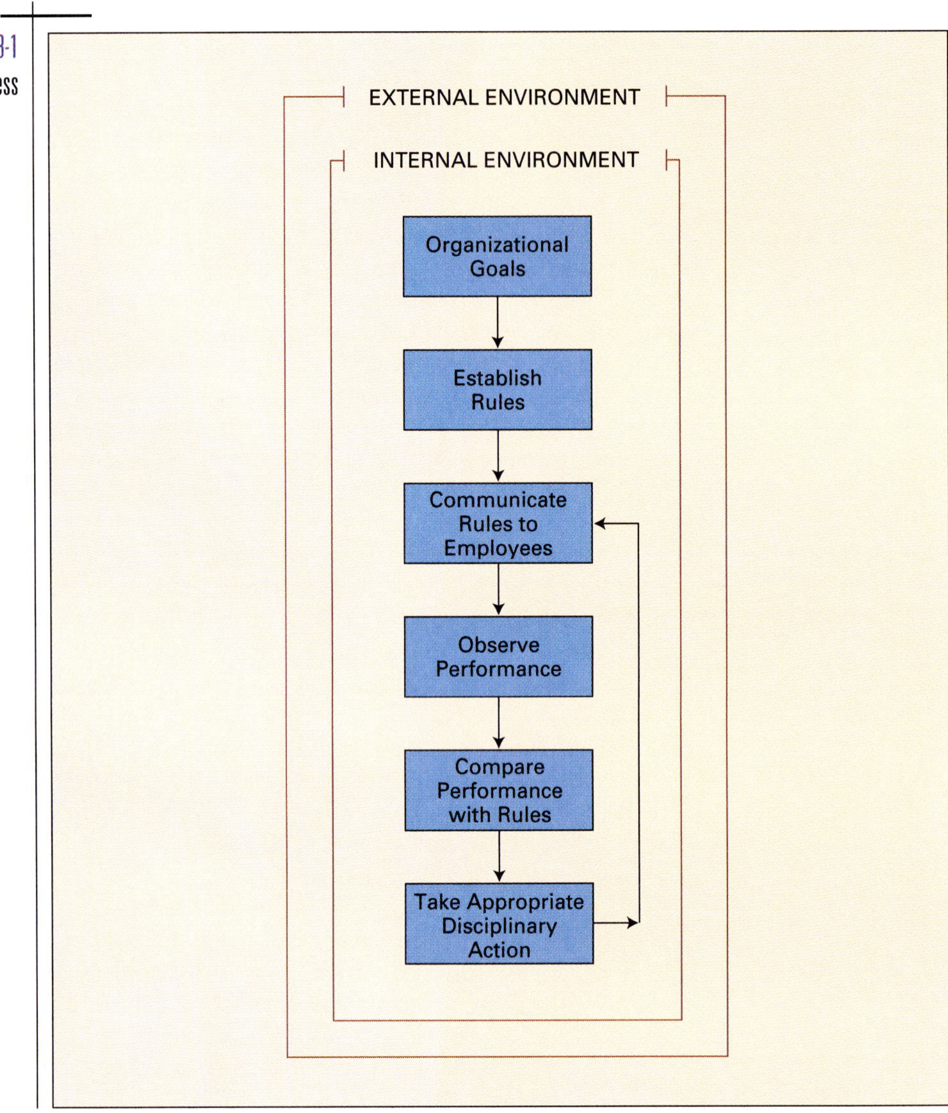

for tardiness before a worker is suspended instead of the two warnings a present contract might require.

Changes in the internal environment of the firm can also alter the disciplinary process. Through organizational development, the firm may alter its culture. This change may result in first-line supervisors handling disciplinary action more positively. Organization policies can also have an impact on the disciplinary action process. For instance, a policy of treating employees as mature human beings would significantly affect the process.

The disciplinary action process deals largely with infractions of rules. Rules are specific guides to behavior on the job. The dos and don'ts associated with accomplishing tasks may be highly inflexible. For example, company rules may prohibit smoking in certain areas and require that hard hats be worn in hazardous areas for safety reasons.

After management has established rules, it must communicate these rules to employees. Individuals cannot obey a rule if they do not know it exists. As long as employee behavior does not vary from acceptable practices, there is no need for disciplinary action. But when an employee's behavior violates a rule, corrective action may be necessary. The purpose of this action is to alter the types of behavior that can have a negative impact on the achievement of organizational objectives—not merely to chastise the violator.

Note that the process shown in Figure 18-1 includes feedback from the point of taking appropriate disciplinary action to communicating rules to employees. When appropriate disciplinary action is taken, employees should realize that certain behaviors are unacceptable and should not be repeated. However, if appropriate disciplinary action is not taken, employees may view the behavior as acceptable and repeat it.

APPROACHES TO DISCIPLINARY ACTION

Several concepts regarding the administration of disciplinary action have been developed. Three of the most important concepts are the hot stove rule, progressive disciplinary action, and disciplinary action without punishment.

The Hot Stove Rule

One approach to administering disciplinary action is referred to as *the hot stove rule*. According to this approach, disciplinary action should have the following consequences, which are analogous to touching a hot stove:

1. *Burns immediately.* If disciplinary action is to be taken, it must occur immediately so that the individual will understand the reason for it. With the passage of time, people have the tendency to convince themselves that they are not at fault, which tends in part to nullify later disciplinary effects.
2. *Provides warning.* It is also extremely important to provide advance warning that punishment will follow unacceptable behavior. As individuals move closer to a hot stove, they are warned by its heat that they will be burned if they touch it; and, therefore, they have the opportunity to avoid the burn if they so choose.
3. *Gives consistent punishment.* Disciplinary action should also be consistent in that everyone who performs the same act will be punished accordingly. As with a hot stove, each person who touches it with the same degree of pressure and for the same period of time is burned to the same extent.
4. *Burns impersonally.* Disciplinary action should be impersonal. The hot stove burns anyone who touches it—without favoritism.

Although the hot stove approach has some merit, it also has weaknesses. If the circumstances surrounding all disciplinary situations were the same, there would be no problem with this approach. However, situations are often quite different, and many variables may be present in each individual disciplinary case. For instance, does the organization penalize a loyal twenty-year employee the same as an individual who has been with the firm less than six weeks? Thus, a supervisor often finds that he or she cannot be completely consistent and impersonal in taking disciplinary action. Because situations do vary, progressive disciplinary action may be more realistic—and more beneficial to both the employee and the organization.

Progressive Disciplinary Action

Progressive disciplinary action is intended to ensure that the minimum penalty appropriate to the offense is imposed. Its use involves answering a series of questions about the severity of the offense. The manager must ask these questions—in sequence—to determine the proper disciplinary action, as illustrated in Figure 18-2. After the manager has determined that disciplinary action is appropriate, the proper question is: "Does this violation warrant more than an oral warning?"[1] If the improper behavior is minor and has not previously occurred, perhaps only an oral warning will be sufficient. Also, an individual may receive several oral warnings before a *yes* answer applies. The manager follows the same procedure for each level of offense in the progressive disciplinary process. The manager does not consider termina-

FIGURE 18-2
The Progressive Disciplinary Approach

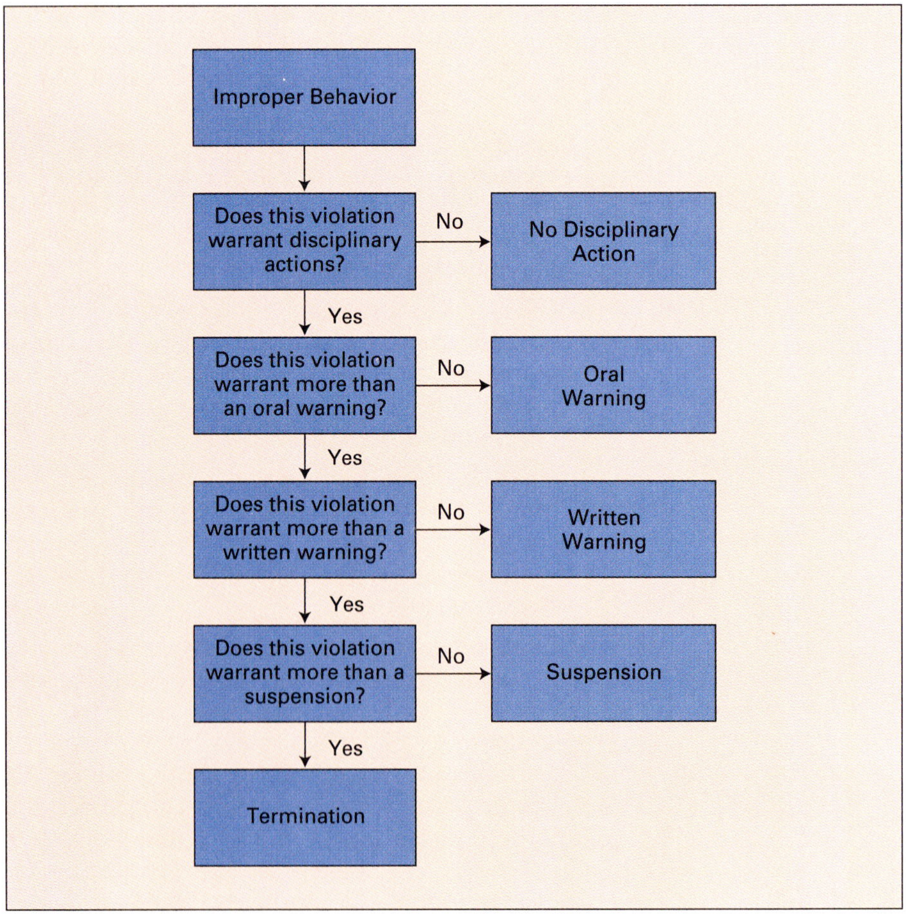

Improper Behavior
Does this violation warrant disciplinary actions?
No
No Disciplinary Action
Yes
Does this violation warrant more than an oral warning?
No
Oral Warning
Yes
Does this violation warrant more than a written warning?
No
Written Warning
Yes
Does this violation warrant more than a suspension?
No
Suspension
Yes
Termination

TABLE 18-1
Suggested Guidelines for Disciplinary Action

Offenses Requiring First, an Oral Warning, Second, a Written Warning, and Third, Termination
Negligence in the performance of duties
Unauthorized absence from job
Inefficiency in the performance of job
Offenses Requiring a Written Warning and Then Termination
Sleeping on the job
Failure to report to work one or two days in a row without notification
Negligent use of property
Offenses Requiring Immediate Discharge
Theft
Fighting on the job
Falsifying time cards
Failure to report to work three days in a row without notification

tion until each lower level question is answered *yes*. However, major violations, such as assaulting a supervisor or another worker, may justify immediate termination of the employee.

In order to assist managers in recognizing the proper level of disciplinary action, some firms have formalized the procedure. One approach is to establish progressive disciplinary action guidelines, as shown in Table 18-1. In this example, a worker who is absent without authorization will receive an oral warning the first time it happens and a written warning the second time; the third time, the employee will be terminated. Fighting on the job is an offense and normally results in immediate termination. However, specific guidelines for various offenses should be developed to meet the needs of the organization. For example, smoking in an unauthorized area may be grounds for immediate dismissal in an explosives factory. On the other hand, the same violation may be less serious in a plant producing concrete products. Basically, the penalty should be appropriate to address the severity of the violation, and no greater.[2]

Disciplinary Action Without Punishment

Disciplinary action without punishment gives a worker time off with pay to think about whether he or she wants to follow the rules and continue working for the company. When an employee violates a rule, the manager issues an *oral* reminder. Repetition brings a written reminder. The third violation results in the worker having to take one, two, or three days off (with pay) to think about the situation. During the first two steps, the manager tries to encourage the employee to solve the problem.[3] If the third step is taken, upon the worker's return, he or she and the supervisor meet to agree that the employee will not violate the rule again or that the employee will leave the firm. When disciplinary action without punishment is used, it is especially important that all rules be explicitly stated in writing. At the time of orientation, new workers should be told that repeated violations of different rules will be viewed in the same way as several violations of the same rule. This approach keeps workers from taking undue advantage of the process.

ADMINISTRATION OF DISCIPLINARY ACTION

As you might expect, disciplinary actions are not pleasant supervisory tasks. Many managers find them to be quite difficult to implement. The reasons for managers wanting to avoid taking disciplinary action include the following:

1. *Lack of training.* The supervisor may not have the knowledge and skill necessary to handle disciplinary problems.
2. *Fear.* The supervisor may be concerned that top management will not support a disciplinary action.
3. *The only one.* The supervisor may think, "No one else is disciplining employees, so why should I?"
4. *Guilt.* The supervisor may think, "How can I discipline someone if I've done the same thing?"
5. *Loss of friendship.* The supervisor may believe that disciplinary action will damage friendship with an employee or the employee's associates.
6. *Time loss.* The supervisor may begrudge the valuable time that is required to administer and explain disciplinary action.
7. *Loss of temper.* The supervisor may be afraid of losing his or her temper when talking to an employee about a rule violation.
8. *Rationalization.* The supervisor may think, "The employee knows it was a wrong thing to do, so why do we need to talk about it?"[4]

These reasons apply to all forms of disciplinary action—from an oral warning to termination. Supervisors often avoid this form of disciplinary action, even when it is in the company's best interest. Such reluctance often stems from breakdowns in other areas of the human resource management function. For instance, if a supervisor has consistently rated an employee high on annual performance appraisals, the supervisor's rationale for terminating a worker for poor performance would be weak. It is embarrassing to decide to fire a worker and then be asked why you rated this individual so highly on the previous evaluation. It could be that the employee's productivity has actually dropped substantially. It could also be that the employee's productivity has always been low but that the supervisor may have had trouble justifying to upper-level management that a person should be terminated. Rather than run the risk of a decision being overturned, the supervisor retains the ineffective worker.

Finally, some supervisors believe that even attempting to terminate women and minorities is useless. However, the statutes and subsequent court decisions associated with women and minorities in the workplace were not intended to protect nonproductive workers. Anyone whose performance is consistently below standard can, and should, be terminated after the supervisor has made reasonable attempts to salvage the employee.

A supervisor may be perfectly justified in administering disciplinary action, but there is usually a proper time and place for doing so. For example, disciplining a worker in the presence of others may embarrass the individual and actually defeat the purpose of the action. Even when they are wrong, employees resent disciplinary action being administered in public. The scenario at the beginning of the chapter, in which Bill Morton quit his job because he was disciplined in front of his peers, provides an excellent illustration. By disciplining employees in private, supervisors prevent them from losing face with their peers.

In addition, many supervisors may be too lenient early in the disciplinary action process and too strict later. This lack of consistency does not give the worker a clear understanding of the penalty associated with the inappropriate action. As a manager of labor relations for Georgia-Pacific Corporation once stated, "A supervisor will often endure an unacceptable situation for an extended period of time. Then, when the supervisor finally does take action, he or she is apt to overreact and come down excessively hard." However, consistency does not necessarily mean that the same penalty must be applied to two different workers for the same offense. For instance, employers would be consistent if they always considered the worker's past record and length of service. For a serious violation, a long-term employee might only receive a suspension, while a worker with only a few months' service might be terminated for the same act. This type of action could reasonably be viewed as being consistent.

In order to assist management in administering discipline properly, a *Code on Discipline Procedure* has been prepared by the Advisory, Conciliation and Arbitration Service. The purpose of the code is to give practical guidance on how to formulate disciplinary rules and procedures and use them effectively. The code recommends the actions shown in Table 18-2. As you can

HRM IN ACTION

—IT IS THE POLICY

As Billy Bowen, a first-line supervisor for Kwik Corporation, entered the office of Sandra Findley, human resource director, he was obviously upset and wanted help. Billy started the conversation by saying, "Allen Smith, one of my employees, violated a serious company policy today by failing to wear his safety glasses on a very dangerous job. The company policy states that any employee who does not follow the stated policy will receive a written reprimand on the first offense and will be terminated on the second violation. Allen has already received one reprimand, and now he has just committed his second violation. However, he has been one of my best workers over five years, and letting him go could have a really negative impact on productivity."

What advice should Sandra provide?

TABLE 18-2
Recommended Disciplinary Procedures

- All employees should be given a copy of the employers' rules on disciplinary procedures. The procedures should specify which employees they cover and what disciplinary actions may be taken, and should allow matters to be dealt with quickly.
- Employees should be told of complaints against them and given an opportunity to state their case. They should have the right to be accompanied by a trade union representative or fellow employee of their choice.
- Disciplinary action should not be taken until the case has been fully investigated. Immediate superiors should not have the power to dismiss without reference to senior management, and, except for gross misconduct, no employee should be dismissed for a first breach of discipline.
- Employees should be given an explanation for any penalty imposed, and they should have a right of appeal, with specified procedures to be followed.
- When disciplinary action other than summary dismissal is needed, supervisors should give a formal oral warning in the case of minor offenses or a written warning in more serious cases.

Source: "Code on Discipline Procedure," *Industrial Management* 7 (August 1977): 7. Used with permission.

see, it stresses communication of rules, telling the employee of the complaint, conducting a full investigation, and giving the employee an opportunity to tell his or her side of the story.

GRIEVANCE HANDLING UNDER A COLLECTIVE BARGAINING AGREEMENT

If employees in an organization are represented by a union, workers who believe they have been disciplined or dealt with unjustly can appeal through the grievance and arbitration procedures of the collective bargaining agreement. The grievance procedure has been described as "one of the truly great accomplishments of the American industrial relations movement. For all its defects . . . it constitutes a social invention of great importance."[5] The grievance system encourages and facilitates the settlement of disputes between labor and management. A grievance procedure permits employees to express complaints without jeopardizing their jobs. It also assists management in seeking out the underlying causes and solutions to grievances.

The Grievance Procedure

Virtually all labor agreements include some form of grievance procedure. A **grievance** can be broadly defined as an employee's dissatisfaction or feeling of personal injustice relating to his or her employment. A grievance under a collective bargaining agreement is normally well defined. It is usually restricted to violations of the terms and conditions of the agreement. There are, however, other conditions that may give rise to a grievance:

- a violation of law
- a violation of the intent of the parties as stipulated during contract negotiations

- a violation of company rules
- a change in working conditions or past company practices
- a violation of health and/or safety standards[6]

Grievance procedures have many common features. However, variations may reflect differences in organizational or decision-making structures or the size of a plant or company. Some general principles based on widespread practice can serve as useful guidelines for effective grievance administration:

- Grievances should be adjusted promptly.
- Procedures and forms used for airing grievances must be easy to utilize and well understood by employees and their supervisors.
- Direct and timely avenues of appeal from rulings of line supervision must exist.[7]

The multiple-step grievance procedure shown in Figure 18-3 is the most common type. In the first step, the employee usually presents the grievance orally and informally to his or her immediate supervisor in the presence of the union steward. This step offers the greatest potential for improved labor relations and a large majority of grievances are settled here. The procedure ends if the grievance can be resolved at this initial step. If the grievance remains unresolved, the next step involves a meeting between the plant manager or human resource manager and higher union officials, such as the grievance committee or the business agent or manager. Prior to this meeting, the grievance is written out, dated, and signed by the employee and the union steward. The written grievance states the events as the employee perceives them, cites the contract provision that allegedly has been violated, and indicates the settlement desired. If the grievance is not settled at this meeting, it is appealed to the third step, which typically involves the firm's top labor representative (such as the vice president of industrial relations) and high-level union officials. At times, depending on the severity of the grievance, the president may represent the firm. A grievance that remains unresolved at the conclusion of the third step may go to arbitration, if provided for in the agreement and the union decides to persevere.

Labor-relations problems can escalate when a supervisor is not equipped to handle grievances at the first step. Although the first step is usually handled informally by the union steward, the aggrieved party, and the supervisor, the supervisor must be fully prepared. The supervisor should obtain as many facts as possible before the meeting, because the union steward is likely to have done his or her homework.

The supervisor needs to recognize that the grievance may not reflect the real problem. For instance, the employee might be angry at the company for modifying its pay policies, even though the change was agreed to by the union. In order to voice discontent, the worker might file a grievance for an unrelated minor violation of the contract.

Arbitration

The grievance procedure has successfully and peacefully resolved many labor-management problems. The final step in most grievance procedures is arbitration. In arbitration, the parties submit their dispute to an impartial third party for resolution. Most agreements restrict the arbitrator's decision to application and interpretation of the agreement and make the decision final and binding on the parties. Although arbitration, at times, is used to settle contract negotiation conflicts, its primary use has been in settling grievances.

FIGURE 18-3
A Multiple-Step Grievance Procedure

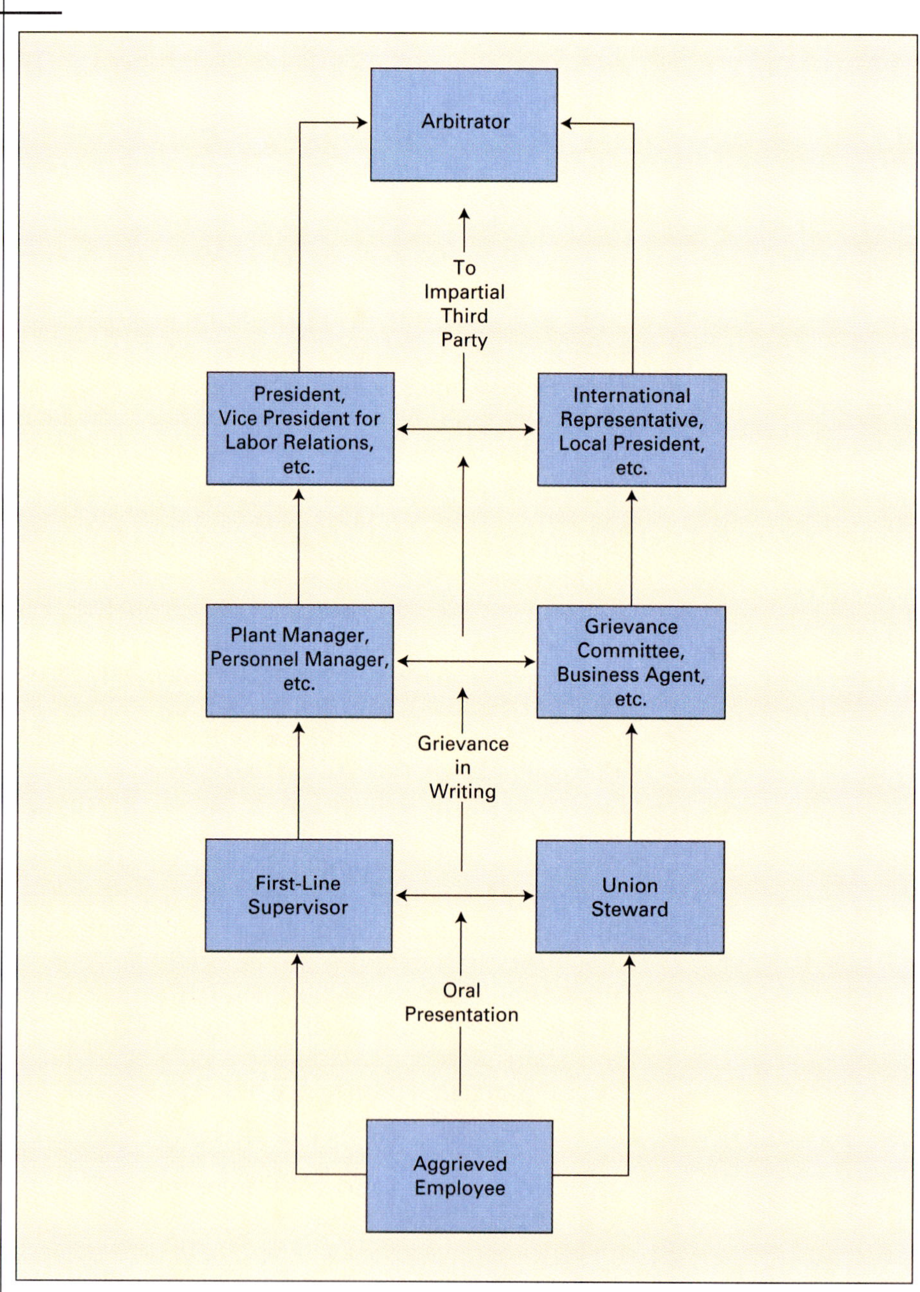

Source: Robert W. Eckles et al., *Essentials of Management for First-Line Supervision* (New York: John Wiley & Sons, 1974): 529. Reprinted by permission of John Wiley & Sons, Inc.

If the union decides in favor of arbitration, it notifies management. At this point, the union and the company select an arbitrator. Most agreements specify the selection method, although it is usually made from a list supplied by the Federal Mediation and Conciliation Service (FMCS) or the American Arbitration Association (AAA), both of which were discussed in Chapter 16. When considering potential arbitrators, both management and labor will study the candidates' previous decisions in an attempt to detect any biases. Obviously, neither party wants to select an arbitrator who might tend to favor the other's position.

When arbitration is used to settle a grievance, a variety of factors may be used to evaluate the fairness of the management actions that caused the grievance. These factors include the following:

- nature of the offense
- due process and procedural correctness
- double jeopardy
- grievant's past record
- grievant's length of service with the company
- knowledge of rules
- warnings
- lax enforcement of rules
- discriminatory treatment

The large number of interacting variables in each case makes the arbitration process difficult. The arbitrator must possess exceptional patience and judgment in rendering a fair and impartial decision.

After the arbitrator has been selected—and has agreed to serve—a time and place for a hearing will be determined. The issue to be resolved will be presented to the arbitrator in a document that summarizes the question(s) to be decided. It will also point out any contract restrictions that prohibit the arbitrator from making an award that would change the terms of the contract.

At the hearing, each side presents its case. Arbitration is an adversarial proceeding, so a case may be lost because of poor preparation and presentation. The arbitrator may conduct the hearing much like a courtroom proceeding. Witnesses, cross-examination, transcripts, and legal counsel may all be used. The parties may also submit, or be asked by the arbitrator to submit, formal written statements. After the hearing, the arbitrator studies the material submitted and testimony given and is expected to reach a decision within thirty to sixty days. The decision is usually accompanied by a written opinion giving reasons for the decision.

The courts will generally enforce an arbitrator's decision unless: (1) the arbitrator's decision is shown to be unreasonable or capricious in that it did not address the issues; (2) the arbitrator exceeded his or her authority; or (3) the award or decision violated a federal or state law.

Proof That Disciplinary Action Was Needed

Any disciplinary action administered may ultimately be taken to arbitration, when such a remedy is specified in the labor agreement. Employers have learned that they must prepare records that will constitute proof of disciplinary action and the reasons for it. Although the format of a written warning may vary, the following information should be included:

1. Statement of facts concerning the offense.
2. Identification of the rule that was violated.
3. Statement of what resulted or could have resulted because of the violation.
4. Identification of any previous similar violations by the same individual.
5. Statement of possible future consequences should the violation occur again.
6. Signature and date.

An example of a written warning is shown in Figure 18-4. In this instance, the worker has already received an oral reprimand. The individual is

FIGURE 18-4
An Example of a Written Warning

Date: August 1, 1995

To: Shane Boudreaux

From: Wayne Sanders

Subject: Written Warning

We are quite concerned because today you were thirty minutes late to work and offered no justification for this. According to our records, a similar offense occurred on July 25, 1995. At that time, you were informed that failure to report to work on time is unacceptable. I am, therefore, notifying you in writing that you must report to work on time. It will be necessary to terminate your employment if this happens again.

Please sign this form to indicate that you have read and understand this warning. Signing is not an indication of agreement.

____
Name

____
Date

also warned that continued tardiness could lead to termination. It is important to document oral reprimands because they may be the first step in disciplinary action leading ultimately to arbitration.

Weaknesses of Arbitration

Arbitration has achieved a certain degree of success in resolving grievances. However, it is not without weaknesses. Some practitioners claim that arbitration is losing its effectiveness because of the length of time between the first step of the grievance procedure and the final settlement. Often, 100-250 days may elapse before a decision is made.[8] The reason for the initial filing of the grievance may actually be forgotten before it is finally settled. Some people object to the cost of arbitration, which has been rising at an alarming rate. The cost of settling even a simple arbitration case can be quite high, even though it is typically shared by labor and management. Forcing every grievance to arbitration could be used as a tactic to place either management or the union in a difficult financial position.

GRIEVANCE HANDLING IN UNION-FREE ORGANIZATIONS

In the past, few union-free firms had formalized grievance procedures. Today this is not the case, as more and more firms have established formal grievance procedures, which they have encouraged employees to use.[9]

While the step-by-step procedure for handling union grievances is common practice, the means of resolving complaints in union-free firms varies. A well-designed grievance procedure ensures that the worker has ample opportunity to make complaints without fear of reprisal. If the system is to work, employees must be well informed about the program and convinced that management wants them to use it. Most employees are hesitant to formalize their complaints and must be constantly urged to avail themselves of the process.[10] The fact that a manager says, "Our workers must be happy because I have received no complaints," does not necessarily mean that employees have no grievances. In a closed, threatening corporate culture, workers may be reluctant to voice their dissatisfaction to management.

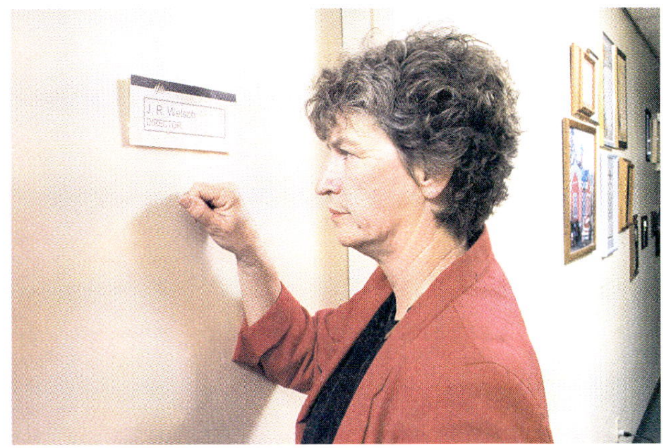

A well-designed grievance procedure ensures that the worker has ample opportunity to make complaints without fear of reprisal.

Typically, an employee initiates a complaint with his or her immediate supervisor. However, if the complaint involves the supervisor, the individual is permitted to bypass the immediate supervisor and proceed to the employee-relations specialist or the manager at the next level. The grievance ultimately may be taken to the organization's top executive for a final decision. Brown & Root, a Houston-based engineering, construction, and maintenance company, has a unique dispute resolution program. Whenever workers feel they need to resolve a dispute, the program allows them to choose one or all of four options: open-door policy, conference, mediation, or arbitration. "We wanted to give our employees several ports of entry to lodge a complaint if they wanted to," says Ralph Morales, manager of employee relations and administrator of the program.[11]

TERMINATION

Termination is the severest penalty that an organization can impose on an employee. Therefore, it should be the most carefully considered disciplinary action. The experience of being terminated is traumatic for employees regardless of their position in the organization. Feelings of failure, fear, disappointment, and anger can occur. It is also a difficult time for the person making the termination decision. Knowing that termination may affect not only the employee but also an entire family increases the trauma. Not knowing how the terminated employee will react also may create considerable anxiety for the manager who must do the firing. Regardless of the similarities in the termination of employees at various levels, distinct differences exist with regard to nonmanagerial/nonprofessional employees, executives, managers, and professionals. Termination is an extremely serious form of discipline and must, therefore, always be carefully considered and appropriate. Furthermore, in today's business environment, companies need to be as concerned with the termination process as with the hiring process.[12] In one survey, company representatives were asked to rank EEO issues according to their seriousness. As Figure 18-5 shows, 34 percent of

FIGURE 18-5
Rank Order of EEO Issues Companies Said Were Most Serious

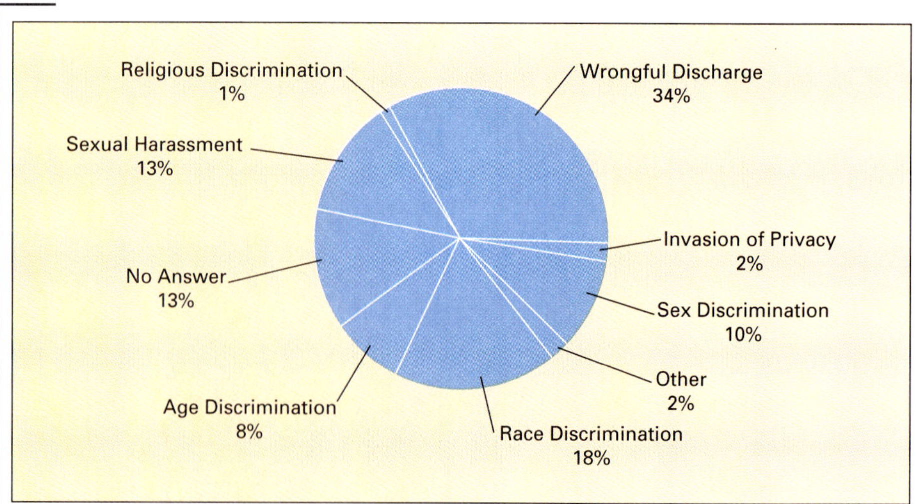

Source: Adapted from Richard T. Reminger, "At Risk," *Personnel Journal* 7 (March 1991): 51–54.

the respondents ranked wrongful discharge as the most serious issue. (Note that 34 percent is about the same as the combined percentages for age, sex, and race discrimination.)[13]

Termination of Nonmanagerial/Nonprofessional Employees

Individuals in this category are neither managers nor professionally trained individuals, such as engineers or accountants. They generally include such employees as steel workers, truck drivers, and waiters. If the firm is unionized, the termination procedure is typically well defined in the labor-management agreement. For example, drinking on the job might be identified as a reason for immediate termination. Excessive absences, on the other hand, may require three written warnings by the supervisor before termination action can be taken.

When the firm is union-free, these workers can generally be terminated more easily. A history of unjustified terminations within a firm, however, may provide an opportunity for unionization. In many union-free organizations, violations justifying termination are included in the firm's employee handbook. At times, especially in smaller organizations, the termination process is informal, with the first-line supervisor advising employees as to what actions warrant termination. Regardless of the size of the organization, employees should be informed by a representative of management of the actions that warrant termination.

Termination of Executives

Executive termination must be viewed from a different perspective. Executives usually have no formal appeal procedure. The decision to terminate an executive has probably been approved by the CEO in the organization. In addition, the reasons for termination may not be as clear as those for lower level employees. Some of the reasons include the following:

1. *Economic.* At times, business conditions may force a reduction in the number of executives.
2. *Reorganization/downsize.* In order to improve efficiency, a firm may reorganize or downsize, resulting in the elimination of some executive positions.
3. *Philosophical differences.* A difference in philosophy of conducting business may develop between an executive and other key company officials. In order to maintain consistency in management philosophy, the executive may be replaced.
4. *Decline in productivity.* The executive may have been capable of performing satisfactorily in the past, but, for various reasons, he or she can no longer perform the job as required.

This list does not include factors related to illegal activities or actions taken that are not in the best interests of the firm. Under those circumstances, the firm has no moral obligation to the terminated executive.

While a company may derive positive benefits from terminating executives, they also present a potentially hazardous situation for the organization. Many corporations are concerned about developing a negative public image that reflects insensitivity to the needs of their employees. They fear that such a reputation would impede their efforts to recruit high-quality managers. Also, terminated executives have, at times, made public statements detrimental to the reputation of the firm.

Termination of Middle and Lower Level Managers and Professionals

In the past, the most vulnerable and perhaps the most neglected group of employees with regard to termination has been middle and lower level managers and professionals, who are generally not union members and, thus, not protected by a labor-management agreement. They also may not have the political clout that a terminated executive has. Termination may have been based on something as simple as the attitude or feelings of an immediate superior on a given day.

EMPLOYMENT AT WILL

Approximately two of every three U.S. workers' jobs depend almost entirely on the continued goodwill of their employers. Individuals falling into this category are known as *at-will employees*. Generally, much of the U.S. legal system presumes that the jobs of such employees may be terminated at the will of the employer and that these employees have a similar right to leave their jobs at any time. **Employment at will** is an unwritten contract created when an employee agrees to work for an employer but no agreement exists as to how long the parties expect the employment to last. Historically, because of a century old common law precedent in the United States, employment of indefinite duration could, in general, be terminated at the whim of either party.

The concept of employment at will has eroded somewhat in recent years. In a current research study, it was found that 41 states had state court decisions recognizing implied contracts.[14] Some courts have decided that terminations of at-will employees are unlawful if they are contrary to general notions of acceptable "public policy" or if they are done in "bad faith." Judges, legislators, and employees are increasingly willing to challenge rigid notions of unlimited employer discretion. In Montana, for instance, the practice of at-will employment effectively ended when the state adopted a law prohibiting the termination of employment except for "good cause."

Employers can do certain things to help protect themselves against litigation for wrongful discharge based on a breach of implied employment contract. In fact, in one survey 60 percent of the companies responding said that they included an employment at will statement on the application blank that applicants are required to sign.[15] Statements in such documents as employment applications and policy manuals that suggest job security or permanent employment should be avoided if employers want to minimize charges of wrongful discharge. Other guidelines that may assist organizations in avoiding wrongful termination suits include clearly defining the worker's duties, providing good feedback on a regular basis, and conducting realistic performance appraisals on a regular basis.[16] However, recent statements in employment contracts aimed at preserving employers' control over at-will decisions do not guarantee employers protection from employment at will liability.[17] For example, in *Criado v*

ITT (SDNY 1993), ITT had disclaimers in its handbook regarding the at-will status of employment. The handbook, however, also contained a corporate code of conduct and an accompanying letter from the president urging all employees who suspect illegal or unethical conduct to come forward without penalty for making a report. Criado, an employee, came forward with suspicions of illegal activity by a vice president and was subsequently fired. The court found that although Criado was an at-will employee, ITT had created an expressed limitation on its right to fire any employee who followed the code of conduct.[18]

DEMOTION AS AN ALTERNATIVE TO TERMINATION

Termination frequently is the solution when a person is not able to perform his or her job satisfactorily. At times, however, demotions are used as an alternative to discharge, especially when a long-term employee is involved. The worker may have performed satisfactorily for many years, but his or her productivity may then begin to decline for a variety of reasons. Perhaps the worker is just not physically capable of performing the job any longer. Or the individual may no longer be willing to work the long hours that the job requires. **Demotion** is the process of moving a worker to a lower level of duties and responsibilities, which typically involves a reduction in pay. Emotions often run high when an individual is demoted. The demoted person may suffer loss of respect from peers and feel betrayed, embarrassed, angry, and disappointed. The employee's productivity may also decrease further. For these reasons, demotion should be used very cautiously.

One means of reducing the trauma associated with a demotion is to establish a probationary period in which a promoted worker is permitted to try out the new job. Should the person not work out, the individual may not view moving back to his or her old job negatively.

If demotion is chosen over termination, efforts must be made to preserve the self-esteem of the individual. The person may be asked how he or she would like to handle the demotion announcement. A positive image of the worker's value to the company should be projected.

The handling of demotions in a unionized organization is usually spelled out clearly in the labor-management agreement. Should a decision be made to demote a worker for unsatisfactory performance, the union should be notified of this intent and given the specific reasons for the demotion. Often the demotion will be challenged and carried through the formal grievance procedure. Documentation is necessary for the demotion to be upheld. Even with the problems associated with demotion for cause, it is often easier to demote than to terminate an employee. In addition, demotion is often less devastating to the employee. For the organization, however, the opposite may be true if the demotion creates lingering ill will and an embittered employee.

Demotion as an Alternative to Layoff

As firms downsize and reduce the number of layers in the organizational structure, positions that may have been held by highly qualified employees may have been eliminated. Rather than lose a valued employee, firms, at times, offer the worker a lower level position, perhaps at the same salary.

LAYOFFS

Historically, the economic well-being of many companies rises and falls in cycles. At times a firm's goods or services may be in great demand; at other times demand falls. Often when demand is low, the firm has no alternative but to lay off workers. Although being laid off is not the same thing as being fired, it has the same effect: The worker is unemployed. And, in today's work environment, there may be little chance of the worker being rehired. Examples of massive layoffs have become commonplace as firms downsize to position themselves to compete in the highly competitive global environment. For example, IBM has cut 170,000 jobs worldwide, and Chevron reduced its workforce by nearly half, to about 50,000 people, after its merger with Gulf Oil Company. Then Chevron cut its staff by another 6,500.[19,20] AT&T has eliminated more than 100,000 jobs in the last ten years.[21] Today only 15 percent of laid-off workers expect to get their jobs back, as compared to 44 percent in past recoveries.[22]

Being laid off can often have extreme psychological consequences. Says an electrical engineer who was laid off in January, after nearly 30 years with Xerox, "Losing my job was the most shocking experience I've ever had in my life. I almost think it's worse than the death of a loved one, because at least we learn about death as we grow up. No one in my age group ever learned about being laid off."[23]

Layoff/Recall Procedures

Even in this rapidly changing environment, at times recalls are necessary. Whether the firm is union-free or unionized, carefully constructed layoff/recall procedures should be developed.[24,25] Workers should understand when they are hired how the system will work in the event of a layoff. When the firm is unionized, the layoff procedures are usually stated clearly in the labor-management agreement. Seniority usually is the basis for layoffs, with the least senior employees laid off first. The agreement may also have a clearly spelled out *bumping procedure*. When senior-level positions are eliminated, the people occupying them have the right to bump workers from lower-level positions, assuming that they have the proper qualifications for the lower-level job. When bumping occurs, the composition of the workforce is altered.

Procedures for recalling laid-off employees are also usually spelled out in labor-management agreements. Again, seniority is typically the basis for worker recall, with the most senior employees being recalled first.

Regardless of a union-free firm's current stand on the issue of layoffs, it should establish layoff procedures prior to facing one. In union-free firms seniority should also be an integral part of any layoff procedure. But, frequently, other factors should be considered. Productivity of the employee is typically an important consideration. When productivity is a factor, management must be careful to ensure that productivity, not favoritism, is the actual basis. Workers may have an accurate perception of their own productivity level and that of their fellow employees. Therefore, it is important to define accurately both seniority and productivity considerations well in advance of any layoffs.

Outplacement

Many organizations have established a systematic means of assisting laid off or terminated employees in locating jobs.[26] The use of outplacement began at the executive level but has recently been used at other organizational levels. In **outplacement**, laid-off employees are given assistance in finding employment elsewhere. In today's environment, mass layoffs have often necessitated group outplacement. Through outplacement, the firm tries to soften the impact of displacement. Some of the services provided by group outplacement are use of a transition center, individual counseling, job fairs, complete access to office equipment (such as computers, fax machines, copy machines), and free postage for mailing application letters and resumes.[27]

TRANSFERS

The lateral movement of a worker within an organization is called a **transfer**. A transfer may be initiated by the firm or by an employee. The process does not, and should not, imply that a person is being promoted or demoted.

Transfers serve several purposes. First, firms often find it necessary to reorganize. Offices and departments are created and abolished in response to the company's needs. In order to fill positions created by reorganization, employee moves not entailing promotion may be necessary. The same is true when an office or department is closed. Rather than terminate valued employees, management may transfer them to other areas within the organization. These transfers may entail moving an employee to another desk in the same office or to a location halfway around the world.

A second reason for transfers is to make positions available in the primary promotion channels. Firms are typically organized into a hierarchical structure resembling a pyramid. Each succeeding promotion is more difficult to obtain because fewer positions exist. At times, very productive but unpromotable workers may clog promotion channels. Other qualified workers in the organization may find their opportunities for promotion blocked. When this happens, a firm's most capable future managers may seek employment elsewhere. In order to keep promotion channels open, the firm may decide to transfer employees who are unpromotable but productive at their present levels.

Another reason for transfers is to satisfy employees' personal desires. The reasons for wanting a transfer are numerous. An individual may need to work closer to home to care for aging parents. Or the worker may dislike the long commuting trips to and from work. Factors such as these may be sufficiently important that employees may resign if a requested transfer is not approved. Rather than risk losing a valued employee, the firm may agree to the transfer.

Transfers may also be an effective means of dealing with personality clashes. Some people just cannot get along with one another. Because each of the individuals may be a valued employee, transfer may be an appropriate solution to the problem. But human resource managers must be cautious regarding the "grass is always greener on the other side of the fence" syndrome. When some workers encounter a temporary setback, they immediately ask for a transfer—before they even attempt to work through the problem.

Finally, because of the downsizing of management levels, it is becoming necessary for managers to have a wide variety of experiences before achieving a promotion. It has been estimated that by the year 2000, the typical large corporation will have half the management levels and one-third the managers that it has today.[28] Individuals who desire upward mobility often explore possible lateral moves so that they can learn new skills.[29]

Before any worker's request for transfer is approved, it should be analyzed in terms of the best interests of both the firm and the individual. Disruptions may occur when the worker is transferred, for example, should a qualified worker not be available to step into the position being vacated.

Management should establish clear policies regarding transfers. Such policies let workers know in advance when a transfer request is likely to be approved and what its ramifications will be. For instance, if the transfer is for personal reasons, some firms do not pay moving costs. Whether the organization will or will not pay should be clearly spelled out.

A GLOBAL PERSPECTIVE

International transfers involve the movement of workers within a multinational organization. A transfer may be initiated by the firm or by an employee, but most international transfers are initiated by the firm. International transfers are used to take advantage of domestic talent in global business operations. Such transfers are often necessary to manage global operations effectively, but inappropriately handled transfers may do personal and career damage to those involved and will not benefit the company.

A well-thought-out expatriate transfer policy can help a company avoid many of the frustrations and pitfalls of sending people abroad while achieving cost savings. When developing an expatriate policy, the first thing the company needs to consider is why it is sending people abroad. The policy should be directed at achieving the company's business objectives. The company must also consider the needs of expatriates. The decision to go overseas, for instance, should be mutually acceptable by the employee and the employer. Working overseas is a big step, and people moving for the first time may have real fears and concerns. It is a good idea to structure the expatriate transfer policy as follows: the preassignment period, the journey out, the assignment itself, the prereturn period, the journey back, and the postassignment period. Establishing the policy is the first part; communicating it is the second.[30] Only by utilizing a well-thought-out expatriate transfer policy can companies avoid the problems of sending people abroad and best utilize the talents of those being transferred.

PROMOTION

A **promotion** is the movement of a person to a higher-level position in the organization. The term promotion is one of the most emotionally charged words in the field of human resource management. An individual who receives a promotion normally receives additional financial rewards and the ego boost associated with achievement and accomplishment. Most employees feel positively about being promoted. But for every individual who gains a promotion, there are probably others who were not selected. If these individuals wanted the promotion badly enough, they may slack off or even resign. If the consensus of employees directly involved is that the wrong person was promoted, considerable resentment may result.

In future promotions will not be as available as they were in the past.[31] For one thing, many firms are reducing the number of levels in their hierarchies. As the number of middle management positions declines, fewer promotional opportunities will be available. The effect of these changes is that more people will be striving for fewer promotion opportunities. Consequently, organizations must look for ways other than promotion to reward employees. One alternative is the dual-track system described in Chapter 10, whereby highly technical individuals can continue to receive financial rewards without progressing into management. Another option, discussed in Chapter 12, is skill-based pay, a system that compensates employees on the basis of job-related skills they acquire.

RESIGNATION

Even when an organization is totally committed to making its environment a good place to work, workers will still resign. Some employees cannot see promotional opportunities—or at least not enough—for themselves and will move on. A certain amount of turnover is healthy for an organization and is often necessary to afford employees the opportunity to fulfill career objectives. But when turnover becomes excessive, something must be done. The most qualified employees are often the ones who resign because they are more mobile. On the other hand, marginally qualified workers seemingly never leave. If excessive numbers of a firm's highly qualified and competent workers are leaving, means must be found to reverse the trend.

Analyzing Voluntary Resignations

A frequently given reason for resignation is the desire to obtain a better salary and/or benefits. However, most firms either conduct salary surveys or keep in touch with what competitors are paying. Research has shown that when workers mention pay as a reason for resigning, they often have other deeper reasons for deciding to leave. The cause may be a department manager with whom no one can work or a corporate culture that is stifling creative employees. Management should identify the causes and correct them as quickly as possible.

When a firm wants to determine the real reasons that individuals decide to leave, it can use the exit interview and/or the postexit questionnaire.[32] In a survey conducted by the HRNews and the Bureau of National Affairs, Inc., 96 percent of respondents indicated that their companies have some form of exit interview program.[33] The exit interview typically is the last major contact the employee has with the company. The exit interview encourages the employee to tell the reasons for resigning openly and freely. A human resource professional usually conducts this interview. An employee is not as likely to respond as freely during an interview with his or her supervisor, reasoning that he or she may need a letter of recommendation from the supervisor in the future. The typical exit interview involves the following:

- establishment of rapport
- purpose of the interview
- attitudes regarding the old job
- exploration of reasons for leaving
- comparing the old and new jobs

- changes recommended
- conclusion[34]

Specific topics that might be covered by the interviewer during the exit interview are listed in Figure 18-6. Note that the interviewer is focusing on job-related factors and probing for the real reasons the person is leaving. Over a period of time, properly conducted exit interviews can provide considerable insight into why employees are leaving. Patterns are often identified that uncover weaknesses in the firm's human resource management system. Knowledge of the problem permits corrective action to be taken.

The postexit questionnaire is sent to former employees several weeks after they leave the organization. Usually, they have already started work at their new companies. The questionnaire is structured to draw out the real reason the employee left. Ample blank space is also provided so that a former employee can express his or her feelings about, and perceptions of, the job and the organization. One strength of this approach is that the individuals are no longer with the firm and may respond more freely to the questions. A weakness is that the interviewer is not present to interpret and probe for the real reasons for leaving.

Advance Notice of Resignation

Most firms would like to have at least two-weeks' notice of resignation from departing workers. However, a month's notice may be desired from professional and managerial employees who are leaving. When notice is desired by the firm, the policy should be clearly communicated to all employees. If they

FIGURE 18-6
Questions Related to General Job Factors

1. Let's begin by your outlining briefly some of the duties of your job.
2. Of the duties you just outlined, tell me three or four that are crucial to the performance of your job.
3. Tell me about some of the duties you liked the most and what you liked about performing those duties.
4. Now, tell me about some of the duties you liked least and what you did not like about performing those duties.
5. Suppose you describe the amount of variety in your job.
6. Let's talk a little bit now about the amount of work assigned to you. For example, was the amount assigned not enough at times, perhaps too much at times, or was it fairly stable and even overall?
7. Suppose you give me an example of an incident that occurred on your job that was especially satisfying to you. What about an incident that was a little less satisfying?
8. Let's talk now about the extent to which you feel you were given the opportunity to use your educational background, skills, and abilities on your job.
9. Tell me how you would assess the quality of training on your job.
10. Suppose you describe the promotional opportunities open to you in your job.

Source: Wanda R. Embrey, R. Wayne Mondy, and Robert M. Noe, "Exit Interview: A Tool for Personnel Development." Reprinted from the May 1979 issue of *Personnel Administrator,* copyright 1979. Reprinted with the permission from *HRMagazine* (formerly *Personnel Administrator*), published by the Society for Human Resource Management, Alexandria, Virginia.

want departing employees to give advance notice, companies have certain obligations. For instance, suppose that a worker gives notice—and then is terminated immediately. Word of this action will spread rapidly to other employees. Later, should other employees decide to resign, they will likely not give any advance notice.

However, permitting a resigned worker to remain on the job once a resignation has been submitted may create some problems. If bad feelings exist between the employee and the supervisor or the company, the departing worker may be a disruptive force. On a selective basis, the firm may wish to pay the employee for the notice time and ask him or her to leave immediately. However, this action should not often be necessary.

RETIREMENT

Most long-term employees leave an organization by retiring. Retirement plans may be based on reaching a certain age or working a certain number of years with the firm, or both. Upon retirement, former employees usually receive a pension each month for the remainder of their lives.

In the past, there were far too many instances of retirement plan failure. Many workers who retired believing that they would receive lifelong pensions were devastated to find that retirement programs had been insufficiently funded by their employers. In 1974, the Employee Retirement Income Security Act (ERISA) was passed for the purpose of protecting employees participating in company-sponsored retirement plans.

Early Retirement

Sometimes employees will retire before reaching the organization's length of service requirement. Often retirement pay is reduced for each year that the retirement date is advanced. From an organization's viewpoint, early employee retirement has both positive and negative aspects.

Because of the large number of staff reductions many firms are now encountering, early retirement is often viewed as an attractive solution.[35] If an extended layoff is expected, a product line is being discontinued, or a plant is being closed, early retirement may be a responsible solution to the problem of surplus employees.

From a negative viewpoint, valued employees may take advantage of the early retirement option and leave the organization. In addition, early retirement is often more expensive to the company than normal retirement. And early retirement decisions are often made on short notice, resulting in some disruption of a company's operations.

Retirement Planning

Strong emotions often accompany anticipation of retirement. As retirement approaches, the individual may be haunted by these and other questions: Do I have enough money? What will I do? Will I be able to adjust? Just as a well-planned orientation program eases the transition of a new hire into the organization, a company-sponsored retirement planning program eases the transition of long-term employees from work to leisure.

Often a firm devotes time, staff, and money to provide useful information to workers approaching retirement. Typically, such information relates to finances, housing, relocation, family relations, attitude adjustment, and legal affairs.

Some firms have taken retirement planning a step further. At times firms consider both the social and psychological implications of the retirement process. Adaptation to retirement living is the focus of this form of planning. Individuals who have already retired are brought to meetings to speak and answer questions regarding retirement life. Managing the change in life-style is often a topic for discussion, which is helpful to all those considering retirement. Retirement is a major event in an individual's life, and employers can often help to smooth the transition from work to leisure.

LEGAL IMPLICATIONS OF INTERNAL EMPLOYEE RELATIONS

Many people believe that equal employment opportunity legislation primarily affects individuals entering the company for the first time. Nothing could be further from the truth. Virtually all phases of internal employee relations are affected. Of special concern to the EEOC are decisions relating to promotion. The Household Finance Corporation (HFC) was required to pay more than $125,000 to white-collar women employees who charged that they were denied promotion because of their gender. Under terms of a consent decree, the company also agreed to hire women for 20 percent of the branch representative openings (subject to availability). HFC was also required to hire 20 percent of its new employees from specified minority groups for clerical, credit, and branch representative jobs, until the total number of such employees reached 65 percent of their population proportion in the labor area. In addition, HFC agreed to train women and minority employees to help them qualify for better jobs where they are underrepresented.[36]

One of the largest payments ever made was under an agreement signed by AT&T with the EEOC and the Department of Labor. It provided for payment of approximately $15 million to employees allegedly discriminated against. The agreement also called for additional affirmative action and for an estimated $50 million in yearly payments for promotion and wage adjustment to minority and women employees.[37]

Termination of workers who have reached a certain age is a major concern in enforcement of the Age Discrimination Act. In *EEOC v Liggett and Myers*, the Equal Opportunity Commission alleged that age was a factor in the discharge of approximately 10 percent of Liggett and Myers' employees during a reduction in force. The court ruled against the company, and back-pay recovery was estimated at $20 million. In *Hagman and EEOC v United Airlines*, a jury awarded $18.2 million to 112 United Airlines' pilots who had been forced to retire at age 60. In *EEOC v Home Insurance Company*, an age discrimination case was won on behalf of 143 employees at Home Insurance Company who had been forced to retire at age 62; back-pay recovery was estimated at $6-8 million.

In 1986, the Age Discrimination in Employment Act was further amended by removing the upper age ceiling for mandatory retirement. Employers who attempt to retire workers systematically for factors other than performance are coming under increased scrutiny by the EEOC. The problem in many cases is that for appraisal periods prior to termination, high-performance evaluations had often been given to the employees involved. These evaluations provided the terminated employees with the data they needed to develop valid cases contending that the reason for termination was age, not declining performance.

Some firms have tried to open avenues for the promotion of younger workers by offering early voluntary retirement. A potential problem with this option is whether the retirement is truly voluntary. Exerting pressure on employees to retire when they really do not want to is beginning to receive considerable EEOC attention.

The thrust of EEO legislation is that women and minorities should receive equal treatment, and internal employee relations must reflect this principle. For instance, are blacks being fired at a higher rate than whites? Are women not receiving promotional opportunities? The same kinds of questions may be asked about demotions and layoffs. As more women and minorities enter the workforce, EEO administration will likely focus increasingly on internal employee relations.

EMPLOYEE RELATIONS IN TIMES OF INTERNATIONAL CRISIS

According to Jay Hornsby, Dow Chemical Company's vice president of human resources, "For an expatriate employee thousands of miles away from home, the company is the family." Therefore, the firm must provide support for an employee in times of international crisis. Hornsby adds, "Whenever something goes wrong, and it will, he or she will naturally turn to the company for help." The key to maintaining good employee relations is for the company to be there when an expatriate employee needs help. Global human resource professionals have been called on to assist employees based abroad with a wide range of often difficult problems. Some of these problems include medical emergencies, natural disasters, revolutions, and other international crises, such as the recent conflict in the Middle East.[38]

Medical emergencies occur fairly frequently. Ralph W. Stevens, vice president of personnel and employee relations for Hamilton Oil Corporation, recalls the case of a high-ranking technical manager who suffered a stroke while on business in Korea, where the company maintains no office. Stevens managed to find a first-rate physician, set the employee up in a well-regarded hospital, and transfer sufficient funds to cover the medical bills, while comforting the manager's frantic family.[39]

Because of its extensive operations in Latin America, Ferro, a $1 billion international manufacturer, has long had contingency plans in place for another kind of emergency: a terrorist kidnapping. Nothing adverse has ever happened, but the company still strives to maintain a politically neutral and noncontroversial image when it operates in potentially dangerous international locations. Various contingency plans, including means and methods to evacuate workers, if necessary, are in place for most U.S. companies currently operating in the Middle East. CPC International, Inc., for example, has a food processing plant in Saudi Arabia. Richard P. Bergeman, the company's vice president of human resources, has stated, "Naturally we have contingency procedures approved and ready, although we would rather not discuss them."[40]

During its more than 100-year history, Fluor Daniel has had to deal with almost every kind of international crisis. "Earthquakes, hurricanes, uprisings—we've probably had employees caught in all of them," says Tom Blackburn, the company's director of international administration. To Blackburn, more difficult and wrenching than politically induced crises are instances when an expatriate employee dies abroad. He once had to coordinate the transport of a worker's coffin from an international site back to the United States, giving what solace he could to the man's grieving widow.[41] As this scenario illustrates, the ultimate test of a company's concern about positive employee relations comes in times of extreme crisis.

SUMMARY

A necessary but often difficult aspect of internal employee relations is disciplinary action. A major purpose of disciplinary action is to ensure that employee behavior is consistent with the firm's policies, rules, and regulations.

The disciplinary action process is dynamic and ongoing. As long as employee behavior does not vary from acceptable practices, disciplinary action is not necessary. But when an employee's behavior violates a rule, corrective action should be taken. The purpose of this action is to alter behavior that can have a negative impact on the organization.

If the employees in an organization are represented by a union, workers who believe that they have been wrongly disciplined or dealt with unjustly can appeal through the grievance procedure of the collective bargaining agreement. A grievance procedure permits employees to express complaints without jeopardizing their jobs.

Termination is the severest penalty that an organization can impose on an employee. The procedure used both to terminate operative employees and to allow them to appeal the decision is usually well-defined. However, executives do not have a formal appeals procedure; and in the past, the most vulnerable and perhaps most neglected groups of employees with regard to termination have been middle- and lower-level managers and professionals.

Employment at will is created when an employee agrees to work for an employer but there is no agreement as to how long the parties expect the employment to last. In the United States, employment at will has been eroded to a certain degree because of various court decisions.

Internal employee relations also pertain to resignation, demotion, layoff, transfer, promotion, and retirement.

Most people believe that equal employment opportunity legislation primarily affects individuals entering the company for the first time. Nothing could be further from the truth. Virtually all phases of internal employee relations are affected. Of special concern to the EEOC are decisions relating to promotion.

A multinational corporation headquartered in the United States often must alter its approach to internal employee relations to address the problems associated with international crises.

QUESTIONS FOR REVIEW

1. Distinguish between discipline and disciplinary action.
2. In progressive disciplinary action, what steps are involved before employee termination?
3. What are the steps that should typically be followed in handling a grievance under a collective bargaining agreement?
4. Why is arbitration often used in the settlement of grievances in a unionized firm?
5. How would grievances typically be handled in a union-free firm? Describe briefly.
6. How does termination often differ with regard to nonmanagerial/nonprofessional employees, executives, managers, and professionals?

7. What is meant by the phrase *employment at will*?
8. Briefly describe the techniques available to determine the real reasons that an individual decides to leave an organization.
9. Distinguish between demotions, transfers, and promotions.
10. What are some legal implications of internal employee relations?

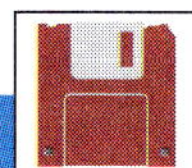

HRM SIMULATION

Incident K in the *Simulation Players Manual* deals with outplacement. Your team has been given the responsibility of formulating a policy on termination and the possibility of using an outplacement service provided by a national consulting firm. Your team has the responsibility of assessing whether or not to offer outplacement services to terminated employees.

Incident N in the *Simulation Players Manual* deals with a promotion decision. Your team will study and make a recommendation on whom to promote.

ABC VIDEO CASE

THE FACTORY OF THE FUTURE
TAPE 2, NUMBER 11

Internal employee relations are changing in today's fast moving world. Now the emphasis is on creativity and teamwork. Square D's Lexington factory has revolutionized the way its employees think about work. A major manufacturer of electrical equipment, the company has divided nearly 300 of its employees into teams of twenty to thirty people. Each team operates like a small business, run by the workers themselves. The transformation of Square D began five years ago when its chairman concluded that the company was spending more on painting its buildings than it was on developing its employees.

When asked how important the retraining of employees, with the emphasis on quality, was to the company's survival, Bill Englehaupt, Square D's quality education manager replied, "I could say if we didn't do it, we could pretty much pick a day, and we'd be out of business. Customer expectations are higher than they've ever been, and we need to continually meet those customer expectations if we expect to stay in business."

HRM INCIDENT 1

—YOU KNOW THE POLICY

Dwayne Alexander is the Dallas-area supervisor for Quik-Stop, a chain of convenience stores. He has full responsibility for managing the seven Quik-Stop stores in Dallas. Each store operates with only one person on duty at a time. Although several of the stores stay open all night, every night, the Center Street store is open all night Monday through Thursday but only from 6:00 a.m. to 10:00 p.m. Friday through Sunday. Because the store is open fewer hours during the weekend, money from sales is kept in the store safe until Monday. Therefore, the time it takes to complete a money count on Monday is greater than normal. The company has a policy that when the safe is being emptied, the manager has to be with the employee on duty, and the employee has to place each $1,000 in a brown bag, mark the bag, and leave the bag on the floor next to the safe until the manager verifies the amount in each bag.

Bill Catron worked the Sunday night shift at the Center Street store and was trying to save his manager time by counting the money prior to his arrival. The store got very busy, and, while bagging a customer's groceries, Bill mistook one of the money bags for a bag containing three sandwiches and put the money bag in with the groceries. Twenty minutes later, Dwayne arrived, and both men began to search for the money. While they were searching, a customer came back with the bag of money. Quik-Stop has a policy that anyone violating the money counting procedure must be fired immediately.

Bill was very upset. "I really need this job," Bill exclaimed. "With the new baby and all the medical expenses we've had, I sure can't stand to be out of a job."

"You knew about the policy, Bill," said Dwayne.

"Yes, I did, Dwayne," said Bill, "and I really don't have any excuse. If you don't fire me, though, I promise you that I'll be the best store manager you've got."

While Bill waited on a customer, Dwayne called his boss at the home office in Houston. With the boss's approval, Dwayne decided not to fire Bill.

Questions

1. Do you agree with Dwayne's decision in view of the discussion on progressive discipline? Discuss.
2. How did Dwayne's decision not to fire Bill serve as a motivational force for Bill?

HRM INCIDENT 2

—SOMETHING IS NOT RIGHT

As Norman Blankenship came to the office at Consolidated Coal Company's Rowland mine, near Clear Creek, West Virginia, he told the mine dispatcher not to tell anyone of his presence. Norman was the general superintendent of the Rowland operation. He had been with Consolidated for more than twenty-three years, having started out as a coal digger.

Norman had heard that one of his section bosses, Tom Serinsky, had been sleeping on the job. Tom had been hired two months earlier and assigned to the Rowland mine by the regional human resource office. He went to work as a section boss, working the midnight to 8:00 a.m. shift. Because of his age and experience, Tom was the senior person in the mine on his shift.

Norman took one of the battery-operated jeeps used to transport workers and supplies in and out of the mine and proceeded to the area where Tom was assigned. Upon arriving, he saw Tom lying on an emergency stretcher. Norman stopped his jeep a few yards away from where Tom was sleeping and approached him. "Hey, you asleep?" Norman asked. Tom awakened with a start and said, "No, I wasn't sleeping."

Norman waited a moment for Tom to collect his senses and then said, "I could tell that you were sleeping. But that's beside the point. You weren't at your work station. You know that I have no choice but to fire you." After Tom had left, Norman called his mine supervisor, who had accompanied him to the dispatcher's office and asked him to complete the remainder of Tom's shift.

The next morning Norman had the mine's human resource officer officially terminate Tom. As part of the standard procedure, the human resource officer notified the regional human resource director that Tom had been fired and gave the reasons for firing him. The regional director asked the human resource officer to put Norman on the line. When he did so, Norman was told, "You know that Tom is the brother-in-law of our regional vice president, Bill Frederick?" "No, I didn't know that," replied Norman, "but it doesn't matter. The rules are clear, and I wouldn't care if he was the regional vice president's son."

The next day the regional director showed up at the mine just as Norman was getting ready to make a routine tour of the mine. "I guess you know what I'm here for," said the regional director. "Yeah, you're here to take away my authority," replied Norman. "No, I'm just here to investigate," said the regional director.

When Norman returned to the mine office after his tour, the regional director had finished his interviews. He told Norman, "I think we're going to have to put Tom back to work. If we decided to do that, can you let him work for you?" "No, absolutely not," replied Norman. "In fact, if he works here, I go." A week later Norman learned that Tom had gone back to work as section boss at another Consolidated coal mine in the region.

Questions

1. What would you do now if you were Norman?
2. Do you believe that the regional director handled the matter in an ethical manner? Explain.

DEVELOPING HRM SKILLS

AN EXPERIENTIAL EXERCISE

Isadore Lamansky is the manager of the machine tooling operations at Lone Star Industries and has five supervisors who report to him. One of his employees is Susie Canton, a supervisor in maintenance. As Isadore comes to work this morning, his thoughts focus on Susie, "Today is the day that I must talk to Susie. I sure hate to do it. I know she is going to take it the wrong way. Ever since Susie was promoted to unit supervisor, she has had trouble maintaining discipline. She tries too hard to keep the men in line because she thinks they are continually trying to push her, and she lets the women get away with murder. Well, I guess I'll get this over with, since that's what I get paid for."

The grapevine is strong at Lone Star Industries, and it didn't take long for Susie to hear rumors. She thinks, "The word is that old Isadore is going to come down on me. He recommended someone else for my job because he doesn't like women in charge. The reason it is so hard to maintain discipline is the fact that the men I supervise intentionally push me to see what I'll do. The women support me, and they are proud of me; the men just want me gone. He is probably going to dredge up some minor stuff to reprimand me about; we need more women in charge, and the boss will have to accept that I'm here for good!"

Who is right? And who is wrong? Can there be a reasonable solution to the problems that exist? This exercise will require two of you to participate. One person will play Susie, and another person will play Isadore. All others should observe carefully. The instructor will provide additional information to participants.

NOTES

1. Arthur R. Pell, "Effective Reprimanding," *Manager's Magazine* 65 (August 1990): 26.

2. Robert N. Lussier, "16 Guidelines for Effective Discipline," *Supervisory Management* 35 (March 1990): 10.

3. David N. Campbell, R.L. Fleming, and Richard C. Grote, "Discipline Without Punishment—At Last," *Harvard Business Review* 63 (July-August 1985): 168.

4. Wallace Wohlking, "Effective Discipline in Employee Relations," *Personnel Journal* 54 (September 1975): 489.

5. Neil W. Chamberlain, *The Labor Sector* (New York: McGraw-Hill, 1985): 240.

6. K.L. Sovereign and Mario Bognanno, "Positive Contract Administration," in Dale Yoder and Herbert S. Heneman, Jr., eds., *ASPA Handbook of Personnel and Industrial Relations: Employee and Labor Relations,* vol. III (Washington, D.C.: The Bureau of National Affairs, 1976): 7-161–7-162.

7. Ibid., 7-164.

8. Lawrence Stessin, "Expedited Arbitration: Less Grief Over Grievances," *Harvard Business Review* 55 (January-February 1977): 129.

9. Paula Eubanks, "Employee Grievance Policy: Don't Discourage Complaints," *Hospitals* 64 (December 20, 1990): 36.

10. James P. Swann, Jr., "Formal Grievance Procedures in Non-Union Plants," *Personnel Administrator* 26 (August 1991): 67.

11. Jennifer Laabs, "Remedies for HR's Legal Headache," *Personnel Journal* 73 (December 1994): 69.

12. Elliot H. Shaller, "Avoid Pitfalls in Hiring, Firing," *Nation's Business* 79 (February 1991): 53.

13. Richard T. Reminger, "At Risk," *Personnel Journal* 70 (March 1991): 51.

14. Richard Edwards, *Rights at Work: Employment Relations in the Post Union Era* (Washington: The Brookings Institution, 1993): Appendix.

15. Raymond L. Hilgert, "Employers Protected by At-Will Statement," *HRMagazine* 36 (March 1991): 60.

16. Clinton O. Longnecker and Frederick R. Post, "The Management Termination Trap," *Business Horizons* 37 (May-June 1994): 71.

17. Lisa Jenner, "Employment-At-Will Liability: How Protected are You?" *HR Focus* 71 (March 1994): 11.

18. Ibid.

19. Stratford Sherman, "Is He Too Cautious to Save IBM?" *Fortune* 130 (October 3, 1994): 82.

20. Brian O'Reilly, "The New Deal: What Companies and Employees Owe One Another," *Fortune* 129 (June 13, 1994): 45.

21. Ibid., 46.

22. Kenneth Labich, "The New Unemployed," *Fortune* 127 (March 8, 1993): 40.

23. Susan Caminiti, "What Happens to Laid-Off Managers," *Fortune* 129 (June 13, 1994): 69.

24. Michael Smith, "Help in Making Those Tough Layoff Decisions," *Supervisory Management* 35 (January 1990): 3.

25. Robert W. Keidel, "Layoffs Take Advance Preparation," *Management Review* 80 (May 1991): 6.

26. Loretta D. Foxman and Walter L. Polsky, "Outplacement Results in Success," *Personnel Journal* 69 (February 1990): 30.

27. Virginia M. Gibson, "In the Outplacement Door," *Personnel* 68 (October 1991): 3–4.

28. David Kirkpatrick, "Is Your Career on Track?" *Fortune* 122 (July 2, 1990): 39.

29. Harvey Mackay, "A Career Roadmap: Getting Started," *Modern Office Technology* 35 (June 1990): 12.

30. Michael J. Kaltz, "How to Establish an Expatriate Policy from Scratch," *Benefits & Compensation International* (January/February 1994): 62–66.

31. Joseph R. Rich and Beth C. Florin-Thuma, "Rewarding Employees in an Environment of Fewer Promotions," *Pension World* 26 (November 1990): 16.

32. Lin Grensing, "Don't Let Them Out the Door Without an Exit Interview," *Management World* 19 (March-April 1990): 11.

33. Robert Wolfe, "Most Employers Offer Exit Interviews," *HRNews* 10 (June 1990): 2.

34. Wanda R. Embrey, R. Wayne Mondy, and Robert M. Noe, "Exit Interview: A Tool for Personnel Development," *Personnel Administrator* 24 (May 1979): 46.

35. Jeffrey S. Hoffman, "Sweetening Early-Retirement Programs," *Personnel* 67 (March 1990): 18.

36. *U.S. v Household Finance Corporation,* 4 EPD para. 7680 (N.D. Ill., 1972)—Consent decree.

37. U.S. Equal Employment Opportunity Commission, *Affirmative Action and Equal Employment: A Guidebook for Employers,* vol. 1 (Washington, D.C.: U.S. Government Printing Office, January 1974): 10.

38. Ellen Brandt, "Global HR," *Personnel Journal* 70 (March 1991): 43.

39. Ibid.

40. Ibid.

41. Ibid.

CHAPTER 19 Human Resource Research

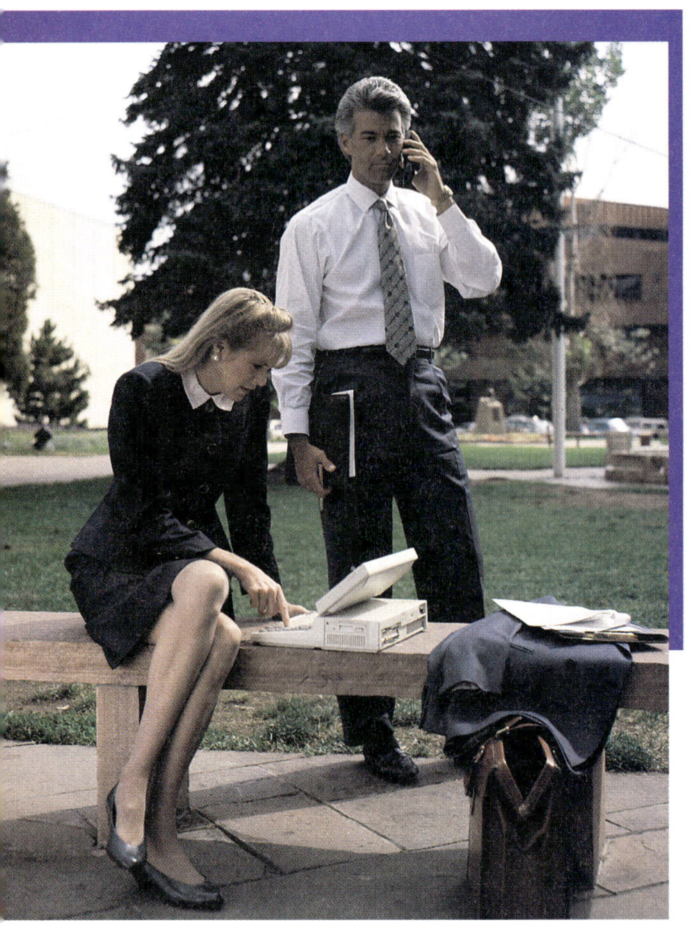

KEY TERMS

CHAPTER OBJECTIVES

1. Explain the importance of research to human resource management, identify the basic methods of inquiry for research, and describe the steps in the research process.
2. Describe how quantitative methods may be used in human resource research and how the human resource function may be evaluated.
3. Describe how technology is affecting human resource management.

Annette Dommert, human resource manager for Saint Joseph Medical Center in Decatur, Illinois, was disturbed as she studied the list of workers who had resigned during the past month. For the sixth month in a row, the number of terminations had increased. To compound the problem, the terminations were in critical areas, such as X-ray and laboratory. Quite a few nurses had also turned in their resignations. Annette had conducted exit interviews with many of the workers who had quit, and most had responded that they were leaving for "more money." However, Annette was well aware of the salary schedules of the other hospitals in the area. Saint Joseph's pay level was well in line overall and even higher than some others in a few categories.

Annette knew that a continued exodus of qualified workers would have a serious impact on patient care at Saint Joseph. She decided to propose a confidential questionnaire to be administered to all employees in the hospital in an attempt to identify reasons for the excessive turnover.

Employee attitudes revealed through human resource research can be of tremendous benefit to managers such as Annette Dommert as they attempt to determine the real reasons for high turnover rates and other indicators of employee dissatisfaction. Without this information, a situation may continue to worsen until the quality of goods and services seriously declines.

We begin this chapter by discussing the benefits of human resource research and the methods of inquiry in human resource research. Then, we describe the research process and quantitative methods in human resource research. Finally, we conclude with sections on evaluating the human resource function and how technology is affecting human resource management.

BENEFITS OF HUMAN RESOURCE RESEARCH

The human resource manager's job, as discussed in Chapter 1, is vastly different from only a few years ago. In order to contend with mounting responsibilities, the human resource manager has discovered that information derived from research is constantly required. **Human resource research** is the systematic study of a firm's human resources for the purpose of maximizing personal and organizational goal achievement.

Applications of human resource research are numerous and increasing rapidly. The potential benefits of sound human resource research are also numerous. Management has begun to realize the full significance of the human component on an organization's ability to achieve its goals. This enlightenment, however belated, has occurred at a time when the competitive nature of business makes it increasingly difficult to obtain and retain qualified individuals.

Specific applications of human resource research depend to a large extent on a firm's needs. As Table 19-1 shows, the type of research presently being conducted overlaps, but differences do exist. These variations reflect the size, goals, and specific problems of particular organizations.

Effective Management

Laws, government regulations, and judicial decisions have called into question many past HRM practices. Managers must now be prepared to prove that their employment decisions are based on valid requirements. However, as Walter Tornow, vice president of research and publications for The Center for Creative Leadership, states, "On the whole, government regulations have had a positive effect because they cause organizations to examine and document their practices in ways that heretofore were not deemed necessary for some."

Another reason for the increased need for human resource research relates to rapid changes in the composition of the workforce. Research is required to determine how the goals of these new workforce members can be integrated with those of the firm.

Largely because of increased educational opportunities, managers and nonmanagers have become more sophisticated in their employment expectations. To respond appropriately, managers may need to modify their approaches to HRM. Although a highly autocratic manager may have been successful in the past, a similar style today may quickly lead to resentment and lower productivity. Also, the organizational structure may need to be

TABLE 19-1
Use of Human Resource Research

COMPANY	RESEARCH AREA
Atlantic Richfield Company	■ Selection test validation Assessment center validation Survey research
Fleming Companies, Inc.	■ Specific emphasis on turnover, turnover reasons, turnover costs Identification of high-potential employees for accelerated development Impact of union contracts on compensation Improving performance appraisal
Control Data Corporation	■ Staffing, compensation, interviewing, performance appraisal, management training, surveys of employee attitudes, productivity enhancement, employee development, selection
Ashland Oil, Inc.	■ Selection at both the exempt and nonexempt levels and also in the early identification of people with potential to become high-level managers
Ford Motor Company	■ Selection, opinion surveys, career progress, performance appraisal, quality motivation, management potential, organization

modified. The means of identifying appropriate managerial styles and organizational structure will continue to be a major task of human resource research.

The nature of work itself has also been changing rapidly. This has caused firms to strive continuously to upgrade their workforces. One of management's most difficult tasks is to get employees to accept change resulting from new technology. The use of robotics in automobile assembly plants has created a tremendous need for retraining, for instance. The General Motors Saturn plant in Springhill, Tennessee, requires many new employee skills. It is not easy for people to accept the fact that their skills are no longer needed and that they must learn new skills. Research may indicate ways in which people may learn to accept change more readily and, thereby, continue to be productive members of the workforce.

Human Resource Planning, Recruitment, and Selection

Plans must be made to recruit, select, and retain productive employees. Each organization has a distinct personality, as does an individual. Thus, organizations must seek to find the best match between their needs and those of their employees. Research can help explain why an individual may be an excellent worker in one firm and a poor worker in another, even though the jobs seem to be similar.

Recruitment research is directed toward determining how individuals with high potential can be encouraged to apply for jobs with a company. Firms need to determine the most likely sources of qualified candidates for their jobs. It does little good to know the qualities that prospective employees should possess and yet not know where and how to recruit them.

The objective of employee selection research is to identify prospective employees with the greatest potential for success. As you might expect, the definition of a successful employee varies from organization to organization. This research often attempts to identify factors (such as background and experience, education, and test scores) that can be used to differentiate successful applicants from less successful ones.[1] Complicating these efforts are variations in the profiles of successful workers by geographic location and gender.

Human Resource Development

Research is also quite important in the area of human resource development. Studies may identify the employees who can benefit from training. For instance, a high error rate associated with certain employees might indicate the need for additional training.

Also, research into the usefulness of the training program may be needed: Are workers better prepared to do their jobs after training, or is the training an exercise in futility? Training and development is expensive, and its costs must be justified.

In addition, the type of training and development that is needed may be identified through human resource research. The productivity of different departments may suggest that certain managers benefit from leadership and communication training. Finally, an analysis of employee performance may suggest additional areas of training and development that are needed.

Compensation

Both actual and perceived inequities in the firm's compensation system can create problems. Managers must be able to identify actual inequities and correct them, as well as provide information to employees to help overcome misconceptions. In order to maintain a fair pay policy, many firms conduct extensive compensation surveys. In addition, in-house surveys are often conducted to determine employee attitudes regarding pay. Compensation research is widely used to identify potential problems before they get out of hand. For instance, if the supply and demand for skilled employees in the labor force is constantly changing, an organization's compensation program can rapidly become outdated and must, therefore, be closely monitored.

Employee and Labor Relations

Research in the area of employee and labor relations focuses primarily on areas that affect individual job performance. Some of this research may be needed to identify factors that will permit the firm to remain union-free. Research may show that internal factors, such as working conditions, may have a detrimental effect on employee productivity and job satisfaction. This type of information can prompt actions that would help an organization remain union-free. When problems are left unsolved, the worker may believe that the only remedy to the situation is to join the union. Continually monitoring factors that affect employee and labor relations will probably always prove beneficial to both the employee and the organization.

Safety and Health

The primary task of research in health and safety relates to the identification of potential problem areas. For instance, research may be conducted to determine the locations and causes of accidents. It also can be used to identify characteristics of workers prone to a higher rate of accidents. Accident patterns may be identified and changes recommended to prevent the occurrence of accidents. Health and safety concerns increased during the 1980s and will probably be the source of even more concern in the future. Therefore, human resource managers must make every attempt to identify health and safety problems and solve them as quickly as possible.

A GLOBAL PERSPECTIVE

Human resource research has expanded dramatically in the past few years. Recent research findings clearly indicate the main global human resource difficulties.[2] In a recent survey, company representatives were asked to name the "most important" issue related to global human resource management (see Table 19-2) and ultimately to corporate success. These twelve issues should probably be the primary focus of international human resource research in the future. However, the ultimate test of

TABLE 19-2
The Most Important Human Resource Issues

HUMAN RESOURCE ISSUE	PERCENTAGE OF RESPONDENTS
Selecting and training local managers	70
Generating companywide loyalty and motivation	70
Speaking and understanding local language and culture	66
Appraising the performances of managers abroad	65
Planning systematic manager development and succession	59
Hiring indigenous sales personnel	57
Compensating foreign managers	54
Hiring/training foreign technical employees	52
Selecting/training U.S. managers overseas	48
Dealing with unions and labor laws abroad	44
Promoting and transferring foreign managers	42
Compensating U.S. nationals abroad	42

Note: The total sample was 95 companies (manufacturing: 51; nonmanufacturing: 44; more profitable: 58; less profitable: 37).

Source: Adapted from Spencer Hayden, "Our Foreign Legions Are Faltering," *Personnel* 67 (August 1990): 42. Used with the permission of The Spencer Hayden Co.

the success of a global operation is the production of a quality product or service at a competitive price. Globally, the quality and cost of a product are determined largely by the effectiveness and efficiency of the production system and the people who run it. In order to be competitive globally, American firms must produce quality products at competitive prices. Manufacturing systems in the United States are now undergoing revitalization to assist American manufacturers in their attempt to be competitive in the global business environment of the next decade. Production systems that will allow American firms to be globally competitive will probably require adaptation to the most recent behavioral and technological changes. Adaptation to these changes will be even more complex overseas, which will present new challenges to human resource managers.

American managers are beginning to balance their capital and human investments to improve their production systems. Human resource managers must ensure that the human component of the organization contributes to productivity. Companies are beginning to follow and extend the Japanese method of worker involvement, which means greater human resource management involvement. American teamwork involves group members in management activities, such as determining the appropriate method of work and rating other group members' performance.[3]

GM Europe is a perfect example of a company that is working in a team environment and where the production system evolves around the concept of teamwork. GM is already the most efficient and profitable automaker in Europe. GM human resource managers recognize that people working in a true team environment is the key to productivity, but the production system must evolve in such a manner to enhance overall productivity. A recent GM Europe car, the Corsa, embodied the latest production and people reforms. The car was designed, engineered, and brought to market in just thirty-six months. The Corsa's design ensured that it was easier to assemble, improving quality and productivity. GM Europe is so successful because the focus is on people, teamwork, and a production system that enhances the productivity of all concerned.[4] Because of the need to compete globally, American firms must reenergize production systems by balancing their capital and human investments and by using new approaches to production. Human resource managers must take the lead in developing and utilizing the human component of these ever-evolving approaches to production.

METHODS OF INQUIRY IN HUMAN RESOURCE RESEARCH

The type of problem and the particular needs of the organization determine, to a large extent, the method of inquiry that will be used. Specific research methods that are particularly useful include the case study, the survey feedback method, and the experiment.

The Case Study

The **case study** is an investigation into the underlying causes of specific problems in a plant, a department, or a work group. The results of the research apply only to that particular set of problems and cannot be generalized. Typical problems that the case study method might be used to investigate include the following:

- an excessively high turnover rate at a particular plant
- a high absenteeism rate in a specific department
- a high accident rate at a certain building site
- low morale in a particular department
- the low number of minority group members in a certain plant
- the underlying reasons for a wildcat strike at a particular location

Naturally, there are many more situations in which the case study method may be appropriate. Although the results cannot be generalized, the results of such studies may suggest possible new management approaches. The human resource management example later in this chapter provides an illustration of a case study provided by an outside consultant for a regional medical center. In other situations, the firm's human resource manager or an HR specialist will conduct the research.

The Survey Feedback Method

A major function of human resource research is to determine periodically the attitudes of employees toward their jobs, pay, and supervision. Typically, this is done by means of survey questionnaires. Responses to questions may also reveal ways to improve productivity. Recall that Annette Dommert, in the example at the beginning of the chapter, is proposing that a confidential questionnaire be administered to all employees in the hospital. In the **survey feedback method**, anonymous questionnaires are used systematically to collect and measure employee attitudes. The Ford Motor Company uses the survey method to obtain the opinions of its salaried workers every other year. The results are published in Ford's in-house publication, *The American Road.*

Surveys may be either of the objective multiple-choice type or the scaled-response type that asks for degrees of agreement or disagreement (see Figure 19-1). Objective analysis of survey results often requires a more detailed study. There are many possible bases for comparison of survey results:

1. Section or department
2. Age
3. Gender
4. Seniority
5. Job level or degree of responsibility
6. Changes in attitudes from previous surveys
7. Comparison with other divisions, departments, or work groups
8. Comparison with a standardized score if a validated instrument is being used

The data become more meaningful to management when analyzed by various subgroups. A major point to consider is that survey responses often identify symptoms rather than causes. For instance, even if the compensation and benefits program is quite competitive, a low evaluation in this area (symptom) may reflect general dissatisfaction with management style rather than an inadequate compensation system. When surveys are administered, the researcher should avoid concentrating on isolated responses. Instead, the data should be viewed from a broader perspective, which may uncover a pattern or general trend. Collectively, the responses will likely reflect this trend if there are difficulties throughout the organization.

When surveys are used to identify employee attitudes and opinions, confidentiality of responses must be ensured.[5] Employees must believe that their specific responses will not be communicated to management. For this reason, outside consultants are often employed to administer the questionnaire. Even if the human resource professionals are completely ethical, employees may still perceive them as a tool of management. Rightly or wrongly,

Why did you decide to do what you are doing now?

a. Desire to aid or assist others
b. Influenced by another person or situation
c. Always wanted to be in this vocation
d. Lack of opportunity or interest in other vocational fields
e. Opportunities provided by this vocation
f. Personal satisfaction from doing this work

What do you like least about your job?

a. Nothing
b. Pay
c. Supervisor relations
d. Problems with fellow workers
e. Facilities
f. Paperwork and reports

Considering all aspects of your job, evaluate your compensation with regard to your contributions to the needs of the organization. Circle the number that best describes how you feel.

Pay Too Low		Pay Low		Pay Average		Pay Above Average		Pay Too High	
1	2	3	4	5	6	7	8	9	10

What are your feelings about overtime work requirements? Circle the number that best indicates how you feel.

	Unnecessary			Necessary on Occasion			Necessary		
1	2	3	4	5	6	7	8	9	10

FIGURE 19-1 Examples of Multiple-Choice and Scaled-Response Survey Questions

employees may always wonder whether the human resource department will succumb to management pressure to reveal specific employee responses.

Confidentiality means more than merely omitting a worker's name on the questionnaire. Even in a large firm, numerous sections consist of only a small number of employees. Or in a large department, a characteristic of a particular worker may make identification easy. For instance, a department might have only one woman in it. Protection of such a person's confidentiality is crucial to obtaining accurate results. The researcher must constantly be alert to these situations and be prepared to consolidate groups when necessary to preserve anonymity.

Survey results must be communicated back to the affected groups. Employees need to see what their collective responses were. And if surveys are to be taken seriously, management must act on the results. When survey results are communicated to management, it is often best for each department or section head to be contacted individually. For instance, if the survey suggests that problems exist in the marketing department, the department head will likely be more receptive to criticism if his or her peers are not listening. Just as workers do not like to be disciplined in the presence of their coworkers, managers do not like to receive survey results in the presence of others. Better results are typically obtained when the data are discussed with each person or group separately.

At times, surveying every employee is not feasible because of time or cost restraints. **Sampling** is a process in which only a portion of the total group is studied, and conclusions are drawn for the entire group. For example, assume that the total number of workers in a firm is 5,000. The time, effort, and cost necessary to survey all 5,000 workers may be prohibitive. If so, the researcher will probably decide to survey a smaller sample group. For example, a sample size of 500 workers may be deemed representative of the entire group. Conclusions are based on the responses from the employees comprising the sample and then applied to the entire group of 5,000 employees.

The Experiment

A method of inquiry that involves the manipulation of certain variables while others are held constant is referred to as an **experiment**. This method utilizes a control group and an experimental group. The control group continues to operate as usual, whereas selected variables are manipulated for the experimental group. For instance, a manager may want to determine the effect that a new training program will have on productivity. The control group would continue to perform tasks in the conventional manner. The experimental group would receive the new training. The assumption is that any change in productivity in the experimental group results from the training. On the surface, the experiment appears to be an excellent means of inquiry. However, isolating the many interrelated variables affecting people and their performance can be extremely difficult.

THE RESEARCH PROCESS

Taking a systematic approach to human resource research is important. The most fruitful research is accomplished by following a logical process, such as that shown in Figure 19-2.

FIGURE 19-2
The Human Resource Research Process

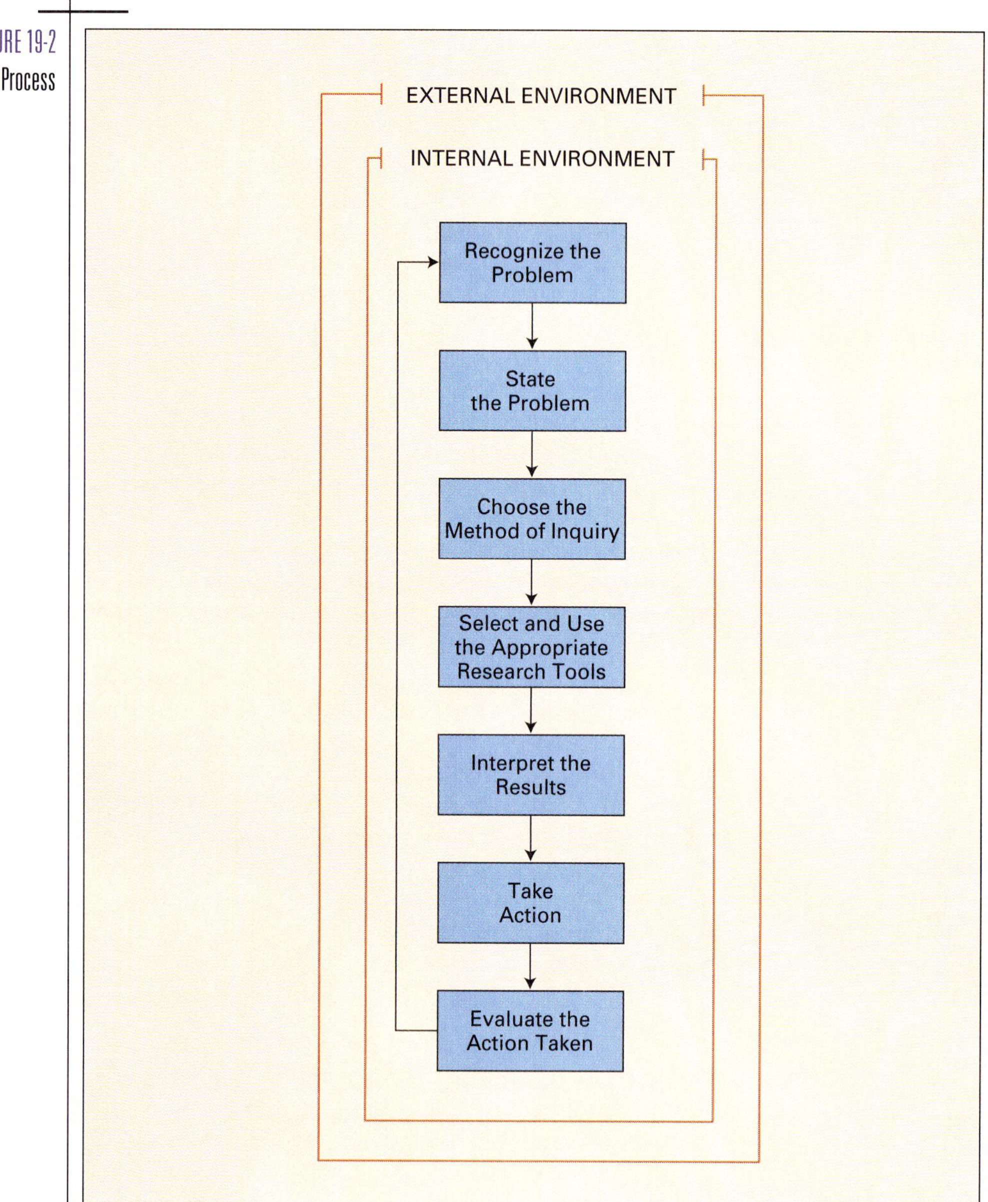

Recognize the Problem

One of the most difficult tasks in the research process is to recognize that a problem exists. For instance, at what point does absenteeism or turnover become excessive? A certain amount of turnover may be healthy for an organization. However, explaining away a potential problem is often convenient. A manager may state, "Even though turnover is high, we really don't have a problem because those people didn't fit into the organization anyway." Such a comment would lead a researcher to suspect that this manager may not be

HRM IN ACTION

—WHY AREN'T THEY HAPPY?

Bob Stephens, president of Queens Manufacturing Company, and Mary Bushnell, the company's human resource director, were engaged in a serious conversation that could have a major impact on the future of the firm. "Mary," said Bob, "I've been hearing rumblings of discontent throughout the organization. For some reason that I can't figure out, people at Queens just don't appear to be as happy as they have been in the past. And it isn't just isolated instances. There is a different attitude everywhere. Any ideas as to how we can determine what's going on so that we can correct the problem?"

If you were Mary, how would you respond?

open to problem recognition. In actuality, the problem may be caused by an inadequate selection process, insufficient managerial training, or any number of other reasons. Or, as the manager suggests, there might not be a problem. Regardless of the situation, openness on the part of the manager is the cornerstone of problem recognition.

State the Problem

The next step in the process is to clearly state the purpose of the research. The major hurdle to overcome is that the problem—not the symptoms—must be identified. As you might expect, this can be difficult. For instance, a manager might maintain that the cause of declining production is low pay when, in fact, the real reason is inadequate supervision or insufficient training. Research may determine that dictatorial supervisors have been exerting so much pressure on employees that they could care less about productivity. If the manager attempted to solve the morale problem through such means as increasing benefits, it is unlikely that conditions would improve. A clear definition of the problem is essential for effective research.

Choose the Method of Inquiry

The method of inquiry chosen depends to a large extent on the nature of the research. The methods of inquiry previously described—the case study, the survey, and the experiment—are all valuable. However, most human resource research involves either the case study or the survey method.

Select and Use the Appropriate Research Tools

Numerous quantitative tools are available for use by the human resource researcher. Managers do not have to be experts in mathematics and statistical theory in order to take advantage of these tools; however, managers do need to know the following:

- availability of quantitative tools
- circumstances under which these tools should be used
- strengths and weaknesses of each method
- how to interpret the results

The selection of a tool depends on the particular purpose for which the research is being conducted.

Interpret the Results

The person closest to the problem should participate in interpreting the results. When outsiders attempt to do this, they often arrive at strange conclusions. For instance, the survey may suggest that major dissatisfaction exists in the engineering department. A person not close to the situation might mistakenly identify the problem as one of inadequate supervision. Actually, the engineers may be voicing dissatisfaction with the condition of their facilities.

Take Action

The most difficult phase of the research process is to take action based on research findings. The results may have identified areas in which changes need to be made. The human resource manager now becomes the catalyst to convince line management that a change is necessary. Many times, this task is quite difficult. Telling a manager that his or her managerial style is causing excessive turnover can be an awkward task. However, the benefits of research are realized only when action is taken to resolve the problem that has been identified.

Evaluate the Action Taken

No research effort is complete until the action has been evaluated. Evaluation requires an objective assessment of whether the action has solved the problem and if so, how. Recall that Figure 19-2 shows a feedback loop from evaluation to problem recognition. Determining whether the problem has been adequately solved will assist in future research efforts. Revisions may be necessary or the entire research approach may need to be rethought, but the information gained through a well-conceived research project almost always proves useful.

QUANTITATIVE METHODS IN HUMAN RESOURCE RESEARCH

Numerous quantitative methods are available to those who conduct human resource research. Most of these tools are available for use on both mainframe and personal computers. Correlation analysis, regression analysis, discriminant analysis, and time series analysis are described here.

Correlation Analysis

Often a researcher would like to know the relative strength of the relationships between variables. Correlation analysis measures the degree of association that exists between two or more variables. For instance, is there a

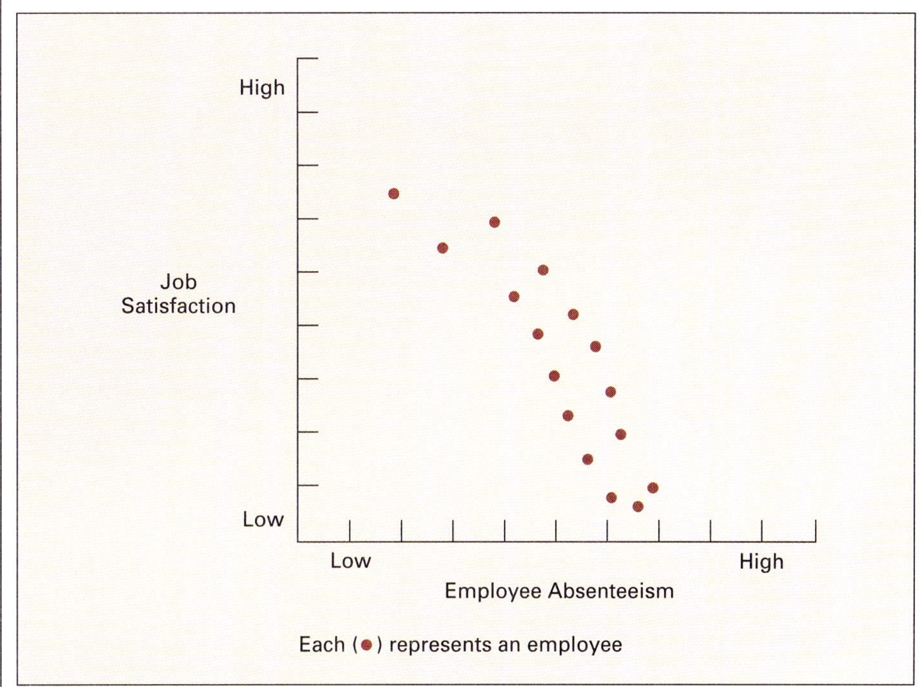

FIGURE 19-3
The Negative Correlation between Job Satisfaction and Employee Absenteeism at a Particular Firm

relationship between job satisfaction and employee absenteeism? Figure 19-3 shows a high *negative* relationship between job satisfaction and employee absenteeism. As job satisfaction goes down, absenteeism goes up. (Employees who have a low level of job satisfaction tend to be absent more often.) Figure 19-4 shows a high *positive* correlation between the level of employee education and productivity: The higher the education level is, the greater the productivity. These correlations are based on data from one firm. They might not hold for another firm and, thus, cannot be universally applied. The benefits of correlation analysis are considerable, but this method must be used with caution. A correlation can be deceptive when the relationship does not reflect cause and effect. A high but meaningless correlation may exist. Human resource managers should be alert to this potential problem and not make decisions based on erroneous interpretations.

Regression Analysis

As discussed in Chapter 5, *regression analysis* is a technique that has proven useful in human resource planning. It has also proven beneficial in human resource research. As previously stated, the purpose of regression analysis is to utilize the relation between two or more quantitative variables so that one variable can be predicted from the other, or others. For instance, a manager might want to determine whether employee productivity can be estimated from educational attainment (refer to Figure 19-4). In regression analysis terminology, the productivity level is referred to as the *dependent* variable. In this example, since there is only one independent variable, the process is re-

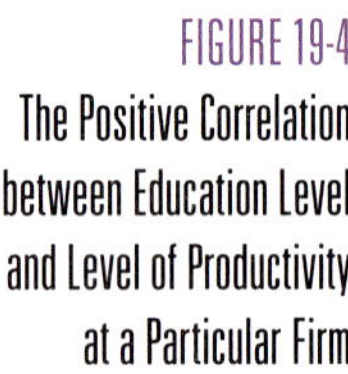

FIGURE 19-4
The Positive Correlation between Education Level and Level of Productivity at a Particular Firm

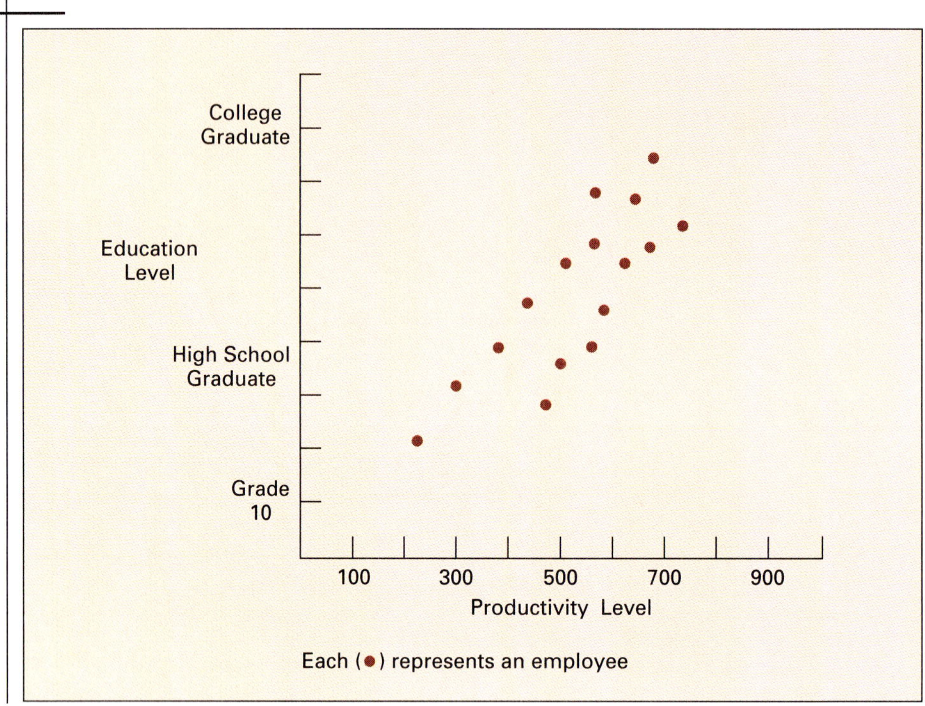

ferred to as *simple linear* regression. The use of two or more independent variables is termed *multiple* regression.

When regression analysis is used in human resource research, some possible dependent variables might be the following:

- satisfaction level of employees
- length of employment of employees
- productivity level of employees
- accident rate of employees

Employment data that might be used as the independent variable include these factors:

- background and biographical data
- work history with the firm
- personal goals and aspirations
- test scores

The researcher might attempt to determine through regression analysis which of the independent variables aid in differentiating between more productive and less productive workers. The regression model developed using these variables may help the manager to identify prospective employees who are likely to become successful workers, thereby improving selection decisions. The model's accuracy must be validated through other statistical means; however, if the model proves appropriate, it can be very useful in the selection process.

Discriminant Analysis

The purpose of discriminant analysis is to identify factors that differentiate between two or more groups in a population. When two-group discriminant analysis is used, an attempt might be made to identify factors that differentiate between these groups:

- satisfied from less satisfied employees
- long-term from short-term employees
- productive from less productive employees
- accident-prone from less accident-prone employees

Only the imagination of the researcher limits the factors that can be used. Some of the factors that the researcher might use to differentiate between two groups include background and biographical data, work history with the firm, personal goals and aspirations, and test scores.

For instance, suppose the researcher was attempting to determine whether certain background or biographical factors differentiated satisfied workers from less satisfied workers. As with regression analysis, the level of satisfaction becomes the dependent variable. However, unlike regression analysis, individuals in the two groups are identified as either satisfied or less satisfied. Throughout the use of discriminant analysis, independent variables capable of distinguishing between the two selected groups are identified. The mechanics of discriminant analysis also permit the researcher to determine the reliability of the model developed.

Time Series Analysis

A technique that has proven quite helpful in making projections is time series analysis. Time series analysis is a variation of regression analysis in which the independent variable is expressed in units of time. As in regression analysis, both a dependent variable and an independent variable are required. However, the independent variable is now associated with time and the dependent variable is associated with demand. When the number of employees required in a company is closely associated with demand for the firm's product, time series analysis may prove useful in forecasting the organization's human resource needs. Using the same general mathematical procedure as in regression analysis, a time series equation can be derived and estimates of future demand calculated.

HUMAN RESOURCE RESEARCH: AN ILLUSTRATION

In order to illustrate how human resource research may be used in an organization, this section presents an actual example. At the firm's request, its name will not be identified. However, the techniques used and the benefits achieved are factual. The organization, a regional medical center in the Southwest, had experienced rapid growth and the accompanying "growing pains." The human resource director and the hospital administrator recognized that problems were developing and called in an outside consultant. The consultant was to work with them in identifying and solving those problems before they became critical.

First, the consultant talked with numerous employees to get a general view of the situation. Hesitancy of employees to talk about certain subjects and their apparent nervousness during the informal interviews suggested the existence of problems.

The next phase of the research project involved developing a survey tailored specifically for the hospital. Sample questions, shown in Figure 19-5,

What do you like most about your job?

a. Helping or providing service for others
b. Learning opportunities
c. Personal satisfaction
d. Being around people
e. The work you perform at this hospital at this job
f. Nothing
g. Other (specify)
h. Other (specify)

What do you like least about your job?

a. Nothing
b. Pay
c. Supervisor relations
d. Problems with fellow workers
e. Facilities
f. Paperwork and reports
g. Patient-related problems
h. Doctor-related problems
i. Other (specify)
j. Other (specify)

How would you describe your overall working environment? Circle the number that best describes how you feel.

Extremely Frustrating		Frustrating		Acceptable		Above Average		Excellent	
1	2	3	4	5	6	7	8	9	10

What do you think of strikes in the health care field? Circle the number that indicates how you feel.

Strongly Favor		Favor		Neutral		Opposed		Strongly Opposed	
1	2	3	4	5	6	7	8	9	10

What do you think about the system of giving pay increases at this hospital? Circle the number that best describes how you feel.

Very Bad		Poor		Satisfied		Good		Excellent	
1	2	3	4	5	6	7	8	9	10

Considering all aspects of your job, evaluate your compensation with regard to your contributions to the needs of the hospital. Circle the number that best describes how you feel.

Pay Too Low		Pay Low		Pay Average		Pay Above Average		Pay Too High	
1	2	3	4	5	6	7	8	9	10

FIGURE 19-5 Sample Survey Questions

were developed, with topics ranging from managerial style to compensation. Administering the questionnaire to all hospital employees and maintaining each participant's confidentiality were both crucial steps. The hospital administrator's role was to notify the employees of the survey. From that point on, the employees would have no further contact with any member of the administration regarding the survey.

Groups of employees met with the consultant in the room where the survey was to be administered. He explained the survey's purpose and then assured the employees of confidentiality. Employees were told that only summary results would be provided to the administration. At this point, it became obvious that problems did exist. Many employees wanted to know in detail the relationship between the consultant and the administration. Continuous assurances of confidentiality had to be given. Because of the nature of hospital work, the researcher had to administer the questionnaire over a forty-eight-hour period. To reinforce confidentiality, the respondents were told that they should put their completed questionnaires in blank envelopes, so that they could not be identified. Some employees even chose to mail their responses to the consultant rather than risk having the questionnaire get lost at the hospital.

The next step entailed analyzing the results. Data from each employee were entered into a computer and analyzed for the entire hospital and for each of its departments. Statistics for the entire hospital proved inconclusive. However, when the survey results were evaluated by departments, some obvious problems began to surface. Employees in certain departments appeared to be more unhappy than workers in other departments. For instance, the levels of satisfaction in the radiology and lab departments appeared to be consistently below the satisfaction level of the hospital in general. Although not as negative, job satisfaction among nurses and aides was also below the hospital average. Figure 19-6 shows the summary of responses by department regarding overall working environment.

At this point, however, only symptoms had been uncovered. Now came the need for identification of specific problems. The results of the survey were presented to each department head individually. They reviewed the results, discussed what the symptoms revealed, and participated in the identification of problems.

The analysis of the radiology department provides an excellent illustration of the difference between the identification of symptoms and the identification of problems. The hospital had experienced rapid growth during the previous few years, and while other departments had increased staff to handle the increased workload, the radiology department had not. This placed considerable pressure on the employees in the department. A mistake made in this department could have serious consequences for patients. Also, questioning of workers revealed that the salary level of the department had not kept pace with radiology departments in nearby hospitals. The combination of these two factors—a department under pressure and an unreasonable salary level—resulted in considerable job dissatisfaction. The cause of the dissatisfaction had now been determined. The same procedure was used in the other departments in which employees had expressed low job satisfaction.

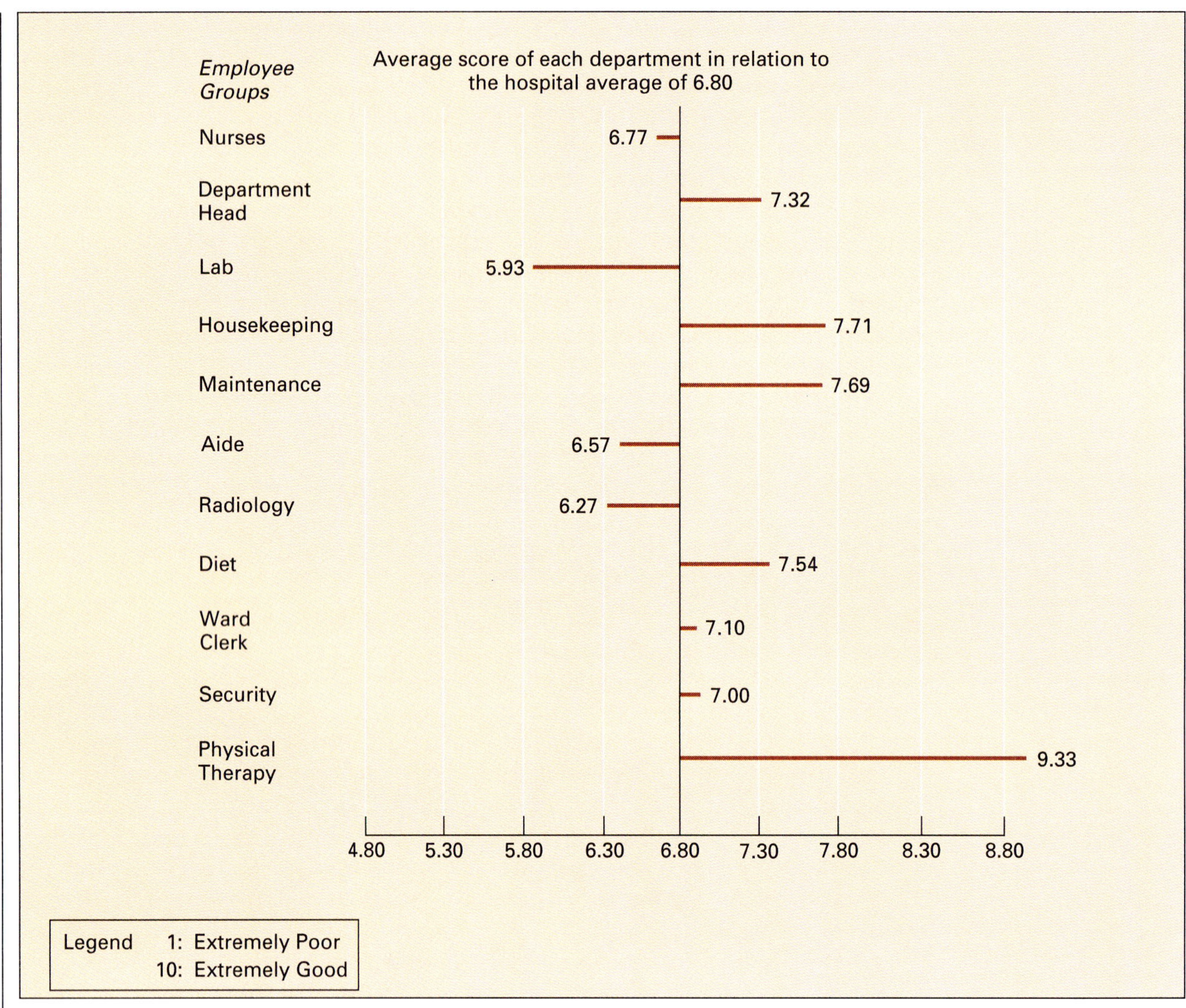

FIGURE 19-6 Descriptions of Overall Working Environment

The consultant was now able to provide the hospital administrator not only with the survey results but also with some sound recommendations. Suggestions for improvement were made for each department, as well as for the entire hospital, including these two steps:

1. Implementation of a management training program emphasizing communication skills, leadership, motivation, and other human relation techniques.
2. Reevaluation of the hospital's compensation program, including reacquainting employees with their benefits package, clarifying the method of granting pay increases, and evaluating new benefits.

The timing of the research and the resulting implementation of the recommendations later proved to be crucial. Within a year, a major attempt at unionizing the hospital was made, but it failed. The research study, which identified human resource problems and proposed solutions, was credited as the major factor in preparing the hospital for its successful efforts to remain union-free.[6]

EVALUATING THE HUMAN RESOURCE MANAGEMENT FUNCTION

The success of any organization depends not only on the formulation and execution of superb plans but also on the continuous evaluation of progress toward the accomplishment of specified objectives. For an organization as a whole, evaluation may be performed in terms of profitability ratios, sales increases, market penetration, and a host of other factors. For individual functional units within the organization, such as the human resource department, evaluation may be more difficult. Some of the perceived obstacles to evaluating the effectiveness of HR departments may be seen in Figure 19-7. Human resource

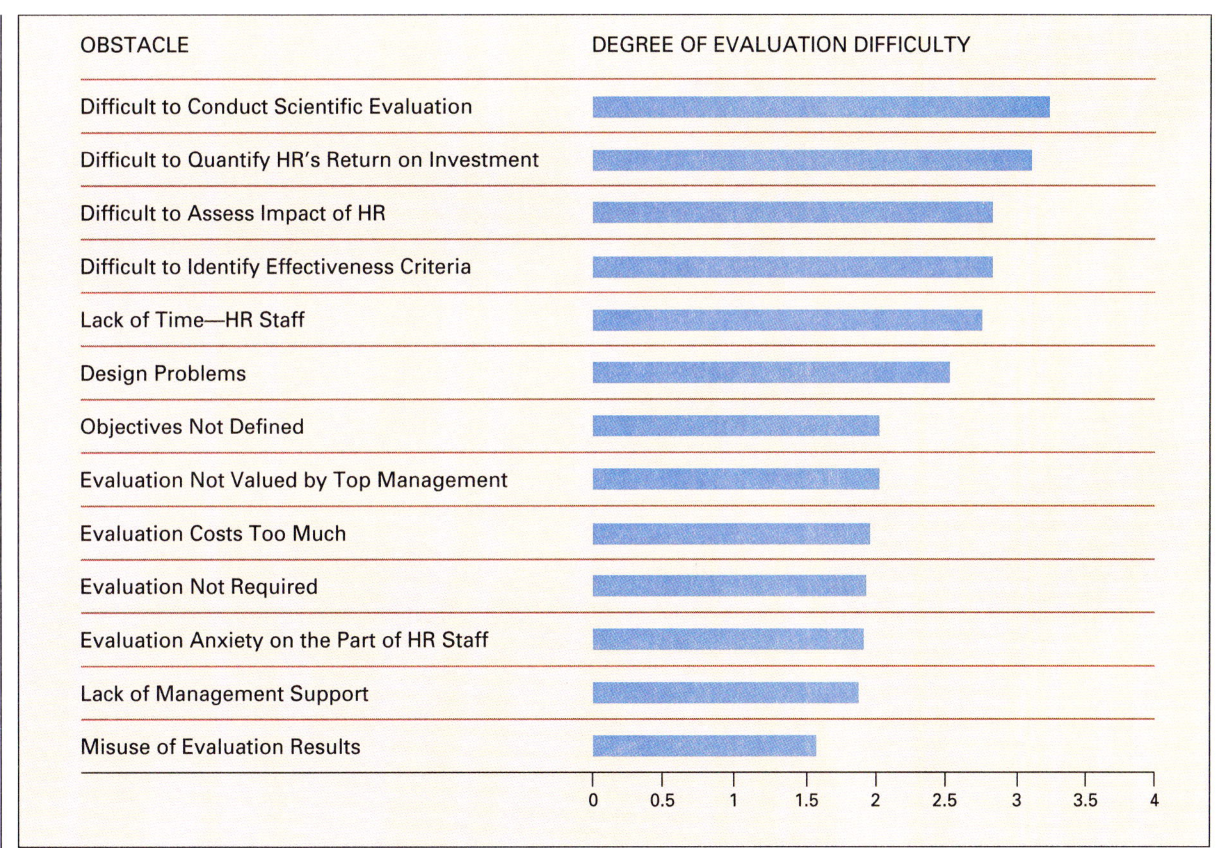

FIGURE 19-7 **Perceived Obstacles to Evaluating the Effectiveness of HR Departments**

Note: 1 = little difficulty and 5 = extreme difficulty

Source: Margaret E. Cashman and James C. McElroy, "Evaluating the HR Function," *HRMagagine* 36 (January 1991): 73. Reprinted with the permission from *HRMagazine* (formerly *Personnel Administrator*), published by the Society for Human Resource Management, Alexandria, VA.

professionals need to make a stronger effort in convincing upper management of the value of their units to the overall mission of the organization.[7]

How should an organization go about evaluating its human resource management function? Are there particular measures or indicators that reveal how well this function is meeting its responsibilities and supporting the organization's efforts to reach its objectives? Two basic methods may be used to evaluate human resource management activities: checklists and quantitative measures.

The checklist approach poses a number of questions that can be answered either *yes* or *no*. This method is concerned with determining whether important activities have been recognized and, if so, whether they are being performed. Essentially, the checklist is an evaluation in terms of what should be done and the extent to which it is being done. Some typical human resource checklist questions are shown in Table 19-3. The more *yes* answers there are, the better the evaluation; *no* answers indicate areas or activities where follow-up or additional work is needed to increase HRM's effectiveness. Organizations deciding to use this evaluation approach will undoubtedly come up with many other questions to ask. The checklist method is purely an internal evaluation device. It is not a vehicle for comparing one company with another.

The other method for evaluating the performance of human resource activities is a quantitative one. It relies on the accumulation of various types of numerical data and the calculation of certain ratios from them. Numerical data are useful primarily as an indicator of activity levels and trends. Ratios show results that are important in themselves but that also reveal (when maintained over a period of time) trends that may be even more important.

In some instances, quantitative measures may be used for external comparisons with other organizations. However, since very few performance standards exist for the HRM function, external comparisons should always

TABLE 19-3
Typical Human Resource Checklist Questions

- Are all legally mandated reports submitted to requiring agencies on time?
- Have formalized procedures and methods been developed for conducting job analysis?
- Are human resource requirements forecasts made at least annually?
- Is the recruiting process effectively integrated with human resource planning?
- Does the application form conform to applicable legal and affirmative action standards?
- Are all employees appraised at least annually?
- Are skills inventories maintained on all employees?
- Are career opportunities communicated clearly to all employees?

TABLE 19-4
Examples of Quantitative Human Resource Management Measures

- Women and minorities selection ratio
- Women and minorities promotion ratio
- Women and minorities termination ratio
- Minority and women hiring percentage
- Minority and women workforce percentage
- Requirements forecast compared to actual human resource needs
- Availability forecast compared to actual availability of human resources
- Average recruiting cost per applicant
- Average recruiting cost per employee hired
- Percentage of positions filled internally
- Average testing cost per applicant
- Percentage of required appraisals actually completed
- Percentage of employees rated in highest performance category
- Percentage of appraisals appealed
- Turnover percentage
- New hire retention percentage
- Percentage of new hires lost

be interpreted with care. For example, the area in which the amount of external comparative data is probably greatest is employee turnover. While it may be tempting to evaluate an organization's turnover in terms of the "industry average" or by size of workforce, such comparisons may be meaningless. There is just too much variation in the factors that affect a specific organization's turnover, such as the nature of the local labor market, the number of long-time employees, the ability of the firm to pay competitive rates, the company's reputation as an employer, and so on.

One measure that can truly be considered a standard is the four-fifths or 80-20 rule, which measures the selection rate of women and minorities against other employees. Generally, this ratio should approximate 80 percent. But even so, there are exceptions to this standard because of the specific situations that organizations face. In short, although quantitative data may be somewhat useful for external comparisons with similar companies, they are probably most helpful in establishing internal baselines (frames of reference) and showing the direction of movement from those baselines.[8] Some examples of quantitative measures for human resource management are listed in Table 19-4.

TECHNOLOGY AFFECTING HUMAN RESOURCE MANAGEMENT[9]

Technological advances in computer hardware and software occur virtually every day. These developments can improve human resource management and raise employee productivity. However, it is impossible to foresee all the new uses for each technological breakthrough. Certainly, managers must be aware of these innovations and their capabilities. Another issue human resource managers must deal with is the rapid rate of technological change. Prior to 1980, significant technological changes occurred every three to five years. Today, major developments are delivered every twelve to eighteen months, and computer systems are now considered evolutionary items as opposed to capital resources. Employees are experiencing changing systems more often than ever before and must continually learn new systems.[10] Still, as an executive for United Services Automobile Association (USAA) noted, even during tough economic times, technological changes must be tracked to maintain a competitive edge.[11]

Application and Communication Hardware and Software

Several types of existing software continue to affect human resource management. This software includes data communication, word processing, computer graphics, spreadsheets, decision support systems, and database management.

Data Communication. The sending of computer data over some form of communication medium, such as phone lines, is referred to as **data communication**. This form of communication is becoming increasingly important in the business world. Caterpillar, Inc., owns its own communications satellite and places a heavy emphasis on advanced data communication to better serve its global market.[12] Human resource managers can transmit documents or messages over phone lines and eliminate wasted time and potential misunderstandings, thus facilitating decision making. For example, prior to a teleconference, it is often useful to utilize electronic mail so that everyone involved can become familiar with the exact nature of the discussion before the conference begins.

Electronic mail users have the capability to schedule a meeting for an entire work group, automatically send messages to meeting attendees, and even check spelling. The use of facsimile (fax) machines to copy a document and send it electronically to another location has been revitalized by faster, lower cost personal computer systems. Cellular radio is another important communications medium for mobile voice and data communications.

In fact, the number of cellular network subscribers (voice and data) is expected to number 22 million in 1996.[13]

Word Processing. A computer application that permits an operator to create and edit written material is referred to as **word processing**. Word processing allows simplified editing of manuscripts and correspondence. For example, inserting a new paragraph at the beginning of a ten-page manuscript no longer requires retyping the entire document. Word processing allows managers to work more efficiently. For example, a manager can type a memo, edit it on the screen, and, with a few commands, print it out or route it to several recipients using electronic mail. Word processing has become one of today's most significant communication enhancement tools. It allows human resource managers to develop sensitive documents, such as workforce reduction plans or performance appraisal reports, without risking a breach of security.

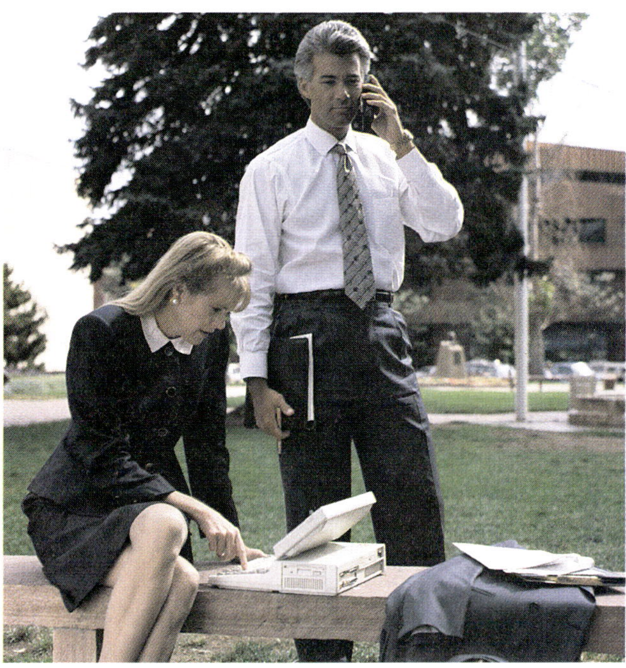

Cellular radio is an important communications medium for mobile voice and data communications.

Computer Graphics. "A picture is worth a thousand words." This adage is certainly applicable to the use of computer graphics. Managers can now use computer programs to produce various kinds of graphs and charts in both black and white and color. These graphics represent a large amount of data reduced to a single image. Human resource managers frequently present data graphically because this method often illustrates a message much more effectively than simple text could.

Spreadsheets. Spreadsheet programs provide a column-row matrix on which numbers or words can be entered, stored, and used for calculations. Predefined statistical, financial, and mathematical functions allow the user to quickly and easily answer *what if* questions. Spreadsheet analysis is particularly beneficial in an activity such as human resource planning.

Decision Support Systems. Computer departments are often backed up with demands for urgently needed information. To overcome this problem, a manager can acquire a **decision support system (DSS)**, an information system that allows users to process and retrieve information quickly. Normally, DSSs are sophisticated database systems capable of retrieving, displaying, and processing a wide variety of information. Graphics, simulation, modeling, and quantitative analysis are also typically available through a DSS. Obviously, DSSs can be very useful in human resource planning.

Database Management. Information subsystems are commonly developed for accounting, office management, manufacturing, marketing, and human resource departments. Often the data in progress in these subsystems are considered to be separate and distinct, resulting in a tremendous amount of redundant data. For example, the accounting subsystem would normally contain the names and Social Security numbers of all employees—and so would the human resource files. The purpose of **database management** is to minimize such redundancies. The term, thus, refers to the integration of information subsystems in order to reduce the duplication of information, effort, and cost and to provide controlled access to this information. For example, when Toyota sought to staff its manufacturing plant in Georgetown, Kentucky, more than 60,000 people applied. An intensive eight-phase hiring process was used and monitored through a computer tracking system.[14]

Teleconferencing

Partly because of the high cost of business travel—in terms of both time and money—teleconferencing is becoming increasingly popular. **Teleconferencing** is a method of conducting or participating in multiparty discussions by telephone or videophone. Teleconferencing may become a major means of improving managerial communication and productivity. Such systems allow human resource managers to resolve many problems without ever meeting in person with the other parties. AT&T's Personal Video System provides a 3 inch by 3 inch window on computer screens to permit desktop videoconferencing characterized as "notes gone visual." Teleconferencing is more expensive than electronic mail, but John Hamilton of Midwest Power Systems in Des Moines, Iowa, justifies the expense in terms of travel payback alone.[15] It has been estimated that videoconferencing will replace 25 percent of all business travel by 2010.

Voice Mail

Voice mail records spoken messages electronically and stores them for delivery to the recipient at a later time. When a voice mail system is used, an individual gains access to his or her account by dialing a special telephone number and providing a password and user-identification number. The user may then listen to any new messages, replay old messages, eliminate messages, and/or record messages for others. Managers can place confidential information in the system and know that the message will be received in the exact manner that it was sent. Voice mail is useful when human resource managers are dealing with sensitive matters, such as layoffs, and want to avoid phone conversations that could be overheard by others.

Expert Systems

An **expert system** is a system that uses knowledge about a narrowly defined, complex area to act as a consultant to a human.[16] In some instances, an organization may rely significantly upon the knowledge of one or more individuals in particular areas that can be captured in an expert system.[17] This captured expertise may then be used for training or may be disseminated throughout the organization for other employees to use. Mrs. Fields Cookies, Inc., uses an expert system to develop a profile of prospective applicants that is compared with the desired employee profile, and reports the results to each of its store managers.[18] Other typical expert systems in the area of human resource management contain data associated with employee performance evaluation, education scheduling, and employee benefits.

Multimedia

Multimedia is a computer application that produces presentations combining automation, stereo sound, full-motion video, and graphics. Users are immediately drawn to these presentations, which makes multimedia very helpful for sales presentations and training and development. Lotus Development Corporation introduced a multimedia version of 1-2-3 that placed all of its program documentation on disk, including interactive instructional "movies."[19] American Airlines uses multimedia to train thousands of employees annually. Human resource managers can incorporate photographs, voice, and document images into database files. A manager can access an employee's photograph, Social Security card, and signed year-end appraisals.[20] In California, kiosks (electronic bulletin boards) are being used to search job opportunities and order birth certificates. To ensure security, the machine reads the magnetic stripe on participants' driver's licenses.[21]

The state of Texas installed multimedia kiosks in shopping malls and grocery stores to provide public information and governmental services. Info/Texas kiosks allow the public to search state and national job banks, retrieve unemployment insurance eligibility information and applications, learn about state labor laws, and get information on job retraining service programs. The kiosks provide full-motion video and bilingual audio and graphics.[22]

Information Utilities/On-Line Services

Commercial communications systems offer the human resource manager a wide range of research tools. Popular information utilities, such as America Online, CompuServe Information Service, and Prodigy, provide a gateway to such data as business demographics, census information, and government publications, as well as popular periodicals such as *Time* and *Business Week*.[23] Another resource is the Internet, a global network used by an estimated 20 million to 25 million users. Human resource managers can access services that include video clips of company facilities or a welcoming message from the chairman. Additional information can be made available regarding product lines, sites, and local lifestyles.[24] Online Career Center, a nonprofit operation listing 10,000 to 12,000 jobs, is one of the most visited locations on the Internet, receiving about 2 million accesses per month.[25]

Human resource managers seeking to hire minority information technology professionals may use private on-line services to access databases and post jobs electronically. Companies, such as IBM, Amoco Corp., AT&T, Kraft General Foods, and Allstate Insurance Co., use these databases, which hold thousands of names of minority candidates.[26]

Virtual HR

Today's human resource managers are faced with the need to cut administrative costs while administering increasingly complex benefits and training programs and regulations. Many companies are using technology, in the form of kiosks and interactive telephone systems, to give employees direct access to human resource information systems that perform routine tasks. Benefits consultant Steve McCormick refers to this trend as *virtual HR*. He cites examples of Apple Computer Inc., Bell Atlantic Corp., and Becton Dickinson & Co. using systems to permit employees to enroll in and monitor 401(k) plans, enroll in benefits programs, and change information about dependents. Merck & Co. uses 25 kiosks to administer its flexible benefits program.[27] Stonybrook Laboratories, Inc., replaced its lobby receptionist with a multimedia kiosk. The kiosk greets visitors and provides such information as safety details, lab data, and employment data, including a company organizational chart. For example, if a visitor is advised to see the safety coordinator, the coordinator's picture is displayed along with directions to her office. If she is unavailable, the visitor is provided with a personnel chart to find another person in the same department.[28]

Virtual Office/Mobile Computing

Mobile computing devices (portable, laptop, notebook, and subnotebook computers) are becoming increasingly common, as well as docking stations that hook such devices to the primary microcomputer network in the office. AT&T's Virtual Office Program, which began in 1991, supplied its commercial account executive with fax-modem-equipped notebook computers, portable printers, telephone calling cards, and even some cellular phones. AT&T managed to eliminate assigned offices and lowered office space, cutting real estate costs by 25 percent.[29] Xerox Corp. gave its sales force notebook computers and pagers, resulting in reduced office space needs and more time spent with customers.[30]

Client/Server System

Client/server systems combine the strengths of various types of computers to split and deliver computer applications and data at reduced costs with greater reliability. These systems utilize networked personal computers (clients) and minicomputers or mainframe computers (server).[31] Eli Lilly and Company, for instance, handles payroll for 15,000 employees and 8,000 retirees on a client/server system.[32]

Groupware

Groupware is software that enables people to work together in groups and assists in decision making, workflow, and work management. Decision-making groupware provides structure for discussing, analyzing, and problem solving by utilizing sophisticated applications of group theory and group dynamics. Activities supported include brainstorming, voting and alternate evaluation, and policy formulation. Workflow groupware helps in managing documents, processes, and information flows throughout an organization. This software enables users to set up routing systems and to establish action and response rules with triggers that release when particular events occur. Work-management groupware assists individuals and teams in communicating (even to the extent of screening out junk electronic mail), scheduling meetings, and managing tasks.[33]

SUMMARY

Human resource research is aimed at maximizing personal and organizational goal achievement. This research should be systematic, with specific applications depending to a large extent on a firm's particular needs. From time to time, all aspects of the HRM functions have needs for research.

The seven basic steps in the research process are (1) recognizing the problem, (2) stating the problem, (3) choosing the method of inquiry, (4) selecting and using the appropriate research tools, (5) interpreting the results, (6) taking action, and (7) evaluating the action taken. Also, numerous quantitative tools are available for use by human resource managers. In addition to the research process and the various quantitative tools, there are the two basic methods of evaluating human resource management activities: checklists and quantitative measures.

Technological advances in computer hardware and software occur virtually every day. These developments can improve human resource management and raise employee productivity. Multimedia is a computer application that produces presentations combining automation, stereo sound, full-motion video, and graphics. Human resource managers are faced with the need to cut administrative costs while administering increasingly complex benefits and training programs and regulations. Many companies are using technology, in the form of kiosks and interactive telephone systems, to give employees direct access to human resource information systems that perform routine tasks.

QUESTIONS FOR REVIEW

1. Describe the general methods of inquiry available for use by the human resource researcher.
2. Why would the experiment rarely be used as a means of inquiry in human resource management?
3. Why has management begun to realize that organizations can benefit from effective human resource research?
4. Briefly describe each of the following quantitative tools as they may be used in human resources:
   a. *Correlation analysis*
   b. *Regression analysis*
   c. *Discriminant analysis*
   d. *Time series analysis*
5. Explain how the human resource management function may be evaluated.
6. Identify and define technological advances affecting human resource management.

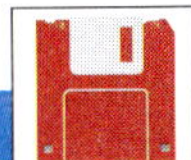

HRM SIMULATION

Your team will have the opportunity to purchase industry research that will aid you in the decision-making process. The surveys that are available include: (1) Industry Average Quality, Morale, Grievances, and Absenteeism; (2) Industry Average and Local Comparable Wage Rates; and (3) Industry Average Training, Safety and Quality Budgets, and Number of Organizations with Employee Participation Programs. If you need this information to help you make better decisions, it may be worth the cost.

ABC VIDEO CASE

QUALITY AND W.E. DEMING TAPE 2, NUMBER 10

Although W.E. Deming has passed away, people are still listening to what he said. Fifty years ago, Deming went to Japan to teach that quality equals success and profit. Making quality products results in satisfied and loyal customers. And quality drastically reduces waste. According to Deming, "You should become partners with your suppliers. If you spend money for quality supplies, fewer products will be defective, and the need for quality inspectors will be reduced. Quality and products will rise."

HRM INCIDENT 1

BEST NOT TO KNOW

Mike Manton is president of Sadler Federal Bank, a Muncie, Indiana, mortgage lender. The company has about 100 employees and assets totaling $250 million. Mike has managed the company since the mid-1950s. He became the principal owner in 1987 when he put together a group of investors to convert Sadler from a saver-owned savings and loan company to a federal bank. Mike had always taken pride in knowing every employee by name, both before and after the management-led buyout. He often remarks that his company is "just one big, happy family."

Last year, however, Mike sensed growing dissatisfaction. Turnover increased, and the workers just didn't seem content anymore. When Mike mentioned this to his office manager, Jeffery Wilson, Jeffery agreed that there had been a change. "I don't know what has caused it," said Jeffery, "but I do know that things are getting worse." Jeffery suggested a professionally conducted attitude survey to identify the problem. Mike agreed, and the survey was conducted with the assistance of a professor from Indiana University. Employees were encouraged to give honest answers and were given the usual assurances of anonymity. They were told that company management would receive only generalized summaries of the survey results.

Mike was shocked by the results. It was evident that a large number of his people were dissatisfied with various aspects of their jobs. Some felt the pay was too low. Others felt that supervision was inadequate or arbitrary. Many objected to harsh working conditions. A few even mentioned the "high and mighty" attitude of the "big boss." Mike told Jeffery, "I simply cannot believe that the people I trusted could be so unappreciative of the jobs Sadler has provided them over the years."

Mike called in his vice presidents, three of whom were co-owners, to discuss the results of the survey. After describing the survey results, he remarked, "We've always provided good jobs for our people and respected their rights. But if I knew who the strongest dissenters were, I don't think we would want them around. If they aren't happy with this company, they can leave."

Questions

1. If you were one of the vice presidents, how would you handle the situation?
2. Discuss Mike's attitude concerning the survey results.

HRM INCIDENT 2

SO WHAT'S THE PROBLEM?

Isabelle Anderson is the Alexandria, Louisiana, plant manager for Hall Manufacturing Company, a company that produces a line of relatively inexpensive painted wood furniture. Six months ago Isabelle became concerned about the turnover rate among workers in the painting department. Manufacturing plant turnover rates in that part of the South generally averaged about 30 percent, which was the case at Hall. The painting department, however, had experienced a turnover of nearly 200 percent in each of the last two years. Because of the limited number of skilled workers in the area, Hall had introduced an extensive training program for new painters, and Isabelle knew that the high turnover rate was proving very costly.

Isabelle conducted exit interviews with many of the departing painters. Some said that they were leaving for more money, others mentioned better benefits, and most cited some kind of personal reason for quitting. Isabelle checked and found that Hall's wages and benefits were competitive with, if not better than, those of other manufacturers in the area. She then called in Nelson Able, the painting supervisor, to discuss the problem. Nelson's response was, "You know how this younger generation is. They work to get enough money to live on for a few weeks and then quit. I don't worry about it. Our old-timers can take up the slack." "But Nelson," Isabelle replied, "we have to worry about the turnover rates. It's really costing the company a lot of money. I'm going to ask Joe Swan in the HR department to administer a survey to get to the bottom of this." Nelson replied, "Do whatever you think is right. I don't see any problem."

Questions

1. Do you agree that a survey of employees is the best way to identify the problem? Explain.
2. If you agree that a survey is needed, what kind of survey do you think should be conducted and how should the results be analyzed?

DEVELOPING HRM SKILLS

AN EXPERIENTIAL EXERCISE

After studying this textbook, students should have a much better appreciation of the type of work human resource managers are involved in. In this exercise, participants will attempt to develop a profile of the attributes a human resource manager should possess. Knowledge gained throughout the course should be used in identifying necessary attributes.

Participants will have a copy of Exhibits 1, 2, and 3. The attributes listed in Exhibit 1 may be more or less important for a human resource manager. Put this list into order by assigning the letter *A* to the five attributes that you think are the most important for a human resource manager to have. Assign a *B* to the five attributes you think are the second most important, *C* to the five attributes third most important, and *D* to the five attributes that you feel are least important. Definitions of each of these attributes are listed in Exhibit 2. You will have ten minutes for this activity.

After doing your individual ranking of these attributes, all students, except six individuals, will be placed into either Group 1 or Group 2. The six people not assigned to Groups 1 or 2 will make up the Review Committee; these individuals will sit together and reach a consensus on the attribute rankings. Groups 1 and 2 will review the individual rankings of each of its members, discuss them, and then agree on a group ranking for the attributes listed. Exhibit 3, a Group Summary Sheet, is provided for this purpose. You will have fifteen minutes for this activity.

After the completion of this exercise, the debriefing will begin with Groups 1 and 2 answering the questions: "What are the top five qualities needed by human resource professionals? Why?"

Then, members of the Review Committee will answer the questions: "Which group identified the most appropriate top five qualities needed by human resource professionals? Why?"

Next, both groups will be asked: "What were the least important qualities needed by human resource professionals? Why?"

Finally, members of the Review Committee will be asked: "Which group identified the most appropriate least important qualities needed by human resource professionals? Why?"

The result of this exercise should be a realistic profile of what attributes an effective human resource manager should possess.

NOTES

1. R. Wayne Mondy, "Job Longevity Differs by Sex," *Convenience Store News* (May 2,1975): 1.

2. Spencer Hayden, "Our Foreign Legions Are Faltering," *Personnel* 67 (August 1990): 42.

3. Work in America Institute, in John Hoerr, "The Payoff from Teamwork," *Business Week* (July 10, 1989): 56–62.

4. Alex Taylor III, "Why GM Leads the Pack in Europe," *Fortune* 127 (May 17, 1993): 83–86.

5. R. Wayne Mondy and Wallace F. Nelson, "Job Satisfaction Among Radiologic Technologies," *Applied Radiology* 7 (July-August 1978): 66.

6. Ibid., 65–67.

7. Margaret E. Cashman and James C. McElroy, "Evaluating the HR Function," *HRMagazine* 36 (January 1991): 73.

8. Donald L. Caruth, Robert M. Noe III, and R. Wayne Mondy, *Staffing the Contemporary Organization* (New York: Praeger Publishers, 1990): 283–299.

9. This section was written by Dr. Judy B. Mondy, Department of General Business, College of Business, McNeese State University.

10. Michael S. Howard, "Welcome to Warp Speed," *Computerworld* 27 (May 17, 1993): 89–93.

11. Alice Laplante, "The Needing Edge," *Computerworld* 25 (March 18, 1991): 65.

12. Michael Fitzgerald, "IS Helps 'Cat' Stay on Its Feet," *Computerworld* 24 (October 9, 1990): 60.

13. Joanie M. Wexler, "Ties That Bind," *Computerworld* 27 (June 28, 1993): 97.

14. Chuck Consentino, John Allen, and Richard Wellins, "Choosing the Right People," *HRMagazine* 35 (March 1990): 66–70.

15. Joanie M. Wexler, "Face-to-Face on the Desktop," *Computerworld* 27 (March 29, 1993): 2.

16. James A. O'Brien, *Introduction to Information Systems in Business Management,* 6th edition (Homewood, Ill.: Richard D. Irwin, 1991): 325.

17. Fritz H. Grupe, "Planning Your Expert System Strategy," *Information Executive* 4 (Winter 1991): 47.

18. Michael Fitzgerald, "Cooking with Expert Systems," *Computerworld* 24 (October 15, 1990): 45.

19. "Issues and Trends: I Want My MPC," *Lotus* 8 (April 1992): 15.

20. Robert Sadarini, "The Art of Imagineering," *Information Executive* 4 (Summer 1991): 6–7.

21. Mitch Betts, "States Redefining Public Service," *Computerworld* 27 (April 19, 1993): 20.

22. Mitch Betts, "Government 'Touch' Aids Citizens," *Computerworld* 28 (April 4, 1994): 51.

23. H.L. Capron, *Essentials of Computing,* 2nd edition (New York, NY: The Benjamin/Cummings Publishing Company, Inc., 1995): 125–127.

24. Ellis Booker, "Job Seekers Scan Electronic Horizon," *Computerworld* 28 (October 3, 1994): 133.

25. Ellis Booker, "Landing a Job Via the 'Net,'" *Computerworld* 28 (October 3, 1994): 133.

26. Jean S. Bozman, "Minority Hiring Getting More Attention," *Computerworld* 27 (November 1, 1993): 101.

27. Mitch Betts, "The Kiosks Are Coming," *Computerworld* 28 (January 24, 1994): 40.

28. Melinda-Carol Ballou, "Lab Adopts Multimedia 'Receptionist,'" *Computerworld* 28 (September 26, 1994): 94.

29. Bryan Hastings, "Pioneers of the Information Age," *PC World* 30 (December 1992): 265–266.

30. Michael Fitzgerald, "Xerox Bets on Virtual Office," *Computerworld* 28 (October 31, 1994): 123.

31. Elizabeth A. Regan and Bridget N. O'Connor. *End-User Information Systems* (New York: Macmillan Publishing Company, 1994): 52.

32. Kim Nash, "New Systems, New Business Practices," *Computerworld* 27 (May 24, 1993): 49.

33. Gary A. Egan, "Groupware: It's for All Companies," *Inside DPMA* 31 (October 1993): 7.

REFERENCES

Chapter 1—Human Resource Management: An Overview

Bavaria, Steve. "Corporate Ethics Should Start in the Boardroom." *Business Horizons* 34 (January-February 1991): 9–12.

Brown, Rick, and Joseph L. Meresman. "Balancing Stability and Innovation to Stay Competitive." *Personnel* 67 (September 1990): 49–52.

Caudron, Shari. "HR Leaders Brainstorm the Profession's Future." *Personnel Journal* 73 (August 1994): 54–61.

Clark, Robert L., and Richard Anker. "Cross-National Analysis of Labor Force Participation of Older Men and Women." *Economic Development and Cultural Change* 41 (April 1993): 489–513.

Cutler, W. Gale. "Jeff Confronts His Boss's Ethics." *Research-Technology Management* 36 (November-December 1993): 48.

Dye, Carson F. "10 Rules Define HR's Role." *Personnel Journal* 69 (June 1990): 46.

Fitz-enz, Jac. "HR's New Score Card." *Personnel Journal* 73 (February 1994): 84–87.

Flynn, Gillian. "HR in Mexico: What You Should Know." *Personnel Journal* 73 (August 1993): 34–41.

Hammmonds, Keith H. "Work: More Complex than We Thought." *Business Week* 3336 (September 13, 1993): 42.

Hyman, Michael R. "Ethical Codes Are Not Enough." *Business Horizons* 33 (March-April 1990): 15–22.

Ireland, Karin. "The Ethics Game." *Personnel Journal* 70 (March 1991): 72–75.

Keaton, Paul N., and Michael J. Semb. "Shaping Up the Bottom Line." *HRMagazine* 35 (September 1990): 81–86.

Knapp, Jeffrey. "Tends in HR Management Systems." *Personnel* 67 (April 1990): 50–55.

Kovach, Kenneth A., and John A. Pearce II. "HR Strategic Mandates for the Future." *Personnel Journal* 69 (January 1990): 57–63.

Laabs, Jennifer. "Employees Manage Conflict and Diversity." *Personnel Journal* 72 (December 1993): 30–34.

Langer, Steven. "Incomes Inch Up." *Personnel Journal* 73 (January 1994): 67–71.

Langer, Steven. "Human Resources: Who Makes What." *Personnel Journal* 69 (February 1990): 102–106.

Levitan, Sar A. "We Can Handle It." *HRMagazine* 35 (April 1990): 39, 42.

Messmer, Max. "Strategic Staffing for the '90s." *Personnel Journal* 69 (October 1990): 92–97.

Pickard, Jane. "A New Institute for a Changing Profession." *Personnel Management* 25 (July 1993): 22–23.

Poole, Jeanne C., William F. Rathgeber III, and Stanley W. Silverman. "Paying for Performance in a TQM Environment." *HRMagazine* 38 (October 1993): 68–72.

Rendero, Thomasine. "HR Panel Takes a Look Ahead." *Personnel* 67 (August 1990): 14–24.

Sheehy, James W. "New Work Ethic Is Frightening." *Personnel Journal* 69 (June 1990): 28–36.

Solomon, Charlene Marmer. "Managing the HR Career of the 90's." *Personnel Journal* 73 (June 1994): 62–69.

Spurgin, Ralph E. "Management in the 90s." *Credit World* 82 (September-October 1993): 24–28.

Thornburg, Linda. "Moving HR to the Head Table." *HRMagazine* 39 (August 1994): 50–51.

Tompkins, Neville. "How to Become a Human Resources Consultant." *HRMagazine* 39 (August 1994): 94–98.

Wagel, William H., and Hermine Zagat Levine. "HR '90: Challenges and Opportunities." *Personnel* 67 (June 1990): 18–42.

Weiss, Alan. "Seven Reasons to Examine Workplace Ethics." *HRMagazine* 36 (March 1991): 69–74.

Chapter 2—Environment of Human Resource Management

Barnum, Cynthia. "U.S. Training Manager Becomes Expatriate." *HRMagazine* 39 (April 1994): 82–84.

Becker, Gary S. "The Long-Term Unemployed Need Long Term Help." *Business Week* (May 20, 1991): 22.

Bernstein, Aaron. "The Case Of the Climbing Welfare Rolls." *Business Week* (May 13, 1991): 40.

Brant, Ellen. "Global HR." *Personnel Journal* 70 (March 1991): 38–44.

Caudron, Shari. "Monsanto Responds to Diversity." *Personnel Journal* 69 (November 1990): 72–80.

Cooper, James C., and Kathleen Madigan. "Downbeat Job Numbers Will Keep the Economy Playing the Blues." *Business Week* (March 25, 1991): 19–20.

D'O'Brian, Joseph. "How to Avoid Temporary Headaches." *Supervisory Management* 39 (March 1994): 1–2.

Foxman, Loretta D., and Walter L. Polsky. "HR Approaches for the Age of Globalization." *Personnel Journal* 70 (April 1991): 38–41.

Howard, Patricia Digh. "Worldshrink." *HRMagazine* 36 (January 1991): 42–43.

Ireland, Karin. "The $100 Billion High." *Personnel Journal* 70 (February 1991): 85.

Jenner, Lisa. "Work-Family Programs: Looking Beyond Written Policies." *HR Focus* 71 (January 1994): 19–20.

King, Albert S., and Terrence R. Bishop. "Human Resource Experience: Survey and Analysis." *Public Personnel Management* 23 (Spring 1994): 165–180.

Losey, Michael R. "Make Changing Workplace Demographics Work for You." *Managing Office Technology* 38 (August 1993): 38.

Messmer, Max. "Strategic Staffing for the '90s." *Personnel Journal* 69 (October 1990): 92–97.

Nelton, Sharon. "A Flexible Style of Management." *Nation's Business* 81 (December 1993): 24–29.

Overman, Stephenie. "Good Faith Is the Answer." *HRMagazine* 39 (January 1994): 74–76.

Packer, Arnold. "Skills Shortage Looms." *HRMagazine* 36 (April 1990): 38, 40.

Platt, Henry A. "Nonsexual Harassment Claims Hit HR's Desk." *HRMagazine* 39 (March 1994): 29–34.

Powell, Gary N. "Upgrading Management Opportunities for Women." *HRMagazine* 35 (November 1990): 67–70.

Recio, Irene. "Beyond Day Care: The Company School." *Business Week* (May 20, 1991): 142.

Reynolds, Calvin, and Rita Bennett. "The Career Couple Challenge." *Personnel Journal* 70 (March 1991): 46–48.

Richman, Louis S. "The Coming World Labor Shortage." *Fortune* 121 (April 9, 1990): 70–77.

Rosen, Benson, and Kay Lovelace. "Fitting Square Pegs into Round Holes." *HRMagazine* 39 (January 1994): 86–91.

Sachs, Robert. "A Productive Workforce: The Final Frontier of Competitive Advantage?" *Business Forum* 15 (Spring 1990): 5–7.

Shaw, Kathy. "It's Not in My Job Description." *CMA—the Management Accounting Magazine* 68 (June 1994): 42.

Wagel, William H. "On the Horizon: HR in the 1990s." *Personnel* 67 (January 1990): 11–16.

Woodford, Karen. "Child Care Sours at America West." *Personnel Journal* 69 (December 1990): 46–47.

Woods, Tom H. "Will the Workforce Be the Focus of the 90s?" *Business Forum* 15 (Spring 1990): 3.

Chapter 3—Equal Employment Opportunity and Affirmative Action

Albert, Rory Judd, and Neal S. Schelberg. "Highlighting the OWBPA." *Pension World* 27 (January 1991): 40–43.

Bequai, August. "The New Office: Personnel Laws in the 1990s." *Risk Management* 39 (January 1992): 40–44.

Biskupic, Joan. "Behind the Fight Over Quotas Lie Divisive Racial Issues." *Congressional Quarterly Weekly Report* 49 (June 1, 1991): 1442–1445.

Biskupic, Joan. "Democrats Scramble for Cover Under GOP 'Quota' Attacks." *Congressional Quarterly Weekly Report* 49 (May 25, 1991): 1378–1380.

Biskupic, Joan. "Lawmakers Seek Bias Shield for Workers Overseas." *Congressional Quarterly Weekly Report* 49 (March 30, 1991): 801.

Biskupic, Joan. "Supporters of Anti-Job-Bias Bill Need a Winning Strategy." *Congressional Quarterly Weekly Report* 49 (March 16, 1991): 683–685.

Blow, Richard. "Stamped Out." *The New Republic* 219 (January 10, 1994): 11–12.

Eastland, Terry. "Discrimination in the Name of Diversity." *The Wall Street Journal* (November 2, 1994): A15.

Flynn, Kelly. "Preventive Medicine for Sexual Harassment." *Personnel* 68 (March 1991): 17.

Galen, Michele et al. "Ending Sexual Harassment: Business Is Getting the Message." *Business Week* (March 18, 1991): 98–100.

Garland, Susan B., and Lisa Driscoll. "Can the Feds Bust Through the 'Glass Ceiling'?" *Business Week* (April 29, 1991): 33.

Israel, David, and Greg McConnell. "New Law Protects Older Workers." *HRMagazine* 36 (March 1991): 77–78.

Krell, Susan K. "Human Resources Employment Law: Keeping Out of Harm's Way." *Journal of Accountancy* 177 (January 1994): 72–75.

Laabs, Jennifer J. "The ADA: Tough Subject, Straight Answers." *Personnel Journal* 73 (February 1994): 25–28.

Lissy, William E. "Workers Compensation and the ADA." *Supervision* 54 (December 1993): 20–21.

McCalla, Robert K. "Stopping Sexual Harassment Before It Begins." *Management Review* 80 (April 1991): 44–46.

Murphy, Betty Southard, Wayne E. Barlow, and D. Diane Hatch. "'Reasonable Woman' is New Standard for Sexual Harassment." *Personnel Journal* 70 (May 1991): 34–36.

Nelson-Horchler, Joani. "The Best Man for a Job Is a Man!" *Industry Week* 240 (January 7, 1991): 50–52.

Nobile, Robert J., Esq. "To Waiver or Not to Waiver Is the Question of OWBWA." *Personnel* 68 (June 1991): 11.

Raisner, Jack. "When Workplace Relationships Cause

Discrimination." *HRMagazine* 36 (January 1991): 75–76.

Reminger, Richard T. "At Risk EEO Complaints Are on the Rise, but Most Companies Are Doing Little to Fight Back." *Personnel Journal* 70 (March 1991): 51–54.

Rosen, Jeffrey. "Is Affirmative Action Doomed? How the Law is Unraveling." *The New Republic* 211 (October 17, 1994): 25–30.

Schiller, Zachary, and Mark Landler. "Ending Sexual Harassment: Business Is Getting the Message." *Business Week* (March 18, 1991): 98–100.

Segal, Jonathan A. "New Rules for Waivers by Older Workers." *HRMagazine* 36 (April 1991): 84–88.

Segal, Jonathan A. "Traps to Avoid in FMLA Compliance." *HRMagazine* 39 (February 1994): 97–101.

Segal, Jonathan A. "When Charles Manson Comes to the Workplace." *HRMagazine* 39 (June 1994): 33–38.

Varca, Phillip E. and Patricia Pattison. "Evidentiary Standards in Employment Discrimination: A View Toward the Future." *Personnel Psychology* 46 (Summer 1993): 239–258.

Wendt, Ann C., and William M. Slonaker. "Confronting and Preventing Employment Discrimination." *Supervision* 52 (March 1991): 3–5.

Chapter 4—Job Analysis

Bergstrom, Robin Yale. "Workforce Obsolescence." *Production* 105 (August 1993): 52–55.

Busi, Donald C. "The Job Description: More Than Bureaucratic Control." *Supervisory Management* 35 (October 1990): 5.

Clifford, James P. "Job Analysis: Why Do It, and How Should It be Done?" *Public Personnel Management* 23 (Summer 1994): 321–340.

Hales, H. Lee, and Brian J. Savoie. "Building a Foundation for Successful Process Reengineering." *Industrial Engineering* 26 (September 1994): 17–19.

Johnston, Sam T. "Work Teams: What's Ahead in Work Design and Rewards Management." *Compensation and Benefits Review* 25 (March-April): 35–41.

Koretz, Gene. "Professional Workers: Can America Keep Its Edge?" *Business Week* (April 2, 1990): 23.

Lawler, Edward E. III. "Let the Workers Make White-Knuckle Decisions." *Fortune* 121 (March 26, 1990): 49–52.

Mondy, R. Wayne, Robert M. Noe, and Robert E. Edwards. "What the Staffing Function Entails." *Personnel* 63 (April 1986): 55–58.

Perlman, Stephen L. "Employees Redesign Their Jobs." *Personnel Journal* 69 (November 1990): 37–40.

Rattner, Steven. "If Productivity's Rising, Why Are Jobs Paying Less?" *The New York Times Magazine* (September 19, 1993): 54.

Rea, Peter, Julie Rea, and Charles Moomaw. "Use Assessment Centers in Skill Development." *Personnel Journal* 69 (April 1990): 126–131.

Smith, Bob. "Business Process Reengineering: More Than a Buzzword." *HR Focus* 71 (January 1994): 17–18.

Solomon, Charlene Marmer. "Success Abroad Depends on More Than Job Skills." *Personnel Journal* 73 (April 1994): 51–58.

Chapter 5—Human Resource Planning

Anthony, Peg, and Lincoln Akin Norton. "Link HR to Corporate Strategy." *Personnel Journal* 70 (April 1991): 75–86.

Arthur, Jeffrey B. "Effects of Human Resource Systems on Manufacturing Performance and Turnover." *Academy of Management Journal* 37 (June 1994): 670–687.

Berry, William E. "Management Accountant's Strategic Asset: The Resource Information System." *Management Accounting (USA)* 75 (January 1994): 56–57.

Brant, Ellen. "Global HR." *Personnel Journal* 70 (March 1991): 38–44.

Cashman, Margaret E., and James C. McElroy. "Evaluating the HR Function." *HRMagazine* 36 (January 1991): 70–73.

Clinton, Roy J., Stan Williamson, and Art L. Bethke. "Implementing Total Quality Management: The Role of Human Resource Management." *SAM Advanced Management Journal* 59 (Spring 1994): 10–16.

Fischer, Robert L. "HRIS Quality Depends on Teamwork." *Personnel Journal* 70 (April 1991): 47–51.

Francis, Barton C. "Succession Planning for Closely Held Business." *Journal of Accountancy* 171 (April 1991): 83–85.

Greengard, Samuel. "HRIS: The Next Generation." *Personnel Journal* 73 (March 1994): 40–45.

Greengard, Samuel. "New Technology is HR's Route to Reengineering." *Personnel Journal* 73 (July 1994): 32C-42C.

Kossek, Ellen Ernst, Willard Young, Debra C. Gash, and Victor Nichol. "Waiting for Innovation in the Human Resources Department: Godot Implements a Human Resource Information System." *Human Resource Management* 33 (Spring 1994): 135–159.

Kovach, Kenneth A., and John A. Pearce II. "HR Strategic Mandates for the 1990s." *Personnel* 67 (April 1990): 50–55.

Kromling, Larry K. "Calcomp Reshapes HR for the Future." *Personnel Journal* 69 (January 1990): 57–63.

Kubiak, Sharon L., Jack L. Simonetti, C. Joseph Sass, and Nick Nykodym. "Making People an Organization's Most Important Resource." *Business* 40 (October-November-December 1990): 33–35.

MacAdam, Maureen. "HRIS: Document What You're Doing." *Personnel Journal* 69 (February 1990): 56–63.

McElwain, James E. "Succession Plans Designed to Manage Change." *HRMagazine* 36 (February 1991): 67–71.

Messmer, Max. "Strategic Staffing for the '90s." *Personnel Journal* 69 (October 1990): 92–97.

Miller, Marc S. "Up & Running." *Personnel* 67 (November 1990): 23.

Moellring, Genevieve. "Integrate HRIS and Payroll." *Personnel Journal* 70 (February 1991): 79–82.

Mondy, R. Wayne, Robert M. Noe, and Robert E. Edwards. "What the Staffing Function Entails." *Personnel* 63 (April 1986): 55–58.

Nardoni, Ren. "Planning Promotes HRIS Success." *Personnel Journal* 70 (January 1991): 61–65.

O'Connell, Sandra E. "Five Principles for Managing Technology Resources." *HRMagazine* 39 (January 1994): 35–36.

O'Connell, Sandra E. "Planning and Setting up a New HRIS." *HRMagazine* 39 (March 1994): 37–39.

Overman, Stephenie. "Different World Brings Challenge." *HRMagazine* 35 (June 1990): 58–60.

Overman, Stephenie. "Is HR a Weak Link in the Global Chain?" *HRMagazine* 39 (June 1994): 67–68.

Pollard, John R. "HRIS: Time Is of the Essence." *Personnel Journal* 69 (November 1990): 42–44.

Shetty, Y.K., and Paul F. Buller. "Regaining Competitiveness Requires HR Solutions." *Personnel* 67 (July 1990): 8–12.

Thornburg, Linda. "The High Cost of Delivering Data." *HRMagazine* 39 (May 1994): 49–53.

Tinsley, Dillard B. "Future Flash: Computer Facilitates HR Function." *Personnel* 67 (February 1990): 32–35.

Vatter, Robert H. "Women in the Work Force." *Statistical Bulletin-Metropolitan Life Insurance Company* 75 (July-September 1994): 2–10.

Chapter 6—Recruitment

Asdorian, Martin. "Drowning in Resumes (Clearly Written and Specifically Defined Employment Ads)." *HRMagazine* 37 (September 1992): 59–60.

Anthony, Peg. "Track Applicants, Track Costs." *Personnel Journal* 69 (April 1990): 75–81.

Avery, Susan. "Shorthanded? Hire a Temp." *Purchasing* 108 (March 22, 1990): 70–71, 75–76.

Barclay, Lizabeth A., and Alan R. Bass. "Get the Most From Recruitment Efforts." *HRMagazine* 39 (June 1994): 70–72.

Bargerstock, Andrew S., and Gerald Swanson. "Four Ways to Build Recruitment Alliances." *HRMagazine* 36 (March 1991): 49–53.

Barsoux, Jean-Louis. "Job Ads: Reading Between the Lines (EC Countries)." *International Management* 48 (May 1993): 65.

Benson, Tracy E. "Ready, Aim, Hire." *Industry Week* 24 (February 4, 1991): 16.

Brady, Teresa. "Genetic Testing: Medical and Legal Issues, and DuPont's Program." *Employment Relations Today* 20 (Autumn 1993): 257–266.

Caudron, Shari. "Team Staffing Requires New HR Role." *Personnel Journal* 73 (May 1994): 88–94.

Caudron, Shari. "Contingent Work Force Spurs HR Planning." *Personnel Journal* 73 (July 1994): 52–58.

D'O'Brian, Joseph. "Beware of False Advertising When Hiring." *Supervisory Management* 38 (November 1993): 1–2.

Fitz-enz, Jac. "Getting—and Keeping—Good Employees." *Personnel* 67 (August 1990): 25–28.

Hahn, Jeffrey M. "Pre-employment Information Services: Employers Beware? (Liability in Screening Applicants)." *Employee Relations Law Journal* 17 (Summer 1991): 45–69.

Halcrow, Allan. "Scaling the Recruitment Wall." *Personnel Journal* 70 (April 1991): 69–72.

Hughes, Johnston. "Recruitment: Don't Search, Research." *Personnel Journal* 73 (January 1994): S2–S3.

Kacmar, K. Michele. "Look at Who's Talking." *HRMagazine* 38 (February 1993): 56–58.

Keaton, Paul N., and Janine Anderson. "Leasing Offers Benefits to Both Sides." *HRMagazine* 35 (July 1990): 53, 55, 56, 58.

Koch, Jennifer. "Apple Ads Target Intellect." *Personnel Journal* 69 (March 1990): 107–114.

Kruger, Pamela. "For Job Seekers, On-line Options." *The New York Times* (August 28 1994): 21 (Sec 3).

Leibowitz, Zandy B., Nancy K. Schlossberg, and Jane E. Shore. "Stopping the Revolving Door." *Training and Development Journal* 45 (February 1991): 43–50.

Leonard, Bill. "Resume Databases to Dominate Field." *HRMagazine* 38 (April 1993): 59–60.

Martucci, William C., and Daniel B. Boatright. "Recent Employment-Related Legislation." *Employment Relations Today* 21 (Summer 1994): 233–239.

Mondy, R. Wayne, Robert M. Noe, and Robert E. Edwards. "What the Staffing Function Entails." *Personnel* 63 (April 1986): 55–58.

Phillips, Douglas J. "The Price Tag on Turnover." *Personnel Journal* 69 (December 1990): 58–61.

Ramsey, Robert D. "How to Hire the Best (Role of Supervisor)." *Supervision* 55 (April 1994): 14–17.

Ross, John. "Effective Ways to Hire Contingent Personnel." *HRMagazine* 36 (February 1991): 52–54.

Springer, Felix J., and Albert Zakarian. "Managing with Legal Employment Background Checks." *Pension World* 26 (June 1990): 15.

Tarrant, Sharon M. "Setting Up an Electronic Job Posting System." *Training and Development* 48 (January 1994): 39–42.

Wymer, John F. "Contract Employees: Yours, Mine, or Ours?" *Employee Relations Law Journal* 19 (Autumn 1993): 247–255.

Chapter 7—Selection

Ambash, Joseph W. "Knowing Your Limits: How Far Can You Go When Checking an Applicant's Background?" *Management World* 19 (March-April 1990): 8–10.

Atwood, Caleb S., and James M. Neel. "New Lawsuits Expand Employer Liability." *HRMagazine* 35 (October 1990): 88–90.

Biddle, Richard E. "How to Set Cutoff Scores for Knowledge Tests Used in Promotion, Training, Certification, and Licensing." *Public Personnel Management* 22 (Spring 1993): 63–79.

Bragg, Arthur. "Checking References." *Sales and Marketing Management* 142 (November 1990): 68–70.

Byrne, John A. "Why Headhunters Are Hunting Each Other." *Business Week* (January 14, 1991): 43.

Cronin, Michael P. "Hiring: This Is a Test." *Inc.* 15 (August 1993): 64–68.

Decker, Kurt H. "The Rights and Wrongs of Screening." *Security Management* 34 (January 14, 1991): 44–49.

Dossin, Milton N., and Nancie L. Merritt. "Sign-On Bonuses Score for Recruiters." *HRMagazine* 35 (March 1990): 42–43.

Fagiano, David. "Interviewing for Style." *Management Review* 79 (November 1990): 4.

Fenton, James W., Jr. "Negligent Hiring/Retention Adds to Human Resources Woes." *Personnel Journal* 69 (April 1990): 62–73.

Fitz-enz, Jac. "Getting—and Keeping—Good Employees." *Personnel* 67 (August 1990): 25–28.

Kluger, Avraham N., and Hannah R. Rothstein. "The Influence of Selection Test Type on Applicant Reactions to Employment Testing." *Journal of Business & Psychology* 8 (Fall 1993): 3–25.

Kowal, Dennis M. "Emphasize Integrity Assessment in Interviews." *Personnel Journal* 69 (June 1990): 66–71.

Krupp, Neil B. "Overseas Staffing for the New Europe." *Personnel* 67 (July 1990): 20–25.

Lowry, Phillip E. "The Structured Interview: An Alternative to the Assessment Center?" *Public Personnel Management* 23 (Summer 1994): 201–15.

McKendrick, Joseph E., Jr. "Latest AMS Foundation Survey Finds: One-Third of Nation's Employers Have or Are Considering Drug Testing." *Management World* 19 (March-April 1990): 2–4.

Martinez, Michelle Nelly. "Creative Ways to Employ People with Disabilities." *HRMagazine* 35 (November 1990): 40–44, 101.

Martinez, Michelle Neely. "Making Room for Work/Family Positions." *HRMagazine* 35 (August 1990): 45–47.

Messmer, Max. "Strategic Staffing for the '90s." *Personnel Journal* 69 (October 1990): 92–97.

"Negligent Hiring Costs Companies." *Supervisory Management* 35 (March 1990): 2.

Overman, Stephenie. "A Delicate Balance Protects Everyone's Rights." *HRMagazine* (November 1990): 36–39.

Segal, Jonathan A. "Follow the Yellow Brick Road." *HRMagazine* 35 (November 1990): 83–86.

Simms, Michele. "Defining Privacy in Employee Health Screening Cases: Ethical Ramifications Concerning the Employee/Employer Relationship." *Journal of Business Ethics* 13 (May 1994): 315–325.

Solomon, Charlene Marmer. "Testing Is Not at Odds With Diversity Efforts." *Personnel Journal* 72 (March 1993): 100–104.

Waerdt, Lois Vander. "Taking Nothing for Granted—Check Applicants' Background and References—Thoroughly." *Management World* 9 (March-April 1990): 5–7.

Chapter 8—Organization Change and Human Resource Development

Anfuso, Dawn. "Company-Union Partnership Turns Xerox Around." *Personnel Journal* 73 (January 1994): 61.

Bridges, William. "The End of the Job." *Fortune* 130 (September 19, 1994): 62–64.

Caudron, Shari. "Team Staffing Requires New HR Role." *Personnel Journal* 73 (May 1994): 88–93.

Estreicher, Samuel. "Laws Promoting Worker Training, Productivity, and Quality." *Labor Law Journal* 44 (February 1993): 110–118.

Foxman, Loretta D., and Walter L. Polsky. "HR Approaches for the Age of Globalization." *Personnel Journal* 70 (April 1991): 38–40.

Giusti, Joseph P., David R. Baker, and Peter J. Graybash. "Satellites Dish Out Global Training." *Personnel Journal* 70 (June 1991): 80–84.

Hamilton, Constance. "Training Is a Vital Link in the Process." *HR Focus* 69 (September 1992): 4–5.

Hanlin, James R., and Nancy J. Johns. "Championship Training." *Training and Development Journal* 45 (February 1991): 56–62.

Hodge, John W. "Restoring U.S. Competitive Advantage." *HRMagazine* 38 (January 1993): 15–16.

Huselid, Mark A. "Documenting HR's Effect on Company Performance." *HRMagazine* 39 (January 1994): 79–84.

Jenkins, Gary E. "Beyond the Borders: The Human Resource Professional in a Global Economy." *Employee Benefit Plan Review* 11 (May 1993): 43–44.

Kanin-Lovers, Jill, and Jeff Boyle. "Team Incentives as a Core Management Process." *Journal of Compensation & Benefits* 10 (July/August 1994): 57–60.

Laabs, Jennifer. "Hewlitt-Packard's Core Values Drive HR Strategy." *Personnel Journal* 72 (December 1993): 38–45.

Lancaster, Hal. "If You Can't Talk the Talk, You Risk Taking a Walk (Management Buzzwords)." *The Wall Street Journal* (October 18, 1994): B1.

McElrath-Slade, Rose. "Caution: Re-Engineering in Progress." *HRMagazine* 39 (June 1994): 54–59.

Mager, Robert F. "No Self-Efficacy, No Performance." *Training* (April 1992): 32–36.

Nowack, Kenneth M. "A True Training Needs Analysis." *Training and Development Journal* 45 (April 1991): 69–73.

Overman, Stephenie. "Big Bang Change: Re-Engineering HR." *HRMagazine* 39 (June 1994): 50–53.

Peak, Martha H. "Coming to Grips With Change." *Management Review* 83 (July 1994): 40–44.

Peters, Tom. "To Forget Is Sublime (Change and Adaptation in Corporate Thinking)." *Forbes* 153 (April 11, 1994 supp): 154.

Silverstein, Neil. "CBT Myths vs. Reality." *Training* 31 (February 1994): 71–72.

Sims, Ronald R. "Human Resource Management's Role in Clarifying the New Psychological Contract." *Human Resource Management* 33 (Fall 1994): 373–382.

Solomon, Charlene Marmer. "Global Operations Demand That HR Rethink Diversity." *Personnel Journal* 73 (July 1994): 48.

Sunoo, Brenda Paik. "HR Positions U.S. Long Distance for Further Growth." *Personnel Journal* 73 (June 1994): 78–87.

Tennesen, Michael. "HR Faces Distinct Issues in Rural Areas." *Personnel Journal* 73 (June 1994): 112–119.

Thompson, Curt M. "Preparation Is Key to Successful Change." *HR Focus* 71 (April 1994): 17–18.

Thornburg, Linda. "Creating a Commitment to Change." *HRMagazine* 6 (January 1991): 54–56.

Turban, Daniel B., and Thomas W. Daugherty. "Role of Protégé Personality in Receipt of Mentoring and Career Success." *Academy of Management Journal* 37 (June 1994): 688–702.

Whittlesey, Fred E., and Carol L. Maurer. "Strategies for Exiting the Recession (Human Resources Program Design)." *Journal of Compensation & Benefits* 9 (May/June 1994): 12–17.

Wilhelm, Paul G. "Employment at Will Harms Productivity." *HRMagazine* 35 (September 1990): 88.

Chapter 9—Corporate Culture and Organization Development

Auteri, Enrico. "Upward Feedback Leads to Culture Change (Management Style Analysis Program at Fiat SpA Redefines Role of Managers)." *HRMagazine* 39 (June 1994): 78–80.

Clement, Ronald W. "Culture, Leadership, and Power: The Keys to Organizational Change." *Business Horizons* 37 (January/February 1994): 33–39.

Dahler-Larsen, Peter. "Corporate Culture and Morality: Durkheim-Inspired Reflections on the Limits of Corporate Culture." *Journal of Management Studies* 31 (January 1994): 1–18.

Dunsing, Dick, and Ken Matejka. "Overcoming the BOHICA Effect (Bend Over, Here It Comes Again)." *Business Horizons* 37 (July/August 1994): 40–42.

Dutton, Gail. "Can California Change Its Corporate Culture?" *Management Review* 83 (June 1994): 49–54.

Elliott, Ronald D. "The Challenge of Managing Change." *Personnel Journal* 69 (March 1990): 40–49.

Gibson, Virginia M. "Organizations Must Adapt to Employees' Changing Needs." *HR Focus* 71 (March 1994): 7.

Jeffcutt, Paul. "The Interpretation of Organization: A Contemporary Analysis and Critique." *Journal of Management Studies* 31 (March 1994): 225–250.

LaBarre, Polly. "The Creative Revolution!" *Industry Week* 243 (May 16 1994): 12–16.

Melum, Mara Minerva. "Total Quality Management: Steps to Success." *Hospitals* 64 (December 5, 1990): 42–44.

Noel, Rita Thomas. "Manager's Toolbox: Five Tools for Better Management." *Supervisory Management* 35 (September 1990): 4–5.

O'Neill, Paul E. "Transforming Managers for Organizational Change." *Training and Development Journal* 44 (July 1990): 87–90.

Overman, Stephenie. "No-Frills HR at Nucor." *HRMagazine* 39 (July 1994): 56–60.

Peak, Martha H. "Coming to Grips With Change." *Management Review* 83 (July 1994): 40–44.

Petrock, Frank. "Corporate Culture Enhances Profits." *HRMagazine* 35 (November 1990): 64–66.

Pines, Ellis. "From Top Secret to Top Priority: The Story of TQM." *Aviation Week & Space Technology* 132 (May 12, 1990): S5–S24.

Redecker, James R. "Code of Conduct as Corporate Culture." *HRMagazine* 35 (July 1990): 83–84, 86–87.

Schneider, Benjamin, Sarah Gunnarson, and Kathryn Niles-Jolly. "Creating the Climate and Culture of Success." *Organizational Dynamics* 23 (Summer 1994): 17–29.

Scott, K. Dow, and Anthony Townsend. "Teams: Why Some Succeed and Others Fail." *HRMagazine* 39 (August 1994): 62–67.

Sharpe, Rochelle, and David Mulholland. "Women Make Strides, but Men Stay Firmly in Top Company Jobs: Female Management Gains Are Impeded by Culture Still Dominated by Males." *The Wall Street Journal* (March 29, 1994): A1.

Sheridan, John H. "A Philosophy for Commitment." *Industry Week* 24 (February 4, 1991): 11–13.

Shilling, Marvina. "Avoid Expatriate Culture Shock." *HRMagazine* 38 (July 1993): 58–63.

Shostak, Arthur B. "The Nature of Work in the

Twenty-First Century: Certain Uncertainties." *Business Horizons* 36 (November-December): 30–34.

Sonnenberg, Frank K. "The Age of Intangibles (Eight Success Factors for Competing Effectively in the 21st Century)." *Management Review* 83 (January 1994): 48–53.

Steingraber, Fred G. "Total Quality Management." *Vital Speeches of the Day* 57 (April 15, 1991): 415–416.

Thornburg, Linda. "Journey Toward a More Inclusive Culture." *HRMagazine* 39 (February 1994): 79–84.

Tosti, Donald, and Stephanie Jackson. "Alignment: How It Works and Why It Matters (Changing Organizational Behavior and Culture)." *Training* 31 (April 1994): 58–60.

Wellins, Richard, and Jill George. "The Key to Self-Directed Teams." *Training and Development Journal* 45 (April 1991): 26–31.

Wilmot, Richard E., and Valorie McClelland. "How to Run a Reality Check." *Training* 27 (May 1990): 66, 68, 71–72.

Wright, Patrick M., and Gary C. McMahan. "Theoretical Perspectives for Strategic Human Resource Management." *Journal of Management* 18 (June 1992): 295–320.

Chapter 10—Career Planning and Development

Arthur, Michael B. "The Boundaryless Career: A New Perspective for Organizational Inquiry." *Journal of Organizational Behavior* 15 (July 1994): 295–306.

Bird, Allan. "Careers as Repositories of Knowledge: A New Perspective on Boundaryless Careers." *Journal of Organizational Behavior* 15 (July 1994): 325–344.

Brown, Tom. "Defining a 'New Social Contract': GTE's Emerging Employee-Partnership Philosophy Reflects New Market Realities." *Industry Week* 243 (August 15, 1994): 52.

Caudron, Shari. "HR Revamps Career Itineraries." *Personnel Journal* 73 (April 1994): 64A-77A.

Deutschman, Alan. "Pioneers of the New Balance." *Fortune* 123 (May 20, 1991): 60–68.

Fierman, Jaclyn. "Beating the Midlife Career Crisis." *Fortune* 128 (September 6, 1993): 52–54, 58–62.

Fitz-enz, Jac. "Getting—and Keeping—Good Employees." *Personnel* 67 (August 1990): 25–28.

Foxman, Loretta D., and Walter L. Polsky. "Aid in Employee Career Development." *Personnel Journal* 69 (January 1990): 22–24.

Gilmore, Gail. "Coping with the Reality of Rightsizing." *Risk Management* 41 (January 1994): 43–47.

Hakim, Cliff. "Boost Morale to Gain Productivity." *HRMagazine* 38 (February 1993): 46–49.

Harrison, Raymond. "Employee Development: Challenge Should Be Linked to Performance." *HR Focus* 70 (October 1993): 9.

Kaye, Beverly, and Zandy Leibowitz. "Career Development: Don't Let It Fizzle." *HRMagazine* 39 (September 1994): 78–83.

Koretz, Gene. "Women Still Earn Less, But They've Come a Long Way." *Business Week* (December 24, 1990): 14.

Leibowitz, Zandy B., Barbara H. Feldman, and Sherry H. Mosley. "Career Development Works Overtime at Corning, Inc." *Personnel* 67 (April 1990): 38–46.

Lentz, Charles W. "Dual Ladders Become Multiple Ladders at Dow Corning." *Research Technology Management* 33 (May-June 1990): 28–34.

McGregor, Elizabeth. "Emerging Careers." *Occupational Outlook Quarterly* 34 (Fall 1990): 22–23.

Mackay, Harvey. "A Career Roadmap: Getting Started." *Modern Office Technology* 35 (June 1990): 12–14.

Martinez, Michelle Neely. "Making Room for Work/Family Positions." *HRMagazine* 35 (August 1990): 45–47.

Matthes, Karen. "Corporate Change and Concern for Employees." *HR Focus* 69 (February 1992): 24.

Mirvis, Phillip H., and Douglas T. Hall. "Psychological Success and the Boundaryless Career." *Journal of Organizational Behavior* 15 (July 1994): 365–380.

Morris, Michelle. "15 Fast-Track Careers." *Money* 19 (June 1990): 108–126.

Reynolds, Calvin, and Rita Bennett. "The Career Couple Challenge." *Personnel Journal* 70 (March 1991): 46–48.

Rieland, Patrick L. "True Professionals Never Stop Learning." *Business Credit* 96 (September 1994): 17.

Rich, Joseph R., and Beth C. Florin-Thuma. "Rewarding Employees in an Environment of Fewer Promotions." *Pension World* 26 (November 1990): 16–17.

Simonsen, Peggy, and Cathy Wells. "African Americans Take Control of Their Careers." *Personnel Journal* 73 (April 1994): 99–105.

Wolff, Michael F. "Building Careers at Procter & Gamble." *Research Technology Management* 33 (September-October 1990): 9–11.

Wooten, William. "Using Knowledge, Skill and Ability." *Public Personnel Management* 22 (Winter 1993): 551–563.

Chapter 11—Performance Appraisal

Antonioni, David. "Improve the Performance Management Process Before Discontinuing Performance Appraisals." *Compensation and Benefits Review* 26 (May/June 1994): 29–37.

Axline, Larry L. "Ethical Considerations of Performance Appraisals." *Management Review* 83 (March 1994): 62.

Bobko, Philip, and Adrienne Colella. "Employee Reactions to Performance Standards: A Review and Research Proposition." *Personnel Psychology* 47 (Spring 1994): 1–29.

Caruth, Donald L., Robert M. Noe III, and R. Wayne Mondy. *Staffing the Contemporary Organization.* (New York: Praeger Publishers, 1990).

Duarte, Neville T., Jane R. Goodson, and Nancy R. Klich. "Effects of Dyadic Quality and Duration on Performance Appraisal." *Academy of Management Journal* 37 (June 1994): 499–521.

English, Gary. "Tuning Up for Performance Management." *Training and Development Journal* 45 (April 1991): 56–60.

Halachmi, Arie. "From Performance Appraisal to Performance Targeting." *Public Personnel Management* 22 (Summer 1993): 323–344.

"How Johnsonville Shares Profits on the Basis of Performance." *Harvard Business Review* 68 (November-December 1990): 27.

Lee, Charles. "Smoothing Out Appraisal Systems." *HRMagazine* 35 (March 1990): 72–74, 76.

Longenecker, Clinton, and Dean Ludwig. "Ethical Dilemmas in Performance Appraisal Revisited." *Journal of Business Ethics* 9 (December 1990): 961–969.

"Making Criticism Pay Off (Supervision of Employees)." *Supervision* 55 (April 1994): 25–26.

Miller, Christopher S., Joan A. Daspin, and Michael H. Schuster. "The Impact of Performance Appraisal Methods on Age Discrimination in Employment Act Cases." *Personnel Psychology* 43 (Autumn 1990): 555–578.

Mondy, R. Wayne, Robert M. Noe III, and Robert E. Edwards. "What the Staffing Function Entails." *Personnel* 63 (April 1986): 55–58.

Moses, Joel, George P. Hollenbeck, and Melvin Sorcher. "Other People's Expectations." *Human Resource Management* 32 (Summer/Fall 1993): 283–297.

Odiorne, George S. "The Trend Toward the Quarterly Performance Review." *Business Horizons* 33 (July-August 1990): 38–41.

"Performance Management: What's Hot—What's Not." *Compensation and Benefits Review* 26 (May/June 1994): 71–75.

Rich, Joseph R., and Beth C. Florin-Thuma. "Rewarding Employees in an Environment of Fewer Promotions." *Pension World* 36 (November 1990): 16–17.

Sahl, Robert J. "Design Effective Performance Appraisals." *Personnel Journal* 69 (October 1990): 53–54, 58, 60.

Sahl, Robert J. "Two Sides of the Coin (Effective Job Appraisals)." *Small Business Reports* 19 (August 1994): 54–57.

Sanchez, Juan I., and Edward L. Levine. "The Impact of Raters' Cognition on Judgment Accuracy: An Extension to the Job Analysis Domain." *Journal of Business & Psychology* 9 (Fall 1994): 47–57.

Scholtes, Peter R. "Total Quality or Performance Appraisal: Choose One." *National Productivity Review* 12 (Summer 1993): 349–363.

Tafti, Peter M. "Face to Face." *Training and Development Journal* 44 (November 1990): 66–71.

Thomas, Steven L., and Robert D. Bretz. "Research and Practice in Performance Appraisal: Evaluating Employee Performance in America's Largest Companies." *Advanced Management Journal* 59 (Spring 1994): 28–34.

Veglahn, Peter A. "Key Issues in Performance Appraisal Challenges: Evidence From Court and Arbitration Decisions." *Labor Law Journal* 44 (October 1993): 595–606.

"What Does Your Boss Really Think of You?" *Supervision* 51 (December 1990): 10.

Yakal, Kathy. "Employee Evaluation Software Creates Thorough, Uniform Review." *PC Magazine* 13 (September 27, 1994): 37–38.

Chapter 12—Financial Compensation

Beatty, Kate. "What's Driving Your Pay?" *HRMagazine* 35 (July 1990): 45–48.

Bergel, Gary I. "Choosing the Right Pay Delivery System to Fit Banding." *Compensation and Benefits Review* 26 (July/August 1994): 34–38.

Britton, Paul B., and Christian M. Ellis. "Designing and Implementing Reward Programs: Finding a Better Way." *Compensation and Benefits Review* 26 (July/August 1994): 39–46.

Brooks, Susan Sonnesyn. "Noncash Ways to Compensate Employees." *HRMagazine* 39 (April 1994): 38–43.

Brown, Tom. "Does Compensation Add Up?" *Industry Week* 239 (August 20, 1990): 13.

Candall, Lin D., and Mark I. Phelps. "Pay for a Global Work Force." *Personnel Journal* 70 (February 1991): 28–33.

Challenger, James E. "Two or More for One." *Manage* 44 (April 1993): 26–27.

Collins, Gail. "Wages and Sin." *Working Woman* 16 (March 1991): 134.

Esquibel, Orlando, Jack Ning, and John Sugg. "New Salary System Supports Changing Culture." *HRMagazine* 35 (October 1990): 43–48.

Fierman, Jaclyn. "The Perilous New World of Fair Pay." *Fortune* 129 (June 13, 1994): 57–61.

Giblin, Edward J., and Leslie G. Kelley. "Three Self-Destructive Pay Mistakes." *Across the Board* 31 (May 1994): 40–43.

Giblin, Edward J., Geoffrey A. Wiegman, and Frank Sanfilippo. "Bringing Pay Up to Date." *Personnel* 67 (November 1990): 17–18.

Langer, Steven F. "What You Earn—and Why." *Personnel Journal* 70 (January 1991): 25–27.

Lopez, Julie Amparano. "A Better Way? Setting Your Own Pay—And Other Unusual Compensation Plans." *The Wall Street Journal* (April 13, 1994): R6.

McKendrick, Joseph E., Jr. "Salary Surveys: Roadmaps for the Volatile Employment Scene of the 1990s." *Management World* 19 (March-April 1990): 18–20.

Meehan, Robert H., and G.V. Lemises. "Compensation Plan Analysis." *HRMagazine* 35 (February 1990): 69–72.

Meng, George J. "All the Parts of Comparable Worth." *Personnel Journal* 69 (March 1990): 98–104.

Nemerov, Donald S. "How to Design a Competency-Based Pay Program." *Journal of Compensation & Benefits* 9 (March/April 1994): 46–53.

Overman, Stephenie. "Selling Your Compensation Plan." *HRMagazine* 39 (July 1994): 49–50.

Overman, Stephenie. "No-Frills HR at Nucor." *HRMagazine* 39 (July 1994): 56–60.

Parnell, John A. "Five Reasons Why Pay Must Be Based on Performance." *Supervision* 52 (February 1991): 6–8.

"The Role of Rewards on a Journey to Excellence." *Personnel Review* 23 (March 1994): 53–55.

Ramsay, Margaret. "Support for Team Works." *CA Magazine* 98 (June 1994): 22–28.

Saunier, Anne M., and Donald D. Gallo. "Use Focus Groups to Support Compensation Change Initiatives." *Journal of Compensation & Benefits* 9 (March/ April 1994): 12–19.

Schraeder, Terry E., and Mark D. Dore. "Compensation a Pay Formula for the '90s." *Personnel Journal* 69 (October 1990): 46–47.

Thornburg, Linda. "Money Is Still the Best Reward." *HRMagazine* 39 (August 1994): 58–59.

Thornburg, Linda. "Business Goals Drive Agenda." *HRMagazine* 39 (April 1994): 49–50.

Weinberg, Ira, and John Hiller. "How to Determine the Reasonableness of Executive Pay." *Journal of Compensation & Benefits* 9 (May/June 1994): 39–44.

Williamson, Paul. "It's What You Do That Counts." *Small Business Reports* 18 (October 1993): 16–20.

Chapter 13—Benefits and Other Compensation Issues

Ackley, Dennis. "What to Say About Pay." *Compensation and Benefits Review* 25 (January/February 1993): 18–21.

Alexander, Michael. "Travel-Free Commuting." *Nation's Business* 78 (December 1990): 33, 36–37.

Anderson, Richard A. "Handling Health-Care Costs in the '90s." *HRMagazine* 35 (June 1990): 89–94.

Belcher, John G. "Gainsharing and Variable Pay: The State of the Art." *Compensation and Benefits Review* 26 (May/June 1994): 50–60.

Byrne, John A. "The Flap Over Executive Pay." *Business Week* (May 6 1991): 90–103.

Candall, Lin D., and Mark I. Phelps. "Pay for a Global Work Force." *Personnel Journal* 70 (February 1991): 28–33.

Cordtz, Dan. "Hire Me, Hire My Family." *Finance World* 159 (September 18, 1990): 76–79.

Deloux, Gene. "Is Your Maternity Policy Ready for the '90s?" *HRMagazine* 35 (November 1990): 57–59.

Epstein, Gene. "Yes, Profit Sharing Spurs Productivity, but Which Method Works Best?" *Barron's* 74 (August 15 1994): 21–22.

Garland, Susan B. "The Retiring Kind Are Getting Militant About Benefits." *Business Week* (May 28, 1990): 29.

Garland, Susan B. "Putting Pension Managers on a Short Leash." *Business Week* (March 26, 1990): 47.

Glassman, David. "Delivering Value to Shareholders—While Making Money at the Same Time." *Financial Management* 22 (Summer 1993): 24–26.

Giblin, Edward J., and Leslie G. Kelley. "Three Self-Destructive Pay Mistakes." *Across the Board* 31 (May 1994): 40–43.

"HR Professionals Sport More Hats Than Ever Before." *Employee Benefits Journal* 15 (September 1990): 9.

Koretz, Gene. "Health Care Keeps Taking Bigger Bites of the Economy." *Business Week* (February 19, 1990): 22.

Kuttner, Robert. "Health Care: Why Corporate America Is Paralyzed." *Business Week* (April 8, 1991): 14.

Leibman, Michael, and Harold P. Weinstein. "Money Isn't Everything." *HRMagazine* 35 (November 1990): 48–51.

Leonard, Bill. "The New Age of Manageable Flexibility." *HRMagazine* 39 (July 1994): 53–54.

McMillan, John D., and Chris Young. "Sweetening the Compensation Package." *HRMagazine* 35 (October 1990): 36–39.

Milkovich, George T., and Jerry M. Newman. *Compensation,* 3rd edition (Homewood, Ill.: Richard D. Irwin, Inc. 1993).

Sibson, Robert E. *Compensation,* 5th edition (New York: American Management Association, 1990).

Stelluto, George L., and Deborah P. Klein. "Compensation Trends Into the 21st Century." *Monthly Labor Review* 113 (February 1990): 38–45.

Sykes, Maurice C. "Pros & Cons of Restricted Bonus Plans." *National Underwriter* 98 (February 28, 1994): 7–9.

"Visions: Funding Retiree Benefits." *HRMagazine* 36 (February 1991): 87–88.

Wilt, Aric T. "Cafeteria Plans Help Meet Needs & Control Costs." *Management Review* 79 (September 1990): 43–46.

Chapter 14—A Safe and Healthy Work Environment

Binion, Janet. "One More Safety Meeting! Safety Meetings Should Be Fun, Not Boring." *Safety & Health* 142 (October 1990): 82, 84.

Bruening, John C. "Risk Communication: A Two-Way Connection." *Occupational Hazards* 52 (October 1990): 76–80.

Caldwell, Dean S., and Douglas M. Ihrke. "Differentiating Between Burnout and Copout in Organizations." *Public Personnel Management* 23 (Spring 1994): 77–84.

Chadd, Charles M. "Managing OSHA Compliance: The Human Resources Issues." *Employee Relations Law Journal* 20 (Summer 1994): 101–113.

Harrinton, Harry, and Nancy Richardson. "Retiree Wellness Plan Cuts Health Costs." *Personnel Journal* 69 (August 1990): 60, 62

Hugh, Sinclair E. "Observations from the Witness Stand." *HRMagazine* 39 (August 1994): 176–177.

Joyce, Marilyn. "Ergonomics Will Take Center Stage During '90s and into New Century." *Occupational Health and Safety* 60 (January 1991): 31–32, 34, 37.

Kohl, John P., Alan N. Miller, and David S. Hames. "AIDS in the Work Place." *Supervision* 51 (November 1990): 11–13.

Kuhar, Mark S. "Worker's Compensation: Is Fraud Flying High?" *Occupational Hazards* 56 (August 1994): 38–41.

Mason, Julie C. "The Cost of Wellness." *Management Review* 83 (July 1994): 29–32.

Moore, R. Henry. "OSHA: What's Ahead for the 1990s." *Personnel* 67 (June 1990): 66–69.

Nelson, Debra L., James Campbell Quick, and Michael A. Hitt. "What Stresses HR Professionals?" *Personnel* 67 (August 1990): 36–39.

Oliver, Bill. "Do You Drug Test Your Employees?" *HRMagazine* 35 (October 1990): 57.

Overman, Stephenie. "Driving the Safety Message Home." *HRMagazine* 39 (March 1994): 58–59.

Pater, Robert. "Safety Leadership Cuts Costs." *HRMagazine* 35 (November 1990): 46–47.

Pope, Tom. "EAPs: Good Idea, But What's the Cost?" *Management Review* 79 (August 1990): 50–53.

Ralfs, Mark, and John Morley. "Turning Employee Problems Into Triumphs." *Training and Development Journal* 44 (November 1990): 73–76.

Ralston, David A. "How Flextime Eases Work/Family Tensions." *Personnel* 67 (August 1990): 45–48.

Reynolds, Larry. "ADA Complaints Are Not What Experts Predicted." *HR Focus* 70 (November 1993): 1–2.

Segal, Jonathan A. "AIDS Education Is a Necessary High-Risk Activity." *HRMagazine* 36 (February 1991): 82–85.

Slater, Robert Bruce. "OSHA Goes on the Offensive (New Regulations and Standards)." *Business and Society Review* 89 (Spring 1994): 44–46.

Smith, R. Blake. "Wellness Administrators Working to Prove Programs Cost-Effective." *Occupational Health & Safety* 59 (October 1990): 100, 102–104.

Stallworth, Hugh F. "Realistic Goals Help Avoid Burnout." *HRMagazine* 35 (June 1990): 169, 171.

Taslitz, Neal. "OSHA, ADA, and the Litigation of CTDs." *Managing Office Technology* 39 (March 1994): 39–46.

Thieme, Cheryl. "Better-Bilt Builds a Substance Abuse Program That Works." *Personnel Journal* 69 (August 1990): 52, 54, 57–58.

Thompson, Brad Lee. "OSHA Bounces Back." *Training* 28 (January 1991): 45–46, 48, 50–51, 53.

Tyson, Patrick R. "OSHA Wins Two Big Ones in Court." *Safety & Health* 150 (July 1994): 25–27.

Watts, Patti. "Are Your Employees Burnout-Proof?" *Personnel* 67 (September 1990): 12–14, 20.

Weinstock, Matthew P. "What Is OSHA Doing?" *Occupational Hazards* 56 (May 1994): 79–82.

Weiss, W. H. "Coping With Work Stress (Supervisors)." *Supervision* 55 (April 1994): 3–5.

Chapter 15—The Labor Union

Bernstein, Aaron. "Bad Connection at AT&T." *Business Week* (April 22, 1991): 32–33.

Bernstein, Aaron. "Been Down So Long . . . But Unions May Ride Out the Recession." *Business Week* (January 14, 1991): 30–31.

Bernstein, Aaron. "Busting Unions Can Backfire on the Bottom Line." *Business Week* (March 18, 1991): 108.

Bernstein, Aaron. "The Teamsters and the Mob: It May Really Be Over." *Business Week* (June 17, 1991): 102–103.

Bernstein, Aaron, and Jim Bartimo. "Wrong Time for Scare Tactics?" *Business Week* (April 16, 1990): 27–28.

Colford, Steven W. "Unions Flock to TV Ads." *Advertising Age* 61 (September 10, 1990): 82.

Eubanks, Paula. "Employee Grievance Policy: Don't Discourage Complaints." *Hospitals* 64 (December 20, 1990): 36–37.

Galand, Susan B. "Why Democrats Still Want to Wear the Union Label." *Business Week* (March 5, 1990): 37.

Hage, David, Robin Knight, and Steven Butler. "Unions Feel the Heat." *U.S. News & World Report* 116 (January 24, 1994): 57–61.

Kelly, Kevin, and Aaron Bernstein. "Why United Is Putting Pilots on the Gravy Train." *Business Week* (April 29, 1991): 32.

Kilgour, John G. "The Odds on White-Collar Organizing." *Personnel* 67 (August 1990): 29–35.

Kirkpatrick, David. "The Union's Role as Co-Manager." *Fortune* 121 (March 26, 1990): 37.

Koretz, Gene, and Celeste Whittaker. "More Picket Lines, Fewer Rank-And-Filers." *Business Week* (May 7, 1990): 24.

Lissy, William E. "Election of 'Financial Core' Union Membership." *Supervision* 51 (September 1990): 22–23.

Lissy, William E. "Management-Sponsored Employees' Committee Not Illegal." *Supervision* 51 (April 1990): 17–19.

Mondy, R. Wayne, and Shane R. Premeaux. "The Labor/Management Power Relationship Revisited." *Personnel Administrator* 30 (May 1985): 52–57.

Ng, Ignace, and Dennis Maki. "Trade Union Influence on Human Resource Management Practices." *Industrial Relations* 33 (January 1994): 121–135.

Premeaux, Shane R., R. Wayne Mondy, and Art L. Bethke. "The Two-Tier Wage System." *Personnel Administrator* 31 (November 1986): 92–100.

Reynolds, Larry. "Management and Labor Draw the Picket Line." *Personnel* 68 (March 1991): 15.

Reynolds, Larry. "Management-Labor Tensions Spell Union Busting." *Personnel* 68 (March 1991): 7–9

Ritter, Anne. "Are Unions Worth the Bargain?" *Personnel* 67 (February 1990): 12–14.

Sanyal, Rajib N. "An Empirical Analysis of the Unionization of Foreign Manufacturing Firms in the U.S." *Journal of International Business Studies* 21 (First Quarter 1990): 119–132.

Solomon, Charlene Marmer. "Nightmare at Nordstrom." *Personnel Journal* 69 (September 1990): 76–83.

Zalusky, John. "Labor Seeks Security, Not Bonuses." *Personnel* 68 (January 1991): 13.

Chapter 16—Collective Bargaining

Anderson, Kay E., Philip M. Doyle, and Albert E. Schwenk. "Measuring Union-Nonunion Earnings Differences." *Monthly Labor Review* 113 (June 1990): 26–38.

Bauman, Alvin. "A New Measure of Compensation Cost Adjustments." *Monthly Labor Review* 113 (August 1990): 11–18.

Bernstein, Aaron. "Bad Connection at AT&T." *Business Week* (April 22, 1991): 32–33.

Bernstein, Aaron. "Been Down So Long . . . But Unions May Ride Out the Recession." *Business Week* (January 14, 1991): 30–31.

Bernstein, Aaron. "Busting Unions Can Backfire on the Bottom Line." *Business Week* (March 18, 1991): 108.

Bernstein, Aaron. "The Teamsters and The Mob: It May Really Be Over." *Business Week* (June, 17, 1991): 102–103.

Bernstein, Aaron, and Jim Bartimo. "Wrong Time for Scare Tactics?" *Business Week* (April 16, 1991): 27–28.

Brown, Marlene. "I'm Overqualified, Bored and Quitting!" *Management World* 19 (March-April 1990): 14–15.

Cimin, Michael. "Collective Bargaining in 1990: Search for Solutions Continues." *Monthly Labor Review* 114 (January 1991): 19–33.

Colford, Steven W. "Unions Flock to TV Ads." *Advertising Age* 61 (September 10, 1990): 82.

"Court Sides With Unions." *Personnel* 67 (June 1990): 6–7.

Eubanks, Paula. "Employee Grievance Policy: Don't Discourage Complaints." *Hospitals* 64 (December 20, 1990): 36–37.

Freedman, Audrey, and William E. Fulmer. "Last Rites for Pattern Bargaining." *Harvard Business Review* 60 (March-April): 39–42ff.

Garland, Susan B. "Why Democrats Still Want to Wear the Union Label." *Business Week* (March 5, 1990): 37

Hoerr, John. "What Should Unions Do?" *Harvard Business Review* 69 (May-June 1991): 30–45.

Kelly, Kevin, and Aaron Bernstein. "Why United Is Putting Pilots on the Gravy Train." *Business Week* (April 29, 1991): 32.

Kilgour, John G. "The Odds on White-Collar Organizing." *Personnel* 67 (August 1990): 29–35.

Kirkpatrick, David. "The Union's Role as Co-Manager." *Fortune* 121 (March 26, 1990): 37

Koretz, Gene, and Celeste Whittaker. "More Picket Lines, Fewer Rank-And-Filers." *Business Week* (May 7, 1990): 24

Lissy, William E. "Election of `Financial Core' Union Membership." *Supervision* 51 (September 1990): 22–23.

Lissy, William E. "Management-Sponsored Employees' Committee Not Illegal." *Supervision* 51 (September 1990): 17–19.

McDonough, Paul S. "Maintain a Union-Free Status." *Personnel Journal* (April 1990): 108–114.

Premeaux, Shane R., R. Wayne Mondy, and Art L. Bethke. "Decertification: Fulfilling Unions' Destiny?" *Personnel Journal* 32 (June 1987): 144–148.

Reynolds, Larry. "Management and Labor Draw the Picket Line." *Personnel* 68 (March 1991): 15.

Reynolds, Larry. "Management-Labor Tensions Spell Union Busting." *Personnel* 68 (March 1991): 7–9.

Ritter, Anne. "Are Unions Worth the Bargain?" *Personnel* 67 (February 1990): 12–14.

Sanyal, Rajib N. "An Empirical Analysis of the Unionization of Foreign Manufacturing Firms in the U.S." *Journal of International Business Studies* 21 (First Quarter 1990): 119–132.

Schiffman, Barry. "Tougher Tactics to Keep Out Unions: Consultants Give Employers a New Bag of Tricks." *The New York Times* 140 (March 3, 1991): sec. 3, F8 (N), col 1.

Solomon, Charlene Marmer. "Nightmare at Nordstrom." *Personnel Journal* 69 (September 1990): 76–83.

Zalusky, John. "Labor Seeks Security, Not Bonuses." *Personnel* 68 (January 1991): 13.

Chapter 17—Union-Free Organizations

Anderson, Kay E., Philip M. Doyle, and Albert E. Schwenk. "Measuring Union-Nonunion Earnings Differences." *Monthly Labor Review* 13 (June 1990): 26–38.

Eubanks, Paula. "Employee Grievance Policy: Don't Discourage Complaints." *Hospitals* 64 (December 20, 1990): 36–37.

Koretz, Gene. "Why Unions Thrive Abroad—But Wither in the U.S." *Business Week* (May 7, 1990): 26.

Lissy, William E. "Election of 'Financial Core' Union Membership." *Supervision* 51 (September 1990): 22–23.

Lissy, William E. "Management-Sponsored Employees' Committee Not Illegal." *Supervision* 51 (April 1990): 17–19.

McDonough, Paul S. "Maintain a Union-Free Status." *Personnel Journal* 69 (April 1990): 108–114.

Premeaux, Shane R., R. Wayne Mondy, and Art L. Bethke. "The Two-Tier Wage System." *Personnel Administrator* 31 (November 1986): 92–100.

Ritter, Anne. "Are Unions Worth the Bargain?" *Personnel* 67 (February 1990): 12–14.

Sanyal, Rajib N. "An Empirical Analysis of the Unionization of Foreign Manufacturing Firms in the U.S." *Journal of International Business Studies* 21 (First Quarter 1990): 119–132.

Schiffman, Barry. "Tougher Tactics to Keep Out Unions: Consultants Give Employers a New Bag of Tricks." *The New York Times* 140 (March 3, 1991): sec. 3, F8 (N), col 1.

Chapter 18—Internal Employee Relations

Barnett, Timothy R., and Daniel S. Cochran. "Making Room for the Whistleblower." *HRMagazine* 36 (January 1991): 58–61.

Bunning, Richard L. "The Dynamics of Downsizing." *Personnel Journal* 69 (September 1990): 69–75.

Capozzi, Lisabeth Eames. "Retaining the Human Potential of Corporate Acquisitions." *HRMagazine* 39 (August 1994): 76–79.

Crane, Donald P., and Paul F. Gerhart. "Wrongful Dismissal Arbitration: What Can the Parties Expect?" *Labor Law Journal* 45 (May 1994): 315–319.

Colon, Robert J. "Grievances Hinge on Poor Contract Language." *Personnel Journal* 69 (September 1990): 32–36.

Davy, Jeanette A., Greg Stewart, and Joe Anderson. "Formalization of Grievance Procedures: A Multi-Firm and Industry Study." *Journal of Labor Research* 13 (Summer 1992): 307–316.

Freedland, Mark. "Performance Appraisal and Disciplinary Action: The Case for Control of Abuses." *International Labour Review* 132 (July-August 1993): 491–506.

Fergus, Mike. "Employees on the Move." *HRMagazine* 36 (May 1990): 44–46.

Foxman, Loretta D., and Walter L. Polsky. "Outplacement Results in Success." *Personnel Journal* 69 (February 1990): 30–37.

Grensing, Lin. "Don't Let Them Out the Door Without an Exit Interview." *Management World* 19 (March-April 1990): 11–13.

Hoffman, Jeffery S. "Sweetening Early-Retirement Programs." *Personnel* 67 (March 1990): 18–20.

Hukill, Craig. "Labor and the Supreme Court: Significant Issues of 1990–1991." *Monthly Labor Review* 114 (January 1991): 34–40.

Karp, Robert E. "Ethical Values Underlying the Termination Process." *Business & Society* 30 (Spring 1991): 1–6.

Laabs, Jennifer J. "Remedies for HR's Legal Headache." *Personnel Journal* 73 (December 1994): 67–76.

Levy, Martin. "Discipline for Professional Employees." *Personnel Journal* 69 (December 1990): 27–28.

Lord, Mary. "Where You Can't Get Fired." *U.S. News & World Report* 110 (January 14, 1991): 46–48.

O'Reilly, Brian. "The New Deal: What Companies and Employees Owe One Another." *Fortune* 129 (June 13, 1994): 44–49.

Pell, Arthur R. "What—No Grievances?" *Manager's Magazine* 68 (October 1993): 29–30.

Pell, Arthur R. "Effective Reprimanding." *Manager's Magazine* 65 (August 1990): 26–27.

Raisner, Jack. "Relocate Without Making False Moves." *HRMagazine* 36 (February 1991): 46–50.

Reynolds, Calvin, and Rita Bennett. "The Career Couple Challenge." *Personnel Journal* 70 (March 1991): 46–48.

Rich, Joseph R., and Beth C. Florin-Thuma. "Rewarding Employees in an Environment of Fewer Promotions." *Pension World* 26 (November 1990): 16–17.

Saltzman, Amy, Anne K. Smith, and Francesca L. Kritz. "Girding for a Pink Slip." *U.S. News & World Report* 110 (January 14, 1991): 54–55.

Shaller, Elliot. "Avoid Pitfalls in Hiring, Firing." *Nation's Business* 79 (February 1991): 51–54.

Smith, Michael. "Help in Making Those Tough Layoff Decisions." *Supervisory Management* 35 (January 1990): 3.

Stroh, Linda K., Anne H. Reilly, and Jeanne M. Brett. "New Trends in Relocation." *HRMagazine* 35 (February 1990): 42–44.

Touby, Laurel Allison. "How to Leave Without Burning Your Bridges." *Working Woman* 16 (April 1991): 30.

Trevino, Linda Klebe. "The Social Effects of Punishment in Organizations: A Justice Perspective." *Academy of Management Review* 17 (October 1992): 647–676.

Wilensky, Ron, and Karen M. Jones. "Quick Response:

Key to Resolving Complaints." *HRMagazine* 39 (March 1994): 42–47.

Wilson, Steve. "Layoffs Take Advance Preparation." *Management Review* 80 (May 1991): 5–6.

Chapter 19—Human Resource Research

Betts, Mitch. "States Redefining Public Service." *Computerworld* 27 (April 19, 1993): 20.

Booker, Ellis. "Job Seekers Scan Electronic Horizon." *Computerworld* 28 (October 3, 1994): 1,133.

Capron, H. L. *Essentials of Computing,* 2nd edition (New York, NY: The Benjamin Cummings Publishing Company, Inc., 1995): 125–127.

Cashman, Margaret E., and James C. McElroy. "Evaluating the HR Function." *HRMagazine* 36 (January 1991): 70–73.

Clark, Robert L., and Richard Anker. "Cross-National Analysis of Labor Force Participation of Older Men and Women." *Economic Development & Cultural Change* 41 (April 1993): 489–513.

Cox, Mark M. "Human Resources' Expanding Role in the Health Care Industry." *Personnel Journal* 69 (May 1990): 41–44.

Estreicher, Samuel. "Laws Promoting Worker Training, Productivity, and Quality." *Labor Law Journal* 44 (February 1993): 110–118.

Fischer, Robert L. "HRIS Quality Depends on Teamwork." *Personnel Journal* 70 (April 1991): 47–51.

Fitz-enz, Jac. "HR's New Score Card." *Personnel Journal* 73 (February 1994): 84–87.

Goodrich, Jonathan N. "Telecommuting in America." *Business Horizons* 33 (July-August 1990): 31–37.

Grupe, Fritz H. "Planning Your Expert System Strategy." *Information Executive* 4 (Winter 1991): 47.

Keaton, Paul N., and Michael J. Semb. "Shaping Up the Bottom Line." *HRMagazine* 36 (September 1990): 81–86.

King, Albert S., and Terrence R. Bishop. "Human Resource Experience: Survey and Analysis." *Public Personnel Management* 23 (Spring 1994): 165–180.

Knapp, Jeffrey. "Trends in HR Management Systems." *Personnel* 67 (April 1990): 56–61.

Koretz, Gene. "A Worker Exodus That Could Weaken Productivity." *Business Week* (July 2, 1990): 22.

Koddek, Ellen Ernst. "Why Many HR Programs Fail." *Personnel* 67 (May 1990): 50–53.

Kromling, Larry K. "Calcomp Reshapes HR for the Future." *Personnel Journal* 69 (January 1990): 57–63.

Sachs, Robert. "A Productive Workforce: The Final Frontier of Competitive Advantage?" *Business Forum* 15 (Spring 1990): 5–7.

Sadarini, Robert. "The Art of Imagineering." *Information Executive* 4 (Summer 1991): 6–7.

Shetty, Y.K., and Paul F. Buller. "Regaining Competitiveness Requires HR Solutions." *Personnel* 67 (July 1990): 8–12.

Tarrant, Sharon M. "Setting Up an Electronic Job Posting System." *Training and Development* 48 (January 1994): 39–42.

Wexler, Joanie M. "Ties That Bind." *Computerworld* 27 (June 28, 1993): 97.

Glossary

Adverse impact: A concept established by the *Uniform Guidelines*; it occurs if women and minorities are not hired at the rate of at least 80 percent of the best achieving group.

Advertising: A way of communicating a firm's employment needs to the public through such media as radio, newspaper, or industry publications.

Affirmative action: Stipulated by EO 11246, it requires employers to take positive steps to ensure employment of applicants and treatment of employees during employment without regard to race, creed, color, or national origin.

Affirmative action program (AAP): A program that an organization develops to employ women and minorities in proportion to their representation in the firm's relevant labor market.

Agency shop: A labor agreement provision requiring, as a condition of employment, that each nonunion member of a bargaining unit pays the union the equivalent of membership dues as a service charge in return for the union acting as the bargaining agent.

AIDS (acquired immune deficiency syndrome): A disease that undermines the body's immune system, leaving the person susceptible to a wide range of fatal diseases.

Aiming: The ability to move one's hands quickly and accurately from one spot to another, which is important in jobs such as electronic parts assembly.

Alcoholism: A treatable disease characterized by uncontrolled and compulsive drinking that interferes with normal living patterns.

Apprenticeship training: A combination of classroom instruction and on-the-job training.

Arbitration: A process in which a dispute is submitted to an impartial third party for a binding decision.

Assessment center: An appraisal approach that requires employees to participate in a series of activities similar to those they might encounter in an actual job.

Authorization card: A document indicating that an employee wants to be represented by a labor organization in collective bargaining.

Availability forecast: A process of determining whether a firm will be able to secure employees with the necessary skills from within the company, from outside the organization, or from a combination of the two sources.

Bargaining unit: A group of employees, not necessarily union members, recognized by an employer or certified by an administrative agency as appropriate for representation by a labor organization for purposes of collective bargaining.

Beachhead demands: Demands that a union does not expect management to meet when they are first made.

Behavior description interview: A structured interview that uses questions designed to probe an applicant's past behavior in specific situations.

Behavior modeling: A training method that utilizes live demonstrations or videotapes to illustrate how managers function in various situations for the purpose of developing interpersonal skills.

Behaviorally anchored rating scale (BARS) method: A performance appraisal method that combines elements of the traditional rating scale and critical incidents methods.

Benchmark job: A well-known job, in which a large percentage of a company's workforce is employed, that represents the entire job structure.

Benefits: All financial rewards that generally are not paid directly to an employee.

Biofeedback: A method of learning to control involuntary bodily processes, such as blood pressure or heart rate.

Board interview: A meeting in which one candidate is interviewed by several representatives of a company.

Bottom-up approach: A forecasting method beginning with the lowest organizational units and progressing upward through an organization ultimately to provide an aggregate forecast of employment needs.

Boycott: A refusal by union members to use or buy their firm's products.

Burnout: A state of fatigue or frustration stemming from devotion to a cause, way of life, or relationship that did not provide the expected reward.

Business games: Simulations that represent actual business situations.

Capitation: An approach to health care where providers negotiate a rate for health care for a covered life over a period of time.

Career: A general course of action a person chooses to pursue throughout his or her working life.

Career anchors: Five different motives identified by Edgar Schein to account for the way people select and prepare for a career.

Career development: A formal approach taken by an organization to ensure that people with the proper qualifications and experience are available when needed.

Career path: A flexible line of progression through which an employee may move during his or her employment with a company.

Career planning: An ongoing process whereby an individual sets career goals and identifies the means to achieve them.

Carpal tunnel syndrome: A condition caused by repetitive flexing and extension of the wrist.

Case study: A training method that utilizes simulated business problems for trainees to solve; also a research method that attempts to uncover the underlying cause of specific problems in a plant, a department, or a work group.

Central tendency: A common error that occurs when employees are incorrectly rated near the average or middle of a scale.

Checkoff of dues: An agreement where a company agrees to withhold union dues from members' paychecks and to forward the money directly to the union.

Classification method: A job evaluation method in which classes or grades are defined to describe a group of jobs.

Client/server systems: Electronic systems that split and deliver computer applications and data at reduced costs with great reliability.

Closed shop: An arrangement whereby union membership is a prerequisite to employment.

Coaching: An on-the-job approach to management development in which a manager is given an opportunity to teach on a one-to-one basis.

Cognitive aptitude tests: Tests that measure an individual's ability to learn, as well as to perform a job.

Collective bargaining: The performance of the mutual obligation of the employer and the representative of the employees to meet at reasonable times and confer in good faith with respect to wages, hours, and other terms and conditions of employment, or the negotiation of an agreement, or any question arising thereunder, and the execution of a written contract incorporating any agreement reached if requested by either party, but such obligation does not compel either party to agree to a proposal or require the making of a concession.

Committee on Political Education (COPE): The political arm of the AFL-CIO.

Comparable worth: A determination of the values of dissimilar jobs (such as company nurse and welder), by comparing them under some form of job evaluation, and the assignment of pay rates according to their evaluated worth.

Compensation: Every type of reward that individuals receive in return for their labor.

Compressed workweek: Any arrangement of work hours that permits employees to fulfill their work obligation in fewer days than the typical five-day workweek.

Computer-based training: A teaching method that takes advantage of the speed, memory, and data manipulation capabilities of the computers for greater flexibility of instruction.

Concurrent validity: A validation method in which test scores and criterion data are obtained at essentially the same time.

Conference method: A widely used instructional approach that brings together individuals with common interests to discuss and attempt to solve problems (also known as the *discussion method*).

Conspiracy: The combination of two or more persons who band together to prejudice the rights of others or of society (such as by refusing to work or demanding higher wages).

Construct validity: A test validation method to determine whether a selection test measures certain traits or qualities that have been identified as important in performing a particular job.

Content validity: A test validation method whereby a person performs certain tasks that are actual samples of the kind of work a job requires or completes a paper-and-pencil test that measures relevant job knowledge.

Corporate culture: The system of shared values, beliefs, and habits within an organization that interacts with the formal structure to produce behavioral norms.

Cost-of-living allowance (COLA): An escalator clause in a labor agreement that automatically increases wages as the U.S. Bureau of Labor Statistics' cost-of-living index rises.

Craft union: A bargaining unit, such as the Carpenters and Joiners union, that is typically composed of members of a particular trade or skill in a specific locality.

Criterion-related validity: A test validation method that compares the scores on selection tests to some aspect of job performance as determined, for example, by performance appraisal.

Critical incident method: A performance appraisal technique that requires a written record of highly favorable and highly unfavorable employee work behavior.

Cumulative trauma disorders: A series of disorders, often associated with using computers, which include injuries to the back and upper extremities.

Cutoff score: The score below which an applicant will not be considered further for employment.

Cyclical variations: Reasonably predictable movements about a trend line that occur over a period of more than a year.

Data communication: The sending of computer data over some form of communication medium, such as telephone lines.

Database management: The integration of information subsystems in order to reduce the duplication of information, effort, and cost and to provide controlled access to this information.

Decertification: Election by a group of employees to withdraw a union's right to act as their exclusive bargaining representative.

Decision support system (DSS): An information system that allows users to process and retrieve information quickly.

Defined benefit plan: A retirement plan in which an employer agrees to provide a specific level of retirement income that is either a fixed dollar amount or a percentage of earnings.

Defined contribution plan: A retirement plan that requires specific contributions by an employer.

Demotion: The process of moving a worker to a lower level of duties and responsibilities, which typically involves a pay cut.

Development: Learning that looks beyond the knowledge and skill needed for a present job.

Direct financial compensation: Pay that a person receives in the form of wages, salaries, bonuses, and commissions.

Disciplinary action: The invoking of a penalty against an employee who fails to meet organizational standards or comply with organizational rules.

Disciplinary action without punishment: A process whereby a worker is given time off with pay to think about whether he or she wants to follow the rules and continue working for a company.

Discipline: The state of employee self-control and orderly conduct.

Downsizing: A reduction in the number of people employed by a firm (also known as *restructuring,* and *rightsizing*).

Dual career path: A method of rewarding technical specialists and professionals who can, and should be allowed to, continue to contribute significantly to a company without having to become managers.

Employee assistance program (EAP): A comprehensive approach that many organizations have taken to deal with burnout, alcohol and drug abuse, and other emotional disturbances.

Employee-centered work redesign: An innovative concept designed to link the mission of a company with the job satisfaction needs of its employees.

Employee equity: Payment of individuals performing similar jobs for the same firm commensurate with factors unique to each employee.

Employee requisition: A document that specifies a particular job title, the appropriate department, and the date by which an open job should be filled.

Employee stock ownership plan (ESOP): A companywide incentive plan in which the company provides its employees with common stock.

Employment agency: An organization that assists

als in their attempts to locate jobs.

Employment at will: An unwritten contract created when an employee agrees to work for an employer but no agreement exists as to how long the parties expect the employment to last.

Employment interview: A goal-oriented conversation in which an interviewer and an applicant exchange information.

Equity: The perception by workers that they are being treated fairly.

Equivalent forms method: A means of verifying selection test reliability by correlating the results of tests that are similar but not identical.

Ergonomics: The study of human interaction with tasks, equipment, tools, and the physical environment.

Essay method: A performance appraisal method whereby the rater writes a brief narrative describing an employee's performance.

Ethics: The discipline dealing with what is good and bad, or right and wrong, or with moral duty and obligation.

Executive orders (EO): Directives issued by the president that have the force and effect of laws enacted by the Congress.

Executive search firms: Organizations retained by a company to search for the most qualified executive for a specific position.

Executives: Top-level managers who report directly to a corporation's chief executive officer or the head of a major division.

Exempt employees: Those categorized as executive, administrative, or professional employees and outside salespersons.

Experiment: A method of inquiry that involves the manipulation of certain variables while others are held constant.

Expert system: A system that uses knowledge about a narrowly defined, complex area to act as a consultant to a human.

External environment: The factors that affect a firm's human resources from outside the organization's boundaries.

External equity: Payment of employees at rates comparable to those paid for similar jobs elsewhere.

Factor comparison method: A job evaluation method in which raters (1) need not keep an entire job in mind as they evaluate it and (2) make decisions based on the assumption that there are five universal job factors.

Finger dexterity: The ability to make precise, coordinated finger movements, such as those performed by an electronics assembler or a watchmaker.

Flexible compensation plans: A method that permits employees to choose from among many alternatives in deciding how their financial compensation will be allocated.

Flextime: The practice of permitting employees to choose, with certain limitations, their own working hours.

Forced-choice performance report: A performance appraisal technique in which the rater is given a series of statements about an individual and indicates which items are most or least descriptive of the employee.

Forced distribution method: An appraisal approach in which the rater is required to assign individuals in a work group to a limited number of categories similar to a normal frequency distribution.

401(k) plan: A defined contribution retirement plan in which employees may defer income up to a certain maximum amount allowed.

Frequency rate: A formula used to calculate the number of lost-time accidents per million person-hours worked.

Functional job analysis (FJA): A comprehensive approach to formulating job descriptions that concentrates on the interactions among the work, the worker, and the work organization.

Generalists: Persons who perform tasks in a wide variety of human resource-related areas.

Glass ceiling: The invisible barrier in organizations that prevents many women and minorities from achieving top level management positions.

Going rate: The average pay that most employers provide for the same job in a particular area or industry.

"Golden parachute" contract: A perquisite provided for the purpose of protecting executives in the event their firm is acquired by another.

Grievance: An employee's dissatisfaction or feeling of personal injustice relating to his or her employment.

Grievance procedure: A formal, systematic process that permits employees to complain about matters affecting them and their work.

Group appraisal: The use of a team of two or more managers who are familiar with an employee's performance to appraise it.

Group interview: A meeting in which several job applicants interact in the presence of one or more company representatives.

Groupware: Software that enables people to work together in groups and assists in decision making, workflow and work management.

Guidelines Oriented Job Analysis (GOJA): A method that responds to the growing amount of legislation affecting employment decisions by utilizing a step-by-step procedure to describe the work of a particular job classification.

Halo error: The perception by an evaluator that one factor is of paramount importance and then gives a good or bad overall rating to an employee based on this particular factor.

Hay Guide Chart-Profile Method (Hay Plan): A highly refined version of the point method of job evaluation that uses the factors of know-how, problem solving, accountability, and, where appropriate, working conditions.

Hazard pay: Additional pay provided to employees who work under extremely dangerous conditions.

Health: An employee's freedom from physical or emotional illness.

Health Maintenance Organizations (HMOs): Insurance programs provided by companies that cover all services for a fixed fee with control being exercised over which doctors and health facilities may be used.

Human resource development (HRD): A planned, continuous effort by management to improve employee competency levels and organizational performance through training, and development programs.

Human resource information system (HRIS): Any organized approach for obtaining relevant and timely information on which to base human resource decisions.

Human resource management (HRM): The utilization of a firm's human resources to achieve organizational objectives.

Human resource managers: Individuals who normally act in an advisory (or staff) capacity when working with other (line) managers regarding human resource matters.

Human resource planning (HRP): The process of systematically reviewing human resource requirements to ensure that the required number of employees, with the required skills, are available when they are needed.

Human resource research: The systematic study of a firm's human resources for the purpose of maximizing personal and organizational goal achievement.

Hypnosis: An altered state of consciousness that is artificially induced and characterized by increased receptiveness to suggestions.

In-basket training: A simulation in which the participant is asked to establish priorities for handling a number of business papers, such as memoranda, reports, and telephone messages, that would typically cross a manager's desk.

Incentive compensation: A payment program that relates pay to productivity.

Indirect financial compensation: All financial rewards that are not included in direct compensation.

Industrial union: A bargaining unit that generally consists of all the workers in a particular plant or group of plants.

Informal organization: The set of evolving relationships and patterns of human interaction within an organization that are not officially prescribed.

Injunction: A prohibiting legal procedure used by employers to prevent certain union activities, such as strikes and unionization attempts.

Internal employee relations: Those human resource management activities associated with promotion, transfer, demotion, resignation, discharge, layoff, and retirement.

Internal environment: The factors that affect a firm's human resources from inside the organization's boundaries.

Internal equity: Payment of employees according to the relative value of their jobs within an organization.

Internship: A special form of recruitment that involves placing students in temporary jobs with no obligation either by the company to hire the student permanently or by the student to accept a permanent position with the firm following graduation.

Job: A group of tasks that must be performed if an organization is to achieve its goals.

Job analysis: The systematic process of determining the skills, duties, and knowledge required for performing specific jobs in an organization.

Job analysis schedule (JAS): A systematic method of

studying jobs and occupations developed by the U.S. Department of Labor.

Job bidding: A technique that permits individuals in an organization who believe they possess the required qualifications to apply for a posted job.

Job description: A document that provides information regarding the tasks, duties, and responsibilities of a job.

Job design: A process of determining the specific tasks to be performed, the methods used in performing these tasks, and how the job relates to other work in an organization.

Job enlargement: A change in the scope of a job so as to provide greater variety to a worker.

Job enrichment: The restructuring of the content and level of responsibility of a job to make it more challenging, meaningful, and interesting to a worker.

Job evaluation: That part of a compensation system in which a company determines the relative value of one job in relation to another.

Job knowledge questions: Questions that probe the knowledge a person possesses for performing a particular job.

Job knowledge tests: Tests designed to measure a candidate's knowledge of the duties of a job for which he or she is applying.

Job overload: A condition that exists when employees are given more work than they can reasonably handle.

Job posting: A procedure for communicating to company employees the fact that job openings exist.

Job pricing: Placing a dollar value on the worth of a job.

Job rotation: A training method that involves moving employees from one job to another for the purpose of giving them broader experience.

Job-sample simulation questions: Situations in which an applicant may be required to actually perform a sample task from a particular job.

Job sharing: The filling of a job by two part-time people who split the duties of one full-time job in some agreed-on manner and are paid according to their contributions.

Job specification: A document that outlines the minimum acceptable qualifications a person should possess in order to perform a particular job.

Job Training Partnership Act (JTPA): A federal law that provides job training and employment services for economically disadvantaged adults and youth, dislocated workers, and other persons who face exceptional employment hurdles.

Labor market: The geographical area from which employees are recruited for a particular job.

Leniency: Giving an undeservedly high performance appraisal rating to an employee.

Likes and dislikes survey: A procedure that helps individuals recognize restrictions they place on themselves.

Local union: The basic element in the structure of the U.S. labor movement.

Lockout: A management decision to keep employees out of the workplace and to operate with management personnel and/or temporary replacements.

Long-term trend: A projection of demand for a firm's products, typically five years or more into the future.

Management by objectives (MBO): A philosophy of management that emphasizes the setting of agreed-on objectives by superior and subordinate managers and the use of these objectives as the primary basis for motivation, evaluation, and self control.

Management development: Learning experiences provided by an organization for the purpose of upgrading skills and knowledge required in current and future managerial positions.

Management inventory: Detailed data regarding each manager in an organization, which is used in identifying individuals possessing the potential to move into higher level positions.

Management Position Description Questionnaire (MPDQ): A form of job analysis designed for management positions that uses a checklist method to analyze jobs.

Managing diversity: Having an acute awareness of characteristics common to a culture, race, gender, age, or sexual orientation while at the same time managing employees with these characteristics as individuals.

Mandatory bargaining issues: Bargaining issues that fall within the definition of wages, hours, and other terms and conditions of employment; refusal to bargain in these areas is grounds for an unfair labor practice charge.

Manual dexterity: The coordinated movements of both hands and arms, such as those required by large assembly jobs.

Media: Special methods of communicating ideas and concepts in training and development.

Mediation: A process whereby a neutral third party enters and attempts to resolve a labor dispute when a bargaining impasse has occurred.

Mentoring: An on-the-job approach to management development in which the trainee is given an opportunity to learn on a one-to-one basis from more experienced organizational members.

Mission: An organization's continuing purpose or reason for being.

Modified retirement: An option that permits older employees to work fewer than regular hours for a certain period of time preceding retirement.

Multimedia: A computer application that produces presentations combining automation, stereo sound, full-motion video, and graphics.

Multinational corporation (MNC): An organization that conducts a large part of its business outside the country in which it is headquartered and has a significant percentage of its physical facilities and employees in other countries.

National union: An organization composed of local unions, which it charters.

Network career path: A method of job progression that contains both vertical and horizontal opportunities.

New collar workers: Young, well educated, independent workers, who appear to be particularly susceptible to issues related to job security.

Nonfinancial compensation: The satisfaction that a person receives from the job itself or from the psychological and/or physical environment in which the job is performed.

Norm: A distribution that provides a frame of reference for comparing an applicant's performance with that of others.

Objectivity: The condition that is achieved when all individuals scoring a given test obtain the same results.

Occupational Measurement System (OMS): A method of job analysis that enables organizations to collect, store, and analyze information pertinent to human resources by means of an electronic database.

Ombudsperson: A complaint officer with access to top management who hears employees' complaints, investigates them, and sometimes recommends appropriate action.

On-the-job training (OJT): An informal approach to training in which an employee learns job tasks by actually performing them.

Open-door policy: A company policy whereby employees have the right to take any grievance to the person next in the chain of command if a satisfactory solution cannot be obtained from their immediate supervisor.

Open shop: Employment that is open on equal terms to union members and nonmembers alike.

Operative employees: All workers in a firm except managers and professionals, such as engineers, accountants, or professional secretaries.

Organization development (OD): An organization-wide application of behavioral science knowledge to the planned development and reinforcement of a firm's strategies, structures, and processes for improving its effectiveness.

Organizational career planning: The process of establishing career paths within a firm.

Orientation: The guided adjustment of new employees to the company, the job, and the work group.

Outplacement: A process whereby a laid-off employee is given assistance in finding employment elsewhere.

Paired comparison: A variation of the ranking method of performance appraisal in which the performance of each employee is compared with that of every other employee in the particular group.

Pay compression: A situation that occurs when workers perceive that the pay differential between their pay and that of employees in jobs above or below them is too small.

Pay followers: Companies that choose to pay below the going rate because of a poor financial condition or a belief that they simply do not require highly capable employees.

Pay grade: The grouping of similar jobs to simplify the job-pricing process.

Pay leaders: Those organizations that pay higher wages and salaries than competing firms.

Pay range: A minimum and maximum pay rate for a job, with enough variance between the two to allow for some significant pay difference.

Performance appraisal (PA): A formal system of periodic review and evaluation of an individual's job performance.

Permissive bargaining issues: Issues that may be raised by management or a union, but that neither side may insist be bargained over.

Perquisites (perks): Special benefits provided by a firm to key executives to give them something extra.

Plateauing: A career condition that occurs when an employee's job functions and work content remain the same because of a lack of promotional opportunities within the a company.

Point method: An approach to job evaluation in which numerical values are assigned to specific job components and the sum of these values provides a quantitative assessment of a job's relative worth.

Policy: A predetermined guide established to provide direction in decision making.

Position: The tasks and responsibilities performed by one person; there is a position for every individual in an organization.

Position Analysis Questionnaire (PAQ): A structured job analysis questionnaire that uses a checklist approach to identify job elements.

Predictive validity: A validation method that involves administering a selection test and later obtaining the criterion information.

Predictor variables: Factors known to have had an impact on a company's employment levels.

Preferred Provider Organizations (PPOs): A flexible managed care system, in which incentives are provided to members to use services within the system and out-of-network providers may be utilied at greater cost.

Premium pay: Compensation paid to employees for working long periods of time or working under dangerous or undesirable conditions.

Proactive response: Taking action in anticipation of environmental changes.

Profession: A vocation characterized by the existence of a common body of knowledge and a procedure for certifying its practitioners.

Profit sharing: A compensation plan that distributes a predetermined percentage of a firm's profits to its employees.

Programmed instruction (PI): A teaching method that requires no intervention by an instructor.

Progressive disciplinary action: An approach to disciplinary action designed to ensure that the minimum penalty appropriate to an offense is imposed.

Prohibited bargaining issues: Those issues that are statutorily outlawed from collective bargaining.

Promotion: The movement of a person to a higher-level position in an organization.

Promotion from within (PFW): The policy of filling vacancies above entry-level positions with employees presently employed by a company.

Psychomotor abilities tests: Aptitude tests that measure strength, coordination, and dexterity.

Quality circles: Groups of employees who meet regularly with their supervisors to identify production problems and recommend solutions.

Quality of work life (QWL): The extent to which employees satisfy significant personal needs through their organizational experiences.

Random variations: Changes for which there are no patterns.

Ranking method: A job evaluation method in which the rater examines the description of each job being evaluated and arrange the jobs in order according to their value to the company; also a performance appraisal method in which the rater places all employees in a given group in rank order on the basis of their overall performance.

Rating scales method: A widely used performance appraisal method that rates employees according to defined factors.

Reactive response: Simply reacting to environmental changes after they occur.

Realistic job preview (RJP): A method of conveying job information to an applicant in an unbiased manner, including both positive and negative factors.

Recruitment: The process of attracting individuals on a timely basis, in sufficient numbers and with appropriate qualifications, and encouraging them to apply for jobs with an organization.

Recruitment methods: The specific means by which potential employees are attracted to an organization.

Recruitment sources: The places where qualified individuals are located.

Reengineering: The fundamental rethinking and radical redesign of business processes to achieve dramatic improvements in critical, contemporary measures of performance, such as cost, quality, service, and speed.

Reference checks: A means of providing additional insight into the information provided by an applicant and a way of verifying the accuracy of the information provided.

Regression analysis: A quantitative technique used to predict one item (known as the dependent variable) through knowledge of other items (known as independent variables).

Reliability: The extent to which a selection test provides consistent results.

Requirement forecast: An estimate of the numbers and kinds of employees an organization will need at future dates in order to realize its stated objectives.

Resume: A common method used by job seekers to present background information.

Right-to-work laws: Laws that prohibit management and unions from entering into agreements requiring union membership as a condition of employment.

Role ambiguity: A condition that exists when employees lack clear information about the content of their jobs.

Role conflict: A condition that occurs when an individual is placed in the position of having to pursue opposing goals.

Role playing: A training method in which participants "act out" job techniques needed in specific situations without the benefit of either a script or a rehearsal.

Safety: The protection of employees from injuries caused by work-related accidents.

Sampling: The process by which only a portion of a total group is studied and from which conclusions are drawn for the entire group.

Scanlon plan: A gain-sharing plan designed to bind employees to their firm's performance.

Seasonal variations: Reasonably predictable changes that occur over a period of a year.

Secondary boycott: The practice of a union attempting to encourage third parties (such as suppliers and customers) to stop doing business with a firm.

Selection: The process of choosing from a group of applicants those individuals best suited for a particular position.

Selection ratio: The number of people hired for a particular job compared to the total number of individuals in the applicant pool.

Self-assessment: The process of learning about oneself.

Sensitivity training: An organizational development technique that is designed to make people aware of themselves and their impact on others.

Severity rate: A formula that is used to calculate the number of days lost because of accidents per million person-hours worked.

Shareholders: The owners of a corporation.

Shift differential: Additional money paid to reward employees for the inconvenience of working undesirable hours.

Simulation: A technique for experimenting with a real-world situation by means of a mathematical model that represents the actual situation.

Simulators: Training devices of varying degrees of complexity that duplicate the real world.

Situational questions: Questions that pose a hypothetical job situation to determine what an applicant would do in such a situation.

Skills inventory: Information maintained on nonmanagerial employees in a company regarding their availability and preparedness to move either into higher level positions or laterally.

Social responsibility: The implied, enforced, or felt obligation of managers, acting in their official capacities, to serve or protect the interests of groups other than themselves.

Special events: A recruitment method that involves an effort on the part of a single employer or group of employers, to attract a larger number of applicants for interviews.

Specialist: An individual who may be a human resource executive, a human resource manager, or a nonmanager and who is typically concerned with only one of the six functional areas of human resource management.

Split-halves method: A means of determining the reliability of a selection test by dividing the results into two parts and then correlating the results of these two parts.

Standard hour plan: An individual incentive plan under which time allowances are calculated for each unit of output.

Standardization: The degree of uniformity of the procedures and conditions related to administering tests.

Stock option plan: An incentive plan in which a managers can buy a specified amount of stock in their company in the future at or below the current market price.

Straight piecework plan: A payment plan in which a predetermined amount of money is paid for each unit produced.

Strategic planning: The determination of overall organizational purposes and goals and how they are to be achieved.

Strength/weakness balance sheet: A self-evaluation procedure, developed originally by Benjamin Franklin, that helps people to become aware of their strengths and weaknesses.

Stress: The body's nonspecific reaction to any demand made on it.

Stress interview: A form of interview that intentionally creates anxiety to determine how a job applicant will react in certain types of situations.

Strictness: Being unduly critical of an employee's work performance.

Strike: An action by union members who refuse to work in order to exert pressure on management in negotiations.

Structured interview: A process in which an interviewer consistently asks each applicant for a particular job the same series of job-related questions.

Survey feedback method: A survey method and research technique that systematically collects information about organizations and employee attitudes and makes the data available in aggregate form to employees and management so that problems can be diagnosed and plans developed to solve them.

Team building: A conscious effort to develop effective work groups throughout an organization.

Team equity: Payment of more productive teams within an organization at a higher rate than less productive teams.

Telecommuting: A procedure whereby workers are able to remain at home or otherwise away from the office and perform their work over data lines tied to a computer.

Teleconferencing: A method of conducting or participating in multiparty discussions by telephone or videophone.

Test-retest method: A means of determining selection test reliability by giving the test twice to the same group of individuals and correlating the two sets of scores.

Total Quality Management (TQM): A top management philosophy that emphasizes the continuous improvement of the processes that result in goods or services.

Traditional career path: A vertical line of career progression from one specific job to the next.

Training: Those activities that permit individuals to acquire knowledge and skill needed for their present jobs.

Transactional analysis (TA): An organizational development method that considers the three ego states of the Parent, the Adult, and the Child in helping people understand interpersonal relations and thus assists in improving an organization's effectiveness.

Transcendental meditation (TM): A stress-reduction technique whereby an individual mentally repeats a secret word or phrase (mantra), provided by a trained instructor, while comfortably seated.

Transfer: The lateral movement of a worker within an organization.

Two-tier wage system: A wage structure that pays newly hired employees less than established employees for performing the same or similar jobs.

Union: A group of employees who have joined together for the purpose of dealing collectively with their employer.

Union shop: A requirement that all employees become members of a union after a specified period of employment (the legal minimum is thirty days) or after a union shop provision has been negotiated.

Unstructured interview: A meeting with a job applicant during which an interviewer asks probing, open-ended questions.

Utility analysis: Determination of the ratio of benefits to costs for any selection technique.

Utilization review: A process that scrutinizes medical diagnoses, hospitalization, surgery, and other medical treatment and care prescribed by doctors.

Validity: The extent to which a test measures what it purports to measure.

Vestibule training: Training that takes place away from the production area on equipment that closely resembles the actual equipment used on the job.

Vocational interest tests: A method of determining the occupation in which a person has the greatest interest and from which the person is most likely to receive satisfaction.

Voice mail: Spoken messages transmitted electronically and stored for delivery to the recipient at a later time.

Wage curve: The fitting of plotted points on a curve in order to create a smooth progression between pay grades (also known as the *pay curve*).

Weighted checklist performance report: A performance appraisal technique in which the rater completes a form similar to a forced-choice performance report except that the various responses have been assigned different weights.

Word processing: A computer application that permits an operator to create and edit written material.

Work-sample tests: Tests requiring the identification of a task or set of tasks that are representative of a particular job.

Work standards method: A performance appraisal method that compares each employee's performance to a predetermined standard or expected level of output.

Worker requirements questions: Questions that seek to determine an applicant's willingness to conform to the requirements of a job.

Workplace flexibility: Various options given to employees designed to provide them with greater control over their jobs and job environments.

Wrist-finger speed: The ability to make rapid wrist and finger movements, such as those required in inspector-packer and assembly operation jobs.

Yellow-dog contract: A written agreement between an employee and a company made at the time of employment, prohibiting a worker from joining a union or engaging in union activities.

Zero-base forecasting: A method for estimating future employment needs using the organization's current level of employment as the starting point.

INDEX

Photo Credits

Chapter 1 © Charles Thatcher/Tony Stone Images; Chapter 2 © Bruce Ayres/Tony Stone Images; Chapter 3 © Bruce Ayres/Tony Stone Images; Chapter 4 © Walter Hodges/Tony Stone Images; Chapter 5 © Terry Vine/Tony Stone Images; Chapter 6 © Michael Newman/PhotoEdit; Chapter 7 © Camerique/H. Armstrong Roberts; Chapter 8 © Walter Hodges/Tony Stone Images; Chapter 9 © Walter Hodges/Tony Stone Images; Chapter 10 © Frank Herholdt/Tony Stone Images; Chapter 11 © Mike Malyszko/FPG International; Chapter 12 © Charles Thatcher/Tony Stone Images; Chapter 13 © Zefa-U.K./H. Armstrong Roberts; Chapter 14 © Mark Richards/PhotoEdit; Chapter 15 © Charles Feil/FPG International; Chapter 16 © Steven Peters/Tony Stone Images; Chapter 17 © Tony Ward/FPG International; Chapter 18 © Tony Freeman/PhotoEdit; Chapter 19 © T. del Amo/H. Armstrong Roberts.